Business Marketing Management: B2B

Business Marketing Management: B2B

10e

MICHAEL D. HUTT
Arizona State University

•

THOMAS W. SPEH
Miami University

SOUTH-WESTERN
CENGAGE Learning™

Australia • Brazil • Japan • Korea • Mexico • Singapore • Spain • United Kingdom • United States

SOUTH-WESTERN
CENGAGE Learning™

**Business Marketing Management:
B2B, Tenth Edition**
Michael D. Hutt and Thomas W. Speh

Vice President of Editorial, Business:
Jack W. Calhoun

Editor-in-Chief: Melissa Acuna

Acquisitions Editor: Mike Roche

Developmental Editor: Erin Berger

Editorial Assistant: Shanna Shelton

Senior Marketing Coordinator: Sarah Rose

Executive Marketing Manager:
Kimberly Kanakes

Content Project Manager: Melissa Sacco

Managing Media Editor: Pam Wallace

Media Editor: John Rich

Website Project Manager: Brent Beck

Frontlist Buyer, Manufacturing: Bev Breslin

Production Service: Pre-Press PMG

Copyeditor: Pamela Rockwell

Compositor: Pre-Press PMG

Senior Art Director: Stacy Jenkins Shirley

Internal Design: Joseph Pagliaro

Cover Design: cmilller design

Cover Image: © Getty Images/Tetra Images

Photography Manager: Deanna Ettinger

Photo Researcher: Pre-PressPMG

To Rita and to Sara, and in memory of Michele

PREFACE

Special challenges and opportunities confront the marketer who intends to serve the needs of organizations rather than households. Business-to-business customers represent a lucrative and complex market worthy of separate analysis. A growing number of collegiate schools of business in the United States, Canada, and Europe have added industrial or business marketing to their curricula. In addition, a large and growing network of scholars in the United States and Europe is actively engaged in research to advance theory and practice in the business marketing field. Both the breadth and quality of this research has increased markedly during the past decade.

The rising importance of the field can be demonstrated by several factors. First, because more than half of all business school graduates enter firms that compete in business markets, a comprehensive treatment of business marketing management appears to be particularly appropriate. The business marketing course provides an ideal platform to deepen a student's knowledge of the competitive realities of the global marketplace, customer relationship management, cross-functional decision-making processes, supply chain management, e-commerce, and related areas. Such core content areas strike a responsive chord with corporate recruiters and squarely address key educational priorities established by the American Assembly of Collegiate Schools of Business (AACSB).

Second, the business marketing course provides a perfect vehicle for examining the special features of high-technology markets and for isolating the unique challenges that confront the marketing strategist in this arena. High-tech markets represent a rapidly growing and dynamic sector of the world economy and a fiercely competitive global battleground but often receive only modest attention in the traditional marketing curriculum. Electronic (e) commerce also falls squarely into the domain of the business market. In fact, the opportunity for e-commerce in the business-to-business market is estimated to be several times larger than the opportunity that exists in the business-to-consumer market.

Third, the Institute for the Study of Business Markets (ISBM) at Pennsylvania State University has provided important impetus to research in the area. ISBM has become a major information resource for researchers and practitioners and has assumed an active role in stimulating and supporting research on substantive business marketing issues. In turn, the number of research studies centered on the business-to-business domain has significantly expanded in recent years, and specialized journals in the area attract a steady stream of submissions. The hard work, multiyear commitments, and leadership of the editors of these journals are worthy of note: *Journal of Business-to-Business Marketing*, J. David Lichtenthal, Baruch College; *Journal of Business & Industrial Marketing*, Wesley J. Johnston, Georgia State University; and *Industrial Marketing Management*, Peter LaPlaca, University of Connecticut.

Three objectives guided the development of this edition:

1. To highlight the similarities between consumer-goods and business-to-business marketing and to explore in depth the points of departure. Particular attention is given to market analysis, organizational buying behavior, customer relationship management, supply chain management, and the ensuing adjustments required in the marketing strategy elements used to reach organizational customers.

2. To present a managerial rather than a descriptive treatment of business marketing. Whereas some descriptive material is required to convey the

dynamic nature of the business marketing environment, the relevance of the material is linked to marketing strategy decision making.

3. To integrate the growing body of literature into a strategic treatment of business marketing. In this text, relevant work is drawn from organizational buying behavior, procurement, organizational behavior, supply chain management, strategic management, and the behavioral sciences, as well as from specialized studies of business marketing strategy components.

The book is structured to provide a complete and timely treatment of business marketing while minimizing the degree of overlap with other courses in the marketing curriculum. A basic marketing principles course (or relevant managerial experience) provides the needed background for this text.

New to This Edition

Although the basic objectives, approach, and style of earlier editions have been maintained, several changes and additions have been made that reflect both the growing body of literature and the emerging trends in business marketing practice. Specifically, the following themes and distinctive features are incorporated into the tenth edition:

- **Relationship Marketing Strategies:** new and expanded coverage of the drivers of relationship marketing effectiveness and the financial impact of relationship marketing programs.

- **Strategic Alliances:** a timely and richly illustrated discussion of the determinants and social ingredients of alliance success.

- **Strong B2B Brands:** specific steps for building and managing a profitable B2B brand.

- **Marketing Performance Measurement:** a timely treatment of specific metrics for measuring the impact of marketing strategy decisions on firm performance.

- **A Value-Based Approach for Pricing:** a timely description of a framework for identifying and measuring value by customer segment.

- **A Customer-Centered Approach to Channel Design:** a fresh approach for designing channels from the bottom up, rather than the top down.

- **Other new topics of interest:** the new edition includes expanded treatment of **customer experience management, corporate entrepreneurship, strategic positioning**, and the emerging trends in **online advertising strategies**.

Organization of the Tenth Edition

The needs and interests of the reader provided the focus in the development of this volume. The authors' goal is to present a clear, timely, and engaging examination of business marketing management. To this end, each chapter provides an overview, highlights key concepts, and includes several carefully chosen examples of contemporary business marketing practice, as well as a cogent summary and a set of provocative discussion questions. Contemporary business marketing strategies and challenges are illustrated with three types of vignettes: "B2B Top Performers," "Inside Business Marketing," and "Ethical Business Marketing."

The book is divided into six parts with a total of 17 chapters. Part I introduces the distinguishing features of the business marketing environment. Careful examination is given to each of the major types of customers, the nature of the procurement function, and key trends that are reshaping buyer-seller relationships. Relationship management establishes the theme of Part II, in which chapter-length attention is given to organizational buying behavior and customer relationship management. By thoroughly updating and illustrating the core content, this section provides a timely and comprehensive treatment of customer profitability analysis and relationship management strategies for business markets. After this important background is established, Part III centers on the techniques that can be applied in assessing market opportunities: market segmentation and demand analysis, including sales forecasting.

Part IV centers on the planning process and on designing marketing strategy for business markets. Recent work drawn from the strategic management and strategic marketing areas provides the foundation for this section. This edition provides an expanded and integrated treatment of marketing strategy development using the balanced scorecard, enriched by strategy mapping. Special emphasis is given to defining characteristics of successful business-to-business firms and to the interfacing of marketing with other key functional areas such as manufacturing, research and development, and customer service. This functionally integrated planning perspective serves as a focal point in the analysis of the strategy development process. Here at the core of the volume, a separate chapter provides an integrated treatment of strategy formulation for the global market arena, giving particular attention to the new forms of competitive advantage that rapidly developing economies present (for example, China).

Next, each component of the marketing mix is examined from a business marketing perspective. The product chapter gives special attention to the brand-building process and to the strategic importance of providing competitively superior value to customers. Adding further depth to this core section are the chapters on managing product innovation and managing services for business markets. In turn, special attention is given to e-commerce and supply chain strategies for business markets. Building on the treatment of customer relationship marketing provided in Part II, the personal selling chapter explores the drivers of relationship marketing effectiveness as well as the financial impact of relationship marketing programs.

Marketing performance measurement provides the central focus for Part V. It provides a compact treatment of marketing control systems and uses the balanced scorecard as an organizing framework for marketing profitability analysis. Special attention is given to identifying the drivers of marketing strategy performance and to the critical area of strategy implementation in the business marketing firm. Part VI includes a collection of cases tailored to the business marketing environment.

Cases

Part VI includes 12 cases, 8 of which are new to this edition. These cases, of varying lengths, isolate one or more business marketing problems. Included among the selections for this edition are cases that raise provocative issues and illustrate the challenges and opportunities that small firms confront and the best practices of leading-edge firms such as Medtronics Corporation, Hewlett-Packard, FedEx, and 3M Canada. Other cases new to this edition provide students with a variety of business marketing strategy applications. A *Case Planning Guide*, which keys the cases to relevant text chapters, provides an organizing structure for Part VI. In addition, a short case, isolating core concepts, is included with each chapter. Two-thirds of the end-of-chapter cases are new to this edition and uncover opportunities and challenges confronting firms such as Apple, Intuit, Sealed Air Corp, SunPower, and Cisco. These cases provide a valuable tool for sparking class discussion and bringing strategy issues to life.

Ancillary Package

We are most indebted to John Eaton, Arizona State University, for his fine work in bringing together all of the elements of the ancillary package so that all supplements work together seamlessly. The ancillary package includes:

Instructor's Resource CD (IRCD)

The Instructor's Resource CD delivers all the traditional instructor support materials in one handy place: a CD. Included on the CD are electronic files for the complete Instructor's Manual, Test Bank, computerized Test Bank and computerized Test Bank software (ExamView), and chapter-by-chapter PowerPoint presentation files that can be used to enhance in-class lectures. PowerPoint files have been thoroughly updated and feature hundreds of new slides that instructors can use to tailor their lectures to their particular needs and preferences. We are indebted to Ray DeCormier, Central Connecticut State University, for developing the PowerPoint files and for contributing his expertise to this project.

Instructor's Manual   The Instructor's Manual for the tenth edition of *Business Marketing Management: B2B* provides a variety of creative suggestions designed to help the instructor incorporate all the materials available to create a dynamic learning environment. A few of the key features available in the Instructor's Manual for this edition include

- course design suggestions
- chapter outlines and supporting chapter materials
- suggested readings listed by chapter
- case analysis suggestions as well as assessment rubrics
- cooperative learning exercises
- ideas for effectively integrating the video package into the classroom discussion

The Instructor's Manual files are located on the IRCD and are also available for download at the text support site, **http://www.cengage.com/marketing/hutt**.

Test Bank   The revised and updated Test Bank includes over 1,500 multiple-choice and true/false questions, emphasizing the important concepts presented in each chapter, along with an average of five essay questions per chapter. The Test Bank questions vary in levels of difficulty so that each instructor can tailor the testing to meet specific needs. Each question is tagged to AACSB standards, discipline guidelines, and Rubin/Dierdorff standards. The Test Bank files are located on the IRCD.

ExamView (Computerized) Test Bank   The Test Bank is also available on the IRCD in computerized format (ExamView), allowing instructors to select problems at random by level of difficulty or type, customize or add test questions, and scramble questions to create up to 99 versions of the same test. This software is available in Mac or Windows formats.

PowerPoint Presentation Slides   The PowerPoint presentation slides bring classroom lectures and discussions to life with the Microsoft PowerPoint presentation tool. These presentations are organized by chapter, helping to create an easy-to-follow lecture, and are extremely professor friendly and easy to read. There are two PowerPoint versions for this edition: the GOLD version includes varying slide background and animation; the SILVER version provides simpler design for professors who would like to add their own material. The PowerPoint presentation slides are available on the IRCD and as downloadable files on the text support site, http://www.cengage .com/marketing/hutt.

Web Site

Visit the text Web site at **http://www.cengage.com/marketing/hutt** to find instructor's support materials as well as study resources that will help students practice and apply the concepts they have learned in class.

Videos

A new video package has been prepared to provide a relevant and interesting visual teaching tool for the classroom. Each video segment applies text materials to the real world, demonstrating how everyday companies effectively deal with business marketing management issues.

Student Resources

Online quizzes for each chapter are available on the Web site for those students who would like additional study materials. After each quiz is submitted, automatic feedback tells the students how they scored and what the correct answers are to the questions they missed. Students are then able to e-mail their results directly to their instructor, if desired.

Acknowledgments

The development of a textbook draws upon the contributions of many individuals. First, we would like to thank our students and former students at Arizona State University,

Miami University, the University of Alabama, and the University of Vermont. They provided important input and feedback when selected concepts or chapters were originally class tested. We would also like to thank our colleagues at each of these institutions for their assistance and support.

Second, we express our gratitude to several distinguished colleagues who carefully reviewed the volume and provided incisive comments and valuable suggestions that improved the tenth edition. They include: Blaine Branchik, *Quinnipiac University*; Brian Brown, *University of Massachusetts, Amherst*; Abbie Griffin, *University of Utah*; Peter A. Reday, *Youngstown State University*; Larry P. Schramm, *Oakland University*; Judy Wagner, *East Carolina University*; and Jianfeng Wang, *Mansfield University of Pennsylvania*.

We would also like to express our continuing appreciation to others who provided important suggestions that helped shape earlier editions: Kenneth Anselmi, *East Carolina University*; Joseph A. Bellizzi, *Arizona State University*; Paul D. Boughton, *Saint Louis University*; Michael R. Czinkota, *Georgetown University*; S. Altan Erdem, *University of Houston–Clear Lake*; Troy Festervand, *Middle Tennessee State University*; Srinath Gopalakrishna, *University of Missouri, Columbia*; Paris A. Gunther, *University of Cincinnati*; Jon M. Hawes, *University of Akron*; Jonathan Hibbard, *Boston University*; Lee Hibbert, *Freed-Hardeman University*; George John, *University of Minnesota*; Joe H. Kim, *Rider University*; Kenneth M. Lampert, *Metropolitan State University, Minnesota*; Jay L. Laughlin, *Kansas State University*; J. David Lichtenthal, *Baruch College*; Gary L. Lilien, *Pennsylvania State University*; Lindsay N. Meredith, *Simon Fraser University*; K. C. Pang, *University of Alabama at Birmingham*; Richard E. Plank, *University of South Florida*; Constantine Polychroniou, *University of Cincinnati*; Bernard A. Rausch, *Illinois Institute of Technology*; David A. Reid, *The University of Toledo*; Paul A. Roobol, *Western Michigan University*; Beth A. Walker, *Arizona State University*; Elizabeth Wilson, *Suffolk University*; James F. Wolter, *Grand Valley State University*; Ugut Yucelt, *Pennsylvania State University at Harrisburg*; and John M. Zerio, *American Graduate School of International Management*.

We are especially indebted to four members of the Board of Advisors for Arizona State University's Center for Services Leadership. Each served as a senior executive sponsor for a funded research study, provided access to the organizations, and contributed valuable insights to the research. Collectively, these studies sharpened the strategy content of the volume. Included here are Michael Daniels, Senior Vice President, Global Technology Services, *IBM Global Services*; Greg Reid, Chief Marketing Officer, *YRC Worldwide Inc.*; Adrian Paull, Vice President, Customer Product Support, *Honeywell Aerospace*; and Merrill Tutton, President, *AT&T UK*, retired. We would like to thank Jim Ryan, President and Chief Executive Officer, *W. W. Grainger*, for his insights and contributions to this edition. We would also like to thank Mohan Kuruvilla, Adjunct Professor, *Indian Institute of Management Kozhikode*, for his keen insights and recommendations. We also extend our special thanks to Dr. Joseph Belonax, *Western Michigan University*, for contributing ideas and content to the teaching package.

The talented staff of South-Western/Cengage Learning displayed a high level of enthusiasm and deserves special praise for their contributions in shaping this edition. In particular, Mike Roche provided valuable advice and keen insights for this edition. In turn, we were indeed fortunate to have Erin Berger, our development editor, on our team. Her steady hand, efficient style, and superb coordinating skills advanced the project. Pamela Rockwell contributed excellent copyediting skills and Melissa Sacco, our Project Manager, provided a confident style and a seasoned approach during the production process. We express our gratitude to Diane A. Davis, Arizona State University, for lending her superb administrative skills and creative talent to the project and for delivering under pressure.

Finally, but most importantly, our overriding debt is to our wives, Rita and Sara, whose encouragement, understanding, and direct support were vital to the completion of this edition. Their involvement and dedication are deeply appreciated.

Michael D. Hutt
Thomas W. Speh

Michael D. Hutt (PhD, Michigan State University) is the Ford Motor Company Distinguished Professor of Marketing at the W. P. Carey School of Business, Arizona State University. He has also held faculty positions at Miami University (Ohio) and the University of Vermont.

Dr. Hutt's teaching and research interests are concentrated in the areas of business-to-business marketing and strategic marketing. His current research centers on the cross-functional role that marketing managers assume in the formation of strategy. Dr. Hutt's research has been published in the *Journal of Marketing*, *Journal of Marketing Research*, *MIT Sloan Management Review*, *Journal of Retailing*, *Journal of the Academy of Marketing Science*, and other scholarly journals. He is also the co-author of *Macro Marketing* (John Wiley & Sons) and contributing author of *Marketing: Best Practices* (South-Western).

Assuming a variety of leadership roles for American Marketing Association programs, he co-chaired the Faculty Consortium on Strategic Marketing Management. He is a member of the editorial review boards of the *Journal of Business-to-Business Marketing*, *Journal of Business & Industrial Marketing*, *Industrial Marketing Management*, *Journal of the Academy of Marketing Science*, and *Journal of Strategic Marketing*. For his 2000 contribution to *MIT Sloan Management Review*, he received the Richard Beckhard Prize. Dr. Hutt has consulted on marketing strategy issues for firms such as IBM, Motorola, Honeywell, AT&T, Arvin Industries, ADT, and Black-Clawson, and for the food industry's Public Policy Subcommittee on the Universal Product Code.

Thomas W. Speh, PhD, is Professor of Marketing Emeritus and Associate Director of MBA Programs at the Farmer School of Business, Miami University (Ohio). Dr. Speh earned his PhD from Michigan State University. Prior to his tenure at Miami, Dr. Speh taught at the University of Alabama.

Dr. Speh has been a regular participant in professional marketing and logistics meetings and has published articles in a number of academic and professional journals, including the *Journal of Marketing*, *Sloan Management Review*, *Harvard Business Review*, *Journal of the Academy of Marketing Sciences*, *Journal of Business Logistics*, *Journal of Retailing*, *Journal of Purchasing and Materials Management*, and *Industrial Marketing Management*. He was the recipient of the Beta Gamma Sigma Distinguished Faculty award for excellence in teaching at Miami University's School of Business and of the Miami University Alumni Association's Effective Educator award.

Dr. Speh has been active in both the Warehousing Education and Research Council (WERC) and the Council of Logistics Management (CLM). He has served as president of WERC and as president of the CLM. Dr. Speh has been a consultant on strategy issues to such organizations as Xerox, Procter & Gamble, Burlington Northern Railroad, Sara Lee, J. M. Smucker Co., and Millenium Petrochemicals, Inc.

CASE CONTRIBUTORS

Erin Anderson, *INSEAD*

Bradley W. Brooks, *Queens University of Charlotte*

Clayton M. Christensen, *Harvard Business School*

Terry H. Deutscher, *Richard Ivey School of Business*

Ali F. Farhoomand, *University of Hong Kong*

John H. Friar, *Northeastern University*

John B. Gifford, *Miami University (Ohio)*

Raymond M. Kinnunen, *Northeastern University*

Marc H. Meyer, *Northeastern University*

David W. Rosenthal, *Miami University (Ohio)*

David V. Rudd, *Lebanon Valley College*

Susan Sieloff, *Northeastern University*

Robert E. Spekman, *Darden School of Business, University of Virginia*

David Weinstein, *INSEAD*

John M. Zerio, *Thunderbird School of Global Management*

CONTENTS IN BRIEF

Preface   vii

PART I   THE ENVIRONMENT OF BUSINESS MARKETING   1

Chapter 1   A Business Marketing Perspective   3

Chapter 2   The Business Market: Perspectives
on the Organizational Buyer   33

PART II   MANAGING RELATIONSHIPS IN BUSINESS MARKETING   61

Chapter 3   Organizational Buying Behavior   63

Chapter 4   Customer Relationship Management
Strategies for Business Markets   91

PART III   ASSESSING MARKET OPPORTUNITIES   121

Chapter 5   Segmenting the Business Market
and Estimating Segment Demand   123

PART IV   FORMULATING BUSINESS MARKETING STRATEGY   151

Chapter 6   Business Marketing Planning:
Strategic Perspectives   153

Chapter 7   Business Marketing Strategies
for Global Markets   180

Chapter 8   Managing Products
for Business Markets   208

Chapter 9   Managing Innovation and New
Industrial Product Development   232

9 Chapter 10 Managing Services
for Business Markets   257

10 Chapter 11 Managing Business
Marketing Channels   281

Chapter 12 E-Commerce Strategies
for Business Markets   303

11 Chapter 13 Supply Chain Management   329

12 Chapter 14 Pricing Strategy for
Business Markets   358

13 Chapter 15 Business Marketing Communications:
Advertising and Sales Promotion   383

14 Chapter 16 Business Marketing Communications:
Managing the Personal
Selling Function   407

PART V   EVALUATING BUSINESS MARKETING
STRATEGY AND PERFORMANCE   **433**

15 Chapter 17 Marketing Performance
Measurement   435

Cases   609

Name Index   609

Subject Index   619

CONTENTS

Preface   vii

PART I   THE ENVIRONMENT OF BUSINESS MARKETING   1

Chapter 1   A Business Marketing Perspective   3

Business Marketing   4

Business Marketing Management   5

Business Market Customers   6

B2B TOP PERFORMERS: Jim Ryan, President and Chief Executive Officer, W.W. Grainger, Inc.   7

Business Markets versus Consumer-Goods Markets   7

B2B TOP PERFORMERS: Career Path for B2B CEOs: For Many, It Began in Marketing!   9

Creating the Customer Value Proposition   10

Marketing's Cross-Functional Relationships   11

Characteristics of Business Markets   13

Business and Consumer Marketing: A Contrast   14

Smucker: A Consumer and Business Marketer   15

Distinguishing Characteristics   16

A Relationship Emphasis   16

The Supply Chain   17

Supply Chain Management   18

Managing Relationships in the Supply Chain   19

Commercial Enterprises as Consumers   21

INSIDE BUSINESS MARKETING: The iPhone: A Triumph of Supply Chain Management Too   22

Classifying Goods for the Business Market   22

Entering Goods   23

Foundation Goods   24

Facilitating Goods   24

Business Marketing Strategy   26

Illustration: Manufactured Materials and Parts   26

Illustration: Installations   26

Illustration: Supplies   26

A Look Ahead   27

Summary   29

Discussion Questions   29

Internet Exercises   30

Case: R.I.M.'s BlackBerry and Apple's iPhone: The Face-Off
in the Business Market   31

New Strategy Directions   31

Discussion Questions   32

Chapter 2   The Business Market: Perspectives on the Organizational Buyer   33

Commercial Enterprises: Unique Characteristics   34

Distribution by Size   35

Geographical Concentration   35

Classifying Commercial Enterprises   36

The Purchasing Organization   37

Goals of the Purchasing Function   38

INSIDE BUSINESS MARKETING: The Supply Chain for McNuggets   39

Strategic Procurement   39

INSIDE BUSINESS MARKETING: Respond with Value-Based Selling Tools   43

E-Procurement   44

Everyone Is Getting Wired   44

Enhancing the Buyer's Capabilities   45

Delivering Measurable Results   45

Buying Direct and Indirect Goods   45

Reverse Auctions   46

ETHICAL BUSINESS MARKETING: Gift Giving: "Buy Me These
Boots and You'll Get My Business"   47

How Organizational Buyers Evaluate Potential Suppliers   47

Governments: Unique Characteristics   47

E-Government   49

Influences on Government Buying   49

Understanding Government Contracts   49

Telling Vendors How to Sell: Useful Publications   50

Purchasing Organizations and Procedures: Government   50

Federal Buying   52

A Different Strategy Required   53

The Institutional Market: Unique Characteristics   53

Institutional Buyers: Purchasing Procedures   54

Dealing with Diversity: A Market-Centered Organization   57

Summary   57
Discussion Questions   58
Internet Exercises   59
Case: Sealed Air Corporation: Delivering Packaging Solutions   60
Discussion Questions   60

PART II   MANAGING RELATIONSHIPS IN BUSINESS MARKETING   61

Chapter 3   Organizational Buying Behavior   63

The Organizational Buying Process   65
The Search Process   66
New Task   67
Straight Rebuy   68
Modified Rebuy   69
Forces Shaping Organizational Buying Behavior   71
Environmental Forces   71
Organizational Forces   73
Strategic Priorities in Purchasing   73
Organizational Positioning of Purchasing   75
INSIDE BUSINESS MARKETING: Go Digital to Target
Buying Influentials   77
Group Forces   77
INSIDE BUSINESS MARKETING: Innovate and Win with BMW   80
Individual Forces   82
B2B TOP PERFORMERS: Delivering Customer Solutions   84
The Organizational Buying Process: Major Elements   85
Summary   86
Discussion Questions   87
Internet Exercises   88
Case: The Tablet PC for Nurses: A Mobile Clinical Assistant   89
Discussion Questions   90

Chapter 4   Customer Relationship Management Strategies for Business Markets   91

Relationship Marketing   92
Types of Relationships   93
Value-Adding Exchanges   94
Nature of Relationships   94
Strategic Choices   94

B2B TOP PERFORMERS: Understanding the Customer's
Business—The Key to Success   95

   Managing Buyer-Seller Relationships   95

   Transactional Exchange   95

   Collaborative Exchange   96

   Switching Costs   96

   Strategy Guidelines   97

   Measuring Customer Profitability   99

   Activity-Based Costing   99

   Unlocking Customer Profitability   99

   The Profitable Few   100

   Managing High- and Low-Cost-to-Serve Customers   101

   Managing Unprofitable Customers   103

   Firing Customers   103

   Customer Relationship Management   104

   Acquiring the Right Customers   104

INSIDE BUSINESS MARKETING: Diversify a Customer Portfolio Too! 106

   Crafting the Right Value Proposition   107

   Instituting the Best Processes   109

   Motivating Employees   110

   Learning to Retain Customers   111

   Strategic Alliances   112

   Accessing Complementary Skills   112

   Benefits of Strategic Alliances   113

   Determinants of Alliance Success   114

   The Social Ingredients of Alliance Success   116

   Summary   118

   Discussion Questions   118

   Internet Exercises   119

   **Case: Hewlett-Packard Challenges from a Diverse Mix
of Demanding Customers**   120

PART III   ASSESSING MARKET OPPORTUNITIES   121

Chapter 5   Segmenting the Business Market and Estimating Segment Demand   123

   Business Market Segmentation Requirements and Benefits   125

   Requirements   125

   Benefits   125

INSIDE BUSINESS MARKETING: How to See What's Next   126

    Bases for Segmenting Business Markets   127

    Macrolevel Bases   128

    Microlevel Bases   131

B2B TOP PERFORMERS: Steering Customers to the
Right Channel   133

    Illustration: Microsegmentation   136

    The Segmentation Process   136

    Choosing Market Segments   136

INSIDE BUSINESS MARKETING: A Fresh Approach to Segmentation:
Customer Service Segmentation   137

    Isolating Market Segment Profitability   138

    Implementing a Segmentation Strategy   139

    Estimating Segment Demand   139

    The Role of the Demand Estimation   140

INSIDE BUSINESS MARKETINGL: Accurate Forecasts
Drive Effective Collaboration between Boeing and Alcoa   141

    Methods of Forecasting Demand   142

    Qualitative Techniques   142

    Quantitative Techniques   144

    CPFR: A New Collaborative Approach to Estimating Demand   145

    Combining Several Forecasting Techniques   146

    Summary   147

    Discussion Questions   147

    Internet Exercises   148

    Case: Federated Insurance: Targeting Small
                 Businesses   149

    Cultivating Business Relationships   149

    Discussion Questions   150

PART IV   FORMULATING BUSINESS MARKETING STRATEGY   151

**Chapter 6   Business Marketing Planning:
Strategic Perspectives   153**

    Marketing's Strategic Role   154

    The Hierarchy of Strategies   154

    Strategy Formulation and the Hierarchy   156

INSIDE BUSINESS MARKETING: From Bullet-Point Plans
to Strategic Stories at 3M   158
    Functionally Integrated Planning: The Marketing Strategy Center   158
B2B TOP PERFORMERS: Cross-Functional Relationships: Effective
Managers Deliver on Promises   159
    The Components of a Business Model   160
    Customer Interface   162
    Core Strategy   163
    Strategic Resources   164
    The Value Network   164
    Strategic Positioning   165
    Strategic Positioning Illustrated   166
    Building the Strategy Plan   167
    The Balanced Scorecard   168
    Financial Perspective   168
    Customer Perspective   170
    Internal Business Process Perspective   171
    Strategy Map   173
    Summary   175
    Discussion Questions   176
    Internet Exercises   177
    Case: Microsoft Targets Small and Mid-Sized Businesses   178
    Challenging Intuit, Inc.   178
    Discussion Questions   179

Chapter 7   Business Marketing Strategies for Global Markets   180

Capturing Global Advantage in Rapidly Developing Economies   181
Mapping Sources of Global Advantage   182
    The Cost Advantage   183
    The Market Access Advantage   186
    The Capabilities Advantage   187
INSIDE BUSINESS MARKETING: How Offshore Outsourcing
Affects Customer Satisfaction—and a Company's Stock Price!   188
    The Outsourcing Decision   189
    Global Market Entry Options   190
    Exporting   190

Contracting   191

Strategic Global Alliances (SGA)   192

Joint Ventures   193

ETHICAL BUSINESS MARKETING: The Bribery Dilemma in
Global Markets   194

Choosing a Mode of Entry   195

Multidomestic versus Global Strategies   195

B2B TOP PERFORMERS: General Electric Aircraft Engines:
Global Strategy Means Help Your Customers   196

Source of Advantage: Multidomestic versus Global   197

Types of International Strategy   198

A Strategic Framework   199

Global Strategy   201

Build on a Unique Competitive Position   201

Emphasize a Consistent Positioning Strategy   201

Establish a Clear Home Base for Each Distinct Business   201

Leverage Product-Line Home Bases at Different Locations   202

Disperse Activities to Extend Home-Base Advantages   202

Coordinate and Integrate Dispersed Activities   202

Managing Risk in Emerging Markets   203

Summary   203

Discussion Questions   204

Internet Exercise   205

Case: Schwinn: Could the Story Have Been Different?   206

Alternative Reality One: Aim High   206

Alternative Reality Two: If You Can't Beat Them, Join Them   206

Discussion Question   207

Chapter 8   Managing Products for Business Markets   208

Building a Strong B2B Brand   209

Brand-Building Steps   210

A Systems Model for Managing a Brand   212

B2B TOP PERFORMERS: Corporate Brand Personality Traits
of a Successful 21st-Century Business   214

Product Quality and Customer Value   215

Meaning of Quality   215

Meaning of Customer Value   216

Product Support Strategy: The Service Connection   218

Product Policy 218
Types of Product Lines Defined 218
Defining the Product Market 219

B2B TOP PERFORMERS: BASF: Using Services to Build a Strong Brand 221
Planning Industrial Product Strategy 221
Product Positioning 221
The Process 221
Isolating Strategy Opportunities 222
Product Positioning Illustrated 223
The Technology Adoption Life Cycle 223
Types of Technology Customers 224

INSIDE BUSINESS MARKETING: The Gorilla Advantage
in High-Tech Markets 225
Strategies for the Technology Adoption Life Cycle 225
The Bowling Alley 226
The Tornado 227
Main Street 228
Summary 228
Discussion Questions 229
Internet Exercise 230
Case: Cisco TelePresence: The "As if you were there" Technology 231
Benefits 231
The Price Tag 231
Discussion Questions 231

**Chapter 9   Managing Innovation and New
Industrial Product Development   232**

The Management of Innovation 233
Induced Strategic Behavior 234
Autonomous Strategic Behavior 234
Product Championing and the Informal Network 236
Conditions Supporting Corporate Entrepreneurship 238
Managing Technology 238
Classifying Development Projects 239
A Product-Family Focus 239
The Disruptive Innovation Model 240
Illustration: A New-Market Disruption 243
Innovation Winners in High-Technology Markets 243

INSIDE BUSINESS MARKETING: Patching: The New Corporate
Strategy in Dynamic Markets   245
    The New-Product-Development Process   246
    What Drives a Firm's New Product Performance?   246
    Anticipating Competitive Reactions   248
    Sources of New Product Ideas   248
B2B TOP PERFORMERS: IDEO: The Hits Just Keep on Coming!   249
    Determinants of New Product Performance and Timeliness   251
    The Determinants of Success   251
    Fast-Paced Product Development   252
    Summary   253
    Discussion Questions   254
    Internet Exercise   255
    Case: Steelcase Inc. Extends Reach to Growing Health-Care Market 256
    Discussion Question   256

**Chapter 10   Managing Services for Business
Markets**   257
    Understanding the Full Customer Experience   258
    The Customer Experience Life Cycle   258
    Applying the Customer Experience Map   260
    Customer Experience Management   260
    A Solution-Centered Perspective   260
INSIDE BUSINESS MARKETING: Do Service Transition Strategies Pay Off? 262
    Benefits of Solution Marketing   262
    Business Service Marketing: Special Challenges   263
    Services Are Different   264
    Tangible or Intangible?   264
    Simultaneous Production and Consumption   265
    Service Variability   265
    Service Perishability   266
    Nonownership   266
INSIDE BUSINESS MARKETING: To Sell Jet Engines, Teach Your Customer
How to Sell Aircraft   267
    Service Quality   268
    Dimensions of Service Quality   268
    Customer Satisfaction and Loyalty   268

Service Recovery   269

Zero Defections   270

Return on Quality   270

Marketing Mix for Business Service Firms   271

Segmentation   271

Service Packages   272

Pricing Business Services   275

Services Promotion   276

Services Distribution   277

Developing New Services   277

Summary   278

Discussion Questions   278

Internet Exercise   279

Case: SafePlace Corporation   280

Discussion Questions   280

Chapter 11   Managing Business Marketing Channels

Chapter 11   Managing Business Marketing
             Channels   **281**

The Business Marketing Channel   282

Direct Channels   283

INSIDE BUSINESS MARKETING: IBM Uses the Internet to Collaborate
with Channel Partners and Build Customer Loyalty   284

Indirect Channels   284

Integrated Multichannel Models   285

Participants in the Business Marketing Channel   287

Distributors   287

Manufacturers' Representatives   290

B2B TOP PERFORMERS: Why Intel Uses Reps   291

Channel Design   292

Step 1: Define Customer Segments   293

Step 2: Customers' Channel Needs by Segment   293

Step 3: Assess the Firm's Channel Capabilities   294

Step 4: Benchmark to Competitors   294

Step 5: Create Channel Solutions for Customers' Latent Needs   295

Step 6: Evaluate and Select Channel Options   295

Crucial Points in Channel Transformation   295

Channel Administration   296

Selection of Channel Members   296

Motivating Channel Members   297

Summary   299

Discussion Questions   299

Internet Exercise   300

Case: SunPower's Go-to-Market Strategy   301

Discussion Questions   301

Chapter 12   E-Commerce Strategies for Business Markets   303

Defining E-Commerce   305

Key Elements Supporting E-Commerce   307

Intranets and Extranets   307

INSIDE BUSINESS MARKETING: Extending the Boundaries of
E-Commerce: B2M (Business to Machines) E-Commerce   308

The Strategic Role of E-Commerce   309

E-Commerce as a Strategic Component   309

INSIDE BUSINESS MARKETING: UPS Delivers the Goods Using Sophisticated
E-Commerce Technology   310

What the Internet Can Do   310

The Internet: Strategy Still Matters   311

Crafting an E-Commerce Strategy   312

Delineating E-Commerce Objectives   314

Specific Objectives of Internet Marketing Strategies   314

B2B TOP PERFORMERS: GE Healthcare: Using the Web to Create New Services   316

Internet Strategy Implementation   316

The Internet Product   316

INSIDE BUSINESS MARKETING: "Borrow Best Tactics From
Consumer E-Commerce To Revamp Your B2B Site"   318

Channel Considerations with Internet Marketing   320

The Internet as a Channel Alternative   321

The Effect of the Internet on Pricing Strategy   322

The Internet and Customer Communication   322

Summary   324

Discussion Questions   325

Internet Exercise   326

Case: Using the Internet at W.W. Grainger   327

Discussion Questions   328

Chapter 13   Supply Chain Management   329

The Concept of Supply Chain Management   331
Partnerships: The Critical Ingredient   332
Supply Chain Management: A Tool for Competitive Advantage   333
Supply Chain Management Goals   335
Benefits to the Final Customer   336
INSIDE BUSINESS MARKETING: When the Chain Breaks   337
The Financial Benefits Perspective   337
Information and Technology Drivers   338
Successfully Applying the Supply Chain Management Approach   339
B2B TOP PERFORMERS: Making Supplier Relationships Work   340
Successful Supply Chain Practices   340
Logistics as the Critical Element in Supply Chain Management   341
Distinguishing Between Logistics and Supply Chain Management   342
Managing Flows   342
The Strategic Role of Logistics   343
Sales-Marketing-Logistics Integration   343
Just-in-Time Systems   343
Total-Cost Approach   344
Calculating Logistics Costs   346
Activity-Based Costing   346
Total Cost of Ownership   346
Business-to-Business Logistical Service   346
Logistics Service Impacts on the Customer   347
Determining the Level of Service   348
Logistics Impacts on Other Supply Chain Participants   348
Business-to-Business Logistical Management   349
Logistical Facilities   349
Transportation   350
Inventory Management   352
INSIDE BUSINESS MARKETING: The Profit Impact of Inventory
Management   353
Third-Party Logistics   353
Summary   355
Discussion Questions   355
Internet Exercise   356
Case: Managing Logistics at Trans-Pro   357
Discussion Question   357

Chapter 14   Pricing Strategy for Business Markets   358

The Meaning of Value in Business Markets	359
Benefits	360
Sacrifices	360
Value-Based Strategies	361
The Pricing Process in Business Markets	362
Price Objectives	362
Demand Determinants	363
Value-Based Pricing Illustrated	365
Cost Determinants	368
Competition	370
Pricing across the Product Life Cycle	371
Pricing New Products	372
INSIDE BUSINESS MARKETING: Understanding the Economic Value of New Products	373
Legal Considerations	373
Responding to Price Attacks by Competitors	374
Evaluating a Competitive Threat	374
Understanding the Rules of Competitive Strategy	376
Competitive Bidding	377
Closed Bidding	377
Open Bidding	378
Strategies for Competitive Bidding	378
Summary	379
Discussion Questions	380
Internet Exercise	381
Case: Price Like a Retailer, Not a Widget Maker	382
Discussion Questions	382

Chapter 15   Business Marketing Communications: Advertising and Sales Promotion   383

The Role of Advertising	385
Integrated Communication Programs	385
Enhancing Sales Effectiveness	385
Increased Sales Efficiency	385
Creating Awareness	386
Interactive Marketing Communications	386

What Business-to-Business Advertising Cannot Do   387
Managing Business-to-Business Advertising   387
Defining Advertising Objectives   387
Written Objectives   388
Determining Advertising Expenditures   389
Developing the Advertising Message   391
Selecting Advertising Media for Business Markets   392

INSIDE BUSINESS MARKETING: Viral Marketing Campaigns Create Buzz   393

B2B TOP PERFORMERS: Search Engine Marketing at Google:
The Right Message, the Right Time   395
Direct Marketing Tools   396
Measuring Advertising Effectiveness   397
Measuring Impacts on the Purchase Decision   398
The Measurement Program   398
Managing Trade Show Strategy   400
Trade Shows: Strategy Benefits   400
Trade-Show Investment Returns   401
Planning Trade-Show Strategy   401
Trade-Show Objectives   402
Selecting the Shows   402
Managing the Trade-Show Exhibit   402
Evaluating Trade-Show Performance   403
Summary   404
Discussion Questions   405
Internet Exercise   405
Case: Johnson Controls, Inc.   406
Discussion Questions   406

Chapter 16   Business Marketing Communications: Managing the Personal Selling Function   407

Relationship Marketing Strategy   409
Drivers of Relationship Marketing Effectiveness   409
Relationship Marketing (RM) Programs   411
Financial Impact of RM Programs   411
Targeting RM Programs   412
Managing the Sales Force   413
Organizing the Personal Selling Effort   413

Key Account Management   414

National Account Success   417

B2B TOP PERFORMERS: Using Customized Strategies
to Outmaneuver Rivals   418

Isolating the Account Management Process   418

Account Management Success   419

Sales Administration   421

Recruitment and Selection of Salespersons   421

Training   421

Supervision and Motivation   422

Evaluation and Control   425

Models for Business-to-Business Sales Force Management   426

Deployment Analysis: A Strategic Approach   426

Summary   429

Discussion Questions   429

Internet Exercise   430

**Case: Account Management at YRC Worldwide: Choosing
Customers Wisely**   431

Discussion Question   431

PART V   EVALUATING BUSINESS MARKETING STRATEGY AND PERFORMANCE   433

Chapter 17   Marketing Performance Measurement   435

A Strategy Map: Portrait of an Integrated Plan   437

Developing the Strategy: The Process   438

Maps: A Tool for Strategy Making   441

Marketing Strategy: Allocating Resources   441

Guiding Strategy Formulation   442

Managing Individual Customers for Profit   442

The Marketing Control Process   443

Control at Various Levels   443

Strategic Control   443

Annual Plan Control   446

Marketing Control: The Marketing Performance Dashboard   446

Efficiency and Effectiveness Control   448

Profitability Control   449

Implementation of Business Marketing Strategy   451

INSIDE BUSINESS MARKETING: Tracking Marketing Success at Siemens   **452**

    The Strategy-Implementation Fit   **452**

    Implementation Skills   **453**

    The Marketing Strategy Center: An Implementation Guide   **454**

    Looking Back   **455**

B2B TOP PERFORMERS: Cross-Functional Relationships:
Effective Managers Deliver on Promises   **456**

    Summary   **457**

    Discussion Questions   **458**

    Internet Exercise   **459**

    Case: Intuit Leads in the Accounting Software Market   **460**

    Discussion Question   **460**

Cases   **461**

    Case Planning Guide   461

    Columbia Industries, Inc.   462

    Clariant Corporation Marketing   471

    Circuit Board Corporation   486

    3M Canada: Industrial Business Division   499

    Fedex Corp.: Structural Transformation through e-business   515

    Clearwater Technologies   535

    Barro Stickney, Inc.   541

    We've Got Rhythm! Medtronic Corporation's
        Cardiac Pacemaker Business   547

    Total Quality Logistics: Sales Force Management   565

    Telezoo (A): Feast or Famine?   583

    Van Leer Packaging Worldwide: The TOTAL Account (A)   595

    Ethical Dilemmas in Business Marketing   607

Name Index   **609**

Subject Index   **619**

THE ENVIRONMENT OF BUSINESS MARKETING

A Business Marketing Perspective

The business market poses special challenges and significant opportunities for the marketing manager. This chapter introduces the complex forces that are unique to the business marketing environment. After reading this chapter, you will understand:

1. the dynamic nature of the business marketing environment and the basic similarities and differences between consumer-goods and business marketing.

2. the underlying factors that influence the demand for industrial goods.

3. the nature of buyer-seller relationships in a product's supply chain.

4. the types of customers in this important market.

5. the basic characteristics of industrial products and services.

Business Marketing

Business marketers serve the largest market of all: The dollar volume of transactions in the industrial or business market significantly exceeds that of the ultimate consumer market. In the business market, a single customer can account for an enormous level of purchasing activity. For example, the corporate procurement department at IBM spends more than $40 billion annually on industrial products and services.[1] Others, such as Procter & Gamble, Apple, Merck, Dell, and Kimberly Clark each spend more than half of their annual sales revenue on purchased goods and services.[2] Indeed, all formal organizations—large or small, public or private, for-profit or not-for-profit—participate in the exchange of industrial products and services, thus constituting the business market.

Business markets are "markets for products and services, local to international, bought by businesses, government bodies, and institutions (such as hospitals) for incorporation (for example, ingredient materials or components), for consumption (for example, process materials, office supplies, consulting services), for use (for example, installations or equipment), or for resale. . . . The only markets not of direct interest are those dealing with products or services which are principally directed at personal use or consumption such as packaged grocery products, home appliances, or consumer banking."[3] The factors that distinguish business marketing from consumer marketing are the nature of the customer and how that customer uses the product. In business marketing, the customers are organizations (businesses, governments, institutions).

Business firms buy industrial goods to form or facilitate the production process or use as components for other goods and services. Government agencies and private institutions buy industrial goods to maintain and deliver services to their own market: the public. Industrial or business marketing (the terms can be used interchangeably) accounts for more than half the economic activity in the United States, Canada, and most other nations. More than 50 percent of all business school graduates join firms that compete directly in the business market. The heightened interest in high-technology markets—and the sheer size of the business market—has spawned increased emphasis on business marketing management in universities and corporate executive training programs.[4]

This book explores the business market's special opportunities and challenges and identifies the new requirements for managing the marketing function in this vital sector of the global economy. The following questions establish the theme of this first chapter: What are the similarities and differences between consumer-goods marketing

---

[1] Tim Ferguson, "IBM Shifts Procurement HQ to China," ZDNet News: October 13, 2006, accessed at http://www.news.zdnet.com on June 1, 2008.

[2] Chip W. Hardt, Nicolas Reinecke, and Peter Spiller, "Inventing the 21st Century Purchasing Organization," *The McKinsey Quarterly* (4, 2007): pp. 115–117.

[3] Prospectus for the Institute for the Study of Business Markets, College of Business Administration, the Pennsylvania State University and J. David Lichtenthal, Venkatapparao Mummaleni, and David T. Wilson, "The Essence of Business Marketing Theory, Research, and Tactics: Contributions from the Journal of Business-to-Business Marketing," *Journal of Business-to-Business Marketing* 15 (2, 2008): pp. 91–123.

[4] J. David Lichtenthal, "Business-to-Business Marketing in the 21st Century," *Journal of Business-to-Business Marketing* 12 (1, 2, 1998): pp. 1–5; J. Lichtenthal, "Advocating Business Marketing Education: Relevance and Rigor—Uttered as One," *Journal of Business-to-Business Marketing* 14 (1, 2007): pp. 1–12; and Michael D. Hutt and Thomas W. Speh, "Business Marketing Education: A Distinctive Role in the Undergraduate Curriculum," *Journal of Business-to-Business Marketing* 12 (1, 2, 1998): pp. 103–126.

FIGURE 1.1 | **POWERFUL B2B BRANDS**

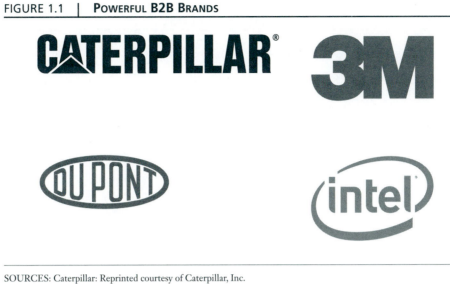

SOURCES: Caterpillar: Reprinted courtesy of Caterpillar, Inc.
3M: Courtesy of 3M.
DUPONT: Copyright © 2005 DuPont. All rights reserved. The DuPont Oval Logo is a registered trademark of DuPont
and its affiliates. Used by permission.
Intel: Reprinted by permission of Intel Corporation.

and business marketing? What customers constitute the business market? How can the
multitude of industrial goods be classified into manageable categories? What forces
influence the behavior of business market demand?

Business Marketing Management

Many large firms that produce goods such as steel, production equipment, or computer-
memory chips cater exclusively to business market customers and never directly
interact with their ultimate consumers. Other firms participate in both the consumer-
goods and the business markets. The introduction of laser printers and personal
computers brought Hewlett-Packard, historically a business-to-business marketer,
into the consumer market. Conversely, lagging consumer markets prompted Sony
Corporation to expand to the business market by introducing office automation products. Both companies had to reorient their marketing strategies dramatically because of
significant differences in the buying behavior of consumer versus business markets.

Products like cell phones, office furniture, personal computers, and software are purchased in both the consumer and the business markets. What distinguishes business marketing from consumer-goods marketing is the *intended use of the product* and the *intended
consumer*. Sometimes the products are identical, but a fundamentally different marketing
approach is needed to reach the organizational buyer. Interestingly, some of the most
valuable brands in the world belong to business marketers: Cisco, Google, BlackBerry,
Caterpillar, IBM, FedEx, GE, DuPont, Intel, Hewlett-Packard, and 3M[5] (Figure 1.1).

---

[5] Frederick E. Webster, Jr. and Kevin Lane Keller, "A Roadmap for Branding in Industrial Markets," *Journal of Brand
Management* 11 (May 2004): pp. 388–402; and Matthew Schwartz, "B to B's Best: Brands," *B to B*, Special Issue (2007),
accessed at http://www.btobonline on May 15, 2008.

FIGURE 1.2 | **THE CONSUMER MARKET (B2C) AND THE BUSINESS MARKET (B2B) AT DELL**

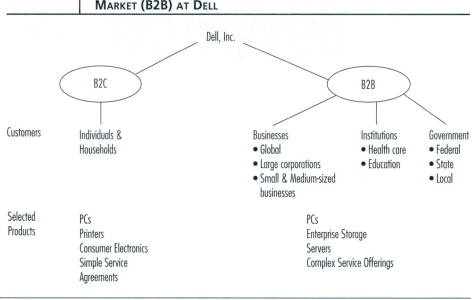

Business Market Customers

Business market customers can be broadly classified into three categories: (1) commercial enterprises—that is, businesses; (2) institutions—for example, universities; and (3) government. Consider Dell, Inc.: The firm serves both the business market (B2B) and the consumer market (B2C) (Figure 1.2). Importantly, however, more than 80 percent of its sales come from B2B customers!

Dell serves each sector of the business market.[6] First, the firm has developed close relationships with large global enterprises, like Boeing, and large corporate customers. These customers purchase thousands of personal computers (PCs) and now turn to Dell for a full range of information technology (IT) products and services. The volume of business coming from a single business customer can be huge: One customer bought 20,000 laptop computers for its global sales organization, and some enterprises have an installed base of more than 100,000 Dell computers. Second, small and medium-sized businesses (SMB) represent a substantial market, and Dell demonstrates special skills in understanding and reaching these customers. SMB firms now represent more than 1 million of Dell's customers in the United States, and this base is growing rapidly around the world. Third, the firm serves the government market at all levels as well as institutional customers like universities and health-care organizations. Across each of its market sectors, a worldwide shift in demand from desktop computers to mobility products, including notebooks, is fueling rapid growth for Dell in India and China as well as in Europe, the Middle East, and Africa.[7] To compensate for the maturing PC business, Dell has also

---

[6] V. Kasturi Rangan and Marie Bell, "Dell—New Horizons," Harvard Business School Case #9–502–022, October 10, 2002 (Boston, MA: Harvard Business School Publishing).

[7] Daniel Workman, "Dell Computer International Sales," *suite101.com*, June 22, 2008, accessed at http://multinationalexpansion.suite101.com/article.cfm/dell_computer_international_sales on June 28, 2008.

B2B TOP PERFORMERS

Jim Ryan, President and Chief Executive Officer, W.W. Grainger, Inc.

W.W. Grainger, Inc. (NYSE: GWW), with sales of $6.5 billion, is the leading broad line supplier of facilities maintenance products serving businesses and institutions throughout North America. Through its network of nearly 600 branches, 18 distribution centers, and multiple Web sites, Grainger helps customers save time and money by providing them with the right products to keep their facilities running.

Jim Ryan was elected to group president of Grainger in 2004, president of Grainger in 2006, chief operating officer in 2007, adding the title of chief executive officer in 2008. Ryan's career at Grainger is testimony to his philosophy that "you prepare to be a leader by deliberately taking on unfamiliar and difficult assignments—those that many shy away from. Challenging assignments are the training ground that provides the highest level of learning, preparing you for leadership at the top levels of large companies." Jim's rise through the ranks of Grainger includes senior assignments in IT, Grainger Parts, Marketing, Sales & Service, and the company's eBusiness. While in IT, Ryan oversaw the implementation of the SAP system and achieved corporate Y2K compliance. Both of these accomplishments reflect Ryan's focus on seeking out challenging undertakings.

Grainger's success is focused on helping its customers reduce the overall acquisition costs for maintenance, repair, and operating (MRO) items. Grainger encourages customers to eliminate their inventories of MRO items and rely on Grainger's responsive distribution systems and expertise to provide these items just when they are needed, reducing the acquisition costs of these indirect materials. Grainger's philosophy is to be "customer intimate," where a customer's and a supplier's (Grainger) processes are fully integrated so that the customer becomes more efficient. Essentially, Grainger seeks to reduce the customer's total costs of acquiring MRO products.

Ryan believes that students preparing to be future leaders of B2B companies can best prepare for that role by developing four skills during their college education: (1) discipline and a strong work ethic; (2) cultivating "people skills"; (3) building analytical skills; and (4) organizational skills. He advises young people to focus on the strong work ethic early in their careers and to accept tough jobs other managers are not interested in tackling. Echoing his own tactics, Ryan advises students that "you learn the critical management skills when you take on those assignments that are unfamiliar and complicated." His accomplishments as a leader of a successful company are testimony to the wisdom of his approach.

SOURCE: Reprinted by permission of Grainger.

expanded the scope of its product offerings to include a broader array of IT products, including servers and data storage for the business market, and a growing list of consumer electronics products, such as flat-screen TVs and Global Positioning Systems (GPS), for the consumer market.

Business Markets versus Consumer-Goods Markets

The basic task of management cuts across both consumer-goods and business marketing. Marketers serving both sectors can benefit by rooting their organizational plan in a *market orientation*, which requires superior proficiency in understanding and satisfying customers.[8] Such market-driven firms demonstrate

- a set of values and beliefs that places the customers' interests first[9];
- the ability to generate, disseminate, and productively use superior information about customers and competitors[10];
- the coordinated use of interfunctional resources (for example, research and development, manufacturing).[11]

Distinctive Capabilities   A close examination of a market-driven firm reveals two particularly important capabilities: market sensing and customer linking.[12] First, the **market-sensing capability** concerns how well the organization is equipped to continuously sense changes in its market and anticipate customer responses to marketing programs. Market-driven firms spot market changes and react well in advance of their competitors (for example, Coca-Cola in the consumer-goods market and 3M in the business market). Second, the **customer-linking capability** comprises the particular skills, abilities, and processes an organization has developed to create and manage close customer relationships.

Consumer-goods firms, such as Procter & Gamble (P&G), demonstrate these capabilities in working with powerful retailers like Wal-Mart. Here, multifunctional teams in both organizations work together by sharing delivery and product-movement information and by jointly planning promotional activity and product changes. Although evident in manufacturer-reseller relations in the consumer-goods market, strong customer-linking capabilities are crucial in the business market, where close buyer-seller relationships prevail. Leading business-to-business firms like IBM and Hewlett-Packard demonstrate distinctive customer-linking skills and Cisco has propelled its legendary record of growth by forging close working relationships with customers and channel partners alike.

Managing Customers as Assets   Marketing expenditures that were once viewed as short-term expenses are now being considered as customer assets that deliver value for the firm and its shareholders.[13] As global competition intensifies, marketing managers are under increasing pressure to demonstrate the return on investment from marketing spending, deliver strong financial performance, and be more accountable to shareholders.[14] To meet these performance standards, firms must develop and

[8]George S. Day, "The Capabilities of Market-Driven Organizations," *Journal of Marketing* 58 (October 1994): pp. 37–52; and Gary F. Gebhardt, Gregory S. Carpenter, and John F. Sherry, Jr., "Creating a Market Orientation: A Longitudinal, Multifirm, Grounded Analysis of Cultural Transformation," *Journal of Marketing* 70 (October 2006): pp. 37–55.

[9]Rohit Deshpande, John U. Farley, and Frederick E. Webster Jr., "Corporate Culture, Customer Orientation, and Innovativeness in Japanese Firms: A Quadrad Analysis," *Journal of Marketing* 57 (January 1993): pp. 23–37.

[10]Ajay K. Kohli and Bernard J. Jaworski, "Market Orientation: The Construct, Research Propositions, and Managerial Implications," *Journal of Marketing* 54 (April 1990): pp. 1–18.

[11]John C. Narver and Stanley F. Slater, "The Effect of a Market Orientation on Business Profitability," *Journal of Marketing* 54 (October 1990): pp. 20–35.

[12]Day, "Capabilities of Market-Driven Organizations," pp. 37–52; and Girish Ramani and V. Kumar, "Interaction Orientation and Firm Performance," *Journal of Marketing* 72 (January 2008): pp. 27–45.

[13]V. Kumar and Werner Reinartz, *Customer Relationship Management* (Hoboken, NJ: John Wiley & Sons, 2006).

[14]Frederick E. Webster, Jr., Alan J. Malter, and Shankar Ganesan, "The Decline and Dispersion of Marketing Competence," *MIT Sloan Management Review* 46 (Summer 2005): pp. 35–43.

B2B TOP PERFORMERS

Career Path for B2B CEOs: For Many, It Began in Marketing!

Executives with a strong background in sales and marketing are taking the top position at leading business marketing firms. Why? Companies now place increased importance on customer relationships. "They've changed their sales strategies to emphasize building long-term partnerships with customers. And they're building profitable businesses on the notion that it's far cheaper to sell to current customers than it is to acquire new ones." Sales and marketing executives understand customers, know the competitive landscape, and have keen insights concerning how to add value to the firm's offerings and to the customer's organization. That is why many firms are tapping sales and marketing executives for the CEO position. Here are three examples:

- Cisco Systems—John Chambers began his career as an IBM salesperson where he learned the importance of listening carefully to customers and delivering on promises.[1]

- Xerox Corporation—Ann Mulcahy spent the majority of her 25 years at the firm in sales positions before being appointed president and CEO.

- GE—In a 20-year career, Jeffrey Immelt held a variety of GE sales and marketing positions before being named to succeed Jack Welch as CEO.

All of these CEOs have taken steps to make their respective organization more customer centered. For example, Jeffrey Immelt's priorities for GE reflect his background in B2B marketing. These are "making sure all the processes work correctly, for example, so deliveries are always on time; ensuring that whatever GE's proposition to the customer is, it will make that customer more money; and increasing the effectiveness of GE's sales force."[2] Looking ahead, he seeks new leaders for growth at GE—people who are passionate about customers and innovation, people who really know markets and products.[3]

---

[1] "Business Biographies: John T. Chambers," http://www.answers.com, accessed on June 29, 2008.

[2] Eilene Zimmerman, "So You Wanna Be a CEO," *Sales & Marketing Management* (January 2002): pp. 31–35.

[3] Patricia O'Connell, "Bringing Innovations to the Home of Six Sigma," *BusinessWeek Online*, August 1, 2005, accessed at http://www.businessweek.com.

---

nurture **customer relationship management capabilities,** which include all the skills required to identify, initiate, develop, and maintain profitable customer relationships.

Marketing Tasks: What Managers Do   To bring the job of business marketing professionals to life, let's examine some of the day-to-day assignments they perform. In customer relationship management, some critical marketing tasks include "identifying and categorizing customer segments; determining a customer's current and potential needs; visiting customers to learn about the uses and applications of individual products; developing and executing the individual components of sales, advertising, promotion, and services programs; assessing price sensitivities; and determining customer response to rivals' current and potential offerings."[15] Research clearly demonstrates that the customer relationship management process has an important impact on a firm's financial performance.

---

[15] Rajendra K. Srivastava, Tasadduq A. Shervauie, and Liam Fahey, "Marketing, Business Processes, and Shareholder Value: An Organizationally Embedded View of Marketing Activities and the Discipline of Marketing," *Journal of Marketing* 63 (Special Issue, 1999): pp. 168–179.

Profit Focus   Developing a firm grasp on the profit impact of marketing strategy actions is fundamental to the job of a business marketing manager. Included here is the need to isolate the forces that drive customer profitability, aligning resources spent on customers to the revenues and profit that will be secured. To this end, Robert S. Kaplan and David P. Norton assert:

> A company that forgets, or never realizes, that it has unprofitable products and customers in the current period will almost surely continue to incur losses in unprofitable products and customers in future periods. Having a clear picture about where the company is making money and losing money should be a vital input to any strategy review.[16]

Partnering for Increased Value   A business marketer becomes a preferred supplier to major customers such as Apple, Texas Instruments, or Procter & Gamble by working closely as a partner, developing an intimate knowledge of the customer's operations, and contributing unique value to that customer's business. Business marketing programs increasingly involve a customized blend of tangible products, service support, and ongoing information services both before and after the sale. Market-driven firms place a high priority on customer-linking capabilities and closely align product decisions—as well as delivery, handling, service, and other supply chain activities—with the customer's operations. For firms like Intel or Boeing to deliver maximum value to their customers, each must receive maximum value from its suppliers. For instance, Intel could not have achieved its commanding global market share without the cost, quality, technology, and other advances its suppliers contribute.[17]

Creating the Customer Value Proposition[18]

Business marketing strategy must be based on an assessment of the company, the competitor, and the customer. A successful strategy focuses on identifying those opportunities in which the firm can deliver superior value to customers based on its distinctive competencies. From this perspective, marketing can be best understood as the process of defining, developing, and delivering value.

Market-driven firms attempt to match their resources, skills, and capabilities with particular customer needs that are not being adequately served. By understanding customer needs, marketing managers can define value from the customer's perspective and convert that information into requirements for creating satisfied customers. In turn, a firm's capabilities and skills determine the degree to which the company can meet these requirements and provide greater value than its competitors.

A business marketing firm's offering includes many technical, economic, service, or social benefits that provide value to customers—but so do the offerings of competitors. So, customers compare the value elements of a firm's offering with those offered

---

[16]Robert S. Kaplan and David P. Norton, *The Execution Premium: Linking Strategy to Operations for Competitive Advantage* (Boston, MA: Harvard Business Press, 2008), p. 258.

[17]Gina Roos, "Intel Corporation: It Takes Quality to Be Preferred by World's Biggest Chipmaker," *Purchasing* 131 (November 15, 2001): pp. 21–22.

[18]James C. Anderson, James A. Narus, and Wouter van Rossum, "Customer Value Propositions in Business Markets," *Harvard Business Review* 84 (March 2006): pp. 91–99.

by the next best alternative.[19] A **customer value proposition** captures the particular set of benefits that a supplier offers to advance the performance of the customer organization. Rather than merely attempting to list more benefits than competitors, "best practice suppliers base their value proposition on the few elements that matter most to target customers, demonstrate the value of this superior performance, and communicate it in a way that conveys a sophisticated understanding of the customer's business priorities."[20] The building blocks of a successful value proposition include:

- *Points of parity*—the value elements with essentially the same performance characteristics as the next best alternative;

- *Points of difference*—the value elements that render the supplier's offering either superior or inferior to the next best alternative.

Value Proposition Illustrated   Sonoco, a global packaging supplier headquartered in South Carolina, approached a large European customer, a producer of consumer goods, about redesigning the packaging for one of its successful product lines. Although the redesigned packaging provided several favorable points of difference relative to the next best alternative, Sonoco executives decided to place special emphasis on one point of parity and two points of difference in the customer value proposition: The redesigned packaging will deliver significantly greater manufacturing efficiency in the customer's fill lines, through higher-speed closing, and provide a distinctive look that customers will find more appealing—all for the same price as the present packaging.

What Matters Most?   A point of parity was included in the value proposition because **key buying influentials** (those who have power in the buying process) within the customer organization would not even consider a packaging redesign if the price increased. The first point of difference in the value proposition (increased efficiency) delivered cost savings, allowing the customer to dramatically streamline its production schedule. The second point of difference (more distinctive customer packaging) enhanced the firm's market position and appeal to its customers, allowing it to realize meaningful growth in its revenues and profit. While the other favorable points of difference were certainly mentioned in discussions with the customer organization, Sonoco executives chose to emphasize those points that mattered most to the customer.

Marketing's Cross-Functional Relationships

Rather than operating in isolation from other functional areas, the successful business marketing manager is an integrator—one who understands manufacturing, research and development (R&D), and customer service and who applies these strengths in developing marketing strategies that respond to customer needs.[21] Close and tightly integrated cross-functional relationships underlie the strategy success stories of firms such as Hewlett-Packard and 3M. As firms adopt leaner and more agile structures and emphasize cross-functional teams, the business marketing manager assumes an important and challenging role in strategy formation.

[19]Wolfgang Ulaga and Andreas Eggert, "Value-Based Differentiation in Business Relationships: Gaining and Sustaining Key Supplier Status," *Journal of Marketing* 70 (January 2006): pp. 119–136.
[20]Anderson, Narus, and van Rossum, "Customer Value Propositions," p. 93.
[21]Michael D. Hutt, "Cross-Functional Working Relationships in Marketing," *Journal of the Academy of Marketing Science* 23 (Fall 1995): pp. 351–357.

FIGURE 1.3 | BUSINESS MARKETING PLANNING: A FUNCTIONALLY INTEGRATED PERSPECTIVE

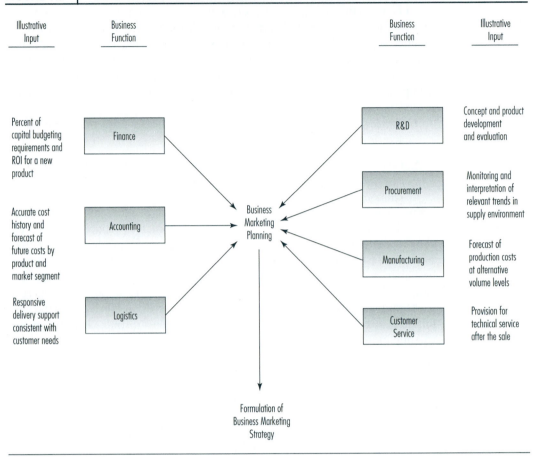

Working Relationships   A day in the life of a business marketing manager centers on building relationships with customers *and* in forging one-to-one relationships with managers in the firm's other functional areas. By building effective cross-functional connections, the marketer is ideally equipped to respond to customers' changing needs.

Business marketing success depends to a large degree on such functional areas in the firm as engineering, R&D, manufacturing, and technical service. Planning in the industrial setting thus requires more functional interdependence and a closer relationship to total corporate strategy than planning in the consumer-goods sector. B. Charles Ames points out that "changes in marketing strategy are more likely to involve capital commitments for new equipment, shifts in development activities, or departures from traditional engineering and manufacturing approaches, any one of which would have companywide implications."[22] All business marketing decisions—product, price, promotion, and distribution—are affected, directly or indirectly, by other functional areas. In turn, marketing considerations influence business decisions in R&D and in manufacturing and procurement, as well as adjustments in the overall corporate strategy. Business marketing planning must be coordinated and synchronized with corresponding planning efforts in R&D, procurement, finance, production, and other areas (Figure 1.3).

---

[22] B. Charles Ames, "Trappings vs. Substance in Industrial Marketing," *Harvard Business Review* 48 (July–August 1976): pp. 95–96.

Characteristics of Business Markets

Business marketing and consumer-goods marketing are different. A common body of knowledge, principles, and theory applies to both consumer and business marketing, but because their buyers and markets function quite differently, they merit separate attention. Consumer and business marketing differ in the nature of markets, market demand, buyer behavior, buyer-seller relationships, environmental influences (economic, political, legal), and market strategy. Yet, the potential payoffs are high for the firm that can successfully penetrate the business market. The nature of the demand for industrial products poses unique challenges—and opportunities—for the marketing manager.

Derived Demand   **Derived demand** refers to the direct link between the demand for an industrial product and the demand for consumer products: *The demand for industrial products is derived from the ultimate demand for consumer products.* Consider the materials and components used in a Harley-Davidson motorcycle. Harley-Davidson manufactures some of the components, but the finished product reflects the efforts of more than 200 suppliers or business marketers who deal directly with the firm. In purchasing a Harley-Davidson motorcycle, the customer is stimulating the demand for a diverse array of products manufactured by business marketing firms—such as tires, electrical components, coil springs, aluminum castings, and other items.

Fluctuating Demand   Because demand is derived, the business marketer must carefully monitor demand patterns and changing buying preferences in the household consumer market, often on a worldwide basis. For example, a decline in mortgage rates can spark an increase in new home construction and a corresponding increase in appliance sales. Retailers generally respond by increasing their stock of inventory. As appliance producers like Maytag increase the rate of production to meet the demand, business marketers that supply these manufacturers with items such as motors, timers, or paint experience a surge in sales. A downturn in the economy creates the opposite result. This explains why the demand for many industrial products tends to *fluctuate* more than the demand for consumer products.

Stimulating Demand   Some business marketers must not only monitor final consumer markets but also develop a marketing program that reaches the ultimate consumer directly. Aluminum producers use television and magazine ads to point out the convenience and recycling opportunities that aluminum containers offer to the consumer—the ultimate consumer influences aluminum demand by purchasing soft drinks in aluminum, rather than plastic, containers. More than 4 billion pounds of aluminum are used annually in the production of beverage containers. Similarly, Boeing promotes the convenience of air travel in a media campaign targeted to the consumer market to create a favorable environment for longer-term demand for its planes; DuPont advertises to ultimate consumers to stimulate the sales of carpeting, which incorporates their product.

Price Sensitivity   **Demand elasticity** refers to the responsiveness of the quantity demanded to a change in price. Demand is elastic when a given percentage change in price brings about an even larger percentage change in the quantity demanded. Inelasticity results when demand is insensitive to price—that is, when the percentage change in demand is less than the percentage change in price. Consider the demand for electronic components that is stimulated by companies making electronic games.

As long as final consumers continue to purchase and upgrade these games and are generally insensitive to price, manufacturers of the equipment are relatively insensitive to the price of electronic components. At the opposite end of the spectrum, if consumers are price sensitive when purchasing soup and other canned grocery products, manufacturers of soup will be price sensitive when purchasing metal cans. Thus, the derived demand indicates that the demand for metal cans is price elastic.

Final consumer demand has a pervasive impact on the demand for products in the business market. By being sensitive to trends in the consumer market, the business marketer can often identify both impending problems and opportunities for growth and diversification.

A Global Market Perspective   A complete picture of the business market must include a horizon that stretches beyond the boundaries of the United States. The demand for many industrial goods and services is growing more rapidly in many foreign countries than in the United States. Countries like Germany, Japan, Korea, and Brazil offer large and growing markets for many business marketers. In turn, China and India represent economies with exploding levels of growth. Countless small firms and many large ones—such as GE, 3M, Intel, Boeing, Dow Chemical, Caterpillar, and Motorola—derive a significant portion of their sales and profits from international markets. For example, China plans to invest more than $300 billion over the next few years in the country's infrastructure, representing an enormous market opportunity for all of GE's industrial businesses, including power generation, health care, and infrastructure (for example, water purification). For cell phone makers such as Motorola, China already represents a fiercely competitive market and features the world's largest base of subscribers—well over 500 million.[23]

Global Challengers   From China's Lenovo (computers) and Baosteel to Brazil's Embraer (light jets) and Petrobras (petroleum) and from India's Infosys Technologies (IT services) to Mexico's Cemex (building materials), a whole host of formidable rivals are emerging. The Boston Consulting Group (BCG) identified the 100 largest, most successful, and most influential firms that have achieved prominence in their rapidly developing markets and beyond.[24] The resulting BCG Challenger 100 list includes firms from 14 countries, including 41 firms from China, 13 from Brazil, 7 from Mexico, and 6 from Russia. Interestingly, 34 provide industrial goods. Total revenue for the BCG 100 is growing over 30 percent a year and profit margins exceed those of large multinational firms in the United States, Japan, and Germany. Business-to-business firms must act decisively, compete aggressively, and seize market opportunities in rapidly developing global economies.

Business and Consumer Marketing: A Contrast

Many consumer-goods companies with a strong reputation in the consumer market decide to capitalize on opportunities they perceive in the business market. The move is often prompted by a maturing product line, a desire to diversify operations, or the strategic

---

[23] Pete Engardio, "A New World Economy," *Business Week*, August 22/29, 2005, pp. 52–58.

[24] Harold L. Sirkin, James W. Hemerling, and Arindam K. Bhattacharya, *Globality: Competing with Everyone from Everywhere for Everything* (New York: Business Plus, 2008), pp. 23–24.

opportunity to profitably apply R&D or production strength in a rapidly growing business market. P&G, departing from its packaged consumer-goods tradition, is using its expertise in oils, fats, and pulps to diversify into fast-growing industries.

The J. M. Smucker Company operates successfully in both the consumer and the business markets. Smucker, drawing on its consumer product base (jellies and preserves), produces filling mixes used by manufacturers of yogurt and dessert items. Marketing strawberry preserves to ultimate consumers differs significantly from marketing a strawberry filling to a yogurt manufacturer. Key differences are highlighted in the following illustration.

Smucker: A Consumer and Business Marketer

Smucker reaches the consumer market with a line of products sold through retail outlets. New products are carefully developed, tested, targeted, priced, and promoted for particular market segments. To secure distribution, the firm employs food brokers who call on both wholesale- and retail-buying units. The company's own sales force reaches selected larger accounts. Achieving a desired degree of market exposure and shelf space in key retail food outlets is essential to any marketer of consumer food products. Promotional plans for the line include media advertising, coupons, special offers, and incentives for retailers. Pricing decisions must reflect the nature of demand, costs, and the behavior of competitors. In sum, the marketer must manage each component of the marketing mix: product, price, promotion, and distribution.

The marketing mix takes on a different form in the business market. Attention centers on manufacturers that potentially could use Smucker products to produce other goods; the Smucker product will lose its identity as it is blended into yogurt, cakes, or cookies. Once Smucker has listed all the potential users of its product (for example, large food processors, bakeries, yogurt producers), the business marketing manager attempts to identify meaningful market segments that Smucker can profitably serve. A specific marketing strategy is developed for each market segment.

When a potential organizational consumer is identified, the company's sales force calls directly on the account. The salesperson may begin by contacting a company president but, at first, generally spends a great deal of time with the R&D director or the product-development group leader. The salesperson is thus challenged to identify the **key buying influentials**—those who have power in the buying process. Senior-level Smucker executives may also assist in the selling process.

Armed with product specifications (for example, desired taste, color, calories), the salesperson returns to the Smucker R&D department to develop samples. Several months may pass before a mixture is finally approved. Next, attention turns to price, and the salesperson's contact point shifts to the purchasing department. Because large quantities (truckloads or drums rather than jars) are involved, a few cents per pound can be significant to both parties. Quality and service are also vitally important.

Once a transaction is culminated, the product is shipped directly from the Smucker warehouse to the manufacturer's plant. The salesperson follows up frequently with the purchasing agent, the plant manager, and other executives. Product movement and delivery information is openly shared, and close working relationships develop between managers at Smucker and key decision makers in the buying organization. How much business can Smucker expect from this account? The performance of the new consumer product in the marketplace determines this: The demand for industrial goods is, as noted, derived from ultimate consumer demand. Note also the importance of (1) developing a close and continuing working relationship with business market customers and (2) understanding the requirements of the total range of buying influentials in the target company.

Distinguishing Characteristics

The Smucker illustration spotlights some of the features that differentiate business marketing strategy from consumer-goods marketing strategy. The business marketer emphasizes personal selling rather than advertising (TV, newspaper) to reach potential buyers. Only a small portion of the business marketer's promotional budget is likely to be invested in advertising, most commonly through trade journals or direct mail. This advertising, however, often establishes the foundation for a successful sales call. The industrial salesperson must understand the technical aspects of the organization's requirements and how those requirements can be satisfied, as well as know who influences the buying decision and why.

The business marketer's product also includes an important service component. The organizational consumer evaluates the quality of the physical product and the quality of the attached services. Attention centers on the total package of benefits the consumer receives. Price negotiation is frequently an important part of the industrial buying/selling process. Products made to particular quality or design specifications must be individually priced. Business marketers generally find that direct distribution to larger customers strengthens relationships between buyer and seller. Smaller accounts can be profitably served through intermediaries—manufacturers' representatives or industrial distributors.

As the Smucker example illustrates, business marketing strategies differ from consumer-goods marketing strategies in the relative emphasis given to certain elements of the marketing mix. It is important to note that the example also highlights fundamental differences between the buyers in each market. In an organization, a variety of individuals influence the purchase decision. Several major questions confront Smucker's business marketing manager: Who are key participants in the purchasing process? What is their relative importance? What criteria does each apply to the decision? Thus, the business marketer must understand the *process* an organization follows in purchasing a product and identify which organizational members have roles in this process. Depending on the complexity of the purchase, this process may span many weeks or months and may involve the participation of several organization members. The business marketer who becomes involved in the purchase process early may have the greatest chance for success.

A Relationship Emphasis

Relationships in the business market are often close and enduring. Rather than constituting the end result, a sale signals the beginning of a relationship. By convincing a large food processor such as General Foods to use its product, Smucker initiates a potential long-term business relationship. More than ringing up a sale, Smucker creates a customer! To maintain that relationship, the business marketer must develop an intimate knowledge of the customer's operations and contribute unique value to its business. **Relationship marketing** centers on all marketing activities directed toward establishing, developing, and maintaining successful exchanges with customers.[25]

---

[25] Robert M. Morgan and Shelby D. Hunt, "The Commitment-Trust Theory of Relationship Marketing," *Journal of Marketing* 58 (July 1994): pp. 20–38.

FIGURE 1.4 | **CHARACTERISTICS OF BUSINESS MARKET CUSTOMERS**

Characteristic	Example
• Business market customers are comprised of commercial enterprises, institutions, and governments.	• Among Dell's customers are Boeing, Arizona State University, and numerous state and local government units.
• A single purchase by a business customer is far larger than that of an individual consumer.	• An individual may buy one unit of a software package upgrade from Microsoft while Citigroup purchases 10,000.
• The demand for industrial products is derived from the ultimate demand for consumer products.	• New home purchases stimulate the demand for carpeting, appliances, cabinets, lumber, and a wealth of other products.
• Relationships between business marketers tend to be close and enduring.	• IBM's relationship with some key customers spans decades.
• Buying decisions by business customers often involve multiple buying influences, rather than a single decision maker.	• A cross-functional team at Procter & Gamble (P&G) evaluates alternative laptop personal computers and selects Hewlett-Packard.
• While serving different types of customers, business marketers and consumer-goods marketers share the same job titles.	• Job titles include marketing manager, product manager, sales manager, account manager.

Building one-to-one relationships with customers is the heart of business marketing. Figure 1.4 provides a recap of key characteristics of business market customers.

The Supply Chain

Figure 1.5 further illuminates the importance of a relationship perspective in business marketing by considering the chain of suppliers involved in the creation of an automobile. Consider Honda Motor Company. At its Marysville, Ohio, auto assembly plant, Honda introduced many new concepts to the U.S. auto industry, including just-in-time parts delivery and a high level of flexible model construction. For instance, the Ohio plant can readily shift from the Acura TL luxury sedan to the Accord, based on customer demand.[26] A new small-car plant in Indiana gives Honda further capacity to make Civic- and Accord-size vehicles—fuel-efficient models particularly coveted by auto buyers as gas prices increase. Across its seven plants in North America, Honda annually purchases more than $17 billion of parts and materials from U.S. suppliers.[27]

The relationships between the auto producers and their suppliers fall squarely into the business marketing domain. Similarly, business marketers such as TRW rely on a

---

[26]Tom Krisher, "Honda Grows While U.S. Auto Industry Falters," accessed at http://biz.yahoo.com on July 2, 2008.

[27]"Honda's First U.S. Auto Plant Celebrates 25 Years of Production," November 1, 2007, accessed at http://www.world.honda.com on July 2, 2008.

FIGURE 1.5 | **THE SUPPLY CHAIN**

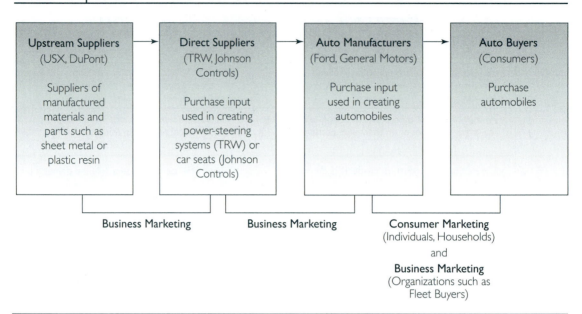

Upstream Suppliers (USX, DuPont)	Direct Suppliers (TRW, Johnson Controls)	Auto Manufacturers (Ford, General Motors)	Auto Buyers (Consumers)
Suppliers of manufactured materials and parts such as sheet metal or plastic resin	Purchase input used in creating power-steering systems (TRW) or car seats (Johnson Controls)	Purchase input used in creating automobiles	Purchase automobiles

Business Marketing   Business Marketing   Consumer Marketing
                                                    (Individuals, Households)
                                                            and
                                                    Business Marketing
                                                    (Organizations such as
                                                        Fleet Buyers)

whole host of others farther back on the supply chain for raw materials, components, and other support. Each organization in this chain is involved in the creation of a product, marketing processes (including delivery), and support and service after the sale. In performing these value-creating activities, each also affects the quality level of the Honda product. Michael Porter and Victor Millar observe that "to gain competitive advantage over its rivals, a company must either perform these activities at a lower cost or perform them in a way that leads to differentiation and a premium price (more value)."[28]

Supply Chain Management

Supply chain management is a technique for linking a manufacturer's operations with those of all of its strategic suppliers and its key intermediaries and customers to enhance efficiency and effectiveness. The Internet allows members of the supply chain all over the world to exchange timely information, exchange engineering drawings during new product development, and synchronize production and delivery schedules. The goal of supply chain strategy is to improve the speed, precision, and efficiency of manufacturing through strong supplier relationships. This goal is achieved through information sharing, joint planning, shared technology, and shared benefits. If the business marketer can become a valued partner in a customer's supply chain, the rewards are substantial: The focus shifts from price to value and from products to solutions.[29] To achieve these results, the business marketing firm must

---

[28]Michael E. Porter and Victor E. Millar, "How Information Gives You Competitive Advantage," *Harvard Business Review* 63 (July–August 1985): pp. 149–160; see also Michael E. Porter, *Competitive Advantage* (New York: The Free Press, 1985).

[29]Marc Bourde, Charlie Hawker, and Theo Theocharides, "Taking Center Stage: The 2005 Chief Procurement Officer Survey" (Sommers, NY: IBM Global Services, 2005), pp. 1–13, accessed at http://www.ibm.com on July 15, 2005.

demonstrate the ability to meet the customer's precise quality, delivery, service, and information requirements.

Managing Relationships in the Supply Chain

Customers in the business market place a premium on the business marketer's supply chain management capabilities. IBM spends 85 percent of its purchasing dollars with 50 suppliers.[30] Of particular importance to IBM is the quality of engineering support it receives from suppliers. IBM actively seeks supplier partners that will contribute fresh ideas, responsive service, and leading-edge technology to attract buyers of future IBM products.

Similarly, Toyota excels at creating and sustaining supplier relationships. In fact, executives across industries want to emulate Toyota's success in creating a base of suppliers who are unshakably loyal, committed to continuous improvement, and drive superior financial performance. Malte Kalkoffen and colleagues at the Boston Consulting Group undertook a broad study to uncover the factors that set Toyota apart from the rest of the industry.[31] The results reveal valuable insights into the strategy path a business marketing manager can follow to develop and sustain a long-term relationship with a world-class customer like Toyota.

How Toyota Builds Distinctive Supplier Relationships   Suppliers consistently rank Toyota as the preferred customer among the auto manufacturers. Why? "Toyota allows them acceptable returns on their investments, is reliable in honoring its contract price agreements, supports suppliers in improving their operations, and provides an equitable split of any cost reductions they achieve. The fundamental principle . . . is simple but profound: treat all suppliers fairly."[32]

Three other principles guide Toyota's approach to supplier relations:

1. The company imposes stringent selection criteria to ensure that every supplier meets Toyota's requirements in terms of cost, quality, and technology. Importantly, Toyota will select only those suppliers that are willing to establish long-term partnerships with the company.

2. The company retains critical new product development (NPD) and design knowledge in-house but uses a streamlined NPD process that features frequent interactions with suppliers to leverage their expertise and increase productivity for Toyota and suppliers alike.

3. Once an ongoing relationship with a supplier has been established, Toyota takes responsibility for helping that supplier firm to develop its capabilities and grow its business. For example, Toyota monitors the performance of its suppliers to an extensive degree, insisting that senior executives of each supplier organization be responsible for quality and performance outcomes. In turn, Toyota performs semiannual quality audits and provides consulting assistance and access to knowledge-sharing networks to enhance its suppliers' capabilities.

---

[30]James Carbone, "Reinventing Purchasing Wins Medal for Big Blue," *Purchasing* 129 (September 16, 1999): pp. 45–46.

[31]The following discussion is based on: Malte Kalkoffen, Zafar Momin, Xavier Mosquet, Jagjit Singh, and George Sticher, "Getting to Win-Win: How Toyota Creates and Sustains Best-Practice Supplier Relationships," The Boston Consulting Group, Inc., September 2007, pp. 1–10, accessed at http://www.bcg.com on May 25, 2008.

[32]Ibid., p. 1.

FIGURE 1.6 | SUPPLIERS' PHILOSOPHY MUST FIT WITH TOYOTA'S

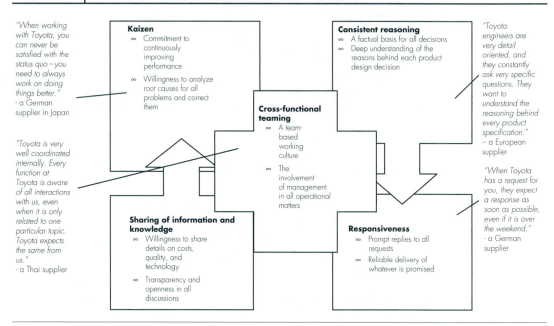

Winning with Toyota   Toyota seeks those suppliers that can provide industry leadership on cost, quality, and technology. Likewise, potential suppliers must demonstrate a willingness to pursue a long-term partnership, and the philosophy that guides the supplier firm must be aligned with Toyota's culture. In evaluating a supplier's philosophical fit, five specific elements are explored: Kaizen (or continuous improvement), consistent reasoning, cross-functional teaming, sharing of information and knowledge, and responsiveness (see Figure 1.6). The selection process is based on Toyota's belief that long-term relationships with familiar suppliers reduces transaction costs and creates more value than short-term ones.

Developing and nurturing close, long-term relationships with customers is an important goal for the business marketer. Built on trust and demonstrated performance, these partnerships require open lines of communication between multiple layers of the buying and selling organizations. Quotes from business marketing executives who count Toyota as a strategic partner (customer), illustrate the nature of long-term relationships:[33]

> "Toyota is tough as hell in negotiations, and we have to share every detail of our data with them—but they are fair, and they know that if we don't make money, we can't innovate for them."

> "Toyota helped us dramatically improve our production system. We started by making one component, and as we improved, Toyota rewarded us with orders for more components. Toyota is our best customer."

---

[33] Ibid., p. 8.

Commercial Enterprises as Consumers

Business market customers, as noted at the outset of the chapter, can be broadly classified into three categories: (1) commercial enterprises, (2) governmental organizations, and (3) institutions. Each is explored in Chapter 2. However, the supply chain concept provides a solid foundation for describing the commercial customers that constitute the business market. Commercial enterprises can be divided into three categories: (1) users, (2) original equipment manufacturers (OEMs), and (3) dealers and distributors.

Users   Users purchase industrial products or services to produce other goods or services that are, in turn, sold in the business or consumer markets. User customers purchase goods—such as computers, photocopiers, or automated manufacturing systems—to set up or support the manufacturing process. When purchasing machine tools from GE, an auto manufacturer is a user. These machine tools do not become part of the automobile but instead help to produce it.

Original Equipment Manufacturers (OEMs)   The OEM purchases industrial goods to incorporate into other products it sells in the business or ultimate consumer market. For example, Intel Corporation produces the microprocessors that constitute the heart of Dell's personal computer. In purchasing these microprocessors, Dell is an OEM. Likewise, Apple is an OEM in purchasing a touch-screen controller from Broadcom Corp.—about \$4 to \$5 of content in every iPhone.[34]

Dealers and Distributors   Dealers and distributors include commercial enterprises that purchase industrial goods for resale (in basically the same form) to users and OEMs. The distributor accumulates, stores, and sells a large assortment of goods to industrial users, assuming title to the goods it purchases. Handling billions of dollars worth of transactions each year, industrial distributors are growing in size and sophistication. The strategic role assumed by distributors in the business market is examined in detail in Chapter 11 (Channels).

Overlap of Categories   The three categories of commercial enterprises are not mutually exclusive. Their classification is based on the intended purpose the product serves for the customer. Ford is a user when purchasing a machine tool for the manufacturing process, but the same company is an OEM when purchasing radios to be installed in the ultimate consumer product.

A marketer must have a good understanding of the diverse organizational consumers that make up the business market. Properly classifying commercial customers as users, OEMs, or dealers or distributors is an important first step to a sharpened understanding of the buying criteria that a particular commercial customer uses in evaluating an industrial product.

Understanding Buying Motivations   Consider the different types of commercial customers that purchase a particular industrial product such as electrical timing mechanisms. Each class of customer views the product differently because each purchases the product for a different reason.

---

[34]Eric J. Savitz, "Battle for Smartphone Market Share Pressures Margins," *Barron's*, June 30, 2008, p. 37.

INSIDE BUSINESS MARKETING

The iPhone: A Triumph of Supply Chain Management Too[1]

Creating an immediate buzz among consumers around the world, Apple's iPhone was judged a triumph of design and flexibility, not to mention a cool, must-have product, before the first unit was sold. However, "a killer product is only successful if it gets to the right customer at the right price at the right time."[2] Many firms fail to reap the rewards of product innovation because they stumble on quality or fail to meet demand, disappointing loyal customers. In addition to demonstrating superior capabilities in new product development and marketing strategy execution, Apple excels at supply chain management.

In its annual Supply Chain Top 25, AMR Research awarded Apple the number-one ranking among a formidable set of top-performing firms, such as Nokia, IBM, Procter & Gamble, Cisco, and Nike. The AMR Research report notes that the leading-edge performance of Apple "signifies an epic shift away from the 20th Century production-efficiency mentality to a new era based on ideas, design, and content. The iPhone maker took the top spot due to a sophisticated mix of brilliant industrial design, transcendent software interfaces, and consumable goods that are entirely digital." This approach provides financial benefits in the form of extremely high inventory turns, minimal material or capacity limitations, and excellent profit margins. By forecasting demand accurately and synchronizing communication across the supply chain, Apple met the demands of its rabid fan base.

[1] Unless otherwise noted, this discussion is based on Thomas Wailgum, "Study: Apple, Nokia, Dell Top Among Global Supply Chains," *CIO*, May 29, 2008, accessed at http://www.cio .com on July 4, 2008.

[2] Bob Trebilcock, "Supply Chain Lessons from iPhone," *Modern Materials Handling*, July 27, 2007, accessed at http://www.mmh .com on July 4, 2008.

A food-processing firm such as Pillsbury buys electrical timers for use in a high-speed canning system. For this customer, quality, reliability, and prompt and predictable delivery are critical. Whirlpool, an OEM that incorporates the industrial product directly into consumer appliances, is concerned with the effect of the timers on the quality and dependability of the final consumer product. Because the timers are needed in large quantities, the appliance manufacturer is also concerned about the producer's production capacity and delivery reliability. Finally, an industrial distributor is most interested in matching the capability of the timing mechanisms to the needs of customers (users and OEMs) in a specific geographical market.

Classifying Goods for the Business Market[35]

Having classified business market customers, we must now ask what type of goods they require, and how each type is marketed. One useful method of classifying industrial goods is to ask the following questions: How does the industrial good or service enter the production process, and how does it enter the cost structure of the firm? The answer enables the marketer to identify those who are influential in the organizational buying process and to understand how to design an effective business marketing strategy. In general, industrial goods can be divided into three broad categories: entering goods, foundation goods, and facilitating goods (Figure 1.7).

[35] Data on the dollar purchases of particular products by selected customers are drawn from Anne Millen Porter and Elena Epatko Murphy, "Hey Big Spender . . . The 100 Largest Industrial Buyers," *Purchasing* (November 9, 1995): pp. 31–42.

FIGURE 1.7 | CLASSIFYING GOODS FOR THE BUSINESS MARKET

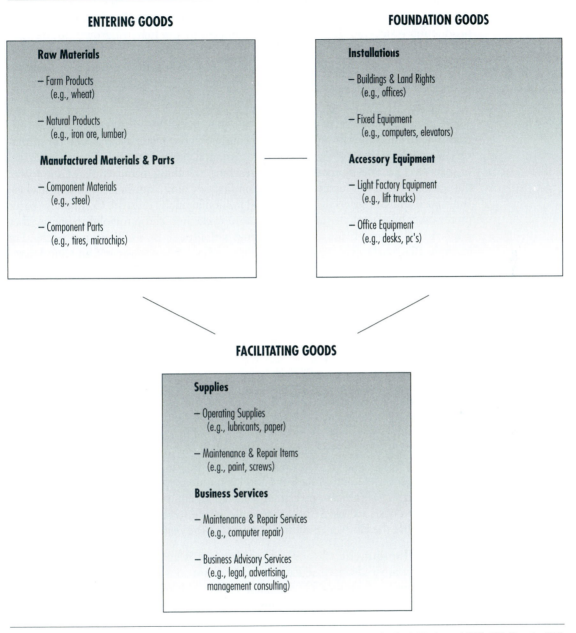

SOURCE: Adapted from Philip Kotler, Marketing Management: Analysis, Planning, and Control, 4th ed. (Englewood Cliffs, N.J.: Prentice-Hall, 1980), p. 172, with permission of Prentice-Hall, Inc.

Entering Goods

Entering goods become part of the finished product. This category of goods consists of raw materials and manufactured materials and parts. Their cost is an expense item assigned to the manufacturing process.

Raw Materials　Observe in Figure 1.7 that **raw materials** include both farm products and natural products. Raw materials are processed only to the level required for economical handling and transport; they basically enter the buying organization's production process in their natural state. Fueled by the massive growth in the Chinese economy, Freeport-McMoRan Copper & Gold Inc., the copper producer, has seen demand surge. McDonald's uses more than 700 million pounds of potatoes each year and dictates the fortunes of many farmers in that agricultural segment. In fact, when attempting to introduce a raspberry sorbet, McDonald's found, to its surprise, that not enough raspberries were being grown![36]

Manufactured Materials and Parts　In contrast to raw materials, **manufactured materials and parts** undergo more initial processing. Component materials such as textiles or sheet steel have been processed before reaching a clothing manufacturer or automaker but must be processed further before becoming part of the finished consumer product. Both Ford and GE spend more than $900 million annually on steel. Component parts, on the other hand, include small motors, motorcycle tires, and automobile batteries; they can be installed directly into another product with little or no additional processing. For example, Black & Decker spends $100 million each year on plastic parts, and Sun Microsystems spends more than $200 million on displays and monitors.

Foundation Goods

The distinguishing characteristic of foundation goods is that they are capital items. As capital goods are used up or worn out, a portion of their original cost is assigned to the production process as a depreciation expense. Foundation goods include installations and accessory equipment.

Installations　**Installations** include the major long-term investment items that underlie the manufacturing process, such as buildings, land rights, and fixed equipment. Large computers and machine tools are examples of fixed equipment. The demand for installations is shaped by the economic climate (for example, favorable interest rates) but is driven by the market outlook for a firm's products. In the face of strong worldwide demand for its microprocessors, Intel is building new plants, expanding existing ones, and making significant investments in capital equipment. A typical semiconductor chip plant costs at least $3 billion to build, equipment accounting for $600 million of the cost and the land and building account for the rest.[37]

Accessory Equipment　**Accessory equipment** is generally less expensive and is short-lived compared with installations, and it is not considered part of the fixed plant. This equipment can be found in the plant as well as in the office. Portable drills, personal computers, and fax machines illustrate this category.

Facilitating Goods

Facilitating goods are the supplies and services (see Figure 1.7) that support organizational operations. Because these goods do not enter the production process or become part of the finished product, their costs are handled as expense items.

---

[36]James Brian Quinn, Intelligent Enterprise: A Knowledge and Service Based Paradigm for Industry (New York: The Free Press, 1992), p. 20.

[37]Dean Takahashi, "Makers of Chip Equipment Beginning to Share the Pain," *The Wall Street Journal*, August 14, 1996, p. B6.

Supplies Virtually every organization requires operating supplies, such as printer cartridges, paper, or business forms, and maintenance and repair items, such as paint and cleaning materials. These items generally reach a broad cross-section of industrial users. In fact, they are very similar to the kinds of supplies that consumers might purchase at a hardware or discount store.

For example, along with products specifically designed for commercial use, Procter & Gamble (P&G) sells adaptations of its well-known consumer products in its professional division.[38] Targeting the business market, customers here include hotels, fast-food restaurants, retailers, and health-care organizations. P&G senses a huge market opportunity—the U.S. market for janitorial and housekeeping cleaning products exceeds $3.2 billion annually.

Services Says analyst James Brian Quinn, "As the service sector has grown to embrace 80 percent of all U.S. employment, specialized service firms have become very large and sophisticated relative to the scale and expertise that individual staff and service groups have within integrated companies."[39] To capture the skills of these specialists and to direct attention to what they do best, many firms are shifting or "outsourcing" selected service functions to outside suppliers. This opens up opportunities for firms that provide such services as computer support, payroll processing, logistics, food operations, and equipment maintenance. These specialists possess a level of expertise or efficiency that organizations can profitably tap. For example, Cisco Systems turned to FedEx to coordinate the movement of parts through its supply chain and on to the customer. By merging the parts shipments in transit for a single customer, the desired product can be assembled at the customer's location, never spending a moment in a Cisco warehouse.[40] Business services include **maintenance and repair support** (for example, machine repair) and **advisory support** (for example, management consulting or information management). Like supplies, services are considered expense items.

Moreover, the explosive growth of the Internet has increased the demand for a range of electronic commerce services, from Web site design to the complete hosting of an e-commerce site. The Internet also provides a powerful new channel for delivering technical support, customer training, and advertising. For example, Intel is shifting over half of its advertising budget to online media and is asking its partners in the "Intel Inside" cooperative ad campaign, like Sony, to increase spending on online media.[41] In turn, the Internet provides the opportunity to manage a particular activity or function from a remote, or even offshore, location. To illustrate, IBM manages the procurement functions for United Technologies Corporation via the Web.[42]

---

[38] Ellen Byron, "Aiming to Clean Up, P&G Courts Business Customers," *The Wall Street Journal*, January 26, 2007, pp. B1–B2.

[39] James Brian Quinn, "Strategic Outsourcing: Leveraging Knowledge Capabilities," *Sloan Management Review* 40 (Summer 1999): p. 9; see also, Mark Gottfredson, Rudy Puryear, and Stephen Phillips, "Strategic Sourcing: From Periphery to Core," *Harvard Business Review* 83 (February 2005): pp. 132–139.

[40] Douglas A. Blackman, "Overnight, Everything Changed for FedEx: Can It Reinvent Itself?" *The Wall Street Journal*, November 4, 1999, pp. A1, A16.

[41] Stuart Elliot, "As Customers Flock to the Web, Intel Gives Chase with Its Ad Budget," *The New York Times*, October 10, 2007, p. C9.

[42] Ira Sager, "Inside IBM: Internet Business Machines," *Business Week E.Biz*, December 13, 1999, pp. ED21–23.

Business Marketing Strategy

Marketing pattern differences reveal the significance of a goods classification system. A marketing strategy appropriate for one category of goods may be entirely unsuitable for another. Often, entirely different promotional, pricing, and distribution strategies are required. The physical nature of the industrial good and its intended use by the organizational customer dictate to an important degree the marketing program's requirements. Some strategy highlights follow.

Illustration: Manufactured Materials and Parts

Recall that manufactured materials and parts enter the buying organization's own product. Whether a part is standardized or customized often dictates the nature of marketing strategy. For custom-made parts, personal selling and customer relationship management activities assume an important role in marketing strategy. The value proposition centers on providing a product that advances the customer's competitive position. The business marketer must also demonstrate strong supply chain capabilities. Standardized parts are typically purchased in larger quantities on a contractual basis, and the marketing strategy centers on providing a competitive price, reliable delivery, and supporting services. Frequently, industrial distributors are used to provide responsive delivery service to smaller accounts.

For manufactured materials and parts, the marketer's challenge is to locate and accurately define the unique needs of diverse customers, uncover key buying influentials, and create solutions to serve these customers profitably.

Illustration: Installations

Installations such as fixed equipment were classified earlier as foundation goods because they are capital assets that affect the buyer's scale of operations. Here the product or technology itself, along with the service capabilities of the firm, are the central factors in marketing strategy, and direct manufacturer-to-user channels of distribution are the norm. Less costly, more standardized installations such as a drill press may be sold through marketing intermediaries.

Once again, personal selling or account management is the dominant promotional tool. The salesperson or account team works closely with prospective organizational buyers. Negotiations can span several months and involve the top executives in the buying organization, especially for buildings or custom-made equipment. Customer buying motives center on economic factors (such as the projected performance of the capital asset) and emotional factors (such as industry leadership). A buyer may be quite willing to select a higher-priced installation if the projected return on investment supports the decision. The focal points for the marketing of installations include a strong customer relationship management effort, effective engineering and product design support, and the ability to offer a product or technology solution that provides a higher return on investment than its competition. Initial price, distribution, and advertising play lesser roles.

Illustration: Supplies

The final illustration centers on a facilitating good: supplies. Again we find different marketing patterns. Most supply items reach a broad market of organizational customers from many different industries. Although some large users are serviced directly, a wide variety of marketing intermediaries are required to cover this broad and diverse market adequately.

The goal of the business marketer is to secure a place on the purchasing function's list of preferred or preapproved suppliers. Importantly, many firms are adopting e-procurement systems to dramatically streamline the process employees follow in buying supplies and other operating resources. From the desktop, an employee simply logs on to the system, selects the needed items from an electronic catalog of suppliers the purchasing function has preapproved, and sends the order directly to the supplier.

For supplies, the marketer's promotional mix includes catalog listings, advertising, and, to a lesser extent, personal selling. Advertising is directed to resellers (industrial distributors) and final users. Personal selling is less important for supplies than it is for other categories of goods with a high unit value, such as installations. Thus, personal selling efforts may be confined to resellers and large users of supplies. Price may be critical in the marketing strategy because many supply items are undifferentiated. However, customized service strategies might be designed to differentiate a firm's offerings from those of competitors. By providing the right product assortment, timely and reliable delivery, and customized services, the business marketer may be able to provide distinctive value to the customer and develop a long-term, profitable relationship.

A Look Ahead

Figure 1.8 shows the chief components of the business marketing management process. Business marketing strategy is formulated within the boundaries established by the corporate mission and objectives. A corporation determining its mission must define its business and purpose, assess environmental trends, and evaluate its strengths and weaknesses. Building e-commerce capabilities and transforming these capabilities into offerings that provide superior customer value constitute vital corporate objectives at leading organizations like GE. Corporate objectives provide guidelines for forming specific marketing objectives. Business marketing planning must be coordinated and synchronized with corresponding planning efforts in R&D, procurement, finance, production, customer service, and other areas. Clearly, strategic plans emerge out of a bargaining process among functional areas. Managing conflict, promoting cooperation, and developing coordinated strategies are all fundamental to the business marketer's interdisciplinary role.

The business marketing management framework (see Figure 1.8) provides an overview of the five major parts of the text. This chapter introduced some of the features that distinguish industrial from consumer-goods marketing; the next chapter explores the major types of customers that make up the business market: commercial enterprises, governmental units, and institutions. Each sector represents a sizable market opportunity, presents special characteristics and needs, and requires a unique marketing strategy response.

Part II examines the organizational buying process and the myriad forces that affect the organizational decision maker. Occupying a central position in Part II is customer relationship management—a managerial process that leading firms in business-to-business marketing have mastered. Here special attention is given to

FIGURE 1.8 | **A FRAMEWORK FOR BUSINESS MARKETING MANAGEMENT**

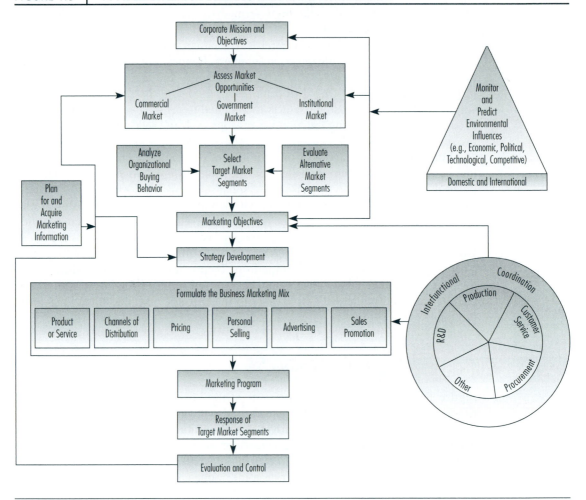

the specific strategies that business marketers can follow in developing profitable relationships with customers. Part III turns to the selection of target segments and specific techniques for measuring the response of these segments. Part IV centers on designing market-driven strategies. Each component of the marketing mix is treated from the business marketing perspective. Special attention is given to creating and managing offerings and managing connections, including treatment of e-commerce and supply chain strategies. Particular emphasis is also given to defining value from the customer's perspective and developing responsive pricing, advertising, and personal selling strategies to deliver that value proposition to target segments.

The processes of implementing, monitoring, and controlling the marketing program are analyzed in Part V. A central theme is how business marketing managers can enhance profitability by maximizing the return on marketing strategy expenditures.

Summary

The business market offers significant opportunities and special challenges for the marketing manager. Market-driven firms in the business market demonstrate superior skill for understanding and satisfying customers. They also possess strong market-sensing and customer-linking capabilities. To deliver strong financial performance, business-to-business firms must also demonstrate customer relationship management skills, which include all the skills required to identify, initiate, develop, and monitor profitable customer relationships. Best-practice marketing strategists base their value propositions on the points of difference that matter the most to target customers, responding clearly and directly to the customer's business priorities. Although a common body of knowledge and theory spans all of marketing, important differences exist between consumer and business marketing, among them the nature of markets, demand patterns, buyer behavior, and buyer-seller relationships.

The dramatic worldwide rise in competition requires a global perspective on markets. To secure a competitive advantage in this challenging environment, business market customers are developing closer, more collaborative ties with fewer suppliers than they have used in the past. They are using the Internet to promote efficiency and real-time communication across the supply chain and demanding quality and speed from their suppliers to an unprecedented degree. These important trends in procurement place a premium on the supply chain management capabilities of the business marketer. Business marketing programs increasingly involve a customized blend of tangible products, service support, and ongoing information services both before and after the sale. Customer relationship management constitutes the heart of business marketing.

The diverse organizations that make up the business market can be broadly divided into (1) commercial enterprises, (2) governmental organizations, and (3) institutions. Because purchases these organizational consumers make are linked to goods and services they generate in turn, derived demand is an important and often volatile force in the business market. Industrial goods can be classified into three categories, based on how the product enters the buying organization's cost structure and the production process: (1) entering goods, (2) foundation goods, and (3) facilitating goods. Specific categories of goods may require unique marketing programs.

Discussion Questions

1. Home Depot is quite busy each morning because local contractors, home remodelers, and other small-business customers are buying the products they require for the day's projects. Such small-business customers represent a huge market opportunity for Home Depot or Lowe's. Describe particular strategies these retailers could follow to target and serve these customers.

2. DuPont, one of the largest industrial producers of chemicals and synthetic fibers, spends millions of dollars annually on advertising its products to final consumers. For example, DuPont invested more than $1 million in a TV advertising blitz that emphasized the comfort of jeans made of DuPont's stretch polyester-cotton blend. DuPont does not produce jeans or market them to final consumers, so why were large expenditures made on consumer advertising?

3. What are the chief differences between consumer-goods marketing and business marketing? Use the following matrix as a guide in organizing your response:

	Consumer-Goods Marketing	Business Marketing
Customers	_____	_____
Buying Behavior	_____	_____
Buyer–Seller Relationship	_____	_____
Product	_____	_____
Price	_____	_____
Promotion	_____	_____
Channels	_____	_____

4. Explain how a company such as GE might be classified by some business marketers as a user customer but by others as an OEM customer.

5. Spending a day in the life of a marketing manager would demonstrate the critical importance of relationship management skills as that manager interacts with employees of other functional areas and, indeed, with representatives from both customer and supplier organizations. Explore the strategic significance of such relationships.

6. Describe the key elements of a customer value proposition. Next, explain how a compelling value proposition might include *points of parity* as well as *points of difference*.

7. Consumer products are frequently classified as convenience, shopping, or specialty goods. This classification system is based on how consumers shop for particular products. Would this classification scheme apply equally well in the business marketing environment?

8. Evaluate this statement: "The ways that leading companies manage time in the supply chain—in new product development, in production, in sales and distribution—are the most powerful new sources of competitive advantage."

9. Evaluate this statement: "The demand for major equipment (a foundation good) is likely to be less responsive to shifts in price than that for materials, supplies, and components." Do you agree or disagree? Support your position.

10. Many firms are shifting selected service functions to outside suppliers. For example, Harley-Davidson recently outsourced its transportation department function to UPS Supply Chain Solutions. What factors would prompt such a decision, and what criteria would a customer like Harley-Davidson emphasize in choosing a supplier?

Internet Exercises

1. Many firms, large and small, have outsourced key functions, like payroll processing to ADP. Go to adp.com and (1) identify the range of services that ADP offers; (2) describe the types of customers the firm serves.

2. BASF "doesn't make the products you buy, but makes them better." Go to http:// www.basf.com and (1) outline the markets that BASF serves and (2) the products it sells.

R.I.M.'s BlackBerry and Apple's iPhone: The Face-Off in the Business Market[43]

Research in Motion Ltd. (R.I.M.), the maker of the BlackBerry, is the North American leader in building smartphones, the versatile handsets that operate more like computers than phones. Once the exclusive domain of e-mail–obsessed professionals and managers across the business market, smartphones are now prized by consumers who want easy access to the Web and digital music and video even more than a mobile connection to their e-mail inbox. The iPhone introduction shifted the contours of the smartphone market toward consumers. An industry once dominated by technical discussions about enterprise security is now dominated by buzz around video games, sleek handset design, and mobile social networks. "That means that R.I.M., which has historically viewed big corporations and wireless carriers as its bedrock customers, needs to alter its DNA in a hurry" in order to retain its leadership position. In the first quarter of 2008, R.I.M. held 45 percent of the U.S. market for smartphones, compared with a nearly 20 percent share for Apple.[44] The breakdown in sales indicates that BlackBerry dominates the corporate market and Apple's iPhone is strong in the consumer market.

New Strategy Directions

To capitalize on its strong brand and leadership position in the smartphone industry, R.I.M. introduced two phones aimed exclusively at the consumer market: the BlackBerry Pearl and the Curve. Well received by consumers, the products met R.I.M.'s performance expectations and now account for a majority of R.I.M.'s device sales. In response, Apple now includes a software upgrade to allow iPhones to connect directly to corporate e-mail systems—a dagger aimed at the heart of R.I.M.'s strength in the business market. The upgrade also allows iPhone users to run customized applications to track inventory, record expenses, and perform other corporate tasks. So, R.I.M. is trying to capture some of the consumer market with the BlackBerry and Apple is attacking R.I.M. on its home turf by driving demand for the iPhone among corporate customers.

Some experts suggest that R.I.M. offers several capabilities that Apple can't yet match, including enhanced security and reliability for corporate users. For example, the company runs its own wireless network so it can make sure e-mails are delivered in a timely fashion.[45] Yet, Apple demonstrates deep skills in product design, innovation, and branding. Simply stated, R.I.M.'s greatest challenge in the consumer-driven smartphone industry may come down to creating devices that people admire and embrace as much as the iPhone.

---

[43] Unless otherwise noted, this discussion is based on Brad Stone, "BlackBerry's Quest: Fend Off the iPhone," *The New York Times*, April 27, 2008, pp. B1 and B4.

[44] Jim Jubak, "New iPhone Shows Apple Still Gets It," accessed at http://www.moneycentral.msn.com on June 6, 2008.

[45] Arik Hesseldahl, "The iPhone Eyes BlackBerry's Turf," *Business Week*, June 23, 2008, p. 38.

Discussion Questions

1. Suggest possible strategies that Apple might follow to strengthen the position of the iPhone in the business market. In turn, what strategies could R.I.M. follow to strengthen the performance of the BlackBerry brand in the consumer market?

2. In your view, which brand will win the battle in the business market? In the consumer market?

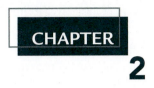

CHAPTER

2

The Business Market: Perspectives on the Organizational Buyer

The business marketer must understand the needs of a diverse mix of organizational buyers drawn from three broad sectors of the business market—commercial enterprises, government (all levels), and institutions—as well as from an expanding array of international buyers. After reading this chapter, you will understand:

1. the nature and central characteristics of each of these market sectors.

2. how the purchasing function is organized in each of these components of the business market.

3. the dramatic role that online purchasing assumes in the business market.

4. the need to design a unique marketing program for each sector of the business market.

Cisco Systems, Inc., provides the networking solutions that are the foundation of the Internet and of most corporate, education, and government networks on a global scale. Today, the Internet and computer networking are a fundamental part of business, education, personal communications, and entertainment. Virtually all messages or transactions passing over the Internet are carried efficiently and securely through Cisco equipment. Cisco provides the hardware and software solutions for transporting data, voice, and video within buildings, across campuses, or around the world.

Rather than serving individuals or household consumers, Cisco is a leading-edge business-to-business firm that markets its products and services to organizations: commercial enterprises (for example, corporations and telecommunications firms), governmental units, and institutions (for example, universities and health-care organizations). Marketing managers at Cisco give special attention to transforming complex technology products and services into concrete solutions to meet customer requirements. For example, when Pep Boys, the leading automotive aftermarket and service chain in the United States wanted to connect its 593 retail store locations across 36 states, Cisco provided the network solution.[1] Likewise, when Procter & Gamble (P&G) wanted to launch a major Internet initiative to meet its aggressive growth targets, the firm turned to Cisco.[2] The sales team from Cisco described how an efficient Internet strategy could improve the way companies interact with employees, suppliers, and customers. Working with Cisco, P&G implemented several initiatives, including an online system called "Web Order Management" that enables retail customers, like Target, to connect to P&G any time to place and manage orders on the Web. In working with Cisco, P&G Chief Information Officer (CIO) Steve David commented: "We like to hook our wagon to people who are the best so they can help us be the best at creating that all-important competitive advantage."[3]

Each of the three business market sectors—commercial firms, institutions, and governments—has identifiable and unique characteristics that business marketers must understand if marketers wish to grow their client bases. A significant first step in creating successful marketing strategy is to isolate the unique dimensions of each major business market sector. How much market potential does each sector represent? Who makes the purchasing decisions? The answers provide a foundation on which managers can formulate marketing programs that respond to the specific needs and characteristics of each business market sector.

Commercial Enterprises: Unique Characteristics

Commercial enterprises include manufacturers, construction companies, service firms (for example, hotels), transportation companies, selected professional groups (for example, dentists), and resellers (wholesalers and retailers purchasing equipment and supplies to use in their operations). Manufacturers are the most important commercial customers: The 100 largest ones purchase more than $1 trillion of goods and services annually.[4]

---

[1] Customer Success Story: "Cisco Helps Pep Boys Improve Point-of-Sale Applications, Security Posture, and Future Flexibility," http://www.cisco.com, accessed June 6, 2008, pp. 1–4.

[2] "Cisco Customer Profile: Procter & Gamble," http://www.cisco.com, accessed July 23, 2002, pp. 1–3.

[3] Ibid., p. 3.

[4] Anne Millen Porter, "Containing Total Spend," *Purchasing* 132 (November 6, 2008): pp. 18–25.

Distribution by Size

A startling fact about the study of manufacturers is that so few of them remain. Available evidence suggests that there are approximately 350,000 manufacturing firms in the United States.[5] And although only 30,000 manufacturing firms (fewer than 10 percent) employ more than 100 workers each, this handful of firms ships more than 75 percent of all U.S. manufactured products. Because manufacturing operations are so concentrated in the United States, the business marketer normally serves far fewer but far larger customers than does a consumer-product marketer. For example, Intel sells microprocessors to a few large manufacturers, like Dell and Hewlett-Packard, who, in turn, target millions of potential computer buyers. Clearly, large buyers are generally vitally important to business marketers. Because each large firm has such vast buying power, business marketers often tailor particular marketing strategies for each customer.

Smaller manufacturing firms also constitute an important business market segment. In fact, more than two-thirds of all U.S. manufacturers employ fewer than 20 people.[6] In addition to small manufacturers, more than 5 million small businesses in the United States employ fewer than 6 people each. Based on sheer numbers, small businesses represent a dominant category of business market customers—but a market that is often difficult to serve.[7] Because the organizational buyer in smaller firms has different needs—and often a very different orientation—astute marketers adjust their marketing programs to this market segment's particular needs. To illustrate, FedEx wanted to increase its share of the small shipper market but recognized that picking up packages at many small businesses is more expensive than picking them up at one larger location.[8] To cost-effectively reach these customers, FedEx encourages small shippers to bring their packages to conveniently located FedEx drop-off points. The strategy has been successful.

Geographical Concentration

Size is not the only concentration factor important to the business marketer: Manufacturers are also concentrated geographically. More than half of all U.S. manufacturers are located in only eight states: California, New York, Ohio, Illinois, Michigan, Texas, Pennsylvania, and New Jersey. Most large metropolitan areas are lucrative business markets. Geographical concentration of industry, however, means only that a large potential volume exists in a given area; each buyer's requirements may still vary significantly.

Geographic concentration has important implications for formulating marketing strategy. First, firms can concentrate their marketing efforts in high-market-potential areas, making effective use of full-time personal sales forces in these markets. Second, distribution centers in large-volume areas can ensure rapid delivery to a large proportion of customers. Finally, firms may not be able to tie their salespeople to specific

---

[5] U.S. Department of Commerce, Bureau of the Census, *2005 County Business Patterns*, accessed at www.censtats.gov, June 6, 2008.

[6] Ibid.

[7] Arun Sharma, R. Krishnan, and Dhruv Grewal, "Value Creation in Business Markets," *Industrial Marketing Management* 30 (June 2001): pp. 391–402.

[8] Thomas H. Davenport, Jeanne G. Harris, and Ajay K. Kohli, "How Do They Know Their Customers So Well?" *MIT Sloan Management Review* 42 (Winter 2001): p. 65.

geographic areas because many large buying organizations entrust the responsibility for purchasing certain products and materials for the entire company to a single individual. For example, Wendy's International, Inc., operates a centralized purchasing system from its Dublin, Ohio, headquarters that supports the entire Wendy's network—all corporate and franchise restaurants on a global basis. The centralized staff purchases all direct materials for all of the restaurants—food, packaging, and supplies. Judith Hollis, vice president of supply chain management at Wendy's, notes:

> We view our job as developing supplier partnerships that are going to assist Wendy's with maintaining our competitive advantage. We look to . . . companies that are involved in technological innovation in quality, food, safety, and preparation efficiency.[9]

By understanding how a potential buyer's purchasing organization is structured, business marketers are better equipped to identify buying influentials and to develop responsive strategy.

Classifying Commercial Enterprises

Marketers can gain valuable strategy insights by identifying the needs and requirements of different types of commercial enterprises or business customers. The **North American Industrial Classification System (NAICS)** organizes business activity into meaningful economic sectors and identifies groups of business firms that use similar production processes.[10] The NAICS is an outgrowth of the North American Free Trade Agreement (NAFTA); it provides for standard economic data reporting among Canada, Mexico, and the United States. Every plant or business establishment receives a code that reflects the primary product produced at that location. The new system, which includes traditional industries while incorporating new and emerging-technology industries, replaces the Standard Industrial Classification (SIC) system that was used for decades.

Figure 2.1 illustrates the building blocks of the system. Observe that the first two digits identify the economic sector and that as more digits are added, the classification becomes finer. For example, all business establishments that create, disseminate, or provide the means to distribute information are included in the Information sector: NAICS Code 51. Nineteen other economic sectors are included in the system. More specifically, U.S. establishments that produce paging equipment are assigned an NAICS Code of 513321. Individual countries customize the six-digit codes for industry subdivisions, but at the five-digit level they are standardized across the three countries.

Using the NAICS   If marketing managers understand the needs and requirements of a few firms within a classification category, they can project requirements for other firms that share that category. Each group should be relatively homogeneous in terms of raw materials required, component parts used, and manufacturing processes employed. The NAICS provides a valuable tool for identifying new customers and for targeting profitable segments of business buyers.

[9] Michael Fredette, "An Interview with Judith Hollis," *Journal of Supply Chain Management* 37 (Summer 2001): p. 3.
[10] www.naics.com, "History of SIC/NAICS," accessed June 15, 2005.

FIGURE 2.1 | **NORTH AMERICAN INDUSTRIAL CLASSIFICATION SYSTEM**

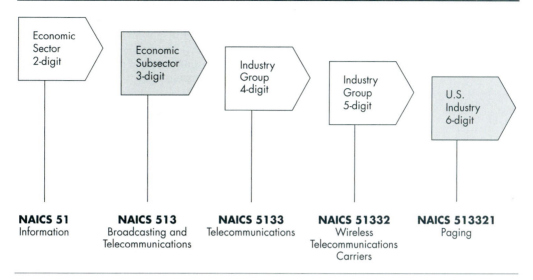

| **NAICS 51** | **NAICS 513** | **NAICS 5133** | **NAICS 51332** | **NAICS 513321** |
| Information | Broadcasting and Telecommunications | Telecommunications | Wireless Telecommunications Carriers | Paging |

SOURCE: Reprinted from K. Douglas Hoffman et al., *Marketing: Best Practices* (Mason, Ohio: South-Western/Thomson Learning, 2003), p. 171.

The Purchasing Organization

Regardless of its organizational characteristics, every firm must procure the materials, supplies, equipment, and services it needs to operate the business successfully. "Spending on purchased goods and services can represent 70 percent of a company's costs, so business leaders have long known that purchasing improvements can directly improve the bottom line."[11] How goods and services are purchased depends on such factors as the nature of the business, the size of the firm, and the volume, variety, and technical complexity of items purchased. Rarely do individual departments in a corporation do their own buying. An individual whose title is director of purchasing or director of procurement usually administers procurement for all departments. Indeed, a decade marked by fierce global competition and rising energy and commodity costs opened the eyes of executives everywhere to the strategic benefits that can be achieved through a best-in-class purchasing and supply management function. So the stature and visibility of corporate buyers has risen in the organization. Alcoa Inc., IBM, and Sarah Lee Corporation, along with a growing list of others, have created chief purchasing officer (CPO) positions, often reporting directly to the chief executive or chief operating officer.[12]

The day-to-day purchasing function is carried out by buyers, each of whom is responsible for a specific group of products. Organizing the purchasing function in this way permits buyers to acquire a high level of technical expertise about a limited number of items. As products and materials become more sophisticated, buyers must

---

[11] Chip W. Hardt, Nicholas Reinecke, and Peter Spiller, "Inventing the 21st Century Purchasing Organization," *The McKinsey Quarterly*, 2007 (4): p. 116.

[12] Timothy Aeppel, "Global Scramble for Goods Gives Corporate Buyers a Lift," *The Wall Street Journal*, October 2, 2007, p. A1; and Shelby D. Hunt and Donna Davis, "Grounding Supply Chain Management in Resource-Advantage Theory," *Journal of Supply Chain Management* 44 (January 2008): pp. 10–21.

TABLE 2.1 | **THE GOALS OF PURCHASING**

Goals	Description
Uninterrupted Flow of Materials	Provide an uninterrupted flow of the materials, supplies, and services required to operate the organization.
Manage Inventory	Minimize the investment in inventory.
Improve Quality	Maintain and improve quality by carefully evaluating and choosing products and services.
Developing and Managing Supplier Relationships	Find competent suppliers and forge collaborative relationships with supply chain.
Achieve Lowest Total Cost	Purchase required products and services at lowest total cost.
Reduce Administrative Costs	Accomplish the purchasing objectives at the lowest possible level of administrative costs.
Advance Firm's Competitive Position	Improve the firm's competitive position by reducing supply chain costs or capitalizing on the capabilities of suppliers.

SOURCE: Adapted with modifications from Michael R. Leenders, Harold E. Fearon, Anna E. Flynn, and P. Fraser Johnson, *Purchasing and Supply Management*, 12th ed. (Chicago: Irwin, 2002), pp. 40–43, and Andrew Bartolini, "CPO Rising: The CPO's Agenda for 2008," Aberdeen Group, February 2008, accessed at http://www.aberdeen.com on June 7, 2008.

become more knowledgeable about material characteristics, manufacturing processes, and design specifications. Frequently, a sizable group is employed to conduct research, evaluate materials, and perform cost studies.

Goals of the Purchasing Function

To address the needs of business customers of all types, the marketer has to understand the purchasing manager's goals and how the purchasing function contributes to the organization's objectives (Table 2.1). The purchasing decision maker must juggle a number of different objectives that often clash. For example, the lowest-priced component part is unacceptable if it does not meet quality standards or is delivered two weeks late. In addition to protecting the cost structure of the firm, improving quality, and keeping inventory investment to a minimum, purchasing assumes a central role in managing relationships with suppliers. Here purchasing assumes a central role in supply chain management.

Supply chain management is a technique for linking a manufacturer's operations with those of all of its strategic suppliers, key intermediaries, and customers. The approach seeks to integrate the relationships and operations of both immediate, first-tier suppliers and those several tiers back in the supply chain, in order to help second-, third-, and fourth-tier suppliers meet requirements like quality, delivery, and the timely exchange of information. Firms that embrace supply chain management also solicit ideas from key suppliers and involve them directly in the new-product-development process. By managing supply chain costs and linking supplier capabilities to new product development, the purchasing function is advancing corporate performance in many organizations.

The Supply Chain for McNuggets

Purchasing managers at McDonald's Corporation have worked closely with suppliers to develop a sophisticated model to reduce the cost of chicken. The model isolates how various feed mixes affect weight gain in chickens, and suppliers are able to optimize chicken weight gain in response to changing food prices.

McDonald's also closely manages and tightly coordinates its supply chain from hatchery to processor and into the restaurants. "McDonald's explicitly orders hatcheries to place eggs in anticipation of the sales forecast for chicken products. Product movement through the supply base is so well orchestrated that a supplier can confidently place the eggs in the hatcheries seventy-five days before McDonald's expects to sell the chicken as McNuggets."

SOURCE: Timothy M. Laseter, Balanced Sourcing: Cooperation and Competition in Supplier Relationships (San Francisco: Jossey-Bass, 1998), p. 14.

Strategic Procurement[13]

Leading-edge organizations like Dell Computer, GE, and Honda demonstrate the critical role that purchasing can assume in creating profit opportunities in their industries. To illustrate, Honda, long recognized for purchasing excellence and its ability to sustain customer loyalty, was able to reduce by 20 percent the costs of external purchases that are embodied in the current Accord. A senior purchasing executive at Honda described how it was done:

> The first thing we did was compile a big list of every possible way we could remove costs from the Accord; most of them, in fact, came from suppliers' work with purchasing and engineering. We studied each idea, prioritized them according to their likelihood of success, and then just started focusing our work on developing them.[14]

Understanding the Total Cost   To unlock savings and growth opportunities, the purchasing function must develop a keen understanding of the total cost and value of a good or service to the firm. Such an approach requires purchasing managers to consider not only the purchase price but also an array of other considerations:

- the factors that drive the cost of the product or service in the supply chain, such as transportation;
- the costs of acquiring and managing products or services;
- quality, reliability, and other attributes of a product or service over its complete life cycle;
- the value of a product or service to a firm and its customers.

[13]This section is based on Matthew G. Anderson and Paul B. Katz, "Strategic Sourcing," *International Journal of Logistics Management* 9 (1, 1998): pp. 1–13.

[14]Timothy M. Laseter, *Balanced Sourcing: Cooperation and Competition in Supplier Relationships* (San Francisco: Jossey-Bass, 1998), p. 224.

Fundamental to this total-system cost perspective is the concept of total cost of ownership. "**Total cost of ownership** considers both supplier and buyer activities, and costs over a product's or service's complete life cycle."[15] For example, a firm can justify buying a higher-quality product and paying a premium price because the initial purchase cost will be offset by fewer manufacturing defects, lower inventory requirements, and lower administrative costs. The total cost of ownership means understanding a range of cost-value relationships associated with individual purchases.

Levels of Procurement Development   In capturing cost savings through improved procurement, Matthew Anderson and Paul Katz of Mercer Management Consulting suggest that firms operate at different levels of development and emphasize different pathways to cost reduction and revenue enhancement (Figure 2.2). Ranging from the least to the most developed, these approaches include (1) Buy for Less; (2) Buy Better; (3) Consume Better; and (4) Sell Better. Note that the most developed strategy—Sell Better—ties purchasing activities directly to strategy. Here procurement builds supplier relationships that ultimately enhance the growth and the market strength of the organization.

Level 1—Leveraged Buy (Buy for Less)   Many firms demonstrate Level 1 procurement practices and achieve cost savings by centralizing decision-making authority, which permits the consolidation of volume and by selecting suppliers that provide the best prices and terms.

Level 2—Linked Buy (Buy Better)   The next level of procurement development is triggered when the procurement organization takes an external view of the supply chain and develops mutually beneficial relationships with suppliers. It achieves cost savings by streamlining the bidding process, optimizing delivery and information flows, and making stable commitments to enable efficient production by suppliers. Incremental cost savings of 5 to 25 percent result from moving from Level 1 to Level 2.

Level 3—Value Buy (Consume Better)   The goal of Level 3 is to advance the performance of the procurement function by optimizing the life cycle costs and value of products and services. Value analysis, complexity management, and early supplier involvement in product design allow buyers and suppliers to uncover added value.

- **Value analysis** is a method of weighing the comparative value of materials, components, and manufacturing processes from the standpoint of their purpose, relative merit, and cost in order to uncover ways of improving products, lowering costs, or both. For example, Ferro Corporation developed a new coating process that allows Whirlpool to paint a refrigerator cabinet in 10 minutes compared with the old process, which took 3 hours.[16] The new process provided significant cost savings for Whirlpool.

- **Complexity management** seeks cost reductions by simplifying the design of products or by using standardized component parts in products and across product lines. Complexity management can also involve the outsourcing of

---

[15] Anderson and Katz, "Strategic Sourcing," p. 3. See also, James Carbone, "Using TCO to Rate Suppliers," *Purchasing* 133 (February 19, 2004): pp. 30–34.

[16] Elizabeth Baatz, "How Purchasing Handles Intense Cost Pressure," *Purchasing* 127 (October 8, 1999): pp. 61–66.

FIGURE 2.2 | LEVELS OF PROCUREMENT DEVELOPMENT AND PATHWAYS TO SAVINGS/REVENUE ENHANCEMENT

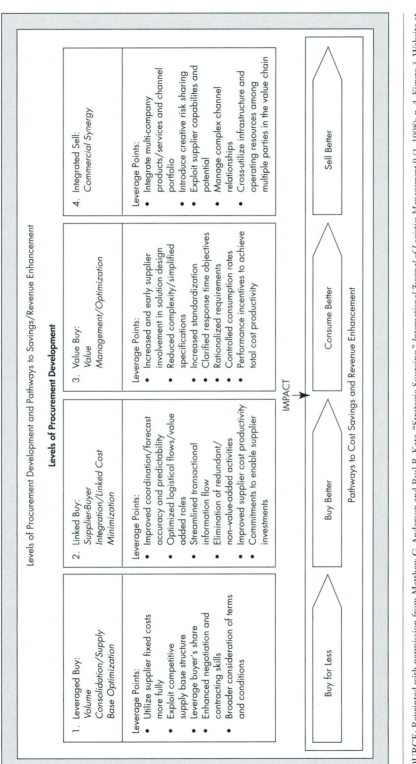

Levels of Procurement Development and Pathways to Savings/Revenue Enhancement

Levels of Procurement Development

1. Leveraged Buy:
Volume Consolidation/Supply Base Optimization

Leverage Points:
- Utilize supplier fixed costs more fully
- Exploit competitive supply base structure
- Leverage buyer's share
- Enhanced negotiation and contracting skills
- Broader consideration of terms and conditions

2. Linked Buy:
Supplier-Buyer Integration/Linked Cost Minimization

Leverage Points:
- Improved coordination/forecast accuracy and predictability
- Optimized logistical flows/value added roles
- Streamlined transactional information flow
- Elimination of redundant/non-value-added activities
- Improved supplier cost productivity
- Commitments to enable supplier investments

3. Value Buy:
Value Management/Optimization

Leverage Points:
- Increased and early supplier involvement in solution design
- Reduced complexity/simplified specifications
- Increased standardization
- Clarified response time objectives
- Rationalized requirements
- Controlled consumption rates
- Performance incentives to achieve total cost productivity

4. Integrated Sell:
Commercial Synergy

Leverage Points:
- Integrate multi-company products/services and channel portfolio
- Introduce creative risk sharing
- Exploit supplier capabilites and potential
- Manage complex channel relationships
- Cross-utilize infrastructure and operating resources among multiple parties in the value chain

IMPACT

Buy for less | Buy Better | Consume Better | Sell Better

Pathways to Cost Savings and Revenue Enhancement

SOURCE: Reprinted with permission from Matthew G. Anderson and Paul B. Katz, "Strategic Sourcing," *International Journal of Logistics Management* 9 (1, 1998): p. 4, Figure 3. Website at http://www.ijlm.org.

FIGURE 2.3 | **SEGMENTING THE BUY**

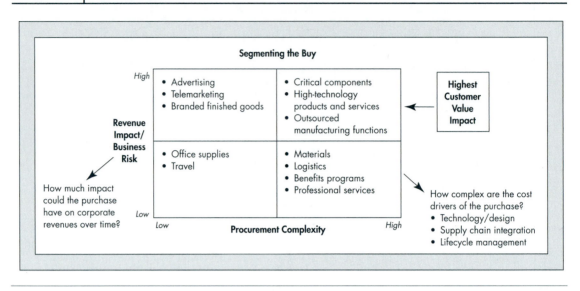

SOURCE: Reprinted with permission from Matthew G. Anderson and Paul B. Katz, "Strategic Sourcing," *International Journal of Logistics Management* 9 (1, 1998): p. 7, Figure 8. Website at http://www.ijlm.org.

production or assembly tasks to supply chain partners. For example, Boeing is taking the concept of supplier collaboration to new heights in the development of the 787 Dreamliner. Rather than integrating supplier parts and materials in its own features, key suppliers assume that responsibility and provide complete subsystems to Boeing. To illustrate, Rockwell Collins provides the major avionics systems—displays, communications, and more—to Boeing for the 787.[17]

- To capture fresh ideas, technologies, and cost savings, leading purchasing organizations emphasize **early supplier involvement in new product development.** At firms like Boeing, Harley-Davidson, Apple, and Honda, key suppliers actively contribute to the new-product-development process from the design stage to the product's introduction, often spending months on-site collaborating with the development team.

By using these methods, Level 3 savings opportunities can be substantial. Research by McKinsey & Company indicates that high-performing purchasing groups generate annual cost savings that are nearly six times greater than those of low performers.[18]

Level 4—Integrated Sell (Sell Better)   Level 4 development applies when specific product and service choices the purchasing organization makes have a significant effect on revenue and also involve a high degree of business risk. For example, the investments of a telecommunications firm such as AT&T in technology products that form its infrastructure have a major effect on the future of the firm. Under such

---

[17] Susan Avery, "Boeing Executive Steven Schaffer is Named Supply Chain Manager of the Year for the 787 Dreamliner Project," October 18, 2007 Issue of *Purchasing*, accessed at http://www.purchasing.com on June 5, 2008.

[18] Hardt, Reinecke, and Spiller, "Inventing the 21st Century Purchasing Organization," p. 116.

INSIDE BUSINESS MARKETING

Respond with Value-Based Selling Tools

Astute B2B marketing strategists use value-based selling to vividly demonstrate the superior value that they provide compared to rivals. For example, Microsoft provides an online tool that potential business customers can use to cost, configure, and compare the Microsoft Windows Server to the whole universe of options, such as Linux. In 5 minutes or less, a business customer can estimate the total cost of ownership of the Microsoft option and then undertake a more detailed business-value study that provides a comprehensive analysis of costs and benefits—tailored to their organization.

To illustrate, when the Linux-based high-performance computing cluster at Callaway Golf reached the end of its useful life, key decision makers decided to examine two options: (1) another Linux-based system or (2) a solution based on Windows Compute Cluster Server running on Hewlett-Packard hardware. Callaway Golf chose the high-performance computing solution based on the Windows server because it offered significant advantages, including manageability, ease of use, and cost. John Loo, design systems senior manager at Callaway Golf, observed: "What really surprised us was the difference in software licensing and maintenance costs. A Linux solution would have been more expensive because we would have needed a separate job scheduler, which is something that Windows Compute Cluster Server provides." Microsoft used value-based selling to demonstrate the points of difference.

SOURCE: "Microsoft Customer Case Study: Callaway Golf," April 11, 2008, accessed at http://www.microsoft.com on June 12, 2008.

conditions, choosing the right technologies and sharing the risks with important suppliers are crucial to the success of AT&T's corporate strategy. Highly skilled and knowledgeable purchasing professionals are required to achieve this advanced level of procurement development, which unites purchasing decisions with corporate growth strategies.

Segmenting Purchase Categories   Each firm purchases a unique portfolio of products and services. Leaders in procurement are giving increased attention to segmenting total purchases into distinct categories and sharpening their focus on those purchases that have the greatest effect on revenue generation or present the greatest risk to corporate performance. From Figure 2.3, observe that various categories of purchases are segmented on the basis of procurement complexity and the nature of the effect on corporate performance (that is, revenue impact/business risk).

Which Purchases Affect Performance?   Procurement complexity considers factors such as the technical complexity, the scope of supply chain coordination required, and the degree to which life cycle costs are relevant. The revenue impact/business risk dimension considers the degree to which a purchase category can influence customers' perceptions of value. For example, purchasing managers at Ford decided that some components are important to brand identity, such as steering wheels, road wheels, and other highly visual parts.

Purchasing managers can use a segmentation approach to isolate those purchase categories that have the greatest effect on corporate revenues. For example, advertising services could have tremendous risk implications relative to customer perceptions of value, whereas office supplies remain a cost issue. Or, in the high-tech arena, the procurement of a new generation of semiconductor technology may essentially be a bet on the company's future.[19]

Business marketers should assess where their offerings are positioned in the port-folio of purchases a particular organization makes. This varies by firm and by indus-try. The revenue and profit potential for the business marketer is greatest in those purchasing organizations that view the purchase as strategic—high revenue impact and high customer-value impact. For example, in the auto industry, electronic braking systems, audio and navigation systems, as well as turbochargers, fit into this category and represent about one-quarter of a passenger vehicle's cost.[20] Here the marketer can contribute offerings directly tied to the customer organization's strategy, enjoy-ing an attractive profit margin. If the business marketer can become a central com-ponent of the customer's supply chain, the effect is even more significant: a valuable, long-term relationship in which the customer views the supplier as an extension of its organization. For categories of goods that purchasing organizations view as less strategic (for example, office supplies), the appropriate marketing strategy centers on providing a complete product assortment, competitive pricing, timely service support, and simplified ordering. By understanding how customers segment their purchases, business marketers are better equipped to target profitable customer groups and de-velop customized strategies.

E-Procurement[21]

Like consumers who are shopping at Amazon (http://www.amazon.com), purchasing managers use the Internet to find new suppliers, communicate with current suppli-ers, or place an order. While providing a rich base of information, purchasing over the Internet is also very efficient: It is estimated that purchase orders processed over the Internet cost only $5, compared with the current average purchase order cost of $100. For example, IBM has moved all of its purchasing to the Web and has created a "private exchange" that links its suppliers. A **private exchange** allows a company like IBM to automate its purchases and collaborate in real time with a specially invited group of suppliers.[22] By handling nearly all its invoices electronically (some 400,000 e-invoices a month), IBM saves nearly $400 million per year using its more efficient Web purchasing strategy.

Everyone Is Getting Wired

Less than a decade ago, pioneering enterprises like IBM, GE, and United Technolo-gies began testing Internet-based negotiations as part of their strategic purchasing programs. Today, more than 80 percent of *Fortune* 1000 enterprises have adopted e-procurement software, and new low-cost, hosted options are driving the adop-tion of e-procurement solutions among medium-sized enterprises. Leading suppliers of

[19]Anderson and Katz, "Strategic Sourcing," p. 7.

[20]Srikant Inampudi, Aurobind Satpathy, and Anant Singh, "Can North American Auto Suppliers Create Value?" *The McKinsey Quarterly*, June 2008, accessed at http://www.mckinsey.com on June 8, 2008.

[21]Tim A. Minahan, "Best Practices in E-Sourcing: Optimizing and Sustaining Supply Savings," September 2004, research report by Aberdeen Group, Inc., Boston, Massachusetts; accessed at http://www.ariba.com on June 15, 2005.

[22]Nicole Harris, "'Private Exchanges' May Allow B-to-B Commerce to Thrive After All," *The Wall Street Journal*, March 16, 2001, p. B4.

e-procurement software include Ariba, Inc. (http://www.ariba.com), Emptoris (http://www.emptoris.com), and Oracle Corporation (http://www.oracle.com). To compete effectively in this information-rich environment, business marketing managers must develop a firm understanding of the e-procurement tools that customers are embracing.

Enhancing the Buyer's Capabilities

Rather than a strategy, e-procurement is a technology platform that enables information to be exchanged efficiently and processes to be automated. E-procurement is "the use of Web-based applications, decision support tools, and associated services to streamline and enhance strategic sourcing processes and knowledge management."[23] Included among the distinguishing components of e-procurement solutions are the following capabilities:

- *online negotiations* that enable the buyer to query suppliers with a request-for-proposal (RFP), request-for-quote (RFQ), or request-for-information (RFI), and to conduct reverse auctions (discussed below);

- *collaboration tools* that enable the purchasing manager to (1) collaborate with internal stakeholders (for example, departments) to develop detailed specifications and priorities for goods or services to be purchased and (2) provide a detailed description of requirements to suppliers through an RFP;

- *knowledge management* capabilities that provide the procurement function and senior management with a central repository of valuable data and information on supplier performance, material and component costs, process flows, and best practices;

- *analytical tools* that support detailed analysis and modeling of purchasing costs and total spending by category across the enterprise.

Delivering Measurable Results

Why are purchasing organizations embracing online purchasing technologies? Because they "deliver measurable benefits in the form of material cost savings, process efficiencies, and performance enhancements" according to Tim Minahan, a supply chain consultant at the Aberdeen Group.[24] Studying procurement processes at sixty companies, including American Express, Motorola, and Alcoa, Aberdeen found that e-procurement cut purchasing cycle time in half, reduced material costs by 14 percent and purchasing administrative costs by 60 percent, and enhanced the ability of procurement units to identify new suppliers on a global scale.

Buying Direct and Indirect Goods

In the United States alone, organizations spend more than $1.4 trillion annually on *indirect* goods or operating resources—items that organizations of all types need to run day-to-day operations. Examples encompass everything from personal computers

---

[23] Minahan, "Best Practices in E-Sourcing," p. 3.

[24] Ibid., p. 3.

and spare parts for factory equipment to office furniture and employee travel, including airline tickets, hotel rooms, and car rental services.[25] Powered by software from Ariba, Motorola has used its global e-requisitioning system to reduce procurement costs and control indirect purchasing, yielding more than $300 million of cost savings in a recent year.[26] During the Internet-boom years, companies invested heavily in e-procurement systems but used them primarily to buy indirect goods. As adopters reaped huge cost savings and began to trust Internet-based purchasing systems, many firms began to use e-procurement to buy *direct* materials or entering goods—the raw materials or component parts that are core to a firm's manufacturing process. As e-procurement systems become more affordable, some experts predict that small and medium-sized firms will soon adopt the purchasing practices of the industry leaders. To illustrate, many suppliers apply what they learn from best-practice firms, like Toyota, to their own purchasing processes and relationship management programs.

Reverse Auctions

One online procurement tool that sparks debate in the business market is the reverse auction. Rather than one seller and many buyers, a **reverse auction** involves one buyer who invites bids from several prequalified suppliers who face off in a dynamic, real-time, competitive bidding process. Reverse auctions are most widely used in the automobile, electronics, aerospace, and pharmaceutical industries. Proponents claim that reverse auctions can lower the cost of procuring products and services by 20 percent or more. A case in point: Sun MicroSystems saved 30 percent on the commodities it purchased through reverse auctions.[27] Critics counter that reverse auctions can inflict real damage on supplier relationships and that the realized savings are often overstated.[28] For example, during the recent economic downturn, many firms used reverse auctions as a tactical weapon to drive supplier prices down but often found that the winning bidder delivered less value—lower quality and poorer service than existing suppliers.

Reverse auctions are best suited for commodity-type items like purchasing materials, diesel fuel, metal parts, chemicals, and many raw materials. On the other hand, reverse auctions are generally *not* appropriate for strategic relationships, where suppliers have specialized capabilities and few suppliers can meet quality and performance standards. Rob Harlan, senior director of e-procurement for Motorola, aptly states: "We pride ourselves on strong supplier relationships. We are not going to jeopardize these for short-term gains with online auctions. You need to ensure the integrity of the bidding environment, educate suppliers on how best to compete, and clearly communicate your intentions and requirements."[29]

[25] Mark Vigoroso, "Buyers Prepare for Brave New World of e-Commerce," *Purchasing* 127 (April 22, 1999): pp. S4–S12; and Mylene Mangalindan, "As Times Get Tough, Firms Buy Online," *The Wall Street Journal*, June 3, 2008, p. B10.

[26] James Carbone, "Motorola Leverages Its Way to Lower Cost," *Purchasing* 133 (September 16, 2004): pp. 31–38.

[27] James Carbone, "Sun's e-Auction Evolution," September 13, 2007 issue of *Purchasing*, accessed at http://www.purchasing.com on June 10, 2008.

[28] Mohanbir Sawhney, "Forward Thinking About Reverse Auctions," June 1, 2003 issue of *CIO Magazine*, accessed at http://www.cio.com on June 20, 2005, pp. 1–6.

[29] Minahan, "Best Practices in E-Sourcing," p. 52.

ETHICAL BUSINESS MARKETING

Gift Giving: "Buy Me These Boots and You'll Get My Business"

Greg Davies, director of sales for Action Printing in Fond du Lac, Wisconsin, encountered this awkward situation. Leaving a restaurant after taking a potential customer to lunch, the prospective client stopped to examine the window display of a country-and-western store located nearby. That's when Davies's prospect turned to him and said very slowly: "I have always wanted a pair of boots like this." "There was no mistaking it: He expected me to buy him the boots," recalls Davies, who simply smiled and began walking again. He declined because company policy, as well as his personal value system, forbids the exchange of expensive personal gifts for business.

As you would imagine, from that day forward, Greg felt awkward around the prospect.

Sales experts suggest that Greg made the right business decision, as well as the right moral decision. He stood behind a well-conceived company policy. In turn, Jacques Werth, a sales consultant, agreed with the decision to walk away. "If your relationship is based on extravagant gifts, entertainment, and other perks, you're likely to lose the business when a bigger bribe comes along, anyway."

SOURCE: Melinda Ligos, "Gimme, Gimme, Gimme!" *Sales & Marketing Management* (March 2002): pp. 33–40.

How Organizational Buyers Evaluate Potential Suppliers

E-procurement systems provide purchasing managers with a rich information environment and a sophisticated set of analytical tools they can use to evaluate the performance of suppliers. Many criteria may be factored into a buyer's ultimate decision: quality, price, delivery reliability, company image, and capability. Buyer perceptions are critical. When products are perceived as highly standardized or commodity-like, price assumes special importance in the purchasing decision and the business marketer faces the intense competitive pressure that reverse auctions impose. On the other hand, when the value offerings of the business marketer are perceived as unique, other criteria dominate and the opportunity exists to develop a strategic relationship with the customer. At a fundamental level, customers in the business market are interested in the total capabilities of a supplier and how those capabilities can assist them in advancing their competitive position—now and in the future.

To this point, the discussion has centered on one sector of the business market—commercial enterprises—and the role the purchasing function assumes. Attention now turns to the government market.

Governments: Unique Characteristics

Federal (1), state (50), and local (87,000) **government units** generate the greatest volume of purchases of any customer category in the United States. Collectively, these units spend more than $1.5 trillion on goods and services each year—the federal government accounts for $400 billion, and states and local government account for the rest.[30] Governmental units purchase from virtually every category of goods

[30] U.S. Census Bureau, *Statistical Abstract of the United States: 2008*, accessed at http://www.census.gov on June 12, 2008.

FIGURE 2.4 | HEWLETT PACKARD'S e-GOVERNMENT STRATEGY

As customers have become adept at shopping online, managing their bank accounts, and requesting services, Internet-savvy citizens now expect the same from their governments. Enabled by information technology, public agencies are giving citizens new tools to access information and services while, at the same time, introducing new efficiencies in government operations.

Hewlett Packard (H-P) has developed a complete portfolio of services tailored to e-government goals:

- Improving quality and ease of access for citizens
- Reducing the cost of service delivery
- Simplifying the implementation of government directives
- Advancing economic growth by stimulating the development of a digital economy

H-P offers targeted solutions that allow citizens to:

- Test for and renew drivers' licenses online
- Purchase decals and permits online
- Access information and services around the clock from public agencies and government departments

H-P has also developed a suite of solutions that governments require for efficient and effective Homeland Security. Included here are:

- Mission-focused technology solutions that protect borders and public transportation systems
- Supportive technologies to enhance the capabilities of law enforcement agencies, firefighters, and emergency response teams
- Security solutions to protect critical infrastructure assets and defend against catastrophic threats.

H-P Success Story:

- Government Customer: Chicago Office of Emergency and Communications (OEMC)
- Mission: The Chicago OEMC is responsible for all 911 communications and emergency operations and for responding to emergency incidents of all types in the city.
- Customer Solution: H-P technologies were applied to support an integrated emergency operation center and are deployed in a Unified Communications Vehicle, which enables city personnel to continue operations from any location. The OEMC also uses surveillance cameras to increase situational awareness when responding to 911 calls.
- Results: The Chicago city government can sustain operations in an alternate location in the event that activities at any of its government buildings are disrupted.

SOURCES: "HP Services: A Comprehensive Managed Services Portfolio," "Homeland Security," and "Public Sector, Health, and Education," accessed at http://www.hp.com on December 4, 2008 and "Securing a City: Chicago Takes a Unified Approach to Emergency Management," accessed at http://www.hp.com on December 26, 2008.

and services—office supplies, personal computers, furniture, food, health care, and military equipment. Business marketing firms, large and small, serve the government market. In fact, 25 percent of the purchase contracts at the federal level are with small firms.[31]

E-Government

Across all levels of government, public officials are embracing the Internet as the best means of delivering services to constituents. E-government, then, involves transferring traditional government operations to an integrated Internet environment to improve public-sector accessibility, efficiency, and customer service. For example, www.govbenefits.com now provides users with access to information about 200 special government benefit programs, and www.recreation.gov provides a description of all publicly managed recreation sites in the United States. Many states, such as Texas, Arizona, Michigan, and Illinois, are launching creative e-government initiatives to deliver service to citizens. For business marketing firms like IBM and Hewlett-Packard that sell information technology products and services, e-government initiatives are sparking a large market opportunity (see Figure 2.4).

Influences on Government Buying

Another level of complexity is added to the governmental purchasing process by the array of influences on this process. In federal, state, and large-city procurement, buyers report to and are influenced by dozens of interested parties who specify, legislate, evaluate, and use the goods and services. Clearly, the range of outside influences extends far beyond the originating agency.

Understanding Government Contracts

Government purchasing is also affected by goals and programs that have broad social overtones, including compliance, set-asides, and minority subcontracting. The **compliance program** requires government contractors to maintain affirmative action programs for minorities, women, and the handicapped. Firms failing to do so are barred from holding government contracts. In the **set-aside program,** a certain percentage of a given government contract is "set aside" for small or minority businesses; no others can participate in that proportion of the contract. The **minority subcontracting program** may require that major contractors subcontract a certain percentage of the total contract to minority firms. For example, Ohio law requires that 7 percent of all subcontractors on state construction projects be minorities. The potential government contractor must understand these programs and how they apply to the firm.

Most government procurement, at any level, is based on laws that establish contractual guidelines.[32] The federal government has set forth certain general contract provisions as part of the federal procurement regulations. These provisions include stipulations regarding product inspection, payment methods, actions as a result of default, and disputes, among many others.

---

[31] Stephanie N. Mehta, "Small Firms Are Getting More Government Contracts," *The Wall Street Journal*, April 27, 1995, p. B2.

[32] Michael R. Leenders and Harold E. Fearon, *Purchasing and Supply Management*, 11th ed. (Chicago: Irwin, 1997), pp. 537–566.

Without a clear comprehension of the procurement laws, the vendor is in an unfavorable position during the negotiation phase. The vendor particularly needs to explore the advantages and disadvantages of the two basic types of contracts:

1. **Fixed-price contracts.** A firm price is agreed to before the contract is awarded, and full payment is made when the product or service is delivered as agreed.

2. **Cost-reimbursement contracts.** The vendor is reimbursed for allowable costs incurred in performance of the contract and is sometimes allowed a certain number of dollars above cost as profit.

Each type of contract has built-in incentives to control costs or to cover future contingencies.

Generally, the fixed-price contract provides the greatest profit potential, but it also poses greater risks if unforeseen expenses are incurred, if inflation increases dramatically, or if conditions change. However, if the seller can reduce costs significantly during the contract, profits may exceed those estimated when the contract was negotiated. The government carefully administers cost-reimbursement contracts because of the minimal incentives for contractor efficiency. Contracts of this type are usually employed for government projects involving considerable developmental work for which it is difficult to estimate efforts and expenses.

To overcome the inefficiencies of both the cost-reimbursement contract (which often leads to cost overruns) and the fixed-price contract (which can discourage firms from bidding because project costs are uncertain), the government often employs incentive contracts. The incentive contract rewards firms when their actual costs on a project are below target costs, and it imposes a penalty when they exceed target costs.

Telling Vendors How to Sell: Useful Publications

Unlike most customers, governments often go to great lengths to explain to potential vendors exactly how to do business with them. For example, the federal government makes available such publications as *Doing Business with the General Services Administration, Selling to the Military,* and *Selling to the U.S. Air Force.* Government agencies also hold periodic seminars to orient businesses to the buying procedures the agency uses. The objective is to encourage firms to seek government business.

Purchasing Organizations and Procedures: Government

Government and commercial purchasing are organized similarly. However, governments tend to emphasize clerical functions because of the detailed procedures the law requires. Although the federal government is the largest single industrial purchaser, it does not operate like a single company but like a combination of several large companies with overlapping responsibilities and thousands of small independent units.[33] The federal government has more than 15,000 purchasing authorities (departments, agencies, and so on). Every government agency possesses some degree of buying influence or authority. Federal government procurement is divided into two categories: defense and nondefense.

---

[33] Ibid., pp. 552–559.

Defense Procurement   The Department of Defense (DOD) spends a large proportion of the federal government's total procurement budget. The DOD's procurement operation is said to be the largest business enterprise in the world. The era of declining budgets for the DOD was quickly reversed with the terrorist attacks on the United States in September 2001. Defense and homeland security became funding priorities in the federal budget.

Each DOD military division—Army, Navy, and Air Force—is responsible for its own major purchases. However, the Defense Logistics Agency (DLA) procures billions of dollars worth of supplies used in common by all branches. The DLA's budget for procurement exceeds $35 billion annually.[34] The purposes of the DLA are to obtain favorable prices through volume purchasing and to reduce duplication of purchasing within the military. Defense-related items may also be procured by other government agencies, such as the General Services Administration (GSA). In fact, the DOD is the GSA's largest customer. Under current agreements between the GSA and the DOD, the military purchases through the GSA many items such as vehicles, desks, office machines, and hand tools.[35] Also, many supplies for military-base operations are procured locally.

Nondefense Procurement   Nondefense procurement is administered by a wide variety of agencies, including cabinet departments (for example, Health and Human Services, Commerce), commissions (for example, the Federal Trade Commission), the executive branch (for example, the Bureau of the Budget), federal agencies (for example, the Federal Aviation Agency), and federal administrations (for example, the GSA). The Department of Commerce centralizes the procurement of supplies and equipment for its Washington office and all local offices. The Department of the Interior, on the other hand, instructs each area and district office of the Mining Enforcement and Safety Administration to purchase mine-safety equipment and clothing locally.

Like the DLA, the GSA centralizes the procurement of many general-use items (for example, office furniture, pens, lightbulbs) for all civilian government agencies. The Federal Supply Service of the GSA is like the purchasing department of a large diversified corporation because it provides a consolidated purchasing, storing, and distribution network for the federal government. The Federal Supply Service purchases many items commonly used by other government agencies, including office supplies, small tools, paint, paper, furniture, maintenance supplies, and duplicating equipment. In some cases, the GSA operates retail-like stores, where any federal buyer can go to purchase equipment and supplies. The GSA has enormous purchasing power, managing more than one-fourth of the government's total procurement dollars.[36]

Under the Federal Supply Schedule Program, departments within the government may purchase specified items from an approved supplier at an agreed-on price. This program provides federal agencies with the sources of products such as furniture, appliances, office equipment, laboratory equipment, and the like. Once a supplier has bid and been approved, the schedule may involve an indefinite-quantity contract for a

---

[34]Defense Logistics Agency, "Facts and Figures," accessed at http://www.dla.mil on June 10, 2008.

[35]U.S. General Services Administration, "Doing Business with the GSA" (Washington, D.C., 1996).

[36]U.S. General Services Administration, "GSA Details FY09 Budget Request," accessed at http://www.gsa.gov on June 10, 2008.

term of 1 to 3 years. The schedule permits agencies to place orders directly with suppliers. Like corporate purchasing units, the GSA is using the Internet to streamline purchasing processes and to facilitate communication with suppliers (see http://www.gsa.gov).

Federal Buying

The president may set the procurement process in motion when he signs a congressional appropriation bill, or an accountant in the General Accounting Office may initiate the process by requesting a new desktop computer. Business marketers can identify the current needs of government buyers by consulting *FedBizOpps (FBO)* at http://www.fbodaily.com. The *FBO*, published by the Department of Commerce, lists all government procurement proposals, subcontracting leads, contract awards, and sales of surplus property. A potential supplier has at least 30 days to respond before bid opening. By law, all intended procurement actions of $10,000 or more, both civilian and military, are published in the *FBO*. Copies of the *FBO* are available at various government field offices, as well as local public libraries.

Once a procurement need is documented and publicly announced, the government follows one of two general procurement strategies: formal advertising (also known as open bid) or negotiated contract.

Formal Advertising   **Formal advertising** means the government solicits bids from appropriate suppliers; usually, the lowest bidder is awarded the contract. This strategy is followed when the product is standardized and the specifications straightforward. The interested supplier must gain a place on a bidder's list (or monitor the *FBO* on a daily basis—which suggests that a more effective approach is to get on the bidder's list by filing forms available from the GSA Business Service Centers). Then, each time the government requests bids for a particular product, the supplier receives an invitation to bid. The invitation to bid specifies the item and the quantity to be purchased, provides detailed technical specifications, and stipulates delivery schedules, warranties required, packing requirements, and other purchasing details. The bidding firm bases its bid on its own cost structure and on the bids it believes its competitors might make.

Procurement personnel review each bid for conformance to specifications. Contracts are generally awarded to the lowest bidder; however, the government agency may select the next-to-lowest bidder if it can document that the lowest bidder would not responsibly fulfill the contract. For example, the Internal Revenue Service (IRS) held a reverse auction for 11,000 desktop PCs and 16,000 notebook PCs. The prebid pricing started at $130 million; when the auction closed, the price was down to $63.4 million.[37]

Negotiated Contract Buying   A negotiated contract is used to purchase products and services that cannot be differentiated on the basis of price alone (such as complex scientific equipment or R&D projects) or when there are few suppliers. There may be some competition because the contracting office can conduct negotiations with several suppliers simultaneously.

---

[37] Richard Walker and Kevin McCaney, "Reverse Auctions Win Bid of Acceptance," *Buyers.Gov* (December 2001): p. 1.

Obviously, negotiation is a much more flexible procurement procedure; the government buyers may exercise considerable personal judgment. Procurement is based on the more subjective factors of performance and quality, as well as on price. The procurement decision for the government is much like that of the large corporation: Which is the best possible product at the lowest price, and will the product meet performance standards?

For example, the U.S. Army and Marines are together planning to replace the Humvee transports used in Iraq with a Joint Light Tactical Vehicle.[38] Lockheed Martin Corporation and Boeing Company, the two largest U.S. defense contractors, are each competing for the contract, along with a formidable set of rival teams led by General Dynamics Corporation, BAE Systems, Northrop Grumman Corporation, and Raytheon Company, respectively. From this field of competitors, three development contracts will be awarded first. That will set the stage for a competition in 2011 where each of the three rivals will demonstrate the performance and reliability of its vehicle. The stakes are high: The winner will receive a $40 billion order to supply 60,000 vehicles over the next decade.

A Different Strategy Required

A marketer positioned to sell to the government has a much different marketing strategy focus than does a firm that concentrates on the commercial sector. The government seller emphasizes (1) understanding the complex rules and standards that must be met; (2) developing a system to keep informed of each agency's procurement plans; (3) generating a strategy for product development and R&D that facilitates the firm's response to government product needs; (4) developing a communications strategy that focuses on how technology meets agency objectives; and (5) generating a negotiation strategy to secure favorable terms regarding payment, contract completion, and cost overruns due to changes in product specifications.

The Institutional Market: Unique Characteristics

Institutional customers comprise the third sector of the business market. Institutional buyers make up a sizable market—total expenditures on public elementary and secondary schools alone exceed $500 billion, and national health expenditures exceed $1.9 trillion.[39] Schools and health-care organizations make up a sizable component of the institutional market, which also includes colleges and universities, libraries, foundations, art galleries, and clinics. On the one hand, institutional purchasers are similar to governments in that the purchasing process is often constrained by political considerations and dictated by law. In fact, many institutions are administered by government units—schools, for example. On the other hand, other institutions are privately operated and managed like corporations; they may even have a broader range of purchase requirements than their large corporate counterparts. Like the commercial enterprise, institutions are ever cognizant of the value of efficient purchasing.

---

[38] Edmond Lococo, "Lockheed, Boeing Brains Fizzle in Humvee-Heir Bid (Updated)," Bloomberg.com June 4, 2008, accessed at http://www.bloomberg.com on June 5, 2008.

[39] U.S. Census Bureau, *Statistical Abstract of the United States: 2008*, accessed at http://www.census.gov on June 12, 2008.

Institutional Buyers: Purchasing Procedures

Diversity is the key element in the institutional market. For example, the institutional marketing manager must first be ready to respond to a school purchasing agent who buys in great quantity for an entire city's school system through a formal bidding procedure and then respond to a former pharmacist who has been elevated to purchasing agent for a small rural hospital.

Health-care institutions provide a good example of the diversity of this market. Some small hospitals delegate responsibility for food purchasing to the chief dietitian. Although many of these hospitals have purchasing agents, the agent cannot place an order unless the dietitian approves it. In larger hospitals, decisions may be made by committees composed of a business manager, purchasing agent, dietitian, and cook. In still other cases, hospitals may belong to buying groups consisting of many local hospitals or meal preparation may be contracted out. In an effort to contain costs, purchasing executives at large hospitals are adopting a supply chain focus and using sophisticated supplier evaluation methods, including e-procurement tools, like their counterparts in the commercial sector. Because of these varied purchasing environments, successful marketers usually maintain a separate marketing manager, staff, and sales force to tailor marketing efforts to each situation.

For many institutions, once a department's budget has been established, the department attempts to spend up to that budget limit. So, institutions may buy simply because there are unused funds in the budget. A business marketer should carefully evaluate the budgetary status of potential customers in the institutional segment of the market.

Because many institutions face strong budgetary pressures, they often outsource segments of their operations to specialists to enhance efficiency and effectiveness. School districts may look to third-party contractors to purchase food and supplies and to manage their meal service operations. For example, in Los Angeles, Marriott Corporation manages food service operations at the city's charter schools, and in Chicago, three different contract companies each operate 10 food-preparation departments.[40] Many universities have turned over operation of their bookstores and beverage contracts and management of their student unions to outside contractors. Business marketers must carefully analyze and understand the operational strategy of their institutional customers. Frequently, extensive sales and marketing attention must center on the third-party contract operators.

Targeted Strategy   The institutional market offers some unique applications for the concept of multiple buying influences (discussed in Chapter 1). Many institutions are staffed with professionals—doctors, professors, researchers, and others. In most cases, depending on size, the institution employs a purchasing agent and, in large institutions, a sizable and skilled purchasing department or materials management department. There is great potential for conflict between those responsible for purchasing and the professional staff for whom the purchasing department is buying. Often, the salesperson must carefully cultivate the professional staff in terms of product benefits and service while developing a delivery timetable, maintenance contract, and price schedule to satisfy the purchasing department. Leading business marketers also use the Internet to provide added value to

---

[40] Susie Stephenson, "Schools," *Restaurants and Institutions* 106 (August 1, 1996): pp. 60–64.

FIGURE 2.5 | **GE HEALTHCARE RE-IMAGINED ADVERTISING: HOW DO YOU CAPTURE A STILL IMAGE OF SOMETHING THAT NEVER SITS STILL?**

SOURCE: © 2008 General Electric Company. All rights reserved. Reprinted by permission from General Electric Company. Accessed at http://www.ge.com/company/advertising/ads_healthcare.html.

their customers. For example, GE Healthcare, a leader in medical imaging and diagnostics equipment (see Figure 2.5), has embraced e-commerce as the centerpiece of its marketing strategy and provides an online catalog, daily Internet specials, and a host of services for its customers—purchasing managers at hospitals and health-care facilities worldwide. In fact, GE and the University of Pittsburgh Medical Center have formed a company to move the laboratory analysis of human tissue into the digital age.[41] Following a routine that has changed little in the past century, the vast majority of tissue samples are viewed individually by doctors using a microscope. The goal of this new venture is to create and market a "virtual microscope" that would scan and store images electronically, improving patient care by making it easier for doctors to share information.

Group Purchasing An important factor in institutional purchasing is group purchasing. Hospitals, schools, and universities may join cooperative purchasing associations to obtain quantity discounts. Universities affiliated with the Education and Institutional Purchasing Cooperative enjoy favorable contracts established by the cooperative and can purchase a wide array of products directly from vendors at the low negotiated prices. The cooperative spends more than $100 million on goods

---

[41] Scott Thurm, "GE Venture to Develop 'Virtual Microscope'," *The Wall Street Journal*, June 5, 2008, p. B5.

FIGURE 2.6 | **A Market-Centered Organization**

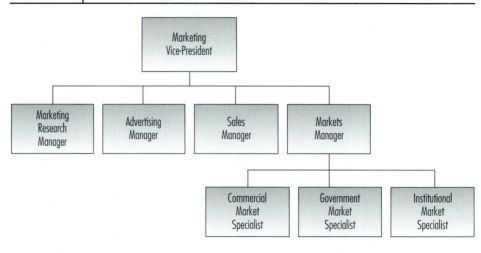

annually. Cooperative buying allows institutions to enjoy lower prices, improved quality (through improved testing and vendor selection), reduced administrative cost, standardization, better records, and greater competition.

Hospital group purchasing represents a significant market exceeding $10 billion. Group purchasing has become widely accepted: More than one-third of public-sector hospitals in the United States are members of some type of affiliated group. Most hospital group purchasing is done at the regional level through hospital associations. However, for-profit hospital chains, which are a growing factor in the health-care field, also engage in group buying. For example, a multihospital system with a $1 billion operating budget spends $300 to $500 million a year on medical supplies and purchased services. By channeling purchases through group purchasing organizations, these large buyers are reaping significant savings.[42]

Group purchasing poses special challenges for the business marketer. The marketer must develop not only strategies for dealing with individual institutions but also unique strategies for the special requirements of cooperative purchasing groups and large hospital chains. The buying centers—individual institution versus cooperative purchasing group—may vary considerably in composition, criteria, and level of expertise. For the purchasing groups, discount pricing assumes special importance. Suppliers who sell through purchasing groups must also have distribution systems that effectively deliver products to individual group members. And even though vendors have a contract with a large cooperative association, they must still be prepared to respond individually to each institution that places an order against the contract.

Institutional Purchasing Practices   In many respects the purchasing practices of large institutions are similar to those of large commercial firms, but there are some important differences. The policies regarding cooperative buying, preference for local vendors, and the delegation of purchasing responsibility for food, pharmaceuticals, and many other

[42]Timothy L. Chapman, Ajay Gupta, and Paul O. Mange, "Group Purchasing Is Not a Panacea for U.S. Hospitals," *McKinsey Quarterly*, no. 1 (1998): p. 160.

items are of particular importance. The business marketer must understand these characteristics to carefully develop effective strategies for these institutional customers.

Dealing with Diversity: A Market-Centered Organization

Because each sector of the business market is unique, many firms have built market specialization into the marketing organization. To illustrate, the industrial products area of the J. M. Smucker Company is organized around market sectors. The institutional, military, and business markets are each managed by different individuals, each thoroughly knowledgeable about one particular market.

Figure 2.6 illustrates one form of a market-centered organizational scheme. Observe that a market manager supervises and coordinates the activities of three market specialists. Each market specialist examines the buying processes, the product preferences, and the similarities and differences between customers in one sector of the business market. Such an analysis enables the market specialist to further categorize customers in a particular sector into meaningful market segments and to design specialized marketing programs for each. A market-centered organization provides the business marketer with a structure for dealing effectively with diversity in the business market.

Summary

In business-to-business marketing, the customers are organizations. The business market can be divided into three major sectors: commercial enterprises, governments (federal, state, and local), and institutions. Many business marketers—for example, Intel, Boeing, and IBM—generate a significant proportion of their sales and profit by serving international customers. Indeed, the demand for many industrial products is growing more rapidly in many foreign countries than in the United States.

Commercial enterprises include manufacturers, construction companies, service firms, transportation companies, selected professional groups, and resellers. Of these, manufacturers account for the largest dollar volume of purchases. Furthermore, although the majority of manufacturing firms are small, buying power is concentrated in the hands of relatively few manufacturers, which are also concentrated geographically.

Commercial enterprises, such as service establishments and transportation or utility companies, are more widely dispersed. A purchasing manager or purchasing agent administers the procurement process. In large firms, the purchasing function has been quite specialized. In addition to protecting the cost structure of the firm, improving quality, and keeping inventory investment to a minimum, purchasing assumes a central role in managing relationships with suppliers. In turn, leading-edge organizations like Dell Computer demonstrate the critical role that purchasing and supply chain management can assume in creating profit opportunities. Rather than devoting exclusive attention to "buying for less," leading organizations tie purchasing activities directly to corporate strategy and use a range of sophisticated e-procurement tools.

Governmental units also make substantial purchases of products. Government buyers use two general purchasing strategies: the formal advertising approach for standardized products and negotiated contracts for those with unique requirements.

Institutional customers, such as health-care organizations and universities, comprise the third sector of the business market. Depending on size, the institution employs a purchasing agent and, in large institutions, a sizable purchasing department. Across business market sectors, purchasing managers are using the Internet to identify potential suppliers, conduct online reverse auctions, and communicate with suppliers.

Diversity is the characteristic that typifies the institutional market. The characteristics, orientations, and purchasing processes of institutional buyers are somewhere between commercial enterprises and government buyers. Cooperative purchasing—a unique aspect of this segment—necessitates a special strategic response by potential suppliers. Many business marketers have found that a market-centered organization provides the specialization required to meet the needs of each market sector.

Discussion Questions

1. A small manufacturer developed a new high-speed packaging system that could be appealing to food-processing firms like Pillsbury and General Mills. This new packaging system is far more efficient but must be priced 15 percent higher than competitors' products. Because purchasing managers evaluate the "total cost of ownership" of major purchases, what selling points should the business marketer emphasize to demonstrate the superiority of this new product?

2. Honda of America relies on 400 suppliers in North America to provide more than 60 percent of the parts and materials for the Accord. What strategies could a business marketer follow in becoming a new supplier to Honda? What criteria would Honda consider in evaluating suppliers?

3. Describe the total-cost-of-ownership orientation that purchasing managers use and illustrate how you could apply it to your next automobile purchase decision.

4. Segmentation is a tool that marketers use to identify target markets. Increasingly, purchasing managers are using the segmentation approach to determine which suppliers are most critical to the goals of the organization. Explain.

5. Compare and contrast the two general procurement strategies employed by the federal government: (1) formal advertising and (2) negotiated contract.

6. Institutional buyers fall somewhere between commercial enterprises and government buyers in terms of their characteristics, orientation, and purchasing process. Explain.

7. Explain how the decision-making process that a university might employ in selecting a new computer would differ from that of a commercial enterprise. Who would be the key participants in the process in each setting?

8. Fearing red tape and mounds of paperwork, Tom Bronson, president of B&E Electric, has always avoided the government market. A recent discussion with a colleague, however, has rekindled Tom's interest in

this sector. What steps should B&E Electric take to learn more about this market?

9. General Electric (GE) has embraced e-purchasing and has saved more than $500 million per year by conducting online reverse auctions in buying a range of goods, including office, computer, and maintenance supplies. What new challenges and opportunities does this auctioning process present for business marketers who serve GE?

10. One purchasing executive observed, "Online auctioning is an appropriate way to buy some categories of products and services but it's entirely inappropriate for others." Agree or disagree? Provide support for your position.

Internet Exercises

1. GE Healthcare has developed an e-commerce initiative to support its marketing strategy, which targets health-care organizations on a worldwide basis. Go to http://www.gemedicalsystems.com and

   a. identify the products and services that the GE unit offers, and

   b. provide a critique of the Web site and consider the degree to which it provides access to the information that a potential buyer might want.

2. Ariba, Inc., is a leading provider of e-procurement software solutions. Go to http://www.ariba.com and

   a. describe the key products and services that the firm offers to its customers, and

   b. review a case history that describes a particular customer and how it has applied one of Ariba's procurement solutions.

Sealed Air Corporation: Delivering Packaging Solutions[43]

Sealed Air Corporation is a global leader in providing business customers with performance solutions for food, protective, and specialty packaging. Best known for its BubbleWrap® cushioning material, the firm has pioneered a number of packaging innovations that have sustained a remarkable pattern of sales growth for more than two decades. Using a consultative selling approach, field sales and technical support specialists at Sealed Air incorporate both packaging materials and specialized equipment to provide a complete packaging solution for customers, providing superior protection against shock, abrasion, and vibration, compared with other forms of packaging. Let's explore the packaging solution that Sealed Air developed for Davis Neon Inc., a wholesale neon sign manufacturer in Heath Springs, South Carolina.

Protecting custom-made neon signs that are shipped worldwide is a challenging problem for Dave Lytle, shipping manager at Davis Neon. "We were using preformed polyethylene foam sheets, which required a lot of storage space and time to unload from the trucks," noted Lytle. "We were keeping our eyes open for an alternative packaging method which would provide comparable protection, yet reduce costs and increase productivity."

After evaluating several alternatives, Dave Lytle chose a solution proposed by Sealed Air to package the neon signs—Instapak Continuous Foam Tubes made by Sealed Air's SpeedyPacker Insight system. Using the SpeedyPacker equipment, now installed in the shipping area at Davis Neon, an operator can create numerous variations of foam bags at the touch of a button. For each neon sign, Davis Neon employees create a custom-made wooden crate with dimensions just large enough to house the sign. The packager then puts a layer of foam tubes, made-to-order by the Speedy Packer equipment, on the bottom of the crate to form a pad. BubbleWrap cushioning is used on the back of the sign, between rows, and on the side to provide surface protection and prevent abrasion of the sign against the crate. Another layer of foam tubes is added on top before the lid is attached to the crate.

Before implementing the Sealed Air solution, packagers used preformed polyethylene foam sheets, each of which had to be cut by hand to fit the crate for the bottom pad and top layer, as well as to fit in between the letters on the neon sign. "The preformed polyethylene foam sheets took a long time to cut, were expensive, and produced significant material waste," stated Lytle. "After working with the new packaging system, the actual savings are 62 percent in material costs. We have also seen productivity increase by 20 percent." Employees at Davis are now able to pack more crates in less time.

Discussion Questions

1. Given the significant value that Sealed Air can provide for a customer, like Davis Neon Inc., what approach should they follow in pricing a particular packaging solution for a customer?

2. Develop a list of other types of customers who face special packaging challenges and may represent promising customer prospects for Sealed Air to target.

---

[43] Case History, "Sealed Air Sheds Light on Davis Neon's Packaging," accessed at www.sealedair.com on June 6, 2008.

PART

II

MANAGING RELATIONSHIPS IN BUSINESS MARKETING

CHAPTER

3

Organizational Buying Behavior

A wide array of forces inside and outside the organization influence the organizational buyer. Knowledge of these forces provides the marketer with a foundation for responsive business marketing strategies. After reading this chapter, you will understand:

1. the decision process organizational buyers apply as they confront differing buying situations and the resulting strategy implications for the business marketer.

2. the individual, group, organizational, and environmental variables that influence organizational buying decisions.

3. a model of organizational buying behavior that integrates these important influences.

4. how a knowledge of organizational buying characteristics enables the marketer to make more informed decisions about product design, pricing, and promotion.

FIGURE 3.1 | **WANT TO WIN THE SUPPORT OF BUYING INFLUENTIALS? ENHANCE THEIR CUSTOMERS' EXPERIENCE**

As a leading supplier to foreign and domestic automakers, Johnson Controls centers marketing research and R&D investments on making the automotive experience safer and more pleasurable for drivers. As a result, design engineers are eager to enhance customer value by incorporating the firm's components in new models.

To spark innovation, Johnson Controls' R&D processes include:

- **Human Factor Studio**, where seating, electronics, and interior components are tested based on ease of reach, usability, and function, giving special attention to ergonomic positioning.

- **Comfort Lab**, which takes vehicle passengers on a road trip via simulator that generates the bumps, dips, and turns of an open-road drive. Here, automakers can even analyze prototype designs before production.

- **Wave Lab**, where the acoustic and vibration properties of automotive interior components can be tested to remove, by design, sounds that cause annoyance or displeasure. The ultimate goal: providing design engineers and their customers—auto buyers—quieter and more comfortable automobile interiors.

SOURCES: "JCI Labs Spark Innovation: Improving the Customer Experience through Research and Development," accessed at http://www.johnsoncontrols.com on December 4, 2008; and "Beyond Bunsen Burners: Science Takes New Forms at Johnson Controls' Innovative Testing Labs," accessed at http://www.johnsoncontrols.com on December 4, 2008.

Market-driven business firms continuously sense and act on trends in their markets. Consider Johnson Controls, Inc., a diverse, multi-industry company that is a leading supplier of auto interiors (including seats, electronics, headliners, and instrument panels) to manufacturers.[1] The striking success of the firm rests on the close relationships that its sales reps and marketing managers have formed with design engineers and purchasing executives in the auto industry. To illustrate, some of Johnson Controls' salespersons work on-site with design teams at Ford, GM, or Honda. To provide added value to the new-product-design process, the firm also invests annually in market research on the needs and preferences of auto buyers—the customer's customer! (Figure 3.1) For example, based on extensive research about how families spend their time in cars, Johnson Controls developed a unique rear seat entertainment system that allows passengers to play video games, watch DVDs, or listen to CDs through wireless headphones or the vehicle's speaker system. Moreover, to enhance the customer experience, technicians at Johnson Controls' research lab test seating and interior components for comfort, safety, ease-of-reach, usability, and function. Using a simulator that generates the bumps, dips, and turns of an open-road drive, scientists can record the passengers' experience and capture valuable information for developing components that improve comfort and safety as well as customer satisfaction. By staying close to the needs of auto buyers, Johnson Controls became the preferred supplier to design engineers who are continually seeking innovative ways to make auto interiors more distinctive and inviting.

---

[1] "JCI Labs Spark Innovation," accessed at http://www.johnsoncontrols.com on June 3, 2008.

FIGURE 3.2 | MAJOR STAGES OF THE ORGANIZATIONAL BUYING PROCESS

Stage	Description
1. Problem Recognition	Managers at P&G need new high-speed packaging equipment to support a new product launch.
2. General Description of Need	Production managers work with a purchasing manager to determine the characteristics needed in the new packaging system.
3. Product Specifications	An experienced production manager assists a purchasing manager in developing a detailed and precise description of the needed equipment.
4. Supplier Search	After conferring with production managers, a purchasing manager identifies a set of alternative suppliers that could satisfy P&G's requirements.
5. Acquisition and Analysis of Proposals	Alternative proposals are evaluated by a purchasing manager and a number of members of the production department.
6. Supplier Selection	Negotiations with the two finalists are conducted, and a supplier is chosen.
7. Selection of Order Routine	A delivery date is established for the production equipment.
8. Performance Review	After equipment is installed, purchasing and production managers evaluate the performance of the equipment and the service support provided by the supplier.

Understanding the dynamics of organizational buying behavior is crucial for identifying profitable market segments, locating buying influences within these segments, and reaching organizational buyers efficiently and effectively with an offering that responds to their needs. Each decision the business marketer makes is based on organizational buyers' probable response. This chapter explores the key stages of the organizational buying process and isolates the salient characteristics of different purchasing situations. Next, attention turns to the myriad forces that influence organizational buying behavior. Knowledge of how organizational buying decisions are made provides the business marketer with a solid foundation for building responsive marketing strategies.

The Organizational Buying Process

Organizational buying behavior is a process, not an isolated act or event. Tracing the history of a procurement decision uncovers critical decision points and evolving information requirements. In fact, organizational buying involves several stages, each of which yields a decision. Figure 3.2 lists the major stages in the organizational buying process.[2]

---

[2] The discussion in this section is based on Patrick J. Robinson, Charles W. Faris, and Yoram Wind, *Industrial Buying and Creative Marketing* (Boston: Allyn and Bacon, 1967), pp. 12–18; see also Jeffrey E. Lewin and Naveen Donthu, "The Influence of Purchase Situations on buying Center Structure and Investment: A Select Meta-Analysis of Organizational Buying Behavior Research," *Journal of Business Research* 58 (October 2005), pp. 1381–1390; and Morry Ghingold and David T. Wilson, "Buying Center Research and Business Marketing Practice: Meeting the Challenge of Dynamic Marketing," *Journal of Business & Industrial Marketing*, 13 (2, 1998): pp. 96–108.

The purchasing process begins when someone in the organization recognizes a problem that can be solved or an opportunity that can be captured by acquiring a specific product. Problem recognition can be triggered by internal or external forces. Internally, a firm like P&G may need new high-speed production equipment to support a new product launch. Or a purchasing manager may be unhappy with the price or service of an equipment supplier. Externally, a salesperson can precipitate the need for a product by demonstrating opportunities for improving the organization's performance. Likewise, business marketers also use advertising to alert customers to problems and demonstrate how a particular product may solve them.

During the organizational buying process, many small or incremental decisions are made that ultimately translate into the final choice of a supplier. To illustrate, a production manager might unknowingly establish specifications for a new production system that only one supplier can meet (Stages 2 and 3). This type of decision early in the buying process dramatically influences the favorable evaluation and ultimate selection of that supplier.

The Search Process

Once the organization has defined the product that meets its requirements, attention turns to this question: Which of the many possible suppliers are promising candidates? The organization invests more time and energy in the supplier search when the proposed product has a strong bearing on organizational performance. When the information needs of the buying organization are low, Stages 4 and 5 occur simultaneously, especially for standardized items. In this case, a purchasing manager may merely check a catalog or secure an updated price from the Internet. Stage 5 emerges as a distinct category only when the information needs of the organization are high. Here, the process of acquiring and analyzing proposals may involve purchasing managers, engineers, users, and other organizational members.

Supplier Selection and Performance Review   After being selected as a chosen supplier (Stage 6) and agreeing to purchasing guidelines (Stage 7), such as required quantities and expected time of delivery, a marketer faces further tests. A performance review is the final stage in the purchasing process. The performance review may lead the purchasing manager to continue, modify, or cancel the agreement. A review critical of the chosen supplier and supportive of rejected alternatives can lead members of the decision-making unit to reexamine their position. If the product fails to meet the needs of the using department, decision makers may give further consideration to vendors screened earlier in the procurement process. To keep a new customer, the marketer must ensure that the buying organization's needs have been completely satisfied. Failure to follow through at this critical stage leaves the marketer vulnerable.

The stages in this model of the procurement process may not progress sequentially and may vary with the complexity of the purchasing situation. For example, some of the stages are compressed or bypassed when organizations make routine buying decisions. However, the model provides important insights into the organizational buying process. Certain stages may be completed concurrently; the process may be discontinued by a change in the external environment or in upper-management thinking. The organizational buying process is shaped by a host of internal and external forces, such as changes in economic or competitive conditions or a basic shift in organizational priorities.

Organizations with significant experience in purchasing a particular product approach the decision quite differently from first-time buyers. Therefore, attention must center on buying situations rather than on products. Three types of buying situations have been delineated: (1) new task, (2) modified rebuy, and (3) straight rebuy.[3]

New Task

In the **new-task buying situation**, organization decisions makers perceive the problem or need as totally different from previous experiences; therefore, they need a significant amount of information to explore alternative ways of solving the problem and searching for alternative suppliers.

When confronting a new-task buying situation, organizational buyers operate in a stage of decision making referred to as **extensive problem solving**.[4] The buying influentials and decision makers lack well-defined criteria for comparing alternative products and suppliers, but they also lack strong predispositions toward a particular solution. In the consumer market, this is the same type of problem solving an individual or household might follow when buying a first home.

Buying-Decision Approaches[5]   Two distinct buying-decision approaches are used: judgmental new task and strategic new task. The greatest level of uncertainty confronts firms in judgmental new-task situations because the product may be technically complex, evaluating alternatives is difficult, and dealing with a new suppliers has unpredictable aspects. Consider purchasers of a special type of production equipment who are uncertain about the model or brand to choose, the suitable level of quality, and the appropriate price to pay. For such purchases, buying activities include a moderate amount of information search and a moderate use of formal tools in evaluating key aspects of the buying decision.

Even more effort is invested in **strategic new-task decisions.** These purchasing decisions are of extreme importance to the firm strategically and financially. If the buyer perceives that a rapid pace of technological change surrounds the decision, search effort is increased but concentrated in a shorter time period.[6] Long-range planning drives the decision process. To illustrate, a large health insurance company placed a $600,000 order for workstation furniture. The long-term effect on the work environment shaped the 6-month decision process and involved the active participation of personnel from several departments.

---

[3] Robinson, Faris, and Wind, *Industrial Buying and Creative Marketing*, chap. 1; see also Erin Anderson, Wujin Chu, and Barton Weitz, "Industrial Purchasing: An Empirical Exploration of the Buyclass Framework," *Journal of Marketing* 51 (July 1987): pp. 71–86; and Morry Ghingold, "Testing the 'Buygrid' Buying Process Model," *Journal of Purchasing and Materials Management* 22 (Winter 1986): pp. 30–36.

[4] The levels of decision making discussed in this section are drawn from John A. Howard and Jagdish N. Sheth, *The Theory of Buyer Behavior* (New York: John Wiley and Sons, 1969), chap. 2.

[5] The discussion of buying decision approaches in this section is drawn from Michele D. Bunn, "Taxonomy of Buying Decision Approaches," *Journal of Marketing* 57 (January 1993): pp. 38–56; see also, Michele D. Bunn, Gul T. Butaney, and Nicole P. Huffman, "An Empirical Model of Professional Buyers' Search Effort," *Journal of Business-to-Business Marketing* 8 (4, 2001): pp. 55–81.

[6] Allen M. Weiss and Jan B. Heide, "The Nature of Organizational Search in High Technology Markets," *Journal of Marketing Research* 30 (May 1993): pp. 230–233. See also, Christian Homburg and Sabine Kuester, "Towards an Improved Understanding of Industrial Buying Behavior: Determinants of the Number of Suppliers," *Journal of Business-to-Business Marketing* 8 (2, 2001): pp. 5–29.

Strategy Guidelines   The business marketer confronting a new-task buying situation can gain a differential advantage by participating actively in the initial stages of the procurement process. The marketer should gather information on the problems facing the buying organization, isolate specific requirements, and offer proposals to meet the requirements. Ideas that lead to new products often originate not with the marketer but with the customer.

Marketers who are presently supplying other items to the organization ("in" suppliers) have an edge over other firms: They can see problems unfolding and are familiar with the "personality" and behavior patterns of the organization. The successful business marketer carefully monitors the changing needs of organizations and is prepared to assist new-task buyers.

Straight Rebuy

When there is a continuing or recurring requirement, buyers have substantial experience in dealing with the need and require little or no new information. Evaluation of new alternative solutions is unnecessary and unlikely to yield appreciable improvements. Thus, a **straight rebuy** approach is appropriate.

Routine problem solving is the decision process organizational buyers employ in the straight rebuy. Organizational buyers apply well-developed choice criteria to the purchase decision. The criteria have been refined over time as the buyers have developed predispositions toward the offerings of one or a few carefully screened suppliers. In the consumer market, this is the same type of problem solving that a shopper might use in selecting 30 items in 20 minutes during a weekly trip to the supermarket. Indeed, many organizational buying decisions made each day are routine. For example, organizations of all types are continually buying **operating resources**—the goods and services needed to run the business, such as computer and office supplies, maintenance and repair items, and travel services. Procter & Gamble alone spends more than $5 billion annually on operating resources.[7]

Buying Decision Approaches   Research suggests that organizational buyers employ two buying-decision approaches: causal and routine low priority. Causal purchases involve no information search or analysis and the product or service is of minor importance. The focus is simply on transmitting the order. In contrast, routine low-priority decisions are somewhat more important to the firm and involve a moderate amount of analysis. Describing the purchase of $5,000 worth of cable to be used as component material, a buyer aptly describes this decision-process approach:

> On repeat buys, we may look at other sources or alternate methods of manufacturing, etc. to make sure no new technical advancements are available in the marketplace. But, generally, a repeat buy is repurchased from the supplier originally selected, especially for low dollar items.

Strategy Guidelines   The purchasing department handles straight rebuy situations by routinely selecting a supplier from a list of approved vendors and then placing an order. As organizations shift to e-procurement systems, purchasing managers retain control of the process for these routine purchases while allowing individual employees to directly

---

[7] Doug Smock, "Strategic Sourcing: P&G Boosts Leverage," *Purchasing* 133 (November 4, 2004): pp. 40–43.

buy online from approved suppliers.[8] Employees use a simple point-and-click interface to navigate through a customized catalog detailing the offerings of approved suppliers, and then order required items. Individual employees like the self-service convenience, and purchasing managers can direct attention to more critical strategic issues. Marketing communications should be designed to reach not only purchasing managers but also individual employees who are now empowered to exercise their product preferences.

The marketing task appropriate for the straight rebuy situation depends on whether the marketer is an "in" supplier (on the list) or an "out" supplier (not among the chosen few). An "in" supplier must reinforce the buyer-seller relationship, meet the buying organization's expectations, and be alert and responsive to the changing needs of the organization.

The "out" supplier faces a number of obstacles and must convince the organization that it can derive significant benefits from breaking the routine. This can be difficult because organizational buyers perceive risk in shifting from the known to the unknown. The organizational spotlight shines directly on them if an untested supplier falters. Buyers may view testing, evaluations, and approvals as costly, time-consuming, and unnecessary.

The marketing effort of the "out" supplier rests on an understanding of the basic buying needs of the organization: Information gathering is essential. The marketer must convince organizational buyers that their purchasing requirements have changed or that the requirements should be interpreted differently. The objective is to persuade decision makers to reexamine alternative solutions and revise the preferred list to include the new supplier.

Modified Rebuy

In the **modified rebuy** situation, organizational decision makers feel they can derive significant benefits by reevaluating alternatives. The buyers have experience in satisfying the continuing or recurring requirement, but they believe it worthwhile to seek additional information and perhaps to consider alternative solutions.

Several factors may trigger such a reassessment. Internal forces include the search for quality improvements or cost reductions. A marketer offering cost, quality, or service improvements can be an external precipitating force. The modified rebuy situation is most likely to occur when the firm is displeased with the performance of present suppliers (for example, poor delivery service).

Limited problem solving best describes the decision-making process for the modified rebuy. Decision makers have well-defined criteria but are uncertain about which suppliers can best fit their needs. In the consumer market, college students buying their *second* computer might follow a limited problem-solving approach.

Buying-Decision Approaches Two buying-decision approaches typify this buying-class category. Both strongly emphasize the firm's strategic objectives and long-term needs. The simple modified rebuy involves a narrow set of choice alternatives and a moderate amount of both information search and analysis. Buyers concentrate on the long-term-relationship potential of suppliers.

[8] Talai Osmonbekov, Daniel C. Bello, and David I Gillilard, "Adoption of Electronic Commerce Tools in Business Procurement: Enhanced Buying Center Structure and Processes," *Journal of Business & Industrial Marketing* 17 (2/3, 2002): pp. 151–166.

The **complex modified rebuy** involves a large set of choice alternatives and poses little uncertainty. The range of choice enhances the buyer's negotiating strength. The importance of the decision motivates buyers to actively search for information, apply sophisticated analysis techniques, and carefully consider long-term needs. This decision situation is particularly well suited to a competitive bidding process. For example, some firms are turning to online reverse auctions (one buyer, many sellers), where the buying organization allows multiple suppliers to bid on a contract, exerting downward price pressure throughout the process. To participate, suppliers must be prepared to meet defined product characteristics, as well as quality and service standards. "And while price will always be an issue, more buyers today use reverse auctions to determine the best value."[9] Rather than being used for specialized products or services where a close working relationship with the supplier is needed, auctions tend to be used for commodities and standardized parts.

Strategy Guidelines   In a modified rebuy, the direction of the marketing effort depends on whether the marketer is an "in" or an "out" supplier. An "in" supplier should make every effort to understand and satisfy the procurement need and to move decision makers into a straight rebuy. The buying organization perceives potential payoffs by reexamining alternatives. The "in" supplier should ask why and act immediately to remedy any customer problems. The marketer may be out of touch with the buying organization's requirements.

The goal of the "out" supplier should be to hold the organization in modified rebuy status long enough for the buyer to evaluate an alternative offering. Knowing the factors that led decision makers to reexamine alternatives could be pivotal. A particularly effective strategy for an "out" supplier is to offer performance guarantees as part of the proposal.[10] To illustrate, the following guarantee prompted International Circuit Technology, a manufacturer of printed circuit boards, to change to a new supplier for plating chemicals: "Your plating costs will be no more than x cents per square foot or we will make up the difference."[11] Given the nature of the production process, plating costs can be easily monitored by comparing the square footage of circuit boards moving down the plating line with the cost of plating chemicals for the period. Pleased with the performance, International Circuit Technology now routinely reorders from this new supplier.

Strategy Implications   Although past research provides some useful guidelines, marketers must exercise great care in forecasting the likely composition of the buying center for a particular purchasing situation.[12] The business marketer should attempt to identify purchasing patterns that apply to the firm. For example, the classes of industrial goods introduced in Chapter 1 (such as foundation goods versus facilitating goods) involve varying degrees of technical complexity and financial risk for the buying organization.

---

[9] James Carbone, "Not Just a Cost Reduction Tool," *Purchasing* 134 (February 17, 2005): p. 43.

[10] Mary Siegfried Dozbaba, "Critical Supplier Relationships: Converting Higher Performance," *Purchasing Today* (February 1999): pp. 22–29.

[11] Somerby Dowst, "CEO Report: Wanted: Suppliers Adept at Turning Corners," *Purchasing* 101 (January 29, 1987): pp. 71–72.

[12] Donald W. Jackson Jr., Janet E. Keith, and Richard K. Burdick, "Purchasing Agents' Perceptions of Industrial Buying Center Influence," *Journal of Marketing* 48 (fall 1984): pp. 75–83.

FIGURE 3.3 | **FORCES INFLUENCING ORGANIZATIONAL BUYING BEHAVIOR**

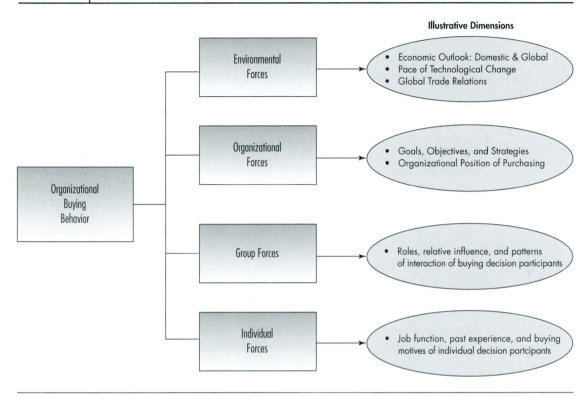

The business marketer must therefore view the procurement problem or need from the buying organization's perspective. How far has the organization progressed with the specific purchasing problem? How does the organization define the task at hand? How important is the purchase? The answers direct and form the business marketer's response and also provide insight into the composition of the decision-making unit.

Forces Shaping Organizational Buying Behavior

The eight-stage model of the organizational buying process provides the foundation for exploring the myriad forces that influence a buying decision by an organization. Observe in Figure 3.3 how organizational buying behavior is influenced by environmental forces (for example, the growth rate of the economy); organizational forces (for example, the size of the buying organization); group forces (for example, patterns of influence in buying decisions); and individual forces (for example, personal preferences).

Environmental Forces

A projected change in business conditions, a technological development, or a new piece of legislation can drastically alter organizational buying plans. Among the environmental forces that shape organizational buying behavior are economic, political, legal, and technological influences. Collectively, such environmental influences define the boundaries within which buyer-seller relationships develop. Particular attention is given to selected economic and technological forces that influence buying decisions.

Economic Influences   Because of the derived nature of industrial demand, the marketer must be sensitive to the strength of demand in the ultimate consumer market. The demand for many industrial products fluctuates more widely than the general economy. Firms that operate on a global scale must be sensitive to the economic conditions that prevail across regions. For example, while the United States, western Europe, and Japan may experience modest increases (for example, 2 or 3 percent) in gross domestic product (GDP) in the years ahead, rapidly developing economies (RDEs) are projected to grow three or four times as fast. In addition to China and India, key RDEs include Mexico, Brazil, central and eastern Europe, and southeast Asia.[13] A wealth of political and economic forces dictate the vitality and growth of an economy. A recent study found that the number of North American companies purchasing goods and services from China, eastern Europe, and India has increased sharply in recent years and will continue to rise.[14] Best-in-class procurement organizations are twice as likely as their competitors to emphasize low-cost-country sourcing strategies.[15] Demonstrating this trend, IBM recently moved its procurement headquarters to Shenzhen, China!

The economic environment influences an organization's ability and, to a degree, its willingness to buy. However, shifts in general economic conditions do not affect all sectors of the market evenly. For example, a rise in interest rates may damage the housing industry (including lumber, cement, and insulation) but may have minimal effects on industries such as paper, hospital supplies, office products, and soft drinks. Marketers that serve broad sectors of the organizational market must be particularly sensitive to the differential effect of selective economic shifts on buying behavior.

Technological Influences   Rapidly changing technology can restructure an industry and dramatically alter organizational buying plans. Notably, the World Wide Web "has forever changed the way companies and customers (whether they be consumers or other businesses) buy and sell to each other, learn about each other, and communicate."[16]

The rate of technological change in an industry influences the composition of the decision-making unit in the buying organization. As the pace of technological change increases, the importance of the purchasing manager in the buying process declines. Technical and engineering personnel tend to be more important when the rate of technological change is great. Recent research also suggests that buyers who perceive the pace of technological change to be more rapid (1) conduct more intense search efforts and (2) spend less time on their overall search processes.[17] Allen Weiss and

[13] Satish Shankar, Charles Ormiston, Nicholas Bloch, Robert Schaus, and Vijay Vishwanath, "How to Win in Emerging Markets," *MIT Sloan Management Review* 49 (Spring 2008): pp. 19–23.

[14] "Global Procurement Study Finds Companies Unprepared to Manage Increased Sourcing from China and India Effectively," accessed at http://www.atkearney.com on May 18, 2005.

[15] Andrew Bartolini, "CPO Rising: The CPO's Agenda for 2008," February 2008, research report by the Aberdeen Group, accessed at http://www.aberdeen.com on May 25, 2008.

[16] Stewart Alsop, "e or Be Eaten," *Fortune*, November 8, 1999, p. 87.

[17] Weiss and Heide, "The Nature of Organizational Search," pp. 220–233; see also Jan B. Heide and Allen M. Weiss, "Vendor Consideration and Switching Behavior for Buyers in High-Technology Markets," *Journal of Marketing* 59 (July 1995): pp. 30–43.

Jan Heide suggest that "in cost-benefit terms, a fast pace of change implies that distinct benefits are associated with search effort, yet costs are associated with prolonging the process" because the acquired information is "time sensitive."[18]

The marketer must also actively monitor signs of technological change and be prepared to adapt marketing strategy to deal with new technological environments. For example, Hewlett-Packard has embraced the Internet in its products, services, practices, and marketing. With search engines, spam filters, iPods, and other technologies, customers now have more control of the information they receive than ever before, notes Scott Anderson, director of enterprise brand communication at Hewlett-Packard. In this dynamic environment, "our strategy is to engage our customers with online interactions and content," he says, pointing to the Web, e-mail, broadband, and blogs as just some of the many electronic tools H-P uses.[19] Similarly, Dell, Inc., now has an entire team dedicated to finding and responding to comments about Dell on the Internet and to creating buzz among bloggers concerning forthcoming product releases.[20] Because the most recent wave of technological change is as dramatic as any in history, the implications for marketing strategists are profound. They involve changing definitions of industries, new sources of competition, changing product life cycles, and the increased globalization of markets.[21]

Organizational Forces

An understanding of the buying organization is based on its strategic priorities, the role of purchasing in the executive hierarchy, and the firm's competitive challenges.

Growing Influence of Purchasing As a rule, the influence of the procurement function is growing. Why? Globalization is upsetting traditional patterns of competition, and companies are feeling the squeeze from rising material costs and stiff customer resistance to price increases. Meanwhile, to enhance efficiency and effectiveness, many firms are outsourcing some functions that were traditionally performed within the organization. As a result, at companies around the world, CEOs are counting on the procurement function to keep their businesses strongly positioned in today's intensively competitive marketplace.[22]

Strategic Priorities in Purchasing

As the influence of purchasing grows, chief procurement officers feel the heat of the spotlight, so they are pursuing an ambitious set of strategic priorities (Table 3.1). They seek cost savings but realize that such savings are only part of what procurement can contribute to the bottom line. More importantly, however, procurement executives are turning to a more strategic question: How can procurement become a stronger competitive weapon? Here attention centers on corporate goals and how procurement can

---

[18] Weiss and Heide, "The Nature of Organizational Search," p. 221.

[19] Kate Maddox, Sean Callahan, and Carol Krol, "Top Trends: B-to-B Marketers Have Proven Remarkably Adaptable in the Last Five Years," *B to B*, June 13, 2005, p. 3, accessed at http://www.BtoBonline.com on July 7, 2005.

[20] Ken Worthen, "Dell, by Going Click for Click with Web Posters, Ensured Bloggers Saw Its New Red Mini Laptop," *Wall Street Journal*, June 3, 2008, p. B6.

[21] Rashi Glazer, "Winning in Smart Markets," *Sloan Management Review* 40 (Summer 1999): pp. 56–69.

[22] Marc Bourde, Charlie Hawker, and Theo Theocharides, "Taking Center Stage: The 2005 Chief Procurement Officer Survey" (Somers, NY: IBM Global Services, May 2005), pp. 1–14, accessed at http://www.ibm.com/bcs on July 1, 2005.

TABLE 3.1 | **STRATEGIC PRIORITIES IN PURCHASING**

Aligning Purchasing with Strategy: *Not Just Buyers*	Shift from an administrative role to a value-creating function that serves internal stakeholders and provides a competitive edge in the market.
Exploring New Value Frontiers: *It's Not Just about Price*	Focus on the capabilities of suppliers emphasizing business outcomes, total cost of ownership, and the potential for long-term value creation.
Putting Suppliers Inside: *The Best Value Chain Wins*	Develop fewer and deeper relationships with strategic suppliers and involve them in decision-making processes, ranging from new product development to cost-reduction initiatives.
Pursuing Low-Cost Sources: *A World Worth Exploring*	Overcome hurdles imposed by geographical differences and seek out cost-effective suppliers around the globe.

SOURCE: Adapted from Marc Bourde, Charlie Hawker, and Theo Theocharides, "Taking Center Stage: The 2005 Chief Procurement Officer Survey," (Somers, N.Y.: IBM Global Services, May 2005), pp. 1–14. Accessed at http://www.ibm.com/bcs on July 1, 2005; and Chip W. Hardt, Nicholas Reinecke, and Peter Spiller, "Inventing the 21st-Century Purchasing Organization," *The McKinsey Quarterly* 2007, No. 4, pp. 115–124.

help their internal customers (that is, other business functions) achieve these goals. As a direct participant in the strategy process, procurement managers are giving increased emphasis to suppliers' *capabilities*, exploring new areas where a strategic supplier can add value to the firm's product or service offerings. Robert K. Harlan, director of e-procurement at Motorola, captures the idea: For new product development, "we bring many suppliers in early to design, simplify, and implement new technologies."[23]

Leading-edge purchasing organizations have also learned that the "best value chain wins," so they are building closer relationships with a carefully chosen set of strategic suppliers and aligning the activities of the supply chain with customers' needs.[24] For example, Honda of America reduced the cost of the Accord's purchased content by setting cost targets for each component—engine, chassis, and so on.[25] Then, purchasing managers worked with global suppliers to understand the cost structure of each component, observe how it is manufactured, and identify ways to reduce costs, add value, or do both.

Offer Strategic Solutions   As purchasing assumes a more strategic role, the business marketer must understand the competitive realities of the customer's business and develop a value proposition—products, services, ideas—that advance its performance goals. For example, IBM centers attention on customer solutions—how its information technology and assorted services can improve the efficiency of a retailer's operations or advance the customer service levels of a hotel chain. Alternatively, a supplier to Hewlett-Packard will strike a responsive chord with executives by offering a new component that will increase the performance or lower the cost of its inkjet printers. To provide such customer solutions, the business marketer needs an intimate understanding of the opportunities and threats that the customer confronts.

[23] Jason Seigel, "Professional Profile: Robert K. Harlan," *Purchasing* 13 (October 7, 2004): p. 32.

[24] Mark Gottfredson, Rudy Puryear, and Stephen Phillips, "Strategic Sourcing: From Periphery to the Core," *Harvard Business Review* 83 (February 2005): pp. 132–139.

[25] Timothy M. Laseter, *Balanced Sourcing: Cooperation and Competition in Supplier Relationships* (San Francisco: Jossey-Bass, 1998), pp. 5–18.

Organizational Positioning of Purchasing

As purchasing moves from a transaction-based support role and assumes a more prominent strategic spot at the executive level, many leading firms are centralizing the procurement function. An organization that centralizes procurement decisions approaches purchasing differently than a company in which purchasing decisions are made at individual user locations. When purchasing is centralized, a separate organizational unit has authority for purchases at a regional, divisional, or headquarters level. For example, by centralizing procurement, American Express realized nearly $600 million in purchasing savings in the first three years.[26] IBM, Sara Lee, 3M, Hewlett-Packard, Wendy's International, and Citicorp are among other corporations that emphasize centralized procurement. A marketer who is sensitive to organizational influences can more accurately map the decision-making process, isolate buying influentials, identify salient buying criteria, and target marketing strategy for both centralized, as well as decentralized, organizations.[27]

Centralization of Procurement: Contributing Factors   Several factors contribute to the trend toward centralizing purchasing. First, centralization can better integrate purchasing strategy with corporate strategy, and e-procurement software tools now enable managers to monitor and analyze corporate spending data in minute detail.[28] Importantly, e-procurement software from firms such as Ariba, Inc. (http://www.ariba.com) now provides buyers with a rich set of new tools to track and manage spending across the entire enterprise. For example, the corporate procurement group at Walt Disney Company manages spending on all items common to the entertainment firm's four business units: media networks, parks and resorts, studio entertainment, and consumer products. These items include such categories as information technology, telecommunications, construction services, and insurance.[29]

Second, an organization with multiple plant or office locations can often cut costs by pooling common requirements. Before Motorola centralized its procurement function, it had 65 different software agreements globally with one supplier for the same software license.[30] By negotiating a global agreement that covers all Motorola operations around the world, the centralized procurement staff saved more than $40 million, or about 50 percent of what the firm had been paying for the 65 different agreements.

Third, the nature of the supply environment also can determine whether purchasing is centralized. If a few large sellers dominate the supply environment, centralized buying may be particularly useful in securing favorable terms and proper service. If the supply industry consists of many small firms, each covering limited geographical areas, decentralized purchasing may achieve better support.

Finally, the location of purchasing in the organization often hinges on the location of key buying influences. If engineering plays an active role in the process, the purchasing function must be in close organizational and physical proximity.

[26] Susan Avery, "American Express Changes Ahead," *Purchasing* 133 (November 4, 2004): pp. 34–38.

[27] E. Raymond Corey, *The Organizational Context of Industrial Buyer Behavior* (Cambridge, MA: Marketing Science Institute, 1978), pp. 99–112.

[28] Tim A. Minahan, "Best Practices in E-Sourcing: Optimizing and Sustaining Supply Savings," September 2004, research report by Aberdeen Group, Inc., Boston, Massachusetts; accessed at http://www.ariba.com on June 15, 2005.

[29] Anne Millen Porter, "Spend a Little, Save a Lot," *Purchasing* 130 (April 4, 2002): pp. 23–34.

[30] James Carbone, "Motorola Leverages Its Way to Lower Cost," *Purchasing* 133 (September 16, 2004): p. 32.

Centralization versus Decentralization Centralized and decentralized procurement differ substantially.[31] Centralization leads to specialization. Purchasing specialists for selected items develop comprehensive knowledge of supply and demand conditions, vendor options, supplier cost factors, and other relevant information. This knowledge, and the significant volume of business that specialists control, enhances their buying strength and supplier options.

The priority given to selected buying criteria is also influenced by centralization or decentralization. By identifying the buyer's organizational domain, the marketer can generally identify the purchasing manager's objectives. **Centralized purchasing** units place more weight on strategic considerations such as long-term supply availability and the development of a healthy supplier complex. Decentralized buyers may emphasize more tactical concerns such as short-term cost efficiency and profit considerations. Organizational buying behavior is greatly influenced by the monitoring system that measures the performance of the unit.

Personal selling skills and the brand preferences of users influence purchasing decisions more at user locations than at centralized buying locations. At user locations, E. Raymond Corey points out that "engineers and other technical personnel, in particular, are prone to be specific in their preferences, while nonspecialized, nontechnical buyers have neither the technical expertise nor the status to challenge them,"[32] as can purchasing specialists at central locations. Differing priorities between central buyers and local users often lead to conflict. In stimulating demand at the user level, the marketer should assess the potential for conflict and attempt to develop a strategy to resolve any differences between the two organizational units.

Strategy Response The organization of the marketer's selling strategy should parallel the organization of the purchasing function of key accounts. To avoid disjointed selling activities and internal conflict in the sales organization, and to serve the special needs of important customers, many business marketers have developed key account management programs to establish a close working relationship that, according to Benson Shapiro and Rowland Moriarty, "cuts across multiple levels, functions, and operating units in both the buying and selling organizations."[33] For example, IBM assigns a dedicated account executive to work with large customers, like Boeing or State Farm Insurance. Thus, the trend toward the centralization of procurement by buyers has been matched by the development of key account management programs by sellers. For large, multinational organizations that have the structure, processes, and information systems to centrally coordinate purchases on a global scale, the customer might be considered for global account management status. A **global account management program** treats a customer's worldwide operations as one integrated account, with coherent terms for pricing, service, and product specifications.[34]

---

[31] Joseph A. Bellizzi and Joseph J. Belonax, "Centralized and Decentralized Buying Influences," *Industrial Marketing Management* 11 (April 1982): pp. 111–115; Arch G. Woodside and David M. Samuel, "Observation of Centralized Corporate Procurement," *Industrial Marketing Management* 10 (July 1981): pp. 191–205; and Corey, *The Organizational Context*, pp. 6–12.

[32] Corey, *The Organizational Context*, p. 13.

[33] Benson P. Shapiro and Rowland T. Moriarty, *National Account Management: Emerging Insights* (Cambridge, MA: Marketing Science Institute, 1982), p. 8; see also James Boles, Wesley Johnston, and Alston Gardner, "The Selection and Organization of National Accounts: A North American Perspective," *Journal of Business & Industrial Marketing* 14 (4, 1999): pp. 264–275.

[34] George S. Yip and Audrey J. M. Bink, "Managing Global Accounts," *Harvard Business Review* 85 (September 2007): pp. 103–111.

For example, Xerox and Hewlett-Packard each have over 100 corporate clients who are given global account status.

Group Forces

Multiple buying influences and group forces are critical in organizational buying decisions. The organizational buying process typically involves a complex set of smaller decisions made or influenced by several individuals. The degree of involvement of group members varies from routine rebuys, in which the purchasing agent simply takes into account the preferences of others, to complex new-task buying situations, in which a group plays an active role.

The industrial salesperson must address three questions.

- Which organizational members take part in the buying process?

- What is each member's relative influence in the decision?

- What criteria are important to each member in evaluating prospective suppliers?

The salesperson who can correctly answer these questions is ideally prepared to meet the needs of a buying organization and has a high probability of becoming the chosen supplier.

The Buying Center　The concept of the buying center provides rich insights into the role of group forces in organizational buying behavior.[35] The buying center

---

[35] For a comprehensive review of buying center research, see Wesley J. Johnston and Jeffrey E. Lewin, "Organizational Buying Behavior: Toward an Integrative Framework," *Journal of Business Research* 35 (January 1996): pp. 1–15; and J. David Lichtenthal, "Group Decision Making in Organizational Buying: A Role Structure Approach," in *Advances in Business Marketing*, vol. 3, ed. Arch G. Woodside (Greenwich, CT: JAI Press, 1988), pp. 119–157.

consists of individuals who participate in the purchasing decision and share the goals and risks arising from the decision. The size of the buying center varies, but an average buying center includes more than 4 persons per purchase; the number of people involved in all stages of one purchase may be as many as 20.[36]

The composition of the buying center may change from one purchasing situation to another and is not prescribed by the organizational chart. A buying group evolves during the purchasing process in response to the information requirements of the specific situation. Because organizational buying is a *process* rather than an isolated act, different individuals are important to the process at different times.[37] A design engineer may exert significant influence early in the process when product specifications are being established; others may assume a more dominant role in later phases. A salesperson must define the buying situation and the information requirements from the organization's perspective in order to anticipate the size and composition of the buying center. Again, the composition of the buying center evolves during the purchasing process, varies from firm to firm, and varies from one purchasing situation to another.

Isolating the Buying Situation   Defining the buying situation and determining whether the firm is in the early or later stages of the procurement decision-making process are important first steps in defining the buying center. The buying center for a new-task buying situation in the not-for-profit market is presented in Table 3.2. The product, intensive-care monitoring systems, is complex and costly. Buying center members are drawn from five functional areas, each participating to varying degrees in the process. A marketer who concentrated exclusively on the purchasing function would be overlooking key buying influentials.

Erin Anderson and her colleagues queried a large sample of sales managers about the patterns of organizational buying behavior their salespeople confront daily. Sales forces that frequently encounter new-task buying situations generally observe that:

> The buying center is large, slow to decide, uncertain about its needs and the appropriateness of the possible solutions, more concerned about finding a good solution than getting a low price or assured supply, more willing to entertain proposals from "out" suppliers and less willing to favor "in" suppliers, more influenced by technical personnel, [and] less influenced by purchasing agents.[38]

By contrast, Anderson and her colleagues found that sales forces facing more routine purchase situations (that is, straight and modified rebuys) frequently observe buying centers that are "small, quick to decide, confident in their appraisals of the problem and possible solutions, concerned about price and supply, satisfied with 'in' suppliers, and more influenced by purchasing agents."[39]

---

[36] For example, see Robert D. McWilliams, Earl Naumann, and Stan Scott, "Determining Buying Center Size," *Industrial Marketing Management* 21 (February 1992): pp. 43–49.

[37] Ghingold and Wilson, "Buying Center Research and Business Marketing Practice," pp. 96–108; see also Gary L. Lilien and M. Anthony Wong, "Exploratory Investigation of the Structure of the Buying Center in the Metalworking Industry," *Journal of Marketing Research* 21 (February 1984): pp. 1–11.

[38] Anderson, Chu, and Weitz, "Industrial Purchasing," p. 82.

[39] Ibid.

TABLE 3.2	THE INVOLVEMENT OF BUYING CENTER PARTICIPANTS AT DIFFERENT STAGES OF THE PROCUREMENT PROCESS

Stages of Procurement Process for a Medical Supplier

Buying Center Participants	Identification of Need	Establishment of Objectives	Identification and Evaluation of Buying Alternatives	Selection of Suppliers
Physicians	High	High	High	High
Nursing	Low	High	High	Low
Administration	Moderate	Moderate	Moderate	High
Engineering	Low	Moderate	Moderate	Low
Purchasing	Low	Low	Low	Moderate

SOURCE: Adapted by permission of the publisher from Gene R. Laczniak, "An Empirical Study of Hospital Buying," *Industrial Marketing Management* 8 (January 1979): p. 61. Copyright © 1979 by Elsevier Science.

Predicting Composition A marketer can also predict the composition of the buying center by projecting the effect of the industrial product on various functional areas in the organization. If the procurement decision will affect the marketability of a firm's product (for example, product design, price), the marketing department will be active in the process. Engineering will be influential in decisions about new capital equipment, materials, and components; setting specifications; defining product performance requirements; and qualifying potential vendors. Manufacturing executives will be included for procurement decisions that affect the production mechanism (for example, materials or parts used in production). When procurement decisions involve a substantial economic commitment or impinge on strategic or policy matters, top management will have considerable influence.

Buying Center Influence Members of the buying center assume different roles throughout the procurement process. Frederick Webster Jr. and Yoram Wind have given the following labels to each of these roles: users, influencers, buyers, deciders, and gatekeepers.[40]

As the role name implies, **users** are the personnel who use the product in question. Users may have anywhere from inconsequential to extremely important influence on the purchase decision. In some cases, the users initiate the purchase action by requesting the product. They may even develop the product specifications.

Gatekeepers control information to be reviewed by other members of the buying center. They may do so by disseminating printed information, such as advertisements, or by controlling which salesperson speaks to which individuals in the buying center. To illustrate, the purchasing agent might perform this screening role by opening the gate to the buying center for some sales personnel and closing it to others.

Influencers affect the purchasing decision by supplying information for the evaluation of alternatives or by setting buying specifications. Typically, those in technical departments, such as engineering, quality control, and R&D, have significant influence on the purchase decision. Sometimes, outside individuals can assume this role.

[40] Frederick E. Webster Jr. and Yoram Wind, *Organizational Buying Behavior* (Englewood Cliffs, NJ: Prentice-Hall, 1972), p. 77. For a review of buying role research, see Lichtenthal, "Group Decision Making in Organizational Buying," pp. 119–157.

INSIDE BUSINESS MARKETING

Innovate and Win with BMW

Leading procurement organizations expect their suppliers to innovate, and they reward them when they do. At firms such as P&G, Coca-Cola, and BMW, purchasing executives use "potential to innovate" as a key criterion for selecting suppliers and evaluate contributions to innovation as part of the supplier development process.

Business marketers who contribute innovative ideas to the new-product-development process at such firms win the support of purchasing managers, marketing executives, design engineers, and other members of the buying center. For example, a salesperson for a top supplier to BMW proposed adding optic-fiber-enabled light rings to headlights to add a distinguishing feature to

the brand. "Drivers on the German autobahn or elsewhere would see the distinctive lights of a high-performance BMW approaching from behind and know to move aside and let it pass. BMW and the supplier jointly developed the idea—and the contract ensures exclusive rights for the automaker." As a result of this collaboration, BMW gained access to new technology that adds value to its brand and the supplier won a lucrative, long-term contract.

SOURCE: A. T. Kearney, "Creating Value through Strategic Supply Management: 2004 Assessment of Excellence in Procurement," (February 2005). Accessed at http://www.atkearney.com on June 25, 2005.

For high-tech purchases, technical consultants often assume an influential role in the decision process and broaden the set of alternatives being considered.[41]

Deciders actually make the buying decision, whether or not they have the formal authority to do so. The identity of the decider is the most difficult role to determine: *Buyers* may have formal authority to buy, but the president of the firm may actually make the decision. A decider could be a design engineer who develops a set of specifications that only one vendor can meet.

The **buyer** has formal authority to select a supplier and implement all procedures connected with securing the product. More powerful members of the organization often usurp the power of the buyer. The buyer's role is often assumed by the purchasing agent, who executes the administrative functions associated with a purchase order.

One person could assume all roles, or separate individuals could assume different buying roles. To illustrate, as users, personnel from marketing, accounting, purchasing, and production may all have a stake in which information technology system is selected. Thus, the buying center can be a very complex organizational phenomenon.

Identifying Patterns of Influence   Key influencers are frequently located outside the purchasing department. To illustrate, the typical capital equipment purchase involves an average of four departments, three levels of the management hierarchy (for example, manager, regional manager, vice president), and seven different individuals.[42]

---

[41] Paul G. Patterson and Phillip L. Dawes, "The Determinants of Choice Set Structure in High-Technology Markets," *Industrial Marketing Management* 28 (July 1999): pp. 395–411; and Philip L. Dawes, Don Y. Lee, and David Midgley, "Organizational Learning in High-Technology Purchase Situations: The Antecedents and Consequences of the Participation of External IT Consultants," *Industrial Marketing Management* 36 (April 2007): pp. 285–299.

[42] Wesley J. Johnston and Thomas V. Bonoma, "The Buying Center: Structure and Interaction Patterns," *Journal of Marketing* 45 (Summer 1981): pp. 143–156; see also Gary L. Lilien and M. Anthony Wong, "An Exploratory Investigation of the Structure of the Buying Center in the Metalworking Industry," *Journal of Marketing Research* 21 (February 1984): pp. 1–11; and Arch G. Woodside, Timo Liakko, and Risto Vuori, "Organizational Buying of Capital Equipment Involving Persons across Several Authority Levels," *Journal of Business & Industrial Marketing* 14 (1, 1999): pp. 30–48.

TABLE 3.3	CLUES FOR IDENTIFYING POWERFUL BUYING CENTER MEMBERS

- *Isolate the personal stakeholders.* Those individuals who have an important personal stake in the decision will exert more influence than other members of the buying center. For example, the selection of production equipment for a new plant will spawn the active involvement of manufacturing executives.

- *Follow the information flow.* Influential members of the buying center are central to the information flow that surrounds the buying decision. Other organizational members will direct information to them.

- *Identify the experts.* Expert power is an important determinant of influence in the buying center. Those buying center members who possess the most knowledge—and ask the most probing questions of the salesperson—are often influential.

- *Trace the connections to the top.* Powerful buying center members often have direct access to the top-management team. This direct link to valuable information and resources enhances the status and influence of the buying center members.

- *Understand purchasing's role.* Purchasing is dominant in repetitive buying situations by virtue of technical expertise, knowledge of the dynamics of the supplying industry, and close working relationships with individual suppliers.

SOURCE: Adapted from John R. Ronchetto, Michael D. Hutt, and Peter H. Reingen, "Embedded Influence Patterns in Organizational Buying Systems," *Journal of Marketing* 53 (October 1989): pp. 51–62.

In purchasing component parts, personnel from production and engineering are often most influential in the decision. It is interesting to note that a comparative study of organizational buying behavior found striking similarities across four countries (the United States, the United Kingdom, Australia, and Canada) in the involvement of various departments in the procurement process.[43]

Past research provides some valuable clues for identifying powerful buying center members (Table 3.3).[44] To illustrate, individuals who have an important personal stake in the decision possess, expert knowledge concerning the choice, and/or are central to the flow of decision-related information tend to assume an active and influential role in the buying center. Purchasing managers assume a dominant role in repetitive buying situations.

Based on their buying center research, Donald W. Jackson Jr. and his colleagues provide these strategy recommendations:

> Marketing efforts will depend upon which individuals of the buying center are more influential for a given decision. Because engineering and manufacturing are more influential in product selection decisions, they may have to be sold on product characteristics. On the other hand, because purchasing is most influential in supplier selection decisions, they may have to be sold on company characteristics.[45]

---

[43] Peter Banting, David Ford, Andrew Gross, and George Holmes, "Similarities in Industrial Procurement across Four Countries," *Industrial Marketing Management* 14 (May 1985): pp. 133–144.

[44] John R. Ronchetto, Michael D. Hutt, and Peter H. Reingen, "Embedded Influence Patterns in Organizational Buying Systems," *Journal of Marketing* 53 (October 1989): pp. 51–62; see also Ajay Kohli, "Determinants of Influence in Organizational Buying: A Contingency Approach," *Journal of Marketing* 53 (July 1989): pp. 50–65; Daniel H. McQuiston and Peter R. Dickson, "The Effect of Perceived Personal Consequences on Participation and Influence in Organizational Buying," *Journal of Business Research* 23 (September 1991): pp. 159–177; and Jerome M. Katrichis, "Exploring Departmental Level Interaction Patterns in Organizational Purchasing Decisions," *Industrial Marketing Management* 27 (March 1998): pp. 135–146.

[45] Jackson, Keith, and Burdick, "Purchasing Agents' Perceptions of Industrial Buying Center Influence," pp. 75–83.

Individual Forces

Individuals, not organizations, make buying decisions. Each member of the buying center has a unique personality, a particular set of learned experiences, a specified organizational function, and a perception of how best to achieve both personal and organizational goals. Importantly, research confirms that organizational members who perceive that they have an important personal stake in the buying decision participate more forcefully in the decision process than their colleagues.[46] To understand the organizational buyer, the marketer should be aware of individual perceptions of the buying situation.

Differing Evaluative Criteria   **Evaluative criteria** are specifications that organizational buyers use to compare alternative industrial products and services; however, these may conflict. Industrial product users generally value prompt delivery and efficient servicing; engineering values product quality, standardization, and testing; and purchasing assigns the most importance to maximum price advantage and economy in shipping and forwarding.[47]

Product perceptions and evaluative criteria differ among organizational decision makers as a result of differences in their educational backgrounds, their exposure to different types of information from different sources, the way they interpret and retain relevant information (perceptual distortion), and their level of satisfaction with past purchases.[48] Engineers have an educational background different from that of plant managers or purchasing agents: They are exposed to different journals, attend different conferences, and possess different professional goals and values. A sales presentation that is effective with purchasing may be entirely off the mark with engineering.

Responsive Marketing Strategy   A marketer who is sensitive to differences in the product perceptions and evaluative criteria of individual buying center members is well equipped to prepare a responsive marketing strategy. To illustrate, a research study examined the industrial adoption of solar air-conditioning systems and identified the criteria important to key decision makers.[49] Buying center participants for this purchase typically include production engineers, heating and air-conditioning (HVAC) consultants, and top managers. The study revealed that marketing communications directed at production engineers should center on operating costs and energy savings; HVAC consultants should be addressed concerning noise level and initial cost of the system; and top managers are most interested in whether the technology is state-of-the-art. Knowing the criteria of key buying center participants has significant operational value to the marketer when designing new products and when developing and targeting advertising and personal selling presentations.

[46] McQuiston and Dickson, "The Effect of Perceived Personal Consequences on Participation and Influence in Organizational Buying," pp. 159–177.

[47] Jagdish N. Sheth, "A Model of Industrial Buyer Behavior," *Journal of Marketing* 37 (October 1973): p. 51; see also Sheth, "Organizational Buying Behavior: Past Performance and Future Expectations," *Journal of Business & Industrial Marketing* 11 (3/4, 1996): pp. 7–24.

[48] Sheth, "A Model of Industrial Buyer Behavior," pp. 52–54.

[49] Jean-Marie Choffray and Gary L. Lilien, "Assessing Response to Industrial Marketing Strategy," *Journal of Marketing* 42 (April 1978): pp. 20–31. For related research, see R. Venkatesh, Ajay K. Kohli, and Gerald Zaltman, "Influence Strategies in Buying Centers," *Journal of Marketing* 59 (October 1995): pp. 71–82; and Mark A. Farrell and Bill Schroder, "Influence Strategies in Organizational Buying Decisions," *Industrial Marketing Management* 25 (July 1996): pp. 293–303.

Information Processing Volumes of information flow into every organization through direct-mail advertising, the Internet, journal advertising, trade news, word of mouth, and personal sales presentations. What an individual organizational buyer chooses to pay attention to, comprehend, and retain has an important bearing on procurement decisions.

Selective Processes Information processing is generally encompassed in the broader term cognition, which U. Neisser defines as "all the processes by which the sensory input is transformed, reduced, elaborated, stored, recovered, and used."[50] Important to an individual's cognitive structure are the processes of selective exposure, attention, perception, and retention.

1. *Selective exposure.* Individuals tend to accept communication messages consistent with their existing attitudes and beliefs. For this reason, a purchasing agent chooses to talk to some salespersons and not to others.

2. *Selective attention.* Individuals filter or screen incoming stimuli to admit only certain ones to cognition. Thus, an organizational buyer is more likely to notice a trade advertisement that is consistent with his or her needs and values.

3. *Selective perception.* Individuals tend to interpret stimuli in terms of their existing attitudes and beliefs. This explains why organizational buyers may modify or distort a salesperson's message in order to make it more consistent with their predispositions toward the company.

4. *Selective retention.* Individuals tend to recall only information pertinent to their own needs and dispositions. An organizational buyer may retain information concerning a particular brand because it matches his or her criteria.

Each of these selective processes influences the way an individual decision maker responds to marketing stimuli. Because the procurement process often spans several months and because the marketer's contact with the buying organization is infrequent, marketing communications must be carefully designed and targeted.[51] Key decision makers "tune out" or immediately forget poorly conceived messages. They retain messages they deem important to achieving goals.

Risk-Reduction Strategies Individuals are motivated by a strong desire to reduce risk in purchase decisions. Perceived risk includes two components: (1) uncertainty about the outcome of a decision and (2) the magnitude of consequences from making the wrong choice. Research highlights the importance of perceived risk and the purchase type in shaping the structure of the decision-making unit.[52] Individual decision making is likely to occur in organizational buying for straight rebuys and for modified rebuys when the perceived risk is low. In these situations, the purchasing agent may initiate action.[53] Modified rebuys of higher risk and new tasks seem to spawn a group structure.

[50] U. Neisser, *Cognitive Psychology* (New York: Appleton, 1966), p. 4.

[51] See, for example, Brent M. Wren and James T. Simpson, "A Dyadic Model of Relationships in Organizational Buying: A Synthesis of Research Results," *Journal of Business & Industrial Marketing* 11 (3/4, 1996): pp. 68–79.

[52] Elizabeth J. Wilson, Gary L. Lilien, and David T. Wilson, "Developing and Testing a Contingency Paradigm of Group Choice in Organizational Buying," *Journal of Marketing Research* 28 (November 1991): pp. 452–466.

[53] Sheth, "A Model of Industrial Buyer Behavior," p. 54; see also W. E. Patton III, Charles P. Puto, and Ronald H. King, "Which Buying Decisions Are Made by Individuals and Not by Groups?" *Industrial Marketing Management* 15 (May 1986): pp. 129–138.

B2B TOP PERFORMERS

Delivering Customer Solutions

If you review the performance of salespersons at most business marketing firms, large or small, you will observe some who consistently perform at a level that sets them apart from their peers. A recent study explores how exceptional performers acquire and use information to manage customer relationships. In-depth interviews were conducted with 60 salespersons at a *Fortune* 500 firm: 20 high-performing, 20 average-performing, and 20 low-performing salespersons.

Sharp differences emerged when the salespersons were asked to categorize their customers into groups based on characteristics they found most useful in managing customer relationships. Here high performers emphasize customer goals, whereas low performers emphasize customer demographics (for example, large versus small firms). In turn,

the study reveals that high performers develop a more extensive network of relationships within the customer organization compared with their colleagues. Importantly, high performers are better able to establish and maintain profitable customer relationships because they align their organization's special capabilities to the customer's primary goals. In other words, top-performing sales specialists provide a solution that advances the performance of the customer organization.

SOURCE: Gabriel R. Gonzalez, Beth A. Walker, Dimitrios Kapelianis, and Michael D. Hutt, "The Role of Information Acquisition and Knowledge Use in Managing Customer Relationships," working paper, Arizona State University, Tempe, Ariz., 2008.

In confronting "risky" purchase decisions, how do organizational buyers behave? As the risk associated with an organizational purchase decision increases, the following occur[54]:

- The buying center becomes larger and comprises members with high levels of organizational status and authority.

- The information search is active and a wide variety of information sources are consulted. As the decision process unfolds, personal information sources (for example, discussions with managers at other organizations that have made similar purchases) become more important.

- Buying center participants invest greater effort and deliberate more carefully throughout the purchase process.

- Sellers who have a proven track record with the firm are favored—the choice of a familiar supplier helps reduce perceived risk.

Rather than price, product quality and after-sale service are typically most important to organizational buyers when they confront risky decisions. When introducing new products, entering new markets, or approaching new customers, the marketing strategist should evaluate the effect of alternative strategies on perceived risk.

---

[54]Johnston and Lewin, "Organizational Buying Behavior: Toward an Integrative Framework," pp. 8–10. See also Puto, Patton, and King, "Risk Handling Strategies in Industrial Vendor Selection Decisions," pp. 89–95.

FIGURE 3.4 | **MAJOR ELEMENTS OF ORGANIZATIONAL BUYING BEHAVIOR**

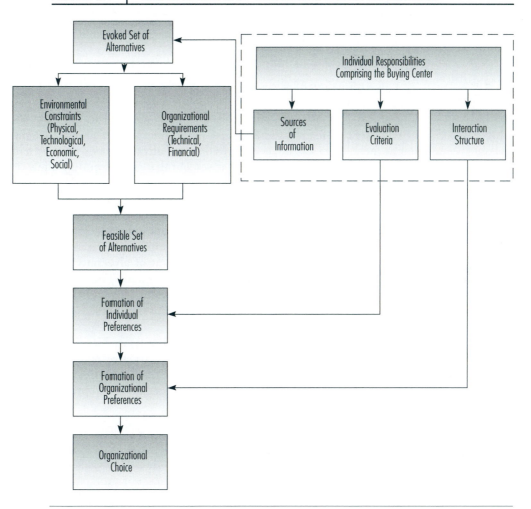

SOURCE: Jean-Marie Choffray and Gary L. Lilien, "Assessing Response to Industrial Marketing Strategy," *Journal of Marketing* 42 (April 1978): p. 22. Reprinted by permission of the American Marketing Association.

The Organizational Buying Process: Major Elements

The behavior of organizational buyers is influenced by environmental, organizational, group, and individual factors. Each of these spheres of influence has been discussed in an organizational buying context, with particular attention to how the industrial marketer should interpret these forces and, more important, factor them directly into marketing strategy planning. A model of the organizational buying process is presented in Figure 3.4, which serves to reinforce and integrate the key areas discussed so far in this chapter.[55]

---

[55] Choffray and Lilien, "Assessing the Response to Industrial Marketing Strategy," pp. 20–31. Other models of organizational buying behavior include Webster and Wind, *Organizational Buying Behavior*, pp. 28–37; and Sheth, "A Model of Industrial Buyer Behavior," pp. 50–56. For a comprehensive review, see Sheth, "Organizational Buying Behavior," pp. 7–24; and Johnston and Lewin, "Organizational Buying Behavior," pp. 1–15.

This framework focuses on the relationship between an organization's buying center and the three major stages in the individual purchase decision process:

1. the screening of alternatives that do not meet organizational requirements;

2. the formation of decision participants' preferences;

3. the formation of organizational preferences.

Observe that individual members of the buying center use various evaluative criteria and are exposed to various sources of information, which influence the industrial brands included in the buyer's **evoked set of alternatives**—the alternative brands a buyer calls to mind when a need arises and that represent only a few of the many brands available.[56]

Environmental constraints and organizational requirements influence the procurement process by limiting the number of product alternatives that satisfy organizational needs. For example, capital equipment alternatives that exceed a particular cost (initial or operating) may be eliminated from further consideration. The remaining brands become the **feasible set of alternatives** for the organization, from which individual preferences are defined. The **interaction structure** of the members of the buying center, who have differing criteria and responsibilities, leads to the formation of organizational preferences and ultimately to organizational choice.

Understanding the organizational buying process enables the marketer to play an active rather than a passive role in stimulating market response. The marketer who identifies organizational screening requirements and the salient evaluative criteria of individual buying center members can make more informed product design, pricing, and promotional decisions.

Summary

Knowledge of the process that organizational buyers follow in making purchasing decisions is fundamental to responsive marketing strategy. As a buying organization moves from the problem-recognition phase, in which a procurement need is defined, to later phases, in which suppliers are screened and ultimately chosen, the marketer can play an active role. In fact, the astute marketer often triggers initial awareness of the problem and helps the organization effectively solve that problem. Incremental decisions made throughout the buying process narrow the field of acceptable suppliers and dramatically influence the ultimate outcome.

The nature of the buying process depends on the organization's level of experience with similar procurement problems. It is thus crucial to know how the organization defines the buying situation: as a new task, a modified rebuy, or a straight rebuy. Each buying situation requires a unique problem-solving approach, involves unique buying influentials, and demands a unique marketing response.

---

[56] Howard and Sheth, *The Theory of Buyer Behavior*, p. 26; see also Ronald P. LeBlanc, "Environmental Impact on Purchase Decision Structure," *Journal of Purchasing and Materials Management* 17 (Spring 1981): pp. 30–36; and Lowell E. Crow, Richard W. Olshavsky, and John O. Summers, "Industrial Buyers' Choice Strategies: A Protocol Analysis," *Journal of Marketing Research* 17 (February 1980): pp. 34–44.

Myriad forces—environmental, organizational, group, and individual—influence organizational buying behavior. First, environmental forces define the boundaries within which industrial buyers and sellers interact, such as general business conditions or the rate of technological change. Second, organizational forces dictate the link between buying activities and the strategic priorities of the firm and the position that the purchasing function occupies in the organizational structure. Third, the relevant unit of analysis for the marketing strategist is the buying center. The composition of this group evolves during the buying process, varies from firm to firm, and changes from one purchasing situation to another. Fourth, the marketer must ultimately concentrate attention on individual members of the buying center. Each brings a particular set of experiences and a unique personal and organizational frame of reference to the buying decision. The marketer who is sensitive to individual differences is best equipped to develop responsive marketing communications that the organizational buyer will remember.

Unraveling the complex forces that encircle the organizational buying process is indeed difficult. This chapter offers a framework that enables the marketing manager to begin this task by asking the right questions. The answers provide the basis for effective and efficient business marketing strategy.

Discussion Questions

1. Ford revamped the way it purchases operating resources such as office, computer, and maintenance supplies. Instead of having employees fill out purchase orders that must be cleared by the boss days later, employees simply log on to an Internet system. They browse through the electronics catalogs of manufacturers, order from a preapproved group of suppliers, and get purchase approval in minutes. What new challenges and opportunities does the e-procurement system present for business marketers who serve Ford?

2. Jim Jackson, an industrial salesperson for Pittsburgh Machine Tool, will call on two accounts this afternoon. The first will be a buying organization Jim has been servicing for the past 3 years. The second call, however, poses more of a challenge. This buying organization has been dealing with a prime competitor of Pittsburgh Machine Tool for 5 years. Jim, who has good rapport with the purchasing and engineering departments, feels that the time may be right to penetrate this account. Recently, Jim learned that the purchasing manager was extremely unhappy with the existing supplier's poor delivery service. Define the buying situations confronting Jim and outline the appropriate strategy he should follow in each case.

3. Karen Weber, the purchasing agent for Smith Manufacturing, views the purchase of widgets as a routine buying decision. What factors might lead her to alter this position? More important, what factors determine whether Karen considers a particular supplier, such as Albany Widget?

4. Harley-Davidson, the U.S. motorcycle producer, recently purchased some sophisticated manufacturing equipment to enhance its position in a very competitive market. First, what environmental forces might have been important in spawning this capital investment? Second, which functional units were likely to have been represented in the buying center?

5. Brunswick Corporation centralizes its procurement decisions at the headquarters level. Discuss how it would approach purchasing differently than a competitor that decentralizes purchasing across various plant locations.

6. The Kraus Toy Company recently decided to develop a new electronic game. Can an electrical parts supplier predict the likely composition of the buying center at Kraus Toy? What steps could an industrial salesperson take to influence the composition of the buying center?

7. Explain how the composition of the buying center evolves during the purchasing process and how it varies from one firm to another, as well as from one purchasing situation to another. What steps can a salesperson take to identify the influential members of the buying center?

8. Carol Brooks, purchasing manager for Apex Manufacturing Co., read the Wall Street Journal this morning and carefully studied, clipped, and saved a full-page ad by the Allen-Bradley Company. Ralph Thornton, the production manager at Apex, read several articles from the same paper but could not recall seeing this particular ad or, for that matter, any ads. How could this occur?

9. Organizations purchase millions of notebook computers each year. Identify several evaluative criteria that purchasing managers might use in choosing a particular brand. In your view, which criteria would be most decisive in the buying decision?

10. The levels of risk associated with organizational purchases range from low to high. Discuss how the buying process for a risky purchase differs from the process for a routine purchase.

Internet Exercises

1. Dell, Inc., has been wildly successful in selling its products over the Internet to customers of all types, including every category of customers in the business market: commercial enterprises, institutions, and government. Assume your university library is planning to purchase 25 new desktop computers. Go to http://www.dell.com and to the Dell Online Store for Higher Education and:

   a. identify the price and product dimensions of two desktop systems that might meet your university's needs, and

   b. provide a critique of the Web site and consider how well it provided access to the information that a potential buyer might want.

The Tablet PC for Nurses: A Mobile Clinical Assistant[57]

Intel Corporation and Motion Computing, Inc., are demonstrating the result of a joint effort to increase the productivity of nurses—the Motion C5 Mobile Clinical Assistant—a tablet-style personal computer designed for use in hospitals and clinics.

The idea for the product emerged from ethnographic studies that Intel conducted in the health-care setting. Here researchers observed the round-the-clock flow of activities in a hospital and meticulously recorded the key tasks performed by the nurses and professional staff, tracing their every movement. The C5 benefited from the rich insights uncovered by Intel's study as well as from similar research that Motion Computing had completed in prior years. The companies believe that the device will help nurses handle chores such as remotely calling up medical records and doctors' orders, charting vital signs, and exchanging information with other professionals.

The Motion C5, which is priced at $2,199, provides a sure-grip handle, a sealed case for easy cleaning and disinfecting, a lightweight design for portability, a 10-inch screen for easily viewing clinical information, rugged construction, and a pen and stylus input so clinicians can enter text and navigate the software without being tied to a keyboard. The innovative device also incorporates such features as integrated bar code and radio frequency identification (RFID) readers for patient identification and/or electronic medication administration, an integrated camera, and built-in wireless connectivity.

When the Motion C5 was released in 2007, about 16 percent of U.S. hospitals were using tablet PCs, and 24 percent had smaller handheld computers. Some hospitals prefer what they call COWs—computers on wheels—that can be rolled into patients' rooms.

One of the first U.S. adopters of the Motion C5 was Island Hospital, located in Anacortes, Washington. Rick Kiser, assistant director of information systems for Island Hospital, was centrally involved in the buying decision. Though Island's buying team had initially recommended adding COWs for every patient room, the nursing staff had concerns about COWs' limitations. Kiser noted: "The single biggest issue was the COWs are impossible to clean. The sanitary aspect was a nightmare."

Holly Hoskinson, RN and clinical infomatics specialist, also noted the COWs were difficult to maneuver from room to room. "We tried a variety of cart styles but they are all still big and heavy." Another Island RN, Chris Storm, agreed: "We wanted a device in each room and based on our budget we would have to move COWs from room to room. That option was not acceptable."

While other brands of PC tablets were evaluated, the buying team determined that the Motion C5 best met Island's needs. Concerning the decision, Rick Kiser observed: "The thing that cinched it was that this tablet was designed for the medical environment. They are drop resistant and easy to clean and other tablets didn't offer anything near what we needed."

---

[57] "The Three M's: Mobility, MEDITECH, and Motion C5," White paper, February 2008, Motion Computing, Inc., accessed at http://www.motioncomputing.com on June 5, 2008; and Don Clark, "Intel, Motion Develop Tablet PC for Nurses," *Wall Street Journal*, February 21, 2007, p. D7.

Discussion Questions

1. Suggest strategies that Motion Computing might follow to speed the adoption of the Motion C5 device by hospitals.

2. Potential members of the buying center for a tablet PC purchasing decision might include hospital administrators, nurses, doctors, information technology (IT) specialists, and purchasing managers. Describe how the buying criteria emphasized by hospital administrators or purchasing managers might differ from those embraced by IT specialists or members of the medical staff.

CHAPTER

4

Customer Relationship Management Strategies for Business Markets

A well-developed ability to create and sustain successful working relationships with customers gives business marketing firms a significant competitive advantage. After reading this chapter, you will understand:

1. the patterns of buyer-seller relationships in the business market.

2. the factors that influence the profitability of individual customers.

3. a procedure for designing effective customer relationship management strategies.

4. the distinctive capabilities of firms that excel at customer relationship management.

5. the critical determinants of success in managing strategic alliances.

Every night, John Chambers, CEO of Cisco Systems, receives a personal update on 15 to 20 major customers via voice-mail. "E-mail would be more efficient but I want to hear the emotion, I want to hear the frustration; I want to hear the caller's level of comfort with the strategy we're employing," says Chambers. "I can't get that through e-mail."[1] In addition to giving day-to-day attention to monitoring relationships with the firm's most valuable customers, John Chambers has personally taken the lead in forging important strategic alliances.[2]

Leading business marketing firms like Cisco succeed by providing superior value to customers, by satisfying the special needs of even the most demanding customers, and by understanding the factors that influence individual customer profitability. Compared with the consumer packaged-goods sector, customer profitability is particularly important in business markets because marketing managers allocate a greater proportion of their marketing resources at the individual customer level.[3] The ability of an organization to create and maintain profitable relationships with these most valuable customers is a durable basis of competitive advantage.

A business marketer who wishes to find a place on Cisco's preferred supplier list must be prepared to help the firm provide more value to its demanding customers. To this end, the marketer must provide exceptional performance in quality, delivery, and, over time, cost competitiveness. The supplier must also understand how Cisco measures value and how its product and service offering can meet or surpass these value expectations. Building and maintaining lasting customer relationships requires careful attention to detail, meeting promises, and swiftly responding to new requirements.

The new era of business marketing is built upon effective relationship management.[4] Many business marketing firms create what might be called a **collaborative advantage** by demonstrating special skills in managing relationships with key customers or by jointly developing innovative strategies with alliance partners.[5] These firms have learned how to be good partners, and these superior relationship skills are a valuable asset. This chapter explores the types of relationships that characterize the business market. What market and situational factors are associated with different types of buyer-seller relationships? What factors influence customer profitability? What strategies can business marketers employ to build profitable relationships with customers? What are the distinctive capabilities of firms that excel at customer relationship management and consistently deliver superior financial performance in managing strategic alliances?

Relationship Marketing[6]

Relationship marketing centers on all activities directed toward establishing, developing, and maintaining successful exchanges with customers and other constituents.[7] Nurturing and managing customer relationships have emerged as an important

---

[1] Frederick E. Reichheld, "Lead for Loyalty," *Harvard Business Review* 79 (July–August 2001): p. 82.

[2] "Cisco: Perspective on Strategic Alliances: An Interview with Greg Fox, Director of Marketing for Cisco's Strategic Alliances," *Leading Edge Newsletter*, Volume 1, No. 5 (May 2006), accessed at http://www.amanet.org on July 5, 2008.

[3] Douglas Bowman and Das Narayandas, "Linking Customer Management Effort to Customer Profitability in Business Markets," *Journal of Marketing Research* 41 (November 2004): pp. 433–447.

[4] For a comprehensive review, see Robert W. Palmatier, *Relationship Marketing* (Boston: Marketing Science Institute, 2008).

[5] Rosabeth Moss Kanter, "Collaborative Advantage," *Harvard Business Review* 72 (July–August 1994): pp. 96–108.

[6] This section is based on George S. Day, "Managing Market Relationships," *Journal of the Academy of Marketing Science* 28 (Winter 2000): pp. 24–30, except when others are cited.

[7] Robert M. Morgan and Shelby D. Hunt, "The Commitment-Trust Theory of Relationship Marketing," *Journal of Marketing* 58 (July 1994): pp. 20–38.

FIGURE 4.1 | **THE RELATIONSHIP SPECTRUM**

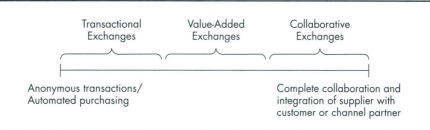

SOURCE: Figure from "Managing Market Relationships" by George S. Day from *Journal of Academy of Marketing Science* 28 (Winter 2000): p. 25. Copyright © 2000. Reprinted by permission of Springer.

strategic priority in most firms. Why? First, loyal customers are far more profitable than customers who are price sensitive and perceive few differences among alternative offerings. Second, a firm that is successful in developing strong relationships with customers secures important and durable advantages that are hard for competitors to understand, copy, or displace.

Types of Relationships

A business marketer may begin a relationship with GE as a supplier (one of many), move to a preferred supplier status (one of a few), and ultimately enter a collaborative relationship with GE (sole source for particular items). Observe in Figure 4.1 that buyer-seller relationships are positioned on a continuum, with transactional exchange and collaborative exchange serving as the endpoints. Central to every relationship is an exchange process where each side gives something in return for a payoff of greater value. **Transactional exchange** centers on the timely exchange of basic products for highly competitive market prices. George Day notes that such exchanges

> include the kind of autonomous encounters a visitor to a city has with the taxi or bus from the airport, as well as a series of ongoing transactions in a business-to-business market where the customer and supplier focus only on the timely exchange of standard products at competitive prices.[8]

Moving across the continuum, relationships become closer or more collaborative. The open exchange of information is a characteristic of collaborative (close) versus transactional (distant) exchange. Likewise, **operational linkages** reflect how much the systems, procedures, and routines of the buying and selling firms have been connected to facilitate operations.[9] These relationship connectors are a feature of a collaborative relationship. For example, such linkages provide the basis for order replenishment or just-in-time deliveries that Honda receives each day from suppliers at its Marysville, Ohio, production facility. **Collaborative exchange** features very close information, social, and operational linkages as well as mutual commitments

[8]Day, "Managing Market Relationships," p. 25.

[9]Joseph P. Cannon and William D. Perreault, Jr., "Buyer-Seller Relationships in Business Markets," *Journal of Marketing Research* 36 (November 1999): pp. 439–460.

made in expectation of long-run benefits. According to James Anderson and James Narus, collaborative exchange involves

> a process where a customer and supplier firm form strong and extensive social, economic, service, and technical ties over time, with the intent of lowering total costs and/or increasing value, thereby achieving mutual benefit.[10]

Value-Adding Exchanges

Between the two extremes on the relationship continuum are value-adding exchanges, where the focus of the selling firm shifts from attracting customers to keeping customers. The marketer pursues this objective by developing a comprehensive understanding of a customer's needs and changing requirements, tailoring the firm's offerings to those needs, and providing continuing incentives for customers to concentrate most of their purchases with them. To illustrate, W.W. Grainger provides a customized Web page for each of its premier corporate customers that individual employees in the customer organization can use to track expenditures on maintenance and operating supplies against key performance benchmarks.

Nature of Relationships

Transactional exchange involves items like packaging materials or cleaning services where competitive bidding is often employed to secure the best terms. Such exchanges are purely contractual arrangements that involve little or no emotional commitment to sustaining the relationship in the future. By contrast, customized, high-technology products—like semiconductor test equipment—fit the collaborative exchange category. Whereas transactional exchange centers on negotiations and an arm's-length relationship, collaborative exchange emphasizes joint problem solving and multiple linkages that integrate the processes of the two parties. Trust and commitment provide the foundation for collaborative exchange.[11] **Relationship commitment** involves a partner's belief that an ongoing relationship is so important that it deserves maximum efforts to maintain it. In turn, **trust** exists when one party has confidence in a partner's reliability and integrity. Recent research highlights the powerful role that contact personnel (for example, salespersons) assume in forging a long-term relationship. "Individuals who build trust in each other will transfer this bond to the firm level."[12]

Strategic Choices

Business marketers have some latitude in choosing where to participate along the relationship continuum. However, limits are imposed by the characteristics of the

---

[10]James C. Anderson and James A Narus, "Partnering as a Focused Market Strategy," *California Management Review* 33 (Spring 1991): p. 96. See also Ven Srivam, Robert Krapfel, and Robert Spekman, "Antecedents to Buyer-Seller Collaboration: An Analysis from the Buyer's Perspective," *Journal of Business Research* (December 1992): pp. 303–320.

[11]Morgan and Hunt, "The Commitment-Trust Theory," pp. 20–38. See also Patricia M. Doney and Joseph P. Cannon, "An Examination of the Nature of Trust in Buyer-Seller Relationships," *Journal of Marketing* 61 (April 1997): pp. 35–51.

[12]Das Narayandas and V. Kasturi Rangan, "Building and Sustaining Buyer-Seller Relationships in Mature Industrial Markets," *Journal of Marketing* 68 (July 2004): p. 74; and Robert W. Palmatier, Lisa K. Scheer, and Jan-Benedict E. M. Steenkamp, "Customer Loyalty to Whom? Managing the Benefits and Risks of Salesperson-Owned Loyalty," *Journal of Marketing Research* 44 (May 2007): pp. 185–199.

B2B TOP PERFORMERS

Understanding the Customer's Business—The Key to Success

To forge a collaborative relationship with a customer, the business marketer requires a deep understanding of the customer's business, its key competitors, and its goals and strategies. In turn, a wealth of communication links are required across the partnering organizations at all levels of management. Salespersons not only work with the purchasing staff but also have close ties to senior executives. For example, for some of IBM's Fortune 500 customers, account executives are direct participants in the customer firm's strategy planning

sessions. Here IBM adds value to the relationship by providing specific recommendations concerning how its products and services can be used to advance the firm's competitive advantage. As a relationship with a large account grows and flourishes, a full-time sales team is often created to serve the needs of that customer. The team comprises sales, service, and technical specialists who have extensive knowledge of the customer's industry. Some team members have worked exclusively with a single customer organization for years.

market and by the significance of the purchase to the buyer. A central challenge for the marketer is to overcome the gravitational pull toward the transaction end of the exchange spectrum. According to Day,

> Rivals are continually working to attract the best accounts away; customer requirements, expectations, and preferences keep changing, and the possibility of friction-free exploration of options in real time on the Web conspire to raise the rate of customer defections.[13]

Managing Buyer-Seller Relationships

Buyers and sellers craft different types of relationships in response to market conditions and the characteristics of the purchase situation. To develop specific relationship-marketing strategies for a particular customer, the business marketer must understand that some customers elect a collaborative relationship, whereas others prefer a more distant or transactional relationship. Figure 4.2 highlights the typical characteristics of relationships at the endpoints of the buyer-seller relationship spectrum.

Transactional Exchange

Customers are more likely to prefer a **transactional relationship** when a competitive supply market features many alternatives, the purchase decision is not complex, and the supply market is stable. This profile fits some buyers of office supplies, commodity chemicals, and shipping services. In turn, customers emphasize a transactional orientation when they view the purchase as less important to the organization's objectives. Such relationships are characterized by lower levels of information exchange and are less likely to involve operational linkages between the buying and selling firms.

---

[13]Day, "Managing Market Relationships," p. 25.

FIGURE 4.2 | THE SPECTRUM OF BUYER-SELLER RELATIONSHIPS

	Transactional Exchange ←→	Collaborative Exchange
Availability of Alternatives	Many Alternatives	Few Alternatives
Supply Market Dynamism	Stable	Volatile
Importance of Purchase	Low	High
Complexity of Purchase	Low	High
Information Exchange	Low	High
Operational Linkages	Limited	Extensive

SOURCE: Adapted from Joseph P. Cannon and William D. Perreault Jr., "Buyer-Seller Relationships in Business Markets," *Journal of Marketing Research* 36 (November 1999): pp. 439–460.

Collaborative Exchange

Buying firms prefer a more **collaborative relationship** when alternatives are few, the market is dynamic (for example, rapidly changing technology), and the complexity of the purchase is high. In particular, buyers seek close relationships with suppliers when they deem the purchase important and strategically significant. This behavior fits some purchasers of manufacturing equipment, enterprise software, or critical component parts. Indeed, say Cannon and Perreault,

> the closest partnerships . . . arise both when the purchase is important and when there is a need—from the customer's perspective—to overcome procurement obstacles that result from fewer supply alternatives and more purchase uncertainty.[14]

Moreover, the relationships that arise for important purchases are more likely to involve operational linkages and high levels of information exchange. Switching costs are especially important to collaborative customers.

Switching Costs

In considering possible changes from one selling firm to another, organizational buyers consider two **switching costs**: investments and risk of exposure. First, organizational buyers invest in their relationships with suppliers in many ways. As Barbara Bund Jackson states:

> They invest *money*; they invest in *people*, as in training employees to run new equipment; they invest in *lasting assets*, such as equipment itself; and they invest in changing basic business *procedures* like inventory handling.[15]

[14]Cannon and Perreault, "Buyer-Seller Relationships," p. 453.

[15]Barbara Bund Jackson, "Build Customer Relationships That Last," *Harvard Business Review* 63 (November–December 1985): p. 125.

Because of these past investments, buyers may hesitate to incur the disruptions and switching costs that result when they select new suppliers.

Risk of exposure provides a second major category of switching costs. Attention centers on the risks to buyers of making the wrong choice. Customers perceive more risk when they purchase products important to their operations, when they buy from less established suppliers, and when they buy technically complex products.

Strategy Guidelines

The business marketer manages a portfolio of relationships with customers—some of these customers view the purchase as important and desire a close, tightly connected buyer-seller relationship; other customers assign a lower level of importance to the purchase and prefer a looser relationship. Given the differing needs and orientations of customers, the business marketer's first step is to determine which type of relationship matches the purchasing situation and supply-market conditions for a particular customer. Second, a strategy must be designed that is appropriate for each strategy type.

Collaborative Customers   Relationship-building strategies, targeted on strong and lasting commitments, are especially appropriate for these customers. Business marketers can sensibly invest resources to secure commitments and directly assist customers with planning. Here sales and service personnel work not only with purchasing managers but also with a wide array of managers on strategy and coordination issues. Regular visits to the customer by executives and technical personnel can strengthen the relationship. Operational linkages and information-sharing mechanisms should be designed into the relationship to keep product and service offerings aligned with customer needs. Given the long time horizon and switching costs, customers are concerned both with the marketers' long-term capabilities and with their immediate performance. Because the customers perceive significant risk, they demand competence and commitment from sellers and are easily frightened by even a hint of supplier inadequacy.

Value Drivers in Collaborative Relationships   A recent study examined this intriguing question: What avenues of differentiation can suppliers of routinely purchased products use to create value in business-to-business relationships, thereby winning key supplier status?[16] From Table 4.1, observe that the study uncovered three sources of value creation—value creation through the core offering, within the sourcing process, and at the level of the customer's operations. The associated relationship benefits and costs for each are listed. Consistent with the total cost of ownership (Chapter 2) perspective that purchasing managers apply, costs as a value driver center on the degree to which the supplier offers a lower price or adds value by taking costs out of the sourcing process or the customer's operations.

The results suggest that relationship benefits display a much stronger potential for differentiation in key supplier relationships than cost considerations. Importantly, service support and personal interaction were identified as the core differentiators,

---

[16]Wolfgang Ulaga and Andreas Eggert, "Value-Based Differentiation in Business Relationships: Gaining and Sustaining Key Supplier Status," *Journal of Marketing* 70 (January 2006): pp. 119–136.

TABLE 4.1 | **Value Drivers in Key Supplier Relationships**

Sources of Value Creation	Relationship Value Dimensions	
	Costs	**Benefits**
Core offering	Product quality	Direct costs
	Delivery performance	
Sourcing process	Service support	Acquisition costs
	Personal interaction	
Customer operations	Supplier know-how	Operation costs
	Time to market	

SOURCE: Wolfgang Ulaga and Andreas Eggert, "Value-Based Differentiation in Business Relationships: Gaining and Sustaining Key Supplier Status," *Journal of Marketing* 70 (January 2006): p. 122. Copyright © 2001. Reprinted by permission of Warren, Gorham, Lamont via Copyright Clearance Center.

followed by a supplier's know-how and its ability to improve a customer's time to market. Product quality and delivery performance, along with cost savings associated with the acquisition process and from operations, display a moderate potential to help a firm gain key supplier status. Finally, price displayed the weakest potential for differentiation. The researchers, Wolfgang Ulaga and Andreas Eggert, conclude: "Whereas cost factors serve as key criteria to get a supplier on the short list of those vendors considered for a relationship, relationship benefits dominate when deciding which supplier" should be awarded key supplier status.[17]

Transaction Customers   These customers display less loyalty or commitment to a particular supplier and can easily switch part or all of the purchases from one vendor to another. A business marketer who offers an immediate, attractive combination of product, price, technical support, and other benefits has a chance of winning business from a transactional customer. The salesperson centers primary attention on the purchasing staff and seldom has important ties to senior executives in the buying organization. M. Bensaou argues that it is unwise for marketers to make specialized investments in transactional relationships:

> Firms that invest in building trust through frequent visits, guest engineers, and cross-company teams when the product and market context calls for simple, impersonal control and data exchange mechanisms are overdesigning the relationship. This path is not only costly but also risky, given the specialized investments involved, in particular, the intangible ones (for example, people, information, or knowledge).[18]

Rather than adopting the approach of "one design fits all," the astute marketer matches the strategy to the product and market conditions that surround a particular customer relationship and understands the factors that influence profitability.

---

[17] Ibid., p. 131.

[18] M. Bensaou, "Portfolio of Buyer-Seller Relationships," *Sloan Management Review* 40 (Summer 1999): p. 43.

Measuring Customer Profitability[19]

To improve customer satisfaction and loyalty, many business-to-business firms have developed customized products and increased the specialized services they offer. Although customers embrace such actions, they often lead to declining profits, especially when the enhanced offerings are not accompanied by increases in prices or order volumes. For a differentiation strategy to succeed, "the value created by the differentiation—measured by higher margins and higher sales volumes—has to exceed the cost of creating and delivering customized features and services."[20] By understanding the drivers of customer profitability, the business marketing manager can more effectively allocate marketing resources and take action to convert unprofitable relationships into profitable ones.

Activity-Based Costing

Most studies of customer profitability yield a remarkable insight: "Only a minority of a typical company's customers is truly profitable."[21] Why? Many firms fail to examine how the costs of specialized products and services vary among individual customers. In other words, they focus on profitability at an aggregate level (for example, product or territory), fail to assign operating expenses to customers, and misjudge the profitability of individual customers. To capture customer-specific costs, many firms have adopted activity-based costing.

Activity-based costing (ABC) illuminates exactly what activities are associated with serving a particular customer and how these activities are linked to revenues and the consumption of resources.[22] The ABC system and associated software link customer transaction data from customer relationship management (CRM) systems with financial information. The ABC system provides marketing managers with a clear and accurate picture of the gross margins and cost-to-serve components that yield individual customer profitability.

Unlocking Customer Profitability

By accurately tracing costs to individual customers, managers are better equipped to diagnose problems and take appropriate action. For example, Kanthal, a heating wire manufacturer, learned to its surprise that one of its largest and most coveted accounts—General Electric's Appliance Division—was also one of its most unprofitable customers.[23] A customer order that normally would cost Kanthal $150 to process cost more than $600 from GE because of frequent order changes, expedited deliveries, and scheduling adjustments. A senior manager at Kanthal suggested to GE that the numerous change orders were costly not only to Kanthal but also to GE. After a quick internal review, GE managers agreed, corrected internal inefficiencies, and then

---

[19]This section, unless otherwise noted, draws on Robert S. Kaplan and V. G. Narayanan, "Measuring and Managing Customer Profitability," *Journal of Cost Management* 15 (5, September–October 2001): pp. 5–15.

[20]Robert S. Kaplan, "Add a Customer Profitability Metric to Your Balanced Scorecard," *Balanced Scorecard Report*, July–August 2005 (Boston: Harvard Business School Publishing Corporation), p. 3.

[21]Kaplan and Narayanan, "Measuring and Managing Customer Profitability," p. 5.

[22]Ibid., p. 7. See also Robert S. Kaplan and Steven R. Anderson, "Time-Driven Activity-Based Costing," *Harvard Business Review* 82 (November 2004): pp. 131–138.

[23]Kaplan and Narayanan, p. 11.

FIGURE 4.3 | **THE WHALE CURVE ILLUSTRATION: 20% OF CUSTOMERS GENERATE 175% OF CUMULATIVE PROFITS**

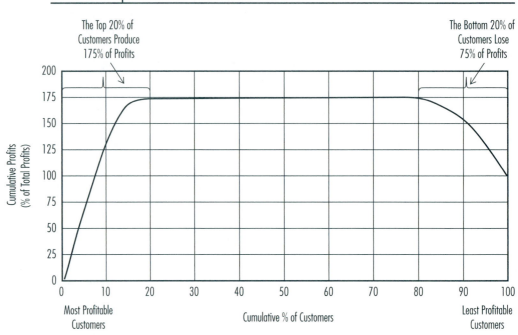

SOURCE: Adapted with modifications from Robert S. Kaplan and V.G. Narayanan, "Measuring and Managing Customer Profitability," *Journal of Cost Management* 15 (September/October 2001): p. 8.

awarded Kanthal with the largest contract in the firm's history. The contract incorporated a surcharge for any change GE made to an existing order and established a minimum order size. By isolating the true cost of serving GE, Kanthal converted an unprofitable relationship to a profitable one and provided further value by helping a key customer reduce costs.

The Profitable Few

Once a firm implements an ABC approach and plots cumulative profitability against customers, a striking portrait emerges that is often referred to as the *whale curve* (Figure 4.3). Robert S. Kaplan, who is codeveloper of activity-based costing, and his colleague, V. G. Narayanan, describe the pattern that many companies find:

> Whereas cumulative sales usually follow the typical 20/80 rule (that is, 20 percent of the customers provide 80 percent of the sales), the whale curve for cumulative profitability usually reveals that the most profitable 20 percent of customers generate between 150 percent and 300 percent of total profits. The middle 70 percent of customers break even and the least profitable 10 percent of customers lose from 50 to 200 percent of total profits, leaving the company with its 100 percent of total profits.[24]

---

[24]Ibid., p. 7. See also Robert S. Kaplan and David P. Norton, *The Execution Premium* (Boston: Harvard Business Press, 2008), pp. 255–261.

TABLE 4.2 | THE CHARACTERISTICS OF HIGH- VERSUS LOW-COST-TO-SERVE CUSTOMERS

	High-Cost-to-Serve Customers	Low-Cost-to-Serve Customers
Presale Costs	Extensive presales support required (i.e., technical and sales resources)	Limited presales support (i.e., standard pricing and ordering)
Production Costs	Order custom products Small order quantities Unpredictable ordering pattern Manual processing	Order standard products Large order quantities Predictable ordering cycle Electronic processing
Delivery Costs	Fast delivery	Standard delivery
Postsale Service Costs	Extensive postsales support required (i.e., customer training, installation, technical support)	Limited postsales support

SOURCE: Adapted, with modifications, from Robert S. Kaplan and V. G. Narayanan, "Measuring and Managing Customer Profitability," *Journal of Cost Management* 15 (September/October 2001): p. 8 and Benson P. Shapiro, V. Kasturi Rangan, Rowland Moriarty, Jr., and Elliot B. Ross, "Manage Customers for Profits (Not Just Sales)," *Harvard Business Review* 65 (September-October 1987): pp. 101–108.

As a rule, large customers tend to be included among the most profitable (see left side of Figure 4.3) or the least profitable (see right side of Figure 4.3)—they are seldom in the middle. Interestingly, some of the firm's largest customers often turn out to be among the most unprofitable. A firm does not generate enough sales volume with a small customer to incur large absolute losses. Only large buyers can be large-loss customers. In Figure 4.3, low-cost-to-serve customers appear on the profitable side of the whale curve and high-cost-to-serve customers end up on the unprofitable side unless they pay a premium price for the specialized support they require.

Managing High- and Low-Cost-to-Serve Customers

What causes some customers to be more expensive than others? Note from Table 4.2 that high-cost-to-serve customers, for example, desire customized products, frequently change orders, and require a significant amount of presales and postsales support. By contrast, low-cost-to-serve customers purchase standard products, place orders and schedule deliveries on a predictable cycle, and require little or no presales or postsales support.

Look Inside First After reviewing the profitability of individual customers, the business marketer can consider possible strategies to retain the most valuable customers and to transform unprofitable customers into profitable ones. However, managers should first examine their company's own internal processes to ensure that it can accommodate customer preferences for reduced order sizes or special services at the lowest cost. For example, a large publisher of business directories reduced the cost of serving its customer base by assigning key account managers to its largest customers (that is, the 4 percent of customers who accounted for 45 percent of its sales)

FIGURE 4.4 | **CUSTOMER PROFITABILITY**

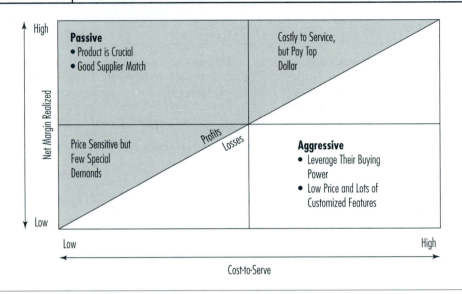

and serving the smallest customers over the Internet and by a telephone sales force.[25] These actions not only cut costs dramatically but also gave each group of customers what they had wanted all along: Large customers wanted a central point of contact where they could secure services customized to their needs; small customers preferred minimal contact with a direct salesperson but wanted the assurance that they could receive advice and support if required.

A Sharper Profit Lens   Business marketing managers can view their customers through the lens of a simple 2 × 2 diagram (Figure 4.4). The vertical axis shows the net margin earned from sales to a particular customer. The **net margin** equals the net price, after all discounts, minus manufacturing costs. The horizontal axis shows the **costs of serving the customer**, including order-related costs plus the customer-specific marketing, technical, and administrative expenses.

Identifying Profitable Customers   Observe from Figure 4.4 that profitable customers can take different forms. To illustrate, a customer like Honda of America would be at the lower left corner of the diagram: demanding low prices, so net margins are low, but also working with its suppliers to streamline activities so that the cost-to-serve is also low. High-cost-to-serve customers who occupy the upper right corner of Figure 4.4 can also be profitable if the net margins earned on sales to them more than compensate the company for the cost of the resources used in serving them.

A company is indeed fortunate if several of its customers occupy the upper left-hand quadrant of the diagram: high margins *and* low cost-to-serve. Because these

[25] George S. Day, "Creating a Superior Customer-Relating Capability," *MIT Sloan Management Review* 44 (Spring 2003): pp. 77–82.

customers represent a valuable asset, marketing managers should forge close relationships with them, anticipate their changing needs, and have protective measures (for example, special services) in place in case competitors attempt to win them away.

Managing Unprofitable Customers[26]

The most challenging set of customers for marketing managers is found in the lower right-hand corner of Figure 4.4: low margins and high cost-to-serve. First, the marketing manager should explore possible ways to reduce the cost of activities associated with serving these customers. For example, perhaps postsales support could be shifted to the Internet. Second, the manager should direct attention to the customer actions that contribute to higher selling costs. To illustrate, the high cost-to-serve may be caused by the customer's unpredictable ordering patterns or by the large demands it places on technical and sales personnel. By detailing the costs of these activities and openly sharing this information with the customer, the business marketing manager can encourage the customer to work with the company more efficiently. From the earlier example, recall that Kanthal used this approach not only to restore profitability but also to help one of its largest customers, General Electric's Appliance Division, refine its internal processes and reduce its costs.

Firing Customers

By improving processes and refining pricing strategies, business marketing managers can transform many, but not all, customers from unprofitable to profitable. What should we do with those unprofitable customers that remain in the high-cost-to-serve quadrant of Figure 4.4? To answer this question, we have to dig deeper into the customer relationship and assess the other benefits that certain customers may provide. Some customers are new and the initial investment to attract them will ultimately be repaid in higher sales volume and profitability. Other customers provide an opportunity for learning. For example, some firms that serve Toyota or Honda incurred initial losses in serving these demanding customers but secured insights into management processes and technology they could effectively apply to all their customers.

Suppose, however, that a customer is unprofitable, not new, and offers little or no opportunity for learning. Furthermore, suppose that the customer resists all attempts to convert the unprofitable relationship into a profitable one. Under these conditions, Robert S. Kaplan and Robin Cooper observe that we might consider firing them, but a more subtle approach will do: "We can, perhaps, let the customer fire itself by refusing to grant discounts and reducing or eliminating marketing and technical support."[27] Customer divestment is a viable strategic option, but one that must be exercised sparingly and only after other options have been thoroughly examined.[28]

[26]This section is based on Robert S. Kaplan and Robin Cooper, *Cost and Effect: Using Integrated Cost Systems to Drive Profitability and Performance* (Boston: Harvard Business School Press, 1998), pp. 193–201.

[27]Ibid., p. 200.

[28]Vikas Mittal, Matthew Sarkees, and Feisal Murshed, "The Right Way to Manage Unprofitable Customers," *Harvard Business Review* 86 (April 2008): pp. 95–102.

Customer Relationship Management

Customer retention has always been crucial to success in the business market, and it now provides the centerpiece of strategy discussions as firms embrace customer relationship management. **Customer relationship management** (CRM) is a cross-functional process for achieving

- a continuing dialogue with customers

- across all their contact and access points, with

- personalized treatment of the most valuable customers,

- to ensure customer retention and the effectiveness of marketing initiatives.[29]

To meet these challenging requirements, business marketing firms, large and small, are making substantial investments in CRM systems—enterprise software applications that integrate sales, marketing, and customer service information. To improve service and retain customers, CRM systems synthesize information from all of a company's contact points or "touch points"—including e-mail, call centers, sales and service representatives—to support later customer interactions and to inform market forecasts, product design, and supply chain management.[30] Salespersons, call center personnel, Web managers, resellers, and customer service representatives all have the same real-time information on each customer.

For an investment in CRM software to yield positive returns, a firm needs a customer strategy. Strategy experts contend that many CRM initiatives fail because executives mistake CRM software for a marketing strategy. Darrell Rigby and his colleagues contend: "It isn't. CRM is the bundling of customer strategy and processes, supported by relevant software, for the purpose of improving customer loyalty and, eventually, corporate profitability."[31] CRM software can help, but only after a customer strategy has been designed and executed. To develop responsive and profitable customer strategies, special attention must be given to five areas: (1) acquiring the right customers, (2) crafting the right value proposition, (3) instituting the best processes, (4) motivating employees, and (5) learning to retain customers (Table 4.3). Observe how CRM technology from leading producers such as Oracle Corporation and Siebel Systems can be used to capture critical customer data, transform it into valuable information, and distribute it throughout the organization to support the strategy process from customer acquisition to customer retention. Thus, a well-designed and executed customer strategy, supported by a CRM system, provides the financial payoff.

Acquiring the Right Customers

Customer relationship management directs attention to two critical assets of the business-to-business firm: its stock of current and potential customer relationships and its collective knowledge of how to select, initiate, develop, and maintain profitable

---

[29]George S. Day, "Capabilities for Forging Customer Relationships," Working Paper, Report No. 00-118, Marketing Science Institute, Cambridge, MA, 2000, p. 4.

[30]Larry Yu, "Successful Customer-Relationship Management," *MIT Sloan Management Review* 42 (Summer 2001): p. 18.

[31]Darrell K. Rigby, Frederick F. Reichheld, and Phil Schefter, "Avoid the Four Perils of CRM," *Harvard Business Review* 80 (January–February 2002): p. 102.

TABLE 4.3 | CREATING A CUSTOMER RELATIONSHIP MANAGEMENT STRATEGY

CRM Priorities				
Acquiring the Right Customers	Crafting the Right Value Proposition	Instituting the Best Processes	Motivating Employees	Learning to Retain Customers
Critical Tasks				
• Identify your most valuable customers. • Calculate your share of their purchases (wallet) for your goods and services.	• Determine the products or services your customers need today and will need tomorrow. • Assess the products or services that your competitors offer today and tomorrow. • Identify new products or services that you should be offering.	• Research the best way to deliver your products or services to customers. • Determine the service capabilities that must be developed and the technology investments that are required to implement customer strategy.	• Identify the tools your employees need to foster customer relationships. • Earn employee loyalty by investing in training and development and constructing appropriate career paths for employees.	• Understand why customers defect and how to win them back. • Identify the strategies your competitors are using to win your high-value customers.
CRM Technology Can Help				
• Analyze customer revenue and cost data to identify current and future high-value customers. • Target marketing communications to high-value customers.	• Capture relevant product and service behavior data from customer transactions. • Create new distribution channels. • Develop new pricing models.	• Process transactions faster. • Provide better information to customer contact employees. • Manage logistics and the supply chain more efficiently.	• Align employee incentives and performance measures. • Distribute customer knowledge to employees throughout the organization.	• Track customer defection and retention levels. • Track customer service satisfaction levels.

SOURCE: Adapted from Darrell K. Rigby, Frederick F. Reichheld, and Phil Schefter, "Avoid the Four Perils of CRM," *Harvard Business Review* 80 (January–February 2002): p. 106.

relationships with these customers.[32] Customer portfolio management, then, is the process of creating value across a firm's customer relationships—from transactional to collaborative—with an emphasis on balancing the customer's desired level of relationship against the profitability of doing so.[33]

[32] Ruth N. Bolton, Katherine N. Lemon, and Peter Verhoof, "Expanding Business-to-Business Customer Relationships," *Journal of Marketing* 72 (January 2008): pp. 46–64.

[33] Michael D. Johnson and Fred Selnes, "Diversifying Your Customer Portfolio," *MIT Sloan Management Review* 46 (Spring 2005): pp. 11–14.

INSIDE BUSINESS MARKETING

Diversify a Customer Portfolio Too!

For an investor, modern portfolio theory demonstrates that optimal performance, for a given level of risk, can best be achieved by building a diversified mix of investment assets that includes the stocks of both large and small firms, representing both U.S. and foreign companies. In building a customer portfolio, similar benefits can be realized by viewing customers as assets and diversifying across categories of customers. For example, after the technology bubble, many information technology (IT) companies, like IBM and Microsoft, were surprised to observe that small and medium-sized businesses (SMB) fueled the recovery in IT spending. Why? Most of the SMB customers did not overindulge in massive hardware and software upgrades to the same extreme extent during the bubble as their large-enterprise counterparts did. So, SMB customers were the first to return and aggressively buy IT products and services. Because Dell, Microsoft, and IBM each have a customer portfolio that includes a strong representation of SMB customers, these firms enjoyed an edge over rivals such as Hewlett-Packard and Sun Microsystems that were less focused on this customer group (that is, asset category) and were "caught waiting" for large-enterprise customers to return.

SOURCE: Mark Veverka, "Little Guys Lead IT Spending Recovery," *Barron's*, October 20, 2003, p. 73.

Account selection requires a clear understanding of customer needs, a tight grasp on the costs of serving different groups of customers, and an accurate forecast of potential profit opportunities. The choice of potential accounts to target is facilitated by an understanding of how different customers define value. **Value**, as defined by James Anderson and James Narus, refers to "the economic, technical, service, and social benefits received by a customer firm in exchange for the price paid for a product offering."[34] By gauging the value of their offerings to different groups of customers, business marketers are better equipped to target accounts and to determine how to provide enhanced value to particular customers.

The account selection process should also consider profit potential. Because the product is critical to their operations, some customers place a high value on supporting services (for example, technical advice and training) and are willing to pay a premium price for them. Other customers are most costly to serve, do not value service support, and are extremely price sensitive. Because customers have different needs and represent different levels of current and potential opportunities, a marketer should divide its customers into groups. The marketer wishes to develop a broader and deeper relationship with the most profitable ones and assign a low priority to the least profitable ones.[35] Frank Cespedes asserts that

> account selection, therefore, must be explicit about which demands the seller
> can meet and leverage in dealings with other customers. Otherwise, the seller

---

[34]Anderson and Narus, p. 98. See also Ajay Menon, Christian Homburg, and Nikolas Beutin, "Understanding Customer Value in Business-to-Business Relationships," *Journal of Business-to-Business Marketing* 12 (2, 2005): pp. 1–33; and Ulaga and Eggert, "Value-Based Differentiation," pp. 119–136.

[35]Frederick F. Reichheld, "Lead for Loyalty," *Harvard Business Review* 79 (July–August 2001): pp. 76–84.

risks overserving unprofitable accounts and wasting resources that might be allocated to other customer groups.[36]

Crafting the Right Value Proposition

A **value proposition** represents the products, services, ideas, and solutions that a business marketer offers to advance the performance goals of the customer organization. Recall from Chapter 1 that the customer value proposition must address this essential question: How do the value elements (benefits) in a supplier's offering compare to those of the next-best alternative? A value proposition may include points of parity (certain value elements are the same as the next-best option) and points of difference (the value elements that make the supplier's offering either superior or inferior to the next-best alternative). For example, a supplier may offer improved technology (positive) at a higher price (negative) and fail to convince customers that the new technology justifies the price increase.

> Best-practice suppliers base their value proposition on the few elements that matter most to target customers, demonstrate the value of this superior performance, and communicate it in a way that conveys a sophisticated understanding of the customer's business priorities.[37]

The Bandwidth of Strategies To develop customer-specific product offerings, the business marketer should next examine the nature of buyer-seller relationships in the industry. The strategies competing firms in an industry pursue fall into a range referred to as the industry bandwidth of working relationships.[38] Business marketers either attempt to span the bandwidth with a portfolio of relationship-marketing strategies or concentrate on a single strategy, thereby having a narrower range of relationships than the industry bandwidth.

Observe in Figure 4.5 how two different industries (medical equipment and hospital supplies) are positioned on the relationship continuum. Because the underlying technology is complex and dynamic, collaborative relations characterize the medical equipment industry. Here, a range of services—technical support, installation, professional training, and maintenance agreements—can augment the core product. By contrast, collaborative relations in the hospital supply industry tend to be more focused and center on helping health-care organizations meet their operational needs (for example, efficient ordering processes and timely delivery).

By diagnosing the spectrum of relationship strategies competitors in an industry follow, a business marketer can tailor strategies that more closely respond both to customers who desire a collaborative emphasis and to those who seek a transaction emphasis. The strategy involves *flaring out* from the industry bandwidth in the collaborative as well as in the transactional direction (see Figure 4.5b).

Flaring Out by Unbundling An unbundling strategy can reach customers who desire a greater transaction emphasis. Here, related services are unbundled to yield the

---

[36]Frank V. Cespedes, *Concurrent Marketing: Integrating Product, Sales, and Service* (Boston: Harvard Business School Press, 1995), p. 193. See also Don Peppers, Martha Rogers, and Bob Dorf, "Is Your Company Ready for One-to-One Marketing?" *Harvard Business Review* 77 (January–February 1999): pp. 151–160.

[37]James C. Anderson, James A. Narus, and Wouter van Rossum, "Customer Value Propositions in Business Markets," *Harvard Business Review* 84 (March 2006): p. 93.

[38]This discussion draws on Anderson and Narus, "Partnering as a Focused Market Strategy," pp. 95–113.

FIGURE 4.5 | **TRANSACTIONAL AND COLLABORATIVE WORKING RELATIONSHIPS**

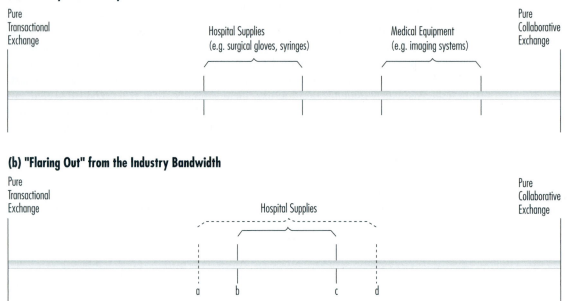

(a) Industry Relationship Bandwidths

Pure
Transactional
Exchange

Hospital Supplies
(e.g. surgical gloves, syringes)

Medical Equipment
(e.g. imaging systems)

Pure
Collaborative
Exchange

(b) "Flaring Out" from the Industry Bandwidth

Pure
Transactional
Exchange

Hospital Supplies

Pure
Collaborative
Exchange

a   b   c   d

SOURCE: Adapted from James C. Anderson and James A. Narus, "Partnering as a Focused Marketing Strategy," *California Management Review* 33 (Spring 1991): p. 97.

core product (**a** in Figure 4.5b), which meets a customer's basic price, quality, and availability requirements. For each service that is unbundled, the price is lowered. Augmented services, such as technical assistance, consulting, and just-in-time delivery, are each offered, but in a menu fashion, on an incremental price basis. Importantly, the price increments for the entire set of unbundled services should be greater than the price premium sought for the collaborative offering. This reflects the efficiencies of providing the complete bundle of services to a collaborative account. This pricing policy is market oriented in that it allows customer firms to choose the product and relationship offering that *they perceive* to provide the greatest value.

Flaring Out with Augmentation   At the other extreme, the collaborative offering (**d** in Figure 4.5b) becomes the augmented product enriched with features the customer values. Augmented features might include coordinated cost-reduction programs, technical assistance, delivery schedule guarantees, and cooperative advertising. Because collaborative efforts are designed to add value or reduce the costs of exchange between partnering firms, a price premium should be received for the collaborative offering.

Allegiance Healthcare Corporation has developed ways to improve hospital supply ordering, delivery, and billing that provide enhanced value to the customer.[39]

---

[39]Valarie A. Zeithaml, Roland T. Rust, and Katherine N. Lemon, "The Customer Pyramid: Creating and Serving Profitable Customers," *California Management Review* 43 (Summer 2001): p. 134.

Instead of miscellaneous supplies arriving in boxes sorted at the convenience of Allegiance's needs, they arrive on "client-friendly" pallets customized to meet the distribution needs of the individual hospital. Moreover, hospitals can secure a structural connection to Allegiance through its ValueLink ordering system for added value and convenience.

Creating Flexible Service Offerings Business marketers can gain a competitive edge by creating a portfolio of service offerings and then drawing on this portfolio to provide customized solutions for groups of customers or even individual customers.[40] First, an offering should be created that includes the bare-bones-minimum number of services valued by all customers in a particular market segment. Microsoft refers to these offerings as "naked solutions." Second, optional services are created that add value by reducing costs or improving the performance of a customer's operations. To meet the needs of particular customers, optional services can then be "custom wrapped" with the core offering to create added value.

Instituting the Best Processes

The sales force assumes a central relationship-management role in the business market. Technical service and customer service personnel also assume implementation roles that are important and visible in buying organizations. Successful relationship strategies are shaped by an effective organization and deployment of the personal selling effort and close coordination with supporting units, such as logistics and technical service. Some firms divide the sales organization into units that each serve a distinct relationship category such as transactional accounts or partnership accounts. Through a careful screening process, promising transaction accounts are periodically upgraded to partnerships.

Best Practices at IBM[41] In serving a particular customer, a number of IBM employees come into contact with the customer organization. To ensure consistent strategy execution, IBM identifies three customer-contact roles for each of its accounts, specifies desired measurable actions for each role, and monitors the customer's degree of satisfaction with each role (Table 4.4). The IBM client representative assigned to the customer is the *relationship owner*, but the account team may include other specialists who complete a project for the customer (*project owner*) or solve a particular customer problem (*problem resolution owner*). Any IBM employee who works on the account can secure timely information from the CRM system to identify recent actions or issues to be addressed. Moreover, for each role, there is an in-process measure and a customer feedback measure.

Consider an IBM technical manager assigned responsibility for installing CRM software for a large bank. As a project owner, this manager's goal is to determine

[40]James C. Anderson and James A. Narus, "Capturing the Value of Supplementary Services," *Harvard Business Review* 73 (January–February 1995): pp. 75–83. See also David Rickard, "The Joys of Bundling: Assessing the Benefits and Risks," The Boston Consulting Group, Inc., 2008, accessed at http://www.bcg.com on May 15, 2008.

[41]This discussion is based on Larry Schiff, "How Customer Satisfaction Improvement Works to Fuel Full Business Recovery at IBM," *Journal of Organizational Excellence* 20 (Spring 2001): pp. 3–18.

TABLE 4.4 | ROLE-BASED STRATEGY EXECUTION AT IBM: MEASURED ACTIONS AND RESULTS

Role	Strategy Goal	Measured Actions	Measured Results (Customer)
Relationship Owner	Improve Customer Relationships	Meet with customer twice per year to identify customer's expectations and set action plan	IBM Customer Satisfaction Survey Results
Project Owner	Exceed Customer Expectations for Each Transaction	Collect conditions of satisfaction, get customer feedback	IBM Transaction Survey Results
Problem Resolution	Fix Customer Problems	Solve in seven days or meet action plan	Customer Satisfaction with Problem Resolution

SOURCE: Adapted from Larry Schiff, "How Customer Satisfaction Improvement Works to Fuel Business Recovery at IBM," *Journal of Organizational Excellence* (Spring 2001): pp. 12–14.

the customer's conditions of satisfaction and then exceed those expectations. When the work is completed, members of the customer organization are queried concerning their satisfaction and the project owner acts on the feedback to ensure that all promises have been kept. Clearly, a sound complaint management process is essential. Recent research found that if a complaint is ineffectively handled, the firm faces a high risk of losing *even* those customers who had previously been very satisfied.[42]

Research suggests that the performance attributes that influence the customer satisfaction of business buyers include:

- the responsiveness of the supplier in meeting the firm's needs,
- product quality,
- a broad product line,
- delivery reliability,
- knowledgeable sales and service personnel.[43]

Motivating Employees

Dedicated employees are the cornerstone of a successful customer relationship strategy. Frederick F. Reichheld notes:

> Leaders who are dedicated to treating people right drive themselves to deliver superior value, which allows them to attract and retain the best employees. That's partly because higher profits result from customer retention, but more important, it's because providing excellent service and value generates pride and a sense of purpose among employees.[44]

[42]Christian Homburg and Andreas Fürst, "How Organizational Complaint Handling Drives Customer Loyalty: An Analysis of the Mechanistic and the Organic Approach," *Journal of Marketing* 69 (July 2005): pp. 95–114.

[43]Bowman and Narayandas, "Linking Customer Management Effort," pp. 433–447.

[44]Reichheld, "Lead for Loyalty," p. 78.

Employee loyalty is earned by investing heavily in training and development, providing challenging career paths to facilitate professional development, and aligning employee incentives to performance measures.[45] For example, Square D, an Illinois-based producer of electrical and industrial equipment, altered its performance-measurement and incentive systems to fit the firm's new customer strategy. Consistent with the goal of attracting high-value customers, salesperson incentives are no longer based on the number of units sold but on the number of customers acquired and on profit margins.

Research clearly demonstrates the link between salespeople's job satisfaction and customer satisfaction in business markets. Christian Homburg and Ruth M. Stock report that the relationship between salespeople's job satisfaction is particularly strong when there is a high frequency of customer interaction, high intensity of customer integration into the value-creating process, and high product or service innovativeness.[46]

Learning to Retain Customers

Business marketers track customer loyalty and retention because the cost of serving a long-standing customer is often far less than the cost of acquiring a new customer.[47] Why? Established customers often buy more products and services from a trusted supplier and, as they do, the cost of serving them declines. The firm learns how to serve them more efficiently and also spots opportunities for expanding the relationship. Thus, the profit from that customer tends to increase over the life of the relationship. To that end, a goal for IBM is to gain an increasing share of a customer's total information technology expenditures (that is, share of wallet). Rather than merely attempting to improve satisfaction ratings, IBM seeks to be recognized as providing superior value to its customers. Larry Schiff, an IBM strategist, notes: "If you delight your customers and are perceived to provide the best value in your market, you'll gain loyalty and market/wallet share."[48] Although loyal customers are likely to be satisfied, all satisfied customers do not remain loyal. Business marketers earn customer loyalty by providing superior value that ensures high satisfaction and by nurturing trust and mutual commitments.

Pursuing Growth from Existing Customers   Business marketers should identify a well-defined set of existing customers who demonstrate growth potential and selectively pursue a greater share of their business. Based on the cost-to-serve and projected profit margins, the question becomes: Which of our existing customers represent the best growth prospects? In targeting individual customers, particular attention should be given to: (1) estimating the current share of wallet the firm has attained; (2) pursuing opportunities to increase that share; and (3) carefully projecting the enhanced customer profitability that will result.[49]

---

[45] Rigby, Reichheld, and Schefter, "Avoid the Perils of CRM," p. 104.

[46] Christian Homburg and Ruth M. Stock, "The Link Between Salespeople's Job Satisfaction and Customer Satisfaction in a Business-to-Business Context: A Dyadic Analysis," *Journal of the Academy of Marketing Science* 32 (Spring 2004): pp. 144–158; and Christian Homburg and Ruth M. Stock, "Exploring the Conditions Under Which Salesperson Work Satisfaction Can Lead to Customer Satisfaction," *Psychology & Marketing* 22 (5, 2005): pp. 393–420.

[47] Reichheld, "Lead for Loyalty," pp. 76–84.

[48] Schiff, "How Customer Satisfaction Improvement Works to Fuel Full Business Recovery at IBM," p. 8.

[49] James C. Anderson and James A. Narus, "Selectively Pursuing More of Your Customer's Business," *MIT Sloan Management Review* 44 (Spring 2003): pp. 42–49.

Evaluating Relationships   Some relationship-building efforts fail because the expectations of the parties do not mesh—for example, when the business marketer follows a relationship approach and the customer responds in a transaction mode. By isolating customer needs and the costs of augmented service features, the marketer is better equipped to profitably match product offerings to the particular customer's needs.

The goal of a relationship is to enable the buyer and seller to maximize joint value. This points to the need for a formal evaluation of relationship outcomes. For example, sales executives at best-practice firms work closely with their partnership accounts to establish mutually defined goals. After an appropriate period, partnerships that do not meet these goals are downgraded and shifted from the strategic market sales force to the geographic sales force.

Business marketers should also continually update the value of their product and relationship offering. Attention here should center on particular new services that might be incorporated as well as on existing services that might be unbundled or curtailed. Working relationships with customer firms are among the most important marketing assets of the firm. They deserve delicate care and continual nurturing!

Strategic Alliances

Not only do business marketing managers form close relationships with customers, they also develop close bonds with other firms. Strategic alliances have become an important tool for achieving a sustainable competitive advantage for leading business firms. To that end, the top 500 global businesses have an average of 60 major strategic alliances each.[50] **Strategic alliances** involve "a formal long-run linkage, funded with direct co-investments by two or more companies, that pool complementary capabilities and resources to achieve generally agreed objectives."[51] In contrast, a **joint venture** involves the formation of a separate, independent organization by the venture partners.

Accessing Complementary Skills

The driving force behind the formation of a strategic alliance is the desire of one firm to leverage its core competencies by linking them with others who have complementary expertise, thereby expanding the product, market, and geographic scope of the organization. Simon Hayes, vice president of Enterprise Strategic Alliances at Cisco Systems, observes: By combining the best that partners have to offer, "strategic alliances are helping companies enhance their strategic presence in the marketplace and develop new solutions to attract new customers or even create whole new market categories."[52] Cisco Systems, a recognized leader in partnering and collaboration, has formed deep, long-term relationships with a host of strategic alliance partners, including Microsoft, IBM, Hewlett-Packard, Nokia, Fujitsu, Accenture, Intel, Italtel,

---

[50]Jeffrey H. Dyer, Prashant Kale, and Habir Singh, "How to Make Strategic Alliances Work," *MIT Sloan Management Review* 42 (Summer 2001): pp. 37–43. See also Fred A. Kuglin and Jeff Hook, *Building, Leading, and Managing Strategic Alliances* (New York: AMACOM, 2007).

[51]George S. Day, *Market Driven Strategy: Processes for Creating Value* (New York: The Free Press, 1990), p. 272.

[52]Simon Hayes, "Getting Strategic Alliances Right," *Synnovation* 3 (May 2008), p. 72, accessed at www.eds.com/synnovation on July 5, 2008.

FIGURE 4.6 | **A Strategic Alliance: Before the Handshake**

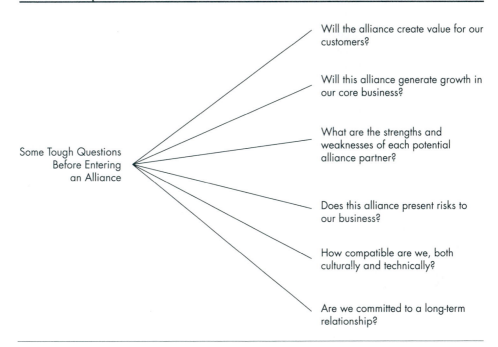

Some Tough Questions Before Entering an Alliance

Will the alliance create value for our customers?

Will this alliance generate growth in our core business?

What are the strengths and weaknesses of each potential alliance partner?

Does this alliance present risks to our business?

How compatible are we, both culturally and technically?

Are we committed to a long-term relationship?

SOURCE: Adapted from Simon Hayes, "Getting Strategic Alliances Right," *Synnovation* 3 (May 2008): p. 74, accessed at www.eds.com.

and many others. For example, the Microsoft–Cisco alliance, formed more than a decade ago, addresses the needs of enterprise and small and medium-size (SMB) customers who need affordable, integrated customer relationship management (CRM) solutions that advance business results and deliver superior customer service. (See Figure 4.6.)

Benefits of Strategic Alliances

Partners to an alliance seek benefits such as (1) access to markets or to technology (a motivating force for General Electric's partnerships in China and India); (2) economies of scale that might be gained by combining manufacturing, R&D, or marketing activities; (3) faster entry of new products to markets (for example, when partners with established channels of distribution in different countries swap new products); and (4) sharing of risk.[53] Simply put, there is a tremendous cost—and risk—when a firm creates its own distribution channels, supply chain network, manufacturing plant, and R&D function in every key market in the world. Also, it takes time to develop relationships with channel members and customers and to develop the skills of employees. Alliances provide an inviting option.

---

[53] Kenneth Ohmae, "The Global Logic of Strategic Alliances," *Harvard Business Review* 67 (March/April 1989): pp. 143–154.

Determinants of Alliance Success

Although offering significant benefits, alliances often fall short of expectations or dissolve. Managing an alliance involves special challenges. Therefore, the ability to form and manage strategic alliances more effectively than rivals can be an important source of competitive advantage.

Building a Dedicated Alliance Function   While many firms generate positive results from strategic alliances, an elite group of firms has demonstrated the capability to generate superior alliance value as measured by the extent to which the alliance met its stated objectives, the degree to which the alliance enhanced the company's competitive position, stock market gains from alliance announcements, and related performance dimensions. Included among the top performers are firms such as Hewlett-Packard, Oracle, Eli Lily & Company, and others. How did they do it? By creating a dedicated strategic alliance function—headed by a vice president or director of strategic alliances with his or her own staff and budget, says Jeffrey H. Dyer and his research team.[54] "The dedicated function coordinates all alliance-related activity within the organization and is charged with institutionalizing processes and systems to teach, share, and leverage prior alliance management experience and know-how throughout the company."[55] Simon Hayes, the Cisco vice president who heads the dedicated alliance function, says:

> At Cisco, we're investing in our alliances with best-practice "videos on demand," strategic alliance leadership-development programs, and strategic scenario-analysis workshops. We believe that the best way to show commitment is with a dedicated, trained, and capable alliance team.[56]

Developing a Joint Value Proposition   Even before negotiations begin, the partners should develop a strategy map that details the shared strategy and the specific value proposition that the partners will deliver to the customer. A close and concise statement of the value proposition is an essential step to getting the organization aligned around a common view of the alliance strategy goals, agreeing upon the unique benefits that the partners will jointly offer to customers.

Developing Close Working Relationships   Rosabeth Moss Kanter emphasizes: "Alliances . . . require a dense web of interpersonal connections and internal infrastructures that enhance learning."[57] Observe the interpersonal connections that unite two *Fortune* 500 firms (referred to as Alpha Communications and Omega Financial Services) in an alliance that markets a cobranded credit and calling card targeted to the business market (see Figure 4.7). The lines connect alliance personnel who have *frequent* and *important* communications and who consider the working relationship to be close. These managers are the **core participants** in the work of the alliance, in contrast to others who are more loosely connected to the alliance team in each

[54]Dyer, Kale, and Singh, "How to Make Alliances Work," p. 37.
[55]Ibid., p. 38.
[56]Hayes, "Getting Strategic Alliances Right," p. 76.
[57]Kanter, "Collaborative Advantage," p. 97.

FIGURE 4.7 | SOCIAL CONNECTIONS IN AN ALLIANCE

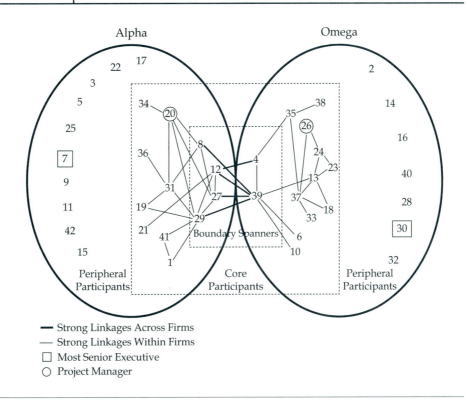

organization (**peripheral participants**). The interpersonal links among the core participants are the circuits through which alliance information flows, decisions are made, and conflicts are resolved.

Boundary-Spanning Connections   Fundamental to the success of the alliance are the working relationships (those connected by the dark lines in Figure 4.7) that span organizational boundaries and unite the partnering firms. These **boundary-spanning** managers (for example, #12 in Alpha and #39 in Omega) have strong communication and friendship links with other managers both within their respective organizations and within the partnering firm. Frequent interactions, the timely exchange of information, and accurate feedback on each partner's actions will minimize misperceptions and strengthen cooperation in an alliance. Likewise, communication among boundary-spanning personnel produces a shared interpretation of goals and common agreement on norms, work roles, and the nature of social relationships.

As close working relationships develop among the alliance participants, psychological contracts, based on trust and shared goals, replace the formal alliance agreement. **Psychological contracts** consist of unwritten and largely nonverbalized sets of congruent expectations and assumptions held by the parties to the alliance about each other's prerogatives and obligations.[58] By promoting openness and flexibility, these interpersonal bonds can speed alliance progress—decisions can be made quickly, unexpected events can be more readily handled, learning is enhanced, and new possibilities for joint action emerge.

Integrating Points of Contact   Firms that are adept at managing strategic alliances use a flexible approach, letting their alliances evolve in form as conditions change over time. They invest adequate resources and management attention in these relationships, and they integrate the organizations so that the appropriate points of contact and communication are managed. Successful alliances achieve five levels of integration:[59]

1. *Strategic integration*, which entails continuing contact among senior executives to define broad goals or discuss changes in each company;

2. *Tactical integration*, which brings middle managers together to plan joint activities, to transfer knowledge, or to isolate organizational or system changes that will improve interfirm connections;

3. *Operational integration*, which provides the information, resources, or personnel that managers require to carry out the day-to-day work of the alliance;

4. *Interpersonal integration*, which builds a necessary foundation for personnel in both organizations to know one another personally, learn together, and create new value; and

5. *Cultural integration*, which requires managers involved in the alliance to have the communication skills and cultural awareness to bridge the differences.

The Social Ingredients of Alliance Success[60]

In a strategic alliance, interpersonal relationships matter. The goals of an alliance cannot be realized in practice until many managers in both organizations know one another personally and take coordinated action to create new value together. Indeed, many alliances that appear to make strategic sense fail to meet expectations because little attention is given to cultivating the interpersonal connections and communication patterns that underlie effective collaboration. Strong interpersonal ties must be forged to unite managers in the partnering organizations and continuing boundary-spanning activity is required at multiple managerial levels as a relationship evolves.

Laying the Foundation   Alliance negotiations set the tone for the relationship. Smooth alliance negotiations rest on finding the proper balance between the formal, legal procedures that establish detailed contractual safeguards for the parties and the informal, interpersonal processes that are crucial in the successful execution of alliance strategy.

---

[58]Peter Smith Ring and Andrew H. Van de Ven, "Developmental Processes of Cooperative Interorganizational Processes," *Academy of Management Review* 19 (January 1992): pp. 90–118.

[59]Kanter, "Collaborative Advantage," pp. 105–107.

[60]This section is based on Michael D. Hutt, Edwin R. Stafford, Beth A. Walker, and Peter H. Reingen, "Defining the Social Network of a Strategic Alliance: A Case Study," *MIT Sloan Management Review* 41 (Winter 2000): pp. 51–62.

Legal documents that establish an alliance and specify the boundaries in elaborate detail are still not complete and exhaustive. Countless ambiguities become evident as middle managers begin to flesh out the specific elements of the alliance plan. To resolve these issues and move the alliance forward, it is here that personal relationships begin to develop and supplement formal role relationships. Alliance negotiations should be structured in a manner that promotes the development of these interpersonal ties.

Experts suggest that more effective transactions are likely to evolve when managers, rather than lawyers, develop and control the negotiation strategy.[61] In turn, "negotiations appear to go more smoothly when parties from different organizations interact with their role counterparts (for example, managers to managers or lawyers to lawyers)."[62] Interactions between lawyers are largely based on institutionalized professional norms, center on a specific activity, and take place over a relatively short period of time. A signed agreement culminates the work of the lawyers; manager-to-manager relationships formed during negotiations provide the social structure through which the goals of the alliance can be realized.

Isolating Top-Management's Role   Beyond establishing joint goals and determining how the alliance fits each firm's total strategy, senior executives define the meaning of the relationship and signal its importance to personnel in the respective firms. Top-management's involvement in a strategic alliance encompasses much more than merely appointing an alliance manager or project leader. In addition to creating a dedicated strategic alliance function, many business-to-business firms, like General Electric and Cisco, appoint an executive sponsor for each alliance. For an alliance-based strategy to succeed, an ongoing level of backing from top management is required.

Executive leadership also assumes a critical role in communicating the strategic role of the alliance and in creating an identity for the alliance within the organization. A senior executive's personal involvement galvanizes support for an alliance throughout the organization. Moreover, direct ties at the top-management level across partnering firms spawn organizational commitment and more active involvement between managers at multiple levels of the hierarchy. If visible participation by senior executives is lacking, the members of the alliance team will begin to question the importance of the initiative to their firm and the value of team membership to their careers.

Cultivating a Network of Relationships   To achieve alliance goals, a well-integrated communication and work-flow network among managers is required within and across firms. A regular audit of evolving social, work, and communication ties can be a valuable tool for management in gauging the health of an alliance and in spotting problem areas. In reviewing the alliance network, attention first should center on relationship patterns at multiple levels. In particular, connections should be examined among **operating personnel** who require timely access to information and resources; between the **project leaders** who establish the climate for the alliance, craft the strategy, and manage execution; and among **senior managers** who signal the importance of the relationship in their respective organizations, lend critical support at key points, and are central to discussions of new opportunities for successful collaboration.

---

[61] Peter Smith Ring and G. Rands, "Sensemaking, Understanding, and Committing: Emergent Transaction Processes in the Evolution of 3M's Microgravity Research Programs," in A.H. Van de Ven, H. Angle, and M. S. Poole, eds., *Research on the Management of Innovation: The Minnesota Studies* (New York: Ballinger/Harper & Row, 1989), pp. 337–366.

[62] Peter Smith Ring and Andrew H. Van de Ven, "Developmental Processes of Cooperative Interorganizational Processes," *Academy of Management Review* 19 (January 1992): p. 109.

Summary

Relationships, rather than simple transactions, provide the central focus in business marketing. By demonstrating superior skills in managing relationships with key customers as well as with alliance partners, business marketing firms can create a collaborative advantage.

To develop profitable relationships with customers, business marketers must first understand the different forms that exchange relationships can take. Transactional exchange centers on the timely exchange of basic products and services for highly competitive market prices. By contrast, collaborative exchange involves very close personal, informational, and operational connections the parties develop to achieve long-term mutual goals. Across the relationship spectrum, different types of relationships feature different relationship connectors. For example, collaborative relationships for important purchases emphasize operational linkages that integrate the operations of the buying and selling organizations and involve high levels of information exchange.

Activity-based costing provides a solid foundation for measuring and managing the profitability of individual customers. When the full costs of serving customers are known, many companies find that 15 to 20 percent of the customers generate 100 percent (or much more) of the profits, a large group of customers break even, and 5 to 10 percent of the customers generate sizable losses. By measuring the cost-to-serve and the net profit from individual customers, business marketing managers can take actions to transform unprofitable relationships into profitable ones through process improvements, menu-based pricing, or relationship management.

Customer relationship management involves aligning customer strategy and business processes for the purpose of improving customer loyalty and, eventually, corporate profitability. To that end, a customer strategy encompasses (1) acquiring the right customers, (2) crafting the right value proposition, (3) instituting the best processes, (4) motivating employees, and (5) learning to retain customers.

The driving force behind the formation of a strategic alliance is the desire of one firm to leverage its core competencies by linking with another firm that has complementary expertise, thereby creating joint value and new market opportunities. Firms adept at managing strategic alliances create a dedicated alliance function, develop a shared strategy map and a clear value proposition that the partners will provide to target customers, and nurture the interpersonal relationships that are crucial to success. A well-integrated communication and work-flow network is required within and across firms. And senior executives' personal involvement galvanizes crucial support. A regular audit of evolving relationship ties can be a valuable tool for gauging an alliance's health.

Discussion Questions

1. A marketing research company found that 6 percent of its clients generated 30 percent of sales and nearly all of its profits. At the other end of the continuum, 70 percent of its clients provided annual billings (revenue) that were below break-even levels, because these customers required an extensive amount of service from research employees. The company took immediate action to terminate relationships with clients who would not give them a higher share of their marketing research expenditures. Evaluate this decision and suggest a set of criteria that the firm might use to screen new clients.

2. Describe how a firm might use menu-based pricing to restore profitability to a high-cost-to-serve customer who demands extensive service and customized support.

3. Evaluate this statement: Large customers tend to be either the most or least profitable in the customer base of a business-to-business firm.

4. Sony develops "collaborative relationships" with some suppliers and "transactional relationships" with other suppliers. What criteria would purchasing executives use in segmenting suppliers into these two categories? Describe the steps a business marketer might take to move the relationship with Sony from a transaction relationship to a more collaborative one.

5. Some consulting organizations persuasively argue that by properly incorporating suppliers into their product-development process, firms can cut their bills for purchased parts and materials by as much as 30 percent. Explore how a buyer-seller partnership might create these cost savings.

6. Concerning buyer-seller relationships, compare and contrast the features of a collaborative relationship versus a transactional relationship in the business market. Describe how the operational linkages might differ by relationship type.

7. Why is the cost of serving a long-standing customer far less than the cost of acquiring a new customer?

8. Discuss the switching costs that Southwest Airlines would incur if it began to phase out its fleet of Boeing airliners with replacements from Airbus. What steps could Airbus take to reduce these switching costs? How might Boeing counter to strengthen its relationship with Southwest?

9. Describe how an office supply firm may have a core offering of products and services for a small manufacturer and an augmented offering for a university.

10. Knowing how to be a good partner is an asset in the business market as Cisco Systems clearly demonstrates. Describe the characteristics of a successful strategic alliance and outline the steps that alliance partners can take to increase the odds that alliance goals will be achieved.

Internet Exercises

1. Oracle Corporation provides customer relationship management software solutions to all sectors of the business market. Go to http://oracle.com and review "success stories" and

   a. identify a particular Oracle customer from the government sector, and

   b. describe the benefits that this government customer received from the software solution.

Hewlett-Packard Challenges from a Diverse Mix of Demanding Customers

Hewlett Packard (H-P) serves a diverse set of customers in the business market and devotes special attention to the Global 1,000—the 1,000 largest enterprises in the world. Across these organizations, however, different perspectives and approaches are used in making information technology (IT) purchases. This diversity across customer groups presents a host of challenges for H-P.

- *Customer Group A* demands a wide variety of IT products, routine maintenance support, and customized services. These customers value the relationship with H-P and are willing to pay a premium for product and service quality.

- *Customer Group B* wants high-quality IT products (e.g., printers, servers) but, most of all, these customers want a rock-bottom price and choose suppliers on that basis.

- *Customer Group C* demands both quality products and extensive service support but wants all of this for a "rock-bottom" price. These customers will freely switch from one supplier to the next. As competition intensifies for H-P and others in the IT sector, more customers are moving into this group each month.

First, describe how H-P might develop a portfolio of relationship strategies to meet the needs of such diverse customer groups. Second, some customers in each group are more costly to serve than others. How should such cost differences be reflected in the particular relationship strategies that H-P follows? Third, what strategies can H-P follow to increase the switching costs of customers in Group B or Group C or increase the profits it derives from these customer groups?

PART

III

ASSESSING MARKET OPPORTUNITIES

CHAPTER

5

Segmenting the Business Market and Estimating Segment Demand

The business marketing manager serves a market comprising many different types of organizational customers with varying needs. Only when this aggregate market is broken down into meaningful categories can the business marketing strategist readily and profitably respond to unique needs. Once the segments are determined, then the marketer must estimate demand for each segment. Accurate projections of future sales are one of the most significant and challenging dimensions of organizational demand analysis. After reading this chapter, you will understand:

1. the benefits of and requirements for segmenting the business market.

2. the potential bases for segmenting the business market.

3. a procedure for evaluating and selecting market segments.

4. the role of market segmentation in the development of business marketing strategy.

5. a process for estimating demand in each market segment.

6. specific techniques to effectively develop a forecast of demand.

A strategist at Hewlett-Packard notes:

> Knowing customers' needs is not enough. . . . We need to know what new products, features, and services will surprise and delight them. We need to understand their world so well that we can bring new technology to problems that customers may not yet truly realize they have.[1]

High-growth companies, large and small, succeed by

- selecting a well-defined group of potentially profitable customers.

- developing a distinctive value proposition (product and/or service offering) that meets these customers' needs better than their competitors.

- focusing marketing resources on acquiring, developing, and retaining profitable customers.[2]

The business market consists of three broad sectors—commercial enterprises, institutions, and government. Whether marketers elect to operate in one or all of these sectors, they encounter diverse organizations, purchasing structures, and decision-making styles. Each sector has many segments; each segment may have unique needs and require a unique marketing strategy. For example, some customers demonstrate attractive profit potential and are receptive to a relationship strategy, whereas others adopt a short-term, transaction focus, suggesting the need for a more streamlined strategy response.[3] The business marketer who recognizes the needs of the various market segments is best equipped to isolate profitable market opportunities and respond with an effective marketing program.

Once market segments are defined, it is then necessary to forecast the expected demand in each segment. In fact, forecasting of demand is an on-going process because forecasts drive so many of the management activities of the business-to-business marketer. Demand forecasts provide the basis on which organizations decide on how to allocate resources, plan manufacturing capacity and output, develop logistics capabilities and strategies, and establish marketing budgets and activities.

The goal of this chapter is to demonstrate how the manager can select and evaluate segments of the business market and then develop accurate estimates of demand. First, the chapter delineates the benefits of and the requirements for successful market segmentation. Second, it explores and evaluates specific bases for segmenting the business market. Third, the chapter provides a framework for evaluating and selecting market segments. Procedures for assessing the costs and benefits of entering alternative market segments and for implementing a segmentation strategy are emphasized. The final section of the chapter examines the demand forecasting process and explains the critical aspects of how business marketers create demand forecasts.

[1] David E. Schnedler, "Use Strategic Market Models to Predict Customer Behavior," *Sloan Management Review* 37 (Spring 1996): p. 92; see also, Eric von Hippel, Stefan Thomke, and Mary Sonnack, "Creating Breakthroughs at 3M," *Harvard Business Review* 77 (September–October 1999): pp. 47–57.

[2] Dwight L. Gertz and João P. A. Baptista, *Grow to Be Great: Breaking the Downsizing Cycle* (New York: The Free Press, 1995), p. 54.

[3] Per Vagn Freytog and Ann Højbjerg Clarke, "Business to Business Market Segmentation," *Industrial Marketing Management* 30 (August 2001): pp. 473–486.

Business Market Segmentation Requirements and Benefits

Yoram Wind and Richard N. Cardozo define a **market segment** as "a group of present or potential customers with some common characteristic which is relevant in explaining (and predicting) their response to a supplier's marketing stimuli."[4] Effective segmentation of markets is the first step in crafting a marketing strategy because the characteristics and needs of each segment will define what elements must be included in how the firm approaches each of the segments in which they choose to do business. Segmentation that is done well provides the necessary information for understanding what elements of the marketing mix are going to be critical in satisfying the target customers in those segments.

Requirements

Potential customers in a market segment have common characteristics that define what things are important to them and how they will respond to various marketing stimuli. The question for the business marketer is: "what are the key criteria for determining which characteristics best define a unique market segment?" A business marketer has four criteria for evaluating the desirability of potential market segments:

1. *Measurability*—The degree to which information on the particular buyer characteristics exists or can be obtained.

2. *Accessibility*—The degree to which the firm can effectively focus its marketing efforts on chosen segments.

3. *Substantiality*—The degree to which the segments are large or profitable enough to be worth considering for separate marketing cultivation.

4. *Responsiveness*—The degree to which segments respond differently to different marketing mix elements, such as pricing or product features.

In summary, the art of market segmentation involves identifying groups of customers that are large and unique enough to justify a separate marketing strategy. The ultimate goal is to have the greatest amount of difference *between* groups (segments) and high similarities *within* them.[5]

Benefits

If the requirements for effective segmentation are met, several benefits accrue to the firm. First, the mere attempt to segment the business market forces the marketer to become more attuned to the unique needs of customer segments. Second, knowing

---

[4]Yoram Wind and Richard N. Cardozo, "Industrial Market Segmentation," *Industrial Marketing Management* 3 (March 1974): p. 155; see also Vincent-Wayne Mitchell and Dominic F. Wilson, "Balancing Theory and Practice: A Reappraisal of Business-to-Business Segmentation," *Industrial Marketing Management* 27 (September 1998): pp. 429–455.

[5]Jessica Tsai, "The Smallest Slice," *CRM Magazine* 12 (2, Feb. 2008): p. 37.

INSIDE BUSINESS MARKETING

How to See What's Next

Strategists falter when they invest too much attention to "what is" and too little to "what could be." For example, by maintaining a strict focus on existing market segments and ignoring new ones, the business marketer may miss important signals of change that customers are sending.

To break this pattern and spot new market opportunities, business marketing strategists should examine three customer groups and the market signals they are sending:

- *Undershot customers*—the existing solutions fail to fully satisfy their needs. They eagerly buy new product versions at steady or increasing prices.

- *Overshot customers*—the existing solutions are too good (for example, exceed the technical performance required). These customers are reluctant to purchase new product versions.

- *Nonconsuming customers*—those who lack the skills, resources, or ability to benefit from existing solutions. These customers are forced

to turn to others with greater skills or training for service.

Although most strategists center exclusive attention on undershot customers, "watching for innovations that have the potential to drive industry change actually requires paying careful attention to the least demanding, most overshot customers and non-consumers seemingly on the fringe of the market." For example, computing jobs that were processed by specialists in the corporate mainframe computer center are now routinely completed by millions of individuals, and corporate photocopying centers were disbanded as low-cost, self-service copiers became a common fixture in offices across organizations.

SOURCE: Clayton M. Christensen and Scott D. Anthony, "Are You Reading the Right Signals?" *Strategy & Innovation Newsletter* (Cambridge, MA.: Harvard Business School Publishing Corporation, September/October 2004), p. 5.

the needs of particular market segments helps the business marketer focus product-development efforts, develop profitable pricing strategies, select appropriate channels of distribution, develop and target advertising messages, and train and deploy the sales force. Thus, market segmentation provides the foundation for efficient and effective business marketing strategies.

Third, market segmentation provides the business marketer with valuable guidelines for allocating marketing resources. Business-to-business firms often serve multiple market segments and must continually monitor their relative attractiveness and performance. Research by Mercer Management Consulting indicates that, for many companies, nearly one-third of their market segments generate no profit and that 30 to 50 percent of marketing and customer service costs are wasted on efforts to acquire and retain customers in these segments.[6] Ultimately, costs, revenues, and profits must be evaluated segment by segment—and even account by account. As market or competitive conditions change, corresponding adjustments may be required in the firm's market segmentation strategy. Thus, market segmentation provides a basic unit of analysis for marketing planning and control.

[6] Gertz and Baptista, *Grow to Be Great*, p. 55.

Bases for Segmenting Business Markets

Whereas the consumer-goods marketer is interested in securing meaningful profiles of individuals (demographics, lifestyle, benefits sought), the business marketer profiles organizations (size, end use) and organizational buyers (decision style, criteria). Thus, the business or organizational market can be segmented on several bases, broadly classified into two major categories: macrosegmentation and microsegmentation.

Macrosegmentation centers on the characteristics of the buying organization and the buying situation and thus divides the market by such organizational characteristics as size, geographic location, the North American Industrial Classification System (NAICS) category, and organizational structure. Such characteristics are important because they often determine the buying needs of the organization. For example, in the plastic packaging industry, a recent study identified seven major packaging and disposable market segments—

1. food packaging;

2. lids, caps, closures, overcaps, and packaging dispensers;

3. preforms;

4. pails;

5. pharmaceutical vials and containers;

6. cosmetics and personal-care items; and,

7. disposable cutlery, bowls, cups, and plates.

Collectively, these segments consumed just over 7.3 billion pounds of plastic resins in 2007.[7]

These macrosegments are significant to the firms that sell materials and components to the plastic packaging industry because each of the major segments has somewhat different needs and requirements for the things that they buy based on the packaging products they are creating. For example, the preform market segment is the fastest-growing segment, which means that competition in this segment will be stiff, requiring a highly responsive marketing approach.

In contrast, **microsegmentation** requires a higher degree of market knowledge, focusing on the characteristics of decision-making units within each macrosegment—including buying decision criteria, perceived importance of the purchase, and attitudes toward vendors. Yoram Wind and Richard Cardozo recommend a two-stage approach to business market segmentation: (1) identify meaningful macrosegments, and then (2) divide the macrosegments into microsegments.[8]

In evaluating alternative bases for segmentation, the marketer is attempting to identify good predictors of differences in buyer behavior. Once such differences are recognized, the marketer can approach target segments with an appropriate marketing strategy. Secondary sources of information, coupled with data in a firm's information

---

[7] Bart Thedinger, "Injection Molders See Growth For Packaging & Disposables," *Plastics Technology* 54 (5, May 2008): p. 98.

[8] Wind and Cardozo, "Industrial Market Segmentation," p. 155; see also Mitchell and Wilson, "Balancing Theory and Practice," pp. 429–455.

TABLE 5.1 | **SELECTED MACROLEVEL BASES OF SEGMENTATION**

Variables	Illustrative Breakdowns
Characteristics of Buying Organizations	
Size (the scale of operations of the organization)	Small, medium, large; based on sales or number of employees
Geographical location	USA, Asia Pacific, Europe, Middle East, and Africa
Usage rate	Nonuser, light user, moderate user, heavy user
Structure of procurement	Centralized, decentralized
Product/Service Application	
NAICS category	Varies by product or service
End market served	Varies by product or service
Value in use	High, low
Characteristics of Purchasing Situation	
Type of buying situation	New task, modified rebuy, straight rebuy
Stage in purchase decision process	Early stages, late stages

system, can be used to divide the market into macrolevel segments. The concentration of the business market allows some marketers to monitor the purchasing patterns of each customer. For example, a firm that sells paper products—tissues, cups, and napkins—to the airlines is dealing with just a handful of potential buying organizations in the U.S. market. There were 12 major airlines operating in the United States in 2007; in comparison, a paper products company selling tissues and the like to ultimate consumers is dealing with literally millions of potential customers. Such market concentration, coupled with rapidly advancing marketing intelligence systems, makes it easier for the business marketer to monitor the purchasing patterns of individual organizations.

Macrolevel Bases

Table 5.1 presents selected macrolevel bases of segmentation. Recall that these are concerned with general characteristics of the buying organization, the nature of the product application, and the characteristics of the buying situation.

Macrolevel Characteristics of Buying Organizations   The marketer may find it useful to partition the market by size of potential buying organization. Large buying organizations may possess unique requirements and respond to marketing stimuli that are different from those responded to by smaller firms. The influence of presidents, vice presidents, and owners declines with an increase in corporate size; the influence of other participants, such as purchasing managers, increases.[9] Alternatively, the

---

[9]Joseph A. Bellizzi, "Organizational Size and Buying Influences," *Industrial Marketing Management* 10 (February 1981): pp. 17–21; see also Arch G. Woodside, Timo Liukko and Risto Vuori, "Organizational Buying of Capital Equipment Involving Persons across Several Authority Levels," *Journal of Business & Industrial Marketing* 14 (1, 1999): pp. 30–48.

marketer may recognize regional variations and adopt geographical units as the basis for differentiating marketing strategies.

Usage rate constitutes another macrolevel variable. Buyers are classified on a continuum ranging from nonuser to heavy user. Heavy users may have needs different from moderate or light users. For example, heavy users may place more value on technical or delivery support services than their counterparts. Likewise, an opportunity may exist to convert moderate users into heavy users through adjustments in the product or service mix.

The structure of the procurement function constitutes a final macrolevel characteristic of buying organizations. Firms with a centralized purchasing function behave differently than do those with decentralized procurement (see Chapter 3). The structure of the purchasing function influences the degree of buyer specialization, the criteria emphasized, and the composition of the buying center. Centralized buyers place significant weight on long-term supply availability and the development of a healthy supplier complex. Decentralized buyers tend to emphasize short-term cost efficiency.[10] Thus the position of procurement in the organizational hierarchy provides a base for categorizing organizations and for isolating specific needs and marketing requirements. Many business marketers develop a national accounts sales team to meet the special requirements of large, centralized procurement units.

Product/Service Application   Because a specific industrial good is often used in different ways, the marketer can divide the market on the basis of specific end-use applications. The NAICS system and related information sources are especially valuable for this purpose (see Chapter 2). To illustrate, the manufacturer of a component such as springs may reach industries incorporating the product into machine tools, bicycles, surgical devices, office equipment, telephones, and missile systems. Similarly, Intel's microchips are used in household appliances, retail terminals, toys, cell phones, and aircraft as well as in computers. By isolating the specialized needs of each user group as identified by the NIACS category, the firm is better equipped to differentiate customer requirements and to evaluate emerging opportunities.

Value in Use   Strategic insights are also provided by exploring the value in use of various customer applications. Recall our discussion of value analysis in Chapter 2. **Value in use** is a product's economic value to the user relative to a specific alternative in a particular application. The economic value of an offering frequently varies by customer application. Milliken & Company, the textile manufacturer, has built one of its businesses by becoming a major supplier of towels to industrial laundries. These customers pay Milliken a 10 percent premium over equivalent towels offered by competitors.[11] Why? Milliken provides added value, such as a computerized routing program that improves the efficiency and effectiveness of the industrial laundries' pick-up and delivery function.

The segmentation strategy adopted by a manufacturer of precision motors further illuminates the value-in-use concept.[12] The firm found that its customers differed in the motor speed required in their applications and that a dominant competitor's new, low-priced machine wore out quickly in high- and medium-speed applications. The marketer concentrated on this vulnerable segment, demonstrating the superior life

---

[10]Timothy M. Laseter, *Balanced Sourcing: Cooperation and Competition in Supplier Relationships* (San Francisco: Jossey-Bass, 1998), pp. 59–86.

[11]Philip Kotler, "Marketing's New Paradigm: What's Really Happening Out There," *Planning Review* 20 (September–October 1992): pp. 50–52.

[12]Robert A. Garda, "How to Carve Niches for Growth in Industrial Markets," *Management Review* 70 (August 1981): pp. 15–22.

TABLE 5.2 | EXAMPLE OF MACROSEGMENTATION: AIRCRAFT INDUSTRY

Macro Segment 1: Civilian Aircraft

Sub-segments

A. Airliners
B. Cargo planes
C. General aviation
D. Agricultural aircraft
E. Business aircraft
F. Civilian Seaplane, Flying Boats, and Amphibious Aircraft
G. Civilian Helicopters
H. Sailplanes
I. Civil Research Aircraft, Prototypes and Specials

Macro Segment 2: Military Aircraft

Sub-segments

A. Bombers, Strike, Ground attack, gunships
B. Patrol, Anti-Submarine and Electronic Warfare aircraft
C. Military transports, tankers, and utility
D. Reconnaissance aircraft
E. Close air support/Counterinsurgency
F. Fighter aircraft, nightfighters and heavy fighters
G. Military Trainers
H. Military Helicopters and autogyros
I. Military Research Aircraft, Prototypes and Specials

SOURCE: http://en.wikipedia.org/wiki/List_of_aircraft_by_category, June 2008.

cycle cost advantages of the firm's products. The marketer also initiated a long-term program to develop a competitively priced product and service offering for customers in the low-speed segment.

Purchasing Situation   A final macrolevel base for segmenting the organizational market is the purchasing situation. First-time buyers have perceptions and information needs that differ from those of repeat buyers. Therefore, buying organizations are classified as being in the early or late stages of the procurement process, or, alternatively, as *new-task*, *straight rebuy*, or *modified rebuy* organizations (see Chapter 3). The position of the firm in the procurement decision process or its location on the buying situation continuum dictates marketing strategy.

These examples illustrate those macrolevel bases of segmentation that business marketers can apply to the organizational market. Other macrolevel bases may more precisely fit a specific situation. A key benefit of segmentation is that it forces the manager to search for bases that explain similarities and differences among buying organizations.

Table 5.2 provides a view of how a manufacturer of aircraft engines might choose to segment the aircraft market from a macrosegmentation vantage point. Note that two very large macro segments exist—civilian and military. Within each of these large

TABLE 5.3 | **Selected Microlevel Bases of Segmentation**

Variables	Illustrative Breakdowns
Key criteria	Quality, delivery, supplier reputation
Purchasing strategies	Single source … multiple sources
Structure of decision-making unit	Major decision participants (for example, purchasing manager and plant manager)
Importance of purchase	High importance … low importance
Organizational innovativeness	Innovator … follower
Personal characteristics	
Demographics	Age, educational background
Decision style	Normative, conservative, mixed mode
Risk	Risk taker, risk avoider
Confidence	High … low
Job responsibility	Purchasing, production, engineering

segments there are several very large macro subsegments. A jet engine manufacturer, like General Electric, would most likely begin the segmentation process in this fashion, looking carefully at the engine requirements for each of the several subsegments. The engine requirements in each segment may turn out to be very different, requiring different-size engines each capable of operating in very different conditions and environments. It could turn out that after detailed analysis of the needs in each subsegment, even further marcosegmentation may be necessary. For example, the "airliner" segment in the civilian macrosegment might be further segmented into regional jets versus full-size passenger jets. And then the full-size passenger jet airplane segment can be divided into specific types of aircraft, such as Boeing 737 or Airbus 340.

Microlevel Bases

Having identified macrosegments, the marketer often finds it useful to divide each macrosegment into smaller microsegments on the basis of the similarities and differences between decision-making units. Often, several microsegments—each with unique requirements and unique responses to marketing stimuli—are buried in macrosegments. To isolate them effectively, the marketer must move beyond secondary sources of information by soliciting input from the sales force or by conducting a special market segmentation study. Selected microbases of segmentation appear in Table 5.3.

Key Criteria   For some business products, the marketer can divide the market according to which criteria are the most important in the purchase decision.[13] Criteria include product quality, prompt and reliable delivery, technical support, price, and supply continuity. The marketer also might divide the market based on supplier profiles

---

[13] Schnedler, "Use Strategic Models," pp. 85–92; and Kenneth E. Mast and Jon M. Hawes, "Perceptual Differences between Buyers and Engineers," *Journal of Purchasing and Materials Management* 22 (Spring 1986): pp. 2–6; Donald W. Jackson Jr., Richard K. Burdick, and Janet E. Keith, "Purchasing Agents' Perceived Importance of Marketing Mix Components in Different Industrial Purchase Situations," *Journal of Business Research* 13 (August 1985): pp. 361–373; and Donald R. Lehmann and John O'Shaughnessy, "Decision Criteria Used in Buying Different Categories of Products," *Journal of Purchasing and Materials Management* 18 (Spring 1982): pp. 9–14.

that appear to be preferred by decision makers (for example, high quality, prompt delivery, premium price versus standard quality, less-prompt delivery, low price).

Illustration: Price versus Service[14]   Signode Corporation produces and markets a line of steel strapping used for packaging a range of products, including steel and many manufactured items. Facing stiff price competition and a declining market share, management wanted to move beyond traditional macrolevel segmentation to understand how Signode's 174 national accounts viewed price versus service trade-offs. Four segments were uncovered:

1. **Programmed buyers** (sales = $6.6 million): Customers who were not particularly price or service sensitive and who made purchases in a routine fashion—product is not central to their operation.

2. **Relationship buyers** (sales = $31 million): Knowledgeable customers who valued partnership with Signode and did not push for price or service concessions—product is moderately important to the firm's operations.

3. **Transaction buyers** (sales = $24 million): Large and very knowledgeable customers who actively considered the price versus service trade-offs but often placed price over service—product is very important to their operations.

4. **Bargain hunters** (sales = $23 million): Large-volume buyers who were very sensitive to any changes in price or service—product is very important to their operations.

The study enabled Signode to sharpen its strategies in this mature business market and to understand more clearly the cost of serving the various segments. Particularly troubling to management was the bargain-hunter segment. These customers demanded the lowest prices and the highest levels of service and had the highest propensity to switch. Management decided to use price cuts only as a defense against competitors' cuts and directed attention instead at ways to add service value to this and other segments.

Value-Based Strategies   Many customers actively seek business marketing firms that can help them create new value to gain a competitive edge in their markets. Based on a comprehensive study of its customer base, Dow Corning identified three important customer segments and the value proposition that customers in each segment are seeking[15]:

innovation-focused customers who are committed to being first to the market with new technologies and who seek new-product-development expertise and innovative solutions that will attract new customers;

customers in fast-growing markets who are pressured by competitive battles over market growth and seek proven performance in technology, manufacturing, and supply chain management;

customers in highly competitive markets who produce mature products, center on process efficiency and effectiveness in manufacturing, and seek cost-effective solutions that keep overall costs down.

---

[14]V. Kasturi Rangan, Rowland T. Moriarty, and Gordon S. Swartz, "Segmenting Customers in Mature Industrial Markets," *Journal of Marketing* 56 (October 1992): pp. 72–82.

[15] Eric W. Balinski, Philip Allen, and J. Nicholas DeBonis, *Value-Based Marketing for Bottom-Line Success* (New York: McGraw-Hill and the American Marketing Association, 2003), pp. 147–152.

B2B TOP PERFORMERS

Steering Customers to the Right Channel

Dow Corning Corporation is the world's largest and most innovative producer of silicone-based products. Although the leader in this large and diverse market, smaller, regional competitors began to take market share away from Dow Corning by selling low-priced silicone products with little or no technical support. Rather than paying for a host of high-quality services such as new-product-development assistance that Dow Corning customarily provides, these customers eagerly sought the lowest price. To meet the challenge, Dow Corning conducted a market segmentation study, isolated the characteristics of this "low-cost" buyer, and created a no-frills Web-based business model to reach this customer segment. To avoid confusion with existing customers and the firm's premium product lines, a new brand was created—Xiameter (http://www .xiameter.com).

To clarify the brand premise and the company connection, the tag line—"The new measure of value from Dow Corning"—was added. By steering price-sensitive customers to the Internet—a low-cost sales channel—the branding strategy allows Dow Corning "to compete head-on with the low-price suppliers of mature product lines, without damaging its position as a value-added leader at the premium price end of the market." Customers, from the United States to high-growth potential countries like China, have responded positively to the Xiameter brand. (See the Dow Corning ad in Figure 5.1.)

SOURCE: Bob Lamons, "Dow Targets Segment to Keep Market Share," *Marketing News*, June 15, 2005, p. 8. See also Randall S. Rozin and Liz Magnusson, "Processes and Methodologies for Creating a Global Business-to-Business Brand," *Journal of Brand Management* 10 (February 2003): pp. 185–207.

The marketer can benefit by examining the criteria decision-making units in various sectors of the business market—commercial, governmental, and institutional—use. As organizations in each sector undergo restructuring efforts, the buying criteria key decision makers use also change. For example, the cost pressures and reform efforts in the health-care industry are changing how hospitals buy medical equipment and pharmaceuticals. To reduce administrative costs and enhance bargaining power, hospitals are following the lead of commercial enterprises by streamlining their operations. Also, they are forming buying groups, centralizing the purchasing function, and insisting on lower prices and better service. Reform efforts are likewise moving government buyers to search for more efficient purchasing procedures and for better value from vendors. Marketers that respond in this challenging environment are rewarded.

Purchasing Strategies   Microsegments can be classified according to buying organizations' purchasing strategy. Some buyers seek to have several suppliers, giving each one a healthy share of their purchase volume; others are more interested in assured supply and concentrate their purchases with one or perhaps two suppliers. Raytheon, the manufacturer of small airplanes for the civilian and business aircraft market decided on a strategy of concentration. They rely on one firm—Castle Metals—to supply all of its needs for the different metals used in an aircraft. The company may reassess its sole supplier every so often, but any "out-supplier" in this situation would have a very difficult time securing some of Raytheon's business. In another case, Toyota looks for suppliers who are able to make suggestions for improving its business operations.

FIGURE 5.1 | **AN AWARD-WINNING AD BY DOW CORNING FOR ITS WEB-BASED BUSINESS MODEL**

Toyota has realized that many of the innovations it has developed in its processes have come from suggestions by their suppliers. So a key strategy for Toyota is to identify suppliers who are creative and invest in new technology for possibly improving Toyota's business.

Structure of the Decision-Making Unit The structure of the decision-making unit, or buying center, likewise provides a way to divide the business market into subsets of customers by isolating the patterns of involvement in the purchasing process of particular decision participants (for example, engineering versus top management). For the medical equipment market, DuPont initiated a formal positioning study among hospital administrators, radiology department administrators, and technical managers to identify the firm's relative standing and the specific needs (criteria) for each level of buying influence within each segment.[16] The growing importance of buying groups, multihospital chains, and nonhospital health-care delivery systems pointed to the need for a more refined segmentation approach.

The study indicates that the medical equipment market can be segmented on the basis of the type of institution and the responsibilities of the decision makers and decision influencers in those institutions. The structure of the decision-making unit and the decision criteria used vary across the following three segments:

- Groups that select a single supplier that all member hospitals must use, such as investor-owned hospital chains;

- Groups that select a small set of suppliers from which individual hospitals may select needed products;

- Private group practices and the nonhospital segment.

Based on the study, DuPont's salespersons can tailor their presentations to the decision-making dynamics of each segment. In turn, advertising messages can be more precisely targeted. Such an analysis enables the marketer to identify meaningful microsegments and respond with finely tuned marketing communications.

Importance of Purchase Classifying organizational customers on the basis of the perceived importance of a product is especially appropriate when various customers apply the product in various ways. Buyer perceptions differ according to the effect of the product on the total mission of the firm. A large commercial enterprise may consider the purchase of consulting services routine; the same purchase for a small manufacturing concern is "an event."

Organizational Innovativeness Some organizations are more innovative and willing to purchase new industrial products than others. A study of the adoption of new medical equipment among hospitals found that psychographic variables can improve a marketer's ability to predict the adoption of new products.[17] These include such factors as an organization's level of change resistance or desire to excel. When psychographic variables are combined with organizational demographic variables (for example, size), accuracy in predicting organizational innovativeness increases.

Because products diffuse more rapidly in some segments than in others, microsegmentation based on organizational innovativeness enables the marketer to identify segments that should be targeted first when it introduces new products. The accuracy

---

[16]Gary L. Coles and James D. Culley, "Not All Prospects Are Created Equal," *Business Marketing* 71 (May 1986): pp. 52–57.

[17]Thomas S. Robertson and Yoram Wind, "Organizational Psychographics and Innovativeness," *Journal of Consumer Research* 7 (June 1980): pp. 24–31; see also Thomas S. Robertson and Hubert Gatignon, "Competitive Effects on Technology Diffusion," *Journal of Marketing* 50 (July 1986): pp. 1–12.

of new product forecasting also improves when diffusion patterns are estimated segment by segment.[18]

Personal Characteristics   Some microsegmentation possibilities deal with the personal characteristics of decision makers: demographics (age, education), personality, decision style, risk preference or risk avoidance, confidence, job responsibilities, and so forth. Although some interesting studies have shown the usefulness of segmentation based on individual characteristics, further research is needed to explore its potential as a firm base for microsegmentation.

Illustration: Microsegmentation[19]

Philips Lighting Company, the North American division of Philips Electronics, found that purchasing managers emphasize two criteria in purchasing light bulbs: how much they cost and how long they last. Philips learned, however, that the price and life of bulbs did not account for the total cost of lighting. Because lamps contain environmentally toxic mercury, companies faced high disposal costs at the end of a lamp's useful life.

New Product and Segmentation Strategy   To capitalize on a perceived opportunity, Philips introduced the Alto, an environmentally friendly bulb that reduces customers' overall costs plus allows the buying organization to demonstrate environmental concern to the public. Rather than targeting purchasing managers, Philips's marketing strategists centered attention on chief financial officers (CFOs), who embraced the cost savings, and public relations executives, who saw the benefit of purchasing actions that protect the environment. By targeting different buying influentials, Philips created a new market opportunity. In fact, the Alto has already replaced more than 25 percent of traditional fluorescent lamps in U.S. stores, schools, and office buildings.

The Segmentation Process

Macrosegmentation centers on characteristics of buying *organizations* (for example, size), *product application* (for example, end market served), and the *purchasing situation* (for example, stage in the purchase decision process). Microsegmentation concentrates on characteristics of organizational decision-making *units*—for instance, choice criteria assigned the most importance in the purchase decision.

Choosing Market Segments

Business marketers begin the segmentation process at the macro level. If they find that the information about the macro segments is sufficient to develop an effective

[18]Yoram Wind, Thomas S. Robertson, and Cynthia Fraser, "Industrial Product Diffusion by Market Segment," *Industrial Marketing Management* 11 (February 1982): pp. 1–8.

[19]W. Chan Kim and Renée Mauborgne, "Creating New Market Space," *Harvard Business Review* 77 (January–February 1999): pp. 88–89. For other segmentation studies, see Mark J. Bennion Jr., "Segmentation and Positioning in a Basic Industry," *Industrial Market Management* 16 (February 1987): pp. 9–18; Arch G. Woodside and Elizabeth J. Wilson, "Combining Macro and Micro Industrial Market Segmentation," in *Advances in Business Marketing*, ed. Arch G. Woodside (Greenwich, CT: JAI Press, 1986), pp. 241–257; and Peter Doyle and John Saunders, "Market Segmentation and Positioning in Specialized Industrial Markets," *Journal of Marketing* 49 (Spring 1985): pp. 24–32.

INSIDE BUSINESS MARKETING

A Fresh Approach to Segmentation: Customer Service Segmentation

Conceptually, customer service segmentation involves identifying groups of customers for which a company will provide types and levels of service. It works on the premise that the service requirements, as well as the associated cost-to-serve and profit potential, vary by customer tier. The exhibit shows the differentiated services that are aligned with each customer segment. The lowest-tier customers require the basic services, some special services are added for mid-tier customers, and top-tier customers get the complete service assortment plus some high-level value-added services.

Service-segment alignments are depicted as double-sided arrows in the exhibit to represent the point that customer needs and service offerings are aligned in accordance with strategic "push-pull" objectives. The goal is to develop a customer service strategy that responds to the unique requirements of particular segments, maintains a tight grasp on costs, and advances profit growth by segment.

SOURCE: Larry Lapide, "Segment Strategically," *Supply Chain Management Review* 12 (5, May/June 2008): pp. 8–9.

Illustrative Customer Segmentation & Differentiated Services Alignment

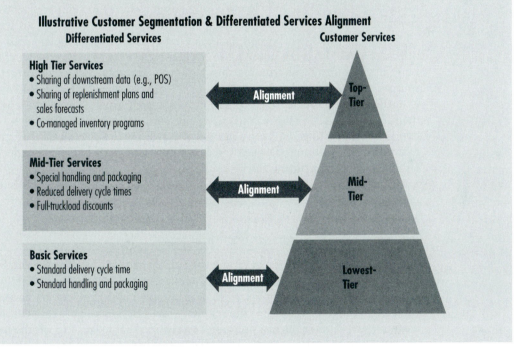

Differentiated Services

High Tier Services
- Sharing of downstream data (e.g., POS)
- Sharing of replenishment plans and sales forecasts
- Co-managed inventory programs

Mid-Tier Services
- Special handling and packaging
- Reduced delivery cycle times
- Full-truckload discounts

Basic Services
- Standard delivery cycle time
- Standard handling and packaging

Customer Services

Top-Tier

Mid-Tier

Lowest-Tier

Alignment

Alignment

Alignment

marketing strategy, then it may not be necessary to go on to any further micrco-segmentation. However, if they cannot develop a distinct strategy based on the macrosegment, then it may be necessary to undertake research on microsegmentation variables within each macrosegment. A marketing research study is often needed to identify characteristics of decision-making units, as the Philips Lighting case illustrated. At this level, chosen macrosegments are divided into microsegments on the basis of similarities and differences between the decision-making units to identify small groups of buying organizations that each exhibit a distinct response to the firm's marketing strategy. As firms develop more segments with special requirements, it then becomes necessary to assess whether the cost of developing a unique strategy for a specific segment is worth the profit to be generated from that segment. The marketer must evaluate the potential profitability of alternative segments before investing in separate marketing strategies. As firms develop a clearer picture of the revenue and costs of serving particular segments and customers, they often find that a small group of customers subsidizes a large group of marginal and, in some cases, unprofitable customers.[20] (See Chapter 4.)

In some cases it may be more effective to examine existing customers in a new light. As A. G. Lafley and Lam Charam note, "segmentation itself can be an innovative act, if we identify a corner of our market that is rarely treated as a segment. Can we look at buyers through some other lens than typical tried and true variables like company size and industry? Identifying an overlooked segment is less expensive than inventing a new technology and may sprout even more opportunities."[21]

One interesting approach in business-to-business marketing today is the rise of account-based marketing (ABM), perhaps the ultimate expression of the trend toward smaller and more precisely targeted marketing strategies. ABM is an approach that treats an individual account as a market in its own right. Done right, it ensures that marketing and sales are fully focused on a target client's most important business issues and that they work collaboratively to create value propositions that specifically address those issues. Far beyond the basics of personalized messaging and segmented offers, true ABM has the potential to deepen relationships with existing clients and build profitability by shortening the sales cycle and increasing win rates and sole-sourced contracts.[22]

ABM is the ultimate in segmentation, as one company is viewed as a separate segment. This approach may become more prevalent in the future as industry consolidation continues to grow. One could see the commercial aircraft industry as a good example of this ultimate level of segmentation—only two companies now produce large, commercial airliners: Boeing and Airbus S.A.S. Similarly, in the diesel locomotive industry in the United States, only General Motors and General Electric make diesel locomotives.

Isolating Market Segment Profitability

To improve on traditional market segmentation, many business marketing firms categorize customers into tiers that differ in current and/or future profitability to the firm. "By knowing the characteristics of profitable customers, companies can direct their marketing efforts to specific segments that are most likely to yield profitable customers."[23] This requires a process of evaluation that makes explicit the near-term potential and the longer-term resource commitments necessary to effectively serve customers in a segment. In particular, special attention is given to the individual drivers of customer profitability, namely the cost-to-serve a particular group of customers and the revenues that result (see Chapter 4).

---

[20]Arun Sharma, R. Krishnan, and Dhruv Grewal, "Value Creation in Markets: A Critical Area of Focus for Business-to-Business Markets," *Industrial Marketing Management* 30 (June 2001): pp. 391–402.

[21]A.G. Lafley and Ram Charan, "Making Inspiration Routine," *Inc* 30 (6, June 2008): pp. 98–101.

[22]Jeff Sands, "Account-Based Marketing," *B to B*, 91 (6, May 8, 2006): p. 11.

[23]Robert S. Kaplan and V. G. Narayanan, "Measuring and Managing Customer Profitability," *Journal of Cost Management* 15 (September–October 2001): p. 13.

FedEx Corporation, for example, categorizes its business customers (for internal purposes) as the good, the bad, and the ugly—based on their profitability.[24] Rather than using the same strategy for all customers, the company assigns a priority to the good, tries to convert the bad to good, and discourages the ugly. Like many other firms, FedEx discovered that many customers are too costly to serve and demonstrate little potential to become profitable, even in the long term. By understanding the needs of customers at different tiers of profitability, service can be tailored to achieve even higher levels of profitability. For example, FedEx encourages small shippers to bring their packages to conveniently located drop-off points and offers a rapid-response pick-up service for large shippers. Once profitability tiers are identified, "highly profitable customers can be pampered appropriately, customers of average profitability can be cultivated to yield higher profitability, and unprofitable customers can be either made more profitable or weeded out."[25]

Implementing a Segmentation Strategy

A well-developed segmentation plan will fail without careful attention to implementing the plan. Successful implementation requires attention to the following issues:

- How should the sales force be organized?

- What special technical or customer service requirements will organizations in the new segment have?

- Who will provide these services?

- Which media outlets can be used to target advertising at the new segment?

- Has a comprehensive online strategy been developed to provide continuous service support to customers in this segment?

- What adaptations will be needed to serve selected international market segments?

The astute business marketing strategist must plan, coordinate, and monitor implementation details. Frank Cespedes points out that "as a firm's offering becomes a product-service-information mix that must be customized for diverse segments, organizational interdependencies increase"[26] and marketing managers, in particular, are involved in more cross-functional tasks. Managing the critical points of contact with the customer is fundamental to the marketing manager's role.

Estimating Segment Demand

Looking back at the Internet boom, executives at telecommunications firms like Alcatel-Lucent and Nortel Networks Corporation now openly acknowledge that they did not see the steep drop in demand coming. Indeed, spending by phone companies

---

[24]R. Brooks, "Alienating Customers Isn't Always a Bad Idea, Many Firms Discover," *The Wall Street Journal*, January 7, 1999, pp. A1 and A12, discussed in Valarie A. Zeithaml, Roland T. Rust, and Katherine N. Lemon, "The Customer Pyramid: Creating and Serving Profitable Customers," *California Management Review* 43 (Summer 2001): p. 118.

[25]Zeithaml, Rust, and Lemon, "The Customer Pyramid," p. 141.

[26]Frank V. Cespedes, *Concurrent Marketing: Integrating Product, Sales, and Service* (Boston: Harvard Business School Press, 1995), p. 271.

on telecommunications gear nearly doubled from 1996 to 2000, to $47.5 billion; all forecasts indicated that this attractive growth path would continue.[27] During this period, telecom equipment makers were dramatically expanding production capacity and aggressively recruiting thousands of new employees. However, in 2001, the demand failed to materialize and the major telecom equipment makers reported significant financial losses. In turn, firms across the industry announced a series of massive job cuts. What happened? "Lousy" sales forecasts played an important role, according to Gregory Duncan, a telecom consultant at National Economic Research Associates.[28]

The Role of the Demand Estimation

Estimating demand within selected market segments is vital to marketing management. The forecast of demand reflects management's estimate of the probable level of company sales, taking into account both potential business and the level and type of marketing effort demanded. Virtually every decision made by the marketer is based on a forecast, formal or informal.

Consider a company that wishes to introduce new telecommunications services to businesses. How large is the market opportunity? An estimate of demand provides the foundation for the planning process. Three broad groups of stakeholders require demand forecasts: engineering design and implementation teams; marketing and commercial development teams; and external entities, such as potential investors, government regulators, equipment and application suppliers, and distribution partners. In the marketing area, commercial questions that must be answered before launch of service and that depend on the estimate of demand include: Where should sales outlets be located? How many are required to cover the target market? What sales levels should be expected from each outlet? What performance targets should be established for each? Demand forecasts are needed to project the company's revenues, profits, and cash flow to assess business viability; to determine cash, equity, and borrowing requirements; and to determine appropriate pricing structures and levels.[29] In short, without knowledge of market demand, marketing executives cannot develop sound strategy and make effective decisions about the allocation of resources.

A primary application of the estimates of demand is clearly in the planning and control of marketing strategy by market segment. Once demand is estimated for each segment, the manager can allocate expenditures on the basis of potential sales volume. Spending huge sums of money on advertising and personal selling has little benefit in segments where the market opportunity is low. Of course, expenditures would have to be based on both expected demand and the level of competition. Actual sales in each segment can also be compared with forecasted sales, taking into account the level of competition, in order to evaluate the effectiveness of the marketing program.

Consider the experience of a Cleveland manufacturer of quick-connective couplings for power transmission systems. For more than 20 years, one of its large distributors had been increasing its sales volume. In fact, this distributor was considered one of the firm's top producers. The manufacturer then analyzed the estimates of demand for each of its 31 distributors. The large distributor ranked thirty-first in

[27]Dennis K. Berman, "'Lousy Sales Forecasts Helped Fuel the Telecom Mess," *The Wall Street Journal*, July 7, 2001, p. B1.
[28]Ibid.
[29]Peter McBurney, Simon Parsons, and Jeremy Green, "Forecasting Market Demand for New Telecommunications Services: An Introduction," *Telematics and Information* 19 (2002): p. 233.

INSIDE BUSINESS MARKETING

Accurate Forecasts Drive Effective Collaboration between Boeing and Alcoa

Alcoa supplies raw aluminum to Boeing for constructing wings for most of Boeing's commercial airplanes. As a result of sharing accurate demand data with Alcoa, Boeing was able to achieve cost reductions and improve delivery-time performance throughout the entire supply chain.

Boeing began by developing an electronic sales forecast to allow Alcoa to receive the forecast file directly into its system. Included in the forecast are all the data Alcoa needed to understand the demand for the raw aluminum to be used in constructing aircraft wings. The forecast data were provided so that they could be loaded into Alcoa's system in an efficient manner, and great emphasis was placed on forecast accuracy. Because forecast errors would totally undermine the supply process, Boeing developed a process to identify errors in demand before communicating the forecasts electronically to Alcoa. Boeing provides Alcoa

with electronic visibility into its ERP (Enterprise Resource Planning) System so that Alcoa can understand when orders will be coming and can thereby respond more effectively to Boeing's needs. In short, Boeing realized that for Alcoa to make decisions on when it should have materials in Boeing's plant, Alcoa had to be given the most accurate forecast data possible.

In working together in the supply chain, the electronic sharing of demand forecasts made it possible for Alcoa to maintain the appropriate levels of aluminum inventory to meet Boeing's requirements.

SOURCE: Adapted from Victoria A. Micheau, "How Boeing and Alcoa Implemented a Successful Vendor Managed Inventory Program," *Journal of Business Forecasting* 24 (Spring 2005): pp. 17–19.

terms of volume relative to potential business, achieving only 15.4 percent of estimated demand. A later evaluation revealed that the distributor's sales personnel did not know the most effective way to sell couplings to its large-customer accounts.

It is important to keep in mind that estimates of probable demand should be made only after the firm has made decisions about its marketing strategy for a particular segment. Only after the marketing strategy is developed can expected sales be forecasted. Many firms are tempted to use the forecast as a tool for deciding the level of marketing expenditures. One study (which sampled 900 firms) found that slightly more than 25 percent of the respondent firms set their advertising budgets after the forecast of demand was developed.[30] Small companies whose budgeting and forecasting decisions were fragmented made up the majority of the firms in this group. Clearly, marketing strategy is a determinant of the level of sales and not vice versa.

Supply Chain Links Sales forecasts are critical to the smooth operation of the entire supply chain. When timely sales forecast information is readily available to all firms in the supply chain, plans can be tightly coordinated and all parties share in the benefits.[31] Sales forecast data is used to distribute inventory in the supply chain, manage stock levels at each link, and schedule resources for all the members of a supply

[30]Douglas C. West, "Advertising Budgeting and Sales Forecasting: The Timing Relationship," *International Journal of Advertising* 14 (1, 1995): pp. 65–77.

[31]John T. Mentzer and Mark A. Moon, "Understanding Demand," *Supply Chain Management Review* 8 (May–June 2004): p. 45.

chain that provide materials, components, and services to a manufacturer. Accurate forecasts go hand-in-hand with good business practices and effective management policies in directing the entire supply chain process. Specific tools are available to develop accurate estimates of market potential; the business marketer must understand the purpose of each alternative technique as well as its strengths and limitations.

Methods of Forecasting Demand

Estimating demand may be highly mathematical or informally based on sales force estimates. Two primary approaches to demand forecasting are recognized: (1) qualitative and (2) quantitative, which includes time series and causal analysis.

Qualitative Techniques

Qualitative techniques, which are also referred to as **management judgment** or **subjective techniques** rely on informed judgment and rating schemes. The sales force, top-level executives, or distributors may be called on to use their knowledge of the economy, the market, and the customers to create qualitative demand estimates. Techniques for qualitative analysis include the executive judgment method, the sales force composite method, and the Delphi method.

The effectiveness of qualitative approaches depends on the close relationships between customers and suppliers that are typical in the industrial market. Qualitative techniques work well for such items as heavy capital equipment or when the nature of the forecast does not lend itself to mathematical analysis. These techniques are also suitable for new-product or new-technology forecasts when historical data are scarce or nonexistent.[32] An important advantage of qualitative approaches is that it brings users of the forecast into the forecasting process. The effect is usually an increased understanding of the procedure and a higher level of commitment to the resultant forecast.

Executive Judgment   According to a large sample of business firms, the **executive judgment method** enjoys a high level of usage.[33] The judgment method, which combines and averages top executives' estimates of future sales, is popular because it is easy to apply and to understand. Typically, executives from various departments, such as sales, marketing, production, finance, and purchasing, are brought together to apply their collective expertise, experience, and opinions to the forecast.

The primary limitation of the approach is that it does not systematically analyze cause-and-effect relationships. Further, because there is no established formula for deriving estimates, new executives may have difficulty making reasonable forecasts. The resulting forecasts are only as good as the executives' opinions. The accuracy of the executive judgment approach is also difficult to assess in a way that allows meaningful comparison with alternative techniques.[34]

The executives' "ballpark" estimates for the intermediate and the long-run time frames are often used in conjunction with forecasts developed quantitatively.

---

[32] A. Michael Segalo, *The IBM/PC Guide to Sales Forecasting* (Wayne, PA: Banbury, 1985), p. 21.

[33] Nada Sanders, "Forecasting Practices in U.S. Corporations: Survey Results," *Interfaces* 24 (March–April 1994): pp. 92–100.

[34] Spyros Makridakis and Steven Wheelwright, "Forecasting: Issues and Challenges for Marketing Management," *Journal of Marketing* 41 (October 1977): p. 31.

However, when historical data are limited or unavailable, the executive judgment approach may be the only alternative. Mark Moriarty and Arthur Adams suggest that executive judgment methods produce accurate forecasts when (1) forecasts are made frequently and repetitively, (2) the environment is stable, and (3) the linkage between decision, action, and feedback is short.[35] Business marketers should examine their forecasting situation in light of these factors in order to assess the usefulness of the executive judgment technique.

Sales Force Composite The rationale behind the **sales force composite** approach is that salespeople can effectively estimate future sales volume because they know the customers, the market, and the competition. In addition, participating in the forecasting process helps sales personnel understand how forecasts are derived and boosts their incentive to achieve the desired level of sales. The composite forecast is developed by combining the sales estimates from all salespeople. By providing the salesperson with a wealth of customer information that can be conveniently accessed and reviewed, customer relationship management (CRM) systems (see Chapter 4) enhance the efficiency and effectiveness of the sales force composite.[36] CRM systems also allow a salesperson to track progress in winning new business at key accounts.

Few companies rely solely on sales force estimates; rather, they usually adjust or combine the estimates with forecasts developed either by top management or by quantitative methods. The advantage of the sales force composite method is the ability to draw on sales force knowledge about markets and customers. This advantage is particularly important for a market in which buyer-seller relationships are close and enduring. The salesperson is often the best source of information about customer purchasing plans and inventory levels. The method can also be executed relatively easily at minimal cost. An added benefit is that creating a forecast forces a sales representative to carefully review these accounts in terms of future sales.[37]

The problems with sales force composites are similar to those of the executive judgment approach: They do not involve systematic analysis of cause and effect, and they rely on informed judgment and opinions. Some sales personnel may overestimate sales in order to look good or underestimate them in order to generate a lower quota. Management must carefully review all estimates. As a rule, sales force estimates are relatively accurate for short-run projections but less effective for long-term forecasts.

Delphi Method In the **Delphi approach to forecasting**, the opinions of a panel of experts on future sales are converted into an informed consensus through a highly structured feedback mechanism.[38] As in the executive judgment technique,

---

[35] Mark M. Moriarty and Arthur J. Adams, "Management Judgment Forecasts, Composite Forecasting Models and Conditional Efficiency," *Journal of Marketing Research* 21 (August 1984): p. 248.

[36] Robert Mirani, Deanne Moore, and John A. Weber, "Emerging Technologies for Enhancing Supplier-Reseller Partnerships," *Industrial Marketing Management* 30 (February 2001): pp. 101–114.

[37] Stewart A. Washburn, "Don't Let Sales Forecasting Spook You," *Sales and Marketing Management* 140 (September 1988): p. 118.

[38] Raymond E. Willis, *A Guide to Forecasting for Planners and Managers* (Englewood Cliffs, NJ: Prentice-Hall, 1987), p. 343.

management officials are used as the panel, but each estimator remains anonymous. On the first round, written opinions about the likelihood of some future event are sought (for example, sales volume, competitive reaction, or technological breakthroughs). The responses to this first questionnaire are used to produce a second. The objective is to provide feedback to the group so that first-round estimates and information available to some of the experts are made available to the entire group.

After each round of questioning, the analyst who administers the process assembles, clarifies, and consolidates information for dissemination in the succeeding round. Throughout the process, panel members are asked to reevaluate their estimates based on the new information from the group. Opinions are kept anonymous, eliminating both "me-too" estimates and the need to defend a position. After continued reevaluation, the goal is to achieve a consensus. The number of experts varies from six to hundreds, depending on how the process is organized and its purpose. The number of rounds of questionnaires depends on how rapidly the group reaches consensus.

Generally, the Delphi technique is applied to long-term forecasting of demand, particularly for new products or situations not suited to quantitative analysis. This approach can provide some good ballpark estimates of demand when the products are new or unique and when there is no other data available. Like all qualitative approaches to estimating demand, it is difficult to measure the accuracy of the estimates.

Qualitative forecasting approaches are important in the process of assessing future product demand, and they are most valuable in situations where little data exists and where a broad estimate of demand is acceptable. New or unique products do not lend themselves to more quantitative approaches to forecasting, so the qualitative methods play a very important role in estimating demand for these items.

Quantitative Techniques

Quantitative demand forecasting, also referred to as systematic or objective forecasting, offers two primary methodologies: (1) time series and (2) regression or causal. **Time series** techniques use historical data ordered chronologically to project the trend and growth rate of sales. The rationale behind time series analysis is that the past pattern of sales will apply to the future. However, to discover the underlying pattern of sales, the analyst must first understand all of the possible patterns that may affect the sales series. Thus, a time series of sales may include trend, seasonal, cyclical, and irregular patterns. Once the effect of each has been isolated, the analyst can then project the expected future of each pattern. Time series methods are well suited to short-range forecasting because the assumption that the future will be like the past is more reasonable over the short run than over the long run.[39]

Regression or **causal** analysis, on the other hand, uses an opposite approach, identifying factors that have affected past sales and implementing them in a mathematical model.[40] Demand is expressed mathematically as a function of the items

---

[39] Spyros Makridakis, "A Survey of Time Series," *International Statistics Review* 44 (1, 1976): p. 63.

[40] Segalo, *Sales Forecasting*, p. 27.

that affect it. A forecast is derived by projecting values for each of the factors in the model, inserting these values into the regression equation, and solving for expected sales. Typically, causal models are more reliable for intermediate than for long-range forecasts because the magnitude of each factor affecting sales must first be estimated for some future time, which becomes difficult when estimating farther into the future.

The specifics of the quantitative approaches to estimating demand are beyond the scope of this chapter. However, the key aspects of these approaches for the business-to-business manager to keep in mind are as follows:

1. To develop an estimate of demand with time series analysis, the analyst must determine each pattern (the trend, cycle, seasonal pattern) and then extrapolate them into the future. This requires a significant amount of historical sales information. Once a forecast of each pattern is developed, the demand forecast is assembled by combining the estimates for each pattern.

2. A critical aspect of regression analysis is to identify the economic variable(s) to which past sales are related. For forecasting purposes, the *Survey of Current Business* is particularly helpful because it contains monthly, quarterly, and annual figures for hundreds of economic variables. The forecaster can test an array of economic variables from the *Survey* to find the variable(s) with the best relationship to past sales.

3. Although causal methods have measurable levels of accuracy, there are some important caveats and limitations. The fact that demand and some causal variables (independent variables) are correlated (associated) does not mean that the independent variable "caused" sales. The independent variable should be logically related to demand.

4. Regression methods require considerable historical data for equations to be valid and reliable, but the data may not be available. Caution must always be used in extrapolating relationships into the future. The equation relates what *has* happened; economic and industry factors may change in the future, making past relationships invalid.

5. A recent study on forecasting methods suggests choosing a methodology based on the underlying behavior of the market rather than the time horizon of the forecast.[41] This research indicates that when markets are sensitive to changes in market and environmental variables, causal methods work best, whether the forecast is short or long range; time series approaches are more effective when the market exhibits no sensitivity to market and/or environmental changes.

CPFR: A New Collaborative Approach to Estimating Demand

CPFR, or Collaborative Planning Forecasting and Replenishment, is a unique approach to forecasting demand that involves the combined efforts of many functions

[41] Robert J. Thomas, "Method and Situational Factors in Sales Forecast Accuracy," *Journal of Forecasting* 12 (January 1993): p. 75.

within the firm as well as with partners in the supply chain. In this approach, one individual in the firm is given the responsibility for coordinating the forecasting process with functional managers across the firm. So sales, marketing, production, logistics, and procurement personnel will be called upon to jointly discuss their plans for the upcoming period. In this way, all the parties who may influence sales performance will participate directly in the demand estimation process.

Once the firm has a good grasp internally of each function's forthcoming strategies and plans, the "demand planner" from the firm will then reach out to customers, distributors, and manufacturers' representatives to assess what their marketing, promotion, and sales plans are for the product in question.

These plans are then shared with the company's functional managers and demand estimates are adjusted accordingly. The demand planner then develops a final demand estimate for the coming period based on this wide array of input. As one might expect, the CPFR approach to estimating demand often results in a very accurate forecast of demand due to the intensive sharing of information among the firm's functional managers and key supply chain and channel partners.

The most practical approach for application of CPFR is for the trading partners to map their partners' forecasts into their own terms, understand where their partners' plans deviate significantly from their own, and then collaborate on the assumptions that may be leading to different estimates. Through this iterative process, intermediaries and manufacturers use collaborative feedback to synchronize their supply chains, while keeping their enterprise planning processes intact.[42]

Combining Several Forecasting Techniques

Recent research on forecasting techniques indicates that forecasting accuracy can be improved by combining the results of several forecasting methods.[43] The results of combined forecasts greatly surpass most individual projections, techniques, and analyses by experts. Mark Moriarty and Arthur Adams suggest that managers should use a composite forecasting model that includes both systematic (quantitative) and judgmental (qualitative) factors.[44] In fact, they suggest that a composite forecast be created to provide a standard of comparison in evaluating the results provided by any single forecasting approach. Each forecasting approach relies on varying data to derive sales estimates. By considering a broader range of factors that affect sales, the combined approach provides a more accurate forecast. Rather than searching for the single "best" forecasting technique, business marketers should direct increased attention to the composite forecasting approach.

---

[42]"Taking It One Step at a Time: Tapping into the Benefits of Collaborative Planning, Forecasting, and Replenishment (CPFR)," *An Oracle White Pape,* (August 2005), http://www.oracle.com/applications/retail/library/white-papers/taking-it-one-step.pdf.

[43]J. Scott Armstrong, "The Forecasting Canon: Nine Generalizations to Improve Forecast Accuracy," *FORESIGHT: The International Journal of Applied Forecasting* 1 (1, June 2005): pp. 29–35.

[44]Moriarty and Adams, "Management Judgment Forecasts," p. 248.

Summary

The business market contains a complex mix of customers with diverse needs and objectives. The marketing strategist who analyzes the aggregate market and identifies neglected or inadequately served groups of buyers (segments) is ideally prepared for a market assault. Specific marketing strategy adjustments can be made to fit the unique needs of each target segment. Of course, such differentiated marketing strategies are feasible only when the target segments are measurable, accessible, compatible, responsive, and large enough to justify separate attention.

Procedurally, business market segmentation involves categorizing actual or potential buying organizations into mutually exclusive clusters (segments), each of which exhibits a relatively homogeneous response to marketing strategy variables. To accomplish this task, the business marketer can draw upon two types of segmentation bases: macrolevel and microlevel. Macrodimensions are the key characteristics of buying organizations and of the purchasing situation. The NAICS together with other secondary sources of information are valuable in macrolevel segmentation. Microlevel bases of segmentation center on key characteristics of the decision-making unit and require a higher level of market knowledge.

This chapter outlined a systematic approach for the business marketer to apply when identifying and selecting target segments. Before a final decision is made, the marketer must weigh the costs and benefits of a segmented marketing strategy. In developing a market segmentation plan, the business marketing manager isolates the costs and revenues associated with serving particular market segments. By directing its resources to its most profitable customers and segments, the business marketer is less vulnerable to focused competitors that may seek to "cherry-pick" the firm's most valuable customers.

The forecasting techniques available to the business marketer are (1) qualitative and (2) quantitative. Qualitative techniques rely on informed judgments of future sales and include executive judgment, the sales force composite, and the Delphi methods. By contrast, quantitative techniques have more complex data requirements and include time series and causal approaches. The time series method uses chronological historical data to project the future trend and growth rate of sales. Causal methods, on the other hand, seek to identify factors that have affected past sales and to incorporate them into a mathematical model. The essence of sound demand forecasting is to combine effectively the forecasts provided by various methods.

Discussion Questions

1. Cogent is a rapidly growing company that makes software which identifies people using biometrics—fingerprints, faces, eyeballs, and other personal characteristics. The firm is making terminals that allow customers to pay for products with their fingerprints. Assess the potential of the "pay by touch" system and suggest possible market segments that might be receptive to the new offering.

2. Automatic Data Processing, Inc. (ADP), handles payroll and tax filing processing for more than 300,000 customers. In other words, firms outsource these functions to ADP. Suggest possible segmentation bases that ADP might employ in this service market. What criteria would be important to organizational buyers in making the decision to turn payroll processing over to an outside firm?

3. FedEx believes that its future growth will come from business-to-business e-commerce transactions where customers demand quick and reliable delivery service. Outline a segmentation plan that the firm might use to become the market leader in this rapidly expanding area.

4. Sara Lee Corporation derives more than $1.5 billion of sales each year from the institutional market (for example, hospitals, schools, restaurants). Explain how a firm such as Sara Lee or General Mills might apply the concept of market segmentation to the institutional market.

5. Some firms follow a single-stage segmentation approach using macrodimensions; others use both macrodimensions and microdimensions. As a business marketing manager, what factors would you consider in making a choice between the two methods?

6. Compare and contrast the sales force composite and the Delphi methods of developing a sales forecast.

7. Although qualitative forecasting techniques are important in the sales forecasting process in many industrial firms, the marketing manager must understand the limitations of these approaches. Outline these limitations.

8. As alternative methods for demand forecasting, what is the underlying logic of (1) time series and (2) regression or causal methods?

9. What limitations must be understood before applying and interpreting the demand forecasting results generated by causal methods?

10. What features of the business market support the use of qualitative forecasting approaches? What benefits does the business market analyst gain by combining these qualitative approaches with quantitative forecasting methods?

Internet Exercises

1. Xerox positions itself as "The Document Company" because the firm provides solutions to help customers manage documents—paper, electronic, online. Go to http://www.xerox.com, click on "Industry Solutions," and

   a. Describe the industry sectors that the firm seems to cover in its market segmentation plan.

   b. Identify the particular product and service that Xerox has developed for bank customers.

Federated Insurance: Targeting Small Businesses[45]

Targeting small and medium-sized business (SMB) customers, Federated Insurance offers clients and prospects a program of complete insurance protection, covering the spectrum from commercial property and casualty insurance and life and disability insurance to group health insurance. Since its founding over a century ago, the market plan for the company has centered on a clear-cut strategy: provide the highest quality, best-value service available to *selected* businesses.

Based in Owatonna, Minnesota, with regional offices in Atlanta and Phoenix, Federated has 2,600 employees and operates in 48 states. Consistent with its heritage and original market plan, the company specializes in business insurance for selected industries:

- Auto dealers and auto parts wholesalers
- Building contractors (for example, electrical, plumbing-heating-cooling)
- Equipment dealers (for example, agricultural, lawn and garden)
- Funeral services
- Jewelers
- Machine shops
- Petroleum marketers and convenience stores
- Tire dealers

Cultivating Business Relationships

Marketing representatives at Federated can tailor insurance protection to meet virtually all of a business owner's insurance needs: property, casualty, health, retirement, and more. They also provide quality risk-management services that respond to the specific needs of business owners. The goal here is to help customers develop procedures and practices that can reduce losses and improve worksite safety conditions.

Federated enjoys a strong reputation among SMB customers, as the following testimonials demonstrate:

> "One of the things Federated does very well is that they have focus. It's not about selling insurance, it's about taking care of your customers, and the businesses that do best are the ones that take care of their customers."
>
> [Tim Smith, President, Bob Smith BMW, Calabasas, California]

---

[45]"About Federated: Our History and Mission," accessed at http://www.federatedinsurance.com on July 10, 2008.

"I've had friends who are in businesses that jump insurance companies all the time and they're price shopping. They don't realize the relationship that you have to build with an insurance company. It's such a close relationship, but yet so secure. With Federated, we don't worry—we don't have to."

[Greg Nesler, President, Rochester Plumbing and Heating, Rochester, Minnesota]

Discussion Questions

1. By directing attention to particular types of businesses (for example, convenience stores or auto dealers), Federated emphasizes macrosegmentation. To further sharpen strategy, suggest possible ways that particular macrosegments could be broken down further into meaningful microsegments.

2. In buying insurance, some SMB customers just want the lowest-priced option for each type of insurance, whereas others want value-added services (for example, risk-management guidance) and a complete, integrated insurance solution. How should Federated respond to customers who are strictly focused on price? In your view, what are the points of difference that Federated should illuminate in the customer value proposition?

PART

IV

FORMULATING BUSINESS MARKETING STRATEGY

CHAPTER

6

Business Marketing Planning:
Strategic Perspectives

To this point, you have developed an understanding of organizational buying behavior, customer relationship management, market segmentation, and a host of other tools managers use. All of this provides a fundamentally important perspective to the business marketing strategist. After reading this chapter, you will understand:

1. marketing's strategic role in corporate strategy development.

2. the multifunctional nature of business marketing decision making.

3. the components of a business model that can be converted into superior positions of advantage in the business market.

4. a valuable framework for detailing the processes and systems that drive strategy success.

Most large corporations implicitly believe that strategy is the province of senior management. This is not so at GE Capital.[1] At a recent planning session, someone suggested that each of its 28 different businesses assemble a team of lower- to mid-level managers, all under the age of 30, and give them the task of finding opportunities that their "older managers" had missed. The young teams returned with a number of fresh ideas, including several focused on how GE Capital could further capitalize on the Internet. New growth strategies come from new ideas. New ideas often come from new voices. Drawing on the collective strengths of the organization is what strategy formulation is all about.

To meet the challenges brought on by growing domestic and global competition, business-to-business firms are increasingly recognizing the vital role of the marketing function in developing and implementing successful business strategies. Effective business strategies share many common characteristics, but at a minimum they are responsive to market needs, they exploit the special competencies of the organization, and they use valid assumptions about environmental trends and competitive behavior. Above all, they must offer a realistic basis for securing and sustaining a competitive advantage.[2] This chapter examines the nature and critical importance of strategy development in the business marketing firm.

First, the chapter highlights the special role of the marketing function in corporate strategy development, with a functionally integrated perspective of business marketing planning. Next, it identifies the sources of competitive advantage by exploring the key components of a business model and how they can be managed to secure distinctive strategic positioning. Finally, a framework is offered for converting strategy goals into a tightly integrated customer strategy. This discussion provides a foundation for exploring business marketing strategy on a global scale—the theme of the next chapter.

Marketing's Strategic Role

Market-driven firms are centered on customers—they take an outside-in view of strategy and demonstrate an ability to sense market trends ahead of their competitors.[3] Many firms—like Johnson & Johnson, Motorola, and Dow Chemical—have numerous divisions, product lines, products, and brands. Policies established at the corporate level provide the framework for strategy development in each business division to ensure survival and growth of the entire enterprise. In turn, corporate and divisional policies establish the boundaries within which individual product or market managers develop strategy.

The Hierarchy of Strategies

Three major levels of strategy dominate most large multiproduct organizations: (1) corporate strategy, (2) business-level strategy, and (3) functional strategy.[4]

---

[1] Gary Hamel, "Bringing Silicon Valley Inside," *Harvard Business Review* 77 (September–October 1999): pp. 78–79. See also Gary Hamel, "The Why, What, and How of Management Innovation," *Harvard Business Review* 84 (February 2006): pp. 72–84.

[2] Eric M. Olson, Stanley F. Slater, and G. Thomas M. Hult, "The Performance Implications of Fit among Business Strategy, Marketing Organization Structure, and Strategic Behavior," *Journal of Marketing* 69 (July 2005): pp. 49–65.

[3] For a comprehensive review, see Ahmet H. Kirca, Satish Jayachandran, and William O. Bearden, "Market Orientation: A Meta Analytic Review of Its Antecedents and Impact on Performance," *Journal of Marketing* 69 (April 2005): pp. 24–41.

[4] This discussion draws on Frederick E. Webster Jr., "The Changing Role of Marketing in the Corporation," *Journal of Marketing* 56 (October 1992): pp. 1–17.

Corporate strategy defines the businesses in which a company competes, preferably in a manner that uses resources to convert distinctive competence into competitive advantage. Essential questions at this level include: What are our core competencies? What businesses are we in? What businesses should we be in? How should we allocate resources across these businesses to achieve our overall organizational goals and objectives? At this level of strategy, the role of marketing is to (1) assess market attractiveness and the competitive effectiveness of the firm, (2) promote a customer orientation to the various constituencies in management decision making, and (3) formulate the firm's overall value proposition (as a reflection of its distinctive competencies, in terms reflecting customer needs) and to articulate it to the market and to the organization at large. According to Frederick Webster Jr., "At the corporate level, marketing managers have a critical role to play as advocates, for the customer and for a set of values and beliefs that put the customer first in the firm's decision making."[5]

Business-level strategy centers on how a firm competes in a given industry and positions itself against its competitors. The focus of competition is not between corporations; rather, it is between their individual business units. A **strategic business unit (SBU)** is a single business or collection of businesses that has a distinct mission, a responsible manager, and its own competitors and that is relatively independent of other business units. The 3M Corporation has defined 40 strategic business units. Each develops a plan describing how it will manage its mix of products to secure a competitive advantage consistent with the level of investment and risk that management is willing to accept. An SBU could be one or more divisions of the industrial firm, a product line within one division, or, on occasion, a single product. Strategic business units may share resources such as a sales force with other business units to achieve economies of scale. An SBU may serve one or many product-market units.

For each business unit in the corporate portfolio, the following essential questions must be answered: How can we compete most effectively for the product market the business unit serves? What distinctive skills can give the business unit a competitive advantage? Similarly, the former CEO at GE, Jack Welch, asks his operating executives to crisply answer the following questions[6]:

- Describe the global competitive environment in which you operate.
- In the last two years, what have your competitors done?
- In the same period, what have you done to them in the marketplace?
- How might they attack you in the future?
- What are your plans to leapfrog them?

The marketing function contributes to the planning process at this level by providing a detailed and complete analysis of customers and competitors and the firm's distinctive skills and resources for competing in particular market segments.

Functional strategy centers on how resources allocated to the various functional areas can be used most efficiently and effectively to support the business-level strategy. The primary focus of marketing strategy at this level is to allocate and coordinate

[5] Ibid.; Webster, "The Changing Role of Marketing," p. 11.

[6] Noel M. Tichy and Stratford Sherman, *Control Your Destiny or Someone Else Will* (New York: Doubleday, 1993), p. 26; see also Jack Welch and John A. Byrne, *Jack: Straight from the Gut* (New York: Warner Books, 2001).

marketing resources and activities to achieve the firm's objective within a specific product market.

Strategy Formulation and the Hierarchy[7]

The interplay among the three levels of the strategy hierarchy can be illustrated by examining the collective action perspective of strategy formulation. This approach applies to strategic decisions that (1) cut across functional areas, (2) involve issues related to the organization's long-term objectives, or (3) involve allocating resources across business units or product markets. Included here are decisions about the direction of corporate strategy, the application of a core technology, or the choice of an alliance partner.

Observe in Figure 6.1 that strategic decision processes often involve the active participation of several functional interest groups that hold markedly different beliefs about the appropriateness of particular strategies or corporate goals. Strategic decisions represent the outcome of a bargaining process among functional interest groups (including marketing), each of which may interpret the proposed strategy in an entirely different light.

Turf Issues and Thought-World Views   Two forces contribute to the conflict that often divides participants in the strategy formulation process. First, different meanings assigned to a proposed strategy are often motivated by deeper differences in what might be called "organizational subcultures." Subcultures exist when one subunit shares different values, beliefs, and goals than another subunit, resulting in different **thought-worlds**.[8] For example, marketing managers are concerned with market opportunities and competitors, whereas R&D managers value technical sophistication and innovation. Second, functional managers are likely to resist strategic changes that threaten their turf. To the extent that the subunit defines the individual's identity and connotes prestige and power, the organizational member may be reluctant to see it altered by a strategic decision.

Negotiated Outcomes   Collective decisions emerge from negotiation and compromise among partisan participants. The differences in goals, thought-worlds, and self-interests across participants lead to conflicts about actions that should be taken. Choices must be negotiated with each interest group attempting to achieve its own ends. The ultimate outcomes of collective decisions tend to unfold incrementally and depend more on the partisan values and influence of the various interest groups than on rational analysis. A study of highly contested strategic decision in a *Fortune* 500 company illustrates the tension that may exist between marketing and R&D.

Two marketing executives describe how the decision was ultimately resolved.[9] According to the marketing manager:

> [Marketing] did an extremely effective job of stepping right in the middle of it and strangling it. . . . What has happened is by laying out the market unit

---

[7]Gary L. Frankwick, James C. Ward, Michael D. Hutt, and Peter H. Reingen, "Evolving Patterns of Organizational Beliefs in the Formation of Marketing Strategy," *Journal of Marketing* 58 (April 1994): pp. 96–110; see also Michael D. Hutt, Beth A. Walker, and Gary L. Frankwick, "Hurdle the Cross-Functional Barriers to Strategic Change," *Sloan Management Review* 36 (Spring 1995): pp. 22–30.

[8]See, for example, Christian Homburg, Ore Jensen, and Harley Krohmer, "Configurations of Marketing and Sales," *Journal of Marketing* 72 (March 2008): pp. 123–154; and Christian Homburg and Ore Jensen, "The Thought Worlds of Marketing and Sales: Which Differences Make a Difference?" *Journal of Marketing* 71 (July 2007): pp. 124–141.

[9]Frankwick, Ward, Hutt, and Reingen, "Evolving Patterns of Organizational Beliefs," pp. 107–108.

FIGURE 6.1 | **A COLLECTIVE ACTION PERSPECTIVE OF THE STRATEGY FORMULATION PROCESS**

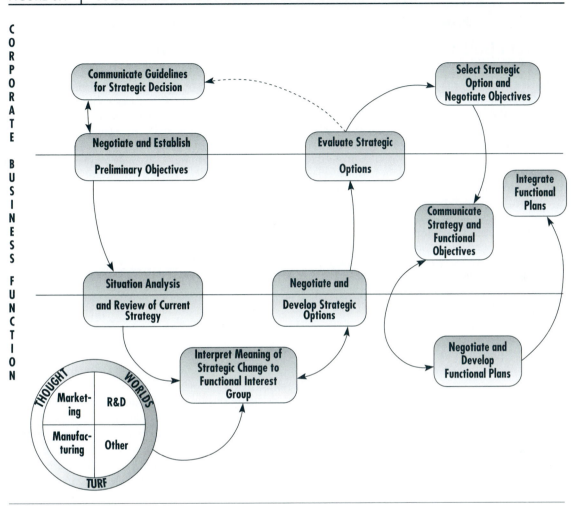

SOURCE: Gary L. Frankwick, James C. Ward, Michael D. Hutt, and Peter H. Reingen, "Evolving Patterns of Organizational Beliefs in the Formation of Strategy," *Journal of Marketing* 58 (April 1994): p. 98. Reprinted with permission by the American Marketing Association.

concerns and again, refocusing on the fact that we are market-based, basically what Marketing did was force the R&D team into submission where they no longer have the autonomy they once had to go about making decisions—they now get input. And whether it's formal or informal, they definitely get the buy-in of marketing before they move forward on what they're doing now.

According to the vice president of marketing:

Before I felt it was technology driving the process. Now I feel that technology is partnering with the marketplace. And the reason I feel that way is because we have [marketing people] in place that are working closely with how the technology develops.

INSIDE BUSINESS MARKETING

From Bullet-Point Plans to Strategic Stories at 3M

After reviewing countless business plans over several years, Gordon Shaw, executive director of planning at 3M, concluded that the firm's business plans failed to reflect deep thought or to inspire commitment and active support. He suspected that the traditional, bullet-list format of the plans was a major part of the problem. Bullet lists are too generic and fail to convey how the business will win in a particular market. To remedy the problem, he turned to strategic narratives—planning through storytelling. Like a good story, a good strategic plan "defines relationships, cause and effect, and a priority among items—*and those elements are likely to be remembered as a complex whole.*"

In using the approach, a strategist at 3M first **sets the stage** by defining the current competitive, market, and company situation in an insightful and coherent manner. Next, the planner must **introduce the dramatic conflict**—the main challenges or critical issues that provide obstacles to success. Finally, the story must **reach resolution** in a satisfying and compelling fashion. Here a logical and concise argument is provided concerning the specific actions the company can take to overcome the obstacles and win. Narrative plans create a rich picture of strategy, bring critical assumptions to the surface, and provide a central message that can motivate and mobilize employees throughout the organization.

SOURCE: Gordon Shaw, Robert Brown, and Philip Bromley, "Strategic Stories: How 3M Is Rewriting Business Planning," *Harvard Business Review* 76 (May/June 1998): pp. 41–50. See also, David J. Collins and Michael G. Rukstad, "Can You Say What Your Strategy Is?" *Harvard Business Review* 86 (April 2008): pp. 82–89.

Implications for Marketing Managers   In advocating a strategic course, marketing managers must be sensitive to the likely response it may arouse in other interest groups. To build pockets of commitment and trust, managers should develop and use a communication network that includes organizational members who have a major stake in the decision. Marketing managers can use these personal networks to understand the interests of other stakeholders, communicate their own interests clearly and sensitively, and thus diffuse the anxiety of others about threats to their turf.

Functionally Integrated Planning: The Marketing Strategy Center[10]

Rather than operating in isolation from other functional areas, the successful business marketing manager is an integrator—one who understands the capabilities of manufacturing, R&D, and customer service and who capitalizes on their strengths in developing marketing strategies that are responsive to customer needs. Marketing managers also assume a central role in strategy implementation.[11] Recent research indicates that in companies found to be strong on strategy execution, over 70 percent of employees affirm that they have a clear idea of the decisions and actions for which they are responsible; that figure drops to 32 percent in organizations weak on execution.[12]

---

[10]Michael D. Hutt and Thomas W. Speh, "The Marketing Strategy Center: Diagnosing the Industrial Marketer's Interdisciplinary Role," *Journal of Marketing* 48 (Fall 1984): pp. 53–61; see also Jeen-Su Lim and David A. Reid, "Vital Cross-Functional Linkages with Marketing," *Industrial Marketing Management* 22 (February 1993): pp. 159–165.

[11]Charles H. Noble and Michael P. Mokwa, "Implementing Marketing Strategies: Developing and Testing a Managerial Theory," *Journal of Marketing*, 63 (October 1999): pp. 57–73.

[12]Gary L. Neilson, Karla L. Martin, and Elizabeth Powers, "The Secrets to Successful Strategy Execution," *Harvard Business Review* 86 (June 2008): p. 63.

B2B TOP PERFORMERS

Cross-Functional Relationships: Effective Managers Deliver on Promises

Ask an R&D manager to identify a colleague from marketing who is particularly effective at getting things done and he or she readily offers a name and a memorable episode to justify the selection. To explore the characteristics of high-performing cross-functional managers, detailed accounts of effective and ineffective interactions were gathered from managers at a *Fortune* 100 high-technology firm. Interestingly, the top-of-mind characteristics that colleagues emphasize when describing high performers are soft skills like openness rather than hard skills like technical proficiency or marketing savvy. Here's a profile:

- High-performing managers are revered by their colleagues for their *responsiveness*. Remembering effective cross-functional episodes, colleagues describe high performers as "timely," "prompt," and "responsive" (for example, "When I need critical information, I turn to him and he gets right back to me").

- Rather than a "functional mindset," high performers demonstrate *perspective-taking* skills—the ability to anticipate and understand the perspectives and priorities of managers from other units (for example, "He's a superb marketing strategist but he also recognizes the special

technical issues that we've been working through to get this product launched on schedule").

- When colleagues describe the *communication style* of their high-performing cross-functional counterparts, they focus on three consistent themes: openness, frequency, and quality. Interactions with high performers are described as "candid," "unencumbered," and characterized by a "free flow of thoughts and suggestions." Such high-quality interactions clarify goals and responsibilities.

By "delivering on their promises," effective managers develop a web of close relationships across functions. "He has really good personal relationships with a lot of people and he has a network—he really understands the mechanisms that you have to use to get things done."

SOURCE: Michael D. Hutt, Beth A. Walker, Edward U. Bond III, and Matthew Meuter, "Diagnosing Marketing Managers' Effective and Ineffective Cross-Functional Interactions," working paper, Tempe, Ariz.: Arizona State University, 2005. See also Edward U. Bond III, Beth A. Walker, Michael D. Hutt, and Peter H. Reingen, "Reputational Effectiveness in Cross-Functional Working Relationships," *Journal of Product Innovation Management* 21 (January 2004): pp. 44–60.

Responsibility charting is an approach that can classify decision-making roles and highlight the multifunctional nature of business marketing decision making. Table 6.1 provides the structure of a responsibility chart. The decision areas (rows) in the matrix might, for example, relate to a planned product-line expansion. The various functional areas that may assume particular roles in this decision process head the matrix columns. The following list defines the alternative roles that participants can assume in the decision-making process.[13]

1. *Responsible* (R): The manager takes initiative for analyzing the situation, developing alternatives, and assuring consultation with others and then makes the initial recommendation. Upon approval of decision, the role ends.

2. *Approve* (A): The manager accepts or vetoes a decision before it is implemented or chooses from alternatives developed by the participants assuming a "responsible" role.

---

[13] Joseph E. McCann and Thomas N. Gilmore, "Diagnosing Organizational Decision Making through Responsibility Charting," *Sloan Management Review* 25 (Winter 1983): pp. 3–15.

3. *Consult* (C): The manager is consulted or asked for substantive input before the decision is approved but does not possess veto power.

4. *Implement* (M): The manager is accountable for implementing the decision, including notifying other relevant participants about the decision.

5. *Inform* (I): Although not necessarily consulted before the decision is approved, the manager is informed of the decision once it is made.

Representatives of a particular functional area may, of course, assume more than one role in the decision-making process. The technical service manager may be consulted during the new-product-development process and may also be held accountable for implementing service-support strategy. Likewise, the marketing manager may be responsible for and approve many of the decisions related to the product-line expansion. For other actions, several decision makers may participate. To illustrate, the business unit manager, after consulting R&D, may approve (or veto) a decision for which the marketing manager is responsible.

The members of the organization involved in the business marketing decision-making process constitute the **marketing strategy center**. The composition or functional area representation of the strategy center evolves during the marketing strategy development process, varies from firm to firm, and varies from one situation to another. Likewise, the composition of the marketing strategy center is not strictly prescribed by the organizational chart. The needs of a particular strategy situation, especially the information requirements, significantly influence the composition of the strategy center. Thus, the marketing strategy center shares certain parallels with the buying center (see Chapter 3).

Managing Strategic Interdependencies   A central challenge for the business marketer in the strategy center is to minimize interdepartmental conflict while fostering shared appreciation of the interdependencies with other functional units. Individual strategy center participants are motivated by both personal and organizational goals. They interpret company objectives in relation to their level in the hierarchy and the department they represent. Various functional units operate under unique reward systems and reflect unique orientations or thought-worlds. For example, marketing managers are evaluated on the basis of sales, profits, or market share; production managers on the basis of manufacturing efficiency and cost-effectiveness. In turn, R&D managers may be oriented toward long-term objectives; customer service managers may emphasize more immediate ones. Strategic plans emerge out of a bargaining process among functional areas. Managing conflict, promoting cooperation, and developing coordinated strategies are all fundamental to the business marketer's interdisciplinary role. By understanding the concerns and orientations of personnel from other functional areas, the business marketing manager is better equipped to forge effective cross-unit working relationships.

The Components of a Business Model[14]

For a strategy to succeed, individuals must understand and share a common definition of a firm's existing business concept. For example, ask any employee at Dell and they

---

[14]Except where noted, this discussion is based on Gary Hamel, *Leading the Revolution* (Boston: Harvard Business School Press, 2000), pp. 70–94.

TABLE 6.1	INTERFUNCTIONAL INVOLVEMENT IN MARKETING DECISION MAKING: AN ILLUSTRATIVE RESPONSIBILITY CHART

Organizational Function

Decision Area	Marketing	Manufacturing	R&D	Logistics	Technical Service	Strategic Business Unit Manager	Corporate Level Planner
PRODUCT							
Design specifications							
Performance characteristics							
Reliability							
PRICE							
List price							
Discount structure							
TECHNICAL SERVICE SUPPORT							
Customer training							
Repair							
LOGISTICS							
Inventory level							
Customer service level							
SALES FORCE							
Training							
ADVERTISING							
Message development							
CHANNEL							
Selection							

NOTE: Decision role vocabulary: R = responsible; A = approve; C = consult; M = implement; I = inform; X = no role in decision.

FIGURE 6.2 | **COMPONENTS OF A BUSINESS MODEL**

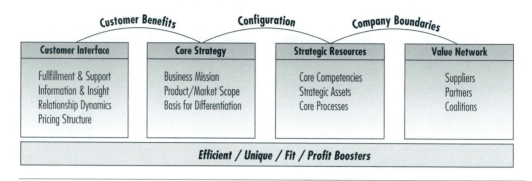

will tell you about the "Dell model" that sets them apart from competitors. A **business concept** or model consists of four major components (Figure 6.2):

- Customer Interface
- Core Strategy
- Strategic Resources
- Value Network

The major components of the business concept are tied together by three important "bridge" elements: customer benefits, configuration, and company boundaries.

Customer Interface

Customer benefits provide the bridge between the core strategy and the customer interface. Customer benefits link the core strategy directly to the needs of customers. The customer interface includes four elements:

1. **Fulfillment and support** refers to the channels a business marketing firm uses to reach customers and the level of service support it provides.

2. **Information and insight** refers to the knowledge captured from customers and the degree to which this information is used to provide enhanced value to the customer.

3. **Relationship dynamics** refers to the nature of the interaction between the firm and its customers (for example, the proportion of relational versus transactional customers; see Chapter 4). Key question: What steps can be taken to raise the hurdle for competitors by exceeding customer expectations or strengthening the customer's sense of affiliation with the firm?

4. **Pricing structure.** A business concept may offer several pricing choices. For example, a firm can bundle products and services or price them on a menu basis.

For example, when airlines buy a Boeing 777, which is equipped with jet engines produced by GE, they pay GE a fee for each flight hour in line with a fixed-priced maintenance agreement. So, rather than products, GE is selling "power by the hour."

Core Strategy

The **core strategy** determines how the firm chooses to compete. From Figure 6.2, observe that three elements are involved in setting a core strategy:

1. The **business mission** describes the overall objectives of the strategy, sets a course and direction, and defines a set of performance criteria that are used to measure progress. The business mission must be broad enough to allow for business concept innovation, and it should be distinguished from the mission of competitors in the industry. For example, by focusing its mission on copiers and copying, Xerox allowed Hewlett-Packard to build a dominant lead in the printer business.

2. **Product/market scope** defines *where* the firm competes. The product markets that constitute the domain of a business can be defined by customer benefits, technologies, customer segments, and channels of distribution.[15] Strategists might consider this question: Are particular customer segments being overlooked by competitors or customers who might welcome a new product-service solution?

3. **Basis for differentiation** captures the essence of how a firm competes differently than its rivals. George Day and Robin Wensley explain:

   A business is differentiated when some value-adding activities are performed in a way that leads to perceived superiority along dimensions that are valued by customers. For these activities to be profitable, the customer must be willing to pay a premium for the benefits and the premium must exceed the added costs of superior performance.[16]

There are many ways for a firm to differentiate products and services:

- Provide superior service or technical assistance competence through speed, responsiveness to complex orders, or ability to solve special customer problems.

- Provide superior quality that reduces customer costs or improves their performance.

- Offer innovative product features that use new technologies.

---

[15] George S. Day, Strategic Market Planning: The Pursuit of Competitive Advantage (St. Paul, MN: West Publishing, 1984).

[16] George S. Day and Robin Wensley, "Assessing Advantage: A Framework for Diagnosing Competitive Superiority," *Journal of Marketing* 52 (April 1988): pp. 3–4. See also Douglas W. Vorhies and Neil A. Morgan, "Benchmarking Marketing Capabilities for Sustainable Competitive Advantage," *Journal of Marketing* 69 (January 2005): pp. 80–94.

Strategic Resources

A business marketing firm gains a competitive advantage through its superior skills and resources. The firm's strategic resources include core competencies, strategic assets, and core processes.

1. **Core competencies** are the set of skills, systems, and technologies a company uses to create uniquely high value for customers.[17] For example, Dell uses its direct-distribution competencies to sell a host of new products to corporate customers, including switches, servers, storage, and a range of peripheral products.[18] Concerning core competencies, the guiding questions for the strategist are: What important benefits do our competencies provide to customers? What do we know or do especially well that is valuable to customers and is transferable to new market opportunities?

2. **Strategic assets** are the more tangible requirements for advantage that enable a firm to exercise its capabilities. Included are brands, customer data, distribution coverage, patents, and other resources that are both rare and valuable. Attention centers on this question: Can we use these strategic assets in a different way to provide new levels of value to existing or prospective customers?

3. **Core processes** are the methodologies and routines companies use to transform competencies, assets, and other inputs into value for customers. For example, drug discovery is a core process at Merck, and delivery fulfillment is a core process at FedEx. Here the strategist considers these questions: Which processes are most competitively unique and create the most customer value? Could we use our process expertise effectively to enter other markets?

From Figure 6.2, note that a configuration component links strategic resources to the core strategy. "Configuration refers to the unique way in which competencies, assets, and processes are interrelated in support of a particular strategy."[19] For example, Honda manages key activities in the new-product-development process differently than its rivals.

The Value Network

The final component of a business concept is the **value network** that complements and further enriches the firm's research base. Included here are suppliers, strategic alliance partners, and coalitions. To illustrate, nimble competitors like Cisco and General Electric demonstrate special skills in forging relationships with suppliers and alliance partners. Concerning the value network, the guiding question for the strategist is: What market opportunities might become available to us "if we could 'borrow' the assets and competencies of other companies and marry them with our own?"[20]

---

[17]James Brian Quinn, "Strategic Outsourcing: Leveraging Knowledge Capabilities," *Sloan Management Review* 40 (Summer 1999): pp. 9–21.

[18]Andy Serwer, "Dell Does Domination," *Fortune*, January 21, 2002, pp. 70–75.

[19]Hamel, Leading the Revolution, p. 78.

[20]Ibid., p. 90.

FIGURE 6.3 | THE PRINCIPLES OF STRATEGIC POSITIONING

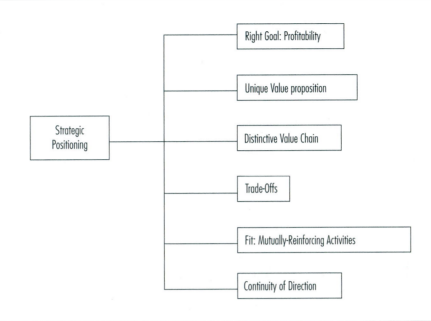

SOURCE: Adapted from Michael E. Porter, "What Is Strategy?" *Harvard Business Review* 74 (November–December 1996): pp. 61–78.

Strategic Positioning[21]

Competitive strategy, at the core, is about being different, choosing to compete in a distinctive way. A business model should reveal the way in which a firm is deliberately emphasizing a different set of activities in order to deliver a unique mix of customer value. Michael Porter asserts that six fundamental principles provide a company with the foundation for establishing and maintaining a distinctive strategic positioning (see Figure 6.3).

- Center on the *right goal*—superior long-term return on investment rather than performance goals defined in terms of sales volume or market share leadership.

- Deliver a *customer value proposition*, or set of benefits, that differs from those of rivals. (For example, Southwest Airlines delivers low-cost, convenient service to customers—particular benefits that full-service rivals cannot match.)

- Create a *distinctive value chain* by performing different activities than rivals or performing similar activities in different ways. (For example, by streamlining the passenger boarding process, Southwest achieves faster turnaround at the gate and can provide more frequent departures with fewer planes.)

---

[21]This section is based on Michael E. Porter, "What Is Strategy?" *Harvard Business Review* 74 (November–December 1996): pp. 61–78.

- Accept *trade-offs* and recognize that a company must forgo some product features or services to remain truly distinctive in others. (For example, Continental Airlines introduced Continental Lite to compete directly against Southwest. By trying to be low cost on some routes and full service on others, Continental lost several hundred million dollars before grounding Continental Lite.)

- Emphasize the way in which all the elements of the strategy *fit* and reinforce one another. (For example, from its standardized fleet of Boeing 737 aircraft to its well-trained ground crews that speed flight turnaround, and its strict limits on the type and length of routes, Southwest's activities complement and reinforce one another, creating a whole system of competing that locks out imitators.)

- Build strong customer relationships and develop unique skills by defining a distinctive value proposition that provides *continuity of direction*. (For example, Southwest continues to pursue its disciplined strategic agenda.)

Michael Porter observes:

> Having a strategy is a matter of discipline. It requires a strong focus on profitability rather than just growth, an ability to define a unique value proposition, and a willingness to make tough trade-offs in choosing what not to do. . . . It involves the configuration of a tailored value chain—the series of activities required to produce and deliver a product or service—that enables a company to offer unique value.[22]

Let's examine how a business-to-business firm has used these principles to establish and maintain a distinctive strategic positioning.

Strategic Positioning Illustrated[23]

Paccar operates in the fiercely competitive heavy-duty truck industry, designing and manufacturing trucks under the Kenworth and Peterbilt brand names. The firm, headquartered in Bellevue, Washington, commands 20 percent of the North American heavy truck market and derives approximately half of its revenues and profits from outside the United States.

A Unique Focus   Rather than centering on large-fleet buyers or large leasing companies, Paccar has chosen to focus on one group of customers—drivers who own their own trucks and contract directly with shippers or serve as contractors to larger trucking companies. Paccar provides an array of specialized services that specifically address the needs of owner-operators: luxurious sleeper cabins, noise-insulated cabins, and sleek interior and exterior options (numbering in the thousands) that prospective buyers can select to put their personal signatures on their trucks. Paccar delivers its products and services to customers through an extensive dealer network of nearly 1,800 locations worldwide.

---

[22]Michael E. Porter, "Strategy and the Internet," *Harvard Business Review* 79 (March 2001): p. 72.

[23]This illustration is based on Michael E. Porter, "The Five Competitive Forces that Shape Strategy," *Harvard Business Review* 86 (January 2008): p. 89.

Distinctive Value Proposition   Built to order, these customized trucks are delivered to customers in six to eight weeks and incorporate features and value-added services that are embraced by owner-operators. Paccar's trucks feature an aerodynamic design that reduces fuel consumption and they maintain resale value better than the trucks offered by rivals. To reduce out-of-service time, Paccar offers a comprehensive roadside assistance program and an information-technology-supported system for expediting and delivering spare parts. According to Michael Porter, "Customers pay Paccar a 10 percent premium, and its Kenworth and Peterbilt brands are considered status symbols at truck stops."[24] Moreover, Paccar has received recognition for consistently leading the heavy-duty truck market in quality, innovation, and customer satisfaction.[25]

By configuring its activities on new product development, manufacturing, and service support differently from rivals, and by tailoring these activities to its customer value proposition, Paccar has achieved an enviable record of financial performance: 68 straight years of profitability, averaging a long-run return on equity above 20 percent.

Building the Strategy Plan

By finding an intricate match between strategy and operations, strategic positioning depends on doing many things well—not just a few. But yet, most companies' underperformance is caused by breakdowns between strategy and operations. Robert S. Kaplan and David P. Norton contend that successful strategy execution involves two basic rules: "understand the management cycle that links strategy and operations, and know what tools to apply at each stage of the cycle."[26] To that end, they propose that companies develop a management system to plan, coordinate, and monitor the links between strategy and operations. This **management system** represents "the integrated set of processes and tools that a company uses to develop its strategy, translate it into operational actions, and monitor and improve the effectiveness of both."[27] (See Figure 6.4.)

Observe that the management system involves five stages, beginning with strategy development (Stage 1) and then moving on to the crucial stage of translating the strategy (Stage 2) into objectives and measures that can be clearly communicated to all functional areas and employees. We will give special attention to two tools: (1) the **balanced scorecard** that provides managers with a comprehensive system for converting a company's vision and strategy into a tightly connected set of performance measures; and (2) the **strategy map**—a tool for visualizing a firm's strategy as a chain of cause-and-effect relationships among strategic objectives. These tools and processes assume a central role in designing key processes (Stage 3), monitoring performance (Stage 4), and adapting the strategy (Stage 5).

---

[24]Ibid.

[25]"Kenworth Wins J.D. Power Awards," August 27, 2007, accessed at http://www.paccar.com/company/jdpower on July 11, 2008.

[26]Robert S. Kaplan and David P. Norton, "Mastering the Management System," *Harvard Business Review* 86 (January 2008): p. 63.

[27]Ibid., p. 64.

FIGURE 6.4 | THE MANAGEMENT SYSTEM: LINKING STRATEGY AND OPERATIONS

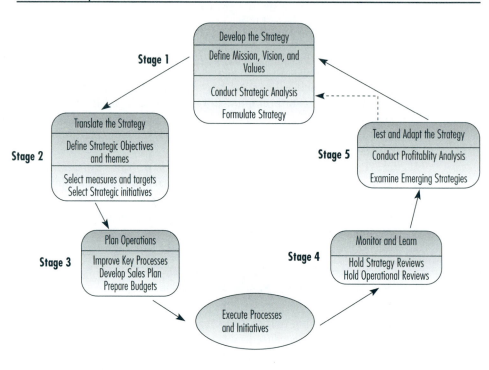

SOURCE: Adapted with modifications from Robert S. Kaplan and David P. Norton, "Mastering the Management System," *Harvard Business Review* 86 (January 2008): p. 65.

The Balanced Scorecard[28]

Measurement is a central element in the strategy process. The balanced scorecard combines financial measures of *past* performance with measures of the drivers of performance. Observe in Figure 6.5 that the scorecard examines the performance of a business unit from four perspectives: (1) financial, (2) customer, (3) internal business processes, and (4) learning and growth.

The architects of the approach, Robert Kaplan and David Norton, emphasize that "the scorecard should tell the story of the strategy, starting with the long-run financial objectives, and then linking them to the sequence of actions that must be taken with financial processes, customers, and finally employees and systems to deliver the desired long-run economic performance."[29]

Financial Perspective

Financial performance measures allow business marketing managers to monitor the degree to which the firm's strategy, implementation, and execution are increasing profits.

---

[28]Except where noted, this discussion is based on Robert S. Kaplan and David P. Norton, *Strategy Maps: Converting Intangible Assets into Tangible Outcomes* (Boston: Harvard Business School Publishing Corporation, 2004). See also Robert S. Kaplan and David P. Norton, *The Balanced Scorecard: Translating Strategy into Action* (Boston: Harvard Business School Press, 1996), chaps. 1–3.

[29]Kaplan and Norton, *The Balanced Scorecard*, p. 47.

THE BALANCED SCORECARD: A FRAMEWORK TO TRANSLATE A STRATEGY INTO OPERATIONAL TERMS

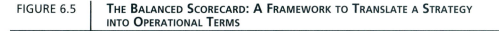

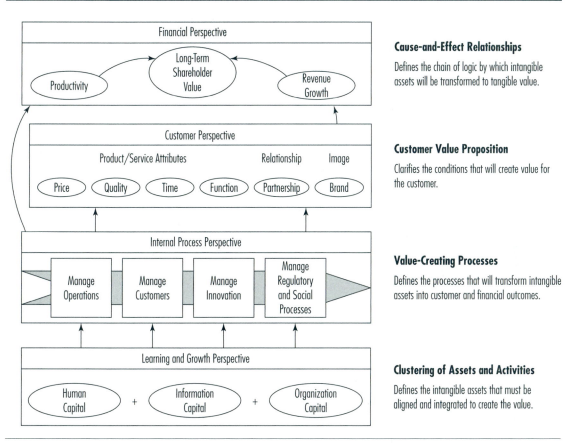

SOURCE: Reprinted by permission of *Harvard Business Review*. From "Balanced Scorecard Framework" by Robert S. Kaplan in *Strategy Maps*, p. 31. Copyright © 2004 by the Harvard Business School Publishing Corporation; all rights reserved.

Measures such as return on investment, revenue growth, shareholder value, profitability, and cost per unit are among the performance measures that show whether the firm's strategy is succeeding or failing. Companies emphasize two basic levers in developing a financial strategy: revenue growth and productivity.[30] The revenue-growth strategy centers on securing sales from new markets and new products or strengthening and expanding relationships with existing customers. The productivity strategy can also take two forms: improve the company's cost structure by reducing expenses and/or use assets more efficiently by decreasing the working and fixed capital needed to support a given level of output.

The balanced scorecard seeks to match financial objectives to a business unit's growth and life cycle stages. Three stages of a business are isolated and linked to appropriate financial objectives:

1. **Growth:** Business units that have products and services with significant growth potential and that must commit considerable resources (for example, production facilities and distribution networks) to capitalize on the market opportunity.

---

[30]Robert S. Kaplan and David P. Norton, "Having Trouble with Your Strategy? Then Map It," *Harvard Business Review* 78 (September–October 2000): pp. 167–176.

Financial Objectives: Sales growth rate by segment; percentage of revenue from new product, services, and customers.

2. **Sustain:** Business units, likely representing the majority of businesses within a firm, that expect to maintain or to perhaps moderately increase market share from year to year.

    Financial Objectives: Share of target customers and accounts; customer and product-line profitability.

3. **Harvest:** Mature business units that warrant only enough investment to maintain production equipment and capabilities.

    Financial Objectives: Payback; customer and product-line profitability.

Customer Perspective

In the customer component of the balanced scorecard, the business unit identifies the market segments it will target (see Chapter 5). Those segments supply the revenue stream that support critical financial objectives. Marketing managers must also identify the value proposition—how the firm proposes to deliver competitively superior and sustainable value to the target customers and market segments. The central element of any business strategy is the value proposition that describes a company's unique product and service attributes, customer relationship management practices, and corporate reputation. Importantly, the value proposition should clearly communicate to targeted customers what the company expects to do *better* and differently than its competitors.

Key Value Propositions and Customer Strategies   Business-to-business firms typically choose among four forms of differentiation in developing a value proposition[31]:

- **Low total cost**—customers are offered attractive prices, excellent and consistent quality, ease of purchase, and responsive service (for example, Dell, Inc.).

- **Product innovation and leadership**—customers receive products that expand existing performance boundaries through new features and functions (for example, Intel and Sony).

- **Complete customer solutions**—customers feel that the company understands them and can provide customized products and services tailored to their unique requirements (for example, IBM).

- **Lock-in**—customers purchase a widely used proprietary product or service from the firm and incur high switching costs (for example, Microsoft's operating system, Cisco's infrastructure products, or Google's search engine).

For the chosen strategy, Table 6.2 presents the core customer outcome measures used to monitor performance in each target segment. The customer perspective complements traditional market share analysis by tracking customer acquisition, customer retention, customer satisfaction, and customer profitability.

---

[31]Kaplan and Norton, *Strategy Maps*, pp. 322–344.

TABLE 6.2	THE CUSTOMER PERSPECTIVE—CORE MEASURES
Market Share	Represents the proportion of business in a given market (in terms of number of customers, dollars spent, or unit volume sold) that a business unit sells.
Customer Acquisition	Tracks, in absolute or relative terms, the rate at which a business unit attracts or wins new customers or business.
Customer Retention	Tracks, in absolute or relative terms, the rate at which a business unit retains customers.
Customer Satisfaction	Matches the satisfaction level of customers on specific performance criteria such as quality, service, or on-time delivery reliability.
Customer Profitability	Assesses the net profit of a customer, or segment, after deducting the unique expenses required to support that customer or segment.

SOURCE: Adapted from Robert S. Kaplan and David P. Norton, *The Balanced Scorecard: Translating Strategy into Action* (Boston: Harvard Business School Press, 1996): p. 68.

Internal Business Process Perspective

To develop the value proposition that will reach and satisfy targeted customer segments and to achieve the desired financial objectives, critical internal business processes must be developed and continually enriched. Internal business processes support two crucial elements of a company's strategy: (1) they create and deliver the value proposition for customers and (2) they improve processes and reduce costs, enriching the productivity component in the financial perspective. Among the processes vital to the creation of customer value are

1. Operations Management Processes,

2. Customer Management Processes,

3. Innovation Management Processes.

Strategic Alignment Robert S. Kaplan and David P. Norton emphasize that "value is created through internal business processes."[32] Table 6.3 shows how key internal processes can be aligned to support the firm's customer strategy or differentiating-value proposition. First, observe that the relative emphasis (see shaded areas) given to a particular process vary by strategy. For example, a firm that actively pursues a product-leadership strategy highlights innovation-management processes, whereas a company adopting a low-total-cost strategy assigns priority to operations-management processes. Second, although the level of emphasis might vary, note how the various processes work together to reinforce the value proposition. For example, a low-total-cost strategy can be reinforced by an innovation-management process that uncovers process improvements and a customer relationship management process that delivers superb postsales support.

From our discussion of strategic positioning, recall that it is much harder for a rival to match a set of interlocked processes than it is to replicate a single process. Michael Porter observes:

> Strategic fit among many activities is fundamental not only to competitive advantage but also to the sustainability of that advantage. . . . Positions built on systems of activities are far more sustainable than those built on individual activities.[33]

---

[32] Ibid., p. 43.

[33] Michael E. Porter, "What Is Strategy?" *Harvard Business Review* 74 (November–December 1996): p. 73.

TABLE 6.3	**ALIGNING INTERNAL BUSINESS PROCESSES TO THE CUSTOMER STRATEGY**

Customer Strategy	The Focus of Internal Business Processes		
	Operations Management	**Customer Relationship Management**	**Innovation Management**
Low-Total-Cost Strategy	Highly Efficient Operating Processes Efficient, Timely Distribution	Ease of Access for Customers; Superb Postsales Service	Seek Process Innovations Gain Scale Economies
Product Leadership Strategy	Flexible Manufacturing Processes Rapid Introduction of New Products	Capture Customer Ideas for New Offering Educate Customers about Complex New Products/ Services	Disciplined, High-Performance Product Development First-to-Market
Complete Customer Solutions Strategy	Deliver Broad Product/ Service Line Create Network of Suppliers for Extended Product/Service Capabilities	Create Customized Solutions for Customers Build Strong Customer Relationships Develop Customer Knowledge	Identify New Opportunities to Serve Customers Anticipate Future Customer Needs
Lock-in Strategies	Provide Capacity for Proprietary Product/ Service Reliable Access and Ease of Use	Create Awareness Influence Switching Costs of Existing and Potential Customers	Develop and Enhance Proprietary Product Increase Breadth/ Applications of Standard

SOURCE: Reprinted by permission of *Harvard Business Review*. From "Customer Objectives for Different Value Propositions" by Robert S. Kaplan in *Strategy Maps*, p. 41. Copyright © 2004 by the Harvard Business School Publishing Corporation; all rights reserved.

Learning and Growth   The fourth component of the balanced scorecard, **learning and growth**, highlights how the firm's intangible assets must be aligned to its strategy to achieve long-term goals. **Intangible assets** represent "the capabilities of the company's employees to satisfy customer needs."[34] The three principal drivers of organizational learning and growth are

1. *human capital*—the availability of employees who have the skills, talent, and know-how to perform activities required by the strategy;

2. *information capital*—the availability of information systems, applications, and information-technology infrastructure to support the strategy;

3. *organization capital*—the culture (for example, values), leadership, employee incentives, and teamwork to mobilize the organization and execute the strategy.

---

[34]Thomas A. Stewart, *Intellectual Capital: The New Wealth of Organizations* (New York: Doubleday, 1998), p. 67, cited in Kaplan and Norton, *Strategy Maps*, pp. 202–203.

Strategic Alignment   To create value and advance performance, the intangible assets of the firm must be aligned with the strategy. For example, consider a company that plans to invest in staff training and has two choices—a training program on total quality management (TQM) or a training initiative on customer relationship management (CRM). A company like Dell, which pursues a low-total-cost strategy, might derive higher value from TQM training, whereas IBM's consulting unit, which pursues a total customer solution strategy, would benefit more from CRM training. Unfortunately, research suggests that two-thirds of organizations fail to create strong alignment between their strategies and their human resources and information technology programs.[35]

Measuring Strategic Readiness   Senior management must ensure that the firm's human resources and information technology systems are aligned with the chosen strategy. To achieve desired performance goals in the other areas of the scorecard, key objectives must be achieved on measures of employee satisfaction, retention, and productivity. Likewise, front-line employees, like sales or technical service representatives, must have ready access to timely and accurate information. However, skilled employees who are supported by a carefully designed information system will not contribute to organizational goals if they are not motivated or empowered to do so. Many firms, such as FedEx and 3M, have demonstrated the vital role of motivated and empowered employees in securing a strong customer franchise.

Now that each of the components of the balanced scorecard have been defined, let's explore a clever tool that can be used to communicate the desired strategy path to all employees while detailing the processes that will be used to implement the strategy.

Strategy Map

To provide a visual representation of the cause-and-effect relationships among the components of the balanced scorecard, Kaplan and Norton developed what they call a strategy map. They say that a strategy must provide a clear portrait that reveals how a firm will achieve its desired goals and deliver on its promises to employees, customers, and shareholders. "A strategy map enables an organization to describe and illustrate, in clear and general language, its objectives, initiatives, and targets; the measures used to assess performance (such as market share and customer surveys); and the linkages that are the foundation for strategic direction."[36]

Key Strategy Principles   Figure 6.6 shows the strategy map template for a firm pursuing a product-leadership strategy. We can use this illustration to review and reinforce the key principles that underlie a strategy map:

- *Companies emphasize two performance levels in developing a financial strategy—a productivity strategy and a revenue-growth strategy.*

- *Strategy involves choosing and developing a differentiated customer value proposition.* Note the value proposition for product leadership: "Products and services that expand existing performance boundaries into the highly desirable." Recall that the other value propositions and customer strategies include low total cost, complete customer solutions, and system lock-in.

---

[35] Kaplan and Norton, *Strategy Maps*, p. 13.

[36] Kaplan and Norton, "Having Trouble with Your Strategy?" p. 170.

FIGURE 6.6 | **STRATEGY MAP TEMPLATE: PRODUCT LEADERSHIP**

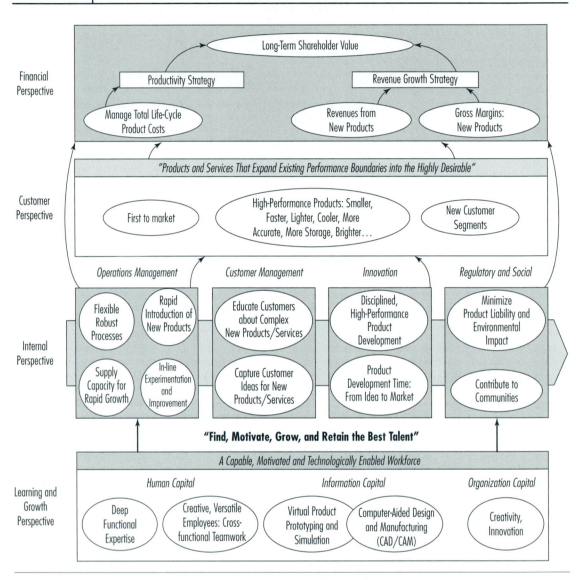

- *Value is created through internal business processes.* The financial and customer perspectives in the balanced scorecard and strategy map describe the performance outcomes the firm seeks, such as increases in shareholder value through revenue growth and productivity improvements, as well as enhanced performance outcomes from customer acquisition, retention, loyalty, and growth.

- *Strategy involves identifying and aligning the critical few processes that are most important for creating and delivering the customer value proposition.* For a product-leadership strategy, observe how each of the internal business processes directly supports the customer value proposition—product leadership.

- *Value is enhanced when intangible assets (for example, human capital) are aligned with the customer strategy.* From Figure 6.6, note the strategic theme for learning and growth: "a capable, motivated, and technologically enabled workforce." When the three components of learning and growth—human, information, and organization capital—are aligned with the strategy, the firm is better able to mobilize action and execute that strategy.

To recap, the balanced scorecard provides a series of measures and objectives across four perspectives: financial, customer, internal business process, and learning and growth. By developing mutually reinforcing objectives across these four areas, a strategy map can be used to tell the story of a business unit's customer strategy and to highlight the internal business processes that drive performance.

Summary

Guided by a deep understanding of the needs of customers and the capabilities of competitors, market-driven organizations are committed to a set of processes, beliefs, and values that promote the achievement of superior performance by satisfying customers better than competitors do. Because many business-to-business firms have numerous divisions, product lines, and brands, three major levels of strategy exist in most large organizations: (1) corporate, (2) business level, and (3) functional. Moving down the strategy hierarchy, the focus shifts from strategy formulation to strategy implementation. Marketing is best viewed as the functional area that manages critical connections between the organization and customers. Business marketing planning must be coordinated and synchronized with corresponding planning efforts in other functional areas. Strategic plans emerge out of a bargaining process among functional areas. Managing conflict, promoting cooperation, and developing coordinated strategies are all fundamental to the business marketer's role.

A business model or concept consists of four major components: (1) a core strategy, (2) strategic resources, (3) the customer interface, and (4) the value network. The core strategy is the essence of how the firm competes, whereas strategic resources capture what the firm knows (core competencies), what the firm owns (strategic assets), and what employees actually do (core processes). Specifying the benefits to customers is a critical decision when designing a core strategy. The customer interface component refers to how customer relationship management strategies are designed and managed, whereas the value network component considers how partners and supply chain members can complement and strengthen the resource base of the firm. To establish and maintain a distinctive strategic positioning, a company should focus on profitability, rather than just revenue growth, deliver a unique value proposition, and configure activities—like new product development or customer relationship management—differently from rivals and in a manner that supports its value proposition.

Successful execution involves linking strategy to operations, using tools and processes like the balanced scorecard and strategy map. The balanced scorecard converts a strategy goal into concrete objectives, and measures are organized into four different perspectives: financial, customer, internal business process, and learning and growth.

The approach involves identifying target customer segments, defining the differentiating customer value proposition, aligning the critical internal processes that deliver value to customers in these segments, and selecting the organizational capabilities necessary to achieve customer and financial objectives. Business marketers primarily emphasize one of the following value propositions or customer strategies: low total cost, product leadership, or system lock-in. A strategy map provides a visual representation of a firm's critical objectives and the cause-and-effect relationships among them that drive superior organizational performance.

Discussion Questions

1. Commenting on the decision-making process of his organization, a senior executive noted: "Sometimes the process is bloody, ugly, just like sausage meat being made. It's not pretty to watch but the end results are not too bad." Why do various functional interest groups often embrace conflicting positions during the strategic decision process? How are decisions ever made?

2. Describe how the primary focus of marketing managers at the corporate level differs from the focus marketing managers take at the business-unit or functional level.

3. A day in the life of a business marketing manager involves interactions with managers from other functions in the firm. First, identify the role of R&D, manufacturing, and logistics functions in creating and implementing marketing strategy. Next, describe some of the common sources of conflict that can emerge in cross-functional relationships.

4. Gary Hamel, a leading strategy consultant, contends that managers as well as Wall Street analysts like to talk about business models but few of them could define "what a business model or business concept really is." Describe the major components of a business model and discuss how these components are linked to the benefits a firm provides to customers.

5. Select a firm such as FedEx, Apple, IBM, Boeing, GE, or Caterpillar and assess its business model. Develop a list of particular skills, resources, and strategies that are especially important to the selected firm's strategic position. Give particular attention to those skills, resources, or characteristics that competitors would have the most difficulty in matching.

6. "Trying to be all things to all customers almost guarantees a weak strategic position for a firm." Agree or disagree? Explain.

7. Strategy experts argue that effective and aligned internal business processes determine how value is created in an organization. Provide an illustration to demonstrate the point.

8. Describe why a business-to-business firm that plans to enter a new market segment may have to realign its internal business processes to succeed in this segment.

9. Describe how the learning and growth objectives in a balanced scorecard might differ for a firm pursuing a low-total-cost strategy versus one that emphasizes complete customer solutions.

10. The fourth component of the balanced scorecard, learning and growth, captures the intangible assets of the firm (for example, human, information, and organization capital). Describe the role these intangible assets might assume in executing strategy at FedEx or Google.

Internet Exercises

1. 3M is a large, diversified, technology company that has numerous business units and manufactures thousands of products. Go to http://www.3m.com and

   a. identify the major market or industry sectors that the firm serves;

   b. describe a new product that 3M has recently introduced for the health-care sector.

Microsoft Targets Small and Mid-Sized Businesses[37]

By targeting small and medium-sized businesses, Microsoft hopes to capture a lucrative market sector, offsetting the slower growth among large-enterprise customers. This large and highly fragmented market includes small businesses with fewer than 50 employees and mid-sized firms with fewer than 500 employees. Microsoft's chief executive, Steve Ballmer, views this market sector as the most vital and fastest-growing segment of the economy. To serve small and mid-market customers, Microsoft has developed a multiyear product plan that calls for increased investment in research and development.

Challenging Intuit, Inc.

Targeting small-business customers, Microsoft recently introduced Microsoft Office Small Business Accounting and Microsoft Office Small Business Management. These offerings are designed to enable small businesses to manage all their sales, marketing, and financial processes within an easy-to-use operating environment. The software is widely available through resellers and retail outlets, including Amazon.com, Best Buy, Office Depot, and Staples. Likewise, Dell offers the software preinstalled on selected Dell small-business computing systems.

By introducing a small-business accounting program, Microsoft is taking direct aim at Intuit, Inc.'s widely used QuickBooks accounting software. Dan Levin, vice president of product management at Intuit, welcomed the competition, adding that the new accounting program "marks the fourth time Microsoft has attempted entry into the small business accounting software market." Intuit is the undisputed leader in this market with its QuickBooks product line, but Microsoft wants to build volume in the small-business accounting market.

Among the key battlegrounds where the two will compete head-to-head are

- first-time accounting software users, most heavily concentrated in the one-to-four-employee segment, that still use basic checkbook accounting and manual processes;

- the one-third of small businesses that upgrade or change their software annually;

- the more than 500,000 new small businesses created in the United States each year.

---

[37]"Microsoft Goes After Small Business," *CNN Money*, September 7, 2005, http://www.cnnmoney.com, and "Cashing in on the U.S. Small Business Accounting Market: Intuit and Microsoft Go Head to Head," Access Markets International Partners, Inc., March 13, 2006, accessed at http://www.ami-partners.com on July 12, 2008.

Discussion Questions

1. To succeed against rivals like Intuit that specialize in small-business customers, describe the differentiating value proposition that Microsoft should offer to customers.

2. Drawing on the balanced scorecard, describe how Microsoft might realign its internal business processes (for example, operations, customer, innovation management) to achieve targeted revenue and profit goals in the small- and mid-sized business segment. What steps might Intuit take to counter Microsoft's challenges?

CHAPTER

7

Business Marketing Strategies for Global Markets

Business marketing firms that restrict their attention to the domestic market are overlooking enormous international market opportunities and a challenging field of competitors. After reading this chapter, you will understand:

1. how to capture the sources of global advantage in rapidly developing economies such as China and India.

2. the spectrum of international market-entry options and the strategic significance of different forms of global market participation.

3. the distinctive types of international strategy.

4. the essential components of a global strategy.

A recent *Business Week* article focused on the significant increase in global competition large U.S. industrial corporations face. Huge but relatively unknown firms from emerging markets are challenging Western firms in almost every global setting.

> From India's Infosys Technologies (IT services) to Brazil's Embraer (light jets), and from Taiwan's Acer (computers) to Mexico's Cemex (building materials), a new class of formidable competitors is rising. There are 25 world-class emerging multinationals today and within 15 years, there will be at least 100 of them. The biggest challenge posed by these up-and-coming rivals will not be in Western markets, but within developing nations. That's the arena of fastest global growth—and home to 80 percent of the world's 6 billion consumers, hundreds of millions of whom have moved into the middle class. . . . The rise of these new multinationals will force American business marketers to rethink strategies for Third World product development, marketing, and links with local companies.[1]

Truly, business-to-business marketing is worldwide in scope, and the very existence of many business marketing firms will hinge on their ability to act decisively, compete aggressively, and seize market opportunities in rapidly expanding global economies. Numerous business marketing firms—such as GE, IBM, Intel, Boeing, and Caterpillar—currently derive much of their profit from global markets. They have realigned operations and developed a host of new strategies to strengthen market positions and compete effectively against the new breed of strong global rivals.

This chapter will examine the need for, and the formulation of, global business marketing strategies. The discussion is divided into four parts. First, attention centers on rapidly developing economies, like China, and the sources of global advantage they can represent for business marketing firms. Second, international market-entry options are isolated and described. Third, "multidomestic" and "global" strategies are compared, and prescriptions provided for where they are most effectively applied. Fourth, the critical requirements for a successful global strategy are explored.

Capturing Global Advantage in Rapidly Developing Economies[2]

A set of rapidly developing economies (RDEs) is reshaping the playing field and forcing business marketing executives to rethink their strategies and the scope of their operations. Key RDEs include, of course, China and India, as well as Mexico, Brazil, central and eastern Europe, and Southeast Asia. Let's put the growth of these economies in perspective. Whereas the United States, western Europe, and Japan are projected to grow by roughly $3 trillion in collective gross domestic product (GDP)

---

[1] Jeffrey E. Garten, "A New Threat to America, Inc.," *Business Week*, July 25, 2005, p. 114. For a review of the top-100 international challengers, see Harold L. Sirkin, James W. Hemerling, and Arindam K. Bhattacharya, *Globality: Competing with Everyone from Everywhere for Everything* (New York: Business Plus, 2008).

[2] This section is based on Arindam Bhattacharya, Thomas Bradtke, Jim Hemerling, Jean Lebreton, Xavier Mosquet, Immo Rupf, Harold L. Sirkin, and Dave Young, "Capturing Global Advantage: How Leading Industrial Companies Are Transforming Their Industries by Sourcing and Selling in China, India, and Other Low-Cost Countries," The Boston Consulting Group, Inc., April 2004, accessed at http://www.bcg.com.

from 2004 to 2010, the key RDEs will grow by more than $2 trillion. Specifically, China's GDP is expected to increase by $750 billion, central and eastern Europe's by $450 billion, Southeast Asia's by $350 billion, India's by $300 billion, Mexico's by $250 billion, and Brazil's by $200 billion. During this period, as highly developed economies like the United States and Japan experience annual GDP growth slightly above 2 percent, China will grow four times as fast, and India, Southeast Asia, and Mexico three times as fast. For example, Vietnam has become an extremely attractive investment opportunity for many business-to-business firms. Vietnam was admitted to the World Trade Organization in 2007, and the country enjoys a solid base of well-educated workers and a government determined to transform the country into a powerful economic entity. It is one of the fastest-growing economies, with a growth in GDP in 2007 of over 8 percent. Not only does Vietnam offer an excellent base for manufacturing operations, it has also become a very attractive market for business-to-business marketers. With a government willing to transform the country into private industrial operations, it is a country that cannot be ignored by firms looking for lower-cost manufacturing opportunities and large markets.

While representing a potentially attractive market opportunity, RDEs also present a formidable competitive challenge to firms in many industries. The migration of sourcing, manufacturing, and service operations from high-cost countries (for example, the United States and western Europe) to low-cost countries (for example, China, Mexico, and India) is well under way and accelerating. In the United States alone, the value of offshore arrangements has increased steadily: The cumulative value of outsourcing contracts rose from $50 billion in 2002 to more than $225 billion in 2007.[3] In turn, imports from these rapidly developing economies are making substantial inroads into core industrial product categories that were historically thought to be protected from such competition. However, leading firms like GE, Microsoft, Cisco, Apple, and Siemens are seizing opportunities by capturing sources of global advantage. In industry after industry, firms are under enormous pressure to make the move to global operations.

Mapping Sources of Global Advantage[4]

A firm can globalize its cost structure through the migration of sourcing, manufacturing, R&D, and service operations from a high-cost country to an RDE. In creating advantaged global operations, companies might conduct R&D in the United States, manufacture some product lines in the United States and others in China and Mexico, and locate customer service in India and Ireland. "Significant portions of manufacturing are expected to remain advantaged in their current locations. Reasons for staying in higher-cost locations might include the need to safeguard intellectual property content, the importance of collocation with customers, or the requirement to use local content."[5]

---

[3] David Jacoby and Bruna Fiqueiredo, "The Art of High-Cost Country Sourcing," *Supply Chain Management Review* 12 (May/June 2008): p. 33.

[4] Unless otherwise noted, this section draws on Jim Hemerling, Dave Young, and Thomas Bradtke, "Navigating the Five Currents of Globalization: How Leading Companies Are Capturing Global Advantage," *BCG Focus* (April 2005), The Boston Consulting Group, Inc., accessed at http://www.bcg.com.

[5] Battacharya et al., "Capturing Global Advantage," p. 7.

Firms that quickly and intelligently seize global opportunities can secure three forms of competitive advantage: (1) a cost advantage, (2) a market access advantage, and (3) a capabilities advantage.

The Cost Advantage

The major driver for a move to RDE sourcing remains very large—and sustainable—cost advantages from two primary sources: lower operating costs and lower capital investment requirements. The savings are striking. Jim Hemerling and his colleagues at the Boston Consulting Group assert that companies that globalize their cost structures by including RDEs can realize savings of 20 to 40 percent in the landed costs of their products. The **landed cost** reflects the realized net savings after logistics costs, other management costs, and import duties involved in moving the product from the RDE (for example, China) to the market destination (for example, the United States). In addition, the capital needed to create a manufacturing facility in an RDE is 20 to 40 percent lower than in a highly developed economy. In addition to the cost and investment advantages, another driver of lower costs has emerged in recent years: government subsidies. Subsidies in the form of direct payment to companies may allow them to price their products below competitive prices and enjoy distinct advantages in other global markets.

Lower Operating Costs   The difference in labor costs is a major component of the RDE cost advantage. Depending on the industry, the factory location, and the nature of employee benefits, a factory worker in the United States or Europe costs $15 to $30 or more per hour. By contrast, a factory worker in China earns $1 per hour, whereas in Mexico and in central and eastern Europe, workers earn $2 to $8 per hour. Figure 7.1 displays the realized cost savings (that is, 30 percent) for industrial products such as electric motors, transformers, and compressors that are manufactured in a RDE. Observe that companies operating in a RDE save not only directly on labor costs but also indirectly on domestic materials and components.

Business Process Outsourcing   When the focus shifts from products to highly labor-intensive sectors, such as services, the cost advantage of outsourcing to a RDE is up to 60 percent. India now represents the global market leader in offshore business-process outsourcing. Included here are not only transactional processes like call centers but also core industrial processes such as R&D and supply chain management. A strong telecommunications infrastructure, coupled with large numbers of highly educated English-speaking managers, engineers, and workers, constitute key advantages for India. By outsourcing call centers to India, General Electric's consumer finance business saved 30 to 35 percent and American Express had savings of more than 50 percent.

Will the Cost Gap Persist?   Experts suggest that the differential in labor rates between RDEs and developed countries will remain substantial for the foreseeable future, even if they grow at dramatically different rates. Wage growth in China and India will be limited by the large number of underemployed people in both countries. Likewise, companies that operate in RDEs have been able consistently to lower purchasing costs over time, achieving cost savings that significantly exceed those that are normally found in the West.

FIGURE 7.1 | **RDEs Offer a Substantial Cost Advantage over Highly Developed Economies**

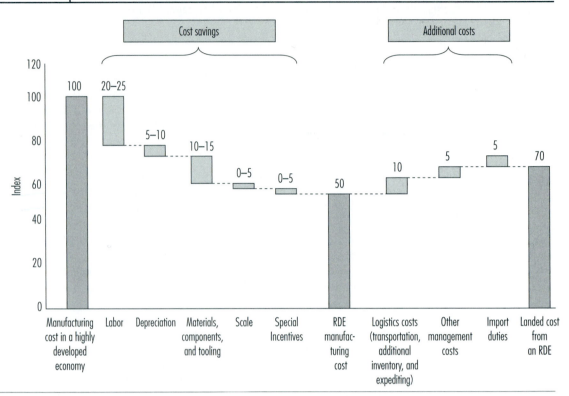

SOURCE: Jim Hemerling, Dave Young, and Thomas Bradtke, "Navigating the Five Currents of Globalization: How Leading Companies Are Capturing Global Advantage," *BCG Focus*, January 2005, The Boston Consulting Group, Inc., accessed at http://www.bcg.com. Copyright © The Boston Consulting Group, Inc. 2005. All rights reserved. Reprinted by permission.

Lower Capital Investment Requirements Another important—and sometimes overlooked—source of the RDE cost advantage is lower capital investment requirements for plants and equipment. While lower operating costs benefit a firm's profit and loss (P&L) statement, lower capital investment requirements also represent significant savings on the balance sheet. The combination of lower product costs and lower capital investment requirements can boost the total return on investment. Figure 7.2 shows the typical cost differential for an industrial installation (for example, factory) in a RDE versus one in a highly developed economy. Observe that a factory in a RDE can be built for just 70 percent of the investment level needed in a highly developed economy. These capital savings result from the lower cost of infrastructure (15 percent savings), the lower cost of local machinery and equipment (10 percent), and the opportunity to substitute labor for costly technology (10 percent). After accounting for the higher costs (5 percent) of imported machinery, the net capital savings are 30 percent in the RDE (see Figure 7.2).

Subsidies Many assume that China's cost advantage in manufacturing comes from cheap labor. But in China's burgeoning steel industry, research suggests that massive government energy subsidies, not other factors, keep prices down. These subsidies have broad implications for how companies compete and collaborate with Chinese

FIGURE 7.2 | **RDEs Offer a Significant Capital Advantage over Highly Developed Economies**

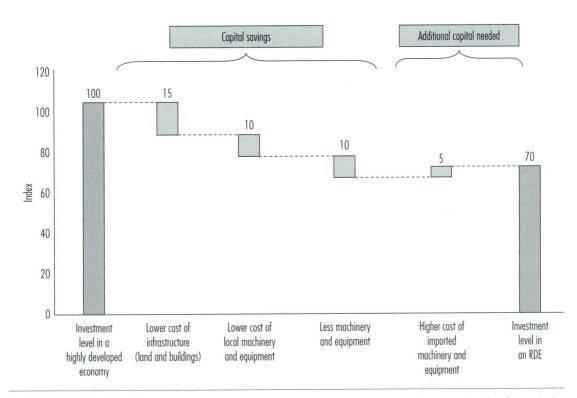

businesses.[6] The country has now become the world's largest steel exporter by volume and it remains the world's largest consumer and producer of steel, with 40 percent of global production. How did China make these astonishing gains so quickly and manage to sell steel for about 19 percent less than steel from U.S. and European companies? Labor accounts for less than 10 percent of the costs of producing Chinese steel, and Chinese steel does not appear to rely on scale economies, supply chain proximities, or technological efficiencies to lower its costs. The answer was a $27 billion energy subsidy (for coal) from the Chinese government. Since energy represents a much larger cost than labor in steel production, the subsidy provides a huge global cost advantage for the Chinese steel industry.

The Hidden Cost of RDE Operations The cost advantages gained through operations in a RDE can be eroded by additional costs if companies fail to recognize them and aggressively control them. Among these hidden costs are[7]

One-time setup costs that include the typical costs of establishing a new business, such as identifying and qualifying suppliers, creating a reliable logistics chain, and training employees;

---

[6] C. V. Usha and George T. Haley, "Subsidies and the China Price," *Harvard Business Review*, 86 (June, 2008): p. 25.

[7] Battacharya et al., "Capturing Global Advantage," pp. 20–21.

Ongoing RDE risk management costs related to monitoring the quality of suppliers, managing inventory in a longer-than-usual logistics chain, and hedging exchange rate fluctuations;

Exit costs related to closing high-cost production or service facilities, including asset write-offs and related restructuring costs, as well as "bad will" costs (for example, damaged relations with unions) in the home country.

A good example of some of the hidden costs in RDE operations is the experience of Intel in China. Intel built a large factory in the central region of China in an effort to accommodate Chinese government pressure to develop the interior of the country. Intel did enjoy the advantage of very low cost labor and lower investment cost, but the huge cost of transportation was not recognized until after the factory was operating. Intel was unable to use large jumbo jets to ship finished computer chips due to the lack of a suitable airport to accommodate Boeing 747s. Moving chips by truck was also challenging because the specialized "air-ride" trucks required for shipping fragile computer chips were not abundant in China. In fact, only 15 air-ride trucks could be found in the entire country! It took many months until more air-ride trucks became available and a new airport could be built. This obvious setback was a costly lesson in dealing with the lack of infrastructure in RDEs. In the truck construction industry, some firms believe that to be able to source in China, they must have a "piece price" savings of at least 20 percent in order to offset the associated costs and risks.[8]

In most cases, business-to-business firms do not exit their home-country operations entirely. They prefer instead to maintain the best home-country operations while moving only the least efficient to RDEs to remain competitive and to secure market access.

The Market Access Advantage

Although companies traditionally relocated manufacturing operations to RDEs to gain cost advantages, once they are established in these countries, they are ideally positioned to serve fast-growing local markets. The striking results that GE Healthcare achieved in China illustrate the market access advantage.

GE Healthcare entered the market by transferring technology to local Chinese R&D centers, which then developed "Chinese" versions of GE medical equipment that offered roughly 80 percent of the performance of Western systems at just 50 percent of the price. Because these products met local needs, GE Healthcare became the market leader in China. Furthermore, the China-developed products also appealed to customers in some Western countries where certain market segments found compelling value in the unique trade-off between the products' price and functionality.

China's Growing Role   For many industrial product categories, China is already the world's largest market. China is the largest market for machine tools, the second largest for power transmissions and distribution equipment, and the second largest

---

[8] Rick Weber, "SC Goes Global," *Body Builders*, 48 (March, 2007): p. 52

for energy consumption. On the consumer product side, China is the world's largest market for cell phones, air conditioners, and refrigerators and represents a large and rapidly growing market for personal computers, automobiles, and consumer electronics products. Other RDEs, like India, are also growing explosively. For Cummins Inc., the diesel engine maker, China and India each represent a lucrative market today. But by 2010, Cummins projects revenues of $2 billion from India and $3 billion from China.[9]

Following Key Customers to RDEs   Many small and mid-sized companies are following their customers to RDEs. For example, Phoenix Electric Manufacturing Company, a Chicago-based producer of electric motors for power tools, kitchen appliances, and other products, added a factory in China.[10] The move enabled Phoenix Electric to retain its largest customers—GE and Emerson Electric—which have shifted most of their consumer-electronics production to the area. Similarly, Hiwasse Manufacturing, an Arkansas-based manufacturer of steel products used in the control panels of refrigerators, ovens, and other appliances, added a facility in Mexico near a GE appliance manufacturing facility.[11]

A Twofold Strategy   As major industrial sectors relocate manufacturing operations to RDEs, business-to-business firms that supply these sectors must take decisive action. Jim Hemerling and his associates at the Boston Consulting Group provide this advice:

> Most companies need to develop a twofold strategic plan: to fill market gaps at home, and to follow selected customers to their new locations. In our experience, it is rarely feasible to pursue only one or the other.[12]

For example, gaps can be filled at home by pursuing new lines of business or new product or service opportunities where the home country advantage can be defended. In turn, when moving to a RDE, suppliers must adjust their operating models to fully capture the cost advantages.

The Capabilities Advantage

To reinforce the cost advantage of operating in RDEs, top-performing global companies capture second-order benefits by tapping into the rapidly developing base of human talent in these countries. China and India each add over 350,000 science and engineering graduates to their talent pool each year. In 2008, at least 5.59 million students will graduate from colleges in China, 13 percent more than last year, according to the Chinese Ministry of Education.[13] In fact, there are so many Chinese students attending college, that 700,000 of the 2007 college graduates were unable to find a job after they graduated, reinforcing the magnitude of the pool of educated talent available to firms locating in China. Many global companies, like GE, Microsoft, Motorola,

---

[9] Pete Engardio and Michael Arndt, "How Cummins Does It," *Business Week*, August 22–29, 2005, pp. 82–83.

[10] Dexter Roberts and Michael Arndt, "It's Getting Hotter in the East," *Business Week*, August 22–29, 2005, pp. 78–81.

[11] Louis Uchitelle, "If You Can Make It Here . . . ," *New York Times*, September 4, 2005, p. B-5.

[12] Hemerling, Young, and Bradtke, "Navigating the Five Currents of Globalization," pp. 9–10.

[13] "Getting a Job May Be Tougher for Graduates," *China Daily*, July 11, 2008, p. 11.

INSIDE BUSINESS MARKETING

How Offshore Outsourcing Affects Customer Satisfaction— and a Company's Stock Price!

Recent research suggests that sending customer service abroad negatively affects customer satisfaction. Jonathan Whitaker and his research colleagues analyzed the outsourcing activities of 150 North American companies and business units. As a group, those firms that outsourced saw a drop in their score on the American Consumer Satisfaction Index. Importantly, the declines in consumer satisfaction scores were roughly the same whether companies outsourced customer service domestically or overseas.

Customer satisfaction scores tend to move in the same direction as companies' stock prices. Based on this historical relationship, the average decline in consumer satisfaction found at companies outsourcing customer service is associated with a roughly 1 to 5 percent decline in a company's market capitalization, depending on the industry in which the company operates. That's a steep price! By the way, market capitalization is a measure of the value of a firm (that is, total outstanding shares × stock price).

To improve the quality of outsourced customer service, special attention should be given to insuring that the provider has all the information required to help the customer and is fully empowered to do so. Interestingly, the researchers found that "back-office offshoring had no effect on overall customer satisfaction. So the savings a company garners this way are not offset by dissatisfaction among customers."

SOURCE: Jonathan Whitaker, M.S. Krishnan, and Claes Fornell, "Customer Service: How Offshore Outsourcing Affects Customer Satisfaction," *The Wall Street Journal*, July 7, 2008, p. R4.

and Siemens, have created R&D centers in both India and China. For example, Motorola employs several thousand engineers in China and operates a large R&D center in Beijing.

Leading companies can make use of this capabilities advantage to accomplish the following:

- *Improve research and development:* The much lower cost of engineers and skilled technicians in RDEs allows companies to increase dramatically the amount of R&D they do for a given budget level.

- *Address unmet customer needs:* The opportunity to make greater use of skilled labor in place of machines allows companies to manufacture customized products less expensively than would be feasible in a more automated setting.

- *Tailor products and services to the burgeoning local markets in RDEs:* To illustrate, Motorola's Beijing R&D center develops cell phones for the local market—the largest handset market in the world.[14]

Unique RDE Risks　　In a remote area of India, a group of gun-wielding commandos emerged from the dense forest in India's Chhattisgarh state. The guerrillas descended on an iron ore processing plant owned by Essar Steel, one of India's biggest companies. There the attackers torched the heavy machinery on the site, plus 53 buses and trucks. The guerrillas left a note that basically said, "Stop shipping local resources out

---

[14] Roberts and Arndt, "It's Getting Hotter in the East," pp. 78–81.

TABLE 7.1	DETERMINING WHICH PRODUCTS TO OUTSOURCE TO RAPIDLY DEVELOPING ECONOMIES (RDEs) AND WHICH TO KEEP AT HOME

Selected Criteria	Maintain Home-Based Manufacturing	Relocate to RDEs
Labor Contract	Low	High
Growth of Demand in Home Market	Low	High
Size of RDE Market	Low	High
Degree of Standardization	Low	High
Intellectual Property Content	High	Low
Logistical Requirements	High	Low

SOURCE: Adapted from Arindam Bhattacharya et al., "Capturing Global Advantage: How Leading Industrial Companies Are Transforming Their Industries by Sourcing and Selling in China, India, and Other Low-Cost Countries," The Boston Consulting Group, Inc., April 2004, pp. 26–30, accessed at http://www.bcg.com.

of the state—or else." The assault on the Essar facility was the work of Naxalites—Maoist insurgents who seek the violent overthrow of the state and who despise India's landowning and business classes. The Naxalites may be a major threat to India's economic power, potentially more damaging to Indian companies, foreign investors, and the state than pollution, crumbling infrastructure, or political gridlock.[15] This is an example of the serious risks that can appear in RDEs.

The Outsourcing Decision[16]

The decision to relocate manufacturing, R&D, or customer service to RDEs is a strategic decision involving a host of economic, competitive, and environmental considerations. Clearly, some products and services are better candidates for outsourcing than others.

What Should Go?   The criteria that favor relocation to RDEs include products or services with high labor content, high growth potential, large RDE markets, and standardized manufacturing or service delivery processes (Table 7.1). These criteria reflect each of the sources of global advantage we have explored. For services, the processes most easily relocated are those that have well-defined process maps or those that are rule-based (for example, the established protocol a customer service call center uses).

What Should Not Go?   Products and services that should remain at home include "those for which protection of intellectual property is critical, those with extreme logistical requirements, those with very high technology content or performance requirements, and those for which customers are highly sensitive to the location of production" (for example, certain military contracts).[17] Concerns about intellectual

---

[15] "In India, Death to Global Business," *Business Week*; May 19, 2008, pp. 44–47.

[16] Battacharya et al., "Capturing Global Advantage," pp. 26–30.

[17] Ibid., p. 29.

FIGURE 7.3 | SPECTRUM OF INVOLVEMENT IN GLOBAL MARKETING

Low Commitment					**High Commitment**
Exporting	Contracting	Strategic Alliance	Joint Venture	Multidomestic Strategy	Global Strategy
Low Complexity					**High Complexity**

property (IP) theft is a major issue in most RDEs, particularly in China. Experts suggest that some multinational companies in China are losing the battle to protect their IP, largely because they emphasize legal tactics rather than including IP directly into their strategic and operational decisions. By carefully analyzing and selecting which products and technologies to sell in China, the best companies reduce the chance that competitors will steal their IP.

Global Market Entry Options[18]

To develop effective global marketing strategy, managers must evaluate the alternative ways that a firm can participate in international markets. The particular mode of entry should consider the level of a firm's experience overseas and the stage in the evolution of its international involvement. Figure 7.3 illustrates a spectrum of options for participating in global markets. They range from low-commitment choices, such as exporting, to highly complex levels of participation, such as global strategies. Each is examined in this section.

Exporting

An industrial firm's first encounter with an overseas market usually involves **exporting** because it requires the least commitment and risk. Goods are produced at one or two home plants, and sales are made through distributors or importing agencies in each country. Exporting is a workable entry strategy when the firm lacks the resources to make a significant commitment to the market, wants to minimize political and economic risk, or is unfamiliar with the country's market requirements and cultural norms. Exporting is the most popular global market entry option among small and medium-sized firms.[19]

Many companies begin export activities haphazardly, without carefully screening markets or options for market entry. These companies may or may not have a measure of success, and they might overlook better export opportunities. If early export

[18] The following discussion is based on Franklin R. Root, *Entry Strategy for International Markets* (Lexington, MA: D. C. Heath, 1987); and Michael R. Czinkota and Ilka A. Ronkainen, *International Marketing*, 2d ed. (Hinsdale, IL: Dryden Press, 1990).

[19] Jery Whitelock and Damd Jobber, "An Evaluation of External Factors in the Decision of UK Industrial Firms to Enter a New Non-Domestic Market: An Exploratory Study," *European Journal of Marketing* 38 (11/12, 2004): p. 1440.

efforts are unsuccessful because of poor planning, the company may be misled into abandoning exporting altogether. Formulating an export strategy based on good information and proper assessment increases the chances that the best options will be chosen, that resources will be used effectively, and that efforts will consequently be carried through to success.

The Commercial Service of the Department of Commerce has developed and maintains a network of international trade specialists in the United States to help American companies export their products and conduct business abroad. Trade specialists operate offices known as Export Assistance Centers (EACs) located in almost 100 cities in the United States and Puerto Rico that assist small and medium-sized companies. EACs are known as "one-stop shops" because they combine the trade and marketing expertise and resources of the Commercial Service along with the finance expertise and resources of the Small Business Administration (SBA) and the Export-Import Bank. Thus they provide companies with a wide array of services in one location, and they also maximize resources by working closely with state and local government as well as with private partners to offer companies a full range of expertise in international trade, marketing, and finance.[20]

Although it preserves flexibility and reduces risk, exporting may limit the future prospects for growth in the country. First, exporting involves giving up direct control of the marketing program, which makes it difficult to coordinate activities, implement strategies, and resolve conflicts with customers and channel members. George Day explains why customers may sense a lack of exporter commitment:

> In many global markets customers are loath to form long-run relationships with a company through its agents because they are unsure whether the business will continue to service the market, or will withdraw at the first sign of adversity. This problem has bedeviled U.S. firms in many countries, and only now are they living down a reputation for opportunistically participating in many countries and then withdrawing abruptly to protect short-run profits.[21]

Contracting

A somewhat more involved and complex form of international market entry is **contracting**. Included among contractual entry modes are (1) licensing and (2) management contracts.

Licensing   Under a **licensing** agreement, one firm permits another to use its intellectual property in exchange for royalties or some other form of payment. The property might include trademarks, patents, technology, know-how, or company name. In short, licensing involves exporting intangible assets.

As an entry strategy, licensing requires neither capital investment nor marketing strength in foreign markets. This lets a firm test foreign markets without a major commitment of management time or capital. Because the licensee is typically a local

[20] *A Basic Guide to Exporting*, the U.S. Department of Commerce with the assistance of Unz & Co., Inc. http://www .export.gov/exportbasics/index.asp, accessed on July 18, 2008.

[21] George S. Day, *Market Driven Strategy: Processes for Creating Value* (New York: The Free Press, 1990), p. 272.

company that can serve as a buffer against government action, licensing also reduces the risk of exposure to such action. With increasing host-country regulation, licensing may enable the business marketer to enter a foreign market that is closed to either imports or direct foreign investment.

Licensing agreements do pose some limitations. First, some companies are hesitant to enter into license agreements because the licensee may become an important competitor in the future. Second, licensing agreements typically include a time limit. Although terms may be extended once after the initial agreement, many foreign governments do not readily permit additional extensions. Third, a firm has less control over a licensee than over its own exporting or manufacturing abroad.

Management Contracts   To expand their overseas operations, many firms have turned to management contracts. In a **management contract** the industrial firm assembles a package of skills that provide an integrated service to the client. When equity participation, either full ownership or a joint venture, is not feasible or is not permitted by a foreign government, a management contract provides a way to participate in a venture. Management contracts have been used effectively in the service sector in such areas as computer services, hotel management, and food services. Michael Czinkota and Ilka Ronkainen point out that management contracts can "provide organizational skills not available locally, expertise that is immediately available rather than built up, and management assistance in the form of support services that would be difficult and costly to replicate locally."[22]

One specialized form of a management contract is a turnkey operation. This arrangement permits a client to acquire a complete operational system, together with the skills needed to maintain and operate the system without assistance. Once the package agreement is online, the client owns, controls, and operates the system. Management contracts allow firms to commercialize their superior skills (know-how) by participating in the international market.

Other contractual modes of entry have grown in prominence in recent years. **Contract manufacturing** involves sourcing a product from a producer located in a foreign country for sale there or in other countries. Here assistance might be required to ensure that the product meets the desired quality standards. Contract manufacturing is most appropriate when the local market lacks sufficient potential to justify a direct investment, export entry is blocked, and a quality licensee is not available.

Strategic Global Alliances (SGA)

A **strategic global alliance** (SGA) is a business relationship established by two or more companies to cooperate out of mutual need and to share risk in achieving a common objective. This strategy works well for market entry or to shore up existing weaknesses and increase competitive strengths. A U.S. firm with a reliable supply base might partner with a Japanese importer that has the established distribution channels and customer base in Japan to form a strong entry into the Japanese market.[23] Alliances

---

[22] Czinkota and Ronkainen, *International Marketing*, p. 493.

[23] Laura Delaney, "Expanding Your Business Globally," *MultiLingual*, 19 (April, 2008): pp. 10–11.

offer a number of benefits, such as access to markets or technology, economies of scale in manufacturing and marketing, and the sharing of risk among partners (see Chapter 4).

Although offering potential, global strategic alliances pose a special management challenge. Among the stumbling blocks are these:[24]

- Partners are organized quite differently for making marketing and product design decisions, creating *problems in coordination and trust.*

- Partners that combine the best set of skills in one country may be poorly equipped to support each other in other countries, leading to *problems in implementing alliances on a global scale.*

- The quick pace of technological change often guarantees that the most attractive partner today may not be the most attractive partner tomorrow, leading to *problems in maintaining alliances over time.*

Jeffrey Dyer and his colleagues conducted an in-depth study of 200 corporations and their 1,572 alliances and found that, on average, the top 500 global companies each participate in 60 major strategic alliances.[25] Fraught with risk, almost half of these alliances fail. Recall from Chapter 4 that firms that excel at generating value from alliances have a dedicated *strategic-alliance function.* A dedicated function acts as a focal point for learning and for leveraging feedback from prior and ongoing alliances. The alliance function ensures that metrics are created and applied to monitor the performance of all of their alliances, domestic and global.

Joint Ventures

In pursuing international entry options, a corporation confronts a wide variety of ownership choices, ranging from 100 percent ownership to a minority interest. Frequently, full ownership may be a desirable, but not essential, prerequisite for success. Thus a joint venture becomes feasible. The **joint venture** involves a joint-ownership arrangement (between, for example, a U.S. firm and one in the host country) to produce and/or market goods in a foreign market. In contrast to a strategic alliance, a joint venture creates a new firm. Some joint ventures are structured so that each partner holds an equal share; in others, one partner has a majority stake. The contributions of partners can also vary widely and may include financial resources, technology, sales organizations, know-how, or plant and equipment. Representing a successful relationship is the 50-50 joint venture between Xerox Corporation and Tokyo-based Fuji Photo Film Company. Through the joint venture, Xerox gained a presence in the Japanese market, learned valuable quality management skills that improved its products, and developed a keen understanding of important Japanese

---

[24] Thomas J. Kosnik, "Stumbling Blocks to Global Strategic Alliances," *Systems Integration Age*, October 1988, pp. 31–39. See also Eric Rule and Shawn Keon, "Competencies of High-Performing Strategic Alliances," *Strategy & Leadership*, 27 (September–October 1998): pp. 36–37.

[25] Jeffrey Dyer, Prashant Kale, and Harbir Singh, *"How To Make Strategic Alliances Work,"* MIT Sloan Management Review 42 (2001): pp. 37–43.

ETHICAL BUSINESS MARKETING

The Bribery Dilemma in Global Markets

Global marketing managers often face a dilemma when home-country regulations clash with foreign business practices. A good case in point is the aerospace industry. U.S. government policies about bribery by private companies have affected aircraft sales in some countries. The U.S. Foreign Corrupt Practices Act (FCPA) of 1977 prohibits payments by U.S. companies and individuals, including exporters of aircraft, to obtain or retain business and has had a major effect on how U.S. companies conduct global business. Until 1999, European laws on transnational bribery were *nonexistent*. Accordingly, some European aerospace manufacturers were widely alleged to have bribed foreign public officials to win sales at the expense of their U.S. competitors.

Currently, the U.S. government and the Organization for Economic Cooperation and Development (OECD) Working Group on Bribery are trying to remove the major obstacles to implementation of the OECD's antibribery convention. The U.S. government is also seeking to strengthen OECD and other multilateral and bilateral disciplines related to bribery and corruption of public officials.

Interestingly, recent press reports allege that European aerospace companies are among the business groups pressing their governments to *relax antibribery rules*. To the extent that bribery and anticorruption disciplines and enforcement in Europe remain weaker than under the U.S. Foreign Corrupt Practices Act, European aerospace companies will enjoy a competitive advantage in sales competitions to foreign governments or government-controlled airlines.

SOURCE: Joseph H. Bogosian, "Global Market Factors Affecting U.S. Jet Producers," Federal Document Clearing House Congressional Testimony, Capital Hill Hearing Testimony, House Transportation and Infrastructure, May 25, 2005.

rivals such as Canon, Inc., and Ricoh Company. This joint venture has thrived for more than three decades.[26]

Advantages   Joint ventures offer a number of advantages. First, joint ventures may open up market opportunities that neither partner could pursue alone. Kenichi Ohmae explains the logic:

> If you run a pharmaceutical company with a good drug to distribute in Japan but have no sales force to do it, find someone in Japan who also has a good product but no sales force in your country. You get double the profit by putting two strong drugs through your fixed cost sales network, and so does your new ally. Why duplicate such high expenses all down the line? . . . Why not join forces to maximize contribution to each other's fixed costs?[27]

Second, joint ventures may provide for better relationships with local organizations (for example, local authorities) and with customers. By being attuned to the host country's culture and environment, the local partner may enable the joint venture to respond to changing market needs, be more aware of cultural sensitivities, and be less vulnerable to political risk.

---

[26] David P. Hamilton, "United It Stands—Fuji Xerox Is a Rarity in World Business: A Joint Venture That Works," *The Wall Street Journal*, September 26, 1996, p. R19.

[27] Kenichi Ohmae, "The Global Logic of Strategic Alliances," *Harvard Business Review* 67 (March–April 1989): p. 147.

The Downside   Problems can arise in maintaining joint-venture relationships. A study suggests that perhaps more than 50 percent of joint ventures are disbanded or fall short of expectations.[28] The reasons involve problems with disclosing sensitive information, disagreements over how profits are to be shared, clashes over management style, and differing perceptions on strategy. Mihir Desai, Fritz Foley, and James Hines studied more than 3,000 American global companies and report that joint ventures appear to be falling out of favor.[29] Why? Increasing forces of globalization such as fragmented production processes make the decision to *not* collaborate pay off. If a firm is considering a joint venture, Desai, Foley, and Hines suggest that they first isolate the reasons for considering a joint venture and make sure that "they can't buy the required services or that knowledge through an arms-length contract that doesn't require sharing ownership. . . . Second, explicitly lay out expectations for the partners in legal and informal documents prior to the creation of the entity so that it's clear what each party is providing. Third, try out partners without setting up a joint venture by conducting business with them in some way. . . . Finally, specify simple exit provisions at the onset and then don't be afraid to walk and go it alone."

Choosing a Mode of Entry

For an initial move into the global market, the full range of entry modes, presented earlier, may be considered—from exporting, licensing, and contract manufacturing to joint ventures and wholly owned subsidiaries. In high-risk markets, firms can reduce their equity exposure by adopting low-commitment modes such as licensing, contract manufacturing, or joint ventures with a minority share. Although nonequity modes of entry—such as licensing or contract manufacturing—involve minimal risk and commitment, they may not provide the desired level of control or financial performance. Joint ventures and wholly owned subsidiaries provide a greater degree of control over operations and greater potential returns.

Once operations are established in a number of foreign markets, the focus often shifts away from foreign opportunity assessment to local market development in each country. This shift might be prompted by the need to respond to local competitors or the desire to more effectively penetrate the local market. Planning and strategy assume a country-by-country focus.

Multidomestic versus Global Strategies

Business marketing executives are under increasing pressure to develop globally integrated strategies to achieve efficiency and rationalization across their geographically dispersed subsidiaries. As such, the challenge of internationalizing the firm is not in providing a homogeneous offering across markets, but rather in finding the best balance between local adaptation (a multidomestic strategy) and global optimization, where one integrated strategy is applied globally.[30] Multinational firms have traditionally managed

[28] Arvind Parkhe, "Building Trust in International Alliances," *Journal of World Business* 33 (Winter 1998): pp. 417–437.

[29] Mihir A. Desai, C. Fritz Foley, and James Hines, "The Costs of Shared Ownership: Evidence From International Joint Ventures," *Journal of Financial Economics* 73 (2004): pp. 323–374.

[30] G. Tomas M. Hult, S. Tamer Cavusgil, Seyda Deligonul, Tunga Kiyak, and Katarina Lagerström, "What Drives Performance in Globally Focused Marketing Organizations? A Three-Country Study," *Journal of International Marketing* 15 (2007): pp. 58–85.

General Electric Aircraft Engines: Global Strategy Means Help Your Customers

General Electric's (GE's) Aircraft Engine Division must maintain a very large global presence, as it markets jet engines to almost every airline in the world. Although most large airlines purchase their aircraft from either Boeing or Airbus, the individual airline makes the choice as to the jet engine manufacturer. Thus, Singapore Air can choose between Pratt & Whitney, Rolls-Royce, or GE. The stakes are high in the industry, given that a particular airline may purchase hundreds of aircraft over a relatively short period of time. The challenges are significant for the jet engine manufacturers: They must have a solid relationship with aircraft manufacturers like Boeing and Airbus, but just as important, they need to expend considerable effort to woo and then keep the airlines as customers. Making GE's job tougher are the global aspects of these relationships. First, Boeing is an American firm and Airbus is a joint venture of firms from several European Union countries. Several other airframe manufacturers are located in Brazil, Canada, and China—and these manufacturers cater to the smaller, regional airlines that fly 50- to 100-seat jets. Even more daunting is the fact that there are close to 80 airlines located all over the world, only a handful of which are U.S.-based.

A major element in GE's marketing strategy is to offer assistance to global customers in creative ways. For example, one new customer is a Chinese airframe manufacturer that had not yet built its first airplane when GE began interacting with company executives! The firm's first airplane would not roll off the assembly line until 2008, yet GE began building relationship ties with this company in 2003—in a subtle way. Because the Chinese airframe manufacturer is a brand-new company, key managers lacked experience in all the key aspects of business-to-business marketing. GE's response: help educate the airframe manufacturer's sales and marketing personnel in all facets of business-to-business marketing. One element of this approach was to invite the entire marketing and sales team to GE's U.S. headquarters for a two-week seminar on B2B marketing. Follow-up would take place in China at a later date to review assignments and projects given to the participants at the first seminar. GE will also work hand-in-hand with the Chinese sales team as they begin making sales calls on the airlines that are potential buyers of their aircraft. GE's efforts illustrate the challenges of selling in rapidly growing global markets where potential customers are rather inexperienced in many facets of business. The challenges for GE are complex, as it must deal with the cultural and business process issues of its Chinese customer, as well as those of all the airlines around the world to whom the Chinese firm will sell the airplanes.

operations outside their home country with **multidomestic strategies** that permit individual subsidiaries to compete independently in their home-country markets. The multinational headquarters coordinates marketing policies and financial controls and may centralize R&D and some support activities. Each subsidiary, however, resembles a strategic business unit that is expected to contribute earnings and growth to the organization. The firm can manage its international activities like a portfolio. Examples of multidomestic industries include most types of retailing, construction, metal fabrication, and many services.

In contrast, a **global strategy** seeks competitive advantage with strategic choices that are highly integrated across countries. For example, features of a global strategy might include a standardized core product that requires minimal local adaptation and that is targeted on foreign-country markets chosen on the basis of their contribution to globalization benefits. Prominent examples of global industries are automobiles, commercial aircraft, consumer electronics, and many categories of industrial machinery.

Major volume and market-share advantages might be sought by directing attention to the United States, Europe, and Japan, as well as to the rapidly developing economies of China and India.

Source of Advantage: Multidomestic versus Global

When downstream activities (those tied directly to the buyer, such as sales and customer service) are important to competitive advantage, a multidomestic pattern of international competition is common. In **multidomestic industries**, firms pursue separate strategies in each of their foreign markets—competition in each country is essentially independent of competition in other countries (for example, Alcoa in the aluminum industry, Honeywell in the controls industry).

Global competition is more common in industries in which upstream and support activities (such as technology development and operations) are vital to competitive advantage. A **global industry** is one in which a firm's competitive position in one country is significantly influenced by its position in other countries (for example, Intel in the semiconductor industry, Boeing in the commercial aircraft industry).

In his book, *Redefining Global Strategy: Crossing Borders in a World Where Differences Still Matter*, Pankaj Ghemawat suggests that most types of economic activity that can be conducted either within or across borders are still quite localized.[31] He argues that firms must be very careful in deciding between a multidomestic or global strategy because the "internationalization of numerous key economic activities, including fixed capital investment, telephone and Internet traffic, tourism, patents, stock investments, etc., remains at around only 10 percent." In his view, national borders are still significant and effective international strategies need to take into account both cross-border similarities and critical differences.[32] In the current global business environment where security is a major issue, intellectual property rights are in question, there are increased threats of economic protectionism, and a number of countries are reasserting national sovereignty, the decision to follow a purely global strategy must be carefully scrutinized.

Coordination and Configuration Further insights into international strategy can be gained by examining two dimensions of competition in the global market: configuration and coordination. **Configuration** centers on where each activity is performed, including the number of locations. Options range from concentrated (for example, one production plant serving the world) to dispersed (for example, a plant in each country—each with a complete value chain from operations to marketing, sales, and customer service). By concentrating an activity such as production in a central location, firms can gain economies of scale or speed learning. Alternatively, dispersing activities to a number of locations may minimize transportation and storage costs, tailor activities to local market differences, or facilitate learning about market conditions in a country.

Coordination refers to how similar activities performed in various countries are coordinated or coupled with each other. If, for example, a firm has three plants—one in the United States, one in England, and one in China—how do the activities in

---

[31] Pankaj Ghemawat, *Redefining Global Strategy: Crossing Borders in a World Where Differences Still Matter* (Boston: Harvard Business School Press, 2007), pp. 9–32.

[32] Ibid., p. 22.

FIGURE 7.4 | **TYPES OF INTERNATIONAL STRATEGY**

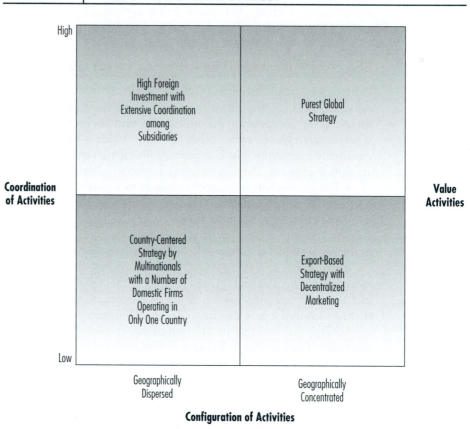

SOURCE: From "Changing Patterns of International Competition" by Michael Porter. Copyright © 1986, by The Regents of the University of California. Reprinted from the *California Management Review*, Vol. 28, No. 2. By permission of The Regents.

these plants relate to one another? Numerous coordination options exist because of the many possible levels of coordination and the many ways an activity can be performed. For example, a firm operating three plants could, at one extreme, allow each plant to operate autonomously (unique production processes, unique products). At the other extreme, the three plants could be closely coordinated, utilizing a common information system and producing products with identical features. Dow Chemical, for example, uses an enterprise software system that allows it to shift purchasing, manufacturing, and distribution functions worldwide in response to changing patterns of supply and demand.[33]

Types of International Strategy

Figure 7.4 portrays some of the possible variations in international strategy. Observe that the purest global strategy concentrates as many activities as possible in one country,

---

[33] Thomas H. Davenport, "Putting the Enterprise into the Enterprise System," *Harvard Business Review*, 76 (July–August 1998): pp. 121–131.

serves the world market from this home base, and closely coordinates activities that must be performed near the buyer (for example, service). Caterpillar, for example, views its battle with the formidable Japanese competitor Komatsu in global terms. As well as using advanced manufacturing systems that allow it to fully exploit the economies of scale from its worldwide sales volume, Caterpillar also carefully coordinates activities in its global dealer network. This integrated global strategy gives Caterpillar a competitive advantage in cost and effectiveness.[34] By serving the world market from its home base in the United States and by closely coordinating sales and service with customers around the world, Boeing also aptly illustrates a pure global strategy. Airbus—the European aerospace consortium—is a strong and clever rival that competes aggressively with Boeing for orders at airlines around the world.[35]

A Global Battle for the PC Market Other interesting global face-offs involve Dell, Inc., versus Lenovo Group, Inc. Dell is now pursuing an integrated global strategy and challenging Lenovo, China's largest producer in its home market.[36] Meanwhile, Lenovo gained worldwide reach when it purchased IBM's PC division. In turn, Hewlett-Packard remains a formidable rival for both.

Other Paths Figure 7.4 illustrates other international strategy patterns. Canon, for example, concentrates manufacturing and support activities in Japan but gives local marketing subsidiaries significant latitude in each region of the world. Thus, Canon pursues an export-based strategy. In contrast, Xerox concentrates some activities and disperses others. Coordination, however, is extremely high: The Xerox brand, marketing approach, and servicing strategy are standardized worldwide. Michael Porter notes:

> Global strategy has often been characterized as a choice between worldwide standardization and local tailoring, or as the tension between the economic imperative (large-scale efficient facilities) and the political imperative (local content, local production). . . . A firm's choice of international strategy involves a search for competitive advantage from configuration/coordination throughout the value chain.[37]

A Strategic Framework

Recall that companies may pursue multidomestic strategies or global strategies. The need for a global strategy is determined by the nature of international competition in a particular industry. On the one hand, many industries are *multidomestic*, and competition takes place on a country-by-country basis with few linkages across operating units (for example, construction and many service offerings). Multidomestic industries do not need a global strategy because the focus should be on developing a series of distinct domestic strategies.

---

[34] Donald V. Fites, "Make Your Dealers Your Partners," *Harvard Business Review* 74 (March–April 1996): pp. 84–95.

[35] Alex Taylor III, "Blue Skies for Airbus," *Fortune*, August 2, 1999, pp. 102–108.

[36] Evan Ramstad and Gary McWilliams, "For Dell, Success in China Tells Tale of Maturing Market," *The Wall Street Journal*, July 5, 2005, pp. A1, A8.

[37] Michael E. Porter, "Changing Patterns of International Competition," *California Management Review* 28 (Winter 1986): p. 25.

FIGURE 7.5 | **A GENERAL FRAMEWORK FOR GLOBAL STRATEGY**

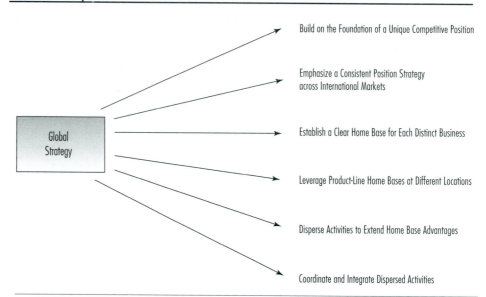

SOURCE: Adapted from Michael E. Porter, "Competing across Locations: Enhancing Competitive Advantage through a Global Strategy," in Michael E. Porter, ed., *On Competition* (Boston: Harvard Business School Press, 1998), pp. 309–350.

Multidomestic Strategy[38]   Pankjak Ghemawat provocatively argues that the world is not flat but semiglobalized, and that borders still exist and they matter when it comes to designing strategy. However, instead of focusing exclusively on the physical boundaries, he suggests that managers look at differences between countries and regions in terms of a framework that includes the following dimensions:

1. Cultural

2. Administrative/Political

3. Geographic

4. Economic

By analyzing these dimensions, a strategist can illuminate country-to-country differences, understand the liability of "foreignness," identify and evaluate foreign competitors, and discount market sizes by distance. Following this assessment, the business-to-business manager is better equipped to develop a responsive strategy for each country.

Global Strategy   For truly global industries, a firm's position in one country significantly affects its position elsewhere, so it needs a *global* strategy. Competing across countries through an integrated global strategy requires a series of choices that are highlighted in Figure 7.5.

---

[38] Ghemawat, *Redefining Global Strategy*, pp. 19–32.

Global Strategy[39]

Build on a Unique Competitive Position

A business marketing firm should globalize first in those business and product lines where it has unique advantages. To achieve international competitive success, a firm must enjoy a meaningful advantage on either cost or differentiation. To this end, the firm must be able to perform activities at a lower cost than its rivals or perform activities in a unique way that creates customer value and supports a premium price. For example, Denmark's Novo-Nordisk Group (Novo) is the world's leading exporter of insulin and industrial enzymes. By pioneering high-purity insulins and advancing insulin delivery technology, Novo achieved a level of differentiation that gave it a strong competitive position in the health-care market in the United States, Europe, and Japan.

Emphasize a Consistent Positioning Strategy

Rather than modifying the firm's product and service offerings from country to country, "a global strategy requires a patient, long-term campaign to enter every significant foreign market while maintaining and leveraging the company's unique strategic positioning."[40] One of the greatest barriers to the success of firms in smaller countries is the perceived need to serve all customer segments and to offer an expanded product assortment to capture the limited market potential. However, by maintaining a consistent position, a firm reinforces its distinctive strategy and keeps its strategic attention focused on the much larger international opportunity.

Establish a Clear Home Base for Each Distinct Business

Although the location of corporate headquarters is less important and may reflect historical factors, a firm must develop a clear home base for competing in each of its strategically distinct businesses. "The **home base** for a business is the location where strategy is set, core product and process technology is created and maintained, and a critical mass of sophisticated production and service activities reside."[41] For example, Japan, Honda's home base for both motorcycles and automobiles, is where 95 percent of its R&D employees are located and all of its core engine research is conducted. For Hewlett-Packard (H-P), the United States hosts 77 percent of the physical space dedicated to manufacturing, R&D, and administration but only 43 percent of H-P's physical space dedicated to marketing. At H-P's home base, R&D managers with specialized expertise are designated worldwide experts; they transfer their knowledge either electronically or through periodic visits to subsidiaries around the world. Regional subsidiaries take responsibility for some process-oriented R&D activities and for local marketing.

The home base should be located in a country or region with the most favorable access to required resources (inputs) and supporting industries (for example, specialized suppliers). Such a location provides the best environment for capturing productivity and innovation benefits. Honda as well as H-P each benefit from a strong supplier network that supports

---

[39] This section is based on Michael E. Porter, "Competing across Locations: Enhancing Competitive Advantage through a Global Strategy," in Michael E. Porter, ed., *On Competition* (Boston: Harvard Business School Press, 1998), pp. 309–350. See also Shaoming Zou and S. Tamer Cavusgil, "The GMS: A Broad Conceptualization of Global Marketing Strategy and Its Effect on Firm Performance," *Journal of Marketing* 66 (October 2002): pp. 40–56.

[40] Porter, "Competing Across Locations," p. 331.

[41] Ibid., p. 332.

each of its principal businesses. The home base should also serve as the central integrating point for activities and have clear worldwide responsibility for the business unit.

Leverage Product-Line Home Bases at Different Locations

As a firm's product line broadens and diversifies, different countries may best provide the home bases for some product lines. Responsibility for leading a particular product line should be assigned to the country with the best locational advantages. Each subsidiary, then, specializes in products for which it has the most favorable advantages (for example, specialized suppliers) and serves customers worldwide. For example, H-P locates many product-line home bases outside the United States, such as its line of compact inkjet printers, which is based in Singapore. In turn, Honda has begun to create a product-line home base for Accord station wagons in the United States. The model was conceived, designed, and developed through the joint efforts of Honda's California and Ohio R&D facilities.

Disperse Activities to Extend Home-Base Advantages

Although the home base is where core activities are concentrated, other activities can be dispersed to extend the firm's competitive position. Potential opportunities should be examined in three areas:

- *Capturing competitive advantages in purchasing.* Inputs that are not central to the innovation process, such as raw materials or general-purpose component parts, must be purchased from the most cost-effective location.

- *Securing or improving market access.* By locating selected activities near the market, a firm demonstrates commitment to foreign customers, responds to actual or threatened government mandates, and may be better equipped to tailor offerings to local preferences. For example, Honda has invested more than $2 billion in facilities in the United States. Likewise, a host of firms, like Honeywell, GE, and Intel, have made large investments in China and India.

- *Selectively tapping competitive advantages at other locations.* To improve capabilities in important skills or technologies at home, global competitors can locate selected activities in centers of innovation in other countries. The goal here is to supplement, but not replace, the home base. To illustrate, Honda gains exposure to California's styling expertise and Germany's high-performance design competencies through small, local, company-financed design centers that transfer knowledge back to the Japanese home base.

Coordinate and Integrate Dispersed Activities

Coordination across geographically dispersed locations raises formidable challenges, among them those of language and cultural differences and of aligning the reward systems for individual managers and subsidiaries with the goals of the global enterprise as a whole. However, successful global competitors achieve unified action by

1. Establishing a clear global strategy that is understood by organizational members across countries;

TABLE 7.2 | **KEY FACTORS FOR MANAGING RISK IN EMERGING MARKETS**

- Understand the individual markets: failing to do so is the fastest route to trouble.
- Use local expertise: there is no substitute for local knowledge.
- Find a partner: strong local relationships are critical.
- Understand the culture: taking a consistent approach in all markets ignores cultural differences with wildly different effects.
- Understand local laws, regulations and ethics: don't assume they are the same as in your home market.
- Be cautious and vigilant; pay attention to details, question, and be skeptical.
- Communicate: open two-way communication is vital, and "gaps" are a crucial cause of misunderstandings.
- Be present: relationships and understanding do not happen remotely.
- Be flexible in response to changing conditions: the pace of change can be dramatic.
- Think long-term: put capacity and resources in place to support the investment over time.

SOURCE: From *Risk Management in Emerging Markets*, p. 6–7. Ernst and Young, 2007. © 2007 EYGM Limited. All rights reserved. Reproduced by permission.

2. Developing information and accounting systems that are consistent on a worldwide basis, thereby facilitating operational coordination;

3. Encouraging personal relationships and the transfer of learning among subsidiary managers across locations;

4. Relying on carefully designed incentive systems that weigh overall contribution to the entire enterprise in addition to subsidiary performance.

Managing Risk in Emerging Markets

Expansion into new global markets or the establishment of manufacturing activities in low-labor-cost markets is not without risk, and the savvy business marketer will carefully assess the risks associated with working in new, global environments (see Table 7.2). Despite the huge market, low-cost labor, and reduced investment cost, there are still many pitfalls associated with both selling and manufacturing in China. These potential threats include: fragmented markets, limited intellectual property protection, an unstructured legal system, the lack of standardized accounting practices, and heavy investment of government in every facet of business.[42]

Summary

Rapidly developing economies (RDEs), like China and India, present a host of opportunities and a special set of challenges for business-to-business firms. Companies that decisively and intelligently pursue RDE strategies can secure three compelling forms of competitive advantage: significantly lower costs; direct access to the fastest-growing markets; and the capabilities for improving R&D, addressing unmet customer needs,

---

[42] Chia Chia Lin and Jason Lin, "Capitalism in Contemporary China: Globalization Strategies, Opportunities, Threats, and Cultural Issues," *Journal of Global Business Issues*, 2 (Winter 2008): pp. 31–40

and increasing overall business effectiveness. The migration of sourcing, manufacturing, R&D, and customer service operations from developed economies to RDEs will continue to accelerate in many industry sectors. However, some products and services are better candidates for relocation or outsourcing than others. For example, those with high labor content and large RDE markets represent solid outsourcing candidates, whereas those for which the protection of intellectual property is critical should stay at home.

Once a business marketing firm decides to sell its products in a particular country, it must select an entry strategy. The range of options includes exporting, contractual entry modes (for example, licensing), strategic alliances, and joint ventures. A more elaborate form of participation is represented by multinational firms that use multidomestic strategies. Here a separate strategy might be pursued in each country served. The most advanced level of participation in international markets is provided by firms that use a global strategy. Such firms seek competitive advantage by pursuing strategies that are highly interdependent across countries. Global competition tends to be more common in industries in which primary activities, like R&D and manufacturing, are vital to competitive advantage.

A global strategy must begin with a unique competitive position that offers a clear competitive advantage. Providing the best odds of global competitive success are businesses and product lines where companies have the most unique advantages. The home base for a business is the location where strategy is set, and the home base for some product lines may be best positioned in other countries. Although core activities are located at the home base, other activities can be dispersed to strengthen the company's competitive position. Successful global competitors demonstrate special capabilities in coordinating and integrating dispersed activities. Coordination ensures clear positioning and a well-understood concept of global strategy among subsidiary managers across countries. Successful global marketers understand the key risks associated with operating in the global environment, and they take steps to mitigate these risks through their strategic approach to different global markets. To create effective global strategies and capture important market opportunities, business-to-business firms must develop a deep understanding of local markets and the special competitive and environmental forces that will drive performance.

Discussion Questions

1. Evaluate this statement: Many business-to-business firms need to fill market gaps at home with new products and services and also follow selected customers to their new locations in rapidly developing economies like India or China.

2. Many observers argue the cost advantage that rapidly developing economies enjoy will evaporate in 5 to 10 years. Agree or disagree? Explain.

3. Describe the characteristics of products and services that would represent poor candidates for outsourcing.

4. In addition to cost advantages, describe the other ways that rapidly developing economies can contribute to competitive advantage.

5. The European aerospace consortium Airbus is a strong competitor to Boeing and is climbing toward its long-stated goal of winning 50 percent

of the over-100-seat airline market. What criteria would a customer like UPS or British Airways consider in choosing aircraft? What are the critical factors that shape competitive advantage in the aircraft market?

6. A small Michigan-based firm that produces and sells component parts to General Motors, Ford, and DaimlerChrysler wishes to extend market coverage to Europe and Japan. What type of market entry strategy would provide the best fit?

7. A major U.S. electronics firm decides the best approach to a global business strategy is to employ a multidomestic strategy. It will focus its efforts on China. Discuss some of the key threats the firm faces as it enters this market. How could it mitigate some of the risks associated with these threats?

8. A supplier of copper tubing and wire has adopted a multidomestic strategy to enter the eastern European market. What factors should it assess in these countries in order to formulate its marketing strategy in each one. Explain.

9. Why would Hewlett-Packard assign product-line responsibility to a subsidiary located outside the United States?

10. A global strategy begins with a unique competitive position that offers a clear competitive advantage. What steps can a global competitor take to ensure that the strategy is implemented in a consistent way in countries around the world?

Internet Exercise

1. General Electric (GE) sells over $5 billion worth of goods and services to Chinese customers in the business market. Go to http://www.ge.com and first identify the various GE divisions, like Healthcare, that contribute to sales volume and then identify a few products from each division that likely address important needs or priorities in China.

Schwinn: Could the Story Have Been Different?[43]

At its peak, Schwinn had more than 2,000 U.S. employees, produced hundreds of thousands of bicycles in five factories, and held 20 percent of the market. Today, however, Schwinn no longer exists as an operating company. The firm, founded in 1895, declared bankruptcy in 1992 and closed its last factory one year later. The Schwinn name is now owned by a Canada-based firm and all of the bikes are manufactured in Asia.

Harold L. Sirkin, a senior vice president at the Boston Consulting Group, argues that Schwinn's story could have been different. He outlines two alternative pathways that might have provided a happier ending to the Schwinn story.

Alternative Reality One: Aim High

Under this scenario, Schwinn decided to center on midrange and premium segments of the market, leaving low-end bicycles for competitors. However, the firm determined that it could substantially reduce costs by turning to low-cost partners in rapidly developing economies for labor-intensive parts. Schwinn interviewed hundreds of potential suppliers and locked the best ones into long-term contracts. Schwinn then reconfigured its operations to perform final assembly and quality inspection in the United States. Still, the changes forced Schwinn to make some painful choices—nearly 30 percent of the workforce was laid off. However, such moves allowed Schwinn to produce bikes at half the previous cost, maintain a significant position in the midrange bicycle market, and leverage its product design capabilities to build a strong position for its brand in the high-end market. As a result, Schwinn is extremely competitive in the U.S. market and is a major exporter of premium bikes to China and Europe. Because of this growth, Schwinn now employs twice as many people in the United States as it did before outsourcing began.

Alternative Reality Two: If You Can't Beat Them, Join Them

Schwinn went on the offensive and moved as quickly as possible to open its own factory in China. By bringing its own manufacturing techniques and by training employees in China, Schwinn was able to achieve high quality and a much lower cost. However, the decision meant that 70 percent of Schwinn's U.S. workers would lose their jobs. But Schwinn kept expanding its China operations and soon started selling bicycles in the Chinese market—not only at the low end but also to the high-end, luxury segment—leveraging its brand name. Schwinn then extended its global operations and reach by adding new facilities in eastern Europe and Brazil. The company has sold over 500,000 bikes in new markets and now has more employees in the United States than it did before deciding to expand into international markets.

---

[43] Harold L. Sirkin, "Don't Be a Schwinn," *BCG/Perspectives*, The Boston Consulting Group, Inc., January 2005, accessed at http://www.bcg.com.

Discussion Question

1. By facing fierce competition from low-cost rivals, many business-to-business firms in the United States and Europe face a situation today similar to Schwinn's. What lessons can they draw from the Schwinn story? How can they strengthen their competitive position?

CHAPTER

8

Managing Products for Business Markets

By providing a solution for customers, the product is the central force of business marketing strategy. The firm's ability to put together a line of products and services that provide superior value to customers is the heart of business marketing management. After reading this chapter, you will understand:

1. how to build a strong business-to-business brand.

2. the strategic importance of providing competitively superior value to customers.

3. the various types of industrial product lines and the value of product positioning.

4. a strategic approach for managing products across the stages of the technology adoption life cycle.

To spur growth at General Electric, CEO Jeffrey Immelt told GE's 11 business unit managers to each take 60 days and return with five ideas for growth that would generate at least $10 million in sales within three years.[1] Of the 55 ideas proposed, 35 were funded, ranging from wind-powered energy systems to sophisticated airport security systems using medical scanning technology. A business marketer's marketplace identity is established through its brand and through the products and services it offers. For example, General Electric's new branding campaign—"Ecomagination"—signals to the market that the firm is very serious about its responsibilities to the environment and is offering solutions such as wind, energy, and water filtration equipment as well as clean-coal services.[2] Because brands constitute one of the most valuable intangible assets that firms possess, branding has emerged as a priority to marketing executives, CEOs, and the financial community.

Product management is directly linked to market analysis and market selection. Products are developed to fit the needs of the market and are modified as those needs change. Drawing on such tools of demand analysis as business market segmentation and market potential forecasting, the marketer evaluates opportunities and selects profitable market segments, thus determining the direction of product policy. Product policy cannot be separated from market selection decisions. In evaluating potential product/market fits, a firm must evaluate new market opportunities, determine the number and aggressiveness of competitors, and gauge its own strengths and weaknesses. The marketing function assumes a lead role in transforming an organization's distinctive skills and resources into products and services that enjoy positional advantages in the market.[3]

This chapter first explores the nature of the brand-building process and the way in which a strong brand can sharpen the focus and energize the performance of the firm. Second, it examines product quality and value from the customer's perspective and directly links them to business marketing strategy. Third, because industrial products can assume several forms, the chapter describes industrial product-line options, while offering an approach for positioning and managing products in high-technology markets.

Building a Strong B2B Brand

Although consumer packaged-goods companies like Procter & Gamble (P&G), Coca-Cola, and Nestle have excelled by developing a wealth of enduring and highly profitable brands, some of the most valuable and powerful brands belong to business-to-business firms: IBM, Microsoft, General Electric, Intel, Hewlett-Packard, Cisco, Google, Oracle, Canon, Siemens, Caterpillar, and a host of others. For most business marketers, the company name is the brand, so the key questions become: "What do you want your company name to stand for? and What do you want it to mean in the mind of the customer?"[4]

[1]Bob Lamons, *The Case for B2B Branding* (Mason, OH: Thomson Higher Education, 2005), pp. 142–144.

[2]Regis McKenna, *Relationship Marketing* (Reading, MA: Addison-Wesley, 1991), p. 7.

[3]Rajan Varadarajan and Satish Jayachandran, "Marketing Strategy: An Assessment of the State of the Field and Outlook," *Journal of the Academy of Marketing Science* 27 (Spring 1999): pp. 120–143.

[4]Frederick E. Webster Jr. and Kevin Lane Keller, "A Roadmap for Branding in Industrial Markets," *Journal of Brand Management* 12 (May 2004): p. 389.

FIGURE 8.1 | **CUSTOMER-BASED BRAND EQUITY PYRAMID**

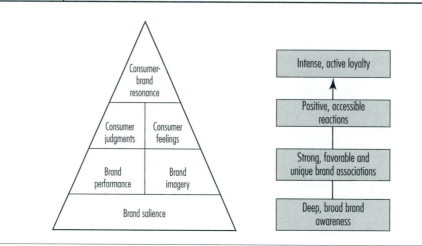

David Aaker says, "**Brand equity** is a set of brand assets and liabilities linked to a brand, its name, and symbol that add to or subtract from the value provided by a product or service and/or to that firm's customers."[5] As we will explore, the assets and liabilities that impact brand equity include brand loyalty, name awareness, perceived quality and other brand associations, and proprietary brand assets (for example, patents). A **brand**, then, is a name, sign, symbol, or logo that identifies the products and services of one firm and differentiates them from competitors.

Providing a rich and incisive perspective, Kevin Lane Keller defines **customer-based brand equity** (CBBE) as the differential effect that customers' brand knowledge has on their response to marketing activities and programs for that brand.[6] The basic premise of his CBBE model is that the power of a brand lies in "what consumers have learned, felt, seen, and heard about the brand over time."[7] So, the power of a brand is represented by all the thoughts, feelings, perceptions, images, and experiences that become linked to the brand in the minds of customers.

Brand-Building Steps[8]

The CBBE model lays out a series of four steps for building a strong brand (see Figure 8.1, right side): (1) develop deep brand awareness or a brand identity; (2) establish the meaning of the brand through unique brand associations (that is, points of difference); (3) elicit a positive brand response from customers through marketing programs; and (4) build brand relationships with customers, characterized by intense loyalty. Providing the foundation for successful brand management is the set of

---

[5]David Aaker, *Managing Brand Equity* (New York: The Free Press, 1991), p. 15.

[6]Kevin Lane Keller, *Strategic Brand Management* (3rd ed., Upper Saddle River, NJ: Prentice Hall, 2007).

[7]Webster and Keller, "A Roadmap for Branding," p. 15.

[8]This section is based on Kevin Lane Keller, "Building Customer-Based Brand Equity," *Marketing Management* 10 (July/August 2001): pp. 15–19.

brand-building blocks (see Figure 8.1, left side) aligned with the branding ladder—salience, performance, imagery, judgments, feelings, and resonance.

Brand Identity   To achieve the right identity for a brand, the business marketer must create brand salience with customers. **Brand salience** is tied directly to brand awareness: How often is the brand evoked in different situations? What type of cues or reminders does a customer need to recognize a brand? **Brand awareness** refers to the customer's ability to recall or recognize a brand under different conditions. The goal here is to ensure that customers understand the particular product or service category where the brand competes by creating clear connections to the specific products or services that are solely under the brand name.

Brand Meaning   **Brand positioning** involves establishing unique brand associations in the minds of customers to differentiate the brand and establish competitive superiority.[9] Although a multitude of different types of brand associations are possible, brand meaning can be captured by examining two broad categories: (1) **brand performance**—the way in which the product or service meets customers' more functional needs (for example, quality, price, styling, and service effectiveness) and (2) **brand imagery**—the ways in which the brand attempts to meet customers' more abstract psychological or social needs.

Brand positioning should incorporate both points of parity and points of difference in the customer value proposition (see Chapter 4). "Points of difference are strong, favorable, unique brand associations that drive customers' behavior; points of parity are those associations where the brand 'breaks even' with competitors and negates their intended points of difference."[10] Strong business-to-business brands like Cisco, IBM, Google, and FedEx have clearly established strong, favorable (that is, valuable to customers), and unique brand associations with customers.

Brand Response   As a branding strategy is implemented, special attention should be directed to how customers react to the brand and the associated marketing activities. Four types of **customer judgments** are particularly vital to the creation of a strong brand (in ascending order of importance):

1. *Quality*—the customer's attitudes toward a brand's perceived quality as well as their perceptions of value and satisfaction;

2. *Credibility*—the extent to which the brand as a whole is perceived by customers as credible in terms of expertise, trustworthiness, and likeability;

3. *Consideration set*—the degree to which customers find the brand to be an appropriate option worthy of serious consideration;

4. *Superiority*—the extent to which customers believe that the brand offers unique advantages over competitors' brands.

Feelings relate to the customers' emotional reaction to the brand and include numerous types that have been tied to brand building, including warmth, fun,

---

[9]Kevin Lane Keller, Brian Sternthal, and Alice Tybout, "Three Questions You Need to Ask About Your Brand," *Harvard Business Review* 80 (September 2002): pp. 80–89.

[10]Webster and Keller, "A Roadmap for Branding," p. 390.

excitement, and security. For example, Apple's brand might elicit feelings of **excitement** (customers are energized by the brand and believe that the brand is cool); IBM or FedEx may evoke feelings of **security** (the brand produces a feeling of comfort or self-assurance); and Cisco's branding campaign, "Welcome to the Human Network," might elicit **warmth** (the brand makes customers feel peaceful). Cisco's vice president–corporate marketing, Marilyn Mersereau, says, "Instead of being a product player with the 'Powered by Cisco' campaign, we're trying to position Cisco to be a platform for your life experience," educating customers about the ways Cisco makes it easier for people to connect with one another via the Web.[11]

Forging Brand Relationships   An examination of the level of personal identification and the nature of the relationship a customer has formed with the brand is the final step in the brand-building process. **Brand resonance** represents the strength of the psychological bond that a customer has with a brand and the degree to which this connection translates into loyalty, attachment, and active engagement with the brand. Keller observes, "Brand resonance reflects a completely harmonious relationship between customers and the brand. . . . The strongest brands will be the ones to which those consumers become so attached that they, in effect, become evangelists and actively seek means to interact with the brand and share their experiences with others."[12]

A Systems Model for Managing a Brand

To build and properly manage brand equity, Kevin Lane Keller and Donald R. Lehman provide an integrative model that can be used to isolate key dimensions of the brand management process.[13] (See Figure 8.2.)

Company Actions   A controllable element for the business marketer in creating brand value concerns the type and amount of marketing expenditures (for example, dollars spent on advertising or channel partner development) as well as the clarity, distinctiveness, and consistency of the marketing strategy, over time and across activities. Strong brands receive proper R&D and marketing support and that support is sustained over time.

What Customers Think and Feel   As we have seen, the "brand ladder" follows an order from awareness and brand associations to attachment and intense, active loyalty. Of course, the actions of competitors as well as environmental conditions can influence how customers feel about a brand (for example, Microsoft poses a challenge to Intuit, UPS challenges FedEx, and Apple's iPhone poses a threat to Research in Motion's BlackBerry). Strong brands stay relevant and excel at providing the benefits that matter the most to customers.[14]

What Customers Do   The primary payoff from positive customer thoughts and feelings is reflected in the purchases they make. Strong brands provide a host of

---

[11]"B to B's Best Brands: Cisco," *B to B's Best, 2007*, accessed at http://www.btobonline.com on July 15, 2008.

[12]Keller, "Building Customer Brand-Based Equity," p. 19.

[13]Kevin Lane Keller and Donald R. Lehman, "Brands and Branding: Research Findings and Future Priorities," *Marketing Science* 25 (November–December 2006): pp. 740–759.

[14]Kevin Lane Keller, "The Brand Report Card," *Harvard Business Review* 78 (January–February 2000): pp. 147–157.

FIGURE 8.2 | **A SYSTEMS MODEL OF BRAND ANTECEDENTS AND CONSEQUENCES**

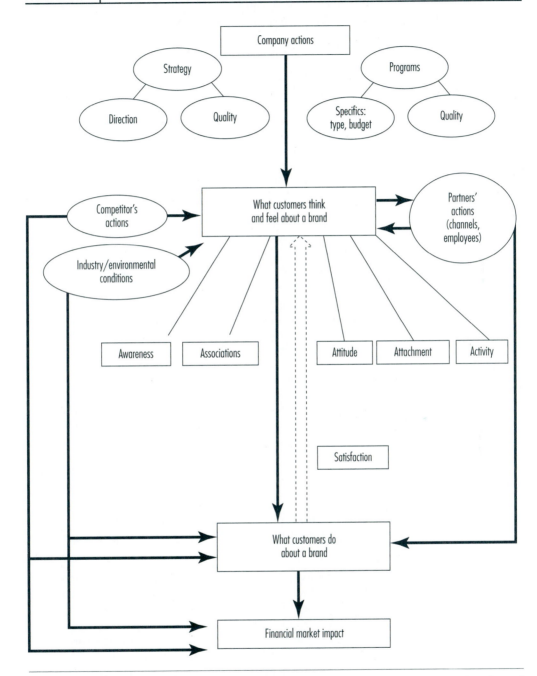

SOURCE: Reprinted by permission, Kevin Lane Keller and Donald R. Lehman, "Brands and Branding: Research Findings and Future Priorities," *Marketing Science* 25 (November/December 2006): p. 753. Copyright © 2006 INFORMS. Institute for Operations Research and the Management Sciences (INFORMS), 7240 Parkway Drive, Suite 300, Hanover, MD 21076 USA.

B2B TOP PERFORMERS

Corporate Brand Personality Traits of a Successful 21st-Century Business

While a product brand personality relates to consumer and user imagery for a specific product, a corporate brand personality centers on the human characteristics or traits of the employees of the corporation as a whole. So, a corporate brand personality is much broader and reflects the values, words, and actions of organizational members, individually and collectively.

Kevin Lane Keller and Keith Richey assert that the corporate brand personality traits of a successful 21st-century business can be defined on three dimensions, thereby guiding employees and influencing how the company will be perceived by customers and key stakeholders:

- The "heart" of the company consists of two traits: *passionate* and *compassionate*. The firm must be passionate about serving customers and demonstrate compassion for employees, suppliers, partners, and members of the communities in which it operates. (Through its customer-centric focus and support of numerous charitable initiatives, Southwest Airlines demonstrates these traits.)

- The "mind" of the company consists of two traits: *creative* and *disciplined*. A successful

firm must develop creative solutions for its customers and display a disciplined approach that is reflected in consistent actions across the organization. (Based on their success in new product development and superior strategy execution, Apple and Intel demonstrate these traits.)

- The "body" of the company includes two traits: *agile* and *collaborative*. The successful firm must have the agility to react quickly to changing market requirements and emphasize a collaborative approach that ensures effective working relationships across functions and with important stakeholders. (By responding quickly to market changes and pursuing relationship marketing strategies that are embraced by customers, channel partners, and alliance partners, Cisco aptly demonstrates these traits.)

SOURCE: Kevin Lane Keller and Keith Richey, "The Importance of Corporate Brand Personality Traits to a Successful 21st Century Business," *The Journal of Brand Management* 14 (September–November 2006): pp. 74–81. Reprinted by permission from Macmillan Publishers Ltd. Copyright 2006.

possible benefits to a firm such as greater customer loyalty, less vulnerability to competitive actions, higher profit margins, and greater cooperation and support from channel partners.

How Financial Markets React A host of business-to-business companies have launched brand-building initiatives, but do such investments generate positive returns? Some recent research on the brand attitude of buyers in evaluating computer-related firms provides some answers.[15] Brand attitude is a component and indicator of brand equity. **Brand attitude** is defined as the percentage of organizational buyers who have a positive image of a company minus those with a negative opinion. This study found that changes in brand attitude are associated with stock market performance and tend to lead accounting financial performance (that is, an increase in brand attitude will be reflected in improved financial performance three to six months later).

[15]David A. Aaker and Robert Jacobson, "The Value Relevance of Brand Attitude in High-Technology Markets," *Journal of Marketing Research* 38 (November 2001): pp. 485–493.

In short, the research demonstrates that investments in building brand attitude for high-technology firms do indeed pay off and increase the firm's value.

In another intriguing study, Thomas J. Madden, Frank Fehle, and Susan Fournier provide empirical evidence of the link between branding and shareholder value creation.[16] They found that a portfolio of brands identified as strong by the Interbrand/*Business Week* valuation method displays significant performance advantages compared to the overall market. "Firms that have developed strong brands create value for their shareholders by yielding returns that are greater in magnitude than a relevant market benchmark, and perhaps more important, do so with less risk."[17]

Product Quality and Customer Value

Rising customer expectations make product quality and customer value important strategic priorities. On a global scale, many international companies insist that suppliers, as a prerequisite for negotiations, meet quality standards set out by the Geneva-based International Standards Organization (ISO). These quality requirements, referred to as **ISO-9000 standards**, were developed for the European Community but have gained a global following.[18] Certification requires a supplier to thoroughly document its quality-assurance program. The certification program is becoming a seal of approval to compete for business not only overseas but also in the United States. For instance, the Department of Defense employs ISO standards in its contract guidelines. Although Japanese firms continue to set the pace in the application of sophisticated quality-control procedures in manufacturing, companies such as Kodak, AT&T, Xerox, Ford, Hewlett-Packard, Intel, GE, and others have made significant strides.

The quest for improved product quality touches the entire supply chain as these and other companies demand improved product quality from their suppliers, large and small. For example, GE has an organization-wide goal of achieving Six Sigma quality, meaning that a product would have a defect level of no more than 3.4 parts per million. Using the Six Sigma approach, GE measures every process, identifies the variables that lead to defects, and takes steps to eliminate them. GE also works directly to assist suppliers in using the approach. Overall, GE reports that Six Sigma has produced striking results—cost savings in the billions and fundamental improvements in product and service quality. Recently, GE has centered its Six Sigma efforts on functions that "teach customers," such as marketing and sales.[19]

Meaning of Quality

The quality movement has passed through several stages.[20] *Stage one* centered on conformance to standards or success in meeting specifications. But conformance quality or zero defects do not satisfy a customer if the product embodies the wrong features.

[16]Thomas J. Madden, Frank Fehle, and Susan Fournier, "Brands Matter: An Empirical Demonstration of the Creation of Shareholder Value Through Branding," *Journal of the Academy of Marketing Science* 34 (2, 2006): pp. 224–235.

[17]Ibid., pp. 232–233.

[18]Wade Ferguson, "Impact of ISO 9000 Series Standards on Industrial Marketing," *Industrial Marketing Management* 25 (July 1996): pp. 325–310.

[19]Erin White, "Rethinking the Quality-Improvement Program," *The Wall Street Journal*, September 19, 2005, p. B3.

[20]Bradley T. Gale, *Managing Customer Value: Creating Quality and Service That Customers Can See* (New York: The Free Press, 1994), pp. 25–30.

Stage two emphasized that quality was more than a technical specialty and that pursuing it should drive the core processes of the entire business. Particular emphasis was given to total quality management and measuring customer satisfaction. However, customers choose a particular product over competing offerings because they perceive it as providing superior *value*—the product's price, performance, and service render it the most attractive alternative. *Stage three*, then, examines a firm's quality performance relative to competitors and examines customer perceptions of the value of competing products. The focus here is on market-perceived quality and value versus that of competitors. Moreover, attention shifts from zero defects in products to zero defections of customers (that is, *customer loyalty*). Merely satisfying customers who have the freedom to make choices is not enough to keep them loyal.[21]

Meaning of Customer Value

Strategy experts Dwight Gertz and Joõa Baptista suggest that "a company's product or service is competitively superior if, at price equality with competing products, target segments always choose it. Thus, value is defined in terms of consumer choice in a competitive context."[22] In turn, the value equation includes a vital service component. For the service component, business marketing strategists must "recognize that specifications aren't just set by a manufacturer who tells the customer what to expect; instead, consumers also may participate in setting specifications." Frontline sales and service personnel add value to the product offering and the consumption experience by meeting or, indeed, exceeding the customer's service expectations.[23] **Customer value,** then, represents a "business customer's overall assessment of a relationship with a supplier based on perceptions of benefits received and sacrifices made."[24]

Benefits   Customer benefits take two forms (Figure 8.3):

1. *Core benefits*—the core requirements (for example specified product quality) for a relationship that suppliers must fully meet to be included in the customer's consideration set;

2. *Add-on benefits*—attributes that differentiate suppliers, go beyond the basic denominator provided by all qualified vendors, and create added value in a buyer-seller relationship (for example, value-added customer service).

Sacrifices   Consistent with the total cost perspective that business customers emphasize (Chapter 2), sacrifices include (1) the purchase price, (2) acquisition costs (for example, ordering and delivery costs), and (3) operations costs (for example, defect-free incoming shipments of component parts reduces operations costs).

[21]Thomas O. Jones and W. Earl Sasser, "Why Satisfied Customers Defect," *Harvard Business Review* 73 (November–December 1995): pp. 88–99; and Richard L. Oliver, "Whence Customer Loyalty," *Journal of Marketing* 63 (Special Issue 1999): pp. 33–44.

[22]Dwight L. Gertz and João P. A. Baptista, *Grow to Be Great: Breaking the Downsizing Cycle* (New York: The Free Press, 1995), p. 128.

[23]C. K. Prahalad and M. S. Krishnan, "The New Meaning of Quality in the Information Age," *Harvard Business Review* 77 (September–October 1999): pp. 109–112. See also, C. K. Prahalad and Venkat Ramaswamy, *The Future of Competition: Co-Creating Unique Value with Customers* (Boston: Harvard Business School Press, 2004).

[24]Ajay Menon, Christian Homburg, and Nikolas Beutin, "Understanding Customer Value in Business-to-Business Relationships," *Journal of Business-to-Business Marketing* 12 (2, 2005): p. 5. See also, Wolfgang Ulaga and Andreas Eggert, "Value-Based Differentiation in Business Relationships: Gaining and Sustaining Key Supplier Status," *Journal of Marketing* 70 (January 2006): pp. 119–136.

FIGURE 8.3 | **WHAT VALUE MEANS TO BUSINESS CUSTOMERS**

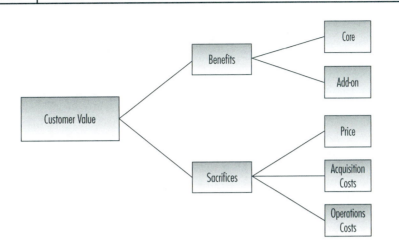

SOURCE: Adapted from Ajay Menon, Christian Homburg, and Nikolas Beutin, "Understanding Customer Value," *Journal of Business-to-Business Marketing* 12 (2, 2005): pp. 4–7.

What Matters Most?   Based on a large study of nearly 1,000 purchasing managers across a wide variety of product categories in the United States and Germany, Ajay Menon, Christian Homburg, and Nikolas Beutin uncovered some rich insights into customer value in business-to-business relationships.[25]

Add-on Benefits   First, the research demonstrates that add-on benefits more strongly influence customer value than do core benefits. Why? All qualified suppliers perform well on core benefits, so add-on benefits tend to be the differentiator for customer value as customers choose among competing offerings. Therefore, business marketers can use value-added services or joint working relationships that influence add-on benefits to strengthen customer relationships. For example, a leading manufacturer of tires for earthmoving equipment offers free consulting services that help customers design maintenance procedures that yield significant cost savings.[26]

Trust   Second, the study reinforces the vital role of trust in a business relationship (see Chapter 4), demonstrating, in fact, that trust has a stronger impact on core benefits than product characteristics.

Reducing Customer's Costs   Third, the results highlight the importance of marketing strategies that are designed to assist the customer in reducing operations costs. The research team observes:

> Ensuring on-time delivery of components and raw materials, getting involved in the customer firm's manufacturing and R&D strategy-making processes, and deploying resources needed to ensure a smooth relationship with the customer will help reduce the customer's operations costs.[27]

[25]Menon, Homburg, and Beutin, "Understanding Customer Value," pp. 1–33.

[26]Das Narayandas, "Building Loyalty in Business Markets," *Harvard Business Review* 83 (September–October 2005): p. 134.

[27]Menon, Homburg, and Beutin, "Understanding Customer Value," p. 25.

By pursuing such initiatives, the business marketer does not have to rely solely on price to demonstrate and deliver value to the customer.

Product Support Strategy: The Service Connection

The marketing function must ensure that every part of the organization focuses on delivering superior value to customers. Business marketing programs involve a number of critical components that customers carefully evaluate: tangible products, service support, and ongoing information services both before and after the sale. To provide value and to successfully implement these programs, the business marketing firm must carefully coordinate activities among personnel in product management, sales, and service.[28] For example, to customize a product and delivery schedule for an important customer requires close coordination among product, logistics, and sales personnel. Moreover, some customer accounts might require special field-engineering, installation, or equipment support, thereby increasing the required coordination between sales and service units.

Post-purchase service is especially important to buyers in many industrial product categories ranging from computers and machine tools to custom-designed component parts. Responsibility for service support, however, is often diffused throughout various departments, such as applications engineering, customer relations, or service administration. Significant benefits accrue to the business marketer who carefully manages and coordinates product, sales, and service connections to maximize customer value.

Product Policy

Product policy involves the set of all decisions concerning the products and services that the company offers. Through product policy, a business marketing firm attempts to satisfy customer needs and to build a sustainable competitive advantage by capitalizing on its core competencies. This section explores the types of industrial product lines and the importance of anchoring product-management decisions on an accurate definition of the product market. A framework is also provided for assessing product opportunities on a global scale.

Types of Product Lines Defined

Because product lines of industrial firms differ from those of consumer firms, classification is useful. Industrial product lines can be categorized into four types[29]:

1. **Proprietary or catalog products.** These items are offered only in certain configurations and produced in anticipation of orders. Product-line decisions concern adding, deleting, or repositioning products in the line.

2. **Custom-built products.** These items are offered as a set of basic units, with numerous accessories and options. For example, NCR offers a line of retail

---

[28]Frank V. Cespedes, *Concurrent Marketing: Integrating Product, Sales, and Service* (Boston: Harvard Business School Press, 1995), pp. 58–85.

[29]Benson P. Shapiro, *Industrial Product Policy: Managing the Existing Product Line* (Cambridge, MA: Marketing Science Institute, 1977), pp. 37–39.

workstations used by large customers like Wal-Mart and 7-Eleven stores as well as by smaller businesses. The basic workstation can be expanded to connect to scanners, check readers, electronic payment devices, and other accessories to meet a business's particular needs. The firm's wide array of products provides retailers with an end-to-end solution, from data warehousing to the point-of-service workstation at checkout. The marketer offers the organizational buyer a set of building blocks. Product-line decisions center on offering the proper mix of options and accessories.

3. **Custom-designed products.** These items are created to meet the needs of one or a small group of customers. Sometimes the product is a unique unit, such as a power plant or a specific machine tool. In addition, some items produced in relatively large quantities, such as an aircraft model, may fall into this category. The product line is described in terms of the company's capability, and the consumer buys that capability. Ultimately, this capability is transformed into a finished good. For example, after canvassing airlines around the world, Airbus detected enough interest in a super jumbo jet to proceed with development.[30]

4. **Industrial services.** Rather than an actual product, the buyer is purchasing a company's capability in an area such as maintenance, technical service, or management consulting. (Special attention is given to services marketing in Chapter 10.)

All types of business marketing firms confront product policy decisions, whether they offer physical products, pure services (no physical product), or a product-service combination.[31] Each product situation presents unique problems and opportunities for the business marketer; each draws on a unique capability. Product strategy rests on the intelligent use of corporate capability.

Defining the Product Market

Accurately defining the product market is fundamental to sound product-policy decisions.[32] Careful attention must be given to the alternative ways to satisfy customer needs. For example, many different products could provide competition for personal computers. Application-specific products, such as enhanced pocket pagers and smart phones that send e-mail and connect to the Web, are potential competitors. A wide array of information appliances that provide easy access to the Internet also pose a threat. In such an environment, Regis McKenna maintains, managers "must look for opportunities in—and expect competition from—every possible direction. A company with a narrow product concept will move through the market with blinders on, and it is sure to run into trouble."[33] By excluding products and technology that compete for the same end-user needs, the product strategist can quickly become out of touch with the market. Both customer needs and the ways of satisfying those needs change.

[30]Alex Taylor III, "Blue Skies for Airbus," *Fortune*, April 1, 1999, pp. 102–108.

[31]Albert L. Page and Michael Siemplenski, "Product-Systems Marketing," *Industrial Marketing Management* 12 (April 1983): pp. 89–99.

[32]For a related discussion on competitive analysis, see Beth A. Walker, Dimitri Kapelianis, and Michael D. Hutt, "Competitive Cognition," *MIT Sloan Management Review* 46 (Summer 2005): pp. 10–12.

[33]McKenna, *Relationship Marketing*, p. 184.

Product Market   A **product market** establishes the distinct arena in which the business marketer competes. Four dimensions of a market definition are strategically relevant:

1. *Customer function dimension.* This involves the benefits that are provided to satisfy the needs of organizational buyers (for example, mobile messaging).

2. *Technological dimension.* There are alternative ways a particular function can be performed (for example, cell phone, pager, notebook computer).

3. *Customer segment dimension.* Customer groups have distinct needs that must be served (for example, sales representatives, physicians, international travelers).

4. *Value-added system dimension.* Competitors serving the market can operate along a sequence of stages.[34] The value-added system for wireless communication includes equipment providers, such as Nokia and Motorola, and service providers, like Verizon and AT&T. Analysis of the value-added system may indicate potential opportunities or threats from changes in the system (for example, potential alliances between equipment and service providers).

Planning for Today and Tomorrow   Competition to satisfy the customer's need exists at the technology level as well as at the supplier or brand level. By establishing accurate product-market boundaries, the product strategist is better equipped to identify customer needs, the benefits sought by the market segment, and the turbulent nature of competition at both the technology and supplier or brand levels. Derek Abell offers these valuable strategy insights:

• Planning for today requires a clear, precise *definition* of the business—a delineation of target customer segments, customer functions, and the business approach to be taken; planning for tomorrow is concerned with how the business should be *redefined* for the future.

• Planning for today focuses on *shaping up* the business to meet the needs of today's customers with excellence. It involves identifying factors that are critical to success and smothering them with attention; planning for tomorrow can entail *reshaping* the business to compete more effectively in the future.[35]

Seeing What's Next   Strategy experts also argue provocatively that many firms are overlooking three important customer groups that may present the greatest opportunity for explosive growth[36]:

• *Nonconsumers* who may lack the specialized skills, training, or resources to purchase the product or service;

• *Undershot customers* for whom existing products are not good enough;

• *Overshot customers* for whom existing products provide more performance than they can use.

---

[34]George S. Day, *Strategic Market Planning: The Pursuit of Competitive Advantage* (St. Paul, MN: West, 1984), p. 73.

[35]Derek F. Abell, "Competing Today While Preparing for Tomorrow," *Sloan Management Review* 40 (Spring 1999): p. 74.

[36]Clayton M. Christensen, Scott D. Anthony, and Erik A. Roth, *Seeing What's Next* (Boston: Harvard Business School Press, 2004), p. 5.

B2B TOP PERFORMERS

BASF: Using Services to Build a Strong Brand

BASF AG, headquartered in Germany, is the world's largest chemical company, with global sales over $33 billion and North American sales of $8 billion. Consistently ranked as one of *Fortune*'s most admired global companies, the firm competes in what many would describe as a commodity business. Rather than pursue a low-total-cost strategy and compete on price, BASF decided to transform itself into an innovative service-oriented company. Services, like R&D support or on-site field services, are hard for rivals to duplicate and when well executed, provide the ultimate differentiation strategy. To communicate its value proposition to customers, the firm launched its advertising campaign with the familiar tag line:

> "We don't make a lot of products you buy.
> We make a lot of the products you buy better."

A senior executive at BASF's ad agency, Tony Graetzer, describes the rationale for this campaign, which has been recognized with numerous awards: "Companies are frequently viewed as tied on the quality of their products, but they are never viewed as tied on the quality of their services." Winning companies provide superior service. By emphasizing how it helps make its customers' products better and delivering on its promises, the BASF brand has become synonymous with customer partnerships and technology leadership.

SOURCE: Bob Lamons, *The Case for B2B Branding* (Mason, Ohio: Thomson, 2005), pp. 91–94.

Planning Industrial Product Strategy

Formulating a strategic marketing plan for an existing product line is the most vital part of a company's marketing planning efforts. Having identified a product market, attention now turns to planning product strategy. Product-positioning analysis provides a useful tool for charting the strategy course.

Product Positioning

Once the product market is defined, a strong competitive position for the product must be secured. **Product positioning** represents the place that a product occupies in a particular market; it is found by measuring organizational buyers' perceptions and preferences for a product in relation to its competitors. Because organizational buyers perceive products as bundles of attributes (for example, quality, service), the product strategist should examine the attributes that assume a central role in buying decisions.

The Process[37]

Observe from Figure 8.4 that the positioning process begins by identifying the relevant set of competing products (Step 1) and defining those attributes that are **determinant** (Step 2)—attributes that customers use to differentiate among the alternatives

---

[37]This section is based on Harper W. Boyd Jr., Orville C. Walker Jr., and Jean-Claude Larréché, *Marketing Management: A Strategic Approach with a Global Orientation* (Chicago: Irwin/McGraw-Hill, 1998), pp. 190–200.

FIGURE 8.4 | **STEPS IN THE PRODUCT-POSITIONING PROCESS**

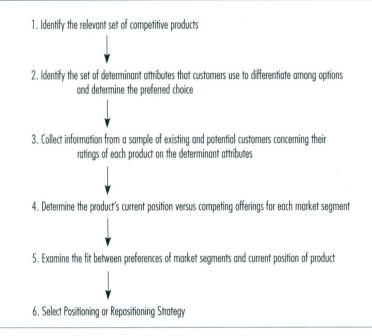

1. Identify the relevant set of competitive products

2. Identify the set of determinant attributes that customers use to differentiate among options and determine the preferred choice

3. Collect information from a sample of existing and potential customers concerning their ratings of each product on the determinant attributes

4. Determine the product's current position versus competing offerings for each market segment

5. Examine the fit between preferences of market segments and current position of product

6. Select Positioning or Repositioning Strategy

SOURCE: Adapted with modifications from Harper W. Boyd Jr., Orville C. Walker Jr., and Jean-Claude Larréché, *Marketing Management: A Strategic Approach with a Global Orientation* (Chicago: Irwin/McGraw-Hill, 1998), p. 197.

and that are important to them in determining which brand they prefer. In short, then, determinant attributes are choice criteria that are both important and differentiating. Of course, some attributes are important to organizational buyers, but they may not be differentiating. For example, safety might be an important attribute in the heavy-duty truck market, but business market customers may consider the competing products offered by Navistar, Volvo, and Mack Trucks as quite comparable on this dimension. Durability, reliability, and fuel economy might constitute the determinant attributes.

Step 3 involves collecting information from a sample of existing and potential customers concerning how they perceive the various options on each of the determinant attributes. The sample should include buyers (particularly buying influentials) from organizations that represent the full array of market segments the product strategist wishes to serve. After examining the product's current position versus competing offerings (Step 4), the analyst can isolate (1) the competitive strength of the product in different segments and (2) the opportunities for securing a differentiated position in a particular target segment (Step 5).

Isolating Strategy Opportunities

Step 6 involves the selection of the positioning or repositioning strategy. Here the product manager can evaluate particular strategy options. First, for some attributes, the product manager may wish to (1) pursue a strategy to increase the importance of an attribute to customers and (2) increase the difference between the competition's and the firm's products. For example, the importance of an attribute such as customer training might be elevated through marketing communications emphasizing how the potential buyer can increase its efficiency and employee performance through the firm's training. If successful, such efforts might move customer training from an important attribute to a determinant attribute in the eyes of customers. Second, if the firm's performance on a determinant product attribute is truly higher than that of competitors—but the market perceives that other alternatives enjoy an edge—marketing communications can be developed to bring perceptions in line with reality. Third, the competitive standing of a product can be advanced by improving the firm's level of performance on determinant attributes that organizational buyers emphasize.

Product Positioning Illustrated[38]

This product positioning approach was successfully applied to a capital equipment product at a major corporation. The product that provided the focus of the analysis is sold in three sizes to two market segments: end users and consulting engineers. Marketing research identified 15 attributes, including reliability, service support, company reputation, and ease of maintenance.

A New Strategy   The research found that the firm's brand enjoyed an outstanding rating on product reliability and service support. Both attributes were generally determinant for the company against most competitors. To reinforce the importance of both attributes, management decided to offer an enhanced warranty program. Both end users and consulting engineers view warranties as important but not a point of differentiation across competing brands. Management surmised, however, that by establishing a new warranty standard for the industry, the attribute could become determinant, adding to the brand's leverage over competitors. In addition, management felt that the new warranty program might also benefit the brand's reputation on other attributes such as reliability and company reputation.

Better Targeting   The study also provided some surprises. Price was not nearly as important to organizational buyers as management had initially believed. This suggested that there were opportunities to increase revenue through product differentiation and service support. Likewise, the research found that the firm's brand dominated all competitors in the large- and medium-sized products, but not in the small-sized products. This particular product had an especially weak competitive position in the consulting engineer segment. Special service support strategies were developed to strengthen the product's standing in this segment. Clearly, product positioning provides a valuable tool for designing creative strategies for business markets.

The Technology Adoption Life Cycle

After decades of being content with letters, telegrams, and telephones, consumers have embraced voice-mail, e-mail, Internet browsers, and a range of information appliances. In each case, the conversion of the market came slowly. Once a particular threshold of consumer acceptance was achieved, there was a stampede. Geoffrey

---

[38]This section is based largely on Behram J. Hansotia, Muzaffar A. Shaikh, and Jagdish N. Sheth, "The Strategic Determinancy Approach to Brand Management," *Business Marketing* 70 (Fall 1985): pp. 66–69.

TABLE 8.1 | THE TECHNOLOGY ADOPTION LIFE CYCLE: CLASSES OF CUSTOMERS

Customer	Profile
Technology enthusiasts (*innovators*)	Interested in exploring the latest innovation, these consumers possess significant influence over how products are perceived by others in the organization but lack control over resource commitments.
Visionaries (*early adopters*)	Desiring to exploit the innovation for a competitive advantage, these consumers are the true revolutionaries in business and government who have access to organizational resources but frequently demand special modifications to the product that are difficult for the innovator to provide.
Pragmatists (*early majority*)	Making the bulk of technology purchases in organizations, these individuals believe in technology evolution, not revolution, and seek products from a market leader with a proven track record of providing useful productivity improvements.
Conservatives (*late majority*)	Pessimistic about their ability to derive any value from technology investments, these individuals represent a sizable group of customers who are price sensitive and reluctantly purchase high-tech products to avoid being left behind.
Skeptics (*laggards*)	Rather than potential customers, these individuals are ever-present critics of the hype surrounding high-technology products.

SOURCE: Adapted from Geoffrey A. Moore, *Inside the Tornado: Marketing Strategies from Silicon Valley's Cutting Edge* (New York: HarperCollins, 1995), pp. 14–18.

Moore defines **discontinuous innovations** as "new products or services that require the end-user and the marketplace to dramatically change their past behavior, with the promise of gaining equally dramatic new benefits."[39] During the past quarter century, discontinuous innovations have been common in the computer-electronics industry, creating massive new spending, fierce competition, and a whole host of firms that are redrawing the boundaries of the high-technology marketplace.

A popular tool with strategists at high-technology firms is the technology adoption life cycle—a framework developed by Geoffrey Moore, a leading consultant to Hewlett-Packard and a host of other Silicon Valley firms.

Types of Technology Customers

Fundamental to Moore's framework are five classes of customers who constitute the potential market for a discontinuous innovation (Table 8.1). Business marketers can benefit by putting innovative products in the hands of **technology enthusiasts**. They serve as a gatekeeper to the rest of the technology life cycle, and their endorsement is needed for an innovation to get a fair hearing in the organization. Whereas technology enthusiasts possess influence, they do not have ready access to the resources needed to move an organization toward a large-scale commitment to the new technology.

---

[39]Geoffrey A. Moore, *Inside the Tornado: Marketing Strategies from Silicon Valley's Cutting Edge* (New York: HarperCollins, 1995), p. 13.

INSIDE BUSINESS MARKETING

The Gorilla Advantage in High-Tech Markets

High-tech companies that can get their products designed into the very standards of the market have enormous influence over the future direction of that market. For example, all PC-based software has to be Microsoft- and Intel-compatible. All networking solutions must be compatible with Cisco Systems' standards; all printers must be Hewlett-Packard–compatible. This is the essence of gorilla power in high-tech markets that firms such as Microsoft, Intel, Cisco, and Hewlett-Packard enjoy. The gorilla advantage allows these market leaders to

- *Attract more customers* by enjoying better press coverage and shorter sales cycles just because information technology managers expect it to be the winner;

- *Keep more customers* because the cost of switching is high for customers and the cost of entry is high for competitors;

- *Drive costs down* by shifting some costly enhancements that customers demand to suppliers while retaining control of the critical components of value creation;

- *Keep profits up* because business partners place a priority on developing complementary products and services that make the *whole product* of the market leader worth more to customers than competing products are worth.

The Internet presents an explosive area of growth in many sectors of the high-tech market as firms square off to gain a leadership position in e-procurement, wireless technologies, supply chain integration, and Web-focused security. The gorilla games are just beginning!

SOURCE: Geoffrey A. Moore, Paul Johnson, and Tom Kippola, *The Gorilla Game: An Investor's Guide to Picking Winners in High-Technology* (New York: HarperBusiness, 1998), pp. 43–70.

By contrast, **visionaries** have resource control and can often be influential in publicizing an innovation's benefits and giving it a boost during the early stages of market development. However, visionaries are difficult for a marketer to serve because each demands special and unique product modifications. Their demands can quickly tax a technology firm's R&D resources and stall the market penetration of the innovation.

The Chasm   Truly innovative products often enjoy a warm welcome from early technology enthusiasts and visionaries, but then sales falter and often even plummet. Frequently, a chasm develops between visionaries who are intuitive and support revolution and the **pragmatists** who are analytical, support evolution, and provide the pathway to the mainstream market. The business marketer that can successfully guide a product across the chasm creates an opportunity to gain acceptance with the mainstream market of pragmatists and conservatives. As Table 8.1 relates, pragmatists make most technology purchases in organizations, and conservatives include a sizable group of customers who are hesitant to buy high-tech products but do so to avoid being left behind.

Strategies for the Technology Adoption Life Cycle

The fundamental strategy for crossing the chasm and moving from the early market to the mainstream market is to provide pragmatists with a 100 percent solution to their problems (Figure 8.5). Many high-technology firms err by attempting to provide something for everyone while never meeting the complete requirements of any

FIGURE 8.5 | THE LANDSCAPE OF THE TECHNOLOGY ADOPTION LIFE CYCLE

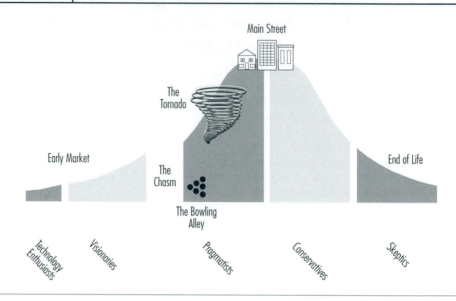

particular market segment. Pragmatists seek the whole product—the minimum set of products and services that provide them with a compelling reason to buy. Geoffrey Moore notes that "the key to a winning strategy is to identify a simple beachhead of pragmatist customers in a mainstream market segment and to accelerate the formation of 100 percent of their whole product. The goal is to win a niche foothold in the mainstream as quickly as possible—that is what is meant by *crossing the chasm*."[40]

The Bowling Alley

In technology markets, each market segment is like a bowling pin, and the momentum from hitting one segment successfully carries over into surrounding segments. The bowling alley represents a stage in the adoption life cycle where a product gains acceptance from mainstream market segments but has yet to be adopted widely.

Consider the evolution of strategy for Lotus Notes.[41] When first introduced, Notes was offered as a new paradigm for corporate-wide communication. To cross into the mainstream market, the Lotus team shifted the product's focus from an enterprise-wide vision of corporate communication to specific solutions for particular business functions. The first niche served was the global account-management function of worldwide accounting and consulting firms. The solution was enhanced account activity coordination for highly visible products. This led to a second niche—global account management for sales teams, where enhanced coordination and information sharing spur productivity.

---

[40]Ibid., p. 22. For a related discussion, see Clayton M. Christensen and Michael E. Raynor, *The Innovator's Solution: Creating and Sustaining Successful Growth* (Boston: Harvard Business School Press, 2003), pp. 73–95.

[41]Moore, *Inside the Tornado*, pp. 35–37.

A Focused Strategy A logical next step for Lotus was movement into the customer service function, where openly sharing information can support creative solutions to customer problems. Successful penetration of these segments created another opportunity—incorporating the customer into the Notes loop. Note the key lesson here: A customer-based, application-focused strategy provides leverage so that a victory in one market segment cascades into victories in adjacent market segments.

The Tornado

Although economic buyers who seek particular solutions are the key to success in the bowling alley, technical or infrastructure buyers in organizations can spawn a tornado (see Figure 8.5). Information technology (IT) managers are responsible for providing efficient and reliable infrastructures—the systems organizational members use to communicate and perform their jobs. They are pragmatists, and they prefer to buy from an established market leader.

IT professionals interact freely across company and industry boundaries and discuss the ramifications of the latest technology. IT managers watch each other closely—they do not want to be too early or too late. Often, they move together and create a tornado. Because a massive number of new customers are entering the market at the same time and because they all want the same product, demand dramatically outstrips supply and a large backlog of customers can appear overnight. At a critical stage, such market forces have surrounded Hewlett-Packard's laser and inkjet printers, Microsoft's Windows products, Intel's Pentium microprocessors, and Research in Motion's BlackBerry device.

Tornado Strategy The central success factors for the tornado phase of the adoption life cycle differ from those that are appropriate for the bowling alley. Rather than emphasizing market segmentation, the central goal is to gear up production to capitalize on the opportunity the broad market presents. In its printer business, Hewlett-Packard demonstrated the three critical priorities during a tornado[42]:

1. "Just ship."
2. Extend distribution channels.
3. Drive to the next lower price point.

First, Hewlett-Packard's quality improvement process allowed it to significantly increase production—first with laser printers, and later with inkjet printers—with few interruptions. Second, to extend market coverage, H-P began to sell its laser printers through PC dealer channels and extended its distribution channels for inkjet printers to computer superstores, office superstores, mail order, and, more recently, to price clubs and other consumer outlets. Third, H-P drove down the price points for its printers—moving inkjet printers below $1,000, then below $500, and then well below that. As this example demonstrates, tornado strategy emphasizes product leadership and operational excellence in manufacturing and distribution.

---

[42]Ibid., p. 81. See also Stephen Kreider Yoder, "Shaving Back: How H-P Used Tactics of the Japanese to Beat Them at Their Game," *The Wall Street Journal*, September 8, 1994, pp. A1, A6.

Main Street

This stage of the technology adoption life cycle represents a period of aftermarket development. The frantic waves of mass-market adoption of the product begin to subside. Competitors in the industry have increased production, and supply now exceeds demand. Moore points out that "the defining characteristic of Main Street is that continued profitable market growth can no longer come from selling the basic commodity to new customers and must come instead from developing niche-specific extensions to the basic platform for existing customers."[43]

Main Street Strategy   The goal here is to develop value-based strategies targeted to particular end-user segments. H-P, for example, matches its printers to the special needs of different segments of home-office users by offering

- A compact portable printer for those users who are space-constrained;
- The OfficeJet printer-fax for those who do not yet own a fax;
- A high-performance color printer for those who create commercial flyers.

Main Street strategy emphasizes operational excellence in production and distribution as well as finely tuned market segmentation strategies. What signals the end of the technology adoption life cycle? A discontinuous innovation appears that incorporates breakthrough technology and promises new solutions for customers.

Summary

Some of the most valuable and enduring global brands belong to business-to-business firms. The power of a brand resides in the minds of customers through what they have experienced, seen, and heard about the brand over time. The customer-based brand equity model consists of four steps: establishing the right brand identity, defining the meaning of the brand through unique brand associations, developing responsive marketing programs to elicit a positive brand response from customers, and building brand relationships with customers, marked by loyalty and active engagement. Research vividly demonstrates that investments in building a strong brand yield a positive payoff in the financial performance of the firm.

Conceptualizing a product must go beyond mere physical description to include all the benefits and services that provide value to customers. The unifying goal for the business marketer: *Provide superior market-perceived quality and value versus competitors.* To a business customer, value involves a trade-off between benefits and sacrifices. Business marketers can strengthen customer relationships by providing value-added services and helping customers reduce operations costs. A carefully coordinated product strategy recognizes the role of various functional areas in providing value to business customers. Special attention should be given to synchronizing the activities among the product-management, sales, and service units.

Industrial product lines can be broadly classified into (1) proprietary or catalog items, (2) custom-built items, (3) custom-designed items, and (4) industrial services.

---

[43]Moore, *Inside the Tornado*, p. 111.

Product management can best be described as the management of capability. In monitoring product performance and in formulating marketing strategy, the business marketer can profitably use product-positioning analysis. By isolating a product's competitive standing in a market, positioning analysis provides strategy insights to the planner. A product attribute is determinant if it is both important and differentiating.

Rapidly changing high-technology markets present special opportunities and challenges for the product strategist. The technology adoption life cycle includes five categories of customers: technology enthusiasts, visionaries, pragmatists, conservatives, and skeptics. New products gain acceptance from niches within the mainstream market, progress from segment to segment like one bowling pin knocking over another, and, if successful, experience the tornado of general, widespread adoption by pragmatists. Importantly, the technology adoption life cycle calls for different marketing strategies at different stages.

Discussion Questions

1. Evaluate this statement: A brand is much more than a name, and branding is a strategy problem, not a naming problem.

2. Identify two business-to-business brands that you would deem to be strong and distinctive. Next, describe the characteristics of each brand that tend to set it apart from rival brands.

3. Using the customer-based brand equity framework as a guide, describe the distinctive components of Apple's brand strategy.

4. Describe why a brand-positioning strategy should include points of difference and points of parity. Provide an illustration to support your case.

5. Regis McKenna notes that "no company in a technology-based industry is safe from unanticipated bumps in the night." In recent years, many industries have been jolted by technological change. In such an environment, what steps can a product strategist take?

6. Bradley Gale, managing director of The Strategic Planning Institute, says: "People systematically knock out income statements and balance sheets, but they often don't monitor the nonfinancial factors that ultimately drive their financial performance. These nonfinancial factors include 'relative customer-perceived quality': how customers view the marketer's offering versus how they perceive competitive offerings." Explain.

7. Distinguish among catalog items, custom-built items, custom-designed items, and services. Explain how marketing requirements vary across these classifications.

8. A particular product strategy will stimulate a response from the market and a corresponding response from competitors. Which specific features of the competitive environment should the business marketing strategist evaluate?

9. Moving across the technology adoption life cycle, compare and contrast technology enthusiasts with pragmatists. Give special attention to the strategy guidelines that the marketing strategist should follow in reaching customers that fall into these two adoption categories.

10. Firms like Microsoft, Apple, Sony, and Intel have experienced a burst of demand for some of their products. During the "tornado" for a high-tech product, the guiding principle of operations for a market leader is "Just ship." Explain and discuss the changes in marketing strategy the firm must follow after the tornado.

Internet Exercise

1. United Technologies Corporation (UTC) provides a broad range of high-technology products and support services to the building systems and aerospace industries. Go to http://www.utc.com and identify UTC's major businesses (product lines).

Cisco TelePresence: The "As if you were there" Technology[44]

Research demonstrates that visual clues—such as raising an eyebrow or slumping the shoulders—comprise more than 50 percent of the information conveyed in a conversation. Unfortunately, until now, video technologies failed to provide the necessary fidelity to transmit these revealing clues effectively. However, Cisco Systems has created a two-way video communications system that preserves all those important nuances, in the process pioneering a new form of digital communications that rivals the effectiveness of in-person meetings. Twenty-five patents are pending for the Cisco TelePresence "as if you were there" technology. One industry analyst observed that video conferencing is like riding a 10-speed bike while TelePresence is like driving a Ferrari.

Benefits

By reducing the need for in-person face-to-face meetings, organizations can reap significant benefits from reduced travel costs, greater productivity, and better relationships with customers and partners. For global companies, executive travel is disruptive, costly, and time-consuming. Why travel to meet in person if you can communicate just as effectively through TelePresence?

The Price Tag

The Cisco TelePresence 3000 costs approximately $300,000 for each installation, or room, plus additional support costs. By contrast, the Cisco TelePresence 1000 is priced at $80,000 per room. As the price of key TelePresence technologies, such as plasma screens and broadband connections, will almost certainly continue to decline rapidly, Cisco believes that the system will enjoy a wider array of applications, making it affordable for more organizations and even for individuals from home.

Discussion Questions

1. Using the technology life cycle as a framework, propose particular marketing strategies that Cisco might employ to "cross the chasm."

2. Identify particular market segments that Cisco might target for the TelePresence product.

---

[44]"Cisco Brings 'In-Person' Realism to Virtual Communications," accessed at http://www.cisco.com/en/US/products/ps7060/index.html on July 15, 2008.

Managing Innovation and New Industrial Product Development

The long-term competitive position of most organizations is tied to their ability to innovate—to provide existing and new customers with a continuing stream of new products and services. Innovation is a high-risk and potentially rewarding process. After reading this chapter, you will understand:

1. the strategic processes, both formal and informal, through which product innovations take shape.

2. the characteristics of innovation winners in high-technology markets.

3. the factors that drive a firm's new product performance.

4. the determinants of new product success and timeliness.

With his American swagger and his hair bleached white, Tony Fadell stood out at button-down Philips Electronics, where he led an in-house operation designing . . . consumer electronics devices. It was there that he came up with the idea of marrying a Napster-like music store with a hard drive-based MP3 player. He shopped the concept around the Valley before Apple's Jon Rubenstein snapped it up and put Fadell in charge of the engineering team that built the first iPod.[1]

Once prototypes were developed, CEO Steve Jobs worked closely with the team and was instrumental in molding the shape, feel, and design of the device.[2] "Ambitious and charismatic (and no longer a bleached blond), Tony now runs the hardware division that makes two of Apple's three product lines: the iPod and the iPhone."[3]

Many firms derive much of their sales and profits from recently introduced products. Indeed, best-practice firms generate about 48 percent of sales and 45 percent of profits from products commercialized in the past five years.[4] But the risks of product innovation are high; significant investments are involved and the likelihood of failure is high. With shortening product life cycles and accelerating technological change, speed and agility are central to success in the innovation battle.

This chapter examines product innovation in the business marketing environment. The first section provides a perspective on the firm's management of innovation. Second, product innovation is positioned within a firm's overall technological strategy. Third, key dimensions of the new-product-development process are examined. Attention centers on the forces that drive successful new product performance in the firm. The final section of the chapter explores the determinants of new product success and timeliness.

The Management of Innovation

Management practices in successful industrial firms reflect the realities of the innovation process itself. James Quinn asserts that "innovation tends to be individually motivated, opportunistic, customer responsive, tumultuous, nonlinear, and interactive in its development. Managers can plan overall directions and goals, but surprises are likely to abound."[5] Clearly, some new-product-development efforts are the outgrowth of deliberate strategies (intended strategies that become realized), whereas others result from emergent strategies (realized strategies that, at least initially, were never intended).[6] Bearing little resemblance to a rational, analytical process, many strategic decisions involving new products are rather messy, disorderly, and disjointed processes around which competing organizational factions contend. In studying

[1]"After Steve Jobs: Apple's Next CEO—Tony Fadell (2)," June 26, 2008, accessed at http://money.cnn.com/galleries/2008/fortune/0806/gallery.apple_jobs_successors.fortune/2.html on July 16, 2008.

[2]Leander Kahney, "Inside Look at Birth of iPod," July 21, 2004, accessed at http://www.wired.com/gadgets/mac/news/2004/07/64286 on June 3, 2008.

[3]"After Steve Jobs: Apple's Next CEO."

[4]John Hauser, Gerald J. Tellis, and Abbie Griffin, "Research on Innovation: A Review and Agenda for *Marketing Science*," *Marketing Science* 25 (November–December 2006): p. 707.

[5]James B. Quinn, "Managing Innovation: Controlled Chaos," *Harvard Business Review* 63 (May–June 1985): p. 83.

[6]Henry Mintzberg and James A. Walton, "Of Strategies, Deliberate and Emergent," *Strategic Management Journal* 6 (July–August 1985): pp. 257–272.

successful innovative companies such as Sony, AT&T, and Hewlett-Packard, Quinn characterized the innovation process as controlled chaos:

> Many of the best concepts and solutions come from projects partly hidden or "bootlegged" by the organization. Most successful managers try to build some slack or buffers into their plans to hedge their bets. . . . They permit chaos and replications in early investigations, but insist on much more formal planning and controls as expensive development and scale-up proceed. But even at these later stages, these managers have learned to maintain flexibility and to avoid the tyranny of paper plans.[7]

Some new products result from a planned, deliberate process, but others follow a more circuitous and chaotic route.[8] Why? Research suggests that strategic activity within a large organization falls into two broad categories: induced and autonomous strategic behavior.[9]

Induced Strategic Behavior

Induced strategic behavior is consistent with the firm's traditional concept of strategy. It takes place in relationship to its familiar external environment (for example, its customary markets). By manipulating various administrative mechanisms, top management can influence the perceived interests of managers at the organization's middle and operational levels and keep strategic behavior in line with the current strategy course. For example, existing reward and measurement systems may direct managers' attention to some market opportunities and not to others. Examples of induced strategic behavior or deliberate strategies might emerge around product-development efforts for existing markets.

Autonomous Strategic Behavior

During any period, most strategic activity in large, complex firms is likely to fit into the induced behavior category. However, large, resource-rich firms are likely to possess a pool of entrepreneurial potential at operational levels, which expresses itself in autonomous strategic initiatives. The 3M Company encourages its technical employees to devote 15 percent of their work time to developing their own ideas. Through the personal efforts of individual employees, new products are born. For example,

- Gary Fadell is the engineering genius behind the iPod.

- Art Fry championed Post-it notes at 3M.

- P. D. Estridge promoted the personal computer at IBM.

- Stephanie L. Kwolek advanced the bulletproof material Kevlar at DuPont.

- Michimosa Fujino championed the HondaJet (see Figure 9.1) that may shake up the small-jet business with the same value proposition—high fuel efficiency and sleek design—that the first-generation Honda Civic used to rattle U.S. auto manufacturers 30 years ago.[10]

---

[7]Quinn, "Managing Innovation," p. 82.

[8]This section is based on Michael D. Hutt, Peter H. Reingen, and John R. Ronchetto Jr., "Tracing Emergent Processes in Marketing Strategy Formation," *Journal of Marketing* 52 (January 1988): pp. 4–19.

[9]Robert A. Burgelman, "A Process Model of Internal Corporate Venturing in the Diversified Major Firm," *Administrative Science Quarterly* 28 (April 1983): pp. 223–244.

[10]This discussion is based on Norihiko Shirouzu, "Mr. Fujino's Bumpy Flight Lands Honda in the Jet Age," *The Wall Street Journal*, June 18, 2007, pp. B1 and B3.

FIGURE 9.1 | CHAMPIONING THE HONDAJET: KEY MILESTONES

Michimasa Fujino, who is now president of Honda Aircraft Company, began work on the project more than two decades ago. He was assigned to a small Honda team that was sent to Mississippi State University to collaborate with the school on advanced aeronautics. By the mid-1990s, the team developed a jet called MH02 that featured a fuselage made of composite materials rather than aluminum. Believing that the design would not be competitive, the company executives killed the project in 1996.

Mr. Fujino then began work on an unorthodox design that would prove critical to the HondaJet's performance: putting the engine above the wing rather than under the wing or at the rear of the fuselage. After presenting the novel design at a critical board meeting, Mr. Fujino rekindled executive support for the project. Key milestones in HondaJet's development process include:

1997	Michimasa Fujino first sketches HondaJet design with unique over-the-wing engine mount
1999	The HondaJet's unique configuration is finalized
2000	Honda establishes a research facility in North Carolina and HondaJet structural design begins
2001	Extensive ground tests validate the HondaJet's innovative design
2003	HondaJet takes its first test flight
2005	Performance tests continue and HondaJet makes its world debut at major Wisconsin air show
2006	Honda Aircraft Company is established and HondaJet begins sales
2007	Honda Aircraft Company announces plans for world headquarters and HondaJet production in North Carolina
2010	Delivery to customers scheduled to begin

SOURCE: Norihiko Shirouzu, "Mr. Fujino's Bumpy Flight Lands Honda in the Jet Age," *Wall Street Journal*, June 18, 2007, p. B1, B3 and the timeline is from http://www.hondajet.com, accessed on November 15, 2008.

"Civic of the Sky"   Senior executives at Honda and industry analysts alike believe that the HondaJet can quickly gain 10 percent of the small-jet market and turn a profit in three to four years. Compared to the popular Cessna Citation CJ1+ that seats four to six passengers, the HondaJet is priced at $3.65 million, $880,000 below the Cessna, uses about 22 percent less fuel, has 20 percent more passenger cabin space, and boasts the fit and finish of a luxury car.

Now in his mid-forties, Mr. Fujino has tirelessly promoted his idea for two decades. He succeeded in keeping the project alive by nurturing ties to senior executives and by tying his risk-taking to Honda's broader efforts to rekindle a spirit of innovation. Although formal reviews of the jet project have been intense and even "ugly" at times, he persevered because, behind the scenes, some senior executives enthusiastically supported his efforts. A crucial turning point for the project came at a critical board meeting where Mr. Fujino was presenting the idea. After an awkward start and what he describes as a "cold glaze" from some board members, "he was able to drive home the jet's potential when he analogized it to Honda's breakthrough car, calling the jet a 'Civic of the sky.'"[11]

Autonomous strategic behavior is conceptually equivalent to entrepreneurial activity and introduces new categories of opportunity into the firm's planning process. Managers at the product-market level conceive of market opportunities that depart from the current strategy course, then engage in product-championing activities to mobilize resources and create momentum for further development of the product. Emphasizing political rather than administrative channels, product champions question the firm's current concept of strategy and, states Robert Burgelman, "provide top management with the opportunity to rationalize, retroactively, successful autonomous strategic behavior."[12] Through these political mechanisms, successful autonomous strategic initiatives, or emergent strategies, can become integrated into the firm's concept of strategy.

Clayton M. Christensen and Michael E. Raynor observe:

> Emergent strategies result from managers' responses to problems or opportunities that were unforeseen in the analysis and planning stages of the deliberate strategy making process. When the efficacy of that strategy . . . is recognized, it is possible to formalize it, improve it, and exploit it, thus transforming an emergent strategy into a deliberate one.[13]

Product Championing and the Informal Network

Table 9.1 highlights several characteristics that may distinguish induced from autonomous strategic behavior. Autonomous strategic initiatives involve a set of actors and evoke strategic dialogue different from that found in induced initiatives. An individual manager, the product champion, assumes a central role in sensing an opportunity and in mobilizing an informal network to explore the idea's technical feasibility and market potential. A **product champion** is an organization member who creates, defines, or adopts an idea for an innovation and is willing to assume significant risk (for example, position or prestige) to successfully implement the innovation.[14]

---

[11]Ibid., p. B3.

[12]Robert A. Burgelman, "Corporate Entrepreneurship and Strategic Management: Insights from a Process Study," *Management Science* 29 (December 1983): p. 1352.

[13]Clayton M. Christensen and Michael E. Raynor, *The Innovator's Solution: Creating and Sustaining Successful Growth* (Boston: Harvard Business School Press, 2003), pp. 215–216.

[14]Modesto A. Maidique, "Entrepreneurs, Champions, and Technological Innovations," *Sloan Management Review* 21 (Spring 1980): pp. 59–70; see also Jane M. Howell, "Champions of Technological Innovation," *Administrative Science Quarterly* 35 (June 1990): pp. 317–341.

TABLE 9.1	INDUCED VERSUS AUTONOMOUS STRATEGIC BEHAVIOR: SELECTED CHARACTERISTICS OF THE MARKETING STRATEGY FORMULATION PROCESS	
	Induced	**Autonomous**
Activation of the strategic decision process	An individual manager defines a market need that converges on the organization's concept of strategy.	An individual manager defines a market need that diverges from the organization's concept of strategy.
Nature of the screening process	A formal screening of technical and market merit is made using established administrative procedures.	An informal network assesses technical and market merit.
Type of innovation	Incremental (e.g., new product development for existing markets uses existing organizational resources).	Major (e.g., new product development projects require new combinations of organizational resources).
Nature of communication	Consistent with organizational work flow.	Departs from organizational work flow in early phase of decision process.
Major actors	Prescribed by the regular channel of hierarchical decision making.	An informal network emerges based on mobilization efforts of the product champion.
Decision roles	Roles and responsibilities for participants in the strategy formulation process are well defined.	Roles and responsibilities of participants are poorly defined in the initial phases but become more formalized as the strategy formulation process evolves.
Implications for strategy	Strategic alternatives are considered and commitment to a particular strategic course evolves.	Commitment to a particular strategic course emerges in the early phases through the sponsorship efforts of the product champion.

SOURCE: Adapted from Michael D. Hutt, Peter H. Reingen, and John R. Ronchetto Jr., "Tracing Emergent Processes in Marketing, Strategy Formation," *Journal of Marketing* 52 (January 1988): pp. 4–19. See also Clayton M. Christensen and Michael E. Raynor, *The Innovator's Solution: Creating and Sustaining Successful Growth* (Boston: Harvard Business School Press, 2003), pp. 213–231.

Senior managers at 3M do not commit to a project unless a champion emerges and do not abandon the effort unless the champion "gets tired." Emphasizing a rich culture of innovation embraced by all employees, senior executives at 3M also encourage product-championing behavior and calculated risk-taking. Moreover, they tolerate what 3M employees call "well-intentioned" failures.[15]

Compared with induced strategic behavior, autonomous or entrepreneurial initiatives are more likely to involve a communication process that departs from the regular work flow and the hierarchical decision-making channels. The decision roles and responsibilities of managers in this informal network are poorly defined in the early phases of the strategy-formulation process but become more formalized as the process evolves. Note in Table 9.1 that autonomous strategic behavior entails a creeping commitment toward a particular strategy course. By contrast, induced strategic initiatives are more likely to involve administrative mechanisms that encourage a more formal and comprehensive assessment of strategic alternatives at various levels in the firm's planning hierarchy.

[15] George S. Day, "Managing the Market Learning Process," *Journal of Business & Industrial Marketing* 17 (4, 2002): p. 246.

Conditions Supporting Corporate Entrepreneurship[16]

Entrepreneurial initiatives cannot be precisely planned but they can be nurtured and encouraged. First, the availability of appropriate rewards can enhance a manager's willingness to assume the risks associated with entrepreneurial activity. Second, as 3M illustrates, senior management can assume an instrumental role in fostering innovation by promoting entrepreneurial initiatives and encouraging calculated risk-taking. Third, resource availability, including some slack time, is needed to provide entrepreneurs with some degrees of freedom to explore new possibilities. 3M encourages scientists to devote up to 15 percent of their time to particular projects that they find personally interesting. Fourth, an organizational structure supporting corporate entrepreneurship provides the administrative mechanisms that bring more voices to the innovation process across the firm and allow ideas to be evaluated, selected, and implemented.[17]

What Motivates Entrepreneurs? Recent research identifies two additional dimensions that motivate corporate entrepreneurs: (1) intrinsic motivation (the drive originating within oneself) and (2) work design (for example, the availability of challenging projects; opportunities to interact directly with customers and other entrepreneurs). Matthew R. Marvel and his research colleagues describe what technical corporate entrepreneurs desire in their job:

> They want their innovative efforts to be connected to customer problems that need to be solved—and important customer problems at that. To understand these problems, they need contact with customers. To get breakthrough ideas on how to solve these problems, they also need contact with other world-class technologists.[18]

Managing Technology

Kodak, Lockheed, IBM, and the management teams of other corporations failed to recognize the major technological opportunity that xerographic copying presented. These firms were among the many that turned down the chance to participate with the small and unknown Haloid Company in refining and commercializing this technology. In the end, Haloid pursued it alone and transformed this one technological opportunity into the Xerox Corporation. Among the "tales of high tech," this remains a classic.[19] Technological change, Michael Porter asserts, is "a great equalizer, eroding the competitive advantage of even well-entrenched firms and propelling others to the forefront. Many of today's great firms grew out of technological changes that they were able to exploit."[20] Clearly, the long-run competitive position of most business-to-business firms depends on their ability to manage, increase, and exploit their technology base. This section explores the nature of development projects, the disruptive

---

[16]This section is based on Matthew R. Marvel, Abbie Griffin, John Hebda, and Bruce Vojak, "Examining the Technical Corporate Entrepreneurs' Motivation: Voices from the Field," *Entrepreneurship Theory and Practice*, 31 (September 2007): pp. 753–768.

[17]Gary Hamel, "The Why, What, and How of Management Innovation," *Harvard Business Review* 84 (February 2006): pp. 72–84.

[18]Marvel, Griffin, Hebda, and Vojak, "Examining the Technical Corporate Entrepreneurs' Motivation," p. 764.

[19]For a related discussion of Xerox's technology blunders, see Andrew Hargadon, *How Breakthroughs Happen: The Surprising Truth about How Companies Innovate* (Boston: Harvard Business School Press, 2003), pp. 168–182.

[20]Michael E. Porter, "Technology and Competitive Advantage," *Journal of Business Strategy* 6 (Winter 1985): p. 60; and Tamara J. Erickson, John F. Magee, Philip A. Roussel, and Komol N. Saad, "Managing Technology as Business Strategy," *Sloan Management Review* 31 (Spring 1990): pp. 73–83.

innovation model, and the defining attributes of successful innovators in fast-changing high-technology markets.

Classifying Development Projects

A first step in exploring the technology portfolio of a firm is to understand the different forms that development projects can take. Some development projects center on improving the manufacturing *process*, some on improving *products*, and others on both process and product improvements. All of these represent commercial development projects. By contrast, research and development is the precursor to commercial development. A firm's portfolio can include four types of development projects.[21]

1. **Derivative projects** center on incremental product enhancements (for example, a new feature), incremental process improvements (for example, a lower-cost manufacturing process), or incremental changes on both dimensions.

   Illustration: A feature-enhanced or cost-reduced Canon color copier.

2. **Platform projects** create the design and components shared by a set of products. These projects often involve a number of changes in both the product and the manufacturing process.

   Illustrations: A common motor in all Black & Decker hand tools; multiple applications of Intel's microprocessor.

3. **Breakthrough projects** establish new core products and new core processes that differ fundamentally from previous generations.

   Illustrations: Computer disks and fiber-optic cable created new product categories.

4. **Research and development** is the creation of knowledge concerning new materials and technologies that eventually leads to commercial development.[22]

   Illustration: Cisco Systems' development of communications technology that underlies its networking systems used by diverse customers like retailers, banks, and hotel chains.

A Product-Family Focus

A particular technology may provide the foundation or platform for several products. For example, Honda applies its multivalve cylinder technology to power-generation equipment, cars, business jets, motorcycles, and lawn mowers.[23] Products that share a common platform but have different specific features and enhancements required for different sets of consumers constitute a **product family**.[24] Each generation of

---

[21]This discussion is based on Steven C. Wheelwright and Kim B. Clark, "Creating Product Plans to Focus Product Development," *Harvard Business Review* 70 (March–April 1992): pp. 70–82.

[22]Ibid., p. 74.

[23]T. Michael Nevens, Gregory L. Summe, and Bro Uttal, "Commercializing Technology: What the Best Companies Do," *Harvard Business Review* 60 (May–June 1990): pp. 154–163; see also C. K. Prahalad, "Weak Signals versus Strong Paradigms," *Journal of Marketing Research* 32 (August 1995): pp. iii–vi.

[24]Marc H. Meyer and James M. Utterback, "The Product Family and the Dynamics of Core Capability," *Sloan Management Review* 34 (Spring 1993): pp. 29–47; see also Dwight L. Gertz and João P. A. Baptista, *Grow to Be Great: Breaking the Downsizing Cycle* (New York: The Free Press, 1995), pp. 92–103.

a product family has a platform that provides the foundation for specific products targeted to different or complementary markets. By expanding on technical skills, market knowledge, and manufacturing competencies, entirely new product families may be formed, thereby creating new business opportunities.

Strategists argue that a firm should move away from planning that centers on single products and focus instead on families of products that can grow from a common platform. Consider the Sony Walkman—one of the most successful products of all time. Based on how different customer segments used the product, Sony developed four basic platforms for the Walkman: playback only, playback and record, playback and tuner, and sports. Then, by applying standard design elements such as color and styling, Sony added an assortment of features and distinctive technical attributes to the basic platforms with relative ease.[25]

The move toward a product-family perspective requires close interfunctional working relationships, a long-term view of technology strategy, and a multiple-year commitment of resources. Although this approach offers significant competitive leverage, Steven Wheelwright and Kim Clark note that companies often fail to invest adequately in platforms: "The reasons vary, but the most common is that management lacks an awareness of the strategic value of platforms and fails to create well-thought-out platform projects."[26]

The Disruptive Innovation Model[27]

Special insights into innovation management come from examining the rate at which products are improving and customers can use those improvements. For example, when personal computers were first introduced in the early 1980s, typists often had to pause for the Intel 286 chip to catch up. But today, only the most demanding customers can fully use the speed and performance of personal computers. For many products, from Excel spreadsheets to application-enriched handsets and information appliances, few customers absorb the performance features that innovating companies include as they introduce new and improved products.

Overshooting   Figure 9.2 shows, first, a rate of improvement in a given product or technology that customers can use, represented by the dotted line, sloping slightly upward across the chart. Second, for a given product, innovating firms offer a trajectory of improvement as they develop new and improved versions over time. The pace of technological progress usually outstrips the ability of many, if not most, customers to keep up with it (see the steeply sloping solid lines in Figure 9.2). Therefore, as companies strive to make better products they can sell at higher profit margins to the most demanding customers, they overshoot and provide much more performance than mainstream customers are able to use.

Sustaining versus Disruptive Innovation   Third, from Figure 9.2, a distinction is made between a sustaining innovation and a disruptive innovation. According to Clayton M. Christensen and Michael E. Raynor, "A sustaining innovation targets

[25]Kathleen M. Eisenhardt and Shona L. Brown, "Time Pacing: Competing in Markets That Won't Stand Still," *Harvard Business Review*, 76 (March–April 1998): p. 67.
[26]Wheelwright and Clark, "Creating Project Plans," p. 74.
[27]This section is based on Christensen and Raynor, *The Innovator's Solution*, pp. 31–65. See also, Ashish Sood and Gerard J. Tellis, "Technological Evolution and Radical Innovation," *Journal of Marketing* 69 (July 2005): pp. 152–168.

FIGURE 9.2 | **THE DISRUPTIVE INNOVATION MODEL**

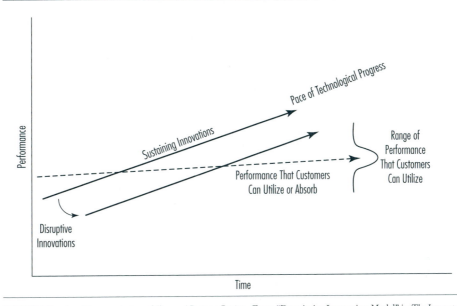

demanding, high-end customers with better performance than what was previously available (for example, incremental product improvements or breakthrough products)."[28] A disruptive innovation represents a product or service that is not as good as currently available alternatives. "But disruptive technologies offer other benefits— typically, they are simpler, more convenient, and less expensive products that appeal to new or less-demanding customers."[29]

Disruptive Strategy Examples Once a disruptive product or service gains a foothold, the improvement cycle begins and eventually it intersects with the needs of more demanding customers. For example, Xerox held a commanding position in the high-speed photocopier business until Canon's simple tabletop copier disrupted that strategy in the early 1980s. Likewise, Southwest Airlines disrupted established airlines; Amazon.com disrupted traditional bookstores; Staples disrupted small stationery stores and distributors of office supplies; and Google disrupted directories of all sorts, including Yellow Pages.

Types of Disruptive Strategies Disruptive strategies can take two forms: low-end disruptions and new-market disruptions. Table 9.2 describes the characteristics of these strategies and contrasts them with a strategy geared to sustaining innovations. Note, for example, that the targeted customers for low-end disruption are *overserved customers*, whereas new-market disruptions target *nonconsumption*—customers who historically lacked the resources to buy and use the product.

---

[28]Christensen and Raynor, *The Innovator's Solution*, p. 34.

[29] Ibid., p. 34.

TABLE 9.2 | **THREE APPROACHES TO CREATING NEW-GROWTH BUSINESSES**

Dimensions	Sustaining Innovations	Low-End Disruptions	New-Market Disruptions
Targeted performance of the product or service	Performance improvement in attributes most valued by the industry's most demanding customers. These improvements may be incremental or breakthrough in character.	Performance that is good enough along the traditional metrics of performance at the low end of the mainstream market.	Lower performance in "traditional" attributes, but *improved performance in new attributes—typically simplicity and convenience.*
Targeted customers or market application	The *most attractive* (i.e., *profitable) customers* in the mainstream markets who are willing to pay for improved performance.	Overserved customers in the low end of the mainstream market.	Targets *nonconsumption:* customers who historically lacked the money or skill to buy and use the product.
Effect on the required business model (processes and cost structure)	Improves or maintains profit margins by exploiting the *existing processes and cost structure* and making better use of current competitive advantages.	Uses a new *operating or financial approach or both*—a different combination of lower gross profit margins and higher asset utilization that can earn attractive returns at the discount prices required to win business at the low end of the market.	Business model must make money at lower price per unit sold and at unit production volumes that initially will be small. Gross margin dollars per unit sold will be significantly lower.

Low-End Strategy Tests   For a low-end disruptive strategy to succeed, two requirements must be met:

1. There should be customers at the low end of the market who are eager to purchase a "good-enough" product if they could acquire it at a lower price.

2. The company must be able to create a business model that can yield attractive profits at the discount prices that are needed to attract customers at the low end of the market.

Example: Southwest Airlines drew customers away from the major carriers.

New-Market Strategy Tests   For new market disruptions, at least one and generally both of these requirements must be met:

1. A large population can be defined who have historically lacked the money, equipment, or skill to acquire this product or service for themselves.

2. Present customers need to go to an inconvenient location to use the product or service.

Examples: Canon desktop photocopiers were a new-market disruption in the 1980s because they enabled employees to make their own copies rather than taking their originals to the corporate high-speed copying center to get help from technical specialists. Also, Research in Motion Limited's BlackBerry is a new-market disruption relative to notebook computers.

A Final Litmus Test Once an innovation passes the tests that apply to low-end or new-market disruptions, a final critical test remains: The innovation must be disruptive to all the significant competitive firms in the industry. If one or more of the significant industry players is pursuing the strategy, the odds will be stacked against the new entrant.

Illustration: A New-Market Disruption[30]

One principle for developing disruptive ideas is to "do what competitors want." For instance, Salesforce.com has pursued a strategy that leaders in the customer relationship (CRM) software market—namely SAP and Oracle—found unappealing. Before Salesforce.com entered the market, both of these formidable rivals sold relatively expensive solutions that required customization and installation to ensure proper integration with the customer's other software packages. Customers also were charged an ongoing fee for maintenance of the installed software.

Adopting a Different Approach Salesforce.com provides customers with access to programs that reside on centralized host computers. Users access these databases through the Web for a modest monthly fee. While customers often find these hosted solutions to be occasionally slower and somewhat more difficult to readily integrate with other applications, they are flexible, easy to use, and quite economical—all defining characteristics of a disruptive innovation.

Scott D. Anthony and his colleagues observe that "Salesforce.com used several tactics that made its competitors unwilling or uninterested in immediately responding:

- It started with nonconsumption (that is, selling to small customers purchasing their first CRM software).

- It targeted a customer its competitors considered undesirable (that is, small and medium-sized businesses that were the least profitable for rivals).

- It used a different distribution channel (that is, on the Web).

- It created a business model that did not depend on a revenue stream of vital importance to incumbents."[31] (By centering on installation and customization fees, SAP and Oracle did not find the fees related to a hosted model to be appealing.)

Innovation Winners in High-Technology Markets

In rapidly changing industries with short product life cycles and quickly shifting competitive landscapes, a firm must continually innovate to keep its offerings aligned with the market. A firm's ability to cope with change in a high-velocity industry is a key

---

[30]Scott D. Anthony, Mark W. Johnson, Joseph V. Sinfield, and Elizabeth J. Altman, *The Innovator's Guide to Growth: Putting Disruptive Innovation to Work* (Boston: Harvard Business Press, 2008), pp. 125–126.

[31]Ibid., p. 126.

to competitive success. Shona Brown and Kathleen Eisenhardt provide an intriguing comparison of successful versus less successful product innovation in the computer industry.[32] Successful innovators were firms that were on schedule, on time to the market, and on target in addressing customer needs. The study found that firms with a successful record of product innovation use different organizational structures and processes than their competitors. In particular, four distinguishing characteristics marked the innovation approach of successful firms.

1. Limited Structure   Creating successful products to meet changing customer needs requires flexibility, but successful product innovators combine this flexibility with a few rules that are never broken. First, strict priorities for new products are established and tied directly to resource allocation. This allows managers to direct attention to the most promising opportunities, avoiding the temptation to pursue too many attractive opportunities. Second, managers set deadlines for a few key milestones and always meet them. Third, responsibility for a limited number of major outcomes is set. For example, at one firm, engineering managers were responsible for product schedules while marketing managers were responsible for market definition and product profitability. Although successful firms emphasized structure for a few areas (for example, priorities or deadlines), less successful innovators imposed more control—lockstep, checkpoint procedures for every facet of new product development—or virtually no structure at all. Successful firms strike a balance by using a structure that is neither so rigid as to stiffly control the process nor so chaotic that the process falls apart.

2. Real-Time Communication and Improvisation   Successful product innovators in the computer industry emphasize real-time communication within new-product-development teams *and* across product teams. Much of the communication occurs in formal meetings, but there is also extensive informal communication throughout the organization. Clear priorities and responsibilities, coupled with extensive communications, allow product developers to improvise. "In the context of jazz improvisation, this means creating music while adjusting to the changing musical interpretations of others. In the context of product innovation, it means creating a product while simultaneously adapting to changing markets and technologies."[33]

More formally, then, **improvisation** involves the design and execution of actions that approach convergence with each other in time.[34] The shorter the elapsed time between the design and implementation of an activity, the more that activity is improvisational. Successful firms expect constant change, and new product teams have the freedom to act. One manager noted: "We fiddle right up to the end" of the new-product-development process. Real-time communications among members of the product development team, coupled with limited structure, provide the foundation for such improvisation.

[32]This section is based on Shona L. Brown and Kathleen M. Eisenhardt, "The Art of Continuous Change: Linking Complexity Theory and Time-Paced Evolution in Relentlessly Shifting Organizations," *Administrative Science Quarterly* 42 (March 1997): pp. 1–34.

[33]Ibid., p. 15.

[34]Christine Moorman and Anne S. Miner, "The Convergence of Planning and Execution: Improvisation in New Product Development," *Journal of Marketing* 62 (July 1998): p. 3.

INSIDE BUSINESS MARKETING

Patching: The New Corporate Strategy in Dynamic Markets

Kathleen M. Eisenhardt and Shona L. Brown contend that traditional corporate planning and resource allocation approaches are not effective in volatile markets. As new technologies, novel products and services, and emerging markets create tempting opportunities, "the clear-cut partitioning of businesses into neat, equidistant rectangles on an organizational chart becomes out of date."

The new corporate-level strategic processes center on managing change and continually realigning the organization to capture market opportunities faster than the competition. Central to this newly defined approach is **patching**—the strategic process corporate executives use routinely to realign or remap businesses to changing market opportunities. Patching can take the form of adding, dividing, transferring, exiting, or combining pieces of businesses. Hewlett-Packard used patching to launch the printer business, create businesses in related products like scanners and faxes, and develop a second printer business built around inkjet technology. Patching is less critical in stable markets but a crucial skill when markets are turbulent. Here a small, agile unit of the firm can be mobilized quickly to capture fresh market opportunities.

SOURCES: Kathleen M. Eisenhardt and Shona L. Brown, "Patching: Restitching Business Portfolios in Dynamic Markets," *Harvard Business Review* 77 (May–June 1999): pp. 72–82; see also, Mark B. Houston, Beth A. Walker, Michael D. Hutt, and Peter H. Reingen, "Cross-Unit Competition for a Market Charter: The Enduring Influence of Structure," *Journal of Marketing* 65 (April 2001): pp. 19–34.

3. Experimentation: Probing into the Future   Some firms make a large bet on one version of the future, whereas others fail to update future plans in light of changing competition. Creators of successful product portfolios did not invest in any one version of the future but, instead, used a variety of low-cost probes to create options. Examples of low-cost probes include developing experimental products for new markets, entering into a strategic alliance with leading-edge customers to better understand future needs, or conducting regular planning sessions dedicated to the future. In turbulent industries, strategists cannot accurately predict which of many possible versions of the future will arrive. Probes create more possible responses for managers when the future does arrive while lowering the probability of being surprised by unanticipated futures.

4. Time Pacing   Successful product innovators carefully managed the transition between current and future projects, whereas less successful innovators let each project unfold according to its own schedule. Successful innovators, like Intel, practice time pacing—a strategy for competing in fast-changing markets by creating new products at predictable time intervals.[35] Organization members carefully choreograph and understand transition processes. For example, marketing managers might begin work on the definition of the next product while engineering is completing work on the current product and moving it to manufacturing. Time pacing motivates managers to anticipate change and can have a strong psychological impact across the organization. "Time pacing creates a relentless sense of urgency around meeting deadlines and concentrates individual and team energy around common goals."[36]

---

[35]Eisenhardt and Brown, "Time Pacing," pp. 59–69.

[36]Ibid., p. 60.

The New-Product-Development Process

To sustain their competitive advantage, leading-edge firms such as Canon, Microsoft, and Hewlett-Packard make new product development a top management priority. They directly involve managers and employees from across the organization to speed actions and decisions. Because new product ventures can represent a significant risk as well as an important opportunity, new product development requires systematic thought. The high expectations for new products are often not fulfilled. Worse, many new industrial products fail. Although the definitions of failure are somewhat elusive, research suggests that 40 percent of industrial products fail to meet objectives.[37] Although there may be some debate over the number of failures, there is no debate that a new product rejected by the market constitutes a substantial waste to the firm and to society.

This section explores (1) the forces that drive a firm's new product performance, (2) the sources of new product ideas, (3) cross-functional barriers to successful innovation, and (4) team-based processes used in new product development. A promising method for bringing the "voice of the consumer" directly into the development process is also explored.

What Drives a Firm's New Product Performance?

A benchmarking study sought to uncover the critical success factors that drive a firm's new product performance.[38] It identified three factors (Figure 9.3): (1) the quality of a firm's new-product-development process, (2) the resource commitments made to new product development, and (3) the new product strategy.

Process   Successful companies use a high-quality new-product-development process—they give careful attention to executing the activities and decision points that new products follow from the idea stage to launch and beyond. The benchmarking study identified the following characteristics among high-performing firms:

- The firms emphasized upfront market and technical assessments before projects moved into the development phase.

- The process featured complete descriptions of the product concept, product benefits, positioning, and target markets before development work was initiated.

- Tough project go/kill decision points were included in the process, and the kill option was actually used.

- The new product process was flexible—certain stages could be skipped in line with the nature and risk of a particular project.

---

[37]Robert G. Cooper, Scott J. Edgett, and Elko J. Kleinschmidt, "Benchmarking Best NPD Practices–I," *Research Technology Management* 47 (January–February 2004): pp. 31–43; see also Robert G. Cooper and Scott J. Edgett, "Maximizing Productivity in Product Innovation," *Research Technology Management* 51 (March–April 2008): pp. 47–58.

[38]Robert G. Cooper and Elko J. Kleinschmidt, "Benchmarking Firms' New Product Performance and Practices," *Engineering Management Review* 23 (Fall 1995): pp. 112–120; see also Robert G. Cooper, Scott J. Edgett, and Elko J. Kleinschmidt, "Benchmarking Best NPD Practices–II," *Research Technology Management* 47 (May–June 2004): pp. 50–59.

FIGURE 9.3 | **THE MAJOR DRIVERS OF A FIRM'S NEW PRODUCT PERFORMANCE**

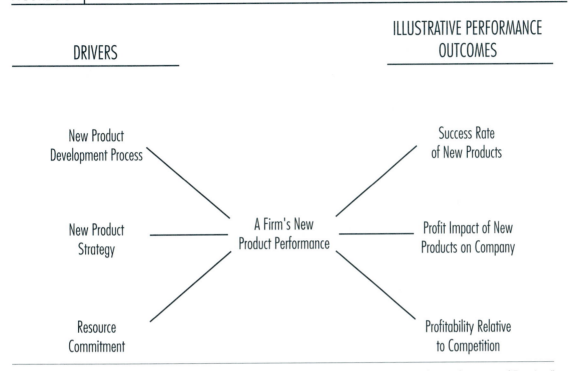

DRIVERS

ILLUSTRATIVE PERFORMANCE OUTCOMES

New Product Development Process

New Product Strategy

Resource Commitment

A Firm's New Product Performance

Success Rate of New Products

Profit Impact of New Products on Company

Profitability Relative to Competition

SOURCE: Adapted from Robert G. Cooper and Elko J. Kleinschmidt, "Benchmarking Firms' New Product Performance and Practices," *Engineering Management Review* 23 (Fall 1995): pp. 112–120.

Detailed upfront homework on the product concept, the likely market response, and the product's technical feasibility, along with a thorough business and financial assessment, are important dimensions of the process successful product creators follow.

Resource Commitments Adequate resources were invested in new product development in top-performing firms. Three ingredients were important here:

1. Top management committed the resources necessary to meet the firm's objectives for the total product effort.

2. R&D budgets were adequate and aligned with the stated new product objectives.

3. The necessary personnel were assigned and were relieved from other duties so that they could give full attention to new product development.

Research suggests that rather than being imposed by top management, the creative potential of new-product-development teams "is likely to be more fully realized when they are given the flexibility—within a broad strategic directive—to determine their own project controls and especially to pursue their own processes and procedures."[39]

---

[39]Joseph M. Bonner, Robert W. Ruekert, and Orville C. Walker Jr., "Upper Management Control of New Product Development Projects and Project Performance," *Journal of Product Innovation Management* 19 (May 2002): p. 243.

New Product Strategy   A clear and visible new product strategy was another driver of a firm's new product performance (see Figure 9.3). Successful firms like 3M set aggressive new product performance goals (for example, *x* percent of company sales and profit from new products) as a basic corporate goal and communicate it to all employees. In turn, Robert Cooper and Elko Kleinschmidt report that successful firms centered development efforts on clearly defined arenas—particular product, market, and technology domains—to direct the new product program:

> The new product strategy specifies "the arenas where we'll play the game," or perhaps more important, where we won't play . . . what's in bounds and out of bounds. Without arenas defined, the search for new product ideas or opportunities is unfocused. . . .[40]

Anticipating Competitive Reactions[41]

Two-thirds of new product introductions trigger reactions by competitors. Consequently, business marketers can improve the odds of new-product-launch success by implementing a strong **competitor orientation** before and during the launch. Here the new product strategist develops detailed scenarios that provide a guide for countering different competitive responses. Competitors are strongly motivated to react when (1) the new product represents a major threat to their market and (2) the market is experiencing a high rate of growth. Competitors are also more inclined to react when extensive marketing communications by the innovating firm enhance the visibility of the new product introduction.

Alternatively, if the new product introduction does not pose a direct challenge to the competitor's market, a reaction is less likely. Recent research suggests that radically new products or products that target niche markets are less likely to spawn competitive responses.

Sources of New Product Ideas

The business marketer should be alert to new product ideas and their sources, both inside and outside the company. Internally, new product ideas may flow from salespersons who are close to customer needs, from R&D specialists who are close to new technological developments, and from top management who know the company's strengths and weaknesses. Externally, ideas may come from channel members, such as distributors or customers, or from an assessment of competitive moves.

Eric von Hippel challenges the traditional view that marketers typically introduce new products to a passive market.[42] His research suggests that the customers in the

---

[40]Cooper and Kleinschmidt, "Benchmarking," p. 117; see also Jean-Marie Choffray and Gary L. Lilien, "Assessing Response to Industrial Marketing Strategy," *Journal of Marketing* 42 (April 1978): pp. 20–31; and Eunsang Yoon and Gary L. Lilien, "New Industrial Product Performance: The Effects of Market Characteristics and Strategy," *Journal of Product Innovation Management* 3 (September 1985): pp. 134–144.

[41]Marion Debruyne, Rudy Moenart, Abbie Griffin, Susan Hart, Erik Jan Hultink, and Henry Robben, "The Impact of New Product Launch Strategies on Competitive Reaction in Industrial Markets," *Journal of Product Innovation Management* 19 (March 2002): pp. 159–170; see also Beth A. Walker, Dimitri Kapelianis, and Michael D. Hutt, "Competitive Cognition," *MIT Sloan Management Review* 46 (Summer 2005): pp. 10–12.

[42]Eric von Hippel, "Get New Products from Customers," *Harvard Business Review* 60 (March–April 1982): pp. 117–122; see also Eric von Hippel, *The Sources of Innovation* (New York: Oxford University Press, 1988); Gerard A. Athaide and Rodney L. Stump, "A Taxonomy of Relationship Approaches during Technology Development in Technology-Based, Industrial Markets," *Journal of Product Innovation Management* 16 (September 1999): pp. 469–482.

B2B TOP PERFORMERS

IDEO: The Hits Just Keep on Coming!

IDEO helps organizations innovate through design. Leading firms like Apple, Research In Motion, Sony, 3M, and others have used product design to define their brands, creating meaningful points of difference over competitors.

Among their greatest hits, IDEO is responsible for designing

- the Microsoft mouse;

- the Swiffer Sweeper for Procter & Gamble;

- mobile sound components for Altec Lansing;

- the coasting bicycle design strategy for Shimano;

- improved patient-provider services for Mayo Clinic;

- "Keep the Change" account service for Bank of America.

FastCompany.com identifies IDEO as one of the world's most innovative companies.

SOURCE: http://www.ideo.com/portfolio/list.asp?p=0&c=&k=40&s=&so=4

business market often develop the idea for a new product and even select the supplier to make that product. The customer is responding to the perceived *capability* of the business marketer rather than to a specific physical product. This points up the need for involving customers in new product development and promoting corporate capability to consumers (idea generators).

Lead Users   Because many industrial product markets for high-technology and, in particular, capital equipment consist of a small number of high-volume buying firms, special attention must be given to the needs of **lead users**. These include a small number of highly influential buying organizations that are consistent early adopters of new technologies.[43] Lead users face needs that are general in the marketplace, but they confront these needs months or years before most of that marketplace encounters them. In addition, they are positioned to benefit significantly by obtaining a solution that satisfies those needs. For example, if an automobile manufacturer wanted to design an innovative braking system, marketing managers might secure insights from auto racing teams, who have a strong need for better brakes. In turn, they might look to a related field like aerospace, where antilock braking systems were first developed so that military aircraft could land on short runways.[44]

The Lead User Method   Lead user projects are conducted by a cross-functional team that includes four to six managers from marketing and technical departments; one member serves as project leader. Team members typically spend 12 to 15 hours per week on the projects, which are usually completed in four to six weeks. Lead user projects proceed through five phases (Figure 9.4). 3M has now successfully used the lead user method in eight different divisions, and support among project teams and divisional managers is strong. For example, the Medical-Surgical Markets Group at

---

[43]von Hippel, "Get New Products," pp. 120–121.

[44]Eric von Hippel, Stefan Thomke, and Mary Sonnack, "Creating Breakthroughs at 3M," *Harvard Business Review* 77 (September–October 1999): pp. 47–57.

FIGURE 9.4 | **THE LEAD USER METHOD**

Phase	Central Focus	Description
Phase 1	Laying the Foundation	The team identifies target markets and secures support from internal stakeholders for the type and level of innovations desired.
Phase 2	Determining the Trends	The team talks to experts in the field who have a broad view of emerging technologies and pioneering applications in the particular area.
Phase 3	Identifying Lead Users	The team begins a networking process to identify lead users at the leading edge of the target market and to gather information that might contribute to breakthrough products.
Phase 4	Developing & Assessing Preliminary Product Ideas	The team begins to shape product ideas and to assess market potential and fit with company interests.
Phase 5	Developing the Breakthroughs	To design final concepts, the team hosts a workshop bringing together lead users with other in-house managers. After further refinement, the team presents its recommendations to senior management.

SOURCE: Adapted with modifications from Eric von Hippel, Stefan Thomke, and Mary Sonnack, "Creating Breakthroughs at 3M," *Harvard Business Review* 77 (September–October 1999), p. 52.

3M used the lead user method to unearth new product ideas and to identify a revolutionary approach to infection control.[45] 3M reports that sales in year 5 for funded lead user project ideas were more than eight times greater than those generated by traditional approaches to idea generation.[46] Other firms adopting a lead user focus include Nortel Networks, Verizon, Nestle, Pitney Bowes, and Philips.

Customer Visits   A popular approach among business marketers for gaining new product insights is customer visits.[47] Here a cross-functional team visits a customer organization to secure a first-hand account of customer needs. Based on a carefully crafted interview guide, in-depth interviews are conducted with key buying influentials to uncover user problems, needs, and desires. For instance, company representatives at Intuit visit customers where they live and work to observe how they use its products such as QuickBooks. After watching many small-business customers struggle with QuickBooks Pro, the firm saw a need and created the solution: QuickBooks Simple Start.[48]

Web-Based Methods for Improving Customer Inputs to Design   Recognizing the ability of customers to innovate, many firms have developed tools that invite

[45]Ibid., p. 56.

[46]"User Innovation: Changing Innovation Focus," *Strategic Direction* 23 (8, 2007): pp. 35–36.

[47]Robert Cooper and Scott Edgett, "Ideation for Product Innovation: What Are the Best Methods?" Product Development Institute, Inc., 2008, accessed at http://www.stage-gate.com on July 10, 2008.

[48]Christopher Meyer and Andre Schwager, "Understanding Customer Experience," *Harvard Business Review* 85 (February 2007): p. 8.

customers to design their own products. With these innovative toolkits, customers are given an array of features that can be configured, as desired, to create their own customized products. These toolkits often incorporate engineering and cost modules. To illustrate, if a customer wishes to change the length of a truck bed, the design tool automatically computes the additional cost and the associated changes that will be required in both the transmission and the engine. For aesthetic compatibility, the design tool might even modify the shape of the cab. Other examples: In its materials business, General Electric provides Web-based tools that customers use for designing better plastics products. Likewise, many software companies encourage users to add custom-designed modules to their standard products and then commercializes the best of those components.[49]

Determinants of New Product Performance and Timeliness

What factors are most important in determining the success or failure of the new product? Why are some firms faster than others in moving projects through the development process? Let's review the available evidence.

The Determinants of Success

Both strategic factors and a firm's proficiency in carrying out the new-product-development process determine new product success.[50]

Strategic Factors   Research suggests that four strategic factors appear to be crucial to new product success. The level of product advantage is the most important. **Product advantage** refers to customer perceptions of product superiority with respect to quality, cost–performance ratio, or function relative to competitors. Successful products offer clear benefits, such as reduced customer costs, and are of higher quality (for example, more durable) than competitors' products. A study of more than 100 new product projects in the chemical industry illustrates the point. Here, Robert Cooper and Elko Kleinschmidt assert, "The winners are new products that offer high relative product quality, have superior price/performance characteristics, provide good value for the money to the customer, are superior to competing products in meeting customer needs, [and] have unique attributes and highly visible benefits that are easily seen by the customer."[51]

Marketing synergy and technical synergy are also pivotal in new product outcomes. **Marketing synergy** is the fit between the needs of the project and the firm's

[49]Stephen Thomke and Eric von Hippel, "Customers as Innovators: A New Way to Create Value," *Harvard Business Review* 80 (April 2002): pp. 74–81.

[50]Mitzi M. Montoya-Weiss and Roger Calantone, "Determinants of New Product Performance: A Review and Meta-Analysis," *Journal of Product Innovation Management* 11 (November 1994): pp. 397–417; see also Robert G. Cooper, Scott J. Edgett, and Elko J. Kleinschmidt, "Benchmarking Best NPD Practices–III," *Research Technology Management* 47 (November–December 2004): pp. 43–55.

[51]Robert G. Cooper and Elko J. Kleinschmidt, "Major New Products: What Distinguishes the Winners in the Chemical Industry?" *Journal of Product Innovation Management* 10 (March 1993): p. 108; see also Tiger Li and Roger J. Calantone, "The Impact of Market Knowledge Competence on New Product Advantage: Conceptualization and Empirical Examination," *Journal of Marketing* 62 (October 1998): pp. 13–29.

resources and skills in marketing (for example, personal selling or market research). By contrast, **technical synergy** concerns the fit between the needs of the project and the firm's R&D resources and competencies. New products that match the skills of the firm are likely to succeed.

In addition to the preceding three factors, an **international orientation** also contributes to the success of product innovation.[52] New products designed and developed to meet foreign requirements and targeted at world or nearest-neighbor export markets outperform domestic products on almost every measure, including success rate, profitability, and domestic and foreign market shares. Underlying this success is a strong international focus in market research, product testing with customers, trial selling, and launch efforts.

Development Process Factors   New product success is also associated with particular characteristics of the development process. **Predevelopment proficiency** provides the foundation for a successful product. Predevelopment involves several important tasks such as initial screening, preliminary market and technical assessment, detailed market research study, and preliminary business/financial analysis. Firms that are skilled in completing these upfront tasks are likely to experience new product success.

Market knowledge and **marketing proficiency** are also pivotal in new product outcomes. As might be expected, business marketers with a solid understanding of market needs are likely to succeed. Robert Cooper describes the market planning for a successful product he examined: "Market information was very complete: there was a solid understanding of the customer's needs, wants, and preferences; of the customer's buying behavior and price sensitivity; of the size and trends of the market; and of the competitive situation. Finally, the market launch was well planned, well targeted, proficiently executed, and backed by appropriate resources."[53]

Technical knowledge and **technical proficiency** are other important dimensions of the new-product-development process. When technical developers have a strong base of knowledge about the technical aspects of a potential new product, and when they can proficiently pass through the stages of the new-product-development process (for example, product development, prototype testing, pilot production, and production start-up), these products succeed.

Fast-Paced Product Development

Rapid product development offers a number of competitive advantages. To illustrate, speed enables a firm to respond to rapidly changing markets and technologies. Moreover, fast product development is usually more efficient because lengthy development processes tend to waste resources on peripheral activities and changes.[54] Of course, although an overemphasis on speed may create other pitfalls, it is becoming an important strategic weapon, particularly in high-technology markets.

---

[52]Elko J. Kleinschmidt and Robert G. Cooper, "The Performance Impact of an International Orientation on Product Innovation," *European Journal of Marketing* 22 (9, 1988): pp. 56–71.

[53]Robert G. Cooper, *Winning at New Products: Accelerating the Process from Idea to Launch* (Reading, Mass: Addison-Wesley, 1993), p. 27; see also Robert G. Cooper, "Perspective: The Stage-Gate® Idea to Launch Process—Update, What's New, and NextGen Systems," *Journal of Product Innovation Management* 25 (May 2008): pp. 213–232.

[54]See, for example, Robert G. Cooper and Elko J. Kleinschmidt, "Determinants of Timeliness in Product Development," *Journal of Product Innovation Management* 11 (November 1994): pp. 381–417.

Matching the Process to the Development Task   How can a firm accelerate product development? A major study of the global computer industry provides some important benchmarks.[55] Researchers examined 72 product development projects of leading U.S., European, and Asian computer firms. The findings suggest that multiple approaches are used to increase speed in product development. Speed comes from properly matching the approach to the product development task at hand.

Compressed Strategy for Predictable Projects   For well-known markets and technologies, a **compression strategy** speeds development. This strategy views product development as a predictable series of steps that can be compressed. Speed comes from carefully planning these steps and shortening the time it takes to complete each one. This research indicates that the compressed strategy increased the speed of product development for products that had predictable designs and that were targeted for stable and mature markets. Mainframe computers fit into this category—they rely on proprietary hardware, have more predictable designs from project to project, and compete in a mature market.

Experiential Strategy for Unpredictable Projects   For uncertain markets and technologies, an **experiential strategy** accelerates product development. The underlying assumption of this strategy, explain Kathleen Eisenhardt and Behnam Tabrizi, is that "product development is a highly uncertain path through foggy and shifting markets and technologies. The key to fast product development is, then, rapidly building intuition and flexible options in order to learn quickly about and shift with uncertain environments."[56]

Under these conditions, speed comes from multiple design iterations, extensive testing, frequent milestones, and a powerful leader who can keep the product team focused. Here real-time interactions, experimentation, and flexibility are essential. The research found that the experiential strategy increased the speed of product development for unpredictable projects such as personal computers—a market characterized by rapidly evolving technology and unpredictable patterns of competition.

Summary

Product innovation is a high-risk and potentially rewarding process. Sustained growth depends on innovative products that respond to existing or emerging consumer needs. Effective managers of innovation channel and control its main directions but have learned to stay flexible and expect surprises. Within the firm, marketing managers pursue strategic activity that falls into two broad categories: induced and autonomous strategic behavior.

New-product-development efforts for existing businesses or market-development projects for the firm's present products are the outgrowth of induced strategic initiatives. In contrast, autonomous strategic efforts take shape outside the firm's current concept of strategy, depart from the current course, and center on new categories of business opportunity; middle managers initiate the project, champion its development, and, if successful, see the project integrated into the firm's concept of strategy.

---

[55]Kathleen M. Eisenhardt and Behnam N. Tabrizi, "Accelerating Adaptive Processes: Product Innovation in the Global Computer Industry," *Administrative Science Quarterly* 40 (March 1995): pp. 84–110.

[56]Ibid., p. 91.

Corporate entrepreneurs thrive in a culture where senior managers promote and reward innovative behavior, encourage risk-taking, and provide the administrative mechanisms to screen, develop, and implement new product ideas.

The long-run competitive position of most business marketing firms depends on their ability to manage and increase their technological base. Core competencies provide the basis for products and product families. Each generation of a product family has a platform that serves as the foundation for specific products targeted at different or complementary market applications. Because companies keep working to make better products, they can sell at higher profit margins to the most demanding customers, and they often overshoot the needs of mainstream customers. A sustaining innovation provides demanding high-end customers with improved performance, whereas disruptive innovations target new or less-demanding customers with an easy-to-use, less-expensive alternative that is "good enough." Disruptive strategies take two forms: low-end and new-market disruptions.

Firms that are successful innovators in turbulent markets combine limited structures (for example, priorities, deadlines) with extensive communication and the freedom to improvise on current projects. These successful product creators also explore the future by experimenting with a variety of low-cost probes and build a relentless sense of urgency in the organization by creating new products at predictable time intervals (i.e., time pacing).

Effective new product development requires a thorough knowledge of customer needs and a clear grasp of the technological possibilities. Lead user analysis and customer visits often uncover valuable new product opportunities. Top-performing firms execute the new-product-development process proficiently, provide adequate resources to support new product objectives, and develop clear new product strategy. Both strategic factors and the firm's proficiency in executing the new-product-development process are critical to the success of industrial products. Fast-paced product development can provide an important source of competitive advantage. Speed comes from adapting the process to the new-product-development task at hand.

Discussion Questions

1. Research by James Quinn suggests that few major innovations result from highly structured planning systems. What does this imply for the business marketer?

2. Compare and contrast induced and autonomous strategic behavior. Describe the role of the product champion in the new-product-development process.

3. The breakthrough products for many companies did not emerge from the formal new-product-development process. Instead, they were championed by a few resourceful employees. What steps can organizations take to motivate and support corporate entrepreneurship?

4. Compare and contrast a low-end versus a new-market disruptive strategy.

5. In many markets, a new entrant might consider a strategy that provides potential customers with a product or technology that is "good enough"

rather than "superior" to existing options. Describe the key tests that a disruptive strategy must pass in order to stack the odds for success in its favor.

6. In fast-changing high-tech industries, some firms have a better record in developing new products than others. Describe the critical factors that drive the new product performance of firms.

7. Rather than planning for and investing in just one version of the future, some firms use low-cost probes to experiment with many possible futures. Evaluate the wisdom of this approach.

8. Describe how Marriott might employ lead user analysis to better align its properties and services with the needs of the executive traveler.

9. New industrial products that succeed provide clear-cut advantages to customers. Define product advantage and provide an example of a recent new product introduction that fits this definition.

10. Evaluate this statement: "To increase the speed of the new-product-development process, a firm might follow one strategy for unpredictable projects and an entirely different one for more predictable ones."

Internet Exercise

1. Years ago, Corning sold dishes and glassware in the consumer market. Today, the firm might be characterized as a high-tech material science company that competes successfully in an array of business markets. Go to http://www.corning.com and identify its major product lines.

Steelcase Inc. Extends Reach to Growing Health-Care Market

Steelcase, a leading office furniture manufacturer, launched a new health-care-focused subsidiary called Nurture. James P. Hackett, president and CEO of Steelcase, had assigned a team to study the health care market, and here is what they concluded:

> We should move into the health-care market by launching a new health care brand. It would expand our current effort "on carpet"—work areas in hospitals that are like the office spaces (nurses' stations, for instance)—but we would also expand "off carpet"—to entirely different areas of the hospital (patients' rooms, examining rooms, café lounges). . . . The brand would draw on technology and products we already had, as well as new products we would manufacture and new customizing services we would provide.[57]

The team got the go-ahead from senior management to launch the new business unit and the Nurture brand.

Given that the cost of hospital care is expected to exceed $1.2 trillion by 2016, Steelcase executives saw the health-care market as a golden opportunity.[58] They were also encouraged to learn that the highest sales volume for the company's Criterion chair—a classic desk seat with adjustable back tension, lumbar-curve support, and wrist rests—was going to health-care customers—hospitals, clinics, and doctors' offices.

John Carlson, vice president of product development and marketing at Nurture, believes that the unit can enjoy a competitive advantage by offering cohesive suites of examination tables, patient beds, nurses' stations, and the like. However, there are some formidable competitors that have deep knowledge of health-care customers, like Hill-Rom, a unit of Hillenbrand Industries. A leading manufacturer of hospital beds, Hill-Rom also offers a limited collection of furniture selections but has been squarely centered on the health-care market for decades and has forged close and enduring relationships with physicians, nurses, and administrators at health-care facilities, large and small.

Discussion Question

1. To develop patient-friendly furnishings or suites of products that boost staff productivity, describe specific steps that marketing strategists at Nurture might take to learn more about the workings of a hospital environment and the needs of different constituents—patients, visitors, nurses, and physicians.

---

[57]James P. Hackett, "Preparing for the Perfect Launch," *Harvard Business Review* 85 (April 2007): p. 49.

[58]Reena Jana, "Steelcase's Medical Breakthrough," March 22, 2007, accessed at http://www.businessweek.com on July 14, 2008.

Managing Services for Business Markets

The important and growing market for business services poses special challenges and meaningful opportunities for the marketing manager. This chapter explores the unique aspects of business services and the special role they play in the business market environment. After reading this chapter, you will understand:

1. the value of systematically monitoring the customer experience and the central role that business services assume in customer solutions.

2. the roles that service quality, customer satisfaction, and loyalty assume in service market success.

3. significant factors to consider in formulating a service marketing strategy.

4. the determinants of new service success and failure.

FedEx Corporation, the global package delivery service, mobilizes for trouble before it occurs: Each night, five empty FedEx jets roam over the United States.[1] Why? So the firm can respond on a moment's notice to unexpected events such as overbooking of packages in Atlanta or an equipment failure in Denver. FedEx excels by making promises to its customers and keeping them. The first major service organization to win the Malcolm Baldrige National Quality Award, FedEx makes specific promises about the timeliness and reliability of package delivery in its advertising and marketing communications. More importantly, FedEx aligns its personnel, facilities, information technology, and equipment to meet those promises. Says Scot Struminger, vice president of information technology at FedEx, "We know that customer loyalty comes from treating customers like you want to be treated."[2]

As this example demonstrates, *services* play a critical role in the marketing programs of many business-to-business firms, whether their primary focus is on a service (FedEx) or whether services provide a promising new path for growth. Indeed, high-tech brands, like IBM or Hewlett-Packard, are built on a promise of value to customers, and service excellence is part of the value package customers demand. In fact, over half of IBM's massive revenue base now comes from services—not products. Clearly, many product manufacturers are now using integrated product and service solutions as a core marketing strategy for creating new growth opportunities; moreover, a vast array of "pure service" firms exist to supply organizations with everything from office cleaning to management consulting and just-in-time delivery to key customers.[3]

This chapter examines the nature of business services, the key buying behaviors associated with their purchase, the major strategic elements related to services marketing, and the new-service-development process.

Understanding the Full Customer Experience

The traditional product-centric mindset rests on the assumption that companies win by creating superior products and continually enhancing the performance of existing products. But services are fundamental to the customer experience that every business-to-business firm provides. Customer experience encompasses every dimension of a company's offering—product and service features, advertising, ease of use, reliability, the process of becoming a customer, or the way problems are resolved—not to mention the ongoing sales relationship.[4]

The Customer Experience Life Cycle

Recent research highlights the importance of examining the customer's experience. A survey of the customers of 362 firms by Bain & Company revealed that only

[1]David Leonhardt, "The FedEx Economy," *New York Times*, October 8, 2005, p. B1.

[2]Don Peppers and Martha Rogers, *Return on Customer: Creating Maximum Value from Your Scarcest Resource* (New York: Currency Doubleday, 2005), p. 144.

[3]Kristian Möller, Risto Rajala, and Mika Westerlund, "Service Innovation Myopia? A New Recipe for Client-Provider Value Creation," *California Management Review* 50 (Spring 2008): pp. 31–48.

[4]Christopher Meyer and Andre Schwager, "Understanding Customer Experiences," *Harvard Business Review* 85 (February 2007): pp. 116–127.

FIGURE 10.1 | THE FIRST STEP IN UNDERSTANDING A CUSTOMER'S EXPERIENCE
IS TO DEVELOP A LIFE CYCLE MAP

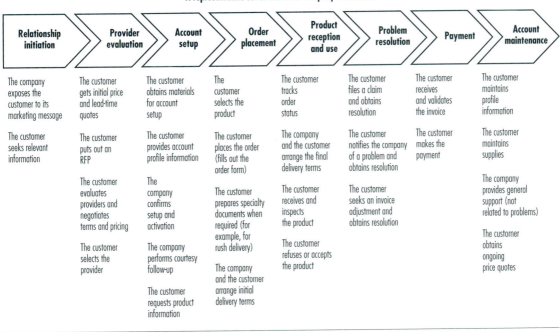

A representative set of customer-company interactions

Relationship initiation	Provider evaluation	Account setup	Order placement	Product reception and use	Problem resolution	Payment	Account maintenance
The company exposes the customer to its marketing message	The customer gets initial price and lead-time quotes	The customer obtains materials for account setup	The customer selects the product	The customer tracks order status	The customer files a claim and obtains resolution	The customer receives and validates the invoice	The customer maintains profile information
The customer seeks relevant information	The customer puts out an RFP	The customer provides account profile information	The customer places the order (fills out the order form)	The company and the customer arrange the final delivery terms	The customer notifies the company of a problem and obtains resolution	The customer makes the payment	The customer maintains supplies
	The customer evaluates providers and negotiates terms and pricing	The company confirms setup and activation	The customer prepares specialty documents when required (for example, for rush delivery)	The customer receives and inspects the product	The customer seeks an invoice adjustment and obtains resolution		The company provides general support (not related to problems)
	The customer selects the provider	The company performs courtesy follow-up	The company and the customer arrange initial delivery terms	The customer refuses or accepts the product			The customer obtains ongoing price quotes
		The customer requests product information					

SOURCE: David Rickard, "Winning by Understanding the Full Customer Experience," The Boston Consulting Group, Inc., 2007, p. 6. Accessed on July 26, 2008 at http://www.bcg.com. All rights reserved. Reproduced by permission.

8 percent described their experience as "superior," yet 80 percent of the companies surveyed believed that the experience that they were delivering was indeed superior.[5] By focusing narrowly only on core-related product elements and overlooking the full customer experience, companies "can end up losing customers without understanding why. Moreover, such companies are missing out on some powerful opportunities to create value and cement their customers' loyalty," says David Rickard, vice president, The Boston Consulting Group.[6]

Customer experience represents the internal and subjective response a business customer has to any direct or indirect contact with a company. We will devote special attention to **touchpoints**—those instances where the customer has direct contact with either the product or service itself or with representatives of it by a third party, such as a channel partner. A customer experience map provides a valuable tool for diagnosing key touchpoints or interactions between the company and the customer from the moment contact is made with a potential customer through the maintenance of an ongoing relationship (see Figure 10.1). Developed from interviews with customers, the map provides a foundation for defining what's most important in your customers' experience.

---

[5]Ibid., p. 117.

[6]David Rickard, "Winning by Understanding the Full Customer Experience," The Boston Consulting Group, Inc., 2006, p. 1, accessed at http://www.bcg.com on May 15, 2008.

Applying the Customer Experience Map

The map was developed by the Boston Consulting Group for a large industrial-goods company that faced this dilemma: Traditional measures of product quality continued to indicate superb performance, but customer satisfaction remained stagnant and the company was losing market share.[7] Once the customer experience map is developed, the next step is to meet with customers and pare down the list to a smaller set of the most critical interactions and product and service characteristics. The ultimate goal of the analysis is to identify (1) the value that customers place on different levels of performance (for example, high, average, low) for each element of their experience, (2) the customers' minimal expectations for each element, and (3) the customers' perception of the firm's performance versus that of key competitors.

Based on the analysis, strategists at the industrial-goods company were surprised to learn that only 40 percent of customers' most critical experiences were tied to the core product, whereas 60 percent were related to softer considerations (for example, the ease of making invoice corrections and resolving problems). This revelation proved crucial to understanding why the company was losing market share even though its customers' ratings of product quality were improving.

Customer Experience Management

Recall from Chapter 4 that customer relationship management captures what a company knows about a particular customer. Christopher Meyer and Andre Schwager persuasively argue that there is a corresponding need for well-developed **customer experience management** processes that capture customers' subjective thoughts about a particular company.[8] Such an approach requires surveys and targeted studies at points of customer interaction that identify gaps between customer expectations and their actual experience. "Because a great many customer experiences aren't the direct consequence of the brand's message or the company's actual offerings . . . the customers themselves . . . must be monitored and probed."[9]

A Solution-Centered Perspective[10]

As global competition intensifies and product differentiation quickly fades, strategists at leading firms from General Electric and IBM to Staples and Home Depot are giving increased attention to services, particularly a solution-centric mindset. Rather than starting with the product, a solution-centered approach begins with an analysis of a *customer problem* and ends by identifying the products and services required to solve the problem. Rather than transaction based, the focus of the exchange process is interaction based, and value is co-created by the firm in concert with the customer (Table 10.1). So, customer offerings represent an "integrated combination of products and services designed to provide customized experiences for specific customer segments."[11] Services, as a critical feature of the solution, become a valuable basis for competitive advantage and an important driver of profitability.

---

[7]This illustration is based on Rickard, ibid., p. 5.

[8]Meyer and Schwager, "Understanding Customer Experiences."

[9]Ibid., p. 116.

[10]Except where noted, this section draws on Mohanbir Sawhney, "Going Beyond the Product: Defining, Designing, and Delivering Customer Solutions," Working Paper, Kellogg School of Management, Northwestern University, December 2004, pp. 1–10.

[11]Ibid., p. 4.

	TABLE 10.1	**FROM A PRODUCT TO A SOLUTIONS PERSPECTIVE**	

	Product Perspective	**Solutions Perspective**
Value Proposition	Win by creating innovative products and enriching features of existing products	Win by creating and delivering superior customer solutions
Value Creation	Value is created by the firm	Value is co-created by the customer and the firm
Designing Offerings	Start with the product or service, and then target customer segments	Start with the customer problem, and then assemble required products and services to solve the problem
Company-Customer Relationship	Transaction-based	Interaction-based and centered on the co-creation of solutions
Focus on Quality	Quality of internal processes and company offerings	Quality of customer–firm interactions

SOURCE: Adapted from Mohanbir Sawhney, "Going Beyond the Product: Defining, Designing, and Delivering Customer Solutions," Working Paper, Kellogg School of Management, Northwestern University, December 2004; and C. K. Prahalad and Venkat Ramaswamy, *The Future of Competition: Co-Creating Unique Value with Customers* (Boston: Harvard Business School Press, 2004).

UPS Solutions   United Parcel Services of America began by mastering a narrow set of activities involved in the package delivery system—picking up, shipping, tracking, and delivering packages. Adopting a solution-centered focus, UPS tapped new market opportunities:[12]

- Designing transportation networks that reduced the time Ford needed to deliver vehicles from its plants to dealers by up to 40 percent;

- Managing the movement of National Semiconductor's products from its manufacturing plants to customers around the world and helping the customer reduce shipping and inventory costs by 15 percent;

- Partnering with Nike and managing all the back-office processes for direct selling from order management and delivery to customer support.

Determine Unique Capabilities   In developing solutions, business marketing firms must define their unique capabilities and determine how to use them to help customers reduce costs, increase responsiveness, or improve quality. In some cases, this may involve taking in some of the work or activities that customers now perform. To illustrate, DuPont first sold paint to Ford but now runs Ford's paint shops. "DuPont, which is paid on the basis of the number of painted vehicles, actually sells less paint than before because it has an incentive to paint cars with the least amount of waste. But the company makes more money as a result of the improved efficiency."[13] The

---

[12]Mohanbir Sawhney, Sridhar Balasubramanian, and Vish V. Krishnan, "Creating Growth with Services," *MIT Sloan Management Review* 45 (Winter 2004): pp. 34–43.

[13]Ibid., p. 39.

INSIDE BUSINESS MARKETING

Do Service Transition Strategies Pay Off?

To improve their competitive position in the era of intense global competition and the increasing commoditization that characterizes many product markets, a host of manufacturing firms have added services to their existing product offerings. If successful, such service transition strategies could make the firm's value proposition more unique, difficult for rivals to duplicate, and valuable to customers, thereby enhancing profitability and firm value. Do these service transition strategies pay off? A recent study by Eric Fang and his colleagues provides the answers.

- Before they can expect positive effects on firm value, business marketing firms should recognize that service transition strategies typically require achieving a critical mass in sales, estimated to be 20 to 30 percent of total sales.

- Transitioning to services is significantly more effective for companies that offer services related to their core product business. Sales of unrelated services demonstrate little impact on firm value.

- Adding services to a core product offering increases firm value for companies in slow growth and turbulent industries. However, "firms in high growth industries can destroy firm value by shifting their focus . . . to service initiatives. In stable (low turbulence) industries, adding services has a negative effect on firm value. . . ."

SOURCE: Eric (Er) Fang, Robert W. Palmatier, and Jan-Benedict E. M. Steenkamp, "Effect of Service Transition Strategies on Firm Value," *Journal of Marketing*, forthcoming.

DuPont example demonstrates a central point about solutions marketing: *Products provide the platform for the delivery of services*.[14]

A recent research study suggests that companies can deliver more effective solutions at profitable prices if they adopt a stronger relationship focus.[15] The authors suggest that business marketers mistakenly view a solution as a customized and integrated combination of products and services for meeting a customer's business needs. In sharp contrast, customers view a solution as a set of customer–company relational processes that involve "(1) customer requirements definition, (2) customization and integration of goods and/or services and (3) their deployment, and (4) postdeployment customer support, all of which are aimed at meeting customers' business needs."[16] Once again, this highlights the importance of moving beyond a mere focus on transactions to consider the full set of customer experiences.

Benefits of Solution Marketing

By shifting from a product to a solutions strategy, business-to-business firms gain two important benefits, namely, new avenues for growth and differentiation.

Creating Growth Opportunities Solutions create fresh opportunities for increasing the amount of business or share-of-wallet that a company receives from its customer base. An expanded portfolio of service-intensive offerings makes this possible. Often, services represent a far larger market opportunity than the core product market.

---

[14]Stephen L. Vargo and Robert F. Lusch, "Evolving to a New Dominant Logic for Marketing," *Journal of Marketing* 68 (January 2004): pp. 1–18.

[15]Kapil R. Tuli, Ajay K. Kohli, and Sundar R. Bharadwaj, "Rethinking Customer Solutions for Product Bundles to Relational Process," *Journal of Marketing* 71 (July 2007): pp. 1–17.

[16]Ibid., p. 1.

To illustrate, Deere & Company, the agricultural equipment manufacturer, found that the proportion of each dollar farmers spend on equipment has been declining for years and that the bulk of that spending now goes for services. Moreover, by centering on that profit pool, Deere is tapping into a market opportunity that is 10 times larger than the equipment market. To that end, Deere provides a range of services for its customers (for example, health insurance and banking) and is employing innovative technologies to make the farmer's life easier and more productive. For example, Deere is experimenting with global positioning systems (GPS) and biosensors on its combines. C. K. Prahalad and Venkat Ramaswamy describe the initiative:

> Imagine driverless combines and tractors with onboard sensors that can measure the oil content of grain or distinguish between weeds and crops. The benefits are enormous. Farmers can ration herbicide according to soil conditions. GPS-guided steering ensures repeatable accuracy, eliminates overtreating of crops . . . thereby reducing time, fuel, labor, and chemical costs. . . . Farmers can be more productive, minimizing the cost per acre.[17]

Sustaining Differentiation and Customer Loyalty As farmers view more and more products as commodities, business marketers who emphasize solutions can sustain differentiation more effectively than rivals who maintain a strict focus on the core product offering. Why? According to Mohanbir Sawhney, "Solutions offer many more avenues for differentiation than products because they include a variety of services that can be customized in many unique ways for individual customers."[18] Likewise, by developing a rich network of relationships with members of the customer organization, co-creating solutions with the customer, and becoming directly connected to the customer's operations, they enhance customer loyalty and throw up severe barriers to competing firms when they attempt to persuade the customer to switch suppliers.

Business Service Marketing: Special Challenges

The development of marketing programs for both products and services can be approached from a common perspective; yet the relative importance and form of various strategic elements differ between products and services. The underlying explanation for these strategic differences, asserts Henry Assael, lies in the distinctions between a product and a service:

> Services are intangible; products are tangible. Services are consumed at the time of production, but there is a time lag between the production and consumption of products. Services cannot be stored; products can. Services are highly variable; most products are highly standardized. These differences produce differences in strategic applications that often stand many product marketing principles on their head.[19]

[17]C. K. Prahalad and Venkat Ramaswamy, *The Future of Competition: Co-Creating Unique Value with Customers* (Boston: Harvard Business School Press, 2004), pp. 93–94.

[18]Mohanbir Sawhney, "Going Beyond the Product," p. 6.

[19]Henry Assael, *Marketing Management: Strategy and Action* (Boston.: Kent Publishing, 1985), p. 693.

FIGURE 10.2 | **BUSINESS PRODUCT—SERVICE CLASSIFICATION BASED ON TANGIBILITY**

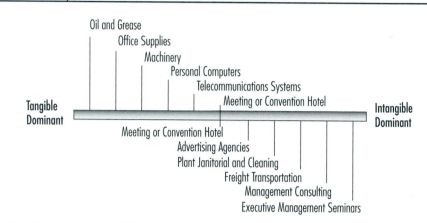

SOURCE: Adapted from G. Lynn Shostack, "Breaking Free from Product Marketing," *Journal of Marketing* 41 (April 1977): p. 77. Published by the American Marketing Association.

Thus, success in the business service marketplace begins with understanding the meaning of *service*.

Services Are Different

There are inherent differences between goods and services, providing a unique set of marketing challenges for service businesses and for manufacturers that provide services as a core offering. Put simply, services are deeds, processes, and performances.[20] For example, a management consultant's core offerings are primarily deeds and actions performed for customers. The most basic, and universally recognized, difference between goods and services is *intangibility*. Services are more intangible than manufactured goods, and manufactured goods are more tangible than services. Because services are actions or performances, they cannot be seen or touched in the same way that consumers sense tangible goods.

Tangible or Intangible?

Figure 10.2 provides a useful tool for understanding the product–service definitional problem. The continuum suggests that there are very few *pure products* or *pure services*. For example, a personal computer is a physical object made up of tangible elements that facilitate the work of an individual and an organization. In addition to the computer's physical design and performance characteristics, the quality of technical service support is an important dimension of the marketing program. Thus, most market offerings comprise a combination of tangible and intangible elements.

Whether an offering is classified as a good or as a service depends on how the organizational buyer views it—whether the tangible or the intangible elements dominate. On one end of the spectrum, grease and oil are tangible-dominant; the essence of what is being bought is the physical product. Management seminars, on the other

---

[20]Valarie A. Zeithaml, Mary Jo Bitner, and Dwayne D. Gremler, *Services Marketing: Integrating Customer Focus across the Firm*, 5th ed. (Boston: McGraw-Hill Irwin, 2009), p. 2.

hand, are intangible-dominant because what is being bought—professional development, education, learning—has few, if any, tangible properties. A convention hotel is in the middle of the continuum because the buyer receives an array of both tangible elements (meals, beverages, notepads, and so on) and intangible benefits (courteous personnel, fast check-ins, meeting room ambiance, and so forth).

The concept of tangibility is especially useful to the business marketer because many business offerings are composed of product and service combinations. The key management task is to evaluate carefully (from the buyer's standpoint) which elements dominate. The more the market offering is characterized by intangible elements, the more difficult it is to apply the standard marketing tools that were developed for products. The business marketer must focus on specialized marketing approaches appropriate for services.

The concept of tangibility also helps the manager focus clearly on the firm's *total market offering*.[21] In addition, it helps the manager recognize that a change in one element of the market offering may completely change the offering in the customer's view. For example, a business marketer who decides to hold spare-parts inventory at a central location and use overnight delivery to meet customer requirements must refocus marketing strategy. The offering has moved toward the intangible end of the continuum because of the intangible benefits of reduced customer inventory and fast transportation. This new "service," which is less tangible, must be carefully explained, and the intangible results of lower inventory costs must be made more concrete to the buyer through an effective promotion program.

In summary, business services are market offerings that are predominantly intangible. However, few services are totally intangible—they often contain elements with tangible properties. In addition to tangibility, business services have other important distinguishing characteristics that influence how they are marketed. Table 10.2 summarizes the core characteristics that further delineate the nature of business services.

Simultaneous Production and Consumption

Because services are generally *consumed as they are produced*, a critical element in the buyer-seller relationship is the effectiveness of the individual who actually provides the service—the IBM technician, the UPS driver, the McKinsey consultant. From the service firm's perspective, the entire marketing strategy may rest on how effectively the individual service provider interacts with the customer. Here the actual service delivery takes place and the promise to the customer is kept or broken. This critical point of contact with the customer is referred to as **interactive** or **real-time marketing**. Recruiting, hiring, and training personnel assume special importance in business service firms.

Service Variability

Observe in Table 10.2 that service is *nonstandardized*, meaning that the quality of the service output may vary each time it is provided.[22] Services vary in the amount of

---

[21]Arun Sharma, R. Krishnan, and Dhruv Grewal, "Value Creation in Markets: A Critical Area of Focus for Business-to-Business Markets," *Industrial Marketing Management* 30 (June 2001): pp. 391–402.

[22]Valarie A. Zeithaml, A. Parasuraman, and Leonard R. Berry, "Problems and Strategies in Services Marketing," *Journal of Marketing* 49 (Spring 1985): p. 34; see also Zeithaml, Berry, and Parasuraman, "Communication and Control Processes in the Delivery of Service Quality," *Journal of Marketing* 52 (April 1988): pp. 35–48.

TABLE 10.2 | **UNIQUE SERVICE CHARACTERISTICS**

Characteristics	Examples	Marketing Implications
Simultaneous production and consumption	Telephone conference call; management seminar; equipment repair	Direct-seller interaction requires that service be done "right"; requires high-level training for personnel; requires effective screening and recruitment
Nonstandardized output	Management advice varies with the individual consultant; merchandise damages vary from shipment to shipment	Emphasizes strict quality control standards; develop systems that minimize deviation and human error; prepackage the service; look for ways to automate
Perishability: inability to store or stockpile	Unfilled airline seats; an idle computer technician; unrented warehouse space	Plan capacity around peak demand; use pricing and promotion to even out demand peaks and valleys; use overlapping shifts for personnel
Lack of ownership	Use of railroad car; use of consultant's know-how; use of mailing list	Focus promotion on the advantages of nonownership: reduced labor, overhead, and capital; emphasize flexibility

equipment and labor used to provide them. For example, a significant human element is involved in teaching an executive seminar compared with providing overnight airfreight service. Generally, the more labor involved in a service, the less uniform the output. In these labor-intensive cases, the user may also find it difficult to judge the quality before the service is provided. Because of uniformity problems, business service providers must focus on finely tuned quality-control programs, invest in "systems" to minimize human error, and seek approaches for automating the service.

Service Perishability

Generally, services *cannot be stored*; that is, if they are not provided at the time they are available, the lost revenue cannot be recaptured. Tied to this characteristic is the fact that demand for services is often unpredictable and widely fluctuating. The service marketer must carefully evaluate capacity—in a service business, **capacity** is a substitute for inventory. If capacity is set for peak demand, a "service inventory" must exist to supply the highest level of demand. As an example, some airlines that provide air shuttle service between New York, Washington, and Boston offer flights that leave every hour. If, on any flight, the plane is full, another plane is brought to the terminal—even for one passenger. An infinite capacity is set so that no single business traveler is dissatisfied. Obviously, setting high capacity levels is costly, and the marketer must analyze the cost versus the lost revenue and customer goodwill that might result from maintaining lower capacity.

Nonownership

The final dimension of services shown in Table 10.2 is that the service buyer uses, but *does not own*, the service purchased. Essentially, payment for a service is a payment for the use of, access to, or hire of items. Renting or leasing is "a way for customers to enjoy use of physical goods and facilities that they cannot afford to buy, cannot justify

INSIDE BUSINESS MARKETING

To Sell Jet Engines, Teach Your Customer How to Sell Aircraft

A major segment of GE Transportation is the General Electric Aircraft Engines division. This unit is the world's largest manufacturer of jet engines, ranging from small 14,000-pound thrust engines up to the giant GE90, a 115,000-pound thrust engine that powers the Boeing 777. As important as these engines are to GE's profitability, the real profits come from the *service package* surrounding the sale of an engine. A jet engine lasts years, and what often clinches a sale and leads to long-term profits for GE is the full-service "package" that accompanies the engine over its lifespan. One GE marketing manager claims that "jet engines are almost commodities; the key differentiator is the lifetime service we offer our customers."

Interestingly, the airline that buys a new aircraft is generally the decision-making unit that chooses the engine brand to be installed—not the aircraft manufacturer, namely Boeing or Airbus. Recognizing the importance of the airline in the purchase process for jet engines, GE embarked on a creative strategy. Several new aircraft manufacturers began operations in China in the early 2000s as a result of that country's major economic growth. One manufacturer, specializing in small, regional jets (50- to 70-passenger capacity), selected GE as the engine supplier in 2004, although the firm

would not produce an airplane until at least 2008. The company was starting from scratch when it selected GE engines for its planes.

GE immediately began working with the firm to refine the plane's design and engineering, and these valuable services were one reason it selected GE as the supplier. More importantly, GE assigned one manager and a team of sales, engineering, and marketing specialists to work with the firm. One of GE's first efforts was to bring 25 sales and marketing managers from the Chinese aircraft company to the United States for two weeks of training. These managers represent the personnel who will be selling the aircraft to airline executives in China, as well as in many other parts of the world. The two-week training program centered on the basics of business-to-business marketing—something the Chinese knew little about. GE brought in experienced faculty to teach the Chinese and provided GE managers to follow up on the training at later dates. What is unique about this approach is that a supplier was actually teaching the customer how to market and sell! Of course, the benefits to GE are huge: If the Chinese aircraft firm is effective at business-to-business selling to airlines, then more GE engines will be demanded in the future.

purchasing, or prefer not to retain after use."[23] The service marketer must feature the advantages of nonownership in its communications to the marketplace. The key benefits to emphasize are reductions in staff, overhead, and capital from having a third party provide the service.

Although there may be exceptions, these characteristics provide a useful framework for understanding the nature of business services and isolating special marketing strategy requirements. The framework suggests that different types of service providers should pursue different types of strategies because of the intangibility and heterogeneity of their services. In this case, providers of professional services (consulting, tax advising, accounting, and so on) should develop marketing strategies that emphasize word-of-mouth communication, provide tangible evidence, and employ value pricing to overcome the issues created by intangibility and heterogeneity.[24]

---

[23] Christopher Lovelock and Evert Gummesson, "Whither Services Marketing? In Search of a New Paradigm and Fresh Perspectives," *Journal of Services Research* 7 (August 2004): p. 36.

[24] Michael Clemes, Diane Mollenkopf, and Darryl Burn, "An Investigation of Marketing Problems across Service Typologies," *Journal of Services Marketing* 14 (no. 6–7, 2000): p. 568; see also, Möllar, Rajala, and Westerlund, "Service Innovation Myopia," pp. 34–46.

Service Quality

Quality standards are ultimately defined by the customer. Actual performance by the service provider or the provider's perception of quality are of little relevance compared with the customer's perception. "Good" service results when the service provider meets or exceeds the customer's expectations.[25] As a result, many management experts argue that service companies should carefully position themselves so that customers expect a little less than the firm can actually deliver. The strategy: underpromise and overdeliver.

Dimensions of Service Quality

Because business services are intangible and nonstandardized, buyers tend to have greater difficulty evaluating services than evaluating goods. Because they are unable to depend on consistent service performance and quality, service buyers may perceive more risk.[26] As a result, they use a variety of prepurchase information sources to reduce risk. Information from current users (word of mouth) is particularly important. In addition, the evaluation process for services tends to be more abstract, more random, and more heavily based on symbology rather than on concrete decision variables.[27]

Research provides some valuable insights into how customers evaluate service quality. From Table 10.3, note that customers focus on five dimensions in evaluating service quality: reliability, responsiveness, assurance, empathy, and tangibles. Among these dimensions, reliability—delivery on promises—is the most important to customers. High-quality service performance is also shaped by the way frontline service personnel provide it. To the customer, service quality represents a responsive employee, one who inspires confidence, and one who adapts to the customer's unique needs or preferences and delivers the service in a professional manner. In fact, the performance of employees who are in contact with the customer may compensate for temporary service quality problems (for example, a problem reoccurs in a recently repaired photocopier).[28] By promptly acknowledging the error and responding quickly to the problem, the service employee may even strengthen the firm's relationship with the customer.

Customer Satisfaction and Loyalty

Four components of a firm's offering and its customer-linking processes affect customer satisfaction:

1. The basic elements of the product or service that customers expect all competitors to provide;

[25] William H. Davidow and Bro Uttal, "Service Companies: Focus or Falter," *Harvard Business Review* 67 (July–August 1989): p. 84.

[26] Valarie A. Zeithaml, "How Consumer Evaluation Processes Differ between Goods and Services," in *Marketing of Services*, James H. Donnelly and William R. George, eds. (Chicago: American Marketing Association, 1981), pp. 200–204.

[27] Ibid.

[28] Christian Gronroos, "Relationship Marketing: Strategic and Tactical Implications," *Management Decision*, 34 (no. 3, 1996): pp. 5–14.

TABLE 10.3 | **THE DIMENSIONS OF SERVICE QUALITY**

Dimension	Description	Examples
Reliability	Delivering on promises	Promised delivery date met
Responsiveness	Being willing to help	Prompt reply to customers' requests
Assurance	Inspiring trust and confidence	Professional and knowledgeable staff
Empathy	Treating customers as individuals	Adapts to special needs of customer
Tangibles	Representing the service physically	Distinctive materials: brochures, documents

SOURCE: Adapted from Valarie A. Zeithaml, Mary Jo Bitner, and Dwayne D. Gremler, *Services Marketing: Integrating Customer Focus across the Firm*, 5th ed. (Boston: McGraw-Hill Irwin, 2009), pp. 116–120.

2. Basic support services, such as technical assistance or training, that make the product or service more effective or easier to use;

3. A recovery process for quickly fixing product or service problems;

4. Extraordinary services that so excel in solving customers' unique problems or in meeting their needs that they make the product or service seem customized.[29]

Leading service firms carefully measure and monitor customer satisfaction because it is linked to customer loyalty and, in turn, to long-term profitability.[30] Xerox, for example, regularly surveys more than 400,000 customers regarding product and service satisfaction using a 5-point scale from 5 (high) to 1 (low). In analyzing the data, Xerox executives made a remarkable discovery: Very satisfied customers (a 5 rating) were far more loyal than satisfied customers. Very satisfied customers, in fact, were *six times* more likely to repurchase Xerox products than satisfied customers.

Service Recovery

Business marketers cannot always provide flawless service. However, the way the firm responds to a client's service problems has a crucial bearing on customer retention and loyalty. **Service recovery** encompasses the procedures, policies, and processes a firm uses to resolve customer service problems promptly and effectively. For example, when IBM receives a customer complaint, a specialist who is an expert in the relevant product or service area is assigned as "resolution owner" of that complaint. On being assigned a customer complaint or problem, the IBM specialist must contact the customer within 48 hours (except in the case of severe problems, where the required

---

[29]Thomas O. Jones and W. Earl Sasser Jr., "Why Satisfied Customers Defect," *Harvard Business Review* 73 (November–December 1995): p. 90.

[30]The Xerox illustration is based on James L. Heskett, Thomas O. Jones, Gary W. Loveman, W. Earl Sasser Jr., and Leonard A. Schlesinger, "Putting the Service-Profit Chain to Work," *Harvard Business Review* 72 (March–April 1994): pp. 164–174.

response is made much faster). Larry Schiff, a marketing strategist at IBM, describes how the process works from there:

> They introduce themselves as owners of the customer's problem and ask: What's it going to take for you to be very satisfied with the resolution of this complaint? . . . Together with the customer, we negotiate an action plan and then execute that plan until the customer problem is resolved. The problem only gets closed when the customer says it is closed, and we measure this [*that is, customer satisfaction with problem resolution*] as well.[31]

Service providers who satisfactorily resolve service failures often see that their customer's level of perceived service quality rises. One study in the ocean-freight-shipping industry found that clients who expressed higher satisfaction with claims handling, complaint handling, and problem resolution have a higher level of overall satisfaction with the shipping line.[32] Therefore, business marketers should develop thoughtful and highly responsive processes for dealing with service failures. Some studies have shown that customers who experienced a service failure and had it corrected to their satisfaction have greater loyalty to the supplier than those customers who did not experience a service failure!

Zero Defections

The quality of service provided to business customers has a major effect on customer "defections"—customers who do not come back. Service strategists point out that customer defections have a powerful effect on the bottom line.[33] As a company's relationship with a customer lengthens, profits rise—and generally rise considerably. For example, one service firm found that profit from a fourth-year customer is triple that from a first-year customer. Many additional benefits accrue to service companies that retain their customers: They can charge more, the cost of doing business is reduced, and the long-standing customer provides "free" advertising. The implications are clear: Service providers should carefully track customer defections and recognize that continuous improvement in service quality is not a cost but, say Frederick Reichheld and W. Earl Sasser, "an investment in a customer who generates more profit than the margin on a one-time sale."[34]

Return on Quality

A difficult decision for the business-services marketing manager is to determine how much to spend on improving service quality. Clearly, expenditures on quality have diminishing returns—at some point, additional expenditures do not increase profits. To make good decisions on the level of expenditures on quality, managers must justify

[31] Larry Schiff, "How Customer Satisfaction Improvement Works to Fuel Business Recovery at IBM," *Journal of Organizational Excellence* 20 (Spring 2001): p. 12.

[32] Srinivas Durvasula, Steven Lysonski, and Subhash C. Mehta, "Business-to-Business Marketing: Service Recovery and Customer Satisfaction Issues with Ocean Shipping Lines," *European Journal of Marketing* 34 (no. 3–4, 2000): p. 441.

[33] Frederick F. Reichheld and W. Earl Sasser, "Zero Defections: Quality Comes to Services," *Harvard Business Review* 68 (September–October 1990): p. 105; see also, Frederick F. Reichheld, *Loyalty Rules! How Today's Leaders Build Lasting Relationships* (Boston: Harvard Business School Press, 2001).

[34] Reichheld and Sasser, "Zero Defections," p. 107.

quality efforts on a financial basis, knowing where to spend on quality improvement, how much to spend, and when to reduce or stop the expenditures. Roland Rust, Anthony Zahorik, and Timothy Keiningham have developed a technique for calculating the "return on investing in quality."[35] Under this approach, service quality benefits are successively linked to customer satisfaction, customer retention, market share, and, finally, to profitability. The relationship between expenditure level and customer-satisfaction change is first measured by managerial judgment and then through market testing. When the relationship has been estimated, the return on quality can be measured statistically. The significant conclusion is that quality improvements should be treated as investments: They must pay off, and spending should not be wasted on efforts that do not produce a return.

Marketing Mix for Business Service Firms

Meeting the needs of service buyers effectively requires an integrated marketing strategy. First, target segments must be selected, and then a marketing mix must be tailored to the expectations of each segment. The business marketing manager must give special consideration to each of the key elements of the service marketing mix: development of service packages, pricing, promotion, and distribution.

In terms of the overall approach that firms develop to interact with their customers, business-to-business service firms are more likely to emphasize *relationship* strategies as opposed to *transactional* strategies.[36] Because the transactional mode involves an arm's-length relationship, success in marketing business services hinges on the business marketer's ability to develop close and long-lasting ties with customers—based on buyer-seller dependence. The emphasis in marketing business services is on managing the total buyer-seller interaction process.

Segmentation

As with any marketing situation, development of the marketing mix is contingent on the customer segment to be served. Every facet of the service, as well as the methods for promoting, pricing, and delivering it, hinges on the needs of a reasonably homogeneous group of customers. The process for segmenting business markets described in Chapter 5 applies in the services market. However, William Davidow and Bro Uttal suggest that customer service segments differ from usual market segments in significant ways.[37]

First, service segments are often narrower, often because many service customers expect services to be customized. Expectations may not be met if the service received is standardized and routine. Second, service segmentation focuses on what

---

[35] Roland T. Rust, Anthony J. Zahorik, and Timothy L. Keiningham, "Return on Quality (ROQ): Making Service Quality Financially Accountable," *Journal of Marketing* 59 (April 1995): pp. 58–70; see also Roland T. Rust, Katherine N. Lemon, and Valarie A. Zeithaml, "Return on Marketing: Using Customer Equity to Focus Marketing Strategy," *Journal of Marketing* 68 (January 2004): pp. 109–127.

[36] Nicole E. Coviello, Roderick J. Brodie, Peter J. Danaher, and Wesley J. Johnston, "How Firms Relate to Their Markets: An Empirical Examination of Contemporary Marketing Practices," *Journal of Marketing* 66 (Summer 2002): p. 38.

[37] Davidow and Uttal, "Service Companies," p. 79.

the business buyers expect as opposed to what they need. Assessing buyer expectations plays a major role in selecting a target market and developing the appropriate service package. This assessment is critical because so many studies have shown large differences between the ways customers and suppliers define and rank different service activities.[38]

Because service-quality expectations play such an important role in determining ultimate satisfaction with a service, they can be used to segment business-to-business markets. One study in the mainframe software industry revealed significant differences between "software specialists" (software experts) and "applications developers" (users of software) in the same firm regarding their expectations of new software. The developers (users) had higher expectations about the quality of a supplier's equipment, its employees' responsiveness, and the amount of personal attention provided.[39] The study concluded that different buying-center members may well have different perspectives and different expectations of service quality. The business marketer should carefully evaluate the possibility of using service-quality expectations as a guide for creating marketing strategy.

Finally, segmenting service markets helps the firm adjust service capacity more effectively. Segmentation usually reveals that total demand is made up of numerous smaller, yet more predictable, demand patterns. A hotel can individually forecast and adjust its capacities to the demand patterns of convention visitors, business travelers, foreign tourists, or vacationers.

Service Packages

The **service package** can be thought of as the product dimension of service, including decisions about the essential concept of the service, the range of services provided, and the quality and level of service. In addition, the service package must consider some unique factors—the personnel who perform the service, the physical product that accompanies the service, and the process of providing the service.[40] A useful way to conceptualize the service product is shown in Figure 10.3.

Customer-Benefit Concept   Services are purchased because of the benefits they offer, and a first step in either creating a service or evaluating an existing one is to define the **customer-benefit concept**—that is, evaluate the core benefit the customer derives from the service. Understanding the customer-benefit concept focuses the business marketer's attention on those attributes—functional, effectual, and psychological—that must be not only offered but also tightly monitored from a quality-control standpoint. For example, a sales manager selecting a resort hotel for an annual sales meeting is purchasing a core benefit that could be stated as "a successful meeting." The hotel marketer must then assess the full range of service attributes and components necessary to provide a successful meeting. Obviously, a wide variety of service elements come into play: (1) meeting-room size, layout, environment,

---

[38]Ibid., p. 83.

[39]Leyland Pitt, Michael H. Morris, and Pierre Oosthuizen, "Expectations of Service Quality as an Industrial Market Segmentation Variable," *Service Industries Journal* 16 (January 1996): pp. 1–9; see also Ralph W. Jackson, Lester A. Neidell, and Dale A. Lunsford, "An Empirical Investigation of the Differences in Goods and Services as Perceived by Organizational Buyers," *Industrial Marketing Management* 24 (March 1995): pp. 99–108.

[40]Donald Cowell, *The Marketing of Services* (London: William Heinemann, 1984), p. 73.

FIGURE 10.3 | CONCEPTUALIZING THE SERVICE PRODUCT

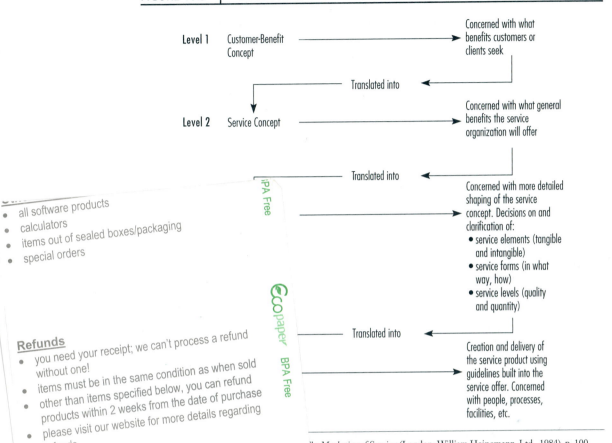

Level 1   Customer-Benefit Concept → Concerned with what benefits customers or clients seek

Translated into

Level 2   Service Concept → Concerned with what general benefits the service organization will offer

Translated into

Concerned with more detailed shaping of the service concept. Decisions on and clarification of:
- service elements (tangible and intangible)
- service forms (in what way, how)
- service levels (quality and quantity)

Translated into

Creation and delivery of the service product using guidelines built into the service offer. Concerned with people, processes, facilities, etc.

The Marketing of Services (London: William Heinemann, Ltd., 1984), p. 100.

...table and quiet sleeping rooms; (4) audiovisual equip-...ss.

...stomer-benefit concept is understood, the next step is ..., which defines the general benefits the service com-...ndle of goods and services it sells to the customer. ...customer-benefit concept into the range of benefits ... For a hotel, the service concept might specify the ...lity, responsiveness, and courteousness in providing ...diovisual equipment; flexible meal schedules; mes-...el; and climate-controlled meeting rooms.

...with the service concept is the **service offer**, which ...services to be offered; when, where, and to whom they ...be provided; and how they will be presented. The service elements that make up the total service package, including both tangibles and intangibles, must be determined. The service offer of the hotel includes a multitude of tangible elements (soundproof meeting rooms, projection equipment, video players, slide projectors, flip charts, refreshments, heating and air-conditioning, meals) and intangible elements (attitude of meeting-room setup personnel, warmth of greetings from desk clerks and bellhops, response to unique requests, meeting-room ambiance). Generally, management finds it easier to manage the tangible (equipment and physical) elements of the service than to control the intangible elements.

Service Delivery System   The final dimension of the service product is the service delivery system—how the service is provided to the customer. The delivery system includes carefully conceived jobs for people; personnel with capabilities and attitudes necessary for successful performance; equipment, facilities, and layouts for effective customer work flow; and carefully developed procedures and processes aimed at a common set of objectives.[41] Thus, the service delivery system should provide a carefully designed blueprint that describes how the service is rendered for the customer.

For physical products, manufacturing and marketing are generally separate and distinct activities; for services, these two activities are often inseparable.[42] The service performance and the delivery system both create the product and deliver it to customers. This feature of services underscores the important role of people, particularly service providers, in the marketing process. Technicians, repair personnel, and maintenance engineers are intimately involved in customer contact, and they decidedly influence the customer's perception of service quality. The business service marketer must pay close attention to both people and physical evidence (tangible elements such as uniforms) when designing the service package.

Lean Consumption   James Womack and Daniel Jones suggest that the concept of "lean consumption" provides an effective way to think about how services are used.[43] **Lean consumption** is focused on providing the full value that buyers desire from their goods and services, with the greatest efficiency and least trouble. When a business buys a computer system, for example, this is not a one-time transaction. The company has embarked on the arduous process of researching, obtaining, integrating, maintaining, upgrading, and finally, disposing of this product. For computer manufacturers (whether employees, managers, or entrepreneurs), developing lean consumption processes requires determining how to configure linked business activities, especially across firms, to meet customer needs without wasting their own—or the customer's—time, effort, and resources. These favorable results are achieved by tightly integrating and streamlining the processes of provision and consumption. This approach has been pursued effectively by Fujitsu Services, a leading global provider of outsourced customer service. Companies that contract with Fujitsu to manage their in-house information technology help desks find that the number of calls their desks receive about a recurring problem—say, malfunctioning printers—often falls to near zero. What Fujitsu does is identify and fix the source of the problem—for example, replace the flawed printers with new ones. By seeking the root cause of the problem somewhere up the value stream (often involving multiple companies), Fujitsu has pioneered a way to eliminate problems and reduce costs.[44]

[41]James L. Heskett, *Managing in the Service Economy* (Boston: Harvard Business School Press, 1986), p. 20.
[42]Cowell, *The Marketing of Services*, p. 110.
[43]James Womack and Daniel Jones, "Lean Consumption," *Harvard Business Review* 83 (March 2005): p. 60.
[44]Ibid., p. 61.

Service Personnel   A first step in creating an effective service package is to ensure that all personnel know, understand, and accept the customer-benefit concept. As Donald Cowell states, "So important are people and their quality to organizations and . . . services that 'internal marketing' is considered to be an important management role to ensure that all staff are customer conscious."[45] In short, the attitudes, skills, knowledge, and behavior of service personnel have a critical effect on the customer's level of satisfaction with the service.

Pricing Business Services

Although product and service pricing policies and strategies share many common threads, the unique characteristics of services create some special pricing problems and opportunities.

Perishability and Managing Demand/Capacity   The demand for services is rarely steady or predictable enough to avoid service perishability. An extremely difficult decision for the business service marketer is to determine the capacity (inventory) of the system: Should it meet peak demand, average demand, or somewhere in between? Pricing can be used to manage the timing of demand and align it with capacity.

To manage demand, the marketer may offer off-peak pricing schemes and price incentives for service orders placed in advance. For example, resort hotels, crowded with pleasure travelers during school vacations and holidays, develop special packages for business groups during the off-season. Similarly, utilities may offer significant rate reductions for off-peak usage. It may also be possible, depending on demand elasticity and competition, to charge premium rates for services provided at peak demand periods. Interestingly, however, a recent study showed that many service firms do not reduce prices to increase business during slow periods.[46]

Service Bundling   Many business services include a core service as well as various peripheral services. How should the services be priced—as an entity, as a service bundle, or individually? **Bundling** is the practice of marketing two or more services in a package for a special price.[47] Bundling makes sense in the business service environment because most service businesses have a high ratio of fixed costs to variable costs and a high degree of cost sharing among their many related services. Hence, the marginal cost of providing additional services to the core service customer is generally low.

A key decision for the service provider is whether to provide pure or mixed bundling.[48] In **pure bundling**, the services are available only in bundled form—they cannot be purchased separately. In **mixed bundling**, the customer can purchase one or more services individually or purchase the bundle. For example, a public warehouse firm can provide its services—storage, product handling, and clerical activities—in a price-bundled form by charging a single rate (8 cents) for each case the warehouse receives from its manufacturer-client. Or the firm may market each service separately and provide a rate for each service individually (3 cents per case for storage, 4 cents

---

[45] Cowell, *The Marketing of Services*, p. 110; see also, Francis X. Frei, "The Four Things a Service Business Must Get Right," *Harvard Business Review* 86 (April 2008): pp. 70–80.

[46] Zeithaml, Parasuraman, and Berry, "Problems and Strategies in Services Marketing," p. 41.

[47] Joseph P. Guiltinan, "The Price Bundling of Services: A Normative Framework," *Journal of Marketing* 51 (April 1987): p. 74.

[48] Ibid., p. 75.

per case for handling, and 1 cent per case for clerical). Additionally, a multitude of peripheral services can be quoted on an individual basis: physical inventory count, freight company selection and routing, merchandise return and repair, and so on. In this way, the customer can choose the services desired and pay for each separately.

Creating a Service-Savvy Sales Force[49] As companies move away from product-related services into more elaborate customer solutions, a new set of challenges are presented to salespeople: Services require a long sales cycle and a complex sales process that often involves the participation of senior executives on both the buying and selling sides. To develop a focused strategy, the sales force at GE Healthcare includes both product and service specialists. The product salespeople are called "hunters," centering their attention on securing customer orders for new equipment. Service salespeople are "farmers"; GE expects them to nurture and develop relationships, growing the service business over time.

Isolate Service Profitability In many industries, firms often supply customers with myriad services such as next-day delivery, customized handling, and specialized labeling. However, not all companies track the real costs of the many services they offer and they have no concrete data on net profit margins. As a result, the high-volume customers who receive the lion's share of these services may be far less profitable than companies think. As business marketers develop and price service offerings, they should give special attention to *cost-to-serve* particular customers and market segments[50] (see Chapter 4). By incorporating cost-to-serve data into the calculation of gross margin, business marketing strategists are better equipped to price services, identify unprofitable customers, and take action to restore profitability.

Services Promotion

The promotional strategies for services follow many of the same prescriptions as those for products. However, the unique characteristics of business services pose special challenges for the business marketer.

Developing Tangible Clues Service marketers must concentrate either on featuring the physical evidence elements of their service or on making the intangible elements more tangible. Physical evidence plays an important role in creating the atmosphere and environment in which a service is bought or performed, and it influences the customer's perception of the service. Physical evidence is the tangible aspect of the service package that the business marketer can control. Attempts should be made to translate the image of a service's intangible attributes into something more concrete.

For business service marketers, uniforms, logos, written contracts and guarantees, building appearance, and color schemes are some of the many ways to make their services tangible. An equipment maintenance firm that provides free, written, quarterly inspections helps make its service more tangible. Xerox, IBM, and FedEx offer service guarantees for selected offerings. The credit card created by car rental companies is another example of an attempt to make a service more tangible. A key concern for the service marketer is to develop a well-defined strategy for managing physical evidence—to enhance and differentiate service evidence by creating tangible clues.

[49]Werner Reinartz and Wolfgang Ulaga, "How to Sell More Services Profitably," *Harvard Business Review* 86 (May 2008): pp. 90–96.

[50]Remko Van Hoek and David Evans, "When Good Customers Are Bad," *Harvard Business Review* 83 (September 2005): p. 9.

Services Distribution

Distribution decisions in the service industry are focused on how to make the service package available and accessible to the user. Direct sale may be accomplished by the user going to the provider (for example, a manufacturer using a public warehouse for storing its product) or, more often, by the provider going to the buyer (for example, photocopier repair). Services can also be delivered over the Internet or provided by channel members.

Delivering Services Through the Internet   The Internet provides a powerful new channel for a host of services. For example, application service providers serve business market customers by allowing them to rent access to computer software and hardware, often providing the access over the Internet.[51] To illustrate, for Dunn and Bradstreet, IBM pulls together credit information on 63 million companies, handles customer support and electronic credit-report distribution, and identifies good customer prospects with its analytic software.[52]

Channel Members   Some manufacturers simply rely on their channel members to provide the services associated with the product. Because wholesalers and distributors are much closer to the customer, this arrangement can be a cost-effective way to deliver installation, repair, and maintenance services. IBM, although well known for its physical products, transformed itself into a services firm as a way to gain competitive advantage. While using a direct sales force to sell its services to large corporate customers, IBM found it difficult to cover the vast middle market in a cost-effective way. The middle market comprises customers with fewer than 2,000 employees or less than $500 million in revenue. IBM's solution was to rely on business partners (channel members) to sell its services to these customers and to provide continuous support to partners and customers via the Internet. In this way, IBM expands its market coverage, responds to the service needs of customers, and increases the profitability and loyalty of its partners.[53]

Developing New Services[54]

In line with our discussion of the new-product-development process (see Chapter 9), research suggests that there are a small set of success factors that drive the outcome of new service ventures. Included here are ensuring an excellent fit to customer needs, involving expert front-line service managers in creating the new service and in helping customers appreciate its distinctive benefits, and implementing a formal and planned launch for the new service offering. Moreover, the study found, for new-to-the-world business services, the primary distinguishing feature impacting performance is the corporate culture—one that actively promotes entrepreneurship, encourages creativity, and includes the direct involvement of senior managers in the new-service-development process.

[51]Jon G. Auerbach, "Playing the New Order: Stocks to Watch as Software Meets the Internet," *The Wall Street Journal*, November 15, 1999, p. R28.

[52]Steve Hamm, "Beyond Blue," *Business Week*, April 18, 2005, pp. 68–76.

[53]Craig Zarley, Joseph Kovar, and Edward Moltzen, "IBM Reaches," *Computer Reseller News* 26 (February 2001): p. 14.

[54]Ulrike de Brentani, "Innovative versus Incremental New Business Services: Different Keys for Achieving Success," *Journal of Product Innovation Management* 18 (no. 3, 2001): pp. 169–187; see also, Adegoke Oke, "Innovation Types and Innovation Management Practices in Service Companies," *International Journal of Operations & Production Management* 27 (no. 6, 2007): pp. 564–587.

Summary

Customer satisfaction represents the culmination of a set of customer experiences with the business-to-business firm. A customer experience map provides a powerful platform for defining the most critical customer–company interactions, uncovering customer expectations, and spotting opportunities to create value and strengthen customer loyalty. Rather than selling individual products and services, leading-edge business-to-business firms focus on what customers really want—solutions. To design a solution, the business marketing manager begins by analyzing a customer problem and then identifies the products and services required to solve that problem. Because solutions can be more readily customized for individual customers, they provide more avenues for differentiation than products can offer.

Business services are distinguished by their intangibility, linked production and consumption, lack of standardization, perishability, and use as opposed to ownership. Together, these characteristics have profound effects on how services should be marketed. Buyers of business services focus on five dimensions of service quality: reliability, responsiveness, assurance, empathy, and tangibles. Because of intangibility and lack of uniformity, service buyers have significant difficulty in comparing and selecting service vendors. Service providers must address this issue in developing their marketing mix.

The marketing mix for business services centers on the traditional elements—service package, pricing, promotion, and distribution—as well as on service personnel, service delivery system, and physical evidence. The goal of the services marketing program is to create satisfied customers. A key first step in creating strategies is to define the customer-benefit concept and the related service concept and offer. Pricing concentrates on influencing demand and capacity as well as on the bundling of service elements. Promotion emphasizes developing employee communication, enhancing word-of-mouth promotion, providing tangible clues, and developing interpersonal skills of operating personnel. Distribution is accomplished through direct means, intermediaries, or the Internet. Firms, large and small, are using the Internet to forge closer relationships with customers and to deliver a vast array of new services. New service marketing can improve effectiveness by creating an organizational culture that fosters risk taking and innovation. Successful new services respond to carefully defined market needs, capitalize on the strengths and reputation of the firm, and issue from a well-planned new-service-development process.

Discussion Questions

1. Local contractors who handle home remodeling and other building projects turn to Home Depot or Lowe's for many products, tools, and materials. Describe how these retailers could adopt a solutions marketing focus to serve those customers.

2. When a company buys a high-end document processor from Xerox or Canon, it is buying a physical product with a bundle of associated services. Describe some of the services that might be associated with such a product. Develop a list of the elements or points of interaction that might be reflected in a customer experience map. How can buyers evaluate the quality or value of these services?

3. Explain why the growth opportunities for many firms, such as IBM or GE, are far greater in services than they are in products.

4. Leading service companies such as American Express and FedEx measure customer satisfaction on a quarterly basis across the global market. Discuss the relationship between customer satisfaction and loyalty.

5. Many firms have a recovery process in place for situations when their products or services fail to deliver what has been promised to the customer. Illustrate how such a process might work.

6. A new firm creates Web sites and electronic commerce strategies for small businesses. Describe the essential elements to be included in its service product.

7. What is the role of physical evidence in the marketing of a business service?

8. As a luxury resort hotel manager, what approaches might you utilize to manage business demand for hotel space?

9. Critique this statement: "A key dimension of success in services marketing, as opposed to products marketing, is that operating personnel in the service firm play a critical selling and marketing role."

10. What steps can a manager take to enhance the chances of success for a new business service?

Internet Exercise

1. Autodesk, Inc., a leading design software and digital content company, provides online collaborative services for the building industry that enables more effective management of all project information. Go to http://www.buzzsaw.com and describe the service solutions Autodesk provides for architects and engineers.

SafePlace Corporation[55]

In February 2002, a guest staying at the Hilton in Cherry Hill, New Jersey, died while attending a convention. Several other guests were sent to the hospital amid fears of an outbreak of Legionnaires' disease or an anthrax attack. Later, it was determined that the guest had died from pneumonia and a blood infection unrelated to the hotel. The alarm surrounding this incident illustrates how important safety has become to a hotel's business.

In response to this need, John C. Fannin III, a fire protection and industrial security expert, formed and is the president of the SafePlace Corporation. The firm is an independent provider of safety accreditation of lodging, health care, educational, and commercial buildings and other occupancies where the safety of people is a concern. Like the "Good Housekeeping Seal of Approval," SafePlace® Accreditation requirements are based on the security, fire protection, and health and life safety provisions of selected nationally recognized codes, standards, and best practices.

The Hotel duPont in Wilmington, Delaware, was the first lodging facility in the United States to receive the SafePlace seal of approval. Such an accreditation process involves a rigorous inspection of the facility and identifies the best practices the hotel should employ, such as the use of key cards (as opposed to keys), self-closing doors, smoke detectors and sprinklers in the guest rooms, throw-bolt locks on the doors, excellent water quality, and safe work and food-handling practices among the hotel staff. The Hotel duPont, which paid a $45,000 fee for the inspection and consulting services, displays the SafePlace seal in the lobby and plans to feature the credential on all of the hotel's marketing materials. Other early adopters of the SafePlace program are New Orleans' Hotel Montcleone and the Sagamore in Bolton Landing, New York. Both report that their approvals have led to increased business.

Tricia Hayes, director of marketing at The Sagamore said that SafePlace has brought meeting-planner attention to her facility and management comfort in adopting best risk-management practices. "Our accreditation has had a big impact on meeting professionals. Our sales managers use it as a sales tool."

Since launching its program, SafePlace is doing particularly well with independent hotels that, according to Fannin, are "quicker to respond to customer preferences than a chain would be." In turn, Fannin feels that there is a huge opportunity in the education market, particularly with colleges and universities (for example, the accreditation of dormitories).

Discussion Questions

1. Describe the core service concept and benefits that SafePlace provides to a hotel and its guests. How would you describe these benefits in the body of an ad?

2. What steps could John Fannin take to fuel the growth of SafePlace?

3. Assess the prospects for SafePlace in the education market and suggest a potential strategy the firm might follow to penetrate this market.

---

[55]Maureen Milford, "Hotel Safety Rises to a New Standard," *The News Journal*, May 13, 2002, p. i, accessed at http:// safeplace.com on September 27, 2002; , and "SafePlace Makes Hospitality Inroads," *Lodging Hospitality*, February 2005, accessed at http://www.safeplace.com on October 15, 2005; and Ruth Hill, "What Hotel Guests Want Today: A Safe Haven in a Secure Property," *HSMAI Marketing Review*, Fall 2005, accessed at http://www.safeplace.com on July 22, 2008.

Managing Business Marketing Channels

The channel of distribution is the marketing manager's bridge to the market. Channel innovation represents a source of competitive advantage that separates market winners from market losers. The business marketer must ensure that the firm's channel is properly aligned to the needs of important market segments. At the same time, the marketer must also satisfy the needs of channel members, whose support is crucial to the success of business marketing strategy. After reading this chapter, you will understand:

1. the alternative paths to business market customers.

2. the critical role of industrial distributors and manufacturers' representatives in marketing channels.

3. the central components of channel design.

4. requirements for successful channel strategy.

Go to Market Strategy, an influential book by Lawrence G. Friedman, aptly describes the central focus of a channel strategy in the business market:

> The success of every go-to-market decision you make, indeed your ability to make smart go-to-market decisions at all, depends on how well you understand your customers. . . . You must build an accurate customer fact-base that clarifies who the customers are in your target market, what they buy, how they buy it, how they want to buy it, and what would motivate them to buy more of it from you.[1]

The channel component of business marketing strategy has two important and related dimensions. First, the channel structure must be designed to accomplish marketing objectives. However, selecting the best channel to accomplish objectives is challenging because (1) the alternatives are numerous, (2) marketing goals differ, and (3) business market segments are so various that separate channels must often be used concurrently. The ever-changing business environment requires managers periodically to reevaluate the channel structure. Stiff competition, new customer requirements, and the rapid growth of the Internet are among the forces that create new opportunities and signal the need for fresh channel strategies.[2]

Second, once the channel structure has been specified, the business marketer must manage the channel to achieve prescribed goals. To do so, the manager must develop procedures for selecting intermediaries, motivating them to achieve desired performance, resolving conflict among channel members, and evaluating performance. This chapter provides a structure for designing and administering the business marketing channel.

The Business Marketing Channel

The link between manufacturers and customers is the **channel of distribution**. The channel accomplishes all the tasks necessary to effect a sale and deliver products to the customer. These tasks include making contact with potential buyers, negotiating, contracting, transferring title, communicating, arranging financing, servicing the product, and providing local inventory, transportation, and storage. These tasks may be performed entirely by the manufacturer or entirely by intermediaries, or may be shared between them. The customer may even undertake some of these functions; for example, customers granted certain discounts might agree to accept larger inventories and the associated storage costs.

Fundamentally, channel management centers on these questions: *Which channel tasks will be performed by the firm, and which tasks, if any, will be performed by channel members?* Figure 11.1 shows various ways to structure business marketing channels. Some channels are **direct**—the manufacturer must perform all the marketing functions needed to make and deliver products. The manufacturer's direct sales force and online marketing channels are examples. Others are **indirect**; that is, some type of intermediary (such as a distributor or dealer) sells or handles the products.

[1]Lawrence G. Friedman, *Go to Market: Advanced Techniques and Tools for Selling More Products, to More Customers, More Profitably* (Boston: Butterworth-Heinemann, 2002), p. 116.
[2]Bert Rosenbloom, "Multi-Channel Strategy in Business-to-Business Markets," *Industrial Marketing Management* 36 (January 2007): pp. 4–7.

FIGURE 11.1 | **B2B MARKETING CHANNELS**

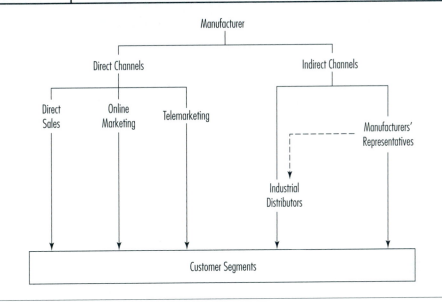

A basic issue in channel management, then, is how to structure the channel so that the tasks are performed optimally. One alternative is for the manufacturer to do it all.

Direct Channels

Direct distribution, common in business marketing, is a channel strategy that does not use intermediaries. The manufacturer's own sales force deals directly with the customer, and the manufacturer has full responsibility for performing all the necessary channel tasks. Direct distribution is often required in business marketing because of the nature of the selling situation or the concentrated nature of industry demand. The direct sales approach is feasible when (1) the customers are large and well defined, (2) the customers insist on direct sales, (3) sales involve extensive negotiations with upper management, and (4) selling has to be controlled to ensure that the total product package is properly implemented and to guarantee a quick response to market conditions.

A direct sales force is best used for the most complex sales opportunities: highly customized solutions, large customers, and complex products. Customized solutions and large customer accounts require professional account management, deep product knowledge, and a high degree of selling skill—all attributes a sales representative must possess. Also, when risk in a purchase decision is perceived as high and significant expertise is required in the sale, customers demand a high level of personal attention and relationship building from the direct sales force as a precondition for doing business. However, according to Lawrence Friedman and Timothy Furey, "in the broad middle market and small-customer market, where transactions are generally simpler, other channels can do a more cost-effective job—and can often reach more customers."[3]

---

[3]Lawrence G. Friedman and Timothy R. Furey, *The Channel Advantage* (Boston: Butterworth-Heinemann, 1999), p. 84.

INSIDE BUSINESS MARKETING

IBM Uses the Internet to Collaborate with Channel Partners and Build Customer Loyalty

The Internet provides a valuable way for business marketers to collaborate with distributors or other resellers, sharing resources and cooperating on electronic marketing initiatives. An excellent example of this channel outreach program is IBM TeamPlayers (http://www.ibm-teamplayers.com). This program uses the Web as a communications and information delivery tool to service the channel members (business partners) of IBM.

IBM TeamPlayers offers channel members customized direct-mail campaigns using mail, fax, and e-mail to reach those customers. The Web site is also an outlet for providing help to channel partners in managing their customer databases, developing

Web pages, executing telemarketing campaigns, and more, with IBM acting as a clearinghouse for other needed resources.

The program strengthens IBM's relationship with its channel partners. Moreover, the initiative allows IBM to identify and reach end users through the partners and helps strengthen customer loyalty to both IBM channel members and to IBM itself.

SOURCE: Barry Silverstein, Business-to-Business Internet Marketing: Five Proven Strategies for Increasing Profits Through Internet Direct Marketing (Gulf Breeze, Fla.: MAXIMUM Press, 1999), p. 307.

Many business marketing firms, such as Xerox, Cisco, and Dell, emphasize e-commerce strategies. Surprisingly, many firms use their Web sites only for promotional purposes and not yet as a sales channel. E-channels can be used by business marketing firms as (1) information platforms, (2) transaction platforms, and (3) platforms for managing customer relationships. The effect on the business increases as a firm moves from level one to level three. E-commerce strategies are fully explored in Chapter 12.

Indirect Channels

Indirect distribution uses at least one type of intermediary, if not more. Business marketing channels typically include fewer types of intermediaries than do consumer-goods channels. Indirect distribution accounts for a large share of sales in the United States. The Gartner Group reports that 60 percent of the U.S. Gross Domestic Product (GDP) is sold through indirect channels.[4] Manufacturers' representatives and industrial distributors account for most of the transactions handled in this way. Indirect distribution is generally found where (1) markets are fragmented and widely dispersed, (2) low transaction amounts prevail, and (3) buyers typically purchase a number of items, often different brands, in one transaction.[5] For example, IBM's massive sales organization concentrates on large corporate, government, and institutional customers. Industrial distributors effectively and efficiently serve literally thousands of other IBM customers—small to medium-sized organizations. These channel partners assume a vital role in IBM's strategy on a global scale.

---

[4]The Gartner Group, "Partnerware Reports, 'Top 10 Tips for Managing Indirect Sales Channels'," http://www.businesswire.com, June 18, 2002.

[5]E. Raymond Corey, Frank V. Cespedes, and V. Kasturi Rangan, *Going to Market: Distribution Systems for Industrial Products* (Boston: Harvard University Press, 1989), p. 26.

FIGURE 11.2 | TYPICAL SALES CYCLE: TASKS PERFORMED THROUGHOUT THE SALES PROCESS

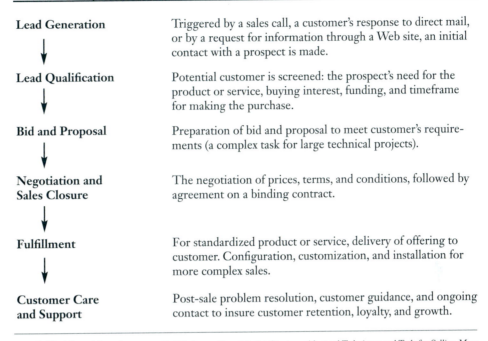

Lead Generation

Triggered by a sales call, a customer's response to direct mail, or by a request for information through a Web site, an initial contact with a prospect is made.

Lead Qualification

Potential customer is screened: the prospect's need for the product or service, buying interest, funding, and timeframe for making the purchase.

Bid and Proposal

Preparation of bid and proposal to meet customer's requirements (a complex task for large technical projects).

Negotiation and Sales Closure

The negotiation of prices, terms, and conditions, followed by agreement on a binding contract.

Fulfillment

For standardized product or service, delivery of offering to customer. Configuration, customization, and installation for more complex sales.

Customer Care and Support

Post-sale problem resolution, customer guidance, and ongoing contact to insure customer retention, loyalty, and growth.

SOURCE: Adapted from Lawrence G. Friedman, *Go to Market Strategy: Advanced Techniques and Tools for Selling More Products, to More Customers, More Profitably* (Boston: Butterworth-Heinemann, 2002), pp. 234–236.

Integrated Multichannel Models[6]

Leading business marketing firms use multiple sales channels to serve customers in a particular market. The goal of a multichannel model is to coordinate the activities of many channels, such as field sales representatives, channel partners, call centers, and the Web, to enhance the total customer experience and profitability. Consider a typical sales cycle that includes the following tasks: lead generation, lead qualification, negotiation and sales closure, fulfillment, and customer care and support (Figure 11.2). In a multichannel system, different channels can perform different tasks within a single sales transaction with a customer. For example, business marketing firms might use a call center and direct mail to generate leads, field sales representatives to close sales, business partners (for example, industrial distributors) to provide fulfillment (that is, deliver or install product), and a Web site to provide postsale support.

Managing Customer Contact Points   Figure 11.3 shows a particular multichannel strategy that a number of leading firms like Oracle Corporation use to reach the vast middle market composed of many small and medium-sized businesses. First, the channels are arranged from top to bottom in terms of their *relative cost of sales* (that is, direct sales is the most expensive, whereas the Internet is the least). By shifting any selling tasks to lower-cost channels, the business marketer can boost profit margins and reach more customers, in more markets, more efficiently.

---

[6]This section is based on Friedman, *Go to Market*, pp. 229–257.

FIGURE 11.3 | **MULTICHANNEL INTEGRATION MAP: SIMPLE EXAMPLE OF HIGH-COVERAGE PARTNERING MODEL**

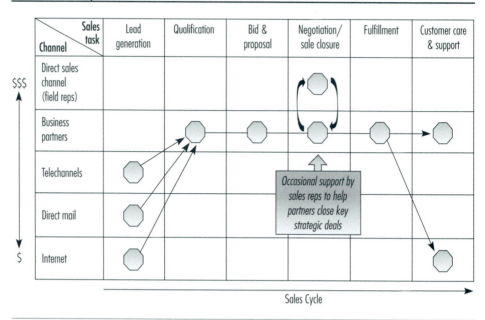

SOURCE: Lawrence G. Friedman, *Go to Market Strategy: Advanced Techniques and Tools for Selling More Products, to More Customers, More Profitably* (Boston: Butterworth-Heinemann, 2002), p. 243. Copyright 2002. Reprinted with permission from Elsevier Science.

Business Partner's Key Role   Returning to Figure 11.3, observe the central role of business partners across the stages of the sales cycle. Low-cost, direct-to-customer channels—like the Internet—are used to generate sales leads, which are then given to channel partners. These partners are then expected to complete the sales cycle but can secure assistance from Oracle's sales representatives to provide guidance and support (when needed) in closing the sale. By emphasizing the partner channel for middle-market customers, Oracle can significantly increase market coverage and penetration while enjoying higher profit margins and lower selling costs. Moreover, this allows the sales force to concentrate on large enterprise customers.

This provides just one example of how a firm can coordinate and configure sales cycle tasks across various sales channels to create an integrated strategy for a particular market. Any firm that serves a variety of markets requires distinctly different multichannel models to serve customers in those markets. To illustrate, a company might serve key corporate accounts through sales representatives and the middle market through channel partners, call centers, and the Internet.

Customer Relationship Management (CRM) Systems   Many business marketing firms pursue very complex market coverage strategies and use *all* of the alternative paths to the market we have discussed. For example, Hewlett-Packard sells directly through a field sales organization to large enterprises; through channel partners and resellers to the government, education, and the midsize business market; and through retail stores to the small business and home market. Notes Lawrence Friedman, a leading sales strategy consultant, "Add in its customer support channels, Web presence, and H-P has an army of channels that it deploys to provide sales, service, and support to its different market segments."[7] This multichannel mix features many points of contact that H-P must manage and coordinate to ensure a "singular" customer experience across channels. CRM systems provide a valuable tool for coordinating sales channel activities and managing crucial connections and handoffs between them (see Chapter 4). Friedman notes:

> Channel coordination used to be a difficult, messy problem involving the tracking and frequent loss of hand-written memos, voice mails, paper lists of sales leads, and dog-eared customer history files. CRM has ushered in a new era of IT-driven channel coordination, enabling electronic transmission of leads and customer histories from one channel to another, with no loss of information or sales information falling through the cracks.[8]

Participants in the Business Marketing Channel

Channel members assume a central role in the marketing strategies of business-to-business firms, large and small. A channel management strategy begins with an understanding of the intermediaries that may be used. Primary attention is given to two: (1) industrial distributors and (2) manufacturers' representatives. They handle a sizable share of business-to-business sales made through intermediaries.

Distributors

Industrial distributors are the most pervasive and important single force in distribution channels. Distributors in the United States number more than 10,000, with sales exceeding $50 billion. Distributors are heavily used for MRO (maintenance, repair, and operations) supplies, with many industrial buyers reporting that they buy as much as 75 percent of their MRO supplies from distributors. Generally, about 75 percent of all business marketers sell *some* products through distributors. What accounts for the unparalleled position of the distributor in the industrial market? What role do distributors play in the industrial distribution process?

Distributors are generally small, independent businesses serving narrow geographic markets. Sales average almost $2 million, although some top $3 billion. Net profits are relatively low as a percentage of sales (4 percent); return on investment averages 11 percent. The typical order is small, and the distributors sell to a multitude of customers in many industries. The typical distributor is able to spread its costs over a sizable group of vendors—it stocks goods from between 200 and 300 manufacturers. A sales force of outside and inside salespersons generates orders. *Outside salespersons* make regular calls on customers and handle normal account servicing and technical assistance. *Inside salespersons* complement these efforts, processing orders and scheduling delivery; their primary duty is to take telephone orders. Most distributors operate from a single location, but some approach the "supermarket" status with as many as 130 branches.

---

[7] Ibid., p. 254.
[8] Ibid., p. 253.

TABLE 11.1 | KEY DISTRIBUTION RESPONSIBILITIES

Responsibility	Activity
Contact	Reach all customers in a de?ned territory through an outside sales force that calls on customers or through an inside group that receives telephone orders
Product availability	Provide a local inventory and include all supporting activities: credit, just-in-time delivery, order processing, and advice
Repair	Provide easy access to local repair facilities (unavailable from a distant manufacturer)
Assembly and light manufacturing	Purchase material in bulk, then shape, form, or assemble to user requirements

Compared with their smaller rivals, large distributors seem to have significant advantages. Small distributors are typically unable to achieve the operating economies larger firms enjoy.[9] Large firms can automate much of their operations, enabling them to significantly reduce their sales and general administrative expenses, often to levels approaching 10 percent of sales.

Distributor Responsibilities Table 11.1 shows industrial distributors' primary responsibilities. The products they sell—cutting tools, abrasives, electronic components, ball bearings, handling equipment, pipe, maintenance equipment, and hundreds more—are generally those that buyers need quickly to avoid production disruptions. Thus, the critical elements of the distributor's function are to have these products readily available and to serve as the manufacturer's selling arm.

Distributors are full-service intermediaries; that is, they take title to the products they sell, and they perform the full range of marketing functions. Some of the more important functions are providing credit, offering wide product assortments, delivering goods, offering technical advice, and meeting emergency requirements. Not only are distributors valuable to their manufacturer-suppliers but their customers generally view them favorably. Some purchasing agents view the distributor as an extension of their "buying arms" because they provide service, technical advice, and product application suggestions.

A Service Focus To create more value for their customers, many large distributors have expanded their range of services. Value is delivered through various supply chain and inventory management services, including automatic replenishment, product assembly, in-plant stores, and design services.[10] The most popular services involve helping customers design, construct, and, in some cases, operate a supply network. Other value-adding activities include partnerships in which the distributor's field application engineers work at a customer's site to help select components for new product designs. To reap the profits associated with these important services, many distributors now charge separate fees for each unique service.

---

[9]Heidi Elliott, "Distributors, Make Way for the Little Guys," *Electronic Business Today* 22 (September 1996): p. 19.

[10]Jim Carbone, "Distributors See Slow Growth Ahead; Expect Electronics Distributors to Offer More Supply Chain and Inventory Services, but Be Prepared to Pay for Them," *Purchasing* 130 (May 16, 2002): p. 27.

Classification of Distributors   To select the best distributor for a particular channel, the marketing manager must understand the diversity of distributor operations. Industrial distributors vary according to product lines and user markets. Firms may be ultraspecialized (for example, selling only to municipal water works), or they may carry a broad line of generalized industrial products. However, three primary distributor classifications are usually recognized.

1. **General-line distributors** cater to a broad array of industrial needs. They stock an extensive variety of products and could be likened to the supermarket in consumer-goods markets.

2. **Specialists** focus on one line or on a few related lines. Such a distributor may handle only power transmission equipment—belts, pulleys, and bearings. The most common specialty is fasteners, although specialization also occurs in cutting tools, power transmission equipment, pipes, valves, and fittings. There is a trend toward increased specialization as a result of increasing technical complexity of products and the need for higher levels of precision and quality control.

3. A **combination house** operates in two markets: industrial and consumer. Such a distributor might carry electric motors for industrial customers and hardware and automotive parts to be sold through retailers to final consumers.

Choosing a Distributor   The selection of a distributor depends on the manufacturer's requirements and the needs of target customer segments. The general-line distributor offers the advantage of one-stop purchasing. If customers do not need a high level of service and technical expertise, the general-line distributor is a good choice. The specialist, on the other hand, provides the manufacturer with a high level of technical capability and a well-developed understanding of complex customer requirements. Specialists handle fasteners, for instance, because of the strict quality-control standards that users impose.

Manufacturers and their distributors are finding the Internet to be a major catalyst for stimulating collaboration. A recent poll asked distributors which business strategies would have the largest effect on them in the future, and the top two were collaboration with supply chain partners and new information technologies.[11] E-collaboration includes sales and services, ordering and billing, technical training and engineering, Internet meetings, auctions, and exchanges. These results suggest that Internet collaboration is a critical strategic force in the business-to-business arena.

The Distributor as a Valuable Partner   The quality of a firm's distributors is often the difference between a highly successful marketing strategy and an ineffective one. Customers prize good distributors, making it all the more necessary to strive continually to engage the best in any given market. Distributors often provide the only economically feasible way of covering the entire market.

In summary, the industrial distributor is a full-service intermediary who takes title to the products sold; maintains inventories; provides credit, delivery, wide product assortment, and technical assistance; and may even do light assembly and manufacturing. Although the distributor is primarily responsible for contacting and supplying

---

[11]Al Tuttle, "E-Collaboration: Build Trust and Success," *Industrial Distribution* 92 (June 1, 2002): p. 59.

present customers, industrial distributors also solicit new accounts and work to expand the market. They generally handle established products—typically used in manufacturing operations, repair, and maintenance—with a broad and large demand.

Industrial distributors are a powerful force in business marketing channels, and all indications point to an expanded role for them. The manufacturer's representative is an equally viable force in the business marketing channel.

Manufacturers' Representatives

For many business marketers who need a strong selling job with a technically complex product, **manufacturers' representatives,** or reps, are the only cost-effective answer. In fact, Erin Anderson and Bob Trinkle note that the one area untouched by the outsourcing boom is field selling in the business-to-business area. They contend that many companies could benefit by using outsourced sales professionals, namely manufacturers' reps, to augment or even replace the field sales force.[12] Reps are salespeople who work independently (or for a rep company), represent several companies in the same geographic area, and sell noncompeting but complementary products.

The Rep's Responsibilities   A rep neither takes title to nor holds inventory of the products handled. (Some reps do, however, keep a limited inventory of repair and maintenance parts.) The rep's forte is expert product knowledge coupled with a keen understanding of the markets and customer needs. Reps are usually limited to defined geographical areas; thus, a manufacturer seeking nationwide distribution usually works with several rep companies. Compared with a distributor channel, a rep generally gives the business marketer more control because the firm maintains title and possession of the goods.

The Rep-Customer Relationship   Reps are the manufacturers' selling arm, making contact with customers, writing and following up on orders, and linking the manufacturer with the industrial end users. Although paid by the manufacturer, the rep is also important to customers. Often, the efforts of a rep during a customer emergency (for example, an equipment failure) mean the difference between continuing or stopping production. Most reps are thoroughly experienced in the industries they serve—they can offer technical advice while enhancing the customer's leverage with suppliers in securing parts, repair, and delivery. The rep also provides customers with a continuing flow of information on innovations and trends in equipment, as well as on the industry as a whole.

Commission Basis   Reps are paid a commission on sales; the commission varies by industry and by the nature of the selling job. Commissions typically range from a low of 2 percent to a high of 18 percent for selected products. The average commission rate is 5.3 percent.[13] Percentage commission compensation is attractive to manufacturers because they have few fixed sales costs. Reps are paid only when they generate orders, and commissions can be adjusted based on industry conditions. Because reps are paid on commission, they are motivated to generate high levels of sales—another fact the manufacturer appreciates.

---

[12] Erin A. Anderson and Bob Trinkle, *Outsourcing the Sales Function: The Real Cost of Field Sales* (Mason, Ohio: Thomson Higher Education, 2005); see also, Daniel H. McQuiston, "A Conceptual Model for Building and Maintaining Relationships between Manufacturers' Reps and Their Principals," *Industrial Marketing Management* 30 (February 2001): pp. 165–181.

[13] Ibid., p. 22.

B2B TOP PERFORMERS

Why Intel Uses Reps

Intel has a strong corporate brand, an experienced corporate sales force, and long-standing relationships with broad-line distributors like Arrow Electronics. Intel also uses manufacturers' representatives. Why?

After purchasing a business unit from Digital Equipment Corporation in 1998, Intel realized that several product lines from the acquired unit provided promising market potential, particularly in networking and communications. Specifically, the product lines could spur profitable growth in embedded applications market segments, such as medical equipment and point-of-sale terminals, where the proper application function is based on microprocessors and network connections. At Intel, however, marketing managers argued that the go-to-market strategy that has proved so successful in the PC market would not be suitable for original equipment manufacturers (OEMs) in these sectors.

George Langer, Intel's worldwide representative program manager, explains:

> There was no sales organization, few customer relationships, and more than a few OEMs who questioned Intel's renewed interest in the embedded segments. Intel did not have existing capability to get these product lines in front of appropriate customers. The customer base was large and diverse. (This was not the PC OEM customer base where Intel had nurtured strong relationships over time.) And, finally, the value of the Intel brand was not clearly associated with communications, embedded, and networking market segments. Intel turned to outsourced selling [that is, manufacturers' reps].

SOURCE: Erin Anderson and Bob Trinkle, *Outsourcing the Sales Function: The Real Cost of Field Sales* (Mason, Ohio: Thomson Higher Education, 2005), pp. 74–75.

Experience   Reps possess sophisticated product knowledge and typically have extensive experience in the markets they serve. Most reps develop their field experience while working as salespersons for manufacturers. They are motivated to become reps by the desire to be independent and to reap the substantial monetary rewards possible on commission.

When Reps Are Used

- *Large and Small Firms:* Small and medium-sized firms generally have the greatest need for a rep, although many large firms—for example, Dow Chemical, Motorola, and Intel—use them. The reason is primarily economic: Smaller firms cannot justify the expense of maintaining their own sales forces. The rep provides an efficient way to obtain total market coverage, with costs incurred only as sales are made. The quality of the selling job is often very good as a result of the rep's prior experience and market knowledge.

- *Limited Market Potential:* The rep also plays a vital role when the manufacturer's market potential is limited. A manufacturer may use a direct sales force in heavily concentrated business markets, where the demand is sufficient to support the expense, and use reps to cover less-dense markets. Because the rep carries several lines, expenses can be allocated over a much larger sales volume.

- *Servicing Distributors:* Reps may also be employed by a firm that markets through distributors. When a manufacturer sells through hundreds of distributors across the United States, reps may sell to and service those distributors.

- *Reducing Overhead Costs:* Sometimes the commission rate paid to reps exceeds the cost of a direct sales force, yet the supplier continues to use reps. This policy is not as irrational as it appears. Assume, for example, that costs for a direct sales force approximate 8 percent of sales and that a rep's commission rate is 11 percent. Using reps in this case is often justified because of the hidden costs of a sales force. First, the manufacturer does not provide fringe benefits or a fixed salary to reps. Second, the costs of training a rep are usually limited to those required to provide product information. Thus, using reps eliminates significant overhead costs.

Multiple Paths to Market   A wide array of factors influences the choice of intermediaries, with the tasks they perform being of prime importance.

Different Market Segments   The primary reason for using more than one type of intermediary for the same product is that different market segments require different channel structures. Some firms use three distinct approaches. Large accounts are called on by the firm's own sales force, distributors handle small repeat orders, and manufacturers' reps develop the medium-sized firm market.

How Customers Buy   Like size of accounts, differences in purchase behavior may also dictate using more than one type of intermediary. If a firm produces a wide line of industrial products, some may require high-caliber selling to numerous buying influences in a single buyer's firm. When this occurs, the firm's own sales force would focus on the more complex buying situations, whereas the distributors would sell standardized products from local stocks.

Channel Design

Channel design is the dynamic process of developing new channels where none existed and modifying existing channels. The business marketer usually deals with modification of existing channels, although new products and customer segments may require entirely new channels. Regardless of whether the manager is dealing with a new channel or modifying an existing one, channel design is an active rather than a passive task. Effective distribution channels do not simply evolve; they are developed by management, which takes action on the basis of a well-conceived plan that reflects overall marketing goals. Business firms formulate their marketing strategies to appeal to selected market segments, to earn targeted levels of profits, to maintain or increase sales and market share growth rates, and to achieve all this within specified resource constraints. Each element of the marketing strategy has a specific purpose.

Channel design is best conceptualized as a series of stages that the business marketing manager must complete to be sure that all important channel dimensions have been evaluated (Figure 11.4). The result of the process is to specify the structure that provides the highest probability of achieving the firm's objectives.[14] Note that the process focuses on channel structure and not on channel participants. **Channel structure** refers to the underlying framework: the number of channel levels, the number and types of intermediaries, and the linkages among channel members. Selection of individual intermediaries is indeed important—it is examined later in the chapter.

---

[14]The discussion that follows is based on V. Kasturi Rangan, *Transforming Your Go-To-Market Strategy: The Three Disciplines of Channel Management* (Boston: Harvard Business Press, 2006), pp. 73–88.

FIGURE 11.4 | **THE CHANNEL DESIGN PROCESS**

Step 1   End-User Focus: Define Customer Segments

Step 2   Identify and Prioritize Customers' Channel Requirements by Segment

Step 3   Assess the Firm's Capabilities to Meet Customers' Requirements

Step 4   Benchmark Channel Offerings of Key Competitors

Step 5   Create Channel Solutions to Customers' Latent Needs

Step 6   Evaluate and Select Channel Options

SOURCE: Adapted from V. Kasturi Rangan, *Transforming Your Go-To-Market Strategy: The Three Disciplines of Channel Management* (Boston: Harvard Business Press, 2006), pp. 73–94.

Step 1: Define Customer Segments

The primary goal of the distribution channel is to satisfy end-user needs, so the channel design process should begin there. Step 1 is about defining target market segments (see Chapter 5) and isolating the customer buying and usage behavior in each segment (what they buy, how they buy, and how they put their purchases to use).

Some business marketers err by considering their channel partners as "customers and rarely looking beyond them." To inform the channel design process, however, the marketing strategist should center on the importance of the product from the customer's perspective. V. Kasturi Rangan observes:

> Producers of agricultural channels, for example, should target farmers and not dealers. Producers of engineering plastics (pellets) for automobile bumpers, on the other hand, should focus on the auto manufacturer and not the consumer, because *that is where the product has value in the eyes of the end user.* . . . Other features of the automobile (not bumpers) are more salient [in the choice decision at the consumer level].[15]

Step 2: Customers' Channel Needs by Segment

Identifying and prioritizing the channel function requirements for customers in each market segment is next. This information should be elicited directly from a sample of present or potential customers from each segment. Table 11.2 provides a representative list of channel functions that may be more or less important to customers in a particular segment. For example, large customers for information-technology products might rank product customization, product quality assurance, and after-sales service as their top three needs. Whereas small customers may prioritize product information, assortment, and availability as their most important needs. The business marketing manager should also probe customers on other issues that might provide strategy

[15] Ibid., p. 76.

TABLE 11.2 | **CHANNEL FUNCTIONS ALIGNED WITH CUSTOMER NEEDS**

Channel Function	Customer Needs
1. Product Information	Customers seek more information for new and/or technically complex products and those that are characterized by a rapidly changing market environment.
2. Product Customization	Some products must be technically modified or need to be adapted to meet the customer's unique requirements.
3. Product Quality Assurance	Because of its importance to the customer's operations, product integrity and reliability might be given special emphasis by customers.
4. Lot Size	For products that have a high unit value or those that are used extensively, the purchase represents a sizable dollar outlay and a significant financial decision for the customer.
5. Assortment	A customer may require a broad range of products, including complementary items, and assign special value to one-stop shopping.
6. Availability	Some customer environments require the channel to manage demand uncertainty and support a high level of product availability.
7. After-Sales Services	Customers require a range of services from installation and repair to maintenance and warranty.
8. Logistics	A customer organization may require special transportation and storage services to support its operations and strategy.

SOURCE: Adapted from V. Kasturi Rangan, Melvyn A. J. Menezes, and E. B. Maier, "Channel Selection for New Industrial Products: A Framework, Method, and Application," *Journal of Marketing* 56 (July 1992): pp. 72–74.

insights. For instance, how sensitive are customers to a two-hour versus six-hour service response time, or how much value do they perceive in a three-year versus one-year warranty?

Step 3: Assess the Firm's Channel Capabilities

Once customer requirements have been isolated and prioritized, an assessment is made of the strengths and weaknesses of the firm's channel. The central focus is on identifying the gaps between what customers in a segment desire and what the channel is now providing. Customers base their choice of a channel not on a single element, but on a complete bundle of benefits (that is, channel functions). To that end, the business-to-business firm should identify particular channel functions, like after-sales support or availability, where action could be taken to enhance the customer value proposition.

Step 4: Benchmark to Competitors

What go-to-market strategies are key competitors using? In designing a channel, cost considerations prevent the business marketer from closing all the gaps on channel capabilities that may appear. However, a clear direction for strategy is revealed by understanding the channel offerings of competitors. For example, an aggressive competitor that goes to market with its own team of account managers and dedicated service specialists might demonstrate special strength in serving large corporate customers. However, countless opportunities exist for smaller rivals to counter this strategy by developing special channel offerings tailored to small and medium-sized customers (for example, Intuit's success in retaining its market leadership position in small-business accounting software despite the aggressive challenge from Microsoft).

Step 5: Create Channel Solutions for Customers' Latent Needs

Sometimes, a review of competitor offerings can alert the marketer to opportunities for new offerings that may have special appeal to customers. "At other times, customers' needs may be latent and unarticulated, and it is the channel steward's responsibility to tap into and surface those requirements."[16] Based on such an assessment, a provider of information-technology equipment created an entirely new channel option for the small and medium-sized customer segment. Rather than selling equipment, this new channel takes responsibility for installing, upgrading, and maintaining the equipment at the customers' locations for an ongoing service fee.

Step 6: Evaluate and Select Channel Options

Channel decisions must ultimately consider the cost-benefit trade-offs and the estimated profitability that each of the viable channel options present.[17] Some of the channel gaps that are uncovered in this assessment can be closed by the independent actions and investments of the business-to-business firm (for example, adding to the service support staff or the sales force). For the most part, however, the greatest progress will come from the channel partners (for example, distributors or reps) working together and discussing how channel capabilities can be aligned to customer needs. "The idea is to enhance the value delivered to customers through collaborative action among channel partners. If the partners can agree on how to pull it off and, indeed, accomplish their redefined tasks,"[18] they will squarely respond to customer needs and advance the performance of the channel. One important implication of the framework is that the design of the channel must change as customer and competitor behavior changes. Rather than a static structure, channel management is an ongoing process involving continuous adjustments and evolution.

Crucial Points in Channel Transformation

Marketing channels are often thought of as a series of product and information flows that originate with the business-to-business firm. In his rich and compelling perspective of the channel design process, V. Kasturi Rangan turns this notion on its head (see Figure 11.5):

> The starting point is the customer, and the customer's demand-chain requirements. The channel is constructed to meet this core need. Roles, responsibilities, and rewards are allocated as a consequence of this need, and not the other way around.[19]

---

[16] Ibid., p. 83.

[17] Arun Sharma and Anuj Mehrotra, "Choosing an Optimal Mix in Multichannel Environments," *Industrial Marketing Management* 36 (January 2007): pp. 21–28.

[18] Rangan, *Transforming Your Go-to-Market Strategy*, p. 88.

[19] Ibid., p. 91.

FIGURE 11.5 | **CUSTOMERS DRIVE THE CHANNEL DESIGN PROCESS**

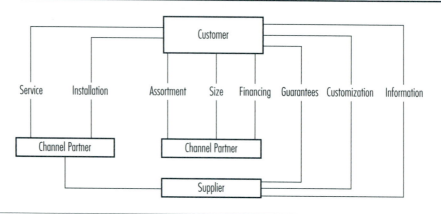

SOURCE: V. Kasturi Rangan, *Transforming Your Go-To-Market Strategy: The Three Disciplines of Channel Management* (Boston: Harvard Business Press, 2006), p. 91.

Channel Administration

Once a particular business-to-business channel structure is chosen, channel partici-pants must be selected, and arrangements must be made to ensure that all obligations are assigned. Next, channel members must be motivated to perform the tasks neces-sary to achieve channel objectives. Third, conflict within the channel must be prop-erly controlled. Finally, performance must be controlled and evaluated.

Selection of Channel Members

Why is the selection of channel members (specific companies, rather than *type*, which is specified in the design process) part of channel management rather than an aspect of channel design? The primary reason is that intermediary selection is an ongoing process—some intermediaries choose to leave the channel, and the supplier terminates others. Thus, selection of intermediaries is more or less continuous. Performance of individual channel members must be evaluated continually. The manufacturer should be prepared to move quickly, replacing poor performers with potentially better ones. Including the selection process in ongoing channel management puts the process in its proper perspective.

Securing Good Intermediaries The marketer can identify prospective channel members through discussions with company salespeople and existing or potential customers, or through trade sources, such as *Industrial Distribution* magazine or the *Verified Directory of Manufacturers' Representatives*. Once the list of potential interme-diaries is reduced to a few names, the manufacturer uses the selection criteria to eval-uate them. For example, the McGraw-Edison Company uses an intensive checklist to compare prospective channel members; important criteria are market coverage, product lines, personnel, growth, and financial standing.

The formation of the channel is not at all a one-way street. The manufacturer must now persuade the intermediaries to become part of the channel system. Some distributors evaluate potential suppliers just as rigorously as the manufacturers rate them—using many of the same considerations. Manufacturers must often demonstrate the sales and profit potential of their product and be willing to grant the intermediaries some territorial exclusivity. Special efforts are required to convince the very best rep in a market to represent a particular manufacturer's product. Those efforts must demonstrate that the manufacturer will treat the rep organization as a partner and support it.

Motivating Channel Members

Distributors and reps are independent and profit oriented. They are oriented toward their customers and toward whatever means are necessary to satisfy customer needs for industrial products and services. Their perceptions and outlook may differ substantially from those of the manufacturers they represent. As a consequence, marketing strategies can fail when managers do not tailor their programs to the capabilities and orientations of their intermediaries. To manage the business marketing channel effectively, the marketer must understand the intermediaries' perspective and devise ways to motivate them to perform in a way that enhances the manufacturer's long-term success. The manufacturer must continually seek support from intermediaries, and the quality of that support depends on the motivational techniques used.

A Partnership   Channel member motivation begins with the understanding that the channel relationship is a *partnership*. Manufacturers and intermediaries are in business together; whatever expertise and assistance the manufacturer can provide to the intermediaries improves total channel effectiveness. One study of channel relationships suggested that manufacturers may be able to increase the level of resources directed to their products by developing a trusting relationship with their reps; by improving communication through recognition programs, product training, and consultation with the reps; and by informing the reps of plans, explicitly detailing objectives, and providing positive feedback.[20]

Another study of distributor-manufacturer working partnerships recommended similar approaches. It also suggested that manufacturers and their distributors engage in joint annual planning that focuses on specifying the cooperative efforts each firm requires of its partner to reach its objectives and that periodically reviews progress toward objectives.[21] The net result is trust and satisfaction with the partnership as the relationship leads to meeting performance goals.

Dealer Advisory Councils   One way to enhance the performance of all channel members is to facilitate the sharing of information among them. Distributors or reps may be brought together periodically with the manufacturer's management to review distribution policies, provide advice on marketing strategy, and supply industry intelligence.[22] Intermediaries can voice their opinions on policy matters and are brought directly into the decision-making process. Dayco Corporation uses a dealer council to

---

[20]Erin Anderson, Leonard M. Lodish, and Barton A. Weitz, "Resource Allocation in Conventional Channels," *Journal of Marketing Research* 24 (February 1987): p. 95; see also McQuiston, "A Conceptual Model for Building and Maintaining Relationships between Manufacturers' Reps and Their Principals," pp. 165–181.

[21]James C. Anderson and James A. Narus, "A Model of Distribution Firm and Manufacturing Firm Working Partnerships," *Journal of Marketing* 54 (January 1990): p. 56.

[22]Doug Harper, "Councils Launch Sales Ammo," *Industrial Distribution* 80 (September 1990): pp. 27–30.

keep abreast of distributors' changing needs.[23] One month after their meeting, council members receive a written report of suggestions they made and of the programs to be implemented as a result. Generally, Dayco enacts 75 percent of distributor proposals. For dealer councils to be effective, the input of channel members must have a meaningful effect on channel policy decisions.

Margins and Commission   In the final analysis, the primary motivating device is compensation. The surest way to lose intermediary support is compensation policies that do not meet industry and competitive standards. Reps or distributors who feel cheated on commissions or margins shift their attention to products generating a higher profit. The manufacturer must pay the prevailing compensation rates in the industry and must adjust the rates as conditions change.

Intermediaries' compensation should reflect the marketing tasks they perform. If the manufacturer seeks special attention for a new industrial product, most reps require higher commissions. As noted earlier in the chapter, many industrial distributors charge separate fees for the value-added services they provide. For this approach to work effectively, it is critical that the client understands the value it is receiving for the extra charges.

Building Trust   The very nature of a distribution channel—with each member dependent on another for success—can invite conflict. Conflict can be controlled in various ways, including channelwide committees, joint goal setting, and cooperative programs involving a number of marketing strategy elements. To compete, business marketers need to be effective at cooperating within a network of organizations—the channel. For example, an IBM executive who led the team that developed the first IBM PC in 1981 also drove the decision to sell it through dealers and later through the channel. Soon after the introduction of the PC, an executive with American Express Travel Related Services approached the IBM executive with an idea to sell the PCs directly to American Express card members. The IBM executive refused—he wanted the *channel* to get the sale. As a result, IBM secured the commitment and trust of its channel partners, setting the stage for many other strategy initiatives.[24]

Successful cooperation results from relationships in which the parties have a strong sense of communication and trust. Robert M. Morgan and Shelby D. Hunt suggest that relationship commitment and trust develop when (1) firms offer benefits and resources that are superior to what other partners could offer; (2) firms align themselves with other firms that have similar corporate values; (3) firms share valuable information on expectations, markets, and performance; and (4) firms avoid taking advantage of their partners.[25] By following these prescriptions, business marketers and their channel networks can enjoy sustainable competitive advantages over their rivals and their networks.

---

[23] James A. Narus and James C. Anderson, "Turn Your Distributors into Partners," *Harvard Business Review* 64 (March–April 1986): p. 68.

[24] Jeff O'Heir, "The Advocates: They Raised Their Voices to Legitimize the Channel," *Computer Reseller News*, June 17, 2002, p. 51.

[25] Robert M. Morgan and Shelby D. Hunt, "The Commitment-Trust Theory of Relationship Marketing," *Journal of Marketing* 58 (July 1994): pp. 20–38.

Summary

Channel strategy is an exciting and challenging aspect of business marketing. The challenge derives from the number of alternatives available to the manufacturer in distributing business products. The excitement results from the ever-changing nature of markets, user needs, and competitors.

Channel strategy involves two primary management tasks: designing the overall structure and managing the operation of the channel. Channel design includes evaluating distribution goals, activities, and potential intermediaries. Channel structure includes the number, types, and levels of intermediaries to be used. A central challenge is determining how to create a strategy that effectively blends e-commerce with traditional channels. Business marketing firms use multiple sales channels to serve customers in a particular market segment: company salespersons, channel partners, call centers, direct mail, and the Internet. The goal of a multichannel strategy is to coordinate activities across those channels to enhance the customer's experience while advancing the firm's performance.

The primary participants in business marketing channels are distributors and reps. Distributors provide the full range of marketing services for their suppliers, although customer contact and product availability are their most essential functions. Manufacturers' representatives specialize in selling, providing their suppliers with quality representation and with extensive product and market knowledge. The rep is not involved with physical distribution, leaving that burden to the manufacturers.

The central objective of channel management is to enhance the value delivered to customers through the carefully orchestrated activities of channel partners. The channel design process hinges on deep knowledge of customer needs, and the channel structure must be adjusted as customer or competitor behavior changes. Selection and motivation of channel partners are two management tasks vital to channel success. The business marketing manager may need to apply interorganizational management techniques to resolve channel conflict. Conflict can be controlled through a variety of means, including channelwide committees, joint goal setting, and cooperative programs that demonstrate trust and commitment.

Discussion Questions

1. Describe the specific tasks in the typical sales cycle and discuss how different channels (for example, business partners versus the Internet) can perform different tasks within a single sales transaction.

2. Using a multichannel integration map (see Figure 11.3), illustrate how a firm might cover small and medium-sized businesses versus large corporate customers.

3. Explain how a direct distribution channel may be the lowest-cost alternative for one business marketer and the highest-cost alternative for another in the same industry.

4. Describe specific product, market, and competitive conditions that lend themselves to (a) a direct channel of distribution and (b) an indirect channel of distribution.

5. Compare and contrast the functions performed by industrial distributors and manufacturers' representatives.

6. What product/market factors lend themselves to the use of manufacturers' representatives?

7. Describe why it might be necessary for a business-to-business firm to serve some customers through reps, some through distributors, others exclusively online, and still others through a direct sales force.

8. Explain how a change in segmentation policy (that is, entering new markets) may trigger the need for drastic changes in the industrial channel of distribution.

9. Both business marketers and distributors are interested in achieving profit goals. Why, then, are manufacturer-distributor relationships characterized by conflict? What steps can the marketer take to reduce conflict and thus improve channel performance?

10. For many years, critics have charged that intermediaries contribute strongly to the rising prices of goods in the American economy. Would business marketers improve the level of efficiency and effectiveness in the channel by reducing as far as possible the number of intermediate links in the channel? Support your position.

Internet Exercise

1. Sysco Corporation is a large distributor of food and food-related products to the food-service industry. The company provides its products and services to approximately 415,000 customers, including restaurants, health-care and educational facilities, lodging establishments, and other food-service customers. Although *Cisco* is most visible in the business press, Sysco generates over $23 billion in sales annually and has more than 45,000 employees. Go to http://www.sysco.com and identify some of the services Sysco provides.

SunPower's Go-to-Market Strategy[26]

SunPower Corporation, a Silicon Valley–based manufacturer of solar cells and solar panels, is emerging as a potential leader in the rapidly growing, but still immature, solar industry. The firm is the leader in cell conversion efficiency, which means that its solar cells generate more electricity at a given size than its rivals. So, when space constraints and aesthetics are important considerations, this attribute makes SunPower an ideal choice for business as well as home installations. To boost energy savings, the company has also developed its own tracking systems that allow its solar panels to follow the sun throughout the day. While costing only 5 percent more to install, this proprietary feature allows for 30 percent more energy generation than traditional solar systems.

SunPower serves all sectors of the business market and its customer list includes Johnson & Johnson, FedEx, Toyota, the U.S. Postal Service, and Microsoft. The company has signed agreements with Macy's, Target, and Wal-Mart to install solar systems at all of their California locations, and this may develop into a much larger opportunity, spreading to those customers' operations across the country.

In serving large corporate customers, like Macy's, SunPower uses a direct channel that controls the complete value chain from the manufacturing of the solar panels to the installation of the system. However, the firm also sees a huge opportunity in selling its solar systems to small and medium-sized businesses (SMBs). For smaller commercial installations (less than 500 kW of peak power), SunPower is developing an indirect channel—a network of commercial dealers that will serve those SMB customers. For customers in this market segment, SunPower emphasizes these benefits:

- lowering the monthly electric bills for your business;
- installing fewer panels that provide more power, thereby reducing your costs;
- taking advantage of government incentives for solar installations;
- supporting the environment and your community.

Discussion Questions

1. Channel design begins with an assessment of customer needs. What benefits or special services should a SunPower commercial dealer provide in order to meet the unique requirements of an SMB customer?

---

[26]Stephen Simko, "Analyst Research: SunPower Corporation," July 22, 2008, Morningstar, Inc., accessed at http://www.morningstar.com on July 26, 2008.

2. Describe the process that SunPower might follow to (a) evaluate potential dealers and (b) select those that will represent them in a particular city or geographical area.

3. To effectively implement channel strategy, what programs or strategies might SunPower take to better prepare and equip commercial dealers to serve SMB customers?

CHAPTER
12

E-Commerce Strategies
for Business Markets

Leading-edge firms are using the Internet to transform the way they do business. The Internet provides a powerful platform for conveying information, conducting transactions, delivering innovative services, and building close customer relationships. After reading this chapter, you will understand:

1. the nature of e-commerce in business markets.

2. the role of e-commerce in a firm's marketing strategy.

3. the key issues involved in designing an e-commerce strategy.

Before the Internet, customers had to call Dow Chemical and request a specification sheet for the products they were considering. The information would arrive a few days later by mail. After choosing a product, the customer could then place an order by calling Dow (during business hours, of course). Now, though, such information is available anytime at Dow.com. In turn, a host of more personalized services are available through MyAccount@Dow, which provides information tailored to the customer's requirements.[1] For example, MyAccount@Dow offers secure internal monitoring of a customer's chemical tank levels. When tanks reach a predetermined level, reordering can be automatically triggered. Similarly, Dell's large-enterprise customers can use its online resources to manage the inventory of personal computers across the organization, properly configure and upgrade them for different departments, and control the purchase order process in line with the customer's own budget restrictions.[2]

Dow Chemical and Dell represent just two of thousands of business marketers who have integrated the Internet and electronic commerce into their corporate strategies. E-commerce not only speeds up and automates a company's internal processes but, just as importantly, spreads the efficiency gains to the business systems of its suppliers and customers. For example, Dell customers can shop online using their own Enterprise Resource Planning (ERP) procurement application, route the electronic requisition through the firm's standard ERP workflow where it can be approved electronically, creating a purchase order that is transmitted instantly to Dell. This order then flows directly into Dell's manufacturing system where the equipment is built immediately and shipped, providing the customer with a timely and efficient solution.[3]

In other applications, e-commerce seamlessly moves data and information over open and closed networks, bringing together previously separate groups inside the organization and throughout the supply chain. By integrating suppliers and customers in this way, the Internet and e-commerce provide powerful tools that are ideally suited to the business-to-business (B2B) arena.

Data on the scope and size of business-to-business transactions on the Internet provide perspective: Compared to B2C volume, the most recent data indicate that B2B activity—transactions by manufacturers and merchant wholesalers—accounted for the most e-commerce (93 percent).[4] Manufacturers lead all industry sectors, with e-commerce accounting for 31.2 percent ($1,568 billion) of total shipments, and merchant wholesalers, including manufacturing sales branches and offices, ranked second, with e-commerce accounting for 20.6 percent ($1,148 billion) of total sales.[5] In contrast, retail e-commerce, the type of Internet sales with which most consumers are familiar, totaled only $107 billion in 2006.[6]

As the massive growth in e-commerce continues, significant opportunities and challenges emerge for all firms that market products and services in the business market. Witness the success of Google's search engine. The Internet is also becoming the main way that managers research B2B purchases.[7] For example, instead of lugging

---

[1]George S. Day and Katrina J. Bens, "Capitalizing on the Internet Opportunity," *Journal of Business & Industrial Marketing* 20 (4–5, 2005): pp. 160–168.

[2]Don Peppers and Martha Rogers, *Return on Customer* (New York: Currency–Doubleday, 2005), p. 42.

[3]"Dell Business to Business Ecommerce Solutions," http://www.dell.com/content/topics/reftopic.aspx/pub/commerce, 2008.

[4]*E-Stats*: Measuring the Electronic Economy, accessed at http://www.census.gov/estats on May 16, 2008, p. 1.

[5]Ibid., p. 3.

[6]Ibid., p. 3.

[7]Jacob Nielsen, "B-to-B Users Want Sites with B-to-C Service, Ease," *B to B* 90 (June 2005): p. 48.

home piles of brochures from a trade show, prospects look up potential suppliers on the Web to learn more about their products and services. Suppliers must change their communication strategy and develop content for the Web first, and print second—if at all. The Web offers interaction and hypertext and a much better way to communicate complex B2B information tailored to the customer's situation.

Firms that can enter the e-commerce marketplace by leveraging Internet capabilities with information processing, delivery capability, interorganizational collaboration, and flexibility may be able to develop important differential advantages in selected market segments. At the same time, major challenges confront organizations attempting to formulate an e-commerce strategy. These firms must craft a comprehensive e-commerce strategy, radically transform their traditional business models, and deal with rapid changes in e-commerce technology.

This chapter examines the nature of e-commerce, the role it can play in the organization's marketing strategy, the key elements in designing an e-commerce strategy, and the future direction and potential for e-commerce in business marketing.

Defining E-Commerce[8]

E-commerce involves "business communications and transmissions over networks and through computers, specifically the buying and selling of goods and services, and the transfer of funds through digital communications."[9] Who is going to gain an advantage in the customer-empowered, competitive markets that are being reshaped by e-commerce? A recent study suggests that firms that already excel at managing customer relationships were best equipped to capitalize on the opportunities of the Internet. According to the researchers, George S. Day and Katrina J. Bens, "Those leaders were able to anticipate earlier how to use the Internet to connect with their customers, exploited it faster, and implemented the initiative better." Such best-of-breed relationship builders like Dell, Cisco Systems, FedEx, GE Healthcare, and Johnson Controls relish the prospects presented by e-commerce.[10]

Alexander Ellinger and his colleagues describe the range of applications that a successful Web site can deliver: Internet applications range from

> . . . basic sites providing customers with general company information to more complex sites where interactive applications offer customers virtual product catalogs, opportunities to provide feedback, and an array of services including the ability to pay for and fulfill orders online. Successful websites add value because of their ability to present fresh, useful, relevant, and comprehensive information. For example, virtual product catalogs on websites are replacing the laborious and expensive necessity of printing and

---

[8]Some authors and business marketing experts have suggested that the more appropriate term is *e-business*, as opposed to *e-commerce*. They reason that *e-commerce* is a broad term that deals with all transactions that are Internet-based, whereas e-business specifically refers to transactions and relationships between organizations. In reality, IBM is given credit for coining the term *e-business* in a major 1997 advertising campaign promoting the notion of e-business. The term was new then but has since become routinely used in the press and marketing campaigns of other companies. This chapter will use *e-commerce*.

[9]David J. Good and Roberta J. Schultz, "E-Commerce Strategies for Business-to-Business Service Firms in the Global Environment," *American Business Review* 14 (June 2002): p. 111.

[10]George S. Day and Katrina J. Bens, "Capitalizing on the Internet Opportunity," p. 164; see also Chuang Ming-Ling and Wade H. Shaw, "A Roadmap for E-Business Implementation," *Engineering Management Journal* 17 (June 2005): pp. 3–13.

updating the physical catalogs that are customarily used in B-to-B sales. Website content can also make information seeking more convenient for customers. Many firms handle common information requests that would normally require access to a service representative by posting customers' most frequently asked questions (FAQs) and the associated answers on their websites.

A major benefit of interactive web-based content is that it makes the provision of customer service less expensive. For example, self-service B-to-B website applications that allow customers automated access to the overall supply chain require fewer service personnel. Interactive web-based applications also facilitate the customization of service and product offerings for individual accounts, creating potential switching costs for customers and offering firms infinite opportunities to learn more about each customer's specific requirements and business operations.[11]

As this discussion suggests, e-commerce is multifaceted and complex. However, the rationale for e-commerce is easy to understand: In certain markets and for selected customers, e-commerce can increase sales volume, lower costs, or provide more real-time information to customers. Ravi Kalkota and Andrew Whinston effectively describe the role of e-commerce for the typical organization:

Depending on how it is applied, e-commerce has the potential to increase revenue by creating new markets for old products, creating new information-based products, and establishing new service delivery channels to better serve and interact with customers. The transaction management aspect of electronic commerce can also enable firms to reduce operating cost by enabling better coordination in the sales, production, and distribution processes (or better supply chain management), and to consolidate operations and reduce overhead.[12]

In short, e-commerce can be applied to almost all phases of business, with the net effect of creating new demand or making most business processes more efficient. E-commerce can be applied to procuring and purchasing products; managing the process for fulfilling customers' orders; providing real-time information on the status of orders, online marketing and advertising; creating online product catalogs and product information data sets; managing the logistics process; and processing the payment of invoices.[13] The applications are limitless, yet not all products and markets can be effectively served through the e-commerce approach. Later in the chapter we will identify situations that offer the greatest potential for effective application of e-commerce. The different applications of e-commerce are depicted in Figure 12.1. Note that e-commerce can play a pivotal role across all functional areas of the business, yet the most important application from the marketing perspective is how e-commerce facilitates interactions with customers.

[11]Alexander E. Ellinger, Daniel F. Lynch, James K. Andzulis, and Ronn J. Smith, "B-to-B e-commerce: A Content Analytical Assessment of Motor Carrier Websites," *Journal of Business Logistics* 24 (2003): p. 32.
[12]Ravi Kalkota and Andrew B. Whinston, *Electronic Commerce* (Reading, MA: Addison-Wesley, 1996), p. 5.
[13]Ming-Ling and Shaw, "A Roadmap for E-Business," p. 5.

FIGURE 12.1 | TYPES OF E-COMMERCE

Interorganizational E-Commerce

1. *Supplier management:* helps to reduce the number of suppliers, lower procurement costs, and increase order cycle time.
2. *Inventory management:* instantaneous transmission of information allows reduction of inventory; tracking of shipments reduces errors and safety stock; out-of-stocks are reduced.
3. *Distribution management:* e-commerce facilitates the transmission of shipping documents and ensures the data are accurate.
4. *Channel management:* rapid dissemination of information to trading partners on changing market and customer conditions. Technical, product, and pricing information can now be posted to electronic bulletin boards. Production information easily shared with all channel partners.
5. *Payment management:* payments can be sent and received electronically among suppliers and distributors, reducing errors, time, and costs.

Intraorganizational E-Commerce

1. *Workgroup communications:* e-mail and electronic bulletin boards are used to facilitate internal communications.
2. *Electronic publishing:* all types of company information, including price sheets, market trends, and product specifications can be organized and disseminated instantaneously.
3. *Sales force productivity:* e-commerce facilitates information flow between production and the sales force and between the sales force and the customer. Firms gain greater access to market and competitor intelligence supplied by the sales force.

Business-to-Customer E-Commerce

1. *Product information:* information on new and existing products is readily available to customers on the firm's Web site.
2. *Sales:* certain products can be sold directly from the firm's Web site, reducing the cost of the transaction and allowing customers to have real-time information about their order.
3. *Service:* customers can electronically communicate about order status, product applications, problems with products, and product returns.
4. *Payment:* payment can be made by the customer using electronic payment systems.
5. *Marketing research:* firms can use e-commerce, the Internet, and their own Web sites to gather significant quantities of information about customers and potential customers.

Key Elements Supporting E-Commerce

Intranets and Extranets

The Internet has become an important element in the marketing strategy of many business marketers; two other very important technological elements, however, are integrated with an Internet strategy. **Intranets** are basically company-specific, internal Internets. An intranet links documents on the organization's scattered internal networks together. A firm's intranet allows different functions and people to share databases, communicate with each other, disseminate timely bulletins, view proprietary information, be trained in various aspects of the firm's business, and share any type of information system the company uses to manage its business. For example,

INSIDE BUSINESS MARKETING

Extending the Boundaries of E-Commerce: B2M (Business to Machines) E-Commerce

E-commerce is multifaceted, as suggested by the use of intranets and extranets, and the applications are growing. A creative and relatively new application of e-commerce—business to machine e-commerce (B2M)—can provide huge savings. B2M e-commerce provides data that help Ryder negotiate with the business marketers that provide them with parts and equipment warranties.

B2M (Business to Machines) e-Commerce is a fast-emerging area within e-commerce. The general idea is that companies can link to remote machines via the Internet. As an example, consider the $5 billion Ryder Truck Company—Ryder System Inc. When a truck rolls into one of the company's maintenance bays, the attendant need only push a button to instantly determine the status of that vehicle. Specifically, a technician simply touches a probe located on the end of a handheld computer to a coin-shaped disk on the truck's cab, capturing information on engine performance and fuel consumption from electronic sensors under the hood. These sensors track information related to 65 different aspects of the truck from oil life and tire wear to filter life, gas mileage, and much more. Prior to the introduction of this B2M system, the company's mechanics were wrong nearly 50 percent of the time when it came to identifying problems with the trucks. Now the sources of trouble are identified more quickly and a truck's downtime is often cut in half. The company manages almost 10,000 technicians and 175,000 trucks, but with the B2M system, inventory tracking, parts ordering, maintenance scheduling, and personnel scheduling are streamlined. Additionally, Ryder uses the information it collects on engine-part wear to negotiate longer warranties from suppliers. According to Chief Information Officer Dennis M. Klinger, the new system cost $33 million but reportedly paid for itself in just a few years!

SOURCE: "The Many Flavors of E-Commerce," Accounting Software Advisor, http://www.accountingsoftwareadvisor.com, accessed 2008.

Boeing, the world's largest commercial aircraft manufacturer, maintains a company intranet that is available to more than 200,000 Boeing employees worldwide. One segment of its intranet contains an online course catalog for company educational programs in supervisor training and quality control. Intranets can also incorporate outside news. For example, Factiva, an information company, streams news into enterprise intranets. Much of the external information can be precisely tailored news, relevant to a particular firm.[14]

Extranets, on the other hand, are links that allow business partners such as suppliers, distributors, and customers to connect to a company's internal networks (intranets) over the Internet or through virtual private networks. An extranet is created when two organizations connect their intranets for business communications and transactions. The purpose of an extranet is to provide a communication mechanism to streamline business processes that normally take place elsewhere. Hewlett-Packard, for example, has established extranet links to its advertising agencies to speed the review of ad campaigns. Business partners access a company's intranet by means of a unique password. Companies in the printing industry, for example, allow customers access to their internal networks to track print jobs as they move through production

---

[14]Marydee Ojola, "Adding External Knowledge to Business Web Sites," *Online* 26 (4, July–August 2002): p. 3.

or to browse databases of images of other media assets.[15] Extranets allow a firm to customize information and interaction with each specific customer who is granted access to its intranet. Hewlett-Packard offers one of the largest medical sites on the Web. To secure customized information, hospital customers have special passwords (based on a profile they provide) that automatically connect them to "special pricing" negotiated through that institution's contracts with Hewlett-Packard.[16]

The Strategic Role of E-Commerce

For the business marketer, the crucial question is: What role does e-commerce assume in the firm's overall marketing strategy? One of the great dangers of e-commerce is the potential for managers to become enamored with the technology and ignore the strategic elements and the role of e-commerce in the firm's overall mission. The Internet and, more specifically, e-commerce are just instruments for accomplishing marketing goals—the need for sound marketing strategy remains.

E-Commerce as a Strategic Component

The use of e-commerce and, more specifically, the Internet is just like any other element the business marketer uses to accomplish the firm's mission: It must be focused, based on carefully crafted objectives, and directed at specific target segments. For the marketer, the Internet can be viewed as:

1. a communication device to build customer relationships;
2. an alternative distribution channel;
3. a valuable medium for delivering services to customers;
4. a tool for gathering marketing research data;
5. a method for integrating supply chain members.

In short, the Internet usually does not replace existing distribution channels; rather, it supports or supplements them. In a similar way, the Internet does not eliminate the selling function; rather, it facilitates the salesperson's efforts and enhances the effectiveness and efficiency of the sales function. Likewise, B2B e-commerce should be viewed as an end-to-end business process, involving the entire supply chain.[17]

According to Hank Barnes, to be successful, business marketers must integrate the Internet and e-commerce into the "fabric of their traditional business operations, leveraging it as a communications tool that can increase sales, satisfaction and service levels."[18] Essentially, e-commerce extends a firm's reach but does not change the fundamentals of how a firm acquires, responds to, and satisfies its customers. Andy Grove, a legendary Intel executive, aptly concludes, "Implementing the new e-commerce model does not mean simply selling something over the Internet, but incorporating

---

[15]"Extranets Enhance Customer Relations," *Graphic Arts Monthly* (January 1999): p. 89.

[16]Curt Werner, "Health Care E-Commerce, Still in Its Infancy, But Growing Fast," *Health Industry Today* 8 (September 1998): p. 9.

[17]Judith Lamont, "Collaborative Commerce Revitalizes Supply Chain," *KM World* 14 (July–August 2005): pp. 16–18.

[18]Hank Barnes, "Getting Past the Hype: Internet Opportunities for B-to-B Marketers," *Marketing News*, February 1, 1999, p. 11.

INSIDE BUSINESS MARKETING

UPS Delivers the Goods Using Sophisticated E-Commerce Technology

UPS (United Parcel Service Inc.) is an express carrier, package delivery company, and a global provider of specialized transportation and logistic services. Over more than 90 years, the firm has expanded from a small regional parcel delivery service into a global company. The company's primary business is the time-definite delivery of packages and documents throughout the United States and more than 200 other countries and territories. UPS is a leading adopter of e-commerce applications, offering new services like UPS online tools and many other service applications to customers through its logistics group at http://www.e-logistics.ups.com and at http://www.upslogistics.com.

As the Internet was taking shape, UPS made a financial commitment to transform its operations to meet the changing needs of the digital economy by establishing electronic connectivity with its extensive base of customers. UPS is responding to the challenge of meeting these changing needs as the e-business evolution continues to unfold. The company has a variety of business solutions that give customers productive ways to manage, grow, and even transform their businesses to stay on course in a fast-changing, competitive market.

UPS uses a carefully crafted e-commerce strategy to deliver the goods quickly, reliably, and securely. Customers can obtain accurate account and shipping information in real time. Consistently meeting or exceeding service expectations enhances customer satisfaction and loyalty. Every day, UPS links 1.8 million sellers to 7 million buyers all over the world and delivers $1.5 billion worth of packages, including more than 55 percent of all the goods ordered online. The company has formed alliances with the leading e-commerce software providers and helps customers build or improve their Web sites so they, in turn, can better serve their customers. UPS e-Logistics, a subsidiary of UPS, provides integrated, end-to-end supply-chain management services to e-commerce businesses and dot.com divisions of established companies. Whether the customers' orders come via Web site, phone, mail, or other channel, UPS e-Logistics can manage the entire fulfillment process from inventory management to shipping—providing clients with new capabilities for managing information, moving inventory, and advancing customer loyalty.

SOURCE: Nabil Alghalith, "Competing with IT: The UPS Case," *Journal of American Academy of Business* 7 (September 2005): pp. 7–15.

the Net into the day-to-day functioning of the company, in particular, as a mode for B2B transactions and for building customer relationships."[19] From the perspective of the entire supply chain, a key issue is to include further use of e-commerce to automate and reduce the cost of transactions and to increase the quality of product data flows throughout the supply chain.[20]

What the Internet Can Do

Before exploring the strategic elements of e-commerce, let's explore the important benefits of an effectively developed e-commerce strategy. The Internet is a powerful tool when used properly, and the advantages are significant in terms of more effectively serving customers, communicating useful information, and lowering the cost of doing business.

[19]As quoted in David Troy, "E-Commerce: Foundations of Business Strategy," Caliber Learning Systems, http://www.caliber.com.

[20]Aislinn McCormick, "Meeting Global Supply Demands," *Bookseller*, September 16, 2005, pp. 12–13.

The Internet: Strategy Still Matters[21]

As an important new technology, many executives, entrepreneurs, and investors assumed that the Internet would change everything and render many of the old rules about competition obsolete. Michael Porter, the noted strategist, argues persuasively that the old rules still apply and the fundamentals of strategy remain unchanged. Indeed, caught up in the excitement over Internet technology, many firms—dot-coms and established firms alike—made bad decisions. For example, some firms have shifted the basis of competition toward price and away from traditional factors like quality, features, and service. Under such conditions, all competitors in an industry struggle to turn a profit. Alternatively, other firms forfeited important proprietary advantages by rushing into misguided partnerships and outsourcing relationships.

The lesson for business marketers is that the Internet is an enabling technology—a powerful set of tools that complements, rather than replaces, traditional ways of competing. So, the key decision is not whether to use Internet technology, but rather how to deploy it. Successful companies integrate Internet initiatives directly into established operations rather than setting these strategies apart in a specialized e-commerce unit. Michael Porter provides this incisive forecast:

> Basic Internet applications will become table stakes—companies will not be able to survive without them, but they will not gain any advantage from them. The more robust competitive advantages will arise from traditional strengths such as unique products, proprietary content, distinctive physical activities, superior product knowledge, and strong service and relationships. . . . Ultimately, strategies that integrate the Internet and traditional competitive advantages and ways of competing should win in many industries.[22]

Enhanced Customer Focus, Responsiveness, and Relationships The Internet allows business marketers to align with their customers on order management and also on product configuration and design, resulting in better customer service and more satisfied customers. Because the Internet creates direct links between customers and factories, corporate buyers can tailor products to meet their exact requirements. Many business marketers now encourage customers to customize products exactly to their specifications right on the Web site.

Reduced Transaction Costs When customers use the Internet to communicate with suppliers, the supplier is able to provide low-cost access to both order entry and order tracking 24 hours a day, seven days a week. Transactions that do not require in-person services can be handled in a cost-effective manner on a Web site, and the firm can devote more staff to working with higher-margin customers requiring personal attention. In effect, e-commerce transfers operations to "self-service," allowing customers to download materials themselves and reducing costs for all involved. Some companies report that by automating transactions over the Internet, the cost of a purchasing transaction has declined from $150 to $25.[23]

---

[21]This section is based on Michael Porter, "Strategy and the Internet," *Harvard Business Review* 79 (March 2001): pp. 63–78.

[22]Ibid., p. 78.

[23]Dave Rumar, "Electronic Commerce Helps Cut Transaction Costs, Reduce Red Tape," *Computing Canada* 25 (32, 1999): p. 24.

Integration of the Supply Chain   The Internet allows companies to electronically link far-flung constituencies, including customers, suppliers, intermediaries, and alliance partners, in spite of organizational, geographical, and functional boundaries. All the supply chain participants can be linked by a common database that is shared over the Internet, making the entire value-adding process seamless and more efficient. The key to effective supply chain operations is the sharing of vital information: sales forecasts, production plans, delivery schedules, tracking of finished product shipments through the distribution network, inventory levels at various points in the supply chain, final sales versus planned sales, and the like.

QAD, Inc., is the developer of *Total eCommerce Solution*, which provides a menu of software and services that help companies more consistently integrate global partners into their back-end systems. The *Total eCommerce Solution* lets users extend supply chain processes to partners, providing the ultimate in business integration. QAD's services include capabilities for communications, translation, application integration, business process management, and business activity management.[24]

Focus on Core Business   The Internet makes it easier for companies to focus on what they do best and spin off or contract out other operations to third parties that are tied to them through the Internet. In this way, the Internet helps companies develop a "virtual company" that contracts with other firms to perform such functions as manufacturing to warehousing. Boeing developed its latest airplane, the Boeing 777, with a portfolio of relationships among subcontractors and lead customers that were linked electronically.[25] This approach allows Boeing to devote more assets and human resources to the critical area of product design.

Access Global Markets   E-commerce provides a powerful means for B2B firms to penetrate far-flung global markets. Using the latest in IT technology, firms can exploit and expand their customer base all over the world by implementing order and procurement management systems, as well as sales, marketing, and customer support functionality.[26] By relying on an e-commerce solution, there is no need to invest in a sales force or "bricks-and-mortar" assets in every potential market—the Web provides the necessary coverage. The approach requires a highly effective Internet strategy and the logistics capacity to efficiently make products available to customers in a timely fashion. Once markets are established through e-commerce, the sales volume in a particular geographic area may, in fact, justify the presence of a sales force, offices, and logistics operations.

Crafting an E-Commerce Strategy

Developing a B2B strategy for e-commerce is no different from developing any other type of marketing strategy. The process begins with an evaluation of the company's products, customers, competitive situation, resources, and operations to better understand how all of these elements mesh with an e-commerce strategy. Figure 12.2 provides a valuable framework that outlines important strategic and tactical questions

---

[24]Renee Boucher Ferguson, "E-com Gets Integration Help," *eWeek*, September 9, 2005, pp. 25–35.

[25]N. Venkatraman and John C. Henderson, "Real Strategies for Virtual Organizing," *Sloan Management Review* 40 (Winter 1999): p. 5.

[26]"E-commerce Market in Asia Still Hot after Dotcom Burst," *Xinhua*, July 31, 2002, accessed at WorldSources, Inc., Online.

FIGURE 12.2 | QUESTIONS TO GUIDE E-COMMERCE STRATEGY FORMULATION

1. Customers and Markets

What are we already doing on the Internet, and how do our activities align with customer needs?

How can we use the Internet to provide better customer service?

How can we use the Internet to make our sales channels more effective?

2. Competitive Threats

How might traditional competitors and e-business startups change market dynamics and take away market share or customers?

Will failure to act now precipitate a crisis within the next two years in any of our lines of business?

Can we ignore the Internet if our competitors are using it to gain attention and pricing advantages?

3. People and Infrastructure

Do our management teams and technical staff have the skills to run an Internet business?

What will it cost to fix weaknesses—exposed by our Internet business strategy—in our processes, infrastructure, and enterprise systems?

What are appropriate business and financial structures for managing Internet business risk?

4. Sources and Operations

Are we blinding ourselves by making assumptions based on our old way of doing business that doesn't fit with the Internet?

What are the Internet-relevant models that match ours, threaten us, or are suitable ways to conduct business?

How can we use the Internet to make supply chains more efficient?

How can we use the Internet to lower our operating costs? How long will it take?

SOURCE: "A CEO's Internet Business Strategy Checklist: The Leading Questions," *Business Technology Journal—Recent Research*, accessed at http://gartner112.gartnerweb.com on April 19, 1999.

that surround e-commerce strategies. Answering these questions helps the business marketing manager to carefully define what the firm hopes to accomplish through an e-commerce strategy and to assess several important resource issues associated with implementing the strategy.

Some business marketers find that e-commerce is becoming so sophisticated and technical that they need assistance in both creating and then managing their e-commerce efforts. As a result, many third-party companies have emerged to provide sophisticated solutions to e-commerce applications, and business marketers may find outsourcing an effective strategy. According to Stanford University's Global Supply Chain Forum, companies using outsourced B2B solutions experience a return nearly 2.5 times their annual investment.[27] A recent study showed that outsourced e-commerce strategies led to marked improvements in customer satisfaction. One other tangible benefit of outsourcing e-commerce applications is that using a single B2B solution helps to provide a single focused approach to e-commerce, thus helping to integrate multidivision companies with a common e-commerce vision.

[27]Frank O. Smith, "Stanford Forum Unearths Big Benefits in B2B Outsourcing," *Manufacturing Business Technology* 25 (December, 2007): p. 11.

Delineating E-Commerce Objectives

A guiding principle in formulating an Internet strategy is to understand that the Internet and the associated technology are nothing more than *tools* the business marketing strategist uses in satisfying the customer at a profit: "It is not a competitive strategy or the capability to deliver the strategy."[28] Often, there is a temptation to think that the Internet can eliminate the need for salespeople, reduce expenditures on trade advertising, or totally replace traditional distribution channels and marketing intermediaries. For most firms, the Internet *supplements* the company's traditional marketing strategy, making it more effective or less costly, or both.

In the channels area, for example, many companies find it beneficial to use the Web to support their dealers' e-business efforts by providing Web-based information to them, offering Web co-op advertising dollars, and allowing the dealers to build a front-end site onto the company's site.[29] Moreover, firms have found that a sales force remains vital in forging customer relationships once an Internet strategy is implemented. In fact, the Internet can make the sales force more productive. For example, PSS WorldMedical is a huge medical products distributor with a sales force of over 700 people. The company developed a closed Customer Link system that allows customers to order products online. The system does not replace the sales force; rather, sales reps continue to earn commissions on Customer Link sales from their accounts. The salespeople can then concentrate more fully on higher-profit capital equipment sales.

Synchronizing the Web with Strategy   Just as important as enhancing effectiveness and efficiency, the Internet is often used to reach an entirely new or different target market. Many experts consider Dell the "poster child for business-to-business e-commerce" because of its legendary success in controlling costs effectively by providing custom-designed personal computers through the Internet.[30] Yet what makes Dell a great Internet marketer is its ability to take its customer-obsessed direct-sales practices and enhance them using the Web. Says Eryn Brown in *Fortune*, "There isn't anything the company does online that it doesn't do in the physical world. Yet Dell and its customers know that nothing beats the Web for taking care of the 'annoying stuff.'"[31] Dell serves as an excellent model for any B2B marketer seeking to fully synchronize an Internet strategy with its traditional salesperson-based strategy. The key to Dell's success is understanding the Internet's role and its relationship to all other elements of the firm's marketing strategy.

Specific Objectives of Internet Marketing Strategies

The Internet can be effective in providing information as well as in stimulating customer action. Internet marketing objectives resemble those of any type of communication strategy in the business marketplace. The Internet can be used to focus on cognitive objectives like stimulating awareness and knowledge of the company, creating a favorable attitude toward the firm, or stimulating the buyer to purchase. Note the Web site for "Custom-Printed Post-it Notes" displayed in Figure 12.3. In this case, 3M allows the customer to use its Web site to create the exact personalized Post-it note desired. This site also illustrates how easy it is for customers to customize the product to their

---

[28]Day and Bens, "Capitalizing on the Internet Opportunity," p. 167.

[29]Ginger Conlon, "Direct Impact," *Sales & Marketing Management* 151 (December 1999): p. 57.

[30]Eryn Brown, "Nine Ways to Win on the Web," *Fortune*, May 17, 1999, p. 114.

[31]Ibid., p. 114.

FIGURE 12.3 | **3M's Web Site Makes It Easy to Personalize Post-it Notes**

requirements and place an order online to create the product. By visiting http://promote.3m.com/index.jsp;jsessionid=akURBYBb9vN8, you can experience firsthand how easy it is to use this online service. The following are some of the most common objectives that business marketers may have for the e-commerce portion of their business:[32]

1. Target a specific market or group of customers.

2. Build recognition of the company name and brands.

3. Convey a cutting-edge image.

4. Conduct market research.

5. Interact with existing customers and cultivate new ones.

6. Provide real-time information on products, services, and company finances to customers and supply chain partners.

[32]Adapted from Neal J. Hannon, *The Business of the Internet* (Cambridge, MA: International Thomson Publishing Company, 1998), p. 210.

B2B TOP PERFORMERS

GE Healthcare: Using the Web to Create New Services

GE Healthcare discovered a way to use the Web to capture data from its medical equipment and create valuable new services for its customers. The resulting service application, called eCenter, monitors and transmits patient data from MRI machines and other GE medical equipment directly to the radiologist (the customer). In addition to enhancing a patient's care, GE can also provide valuable information that can enhance the productivity of a health-care organization. GE can analyze the data from one customer and compare it to that of other customer sites to see how productive a specific radiology department is compared with others that use the same equipment.

Building on the success of this initiative, GE has developed similar eCenter applications for other GE divisions. To illustrate, GE Power Systems customers, such as utilities, can analyze the performance of their turbines versus others in the industry. By viewing information technology as a strategic capability rather than a support function, GE is enhancing its products and co-creating new value with customers.

SOURCE: C. K. Prahalad and Venkat Ramaswamy, *The Future of Competition: Co-Creating New Value with Customers* (Boston: Harvard Business School Press, 2004), p. 223.

7. Sell products and services.

8. Sell in a more efficient manner.

9. Advertise in a new medium.

10. Generate leads for the sales force.

11. Provide a medium for customer service.

12. Build strong relationships with customers.

The specific objectives for a firm's Internet business dictate the issues it must deal with in formulating its strategy. For example, if the objective is to create new sales volume, critical attention must be given to creating systems for handling transactions and providing logistical and service support. Internet strategies vary dramatically based on the objectives.

Internet Strategy Implementation

With the Internet objectives fully delineated, the business marketer is positioned to develop an Internet strategy. As with any marketing process, the Internet strategy must carefully address product, promotion, channels, and pricing. Discussion of strategy implementation begins by examining the important product-related dimensions.

The Internet Product

The Internet product is a complex array of physical elements, software, hardware, extranets, intranets, services, and information. The Web site is the major product element in a company's e-commerce strategy. Even though it may include other dimensions, the heart of an e-commerce strategy is the company's Web site, for here all interactions with the customer are most cost-effectively handled.

FIGURE 12.4 | W.W. GRAINGER MAKES IT EASY TO FIND PRODUCTS AND PLACE ORDERS

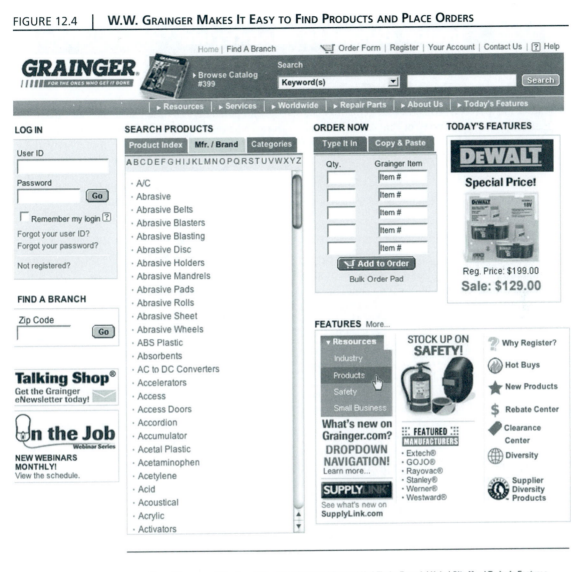

As indicated, a Web site has to be developed on the basis of a careful delineation of company objectives, and it is rare that a Web site is developed on the basis of a single objective. Thus, the design of the Web site becomes more complicated as top management articulates additional objectives. Other obvious ingredients in the planning process are the needs of the targeted Web site visitors. A focus on both dimensions assures that both the company and the customer are accommodated.

Observe from Figure 12.4 how W. W. Grainger uses its Web site to make it easy for customers to look for products and place an order. If the customer wants to browse through different product lines, that can be done with a single click. For a

INSIDE BUSINESS MARKETING

"Borrow Best Tactics From Consumer E-Commerce To Revamp Your B2B Site"

Stuck in a B2B rut? To boost lead generation and e-Commerce transactions, one marketer looked at best practices in consumer marketing. When they retooled their site, changes included:

- Adding lots more images

- Creating unique landing pages for top brand name searches

- Calculating shipping costs

The result is that site traffic increased 587%, and the new lead generation feature created millions of dollars in additional revenue. In turn, new customer segments were identified, such as universities and research labs. When Bob Schneider redesigned the Web site for Ellsworth Adhesives, an industrial adhesive and specialty chemical distributor, his goal was to boost e-commerce sales and lead generation for their field sales reps. But to achieve those B2B goals, Schneider and his team borrowed techniques from the most successful *consumer* e-commerce sites. "If you aren't thinking B2C and are just thinking you're a B2B site, you're not going to be everything you can be. A lot of the B2B sites that we looked at expected a lot of their users," says Schneider, the company's former Webmaster who now consults for Ellsworth Adhesives.

B2B purchasers are also consumers, who likely have come to expect certain things from the online shopping experience based on their personal purchases at Amazon.com and other top consumer sites. Keeping those shoppers in mind during the redesign, Schneider's team applied a consumer focus to the site's design, content, features, and search engine optimization strategy.

Tactic 1. Provide full product information and supporting documents

Tactic 2. Calculate actual shipping costs for orders

Tactic 3. Show photographs of every product

Tactic 4. Provide experts to answer questions

Tactic 5. Create unique landing pages for top brand name searches

Tactic 6. Use negative keywords to filter out consumers

SOURCE: Marketing Sherpa, accessed at http://www.marketing sherpa.com/article.php?ident=30113 on August 30, 2007.

---

repetitive order, the customer simply types in the product number and quantity desired. To pick up a product immediately at a Grainger location, the customer only needs to click on "find a branch."

Successful Web Site Design   To effectively develop a Web site, the designer needs to think like a user—to anticipate how the customer will use the site and the features that will make it easy to use. To use the Internet as a marketing tool, the Web site should allow customers to easily move along the sales process, provide a quick and easy way to find the product they desire, and determine whether the products fit their needs. If the site can accomplish these goals, then the next function is to ease the financial transaction. Speed, ease of use, and security are central to completing the sales transaction and meeting the customer's service expectations.

Internet Catalogs   One of the first applications of e-commerce for many business marketers that sell components, materials, and maintenance and operating resources is to develop an electronic catalog on their Web sites. Rather than leafing through thousands of pages, the user can define exact requirements and easily locate the appropriate item in the catalog. Moreover, the catalog can be continuously updated.

As Chapter 3 indicated, many firms have embraced e-purchasing applications. They have found that electronic purchasing dramatically enhances the effectiveness of buyers and reduces the time and expense they spend searching for operating resources or non-production goods. Firms without Internet catalogs will probably be unable to compete in the future because of the great savings buyers can glean through e-purchasing.

Reverse Auctions   Reverse auctions, which involve one buyer and many sellers, have been embraced by purchasing managers across business market sectors, including government. Why? Many companies such as Quaker Oats and GlaxoSmithKline report millions of dollars of savings with reverse auctions compared with traditional buying methods. FreeMarkets, Inc.—now a part of Ariba—organizes reverse auctions for manufacturers like United Technologies. Here suppliers bid on purchase contracts for component parts, raw materials, and commodities. Firms that sell commodity items face the greatest threat. Experts suggest that reverse auctions can damage long-standing buyer-seller relationships.

Some purchasers have realized that continuously pressing for deeper price cuts might backfire by inhibiting collaboration. If profit margins continually decline, suppliers might be forced to consolidate, thereby enhancing their power.[33] Chapter 14 details particular strategies that the business marketer can implement with customers that utilize reverse auctions.

Private Exchanges[34]   A new form of reverse auction has emerged—private exchanges, which are invitation-only networks that connect a single company to its customers, suppliers, or both. Private exchanges can do what open exchanges (reverse auctions) could not: Since they provide secure, one-on-one communication, they enhance shared supply chain processes, such as inventory management, production planning, and order fulfillment. Some suppliers are using the process improvements generated by their participation in exchanges to build closer relationships with customers. Research suggests that private exchanges can offer competitive advantages to most large suppliers if companies understand what these networks offer and what they demand in return. Unlike open B2B marketplaces and industry consortia, private exchanges keep control in the hands of an active participant—an arrangement that helps focus activity on process rather than price. Because suppliers on a private exchange are either invited guests or hosts, buyers have already chosen to do business with them and often have completed price negotiations. In fact, a private exchange is chiefly an information exchange: Though buyers can shop for a better price elsewhere, it has been shown that they are rarely inclined to do so. Customer relationships built on trust (and supported by nondisclosure agreements) are essential if, for example, suppliers are given access to a customer's sales and inventory information and forecast product demand for that customer, assuring the delivery of goods or services as needed. Private exchanges offer promise for enhancing buyer-supplier relationships and for improving the efficiency of supply chains.

---

[33]Sandy D. Jap, "An Exploratory Study of the Introduction of Online Reverse Auctions," *Journal of Marketing* 67 (July 2003): pp. 96–107.

[34]William Hoffman, Jennifer Keedy, and Karl Roberts, "The Unexpected Return of B2B," *The McKinsey Quarterly*, July 25, 2008, p. 1.

Channel Considerations with Internet Marketing

Firms that develop an Internet strategy must consider several important distribution channel issues. An Internet marketing presence requires the manager to evaluate the following: the effect on channel efficiencies, current marketing intermediaries, and information sharing among channel members; the ability to rapidly deliver product; and the need to consider the outsourcing of some key channel functions.

Channel Efficiencies   One significant benefit of B2B Internet marketing is its positive impact on efficiency in the channels of distribution. The Internet uses low-cost communications technology to automate all kinds of business transactions. As a result, much of the back-office paperwork and tasks required in dealing with channel members that once occupied the time of several employees can now be automated. By linking information systems with channel members through the Web, a firm helps intermediaries more effectively monitor inventory and the flow of goods through their warehouses.

For example, a large tool distributor uses an e-commerce platform from *PartsWatch*.[35] The architecture enables many innovative benefits like central price updating and automatic catalog updates—without the need to send or receive disks. The primary effect on the channel is that a company has real-time information on demand at every level of distribution. Customers can use the system to direct and manage the channel and efficiently provide real-time central services for all channel partners. These types of networks allow purchase order transactions, order acknowledgments, and shipment notices to flow seamlessly between distributors and their suppliers.

Effect on Current Intermediaries   Internet strategies pose interesting questions about the structure of a firm's distribution channel. Depending on the nature of the manufacturer's Internet strategy, the role of current channel members may be expanded, unchanged, or dramatically reduced. The key variable is how much value the channel member adds to the process of marketing and physically distributing products. In some instances, the channel members may be called on to serve target markets that cannot be effectively covered through an Internet approach. Traditional channel members have often been relegated to the role of serving very small niche markets that cannot be efficiently served through direct or Internet marketing approaches. Others have been able to expand their role because of a manufacturer's new Internet strategy. Because many Internet transactions involve one or a few items, a real need exists for someone to handle the process of physically fulfilling orders, and hence a new opportunity is presented to a distributor who can perform this function effectively.

Disintermediation   Because the Internet improves connectivity among firms, it dramatically reduces the cost of communication and coordination in exchange transactions. In a networked channel, firms can bypass intermediaries who have traditionally facilitated the flow of information and goods between firms and their customers. This situation is referred to as **disintermediation**, and indications are that it is taking hold in several B2B sectors. Large travel agencies that sell airline tickets to corporate accounts are experiencing disintermediation as airlines have created their own Web sites that provide as much or more information to the corporate traveler as did the

---

[35]Chris Miller, "E-commerce Advances," *Aftermarket Business* 115 (September 2005): p. 14.

agencies. Itineraries, including hotels, rental cars, and airline tickets, can be arranged with the click of a mouse, and payment can be processed through a secure channel right on the Web site. In fact, because of the success of these Internet strategies, the airlines have reduced or eliminated travel agent commissions, forcing many to either go out of business or focus on leisure travel segments.

The Internet as a Channel Alternative

The Internet can be a very effective "channel" of distribution for reaching selected target markets. Rarely do business marketers rely solely on the Internet as their only approach for contacting customers and consummating sales. Rather, the Internet is but one channel or method for doing business with target markets. At AMP, the large manufacturer of electronic connectors, its Internet catalog complements traditional channels such as the sales force, distributors, and in-house customer service representatives. The catalog simply gives customers another avenue for doing business with the company.[36]

In some cases, the Internet is particularly effective for "distributing" certain types of products like software and written material. The software industry pioneered the use of the Internet for product distribution. Computer software firms like Adobe Systems and Microsoft take advantage of the new Web distribution channels to sell and distribute software electronically. The advantage is that companies of any size, with very small marketing budgets, can take advantage of the Web to create and distribute new products. Anything that can be digitized can be transmitted over the Internet, which offers numerous advantages to marketers desiring to distribute printed materials. In short, the Internet broadens the reach of marketers, providing them with an efficient channel to serve customers on a global scale.

Digital Channel Advantages   By providing an effective mechanism for contacting potential buyers, the Internet offers some advantages over traditional channels of distribution for business products. According to Judy Strauss and Raymond Frost, the Internet adds value for several reasons:[37]

1. The contact can be customized to the buyer's needs.

2. The Internet provides a wide range of referral sources such as Web pages, search engines, shopping agents, newsgroups, chat rooms, and e-mail.

3. The Internet is always open for business: Buyers can contact the site 24 hours a day, seven days a week.

Using the Internet, business marketers can create customized solutions for customers. For example, Staples (http://www.staples.com) offers customized catalogs for its corporate clients. Such a strategy would be costly to implement through traditional channels. The Internet provides Staples with unparalleled flexibility in creating just the type of catalog a particular organization desires. Other firms have developed

[36]Jim Kesseler, "Defining the Future of Business-to-Business Electronic Commerce," *Journal of Global Information Management* 6 (1, 1999): p. 43.

[37]Judy Strauss and Raymond Frost, *Marketing on the Internet* (Upper Saddle River, NJ: Prentice Hall, 1997), p. 168.

online stores to more efficiently reach small and medium-sized businesses that are unprofitable for resellers. The Internet channel, if targeted properly and integrated with traditional channel partners, can be a cost-effective approach for serving selected business market segments.

The Effect of the Internet on Pricing Strategy

By providing buyers with easier access to information about products and suppliers, the Internet bolsters the buyer's bargaining power. The major impact has been to substantially reduce the business marketer's control over price. Says Michael Porter,

> The great paradox of the Internet is that its very benefits—making information widely available; reducing the difficulty of purchasing, marketing, and distribution; allowing buyers and sellers to find and transact business with one another more easily—also makes it more difficult for companies to capture these benefits as profits.[38]

Where sellers may have enjoyed selected geographical advantages because of the lack of nearby competition, the Internet has opened up markets to many new suppliers, resulting in downward pressure on prices. The pressure on price is particularly severe for any products or services that buyers perceive as "commodities." These are precisely the types of items for which buyers are using reverse auctions. The net effect is that business marketers of raw materials, components, and supplies that can be priced and sold on the Internet must carefully rethink their pricing approach by developing a more efficient way of competing on price or by creating new service-enriched offerings that add value in the eyes of potential customers.

The Internet and Customer Communication

The Internet expands the business marketer's communication capabilities. Providing real-time, up-to-date, low-cost information is one of the salient features of an Internet strategy. Within seconds and with a few keystrokes, an entire database can be corrected, updated, and appended, and the information can be shared with potential buyers all over the world. The scope of the communications capability of the Internet is illustrated by the different phases of electronic commerce through which companies typically move.[39] At the most basic level, a firm might offer simple *online information*, like their product catalog, facilitating access to information and enhancing product search capabilities. The limitation is the inability to help the user search for information on the basis of predefined criteria—the catalog simply exists in an electronic format. In the next phase of e-commerce, *database publishing*, the user is provided with search capabilities. Using a search engine, the customer can scan the catalog database and target particular requirements. The third phase, *customer self-service*, provides customized information for specific users. Here customers can download search-assisted catalogs and service diagnostics, along with information on

---

[38]Porter, "Strategy and the Internet," p. 66.

[39]Kesseler, "Defining the Future of Business-to-Business Electronic Commerce," p. 43; see also, D. Eric Boyd and Robert Spekman, "Internet Usage Within B2B Relationships and Its Impact on Value Creation: A Conceptual Model and Research Propositions," *Journal of Business-to-Business Marketing* 11 (1–2, 2004): pp. 9–32.

price and product availability. The final, and most complex, phase of e-commerce, *transactions*, provides for full transactions, from information gathering to purchase to fulfillment to billing to secure payment, all in a single environment.

These categories of Internet communication capability match directly with a recent study of what typical engineers look for when browsing the Web. According to a GlobalSpec Engineering Trends Survey, 91 percent of engineers use the Internet to find components and suppliers, 87 percent use it to obtain product specifications, 72 percent use it for news and information, 68 percent use it for research, 64 percent use it to find pricing information, and 60 percent use it to search for technical application ideas.[40] As this study demonstrates, the Internet is a powerful communication tool that can deliver desired information to customers at a critical point in the purchase decision-making process.

Meet the Customer's Requirements   Compared with traditional, paper-based approaches, each phase or level of e-commerce improves the way business marketers interact with their customers and potential customers. Reflecting this fact is the recent move of the venerable *Thomas Register* to online availability *only*.[41] The Thomas Publishing Company will no longer print its multivolume directories—the *Thomas Register of American Manufacturers* and *The Thomas Register of Regional Buying Guides*—which have been staples for decades at North American industrial facilities. After 2006, Thomas—which was founded more than 100 years ago—will make these directories available exclusively online at http://www.thomasnet.com. The move to online directories resulted from requests from customers. Increasingly, users were opting against the print format and for the online version because the online directories offer search functionality, immediate access to vendor catalogs, direct links to vendor Web sites, e-commerce capability, and a library of CAD drawings. ThomasNet.com contains information on more than 650,000 manufacturers, distributors, and service companies indexed by 67,000 product and service categories.

Of course, Internet communication often merely complements personal contact between buyers and sellers, particularly for complex, expensive products that require customer-specific engineering and customization, extensive negotiations, and long-term contractual arrangements. For example, Boeing's Web site is used more to describe the company and how it is organized, explain each of its aircraft models, describe and explain the firm's full range of services, and outline how potential buyers can work with the company in creating a product for their specific requirements. However, for many firms that market supplies, standard components, repair parts, and the like, e-commerce provides the greatest potential for reducing transaction costs while making marketing communications more efficient and effective.

To recap, the Internet is just one component of the business marketer's overall strategy: It simply extends the firm's reach, and it must be integrated into the overarching strategy the firm uses to reach and interact with its customers. Even at Dell, where the firm operates at the phase-four level of e-commerce—full transaction capability—the Internet is just one approach to the marketplace. According to Chairman Michael Dell, "We work with customers face-to-face, on the telephone,

---

[40]Greg Jarboe, "Meet The B2B Search Engines," *Search Engine Watch*, September 29, 2005, p. 1.

[41]Sean B. Callahan, "Thomas Plans to Drop Print Directories," *B to B* 90 (June 2005): p. 6.

or over the Internet. Depending on the customer, some or all of those techniques will be used; they're all intertwined."[42]

The Role of the Sales Force   Many firms find that the Internet simply makes sales representatives more effective because they can concentrate on solving customer problems and building customer relationships. The Internet streamlines the sales process and eliminates order-processing details for customers and salespersons alike. Although the Internet will supplant some sales that were once the province of the sales force, Internet strategies generally *support* sales-force efforts. By using customer relationship management systems (CRM) (see Chapter 4), the salesperson can customize presentations, respond to specific customer idiosyncrasies, and fend off competitive challenges. Successful companies have developed approaches for integrating sales-force strategies with Internet strategies and for compensating salespeople so that they support online initiatives.[43]

Promotion   To capitalize on the investment in creating and maintaining a Web site, promotions highlighting a site need to be run frequently and in a variety of media to stimulate use. An 18-month analysis of small-, medium-, and large-company B2B Web sites indicated that the number of hits is directly related to the amount of offline advertising and sales promotion.[44] Advertising in trade publications and handouts at trade shows and conferences appear to be especially effective in stimulating the use of business Web sites. Based on the success of leading search engines like Google and Yahoo, keyword advertising has also become a central element in the promotional budgets of B2B firms—reaching potential customers at a critical point in the purchase decision process. Search-engine marketing and other interactive marketing communication tools are examined in Chapter 15.

For business marketers, the Internet provides a powerful vehicle for demonstrating the value of offerings and customizing them for individual customers. Rosabeth Moss Kanter states that e-commerce pacesetters "embrace the Internet as an opportunity for questioning their existing models and experimenting with new ways technology can improve their businesses."[45]

Summary

Business marketers of all types, whether manufacturers, distributors, or service providers, are integrating the Internet and electronic communications into the core of the business marketing strategies. *E-commerce* is the broad term applied to communications, business processes, and transactions that are carried out through electronic technology—mainly the Internet. E-commerce can be applied to almost any aspect of business to make all processes more efficient. Based on Internet technologies, an intranet is an internal network accessible only to company employees and other authorized users. By contrast, an extranet is a private network that uses Internet-based

---

[42]*Financial Times Guide to Digital Business* (Autumn 1999), p. 11.

[43]Stewart Alsop, "E or Be Eaten," *Fortune*, November 8, 1999, p. 87.

[44]Carol Patten, "Marketers Promote Online Traffic through Traditional Media, with a Twist," *Business Marketing* 84 (August 1999): p. 40.

[45]Rosabeth Moss Kanter, "The Ten Deadly Mistakes of Wanna-dots," *Harvard Business Review* 79 (January 2001): p. 99.

technology to link companies with suppliers, customers, and other partners. Extranets allow the business marketer to customize information for a particular customer and to seamlessly share information with that customer in a secure environment.

For business marketers, the Internet has been effective as a powerful communication medium, an alternative channel, a new venue for a host of services, a data-gathering tool, and a way to integrate the supply chain. To be successful, the Internet strategy must be carefully woven into the fabric of the firm's overall marketing strategy. The Internet offers important benefits, including reduced transaction costs, reduced cycle time, supply chain integration, access to information, and closer customer relationships. Given the failure of many dot-com companies, the lesson for business marketers is that the Internet is an enabling technology—a powerful set of tools that complements, rather than replaces, traditional ways of competing.

The e-commerce strategy must be carefully crafted, beginning with a focus on objectives. Once a firm has established objectives, it can formulate an Internet strategy. Included in the strategy is a consideration of the product-related dimensions of the Internet offering, the most visible of which is the firm's Web site. Extranets, electronic catalogs, and customer information must also be integrated into the "product." Several fundamental channel-of-distribution issues must be evaluated, including the effect of the Internet on present channels and channel partners, channel efficiencies, and the Internet as a separate channel to the market. Pricing issues are also significant, particularly in light of the effect of trading communities and auction sites. Finally, marketing communication strategies consider the extent to which the firm provides transactional capabilities on the Web site and how the Internet strategy is integrated with other promotional vehicles. To an important degree, the Internet provides a powerful medium for developing a one-to-one relationship with business market customers.

Discussion Questions

1. How do the different definitions of e-commerce apply to the marketing tasks of a typical business marketer?

2. Discuss how Internet buying may lower the cost of procurement for a large company like Raytheon, the manufacturer of business aircraft.

3. What advantages do Internet marketing strategies have over traditional strategies?

4. A large industrial distributor of power transmission equipment embarks on a project to develop an e-commerce strategy. What lessons could it learn from consumer marketers in the design and operation of its Internet site?

5. The Crespy Company makes control systems that regulate large gas turbine engines. Describe the key elements of the Internet product Crespy might develop for its customers.

6. Find a business marketing company's Web site and evaluate how easy it is for a potential customer to move through the site and eventually purchase a product.

7. What are the key challenges that electronic purchasing via electronic catalogs pose for the typical marketer of office products?

8. Evaluate this statement: The most important determinant of the profit potential of a digital marketplace is the power of buyers and sellers in the particular product arena. Agree or disagree? Explain.

9. Comment on the following: Internet marketing strategies will eventually wipe out most business-to-business intermediaries.

10. Will the Internet result in stiffer price competition in the business-to-business marketplace? Explain.

Internet Exercise

1. Many B2B firms use Google's AdWords product as a component of their integrated marketing communications strategy. Go to http://www.google.com and describe the benefits this product might offer to a B2B firm. Describe how Xerox Corporation might use AdWords to reach prospective customers for its new line of network color printers.

Using the Internet at W. W. Grainger

W. W. Grainger is one of the largest B2B distributors in the world. With nearly 600 branch locations throughout North America, over 2 million customers, 1,900 customer service associates, and a robust line of 500,000 products (tools, pumps, motors, safety and material handling products, and lighting, ventilation, and cleaning items), Grainger is the leading industrial distributor of products that allow organizations of all types to keep their facilities and equipment running smoothly. Grainger's objective is to grow by capturing market share in the highly fragmented North American facilities maintenance market. For the longer term, the company is focused on these goals:

Accelerate sales growth and increase market share by

- capturing a greater share of the business of existing accounts;
- targeting high-potential customer segments.

Increase operating leverage through

- accelerating sales growth;
- targeting high-potential customer segments;
- reconfiguring the logistics network to improve efficiency and customer service;
- enhancing internal processes with technology.

Improve return on invested capital by

- growing those business units that earn more than the cost of capital;
- improving the profitability of business units that earn less than the cost of capital.

Its large sales force and product line allow Grainger to meet customer needs in a highly responsive manner. From its nearly 600 branch locations, products can be delivered to customers within hours of a call. In 2008, the company's major strategic focus was on offering a multichannel approach for purchasing maintenance and operating supplies. This involved providing consistent service through its branches, service centers, and distribution centers. Investments in sales training and a revamped logistics/distribution network were at the heart of this effort. The company's goal of "zero carryovers"— meaning that all orders received by 5:00 p.m. are shipped that day—is very demanding and provides a severe challenge to regularly achieve. Grainger was recently cited by *Industrial Distribution Magazine* as "the strongest brand in the industrial distribution industry—because customers believe Grainger can get them what they need when they need it, you can find a Grainger catalog in virtually every purchasing agent's office in North America." In 2007, Grainger was ranked 375th on the *Fortune* 500 list and was included in *Fortune*'s list of "Most Admired Companies."

Discussion Questions

1. What role would the Internet play in Grainger's strategy, given the firm's past success, the nature of its product line (rather "'stodgy" basic industrial items), the organization of the firm (a 500,000-item catalog, a 1,900-person sales force, and 600 branch locations), and 2 million customers? Visit http://www.grainger.com to see the special services that Grainger offers on its Web site.

2. By providing a very brief description of 500,000 items, a Grainger catalog is massive—weighing several pounds. In the past, Grainger executives worried that the catalog could get too heavy for the average person to lift and, therefore, limited product descriptions to a couple of lines. Go to the firm's Web site, select a particular item, and evaluate the extensive amount of information that is now accessible for each item on the Web.

3. Internet sales for Grainger are the most profitable of all types of sales in its business. In addition, Internet sales account for about 20 percent of its total volume. Explain why Grainger would have such high volume for Internet sales and why these sales are more profitable than those made through conventional methods.

Supply Chain Management

When suppliers fail to deliver products or services as promised, buyers search for a new supplier. Organizational buyers assign great importance to supply chain processes that eliminate the uncertainty of product delivery. Supply chain management assures that product, information, service, and financial resources all flow smoothly through the entire value-creation process. Business marketers invest considerable financial and human resources in creating supply chains to service the needs and special requirements of their customers. After reading this chapter, you will understand:

1. the role of supply chain management in business marketing strategy.

2. the importance of integrating both firms and functions throughout the entire supply chain.

3. the critical role of logistics activities in achieving supply chain management goals.

4. the importance of achieving high levels of logistics service performance while simultaneously controlling the cost of logistics activities.

Johnson Controls is a major supplier to the automotive industry of a variety of components, including dashboards, seats, and consoles. For Chrysler's Jeep Liberty, for example, Johnson Controls supplies complete cockpit modules, seating systems, overhead consoles, and several electronic components. The cockpit module alone consists of 11 major components—from mechanical, electrical, and audio systems to the instrument panel trim. The company integrates parts from 35 suppliers, assembles the complete cockpit, and delivers it to Chrysler as one module—all within what is called the "204-minute broadcast window." As soon as Chrysler notifies the company that it has received an order for a Jeep Liberty, Johnson Controls has 204 minutes to build and deliver that cockpit to the Chrysler plant 9 miles away with any one of 200 different color and interior combinations or options.[1] The company performs that operation 900 times a day, just for that one model.

Interestingly, this choreographed supply chain sequence takes place daily at several Johnson Controls plants around the world for a number of auto manufacturers, such as Mercedes, Buick, and Pontiac. How does Johnson Controls make this happen? The firm applies effective *supply chain management processes* that include (1) integrated computer systems that provide production schedules and demand forecasts to all supply chain members, and (2) collaborative program-management tools that allow manufacturers and suppliers to synchronize activities and respond to events in real time. From the time a component system is engineered to when it is sold, Johnson Controls has adopted processes that tightly connect engineering, manufacturing, procurement, marketing, and sales. Because supply chain partners manufacture components of the firm's interior modules, Johnson Controls works closely with them to design the right product, at the right cost, and deliver it at the right time.

These efforts at Johnson Controls are part of an innovative approach to tightening distribution processes, bolstering links with suppliers and customers, and integrating production and marketing that is referred to as **supply chain management (SCM)**. As new business strategies evolve, SCM is one of the predominant management approaches driving many organizations.[2] Bill Copacino, a noted supply chain consultant, puts the importance of SCM in focus:[3]

> In almost every industry, supply chain management has become a much more important strategic and competitive variable. It affects all of the shareholder value levers—cost, customer service, asset productivity, and revenue generation. Yet we are seeing a growing gap in performance between the leading and the average companies. The best are getting better faster than the average companies across almost every industry. For instance, Dell operates with 60 to 100 inventory turns, more than two or three times most of its competitors. So, clearly, the performance gap is widening, and we see this happening in almost every industry segment. The leading *supply chain* performers are applying new technology, new innovations, and new process thinking to great advantage. The average-performing companies and the laggards have a limited window of opportunity in which to catch up.

---

[1] Lorie Toupin, "Needed: Suppliers Who Can Collaborate throughout the Supply Chain," Supply Chain Automotive Supplement to *Supply Chain Management Review* 6 (July–August, 2002): p. 6.

[2] Peter C. Brewer and Thomas W. Speh, "Using the Balanced Scorecard to Measure Supply Chain Performance," *Journal of Business Logistics* (Spring 2000): p. 75.

[3] Bill Copacino, "Supply Chain Challenges: Building Relationships," *Harvard Business Review* 81 (July 2003): p. 69.

This chapter describes the nature of SCM, explains its important goals, discusses the factors that lead to successful supply chain strategies, and demonstrates how logistics management is a key driver of supply chain success. Once SCM has been defined, the chapter highlights how the business marketer's logistics processes form the core of the SCM strategy. The logistical elements are described in terms of their interface within the distribution channel and how they must be integrated to create desired customer service standards. The chapter then addresses the role of logistics in purchasing decisions, the types of logistics services buyers seek, and the design of effective logistics processes.

The Concept of Supply Chain Management

A supply chain encompasses all the activities associated with moving goods from the raw materials stage through to the end user (for example, a personal computer buyer). A formal definition of SCM is:

> Supply chain management encompasses the planning and management of all activities involved in sourcing and procurement, conversion, and all logistics management activities. Central to SCM are the coordination and collaboration activities performed with channel partners, which may include suppliers, intermediaries, third party service providers, and customers. In essence, supply chain management integrates supply and demand management within and across companies.[4]

The supply chain includes a variety of firms, ranging from those that process raw materials to make component parts to those engaged in wholesaling. Included also are organizations engaged in transportation, warehousing, information processing, and materials handling. The critical processes involved in SCM include the following:

1. Customer Relationship Management
2. Supplier Relationship Management
3. Customer Service Management
4. Demand Management
5. Order Fulfillment
6. Manufacturing Flow Management
7. Product Development and Commercialization
8. Returns Management[5]

Successful SCM coordinates and integrates these processes into a seamless level of performance. Effective supply chain management requires the careful integration of these processes across several different organizations in the supply chain.

[4]CSCMP Definition of Supply Chain Management, accessed at http://cscmp.org/aboutcscmp/definitions/definitions.asp, August 2008.
[5]Douglas Lambert (ed.), *Supply Chain Management* (Sarasota, FL: Supply Chain Management Institute, 2008), p. 10.

Importantly, supply chain management can improve overall company performance in two fundamental ways: revenue enhancement and cost reduction. Supply chain management can—and should—play an important role in each of those areas. For example, supply chain management can play a leadership role in creating a more responsive supply chain, thereby helping the company to win more business (and increase revenues) from customers. Similarly, supply chain management can take the lead in applying good processes to better manage and lower costs across the entire enterprise, not just those typically assigned to procurement, manufacturing, or logistics.[6]

Supply chains should be managed in an integrated manner. Integrated SCM focuses on managing relationships, information, and material flow across organizational borders to cut costs and enhance flow. When the multicompany nature of the supply chain focus is combined with a process-flow approach to business, the critical role that SCM assumes becomes clear. Rather than merely handling order fulfillment, SCM is instrumental in a full range of activities from product development and new-product-launch strategies to fulfillment and recycling. To that end, SCM must be fully integrated into business strategy and fine-tuned throughout the product's life cycle.[7] Leading supply chain–oriented firms focus intensely on monitoring actual user demand instead of forcing into markets products that may or may not sell quickly. In so doing, they minimize the flow of raw materials, finished product, and packaging materials, thereby reducing inventory costs across the entire supply chain.

Partnerships: The Critical Ingredient

Thomas Stalkamp, former CEO of Chrysler, notes that many old-line U.S. industrial firms are hampered by the fact that the atmosphere between the parties in supply chains is more adversarial than it needs to be. He refers to this old-line, nonintegrated approach to business as "adversarial commerce."[8] Fueling the movement to SCM has been the recognition by many firms that adversarial commerce is costly and limits the ability of all supply chain members to compete in the global marketplace.

Integrating activities across the supply chain requires close working relationships. SCM may require that all firms in the supply chain share sensitive and proprietary information about customers, actual demand, point-of-sale transactions, and corporate strategic plans. SCM involves significant joint planning and communication; firms often create teams of personnel that cut across functional and firm boundaries to coordinate the movement of product to market. In other words, achieving the real potential of SCM requires integration not only among departments within the organization but also with external partners.

A wonderful example of the effect of integration among supply chain partners is the case of Avnet, a huge electronics distributor. Avnet developed a program to integrate its supply chain processes with those of a major manufacturer supplier and with the major component supplier to that manufacturer. By sharing demand and production information, the participants raised on-time delivery from 80 percent to

---

[6]Robert A. Rudzki, "Supply Chain Management Transformation: A Leader's Guide," *Supply Chain Management Review* 12 (March, 2008): p. 14.

[7]Laura Rock Kopczak and M. Eric Johnson, "The Supply Chain Management Effect," *MIT Sloan Management Review* 44 (Spring 2003): p. 28.

[8]Thomas T. Stallkamp, "Ending Adversarial Commerce," *Supply Chain Management Review* 9 (October 2005): pp. 46–52.

100 percent of all orders, increased inventory turnover by a factor of 5, and tripled the return on materials! The collaboration of all supply chain partners is required to achieve such performance results.

Traditional, nonintegrated approaches to managing product and information flows are expensive and time-consuming. Such approaches often involve much higher transportation and handling costs, and they demand considerable time from salespeople, buyers, and others in the organization. For example, material is often moved around too much—one major computer manufacturer reported that some of the components it used had traveled 250,000 miles before they reached the ultimate buyer. Furthermore, traditional transactions processes create excess inventory in the pipeline leading to the customer. In the pharmaceutical industry, for example, firms that have not adopted SCM incur higher inventory-carrying costs and provide lower levels of customer service than their competitors.

Firms and their suppliers can create highly competitive supply chains by collaborating. Failure to collaborate can result in inefficiencies such as increases in material cost, distortion of information as it moves through a supply chain, or slow response to product design and development. By entering into long-term supply chain partnerships, firms can eliminate many of these problems and ensure ongoing improvement.[9] Until some type of partnership is in place, the true benefits of supply chain integration cannot be achieved. Dell, for example, strives to maintain long-term relationships with high-reliability suppliers, such as Sony, so that items like monitors can be shipped from the supplier (Sony's factory) directly to the customer. The result is that Dell is able to fulfill customer orders in real time.[10] Industry experts recognize Dell as an elite performer in SCM.[11]

Not only do effective supply chains conduct business as partners, they also openly share information. Intelligence about the customer and what the customer has ordered is transmitted upstream so that every organization in the supply chain has it and can respond accordingly. When information is made immediately available to supply chain members, Tier 1 and Tier 2 suppliers can act immediately, eliminating the delays that created inefficiencies in the past. This allows the supply chain to reduce inventories (safety stocks) and speed up cash flow. Figure 13.1 depicts the stages that companies go through when forming intercompany networks. Note that in Stage 3, the "Extended Enterprise," companies have successfully aligned both their internal and external processes. This is the ultimate goal of SCM.

Supply Chain Management: A Tool for Competitive Advantage

The supply chain can be a powerful competitive weapon, as market leaders like Dell, Grainger, and Hewlett-Packard have demonstrated. Other best-in-class supply chain performers include Johnson Controls, Inc. (JCI), profiled at the outset of this chapter, and Motorola. In recognizing Johnson Controls as a world-class supply chain performer, AMR Research observed: "JCI's continued success proves demand-driven supply chain

[9]Anupam Agrawal and Arnoud De Meyer, "Managing Value in Supply Chain—Case Studies on Alternate Structures," *INSEAD Working Papers Collection* (28, 2008): p. 1.

[10]S. Chopra and J. A. Van Mieghan, "Which e-Business Is Right for Your Supply Chain?" *Supply Chain Management Review* 4 (July–August 2000): p. 34.

[11]Thomas A. Stewart and Louise O'Brien, "Execution Without Excuses," *Harvard Business Review* 83 (March 2005): p. 110.

FIGURE 13.1 | STAGES FIRMS GO THROUGH IN ADOPTING SUPPLY CHAIN MANAGEMENT

The Supply Chain Stages

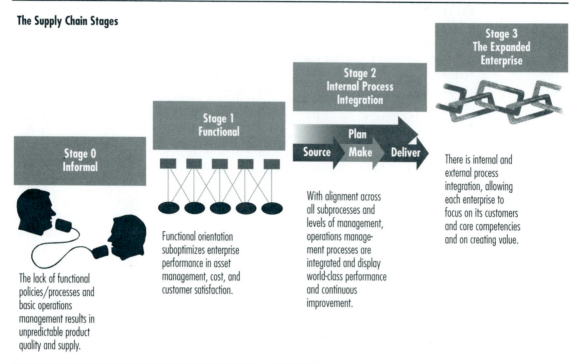

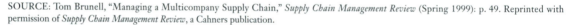

SOURCE: Tom Brunell, "Managing a Multicompany Supply Chain," *Supply Chain Management Review* (Spring 1999): p. 49. Reprinted with permission of *Supply Chain Management Review*, a Cahners publication.

can work anywhere in the supply chain, provided outside-in thinking is applied from the customer backward into manufacturing and engineering."[12] For Motorola, incorporating supply chain management into all phases of the design, sourcing, manufacturing, and distribution processes helped the company to enhance its market position across sectors. Supply chain management is now recognized by Motorola's top management as an important source of competitive advantage and shareholder value creation.[13]

As a primary interface point with the customer, SCM can offer value in the form of competitively superior delivery and value-added services, as defined by customers. Best-in-class SCM practices provide advantages, including 10 to 30 percent higher on-time delivery performance, a 40 to 65 percent (or 1- to 2-month) advantage in cash-to-cash cycle time, and 50 to 80 percent less standing inventory, which all translates into 3 to 6 percent of a company's revenue. For a $100 million company, earnings improvements of up to $6 million are achievable by thoroughly adopting SCM practices.[14] However, SCM, as a source of competitive advantage, is not simply a way to reduce cost, but also a way to boost revenues.[15]

---

[12]Tony Friscia, Kevin O'Marah, Debra Hofman, and Joe Souza, "The AMR Research Supply Chain Top 25 for 2007," accessed at http://www.amrresearch.com/content/ on May 31, 2007.

[13]William Hoffman, "Squeezing Supply Chains," *Traffic World* 127 (July 7, 2007): p. 16.

[14]Bill Faherenwald, "Supply Chain: Managing Logistics for the 21st Century," *Business Week*, December 28, 1998, Special Section, p. 3.

[15]Charles Batchelor, "Moving Up the Corporate Agenda," *The Financial Times*, December 1, 1998, p. 1.

Supply Chain Management Goals

SCM is both a boundary- and function-spanning endeavor. The underlying premise of SCM is that waste reduction and enhanced supply chain performance come only with both intrafirm and interfirm functional integration, sharing, and cooperation. Thus, each firm within the supply chain must tear down functional silos and foster true coordination and integration of marketing, production, procurement, sales, and logistics. Furthermore, actions, systems, and processes among *all* the supply chain participants must be integrated and coordinated. Firmwide integration is a necessary, but not sufficient, condition for achieving the full potential benefits of SCM. Integration must be taken to a higher plane so that functions and processes are coordinated across all the organizations in the supply chain. SCM is undertaken to achieve four major goals: waste reduction, time compression, flexible response, and unit cost reduction.[16] These goals have been articulated in several contexts associated with SCM, and they speak to the importance of both interfunctional and interfirm coordination.

Waste Reduction   Firms that practice SCM seek to reduce waste by minimizing duplication, harmonizing operations and systems, and enhancing quality. With respect to duplication, firms at all levels in the supply chain often maintain inventories. Efficiencies can be gained for the chain as a whole if the inventories can be centralized and maintained by just a few firms at critical points in the distribution process. With a joint goal of reducing waste, supply chain partners can work together to modify policies, procedures, and data-collection practices that produce or encourage waste.[17] Typically, waste across the supply chain manifests itself in excess inventory. Effective ways to address this are through postponement and customization strategies, which push the final assembly of a completed product to the last practical point in the chain. Dell provides an excellent illustration of how to reduce waste through effective "waste" management strategies. The company's build-to-order model produces a computer only when there is an actual customer order. Dell works with its suppliers to achieve a system where inventory turns are measured in hours rather than days. Because Dell does not maintain stocks of unsold finished goods, it has no need to conduct "fire sales." The result: Waste has been eliminated both on the component side and on the finished-goods side.

Time Compression   Another critical goal of SCM is to compress order-to-delivery cycle time. When production and logistics processes are accomplished in less time, everyone in the supply chain is able to operate more efficiently, and a primary result is reduced inventories throughout the system. Time compression also enables supply chain partners to more easily observe and understand the cumulative effect of problems that occur anywhere in the chain and respond quickly. Reduced cycle time also speeds the cash-to-cash cycle for all chain members, enhancing cash flow and financial performance throughout the system. Time compression means that information and products flow smoothly and quickly, thus permitting all parties to respond to customers in a timely manner while maintaining minimal inventory. Many industrial distributors like W.W. Grainger have designed supply chains that are able to respond

[16]Brewer and Speh, "Using the Balanced Scorecard," p. 76.

[17]Kate Vitasek, Karl B. Manrodt, and Jeff Abbott, "What Makes a LEAN Supply Chain?" *Supply Chain Management Review* 9 (October 2005): pp. 39–45.

to customer orders with "same-day" delivery, allowing customers to reduce inventories and to rest assured that timely delivery support is available to solve unexpected problems.

Flexible Response   The third goal of SCM is to develop flexible response throughout the supply chain. Flexible response in order handling, including how orders are handled, product variety, order configuration, order size, and several other dimensions, means that a customer's unique requirements can be met cost-effectively. To illustrate, a firm that responds flexibly can configure a shipment in almost any way (for example, different pallet patterns or different product assortments) and do it quickly without problems for the customer. Flexibility also may mean customizing products in the warehouse to correspond to a customer's need for unique packaging and unitization. The key to flexibility is to meet individual customer needs in a way that the customer views as cost-effective and the supply chain views as profitable.

Unit Cost Reduction   The final goal of SCM is to operate logistics in a manner that reduces cost per unit for the end customer. Firms must determine the level of performance the customer desires and then minimize the costs of providing that service level. The business marketer should carefully assess the balance between level of cost and the degree of service provided. The goal is to provide an appropriate value equation for the customer, meaning that cost in some cases is higher for meaningful enhancements in service. Cost cutting is not an absolute, but the SCM approach is focused on driving costs to the lowest possible level for the level of service requested. For example, shipping product in full truckload quantities weekly is less expensive than shipping pallet quantities every day; however, when a customer like Honda wants daily deliveries to minimize inventories, the SCM goal is to offer daily shipments at the lowest possible cost. SCM principles drive down costs because they focus management attention on eliminating activities that unnecessarily add cost, such as duplicate inventories, double and triple handling of the product, unconsolidated shipments, and uncoordinated promotions, such as special sales.

Hau Lee, an internationally recognized expert, points out that supply chain efficiency is necessary, but it is not enough to ensure that firms do better than their rivals. Only companies that build agile, adaptable, and aligned supply chains get ahead of the competition.[18] Efficient supply chains often become uncompetitive because they do not adapt to changes in market structures: Supply chains need to keep adapting so they can adjust to changing customer needs. In addition, low-cost supply chains are not always able to respond to sudden and unexpected changes in markets—like a shift in resource availability or the effect of a natural disaster. Finally, excellent supply chain companies align the interests of all the firms in their supply chain with their own—if any company's interests differ from those of the other organizations in the supply chain, its actions do not maximize the chain's performance.

Benefits to the Final Customer

A well-managed supply chain ultimately creates tangible benefits for customers throughout the supply chain. When the supply chain reduces waste, improves cycle

---

[18] Hau L. Lee, "The Triple-A Supply Chain," *Harvard Business Review* 82 (October 2004): pp. 102–112.

INSIDE BUSINESS MARKETING

When the Chain Breaks

It began on a stormy evening in New Mexico in March 2000 when a bolt of lightning hit a power line. The temporary loss of electricity knocked out the cooling fans in a furnace at a Philips semiconductor plant in Albuquerque. A fire started, but was put out by staff within minutes. The damage seemed to be minor: eight trays of wafers containing the miniature circuitry to make several thousand chips for mobile phones had been destroyed. After a good clean-up, the company expected to resume production within a week. That is what the plant told its two biggest customers, Sweden's Ericsson and Finland's Nokia, who were vying for leadership in the booming mobile-handset market. Nokia's *supply-chain* managers had realized within two days that there was a problem when their computer systems showed some shipments were being held up. Delays of a few days are not uncommon in manufacturing and a limited number of back-up components are usually held to cope with such eventualities. But whereas Ericsson was content to let the delay take its course, Nokia immediately put the Philips plant on a watch list to be closely monitored in case things got worse.

They did. Semiconductor fabrication plants have to be kept spotlessly clean, but on the night of the fire, smoke and soot had contaminated a much larger area of the plant than had first been thought. Production would be halted for weeks. By the time the full extent of the disruption became clear, Nokia had already started locking up all the alternative sources for the chips.

That left Ericsson with a serious parts shortage. The company, having decided some time earlier to simplify its supply chain by single-sourcing some of its components, including the Philips chips, had no plan B. This severely limited its ability to launch a new generation of handsets, which in turn contributed to huge losses in the Swedish company's mobile-phone division. This has become a classic case study for supply-chain experts and risk consultants.

SOURCE: Adapted from "When the Chain Breaks," *The Economist*, 379 (June 17, 2006): p. 18.
Parts of this article were taken from Yossi Sheffi, *The Resilient Enterprise*, (Boston: MIT Press, 2005) and Martin Christopher, *Logistics and Supply Chain Management* (London: Financial Times Prentice Hall, 2005).

time and flexible response, and minimizes costs, these benefits should flow through to ultimate customers. Thus, a key focus of the supply chain members is monitoring how much the customer is realizing these important benefits and assessing what may be preventing them from doing so. A supply chain's customer can be viewed on several dimensions, and it is important to focus on each. A producer of electronic radio parts views the radio manufacturer as an absolutely critical customer, but the auto manufacturer that installs the radio in a car is equally important, if not more so, and ultimately the final buyer of the automobile must be satisfied. Thus, different demands, desires, and idiosyncrasies of customers all along the supply chain must be understood and managed effectively. As the Inside Business Marketing example at the Phillips semiconductor plant suggests, uncontrollable events can create havoc in a supply chain, and both suppliers and customers need to focus attention on creating detailed contingency plans for overcoming unplanned disruptions.

The Financial Benefits Perspective

Innovative supply chain strategies that couple physical goods movement with financial information sharing can open the door to greater end-to-end supply chain cost savings, better balance sheets, lower total costs, higher margins, and a more stable supply chain with everyone sharing the savings.[19] When supply chain partners are achieving their goals and the benefits are flowing through to customers, supply chain members should succeed financially. The most commonly reported benefits for firms that adopt SCM are lower costs, higher profit margins, enhanced cash flow, revenue growth, and a higher rate of return on assets. Because activities are harmonized and unduplicated, the cost of transportation, order processing, order selection, warehousing, and inventory is usually reduced. A study to validate the correlation between supply chain integration and business success shows that best-practice SCM companies have a 45 percent total supply chain cost advantage over their median supply chain competitors.[20] Cash flows are improved because the total cycle time from raw materials to finished product is reduced. The leading firms also enjoy greater cash flow—they have a cash-to-order cycle time exactly half that of the median company. On the other hand, recent evidence suggests that the stock market punishes firms that stumble in SCM. For example, one study showed that supply chain glitches can result in an 8.6 percent drop in stock price on the day the problem is announced and up to a 20 percent decline within 6 months.[21]

Information and Technology Drivers

Supply chains could not function at high levels of efficiency and effectiveness without powerful information systems. Many of the complex Internet supply chains maintained by companies like Hewlett-Packard and Cisco could not operate at high levels without sophisticated information networks and interactive software. The Internet—and Internet technology—is the major tool business marketers rely on to manage their lengthy and integrated systems. In addition, a host of software applications play a key role in helping a supply chain operate at peak efficiency.

Supply Chain Software   SCM software applications provide real-time analytical systems that manage the flow of products and information through the supply chain network.[22] Of course, many supply chain functions are coordinated, including procurement, manufacturing, transportation, warehousing, order entry, forecasting, and customer service. Much of the software is focused on each one of the different functional areas (for example, inventory planning or transportation scheduling). However, the trend is to move toward software solutions that integrate several or all of these functions. The result is that firms can work with a comprehensive "supply chain suite" of software that manages flow across the supply chain while including all of the key functional areas. Several firms producing Enterprise Resource Planning (ERP) software—such as SAP or Oracle—have developed applications that attempt to integrate functional areas and bridge gaps across the supply chain.

[19]Aura Drakšaitė and Vytautas Snieška, "Advanced Cost Saving Strategies of Supply Chain Management in Global Markets," *Economics and Management* (2008): p. 113

[20]Brad Ferguson, "Implementing Supply Chain Management," *Production and Inventory Management Journal* (Second Quarter, 2000): p. 64.

[21]Robert J. Bowman, "Does Wall Street Really Care about the Supply Chain?" *Global Logistics and Supply Chain Strategies* (April 2001): pp. 31–35.

[22]Steven Kahl, "What's the 'Value' of Supply Chain Software?" *Supply Chain Management Review* 3 (Winter 1999): p. 61.

SCM software creates the ability to transmit data in real time and helps organizations *transform* supply chain processes into competitive advantages. Equipping employees with portable bar code scanners that feed a centralized database, FedEx is a *best-practices* leader at seamlessly integrating a variety of technologies to enhance all processes across an extended supply chain.[23] The company uses a real-time data transmission system (via the bar code scanners used for every package) to assist in routing, tracking, and delivering packages. The information recorded by the scanners is transmitted to a central database and is made available to *all* employees and customers. Each day FedEx's communications network processes nearly 400,000 customer service calls and tracks the location, pickup time, and delivery time of 2.5 million packages! FedEx is electronically linked so tightly with some customers that when the customer receives an order, FedEx's server is notified to print a shipping label, generate an internal request for pickup, and then download the label to the customer's server. The label, with all the needed customer information, is printed at the customer's warehouse and applied to the package just before FedEx picks it up. This tight electronic linkage adds significant efficiency to the customer's supply chain process and allows FedEx to deliver on its promises.[24]

Successfully Applying the Supply Chain Management Approach

The nature of the firm's supply chain efforts often depends on the nature of the demand for its products. Marshall Fisher suggests that products can be separated into two categories: "functional" items, like paper, maintenance supplies, and office furniture, for example; or "innovative" items, like cell phones, the BlackBerry, or other high-tech products. The importance of this distinction is that functional items require different supply chains than do innovative products.[25]

Functional products typically have predictable demand patterns, whereas innovative products do not. The goal for functional products is to design a supply chain with efficient physical distribution; that is, it minimizes logistics and inventory costs and assures low-cost manufacturing. Here, the key information sharing takes place within the supply chain so that all participants can effectively orchestrate manufacturing, ordering, and delivery to minimize production and inventory costs.

Innovative products, on the other hand, have less predictable demand, and the key concern is reacting to short life cycles, avoiding shortages or excess supplies, and taking advantage of high profits during peak demand periods. Rather than seeking to minimize inventory, supply chain decisions center on the questions of where to *position* inventory, along with production capacity, in order to hedge against uncertain demand. The critical task is to capture and distribute timely information on

---

[23] Sandor Boyson and Thomas Corsi, "The Real-Time Supply Chain," *Supply Chain Management Review* 5 (January–February 2001): p. 48.

[24] For a related discussion, see Pierre J. Richard and Timothy M. Devinney, "Modular Strategies: B2B Technology and Architectural Knowledge," *California Management Review* 47 (Summer 2005): pp. 86–113.

[25] Marshall Fisher, "What Is the Right Supply Chain for Your Product?" *Harvard Business Review* 75 (March–April 1997): p. 106.

B2B TOP PERFORMERS

Making Supplier Relationships Work

During the past decade, Toyota and Honda have struck remarkable partnerships with some of the same suppliers who describe their relationships with the Big Three U.S. automakers as adversarial. Of the 2.1 million Toyota/Lexuses and the 1.6 million Honda/Acuras sold in North America in 2003, Toyota manufactured 60 percent and Honda 80 percent in North America. Moreover, the two companies source about 70 to 80 percent of the costs of making each automobile from North American suppliers. Despite the odds, Toyota and Honda have managed to replicate in an alien Western culture the same kind of supplier webs they developed in Japan. Consequently, they enjoy the best supplier relations in the U.S. automobile industry, have the fastest product development processes, and reduce costs and improve quality year after year. Toyota claims that over 60 percent of its innovations come from ideas provided by their suppliers! Hence, they understand the importance of maintaining excellent supplier relationships.

Both firms:

- understand how their suppliers work and develop deep knowledge of the degree of efficiency and effectiveness that particular suppliers demonstrate.
- turn supplier rivalry into an opportunity by rewarding quality, innovation, and cost-reduction initiatives.
- actively supervise suppliers and help them improve their operational capabilities.
- continuously and intensively share information with suppliers.
- conduct joint improvement activities to advance mutual goals.

Rather than excelling on one dimension, Toyota and Honda win by applying all of them as a system for continuously improving supplier relationships.

SOURCE: Jeffrey K. Liker and Thomas Y. Choi, "Building Deep Supplier Relationships," *Harvard Business Review* 82 (December 2004): pp. 104–113.

---

customer demand to the supply chain. When designing the supply chain, firms should concentrate on creating *efficient* processes for functional products and *responsive* processes for innovative products.

Successful Supply Chain Practices

Most successful supply chains have devised approaches for participants to work together in a partnering environment. Supply chains are not effective and, in reality, are *not* supply chains when the participants are adversaries. Supply chain partnerships form the foundation. Highly effective supply chains feature integrated operations across supply chain participants, timely information sharing, and delivering added value to the customer. As testimony to the importance of supply chain partnerships, the Malcolm Baldrige National Quality Award Committee recently made "key supplier and customer partnering and communication mechanisms" a separate category it would use to recognize the best companies in the United States.[26] In considering the economic value created across *the supply chain*, one expert observes, "You should

---

[26]Jeffrey K. Liker and Thomas Y. Choi, "Building Deep Supplier Relationships," *Harvard Business Review* 82 (December 2004): p. 104.

go for the best return on net assets for the supply chain, and trade off costs between income statements and balance sheets to see that *everybody* shares in that gain."[27] For the supply chain partners to work as a unit, this enlightened perspective of collaboration is mandatory.

For the supply chain partnership to succeed, the partners need to clearly define their strategic objectives, understand where their objectives converge (and perhaps diverge), and resolve any differences.[28] Because the supply chain strategy drives all the important processes in each firm as well as those that connect the firms, managers in both organizations must participate in key decisions and support the chosen course. Once key participants specify and endorse supply chain strategies, performance metrics can be established to track how well the supply chain is meeting its common goals. The metrics used to measure performance are tied to the strategy and must be linked to the performance evaluation and reward systems for employees in each of the participating firms. Without this step, individual managers would not be motivated to accomplish the broad goals of the supply chain.

Logistics as the Critical Element in Supply Chain Management

Nowhere in business marketing strategy is SCM more important than in logistics.

> Logistics management is that part of supply chain management that plans, implements, and controls the efficient, effective forward and reverse flow and storage of goods, services and related information between the point of origin and the point of consumption in order to meet customers' requirements. Logistics management activities typically include inbound and outbound transportation management, fleet management, warehousing, materials handling, order fulfillment, logistics network design, inventory management, supply/demand planning, and management of third-party logistics services providers. To varying degrees, the logistics function also includes sourcing and procurement, production planning and scheduling, packaging and assembly, and customer service. It is involved in all levels of planning and execution—strategic, operational and tactical. Logistics management is an integrating function, which coordinates and optimizes all logistics activities, as well as integrates logistics activities with other functions including marketing, sales, manufacturing, finance, and information technology.[29]

Effective business marketing demands efficient, systematic delivery of finished products to channel members and customers. The importance of this ability has elevated the logistics function to a place of prominence in the marketing strategy of many business marketers.

---

[27] Richard H. Gamble, "Financing Supply Chains," *businessfinancemag.com* (June 2002): p. 35.

[28] Peter C. Brewer and Thomas W. Speh, "Adapting the Balanced Scorecard to Supply Chain Management," *Supply Chain Management Review* 5 (March–April 2001): p. 49.

[29] CSCMP Definition of Logistics, accessed at http://cscmp.org/aboutcscmp/definitions/definitions.asp on August 2008.

FIGURE 13.2 | SUPPLY CHAIN FOR ELECTRIC MOTORS

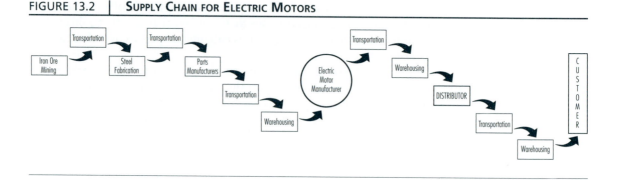

Distinguishing Between Logistics and Supply Chain Management

Logistics is the critical element in SCM. In fact, there is considerable confusion over the difference between the discipline of SCM and logistics. As our definition stated, SCM is focused on the *integration of* all *business processes* that add value for customers.

The 1990s witnessed the rising importance of time-based competition, rapidly improving information technology, expanding globalization, increasing attention to quality, and the changing face of interfirm relationships. These trends combined to cause companies to expand their perspective on logistics to include all the firms involved in creating a finished product and delivering it to the buyer or user on time and in perfect condition. For example, the supply chain for electric motors would include raw material suppliers, steel fabricators, component parts manufacturers, transportation companies, the electric motor manufacturer, the distributor of electric motors, the warehouse companies that store and ship components and finished products, and the motor's ultimate buyer. Figure 13.2 graphically depicts such a supply chain. The SCM concept is an integrating philosophy for coordinating the total flow of a supply channel from supplier to ultimate user. Logistics is critical, however, to business marketers, because regardless of the orientation to the entire supply chain, the firm relies on its logistics system to deliver product in a timely, low-cost manner.

Managing Flows

The significance of the supply chain perspective in logistical management is that the business marketing manager focuses attention on the performance of *all participants* in the supply chain. The manager also coordinates their efforts to enhance the timely delivery of the finished product to the ultimate user at the lowest possible cost. Inherent in the supply chain approach is the need to form close *relationships* with the supply chain participants, including vendors, transportation suppliers, warehousing companies, and distributors. The focus of logistics in the SCM for business marketers is the *flow of product* through the supply chain, with *timely information* driving the entire process.

Product flow in the reverse direction is also important in business supply chains. Many companies, like Xerox and Canon, routinely remanufacture products that are worn out or obsolete. Effective linkages and processes must be in place to return such products to a facility in order to remanufacture or retrofit them. If the reverse supply chains are operating effectively, companies can sometimes realize higher margins on the remanufactured products than they do on new items.[30]

The Strategic Role of Logistics

In the past, logistics was viewed simply as a cost of doing business and a function whose only goal was higher productivity. Today, many companies view logistics as a critical strategic weapon because of its tremendous effect on a customer's operation. For many business marketers, logistics is their *primary* marketing tool for gaining and maintaining competitive superiority. These firms typically recognize that logistics performance is an important part of marketing strategy, and they exploit their logistics competencies. Companies that incorporate logistics planning and management into long-term business strategies can achieve significant benefits, which create real value for the company. Nucor Steel enjoys strong customer loyalty because it can deliver steel to a construction site within a 2- to 4-hour window and offload the truck in the sequence in which the steel beams will be used on the job! This advantage is significant because storage space is limited at most construction sites in urban areas. This strong value-added service allows Nucor to achieve higher levels of profitability than its competitors.

Sales-Marketing-Logistics Integration

The rising value of logistics as a strategic marketing weapon has fostered the integration of the sales, marketing, and logistics functions of many business marketers. In progressive firms, unified teams of sales, production, logistics, information systems, and marketing personnel develop integrated logistics programs to offer to potential customers. Sales calls are made by teams of specialists from each area, and the teams tailor logistics solutions to customer problems. United Stationers, one of the largest U.S. office products distributors, brings operations and salespeople together to meet with the company's resellers in an effort to create customer-responsive logistics service. As a result of its efforts, United guarantees customers that orders placed by 7:00 p.m. will be received before noon on the following day. Customers can dial into United's mainframe computer and place orders electronically. The company considers all of its logistics people to be part of the sales function. Some firms have taken the integration even further. Baxter Healthcare warehouse workers team up with warehouse personnel at the hospitals that Baxter serves. During visits to the customer warehouse, the Baxter warehouser evaluates the operation, looking for ways to improve packing so shipments are easier to unload and unpack. As a result, Baxter warehousers have become salespeople.

Just-in-Time Systems

To serve a customer, business marketers must be prepared to deliver their products frequently and with precise timing. The reason is the widespread adoption by manufacturing firms, like Honda of America, of the **just-in-time (JIT)** inventory principle. Under this principle, suppliers carefully coordinate deliveries with the manufacturer's

---

[30]James Stock, Thomas W. Speh, and Herbert Shear, "Many Happy (Product) Returns," *Harvard Business Review* 80 (July 2002): p. 14.

production schedule—often delivering products just hours before they are used. The objective of a JIT system is to eliminate waste of all kinds from the production process by requiring the delivery of the specified product at the precise time, and in the exact quantity needed. Importantly, the quality must be perfect—there is no opportunity to inspect products in the JIT process. Because JIT attempts to relate purchases to production requirements, the typical order size shrinks, and more frequent deliveries are required. Increased delivery frequency presents a challenge to the business marketing production and logistics system. However, business marketers will have to meet this challenge, as many competitors now compete on the basis of inventory turns and speed to market.[31]

Just-in-Time Relationship A significant effect of JIT purchasing has been to drastically reduce the number of suppliers manufacturers use. Suppliers who are able to meet customers' JIT requirements find their share of business growing.[32] Meeting JIT requirements often represents a marketing edge and may mean survival for some suppliers. The relationship between JIT suppliers and manufacturers is unique and includes operational linkages that unite the buyer and seller. As a result, suppliers find that the relationships are longer lasting and usually formalized with a written contract that may span up to 5 years.

Elements of a Logistical System Table 13.1 presents the controllable variables of a logistical system. Almost no decision on a particular logistical activity can be made without evaluating its effect on other areas. The system of warehouse facilities, inventory commitments, order-processing methods, and transportation linkages determines the supplier's ability to provide timely product availability to customers. As a result of poor supplier performance, customers may have to bear the extra cost of higher inventories, institute expensive priority-order-expediting systems, develop secondary supply sources, or, worst of all, turn to another supplier.

Total-Cost Approach

In the management of logistical activities, two performance variables must be considered: (1) total distribution costs and (2) the level of logistical service provided to customers. The logistical system must be designed and administered to achieve that combination of cost and service levels that yields maximum profits. Logistical costs vary widely for business marketers, depending on the nature of the product and on the importance of logistical service to the buyer. Logistical costs can consume 16 to 36 percent of each sales dollar at the manufacturing level, and logistical activities can consume more than 40 percent of total assets. Thus, logistics can have a significant effect on corporate profitability. How, then, can the marketer manage logistical costs?

The **total-cost**, or trade-off, **approach** to logistical management guarantees to minimize total logistical costs in the firm and within the channel. The assumption is that costs of individual logistical activities are interactive; that is, a decision about one logistical variable affects all or some of the others. Management is thus concerned

---

[31] Andrew Tanzer, "Warehouses That Fly," *Forbes*, October 18, 1999, p. 121.

[32] Peter Bradley, "Just-in-Time Works, but. . . ." *Purchasing* 118 (September 1995): p. 36.

TABLE 13.1 | **CONTROLLABLE ELEMENTS IN A LOGISTICS SYSTEM**

Elements	Key Aspects
Customer service	The "product" of logistics activities, *customer service* relates to the effectiveness in creating time and place utility. The level of customer service provided by the supplier has a direct impact on total cost, market share, and profitability.
Order processing	Order processing triggers the logistics process and directs activities necessary to deliver products to customers. Speed and accuracy of order processing affect costs and customer service levels.
Logistics communication	Information exchanged in the distribution process guides the activities of the system. It is the vital link between the firm's logistics system and its customers.
Transportation	The physical movement of products from source of supply through production to customers is the most significant cost area in logistics, and it involves selecting modes and specific carriers as well as routing.
Warehousing	Providing storage space serves as a buffer between production and use. Warehousing may be used to enhance service and to lower transportation costs.
Inventory control	Inventory is used to make products available to customers and to ensure the correct mix of products is at the proper location at the right time.
Packaging	The role of packaging is to provide protection to the product, to maintain product identity throughout the logistics process, and to create effective product density.
Materials handling	Materials handling increases the speed of, and reduces the cost of, picking orders in the warehouse and moving products between storage and the transportation carriers. It is a cost-generating activity that must be controlled.
Production planning	Utilized in conjunction with logistics planning, production planning ensures that products are available for inventory in the correct assortment and quantity.
Plant and warehouse location	Strategic placement of plants and warehouses increases customer service and reduces the cost of transportation.

SOURCE: Adapted from James R. Stock and Douglas M. Lambert, *Strategic Logistics Management*, 5th ed. (Homewood, IL: McGraw-Hill, 2000).

with the efficiency of the entire system rather than with minimizing the cost of any single logistical activity. The interactions among logistical activities (that is, transportation, inventory, warehousing) are described as cost trade-offs because a cost increase in one activity is traded for a large cost decrease in another activity, the net result being an overall cost reduction.

Calculating Logistics Costs

Activity-Based Costing

The activity-based costing (ABC) technique is used to precisely measure the costs of performing specific activities and then trace those costs to the products, customers, and channels that consumed the activities.[33] This is a powerful tool in managing the logistics operations of a supply chain. ABC provides a mechanism to trace the cost of performing logistics services for the customers that use these services, making it easier to assess the appropriate level of customer service to offer. Firms using ABC analysis can obtain more accurate information about how a particular customer or a specific product contributes to overall profitability.[34]

Total Cost of Ownership

Total cost of ownership (TCO) determines the total costs of acquiring and then using a given item from a particular supplier (see Chapter 2). The approach identifies costs—often buried in overhead or general expenses—that relate to the costs of holding inventory, poor quality, and delivery failure.[35] A buyer using TCO explicitly considers the costs that the supplier's logistics system either added to, or eliminated from, the purchase price and would take a long-term perspective in evaluating cost.[36] Thus, a supplier particularly efficient at logistics might be able to reduce the buyer's inventory costs and the buyer's expenses of inspecting inbound merchandise. As a result, the total cost of ownership from that supplier would be lower than the cost from other suppliers that were not able to rapidly deliver undamaged products. Increasing acceptance of the TCO approach will cause logistics efficiency to become an even more critical element of a business marketer's strategy.

Business-to-Business Logistical Service

Many studies have shown that logistics service is often just as important as product quality as a measure of supplier performance. In many industries, a quality product at a competitive price is a given, so customer service is the key differentiator among competitors. In one industry, for example, purchasing agents begin the buying process by calling suppliers with the best delivery service to see whether they are willing to negotiate prices. Because it is so important to customers, reliable logistics service can lead to higher market share and higher profits. A study by Bain and Company showed that companies with superior logistics service grow 8 percent faster, collect a 7 percent price premium, and are 12 times as profitable as firms with inferior service levels.[37]

---

[33] Bernard J. LaLonde and Terrance L. Pohlen, "Issues in Supply Chain Costing," *International Journal of Logistics Management* 7 (1, 1996): p. 3.

[34] Thomas A. Foster, "Time to Learn the ABCs of Logistics," *Logistics* (February 1999): p. 67.

[35] Lisa Ellram, "Activity-Based Costing and Total Cost of Ownership: A Critical Linkage," *Journal of Cost Management* 8 (Winter 1995): p. 22.

[36] Bruce Ferrin and Richard E. Plank, "Total Cost of Ownership Models: An Exploratory Study," *Journal of Supply Chain Management* 38 (Summer 2002): p. 18.

[37] Mary Collins Holcomb, "Customer Service Measurement: A Methodology for Increasing Customer Value through Utilization of the Taguchi Strategy," *Journal of Business Logistics* 15 (1, 1994): p. 29.

TABLE 13.2 | **COMMON ELEMENTS OF LOGISTICS SERVICE**

Elements	Description
Delivery time	The time from the creation of an order to the fulfillment and delivery of that order encompasses both order-processing time and delivery or transportation time.
Delivery reliability	The most frequently used measure of logistics service, delivery reliability focuses on the capability of having products available to meet customer demand.
Order accuracy	The degree to which items received conform to the specification of the order. The key dimension is the incidence of orders shipped complete and without error.
Information access	The firm's ability to respond to inquiries about order status and product availability.
Damage	A measure of the physical conditions of the product when received by the buyer.
Ease of doing business	A range of factors, including the ease with which orders, returns, credits, billing, and adjustments are handled.
Value-added services	Such features as packaging, which facilitates customer handling, or other services such as prepricing and drop shipments.

SOURCE: Reprinted with permission from Jonathon L. S. Byrnes, William C. Copacino, and Peter Metz, "Forge Service into a Weapon with Logistics," *Transportation & Distribution, Presidential Issue* 28 (September 1987): p. 46.

These facts, together with the extensive spread of just-in-time manufacturing, make it clear that logistical service is important to organizational buyers.

Logistical service relates to the availability and delivery of products to the customer. It comprises the series of sales-satisfying activities that begin when the customer places the order and that end when the product is delivered. Responsive logistical service satisfies customers and creates the opportunity for closer and more profitable buyer-seller relationships.[38] Logistical service includes whatever aspects of performance are important to the business customer (Table 13.2). These service elements range from delivery time to value-added services, and each of these elements can affect production processes, final product output, costs, or all three.

Logistics Service Impacts on the Customer

Supplier logistical service translates into product availability. For a manufacturer to produce or for a distributor to resell, industrial products must be available at the right time, at the right place, and in usable condition. The longer the supplier's delivery time, the less available the product; the more inconsistent the delivery time, the less available the product. For example, a reduction in the supplier's delivery time permits a buyer to hold less inventory because needs can be met rapidly. The customer

[38] Arun Sharma, Dhruv Grewal, and Michael Levy, "The Customer Satisfaction/Logistics Interface," *Journal of Business Logistics* 16 (2, 1995): p. 1.

reduces the risk that the production process will be interrupted. Consistent delivery enables the buyer to program more effectively—or routinize—the purchasing process, thus lowering buyer costs. Consistent delivery-cycle performance allows buyers to cut their level of buffer or safety stock, thereby reducing inventory cost. However, for many business products, such as those that are low in unit value and relatively standardized, the overriding concern is not inventory cost but simply having the products. A malfunctioning $0.95 bearing could shut down a whole production line.

Determining the Level of Service

Buyers often rank logistics service right behind "quality" as a criterion for selecting a vendor. However, not all products or all customers require the same level of logistical service. Many made-to-order products—such as heavy machinery—have relatively low logistical service requirements. Others, such as replacement parts, components, and subassemblies, require extremely demanding logistical performance. Similarly, customers may be more or less responsive to varying levels of logistical service.

Profitable Levels of Service   In developing a logistical service strategy, business marketing strategists should assess the profit impact of the service options that they provide to customers. In nearly all industries, firms provide numerous supply chain services such as next-day delivery, customized handling, and specialized labeling. However, few companies actually trace the true costs of specialized services and the resulting effect on customer profitability (see Chapter 4).

To combat this unhealthy situation, some companies are now using *cost-to-serve* analytics to address the problem—among them are Dow Chemical, Eastman Chemical, and Georgia-Pacific (GP). GP used total-delivered-cost analysis to improve the performance of a major customer account.[39] By incorporating cost-to-serve data into the calculation of gross margin, GP's supply chain team determined that the costs to provide this customer with expedited transportation and distribution services were significantly reducing the account's profitability. In a top-to-top meeting with the customer, GP used the data to expose the root causes of the high costs and poor service, which included last-minute, uncoordinated promotional planning and purchasing across the customer's major business units and the customer's unwillingness to share inventory levels and positioning. Customers, once confronted with the data, are often willing to collaborate on ways to improve service, reduce costs, and restore profitability.

To recap, service levels are developed by assessing customer service requirements. The sales and cost of various service levels are analyzed to find the service level generating the highest profits. The needs of various customer segments dictate various logistical system configurations. For example, when logistical service is critical, industrial distributors can provide the vital product availability, whereas customers with less rigorous service demands can be served from factory inventories.

Logistics Impacts on Other Supply Chain Participants

A supplier's logistical system directly affects a distributor's ability to control cost and service to end users. Delivery time influences not only the customer's inventory

---

[39]Remko Van Hoek, "When Good Customers Are Bad," *Harvard Business Review* 83 (September 2005): p. 19.

requirements but also the operations of channel members. If a supplier provides erratic delivery service to distributors, the distributor is forced to carry higher inventory in order to provide a satisfactory level of product availability to end users.

Inefficient logistics service to the distributors either increases distributor costs (larger inventories) or creates shortages of the supplier's products at the distributor level. Neither result is good. In the first instance, distributor loyalty and marketing efforts will suffer; in the second, end users will eventually change suppliers. When Palm, Inc., developed the Palm Pilot, the firm created such an effective logistics system that its distributors in Latin America were able to offer the same level of after-sales service available in the United States, allowing Palm to reach sales exceeding $250 million in Latin America in a short time frame.[40] In some industries, distributors are expanding their role in the logistics process, which makes them even more valuable to their suppliers and customers. In the chemical industry, for example, the role of distributors is completely transforming as they offer logistics solutions—JIT delivery, repackaging, inventory management—to their customers.[41] The logistics expertise distributors provide enables their vendors (manufacturers) to focus on their own core competencies of production and marketing.

Business-to-Business Logistical Management

The elements of logistics strategy are part of a system, and as such, each affects every other element. The proper focus is the total-cost view. Although this section treats the decisions on facilities, transportation, and inventory separately, these areas are so intertwined that decisions in one area influence the others.

Logistical Facilities

The strategic development of a warehouse provides the business marketer with the opportunity to increase the level of delivery service to buyers, reduce transportation costs, or both. Business firms that distribute repair, maintenance, and operating supplies often find that the only way to achieve desired levels of delivery service is to locate warehouses in key markets. The warehouse circumvents the need for premium transportation (air freight) and costly order processing by keeping products readily available in local markets.

Serving Other Supply Chain Members   The nature of the business-to-business (B2B) supply chain affects the warehousing requirements of a supplier. Manufacturers' representatives do not hold inventory, but distributors do. When manufacturers' reps are used, the supplier often requires a significant number of strategically located warehouses. On the other hand, a supply chain using distributors offsets the need for warehousing. Obviously, local warehousing by the distributor is a real service to the supplier. A few well-located supplier warehouses may be all that is required to service the distributors effectively.

---

[40]Toby Gooley, "Service Stars," *Logistics* (June 1999): p. 37.

[41]Daniel J. McConville, "More Work for Chemical Distributors," *Distribution* 95 (August 1996): p. 63.

Outsourcing the Warehousing Function   Operating costs, service levels, and investment requirements are essential considerations regarding the type of warehouse to use. The business firm may either operate its own warehouses or turn them over to a "third party"—a company that specializes in performing warehousing services. The advantages of third-party warehousing are flexibility, reduced assets, and professional management—the firm can increase or decrease its use of space in a given market, move into or out of any market quickly, and enjoy an operation managed by specialists. Third-party warehousing may sometimes supplement or replace distributors in a market.

Many third-party warehouses provide a variety of logistical services for their clients, including packaging, labeling, order processing, and some light assembly. Saddle Creek Corporation, a third-party warehouse company based in Lakeland, Florida, maintains warehouse facilities in a number of major markets. Clients can position inventories in all these markets while dealing with only one firm. Also, Saddle Creek can link its computer with the suppliers' computers to facilitate order processing and inventory updating. The Saddle Creek warehouse also repackages products to the end-user's order, label, and arrange for local delivery. A business marketer can ship standard products in bulk to the Saddle Creek warehouse—gaining transportation economies—and still enjoy excellent customer delivery service. The public or contract warehouse is a feasible alternative to the distributor channel when the sales function can be economically executed either with a direct sales force or with reps.

Transportation

Transportation is usually the largest single logistical expense, and with continually rising fuel costs, its importance will probably increase. Typically, the transportation decision involves evaluating and selecting both a mode of transportation and the individual carrier(s) that will ensure the best performance at the lowest cost. Mode refers to the type of carrier—rail, truck, water, air, or some combination of the four. Individual carriers are evaluated on rates and delivery performance.[42] The supply chain view is important in selecting individual carriers. Carriers become an integral part of the supply chain, and close relationships are important. One study found evidence that carriers' operating performance improved when they were more involved in the relationship between buyer and seller.[43] By further integrating carriers into the supply chain, the entire supply chain can improve its competitive position. In this section we consider (1) the role of transportation in industrial supply chains and (2) the criteria for evaluating transportation options.

Transportation and Logistical Service   A business marketer must be able to effectively move finished inventory between facilities, to channel intermediaries, and to customers. The transportation system is the link that binds the logistical network together and ultimately results in timely delivery of products. Efficient warehousing does not enhance customer service levels if transportation is inconsistent or inadequate.

---

[42] For example, see James C. Johnson, Donald F. Wood, Danile L. Warlow, and Paul R. Murphy, *Contemporary Logistics*, 7th ed. (Upper Saddle River, NJ: Prentice Hall, 1998).

[43] Julie Gentry, "The Role of Carriers in Buyer-Supplier Strategic Partnerships: A Supply Chain Management Approach," *Journal of Business Logistics* 17 (2, 1996): p. 52.

Effective transportation service may be used in combination with warehouse facilities and inventory levels to generate the required customer service level, or it may be used in place of them. Inventory maintained in a variety of market-positioned warehouses can be consigned to one centralized warehouse when rapid transportation services exist to deliver products from the central location to business customers. Xerox is one company that uses premium airfreight service to offset the need for high inventories and extensive warehouse locations. The decision on transportation modes and particular carriers depends on the cost trade-offs and service capabilities of each. It is interesting that in the age of next-day delivery and express airfreight services, barges that weave their way through a maze of rivers, lakes, and channels are thriving.[44] A barge trip that takes 17 hours would take a train 4 hours and a truck 90 minutes for a similar trip. Although very slow (averaging 15 miles per hour), the barge offers huge cost advantages compared with truck and rail. For products like limestone, coal, farm products, and petroleum, the slow and unglamorous barge is an effective logistics tool.

Transportation Performance Criteria   **Cost of service** is the variable cost of moving products from origin to destination, including any terminal or accessory charges. The cost of service may range from as little as $0.25 per ton-mile via water to as high as $0.50 per ton-mile via airfreight. The important aspect of selecting the transportation mode is not cost per se but cost relative to the objective to be achieved. Bulk raw materials generally do not require prepaid delivery service, so the cost of anything other than rail or water transportation could not be justified. On the other hand, although airfreight may be almost 10 times more expensive than motor freight, the cost is inconsequential to a customer who needs an emergency shipment of spare parts. The cost of premium (faster) transportation modes may be justified by the resulting inventory reductions.

Speed of service refers to the elapsed time to move products from one facility (plant or warehouse) to another facility (warehouse or customer plant). Again, speed of service often overrides cost. Rail, a relatively slow mode used for bulk shipments, requires inventory buildups at the supplier's factory and at the destination warehouse. The longer the delivery time, the more inventory customers must maintain to service their needs while the shipment is in transit. The slower modes involve lower variable costs for product movement, yet they result in lower service levels and higher investments in inventory. The faster modes produce just the opposite effect. Not only must a comparison be made between modes in terms of service but various carriers within a mode must be evaluated on their "door-to-door" delivery time.

Service consistency is usually more important than average delivery time, and all modes of transportation are not equally consistent. Although air provides the lowest average delivery time, generally it has the highest variability in delivery time relative to the average. The wide variations in modal service consistency are particularly critical in business marketing planning. The choice of transportation mode must be made on the basis of cost, average transit time, and consistency if effective customer service is to be achieved.

In summary, because business buyers often place a premium on effective and consistent delivery service, the choice of transportation mode is an important one—one

---

[44]Anna Wilde Mathews, "Jet-Age Anomalies, Slowpoke Barges Do Brisk Business," *The Wall Street Journal*, May 15, 1998, p. B1.

where cost of service is often secondary. However, the best decision on transportation carriers results from a balancing of service, variable costs, and investment requirements. The manager must also consider the transportation requirements of ordinary, versus expedited (rush order), shipments.

Inventory Management

Inventory management is the buffer in the logistical system. Inventories are needed in business channels because

1. Production and demand are not perfectly matched;

2. Operating deficiencies in the logistical system often result in product unavailability (for example, delayed shipments, inconsistent carrier performance);

3. Business customers cannot predict their product needs with certainty (for example, because a machine may break down or there may be a sudden need to expand production).

Inventory may be viewed in the same light as warehouse facilities and transportation: It is an alternative method for providing the level of service customers require, and the level of inventory is determined on the basis of cost, investment, service required, and anticipated revenue.

Quality Focus: Eliminate Inventories   Today's prevalent total-quality-management techniques and just-in-time management principles emphasize the reduction or outright elimination of inventories. Current thinking suggests that inventories exist because of inefficiencies in the system: Erratic delivery, poor forecasting, and ineffective quality-control systems all force companies to hold excessive stocks to protect themselves from delivery, forecasting, and product failure. Instead, improved delivery, forecasting, and manufacturing processes should eliminate the need to buffer against failures and uncertainty. Information technology involving bar coding, scanner data, total quality processes, better transportation management, and more effective information flow among firms in the supply chain have made it possible to more carefully control inventories and reduce them to the lowest possible levels.

The Internet connectivity that unites the supply chain from an information standpoint has permitted substantial inventory reductions in several industries. One recent study showed that average inventory turnover for manufacturers has increased from 8 to more than 12 times per year.[45] Much of the credit for this improvement is attributed to more information sharing among the supply chain members, sophisticated inventory management software, and generally higher levels of supply chain coordination. Successful business marketing managers must develop quality processes that in themselves reduce or eliminate the need to carry large inventories, while coordinating and integrating a supply chain system that can function effectively with almost no inventory.

---

[45] Thomas W. Speh, *Changes in Warehouse Inventory Turnover* (Chicago: Warehousing Education and Research Council, 1999).

INSIDE BUSINESS MARKETING

The Profit Impact of Inventory Management

Deere & Company's core business is manufacturing equipment: agricultural, construction, commercial, and consumer equipment. For its supply chain practices, the firm enjoys an edge over its competitors in the industry, particularly in inventory management. The following illustration demonstrates the significance of this advantage.

On average, assume that Deere maintains 59 days' worth of sales in inventory and the worst firm in the industry maintains 137 days' worth of sales in inventory. Each 30 days' worth of inventory translates to a profit difference of 1.66 percent of sales in the industry. The difference between Deere and the worst competitor is 78 days' worth of inventory. To calculate the profit difference, the following calculations can be made:

Worst firm, inventories:	137 days
Deere & Company, inventories:	59 days
Difference:	*78 days*

Each *30 days* is worth *1.66 percent of sales* in profits. The difference between Deere and its "worst" competitor is 78/30 = *2.6 times.*

The difference in profitability is: 2.6 × 1.66% = *4.3% of sales.*

The difference between the worst firm and the best firm as a result of effectively managing inventories is equal to 4.3 percent of sales. If each firm has $1 billion in sales, the best-managed firm would have *$43 million more profits*, all other things being equal!

Inventory in Rapidly Changing Markets Many companies in rapidly changing high-tech industries must look at inventory characteristics like obsolescence, devaluation, price protection, and return costs.[46] For a company like Hewlett-Packard, with products that have very fast product life cycles, all four of these factors can significantly reduce profits if inventories are not managed effectively. H-P refers to these costs as "inventory-driven costs" (IDCs). In 1995, for example, H-P found that costs related to inventory equaled their PC business's *total operating margin*! For many of their products that are held in the supply chain by various resellers, the major inventory costs to H-P are price protection costs, as they must reimburse resellers for any loss in the market value of the products kept in inventory. Because the inventories of channel partners represent the largest component of inventory costs to H-P, managers are taking steps to improve SCM practices downstream in the channel. For example, H-P has introduced new processes such as vendor-managed inventory (VMI)—where H-P assists resellers in planning inventories and works with the marketing managers of those resellers to estimate and manage demand.

Third-Party Logistics

Using **third-party logistics firms** to perform logistics activities represents an important trend among business-to-business firms. These external firms perform a wide range of logistics functions traditionally performed within the organization.

---

[46]Gianpaolo Callioni, Xavier de Montgros, Regine Slagmulder, Luk N. Van Wassenhove, and Linda Wright, "Inventory-Driven Costs," *Harvard Business Review* 83 (March 2005): pp. 135–141.

Most companies use some type of third-party firm, whether for transportation, warehousing, or information processing. The strategic decision to outsource logistics is often made by top management. The functions the third-party company performs can encompass the entire logistics process or selected activities within that process. Third parties can perform the warehousing; they may perform the transportation function (for example, a truck line like Schneider National); or they may perform the entire logistics process from production scheduling to delivery of finished products to the customer (for example, Ryder Dedicated Logistics). Third parties enable a manufacturer or distributor to concentrate on its core business while enjoying the expertise and specialization of a professional logistics company. The results are often lower costs, better service, improved asset utilization, increased flexibility, and access to leading-edge technology. Recently, some firms have advocated the use of "Fourth-Party Logistics"—firms that own no assets but serve to manage several third parties that are employed to perform various logistics functions.[47]

Despite the advantages of third-party logistics firms, some firms are cautious because of reduced control over the logistics process, diminished direct contact with customers, and the problems of terminating internal operations. In analyzing the most effective and efficient way to accomplish logistics cost and service objectives, the business marketing manager should carefully consider the benefits and drawbacks of outsourcing part or all logistics functions to third-party providers. In an interesting application of third-party logistics, Caterpillar (the manufacturer of earthmoving equipment) formed a logistics services company to manage the parts distribution for other manufacturers.[48] The company applies the knowledge gained from its own experiences in distributing 300 families of products that require over 530,000 spare parts. Caterpillar transfers knowledge from the company's internal operations to customers and vice versa.

Future Focus: The Green Supply Chain   Many experts predict that we will see a major expansion in "green" supply chain initiatives whereby companies are committing to design, source, manufacture, and manage the end-of-life stage for all of their products in an environmentally and socially responsible manner.[49] Other initiatives include developing green packaging and refurbishing products to avoid or minimize landfill waste. One study showed that for many manufacturers, between 40 and 60 percent of a company's carbon footprint resides upstream in its supply chain—from raw materials, transport, and packaging to the energy consumed in manufacturing processes. Therefore, any significant carbon-abatement activities will require collaboration with supply chain partners, first to comprehensively understand the emissions associated with products, and then to analyze abatement opportunities systematically.[50] A carefully orchestrated and cooperative approach among supply chain partners provides the foundation for tackling and solving these challenging environmental issues.

[47]"Fourth Party Logistics: An Analysis," *Logistics Focus* 1 (3, Summer 2002): p. 16.

[48]Peter Marsh, "A Moving Story of Spare Parts," *The Financial Times*, August 29, 1997, p. 8.

[49]"Leading the Charge in Multi-Enterprise Supply Chains," *Global Logistics & Supply Chain Strategies* (January 17, 2008).

[50]Chris Brickman and Drew Ungerman, "Climate Change and Supply Chain Management," McKinsey Quarterly, accessed at http://www.mckinseyquarterly.com/Operations/Supply_Chain_Logistics on August 5, 2008.

Summary

Leading business marketing firms demonstrate superior capabilities in supply chain management. SCM focuses on improving the flow of products, information, and services as they move from origin to destination. A key driver to SCM is coordination and integration among all the participants in the supply chain, primarily through sophisticated information systems and management software. Reducing waste, minimizing duplication, reducing cost, and enhancing service are the major objectives of SCM. Firms successful at managing the supply chain understand the nature of their products and the type of supply chain structure required to meet the needs of their customers. In particular, effective supply chains integrate operations, share information, and above all, provide added value to customers.

Logistics is the critical function in the firm's supply chain because logistics directs the flow and storage of products and information. Successful supply chains synchronize logistics with other functions such as production, procurement, forecasting, order management, and customer service. The systems perspective in logistical management cannot be stressed enough—it is the only way to assure management that the logistical function meets prescribed goals. Not only must each logistical variable be analyzed in terms of its effect on every other variable but the sum of the variables must be evaluated in light of the service level provided to customers. Logistics elements throughout the supply chain must be integrated to assure smooth product flow. Logistical service is critical in the buyer's evaluation of business marketing firms and generally ranks second only to product quality as a desired supplier characteristic.

Logistics decisions must be based on cost trade-offs among the logistical variables and on comparisons of the costs and revenues associated with alternative levels of service. The optimal system produces the highest profitability relative to the capital investment required. Three major variables—facilities, transportation, and inventory—form the basis of logistical decisions B2B logistics managers face. The business marketer must monitor the effect of logistics on all supply chain members and on overall supply chain performance. Finally, the strategic role of logistics should be carefully evaluated: Logistics can often provide a strong competitive advantage.

Discussion Questions

1. What is supply chain management and what are the types of functions and firms that make up the typical supply chain?

2. Explain how an effective supply chain can create a strong competitive advantage for the firms involved in it.

3. Explain why cooperation among supply chain participants determines whether the supply chain is effective.

4. Explain the different elements of "waste" that exist in supply chains and how supply chain management focuses on eliminating the various elements of waste.

5. Describe the role the Internet plays in enhancing supply chain management operations.

6. Adopting the perspective of an organizational buyer, carefully illustrate how the most economical source of supply might be the firm that offers the highest price but also the fastest and most reliable delivery system.

7. Describe a situation in which total logistical costs might be reduced by doubling transportation costs.

8. A key goal in logistical management is to find the optimum balance of logistical cost and customer service that yields optimal profits. Explain.

9. Explain how consistent delivery performance gives the organizational buyer the opportunity to cut the level of inventory maintained.

10. An increasing number of manufacturers are adopting more sophisticated purchasing practices and inventory control systems. What are the strategic implications of these developments for business marketers wishing to serve these customers?

Internet Exercise

1. YRC Worldwide Inc. is a *Fortune* 500 transportation company and one of the largest transportation firms in the world. Go to http://www.yrcw.com/ and examine the online tools available on the Web site. Discuss how the various tools would help a B2B marketer enhance the logistics services that they provide to customers.

Managing Logistics at Trans-Pro

Logistics management is critical in determining the profitability of B2B channel members like industrial distributors. To be successful, the industrial distributor must maintain a very large inventory of its full product line and be able to deliver products promptly when a customer places an order—the major value-added service that the distributor provides to customers is product availability. By having an extensive variety of components and replacements parts available on a round-the-clock basis, the distributor's customers are able to minimize investments in inventory. In addition, customer firms can be certain that their operations will never be shut down because they cannot get a critical component. Because of the nature of the distributor's business, inventory costs often become the single largest expense and, as such, effective inventory management is a key driver of profitability.

Trans-Pro is a large industrial distributor of power transmission equipment— bearings, gears, v-belts, and the like. The company's management, cognizant of the criticality of effective inventory management, developed an incentive scheme for its 50 branch managers to minimize inventories. Each month, average inventory in the warehouse was measured and the branch managers were assessed a penalty for inventory levels that exceeded $2.5 million. For each increment of dollars above the threshold figure, the manager would be docked 1 percent of his or her monthly salary—a very strong incentive to carefully control inventory levels! In addition, Trans-Pro also demanded that customer service be absolutely outstanding. The goal was to deliver an order within 24 hours of receiving it. As might be expected, the managers did a superlative job in managing average monthly inventories. Rarely were any of the branches in excess of the mandated maximum level. Customer service levels approached 98 percent—that is, 98 percent of all orders were delivered within the 24-hour time period.

Discussion Question

1. Critique Trans-Pro's approach to managing logistics.

CHAPTER

14

Pricing Strategy for Business Markets

Understanding how customers define value is the essence of the pricing process. Pricing decisions complement the firm's overall marketing strategy. The diverse nature of the business market presents unique problems and opportunities for the price strategist. After reading this chapter, you will understand:

1. a value-based approach for pricing.

2. the central elements of the pricing process.

3. how effective new-product prices are established and the need to periodically adjust the prices of existing products.

4. how to respond to a price attack by an aggressive competitor.

5. strategic approaches to competitive bidding.

Customer value represents the cornerstone of business-to-business (B2B) marketing in the 21st century.[1] Thus, business marketers must pursue this unifying strategic goal: Be better than your very best competitors in providing customer value.[2] According to Richard D'Aveni:

> While the average competitor fights for niches along a common ratio of price and value ("You get what you pay for"), innovative firms can enter the market by providing better value to the customer ("You can get more than what you pay for"). These companies offer lower cost *and* higher quality. This shift in value is like lowering the stick while dancing the limbo. All the competitors have to do the same dance with tighter constraints on both cost and quality.[3]

The business marketing manager must blend the various components of the marketing mix into a value proposition that responds to the customer's requirements and provides a return consistent with the firm's objectives. Price must be carefully meshed with the firm's product, distribution, and communication strategies. Thomas Nagle points out, "If effective product development, promotion, and distribution sow the seeds of business success, effective pricing is the harvest. Although effective pricing can never compensate for poor execution of the first three elements, ineffective pricing can surely prevent these efforts from resulting in financial success. Regrettably, this is a common occurrence."[4]

This chapter is divided into five parts. The first defines the special meaning of customer value in a business marketing context. The second analyzes key determinants of the industrial pricing process and provides an operational approach to pricing decisions. The third examines pricing policies for new and existing products, emphasizing the need to actively manage a product throughout its life cycle. The fourth provides a framework to guide strategy when a competitor cuts prices. The final section examines an area of particular importance to the business marketer: competitive bidding.

The Meaning of Value in Business Markets

When members of a buying center select a product, they are buying a given level of product quality, technical service, and delivery reliability. Other elements may be important—the reputation of the supplier, a feeling of security, friendship, and other personal benefits flowing from the buyer-seller relationship. Value represents a trade-off between benefits and sacrifices. **Customer value**, then, represents a business customer's overall assessment of the utility of a relationship with a supplier based on benefits received and sacrifices made[5] (Figure 14.1).

---

[1]Ajay Menon, Christian Homburg, and Nikolas Beutin, "Understanding Customer Value in Business-to-Business Relationships," *Journal of Business-to-Business Marketing* 12 (2, 2005): pp. 1–33; see also James C. Anderson, Nirmalya Kumar, and James A. Narus, *Value Merchants: Demonstrating and Documenting Superior Value in Business Markets* (Boston: Harvard Business School Press, 2007).

[2]Bradley T. Gale, *Managing Customer Value: Creating Quality and Service That Customers Can See* (New York: The Free Press, 1994), pp. 73–75.

[3]Richard A. D'Aveni, *Hypercompetitive Rivalries* (New York: The Free Press, 1995), p. 27.

[4]Thomas T. Nagle, *The Strategy and Tactics of Pricing: A Guide to Profitable Decision Making* (Englewood Cliffs, NJ: Prentice-Hall, 1987), p. 1.

[5]This discussion is based on Menon, Homburg, and Beutin, "Understanding Customer Value," pp. 1–33.

FIGURE 14.1 | CUSTOMER VALUE IN BUSINESS MARKETS

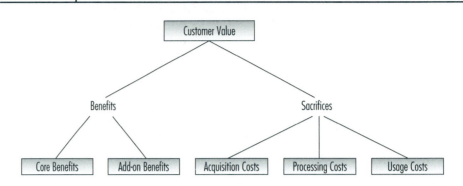

SOURCE: Adapted with modifications from Ajay Menon, Christian Homburg, and Nikolas Beutin, "Understanding Customer Value in Business-to-Business Relationships," *Journal of Business-to-Business Marketing* 12 (2, 2005): pp. 1–33.

Benefits

Two types of benefits can contribute to customer value in business markets: core benefits and add-on benefits (see Chapter 8).

Core Benefits   **Core benefits** are the basic requirements the business marketer must meet to be included in the customer's consideration set. Represented here would be a specific level of product quality and performance, as well as expected levels of pre- and postsales service. Likewise, by enhancing problem solving and the open sharing of ideas, a trust-based relationship adds value and the customer sees it as a core benefit.

Add-on Benefits   **Add-on benefits** are those "attributes, typically not required, that assist the customer in selecting a supplier from among a qualified set of potential suppliers."[6] These are relational characteristics or services that differentiate suppliers and focus on "attractor" attributes in buyer-seller relationships.

Examples of add-on benefits would be *joint working relationships* in product development, quality control, logistics, and delivery systems. **Supplier flexibility**, or the willingness of a business marketer to accommodate a customer's unique business needs, likewise adds customer value. The supplier's **commitment**, namely the desire to make the relationship work, can also provide an add-on benefit to the customer. Supplier commitment "takes into account the supplier's willingness to make short-term sacrifices, invest in the relationship, and be tolerant of buyer's mistakes (for example, mistakes in ordering or outlining product specifications)."[7]

Sacrifices

A broad perspective is likewise needed in examining the sacrifices, or costs, a particular alternative may present for the buyer. When purchasing a product or service, a business customer always assumes various costs above and beyond the actual purchase price.

---

[6]Ibid., p. 6; see also Das Narayandas, "Building Loyalty in Business Markets," *Harvard Business Review* 83 (September 2005): pp. 131–139.

[7]Menon, Homburg, and Beutin, "Understanding Customer Value," p. 15.

TABLE 14.1 | CUSTOMERS' COST-IN-USE COMPONENTS

Acquisition Costs	+	Possession Costs	+	Usage Costs	=	Total Cost in Use
Price		Interest cost		Installation costs		
Paperwork cost		Storage cost		Training cost		
Transportation costs		Quality control		User labor cost		
Expediting cost		Taxes and insurance		Product longevity		
Cost of mistakes in order		Shrinkage and obsolescence		Replacement costs		
Prepurchase product evaluation costs		General internal handling costs		Disposal costs		

SOURCE: Adapted from Frank V. Cespedes, "Industrial Marketing: Managing New Requirements," *Sloan Management Review* 35 (Spring 1994): p. 46.

Many businesses buy products online to reduce paperwork and lower transaction and search costs.[8] Rather than making a decision on the basis of price alone, organizational buyers emphasize the **total cost in use** of a particular product or service.[9] Observe in Table 14.1 that an organizational customer considers three different types of costs in a total cost-in-use calculation:

1. **Acquisition costs** include not only the selling price and transportation costs but also the administrative costs of evaluating suppliers, expediting orders, and correcting errors in shipments or delivery.

2. **Possession costs** include financing, storage, inspection, taxes, insurance, and other internal handling costs.

3. **Usage costs** are those associated with ongoing use of the purchased product such as installation, employee training, user labor, and field repair, as well as product replacement and disposal costs.

Value-Based Strategies

Aided by sophisticated supplier evaluation systems, buyers can measure and track the total cost/value of dealing with alternative suppliers. In turn, astute business marketers can pursue value-based strategies that provide customers with a lower cost-in-use solution. For example, the logistical expenses of health-care supplies typically account for 10 to 15 percent of a hospital's operating costs. Medical products firms, like Becton, Dickinson and Company, develop innovative product/service packages that respond to each component of the cost-in-use equation. Such firms can reduce a hospital's acquisition costs by offering an electronic ordering system, possession costs by emphasizing just-in-time service, and usage costs by creating an efficient system for disposing of medical supplies after use.

[8]Walter Baker, Mike Marn, and Craig Zawada, "Price Smarter on the Net," *Harvard Business Review* 79 (February 2001): pp. 122–127.

[9]Frank V. Cespedes, "Industrial Marketing: Managing New Requirements," *Sloan Management Review* 35 (Spring 1994): pp. 45–60.

Differentiating Through Value Creation   Value-based strategies seek to move the selling proposition from one that centers on current prices and individual transactions to a longer-term relationship built around value and lower total cost in use. Importantly, recent research suggests that benefits have a greater effect on perceived value to business customers than sacrifices (price and costs). Ajay Menon, Christian Homburg, and Nikolas Beutin note: Contrary to the general belief in a cost-driven economy, "we encourage managers to emphasize benefits accruing from a relationship and not focus solely on lowering the price and related costs when managing customer value."[10] A better way is to provide unique add-on benefits by building trust, demonstrating commitment and flexibility, and initiating joint working relationships that enhance customer value and loyalty.

In support, recent research by Wolfgang Ulaga and Andreas Eggert indicates that relationship benefits display a stronger potential for differentiation in key supplier relationships than cost considerations.[11] Based on a best-practice profile for companies seeking key supplier status, the researchers identify service support and personal interaction as core differentiators, followed by a supplier's know-how and its ability to improve a customer's time to market. Product quality and delivery performance, along with acquisition cost and operation costs, display a moderate potential to help the awarding of key supplier status to a business-to-business firm by a customer. Interestingly, price shows the weakest potential for differentiation. A specific approach for designing value-based strategies is highlighted in the next section.

The Pricing Process in Business Markets

There is no easy formula for pricing an industrial product or service. The decision is multidimensional: The interactive variables of demand, cost, competition, profit relationships, and customer usage patterns each assumes significance as the marketer formulates the role of price in the firm's marketing strategy. Pertinent considerations, illustrated in Figure 14.2, include (1) pricing objectives, (2) demand determinants, (3) cost determinants, and (4) competition.

Price Objectives

The pricing decision must be based on objectives congruent with marketing and overall corporate objectives. The marketer starts with principal objectives and adds collateral pricing goals: (1) achieving a target return on investment, (2) achieving a market-share goal, or (3) meeting competition. Many other potential pricing objectives extend beyond profit and market-share goals, taking into account competition, channel relationships, and product-line considerations.

Because of their far-reaching effects, pricing objectives must be established with care. Each firm faces unique internal and external environmental forces. Contrasting the strategies of DuPont and Dow Chemical illustrates the importance of a unified corporate direction. Dow's strategy focuses first on pricing low-margin commodity

---

[10]Menon, Homburg, and Beutin, "Understanding Customer Value," p. 25.

[11]Wolfgang Ulaga and Andreas Eggert, "Value-Based Differentiation in Business Relationships: Gaining and Sustaining Key Supplier Status," *Journal of Marketing* 70 (January 2006): pp. 119–136.

FIGURE 14.2 | **KEY COMPONENTS OF THE PRICE-SETTING DECISION PROCESS**

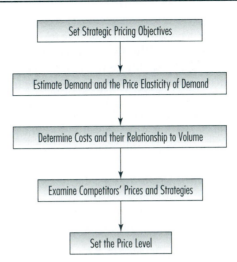

goods *low* to build a dominant market share and then on maintaining that dominant share. DuPont's strategy, on the other hand, emphasizes higher-margin specialty products. Initially, these products are priced at a *high* level, and prices are reduced as the market expands and competition intensifies. Each firm requires explicit pricing objectives that are consistent with its corporate mission.

Demand Determinants

A strong market perspective is fundamental in pricing. The business market is diverse and complex. A single industrial product can be used in many ways; each market segment may represent a unique application for the product and a separate usage level. The importance of the industrial good in the buyer's end product also varies by market segment. Therefore, potential demand, sensitivity to price, and potential profitability can vary markedly across market segments. To establish an effective pricing policy, marketers should focus first on the value a customer places on a product or service. This reverses the typical process that gives immediate attention to the product cost and the desired markup.[12]

Assessing Value[13] How organizational buyers evaluate the economic value of the total offering determines the appropriateness of a pricing strategy. Two competitors with similar products may ask different prices because buyers perceive their total offerings as unique. In the eyes of the organizational buyer, one firm may provide more value than another.

 Economic value represents the cost savings and/or revenue gains that customers realize by purchasing the firm's product instead of the next-best alternative. Some

---

[12]Robert J. Dolan, "How Do You Know When the Price Is Right?" *Harvard Business Review* 73 (September–October 1995): pp. 174–183; see also Thomas T. Nagle and George E. Cressman Jr. "Don't Just Set Prices, Manage Them," *Marketing Management* 11 (November–December 2002): pp. 29–34.

[13]This section is based on Gerald E. Smith and Thomas T. Nagle, "A Question of Value," *Marketing Management* 14 (July/August 2005): pp. 38–43.

product or service features are quite similar across competitive offerings in a category (that is, points of parity) whereas others might be unique to a particular firm's brand (that is points of differentiation). **Commodity value,** then, is the value that a customer assigns to product features that resemble those of competitors' offerings. By contrast, **differentiation value** is the value associated with product features that are unique and different from competitors'. Importantly, the price-per-unit of value that organizational buyers are willing to pay a firm for differentiating features is greater than the price-per-unit of value that they would pay for commodity features. "That's because refusal to pay a supplier's price for differentiating features means that the buyer must forgo those features. Refusal to pay a supplier's price for commodity features means simply that the customer must buy them elsewhere," says Gerald E. Smith and Thomas T. Nagle.[14] Recall that best-practice business-to-business firms create distinctive value propositions (see Chapter 4) that isolate those product and service features that matter the most to customers, demonstrate the value of their unique elements, and communicate that value in a manner that clearly conveys a deep understanding of the customer's business priorities.[15]

Isolating Value Drivers in Key Customer Segments   Exploratory methods such as depth interviews are required for identifying and measuring value. For example, depth interviews can be used to probe customer needs and problems and for learning how your products or services could address these problems. The goal here is to first identify the most significant drivers of value for customers in each market segment (see Figure 14.3). Economic value embodies both cost and revenue drivers. **Cost drivers** create value by providing economic savings while **revenue drivers** add incremental value by facilitating revenue or margin expansion.[16] For example, consider the value that Sonoco, a packaging supplier, provided for Lance, the snack food maker. One improvement involved the use of flexographic painted packaging film on some of Lance's key brands.[17] These efforts drastically reduced Lance's packaging costs (cost driver) and, by enhancing the appeal of the products, spawned a growth in sales (revenue driver).

Second, once the business marketing strategist has identified the most important value drivers for customers, attention then turns to quantifying the impact of the firm's product or service on the customer's business model. To illustrate, a medical equipment company developed a new surgical product. Based on depth interviews with surgical teams at key hospitals, value research found that this product could reduce the length of a particular surgical procedure from 55 minutes to 40 minutes, freeing up precious time in capacity-constrained operating rooms.[18] In addition to estimating the value of the product, the study also revealed ways in which surgical procedures could be more tightly scheduled to capture the full value potential of the new product.

Third, the strategist should compare the firm's product or service to the next-best alternative, isolating those features that are unique and different from competitors.

---

[14]Ibid., p. 40.

[15]James C. Anderson, James A. Narus, and Wouter van Rossum, "Customer Value Propositions in Business Markets," *Harvard Business Review* 86 (March 2006): p. 93.

[16] Gerald E. Smith and Thomas T. Nagle, "How Much Are Customers Willing to Pay?" *Marketing Research* 14 (Winter 2002): pp. 20–25.

[17]Maryanne Q. Hancock, Roland H. John, and Philip J. Wojcik, "Better B2B Selling," *The McKinsey Quarterly* (June 2005): pp. 1–8.

[18]Smith and Nagle, "How Much Are Customers Willing to Pay?" p. 23.

FIGURE 14.3 | **A VALUE-BASED APPROACH FOR PRICING**

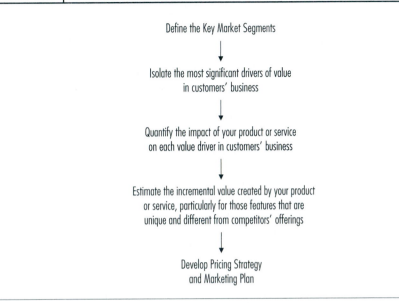

SOURCE: Adapted from Gerald E. Smith and Thomas T. Nagle, "How Much Are Customers Willing to Pay," *Marketing Research* 14 (Winter 2002): pp. 20–25.

Does the product provide favorable points of difference that provide value that a customer cannot access elsewhere? How much value does each of these features create for the customer? Finally, by understanding how customers actually use a product or service and realize value from its use, the business marketer is ideally equipped to set the price and develop a responsive marketing strategy.

Value-Based Pricing Illustrated[19]

DataCare was planning to introduce a new data-based service targeting subacute hospitals where patients stay for longer recovery periods. Drawing on extensive operating data gathered from 300 hospitals throughout North America, DataCare developed software that enabled hospital administrators to make benchmarking comparisons with best-in-class institutions using the data. By subscribing to the service, customers could input their operating data into the firm's central operating database and, in return, would have access to the benchmarking capabilities and expert consultation from the nationally recognized physicians who founded the firm. Before introducing the service, the founders asked consultants at Strategic Pricing Research to examine this question: "Would the market be willing to pay a price of $2,000 per year?"

Value Research In addition to measuring willingness to pay, the consultants also calculated the value that DataCare's customers would receive from the new service. First, different market segments were identified and a customer interview guide was

---

[19]This illustration is drawn from Smith and Nagle, "How Much Are Customers Willing to Pay?" p. 23.

developed: nonprofit hospitals, for-profit hospitals, and hospital chains. Second, several value drivers emerged from the customer interviews: nurse turnover, Health Care Financial Administration (HCFA) violations (that is, an oversight agency for Medicare and Medicaid), patient mix, and infection rates. Third, the potential impact of DataCare's new service on each of these value drivers was quantified. To illustrate, the database indicated that best-in-class institutions have nurse turnover rates of 30 percent. In turn, the analysis revealed that a hospital incurs a cost of $2,200 to $2,800 each time a nurse leaves. Assume that a hospital with a nursing staff of 50 has a turnover rate of 44 percent. A reduction in nurse turnover rate to the best-in-class level would be worth 14% $\times$ 50 $\times$ ($2,200 to $2,800), or $15,400 to $19,600. After providing this calculation, the customer was asked: Does this sound correct?

By repeating this process for each of the value drivers, the consultants concluded the interviews by summarizing the potential impact of the new service on each of the value drivers: $15,400 to $19,000 for nurse turnover; $9,000 to $12,000 for lower infection rates; and $4,000 for fewer HCFA violations.

In describing the study's conclusions, Gerald E. Smith and Thomas T. Nagle observe:

> The price DataCare originally proposed was well below the estimated value the customer would receive by adopting the new service, and well below the approximate price customers would be willing to pay if they were fully informed of the value of the new service. The study led to a substantial revision in pricing strategy and the marketing plan of DataCare's new service.[20]

As the DataCare case illustrates, the business marketing strategist can secure a competitive advantage by emphasizing a value-based approach and by developing the tools to document and communicate the unique value that its products and services create for customers in each market segment.[21]

Elasticity Varies by Market Segment   Price elasticity of demand measures the degree to which customers are sensitive to price changes. Specifically, **price elasticity of demand** refers to the rate of percentage change in quantity demanded attributable to a percentage change in price. Price elasticity of demand is not the same at all prices. A business marketer contemplating a change in price must understand the elasticity of demand. For example, total revenue (price times quantity) *increases* if price is decreased and demand is price elastic, whereas revenue *falls* if the price is decreased and demand is price inelastic. Many factors influence the price elasticity of demand—the ease with which customers can compare alternatives and switch suppliers, the importance of the product in the cost structure of the customer's product, and the value that the product represents to a customer.

Satisfied Customers Are Less Price Sensitive   Recent research demonstrates that highly satisfied customers are less sensitive to prices, compared with those who have a moderate level of customer satisfaction.[22] This relationship is particularly strong

---

[20]Ibid., p. 23.

[21]Werner Reinartz and Wolfgang Ulaga, "How to Sell Services More Profitability," *Harvard Business Review* 86 (May 2008): pp. 91–96.

[22]Ruth Maria Stock, "Can Customer Satisfaction Decrease Price Sensitivity in Business-to-Business Marketing?" *Journal of Business-to-Business Marketing* 12 (3, 2005): pp. 59–85.

for purchase decisions that involve a high level of product/service complexity and a high degree of customization. Thus, reduced customer price sensitivity represents an important payoff to a business marketer for developing a customized solution for the customer.

Search Behavior and Switching Costs The price sensitivity of buyers increases— and a firm's pricing latitude decreases—to the degree that

- Organizational buyers can easily shop around and assess the relative performance and price of alternatives. Purchasing managers in many firms use information technology to track supplier prices on a global basis.

- The product is one for which it is easy to make price comparisons. For example, it is easier to compare alternative photocopiers than it is to compare specialized manufacturing equipment options.

- Buyers can switch from one supplier to another without incurring additional costs. As Chapter 4 highlights, low switching costs allow a buyer to focus on minimizing the cost of a particular transaction.[23]

End Use Important insights can be secured by answering this question: How important is the business marketer's product as an input into the total cost of the end product? If the business marketer's product has an insignificant effect on cost, demand is likely inelastic. Consider this example:

> A manufacturer of precision electronic components was contemplating an across-the-board price decrease to increase sales. However, an item analysis of the product line revealed that some of its low-volume components had exotic applications. A technical customer used the component in an ultrasonic testing apparatus that was sold for $8,000 a unit. This fact prompted the electronics manufacturer to raise the price of the item. Ironically, the firm then experienced a temporary surge of demand for the item as purchasing agents stocked up in anticipation of future price increases.[24]

Of course, the marketer must temper this estimate by analyzing the costs, availability, and suitability of substitutes. Generally, when the industrial product is an important but low-cost input into the end product, price is less important than quality and delivery reliability. When, however, the product input represents a larger part of the final product's total cost, changes in price may have an important effect on the demand for both the final product and the input. When demand in the final consumer market is price elastic, a reduction in the price of the end item (for example, a personal computer) that is caused by a price reduction of a component (for example, a microprocessor) generates an increase in demand for the final product (personal computer) and, in turn, for the industrial product (microprocessor).

End-Market Focus Because the demand for many industrial products is derived from the demand for the product of which they are a part, a strong end-user focus

---

[23]Dolan, "How Do You Know When the Price Is Right?" pp. 178–179.

[24]Reed Moyer and Robert J. Boewadt, "The Pricing of Industrial Goods," *Business Horizons* 14 (June 1971): pp. 27–34; see also George Rostky, "Unveiling Market Segments with Technical Focus Research," *Business Marketing* 71 (October 1986): pp. 66–69.

is needed. The marketer can benefit by examining the trends and changing fortunes of important final consumer markets. Different sectors of the market grow at different rates, confront different levels of competition, and face different short-run and long-run challenges. A downturn in the economy does not fall equally on all sectors. Pricing decisions demand a two-tiered market focus—on organizational customers and on final-product customers. Thus, business marketers will have more success in raising prices to customers who are prospering than to customers who are hard pressed.

Value-Based Segmentation   The value customers assign to a firm's offering can vary by market segment because the same industrial product may serve different purposes for different customers. This underscores the important role of market segmentation in pricing strategies. Take Sealed Air Corporation, the innovative supplier of protective packaging, including coated air bubbles.[25] The company recognized that for some applications, substitutes were readily available. But for other applications, Sealed Air had an enormous advantage—for example, its packaging materials offered superior cushioning for heavy items with long shipping cycles. By identifying those applications where the firm had a clear advantage and understanding the unique value differential in each setting, marketing managers were ideally equipped to tackle product-line expansion and pricing decisions and to ignite Sealed Air's remarkable revenue growth for nearly two decades.

Cost Determinants

Business marketers often pursue a strong internal orientation; they base prices on their own costs, reaching the selling price by calculating unit costs and adding a percentage profit. A strict cost-plus pricing philosophy overlooks customer perceptions of value, competition, and the interaction of volume and profit. Many progressive firms, such as Canon, Toyota, and Hewlett-Packard (H-P), use target costing to capture a significant competitive advantage.

Target Costing[26]   **Target costing** features a design-to-cost philosophy that begins by examining market conditions: The firm identifies and targets the most attractive market segments. It then determines what level of quality and types of product attributes are required to succeed in each segment, given a predetermined target price and volume level. According to Robin Cooper and Regine Slagmulder, to set the target price, the business marketer has to understand the customer's perception of value: "A company can raise selling prices only if the perceived value of the new product exceeds not only that of the product's predecessor, but also that of competing products."[27]

Once the target selling price and target profit margins have been established, the firm calculates the allowable cost. The strategic cost-reduction challenge isolates the profit shortfall that occurs if the product designers are unable to achieve the allowable cost. The value of distinguishing the allowable cost from the target cost lies in the pressure that this exercise exerts on the product-development team and the company's suppliers. To transmit the competitive cost pressure *it* faces to its suppliers, the firm then breaks down the target price of a new product into a cascade of

[25]Dolan, "How Do You Know When the Price Is Right?" pp. 176–177.

[26]This section is based on Robin Cooper and Regine Slagmulder, "Develop Profitable New Products with Target Costing," *Sloan Management Review* 40 (Summer 1999): pp. 23–33.

[27]Ibid., p. 26.

target costs for each component or function. For example, the major functions of an automobile include the engine, transmission, cooling system, and audio system.

A Profit-Management Tool   Toyota used target costing to reduce the price of its recently modified Camry model and did so while offering as standard equipment certain features that were expensive options on the model it replaced. Similarly, Canon used target costing to develop its breakthrough personal copier that transformed the photocopier industry.[28] Rather than a cost-control technique, Japanese managers who pioneered the approach view target costing as a profit-management tool. As Robin Cooper and W. Bruce Chew assert, "The task is to compute the costs that must not be exceeded if acceptable margins from specific products at specific price points are to be guaranteed."[29]

Classifying Costs[30]   The target costing approach stresses why the marketer must know which costs are relevant to the pricing decision and how these costs fluctuate with volume and over time; they must be considered in relation to demand, competition, and pricing objectives. Product costs are crucial in projecting the profitability of individual products as well as of the entire product line. Proper classification of costs is essential.

The goals of a cost classification system are to (1) properly classify cost data into their fixed and variable components and (2) properly link them to the activity causing them. The manager can then analyze the effects of volume and, more important, identify sources of profit. The following cost concepts are instrumental in the analysis:

1. **Direct traceable or attributable costs:** Costs, fixed or variable, are incurred by and solely for a particular product, customer, or sales territory (for example, raw materials).

2. **Indirect traceable costs:** Costs, fixed or variable, can be traced to a product, customer, or sales territory (for example, general plant overhead may be indirectly assigned to a product).

3. **General costs:** Costs support a number of activities that cannot be objectively assigned to a product on the basis of a direct physical relationship (for example, the administrative costs of a sales district).

General costs rarely change because an item is added or deleted from the product line. Marketing, production, and distribution costs must all be classified. When developing a new line or when deleting or adding an item to an existing line, the marketer must grasp the cost implications:

- What proportion of the product cost is accounted for by purchases of raw materials and components from suppliers?

- How do costs vary at differing levels of production?

[28]Jean-Phillipe Deschamps and P. Ranganath Nayak, *Product Juggernauts: How Companies Mobilize to Generate a Stream of Market Winners* (Boston: Harvard Business School Press, 1995), pp. 119–149.

[29]Robin Cooper and W. Bruce Chew, "Control Tomorrow's Costs through Today's Designs," *Harvard Business Review* 74 (January–February 1996): pp. 88–97.

[30]Kent B. Monroe, *Pricing: Making Profitable Decisions* (New York: McGraw-Hill, 1979), pp. 52–57; see also Nagle, *The Strategy and Tactics of Pricing*, pp. 14–43.

- Based on the forecasted level of demand, can economies of scale be expected?

- Does our firm enjoy cost advantages over competitors?

- How does the "experience effect" impact our cost projections?

Competition

Competition establishes an upper limit on price. An individual industrial firm's degree of latitude in pricing depends heavily on how organizational buyers perceive the product's level of differentiation. Price is only one component of the cost/benefit equation; the marketer can gain a differential advantage over competitors on many dimensions other than physical product characteristics—reputation, technical expertise, delivery reliability, and related factors. Regis McKenna contends, "Even if a company manufactures commodity-like products, it can differentiate the products through the service and support it offers, or by target marketing. It can leave its commodity mentality in the factory, and bring a mentality of diversity to the marketplace."[31] In addition to assessing the product's degree of differentiation in various market segments, one must ask how competitors will respond to particular pricing decisions.

Hypercompetitive Rivalries   Some strategy experts emphasize that traditional patterns of competition in stable environments is being replaced by hypercompetitive rivalries in a rapidly changing environment.[32] In a stable environment, a company could create a fairly rigid strategy designed to accommodate long-term conditions. The firm's strategy focused on sustaining its own strategic advantage and establishing equilibrium where less-dominant firms accepted a secondary status.

In hypercompetitive environments, successful companies pursue strategies that create temporary advantage and destroy the advantages of rivals by constantly disrupting the market's equilibrium. For example, Intel continually disrupts the equilibrium of the microprocessor industry sector, and Hewlett-Packard stirs up the computer printer business by its consistent drives to lower price points. Moreover, the Internet provides customers with real-time access to a wealth of information that drives the prices of many products lower. Leading firms in hypercompetitive environments constantly seek out new sources of advantage, further escalating competition and contributing to hypercompetition.

Consider the hypercompetitive rivalries in high-technology markets. Firms that sustain quality and that are the first to hit the next-lower strategic price point enjoy a burst of volume and an expansion of market share. For example, Hewlett-Packard has ruthlessly pursued the next-lower price point in its printer business, even as it cannibalized its own sales and margins.[33]

Gauging Competitive Response   To predict the response of competitors, the marketer can first benefit by examining the cost structure and strategy of both direct competitors and producers of potential substitutes. The marketer can draw on public statements and records (for example, annual reports) to form rough estimates.

[31]Regis McKenna, *Relationship Marketing* (Reading, MA: Addison-Wesley, 1991), pp. 178–179.

[32]D'Aveni, *Hypercompetitive Rivalries*, pp. 149–170.

[33]Geoffrey A. Moore, *Inside the Tornado: Marketing Strategies from Silicon Valley's Cutting Edge* (New York: HarperCollins, 1995), pp. 84–85.

TABLE 14.2	SELECTED COST COMPARISON ISSUES: FOLLOWERS VERSUS THE PIONEER
Technology/economies of scale	Followers may benefit by using more current production technology than the pioneer or by building a plant with a larger scale of operations.
Product/market knowledge	Followers may learn from the pioneer's mistakes by analyzing the competitor's product, hiring key personnel, or identifying through market research the problems and unfulfilled expectations of customers and channel members.
Shared experience	Compared with the pioneer, followers may be able to gain advantages on certain cost elements by sharing operations with other parts of the company.
Experience of suppliers	Followers, together with the pioneer, benefit from cost reductions achieved by outside suppliers of components or production equipment.

SOURCE: Adapted from George S. Day and David B. Montgomery, "Diagnosing the Experience Curve," *Journal of Marketing* 47 (Spring 1983): pp. 48–49.

Competitors that have ascended the learning curve may have lower costs than those just entering the industry and beginning the climb. An estimate of the cost structure is valuable when gauging how well competitors can respond to price reductions and when projecting the pattern of prices in the future.

Under certain conditions, however, followers into a market may confront lower initial costs than did the pioneer. Why? Some of the reasons are highlighted in Table 14.2. By failing to recognize potential cost advantages of late entrants, the business marketer can dramatically overstate cost differences.

The market strategy competing sellers use is also important here. Competitors are more sensitive to price reductions that threaten those market segments they deem important. They learn of price reductions earlier when their market segments overlap. Of course, competitors may choose not to follow a price decrease, especially if their products enjoy a differentiated position. Rather than matching competitors' price cuts, one successful steel company reacts to the competitive challenge by offering customized products and technical assistance to its customers.[34] Later in the chapter, special attention is given to this question: How should you respond to price attacks by competitors?

The manager requires a grasp of objectives, demand, cost, competition, and legal factors (discussed later) to approach the multidimensional pricing decision. Price setting is not an act but an ongoing process.

Pricing across the Product Life Cycle

What price should be assigned to a distinctly new industrial product or service? When an item is added to an existing product line, how should it be priced in relation to products already in the line?

---

[34]Arun Sharma, R. Krishnan, and Dhruv Grewal, "Value Creation in Markets: A Critical Area of Focus for Business-to-Business Markets," *Industrial Marketing Management* 30 (June 2001): pp. 397–398.

Pricing New Products

The strategic decision of pricing new products can be best understood by examining the policies at the boundaries of the continuum—from **skimming** (high initial price) to **penetration** (low initial price). Consider again the pricing strategies of DuPont and Dow Chemical. Whereas DuPont assigns an initial high price to new products to generate immediate profits or to recover R&D expenditures, Dow follows a low-price strategy with the objective of gaining market share.

In evaluating the merits of skimming versus penetration, the marketer must again examine price from the buyer's perspective. This approach, asserts Joel Dean, "recognizes that the upper limit is the price that will produce the minimum acceptable rate of return on the investment of a sufficiently large number of prospects."[35] This is especially important in pricing new products because the potential profits to buyers of a new machine tool, for example, will vary by market segment, and these market segments may differ in the minimum rate of return that will induce them to invest in the machine tool.

Skimming   A skimming approach, appropriate for a distinctly new product, provides an opportunity to profitably reach market segments that are not sensitive to the high initial price. As a product ages, as competitors enter the market, and as organizational buyers become accustomed to evaluating and purchasing the product, demand becomes more price elastic. Joel Dean refers to the policy of skimming at the outset, followed by penetration pricing as the product matures, as **time segmentation**.[36] Skimming enables the marketer to capture early profits, then reduce the price to reach more price-sensitive segments. It also enables the innovator to recover high developmental costs more quickly.

Robert Dolan and Abel Jeuland demonstrate that during the innovative firm's monopoly period, skimming is optimal if the demand curve is stable over time (no diffusion) and if production costs decline with accumulated volume. A penetration policy is optimal if there is a relatively high repeat purchase rate for nondurable goods or if a durable good's demand is characterized by diffusion.[37]

Penetration   A penetration policy is appropriate when there is (1) high price elasticity of demand, (2) strong threat of imminent competition, and (3) opportunity for a substantial reduction in production costs as volume expands. Drawing on the experience effect, a firm that can quickly gain substantial market share and experience can gain a strategic advantage over competitors. The feasibility of this strategy increases with the potential size of the future market. By taking a large share of new sales, a firm can gain experience when the growth rate of the market is large. Of course, the value of additional market share differs markedly between industries and often among products, markets, and competitors in an industry.[38] Factors to be assessed

---

[35]Joel Dean, "Pricing Policies for New Products," *Harvard Business Review* 54 (November–December 1976): p. 151.

[36]Ibid., p. 152.

[37]Robert J. Dolan and Abel P. Jeuland, "Experience Curves and Dynamic Demand Models: Implications for Optimal Pricing Strategies," *Journal of Marketing* 45 (Winter 1981): pp. 52–62; see also, Paul Ingenbleek, Marion Debruyne, Rudd T. Frambach, and Theo M. Verhallen, "Successful New Product Pricing Practices: A Contingency Approach," *Marketing Letters* 14 (December 2004): pp. 289–304.

[38]Robert Jacobson and David A. Aaker, "Is Market Share All that It's Cracked Up to Be?" *Journal of Marketing* 49 (Fall 1985): pp. 11–22; and Yoram Wind and Vijay Mahajan, "Market Share: Concepts, Findings, and Directions for Future Research," in *Review of Marketing 1981*, Ben M. Enis and Kenneth J. Roering, eds. (Chicago: American Marketing Association, 1981), pp. 31–42.

INSIDE BUSINESS MARKETING

Understanding the Economic Value of New Products

Measuring the economic value that a product delivers to different customer segments is an essential ingredient in launching successful new products. Because customers will compare a new product offering to the next-best alternative, the marketing strategist must also understand the value delivered by competitors. Experts suggest that the most effective way to determine the value of a new product is through in-depth surveys. Here central attention is given to learning how a company's product affects the customer's business by reducing costs and/or by increasing revenue. The results provide an important foundation for effective pricing and responsive sales strategies. For example, after uncovering the value of a new software product, the firm, which was planning on a $99 price, decided the correct price was $349. Sales results exceeded expectations.

SOURCE: John Hogan and Tom Lucke, "Driving Growth with New Products: Common Pricing Traps to Avoid," *Journal of Business Strategy* 27 (1, 2006): pp. 54–58.

in determining the value of additional market share include the investment requirements, potential benefits of experience, expected market trends, likely competitive reaction, and short- and long-term profit implications.

Product Line Considerations   The contemporary industrial firm with a long product line faces the complex problem of balancing prices in the product mix. Firms extend their product lines because the demands for various products are interdependent, because the costs of producing and marketing those items are interdependent, or both.[39] A firm may add to its product line—or even develop a new product line—to fit more precisely the needs of a particular market segment. If both the demand and the costs of individual product-line items are interrelated, production and marketing decisions about one item inevitably influence both the revenues and costs of the others.

Are specific product-line items substitutes or complements? Will changing the price of one item enhance or retard the usage rate of this or other products in key market segments? Should a new product be priced high at the outset to protect other product-line items (for example, potential substitutes) and to give the firm time to revamp other items in the line? Such decisions require knowledge of demand, costs, competition, and strategic marketing objectives.

Legal Considerations

Because the business marketer deals with various classifications of customers and intermediaries as well as various types of discounts (for example, quantity discounts), an awareness of legal considerations in price administration is vital. The **Robinson-Patman Act** holds that it is unlawful to "discriminate in price between different purchasers of commodities of like grade and quality . . . where the effect of such discrimination may be substantially to lessen competition or tend to create a monopoly, or to injure, destroy, or prevent competition. . . ." Price differentials are permitted,

[39]Monroe, *Pricing*, p. 143; see also Robert J. Dolan, "The Same Make, Many Models Problem: Managing the Product Line," in *A Strategic Approach to Business Marketing*, Robert E. Spekman and David T. Wilson, eds. (Chicago: American Marketing Association, 1985), pp. 151–159.

but they must be based on cost differences or the need to "meet competition."[40] Cost differentials are difficult to justify, and clearly defined policies and procedures are needed in price administration. Such cost-justification guidelines are useful not only when making pricing decisions but also when providing a legal defense against price discrimination charges.

Responding to Price Attacks by Competitors[41]

Rather than emphasizing the lowest price, most business marketers prefer to compete by providing superior value. However, across industries, marketing managers face constant pressure from competitors who are willing to use price concessions to gain market share or entry into a profitable market segment. When challenged by an aggressive competitor, many managers immediately want to fight back and match the price cut. However, because price wars can be quite costly, experts suggest a more systematic process that considers the long-run strategic consequences versus the short-term benefits of the pricing decision. Managers should never set the price simply to meet some immediate sales goal, but, instead, to enhance long-term project goals. George E. Cressman Jr. and Thomas T. Nagle, consultants from the Strategic Pricing Group, Inc., observe: "Pricing is like playing chess; players who fail to envision a few moves ahead will almost always be beaten by those who do."[42]

Evaluating a Competitive Threat

Figure 14.4 provides a systematic framework for developing a strategy when one or more competitors have announced price cuts or have introduced new products that offer more value to at least some of your customers. To determine whether to reduce price to meet a competitor's challenge, four important questions should be addressed.

1. *Is there a response that would cost you less than the preventable sales loss?* (See center of Figure 14.4.) Before responding to a competitor's price reduction, the marketing strategist should ask: Do the benefits justify the costs? If responding to a price change is less costly than losing sales, a price move may be the appropriate decision. On the other hand, if the competitor threatens only a small slice of expected sales, the revenue loss from ignoring the threat may be much lower than the costs of retaliation. Indeed, when the threat centers on a small segment of customers, the cost of reducing prices for *all* customers to prevent the small loss is likely to be prohibitively expensive.

   If a price response is required, the strategist should focus the firm's competitive retaliation on the most cost-effective actions. The cost of retaliating to a price

[40]For a comprehensive discussion of the Robinson-Patman Act, see Monroe, *Pricing*, pp. 249–267; see also James J. Ritterskamp Jr. and William A. Hancock, "Legal Aspects of Purchasing," in *The Purchasing Handbook*, Harold E. Fearon, Donald W. Dobler, and Kenneth H. Killen, eds. (New York: McGraw-Hill, 1993), pp. 529–544.

[41]This section is based on George E. Cressman Jr. and Thomas T. Nagle, "How to Manage an Aggressive Competitor," *Business Horizons* 45 (March–April 2002), pp. 23–30.

[42]Ibid., p. 24.

FIGURE 14.4 | **EVALUATING A COMPETITIVE THREAT**

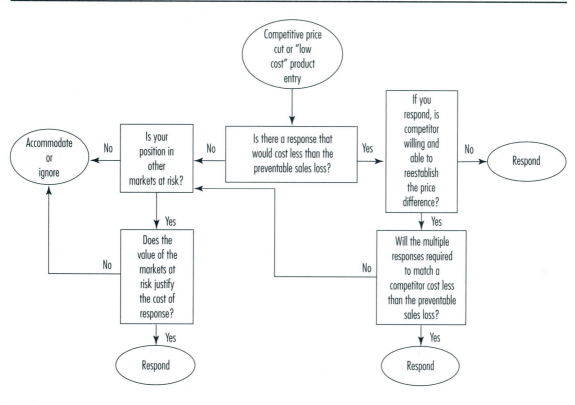

SOURCE: Reprinted from George E. Cressman, Jr. and Thomas T. Nagle, "How to Manage an Aggressive Competitor," *Business Horizons* 45 (March–April 2002): p. 25, Copyright © 2002, with permission from Elsevier.

threat can be reduced by incorporating one or more of the following elements into the pricing action:

- Center reactive price cuts only on those customers likely to be attracted to the competitor's offer (for example, rather than cutting the price of its flagship Pentium chip, Intel offered the lower-priced Cerrus chip for the cost-conscious market segment).

- Center reactive price cuts on a particular geographic region, distribution channel, or product line where the competitor has the most to lose from a price reduction (for example, Kodak might respond to a challenge from Fuji with price promotions in Japan where Fuji enjoys attractive margins and a larger market share).

- Capitalize on any competitive advantages to increase the value of your offer as an alternative to matching the price (for example, a firm that has better-quality products can respond by offering a longer warranty period to customers).

2. *If you respond, is the competitor willing and able to merely reduce the price again to restore the price difference?* Matching a price cut will be ineffective if the

competitor simply reestablishes the differential by a further price reduction. According to Cressman and Nagle, to determine the appropriate course, the strategist should attempt to understand why the competitor chose to compete on price in the first place: "If the competitor has little market share relative to the share that could be gained with a price advantage, and has no other way to attract customers, then there is little to lose from bringing the price down as low as necessary to gain sales."[43] This is especially true when competitors have made huge investments in areas such as R&D that largely represent sunk costs. Under such conditions, accommodation—market share loss—is less costly than fighting a price war.

3. *Will the multiple responses that may be required to match the competitor's price still cost less than the avoidable sales loss?* A single response is rarely enough to stop price moves by competitors that are struggling to establish a market position. Price competition is particularly likely in industries where entry requires a significant investment in fixed manufacturing capacity. Rather than idling manufacturing capacity, a competitor may be willing to aggressively pursue sales that will make at least some contribution to covering fixed costs. If competitors are likely to continue to cut prices, the best strategy for the defender is to:

   • Allow the competitor to win where it is least damaging to profitability, such as in more price-sensitive, lower-margin customer segments (for example, government contracts).

   • Create barriers that make it more difficult for competitors to reach less price-sensitive, more profitable customer segments (for example, build switching costs by developing unique solutions for the most valued customers).

4. *Is your position in other markets (product or geographic) at risk if the competitor increases market share? Does the value of all the markets that are at risk justify the cost of the strategy response?* Before responding with a price reduction, the business marketer must clearly define the long-run strategic benefits as well as the risks of a particular strategy response. The benefits might include additional sales in a particular market in the future, or immediate sales gains of complementary products (such as software, peripherals, and services associated with the sale of a computer), or a lower cost of future sales resulting from increased volume.

Understanding the Rules of Competitive Strategy

Dealing effectively with an aggressive competitor requires more than a willingness to fight—it requires a competitive strategy and an understanding of when the appropriate response to a competitor's price cut is to ignore it, accommodate it, or retaliate. George E. Cressman and Thomas T. Nagle offer these guidelines for competitive strategy development:

• Never participate in a competitive engagement you cannot win. Fight those battles where you have competitive strength, and avoid those where you are clearly at a disadvantage. . . .

[43]Ibid., p. 27.

- Always participate in competitive engagements from a position of advantage. Don't fight by competitors' rules (which they select for their advantage); use what is advantageous for you.[44]

Competitive Bidding

A significant volume of business commerce is transacted through competitive bidding. Rather than relying on a specific list price, the business marketer must develop a price, or a bid, to meet a customer's particular product or service requirements.

Government and other public agencies buy almost exclusively through competitive bidding. Competitive bidding in private industry centers on two types of purchases. One is nonstandard materials, complex fabricated products where design and manufacturing methods vary, and products made to the buyer's specifications. These types of items have no generally established market level. Competitive bids enable the purchaser to evaluate the appropriateness of the prices.[45] Second, many firms are using reverse auctions, where many sellers bid for an order from a single buyer (see Chapter 2). GE, for example, uses reverse auctions to buy both direct (for example, standard component parts) and indirect materials (for example, maintenance items, office supplies), making roughly a third of its total purchasing expenditures in this fashion. Typically, reverse auctions are best suited for product categories that buyers view as commodities.[46] Competitive bidding may be either closed or open.

Closed Bidding

Closed bidding, often used by business and governmental buyers, involves a formal invitation to potential suppliers to submit written, sealed bids. All bids are opened and reviewed at the same time, and the contract is generally awarded to the lowest bidder who meets desired specifications. The low bidder is not guaranteed the contract—buyers often make awards to the lowest responsible bidder; the ability of alternative suppliers to perform remains part of the bidding process.

Online Sealed Bid Format   There is also a sealed bid format used for online auctions. The term *sealed* means that only one supplier and the buyer have access to the details of the bid. According to Sandy Jap:

> The bid process is asynchronous in the sense that the buyer and supplier take turns viewing the bid. The buyer posts the RFP (request for purchase) electronically, the supplier submits a bid, and the buyer views the submitted bid. The buyer then either makes a decision after viewing all bids or, if multiple rounds of bidding are involved, may respond to the supplier, who then resubmits a new bid.[47]

[44]Ibid., p. 30.

[45]Stuart St. P. Slatter, "Strategic Marketing Variables under Conditions of Competitive Bidding," *Strategic Management Journal* 11 (May–June 1990): pp. 309–317; see also Arthur H. Mendel and Roger Poueymirou, "Pricing," in *The Purchasing Handbook*, Harold E. Fearon, Donald W. Dobler, and Kenneth H. Killen, eds. (New York: McGraw-Hill, 1993), pp. 201–227.

[46]See, for example, C. M. Sashi and Bay O'Leary, "The Role of Internet Auctions in the Expansion of B2B Markets," *Industrial Marketing Management* 31 (February 2002): pp. 103–110.

[47]Sandy D. Jap, "Online Reverse Auctions: Issues, Themes, and Prospects for the Future," *Journal of the Academy of Marketing Science* 30 (fall 2002): p. 507.

Open Bidding

Open bidding is more informal and allows suppliers to make offers (oral and written) up to a certain date. The buyer may deliberate with several suppliers throughout the bidding process. Open bidding may be particularly appropriate when specific requirements are hard to define rigidly or when the products and services of competing suppliers vary substantially.

In some buying situations, prices may be negotiated. Complex technical requirements or uncertain product specifications may lead buying organizations first to evaluate the capabilities of competing firms and then to negotiate the price and the form of the product-service offering. Negotiated pricing is appropriate for procurement in both the commercial and the governmental sectors of the business market (see Chapter 2).

Online Open Bid Format   When conducted online, open bidding takes a different form. Here suppliers are invited to bid simultaneously during a designated time period for the contract. In contrast to the sealed-bid format, all suppliers and the buyer view the bids at the same time. The goal, of course, is to push the price down. Sandy Jap, who has conducted extensive research on reverse auctions, argues that the open-bid format, when used regularly, can damage buyer-supplier relationships:

> This harm occurs because open-bid formats reveal pricing information to competition, which erodes the supplier's bargaining power. Open-bid formats also place a more explicit focus on price, a short-term variable that is usually the focus of transaction-oriented exchanges rather than relational exchanges. When buyers use an open-bid format amid a context in which relational exchanges are emphasized, they send an inconsistent message to suppliers and may foster distrust.[48]

Recent research on the use of online reverse auctions suggests that the larger the number of bidders, the larger the economic stakes, and the less visible the price in an auction, the more positive is the impact on the buyer-seller relationship.[49] However, large price drops over the course of the event have a detrimental effect on the buyer-seller relationship.

Strategies for Competitive Bidding

Because making bids is costly and time-consuming, firms should choose potential bid opportunities with care. Contracts offer differing levels of profitability according to the bidding firm's related technical expertise, past experience, and objectives. Therefore, careful screening is required to isolate contracts that offer the most promise.[50] Having isolated a project opportunity, the marketer must now estimate the probabilities of winning the contract at various prices. Assuming that the contract is awarded to the lowest bidder, the chances of the firm winning the contract decline as the bid price increases. How will competitors bid?

---

[48]Ibid., p. 514.

[49]Sandy Jap, "The Impact of Online Reverse Auction Design on Buyer-Seller Relationships," *Journal of Marketing* 71 (January 2007): pp. 146–159.

[50]For example, see Paul D. Boughton, "The Competitive Bidding Process: Beyond Probability Models," *Industrial Marketing Management* 16 (May 1987): pp. 87–94.

A Strategic Approach to Reverse Auctions[51]   Pricing experts suggest that customers use reverse auctions for two purposes: (1) to purchase commodity products at the lowest possible price and (2) to tempt suppliers of differentiated products to sacrifice their profit margins in the heat of bidding. If a firm's offering is not highly differentiated from competition, participating in an auction may represent the only choice. However, to minimize the risk of winning an unprofitable bid, a careful estimate should be made of the true incremental cost of supplying the customer, including the costs associated with special terms and conditions as well as unique technical, marketing, and sales support. This analysis will provide the business marketing strategist with a "walk-away" price.

In contrast, if a firm's offering provides significant value to customers relative to competition, John Bloomer, Joe Zale, and John Hogan, consultants at the Strategic Pricing Group, recommend the following decisive tactics:[52]

1. "Preempt the auction: convince the buyer not to go forward with the auction because you have a unique value proposition and are not inclined to participate.

2. Manage the process: influence bid specifications and vendor qualification criteria.

3. Walk away: simply refuse to participate. . . ."

A strategic approach to reverse auctions, then, defines success as winning only those bids that are profitable and that do not undermine pricing for other products or for other customers.

Summary

At the outset, the business marketer must assign pricing its role in the firm's overall marketing strategy. Giving a particular industrial product or service, an "incorrect" price can trigger a chain of events that undermines the firm's market position, channel relationships, and product and personal selling strategies. Customer value represents a business customer's overall assessment of the utility of a relationship with a supplier based on benefits received and sacrifices made. Price is but one of the costs that buyers examine when considering the value of competing offerings. Thus, the marketer can profit by adopting a strong end-user focus that gives special attention to the way buyers trade off the costs and benefits of various products. Responsive pricing strategies can be developed by understanding the economic value that a product provides for a customer. Economic value represents the cost savings and/or revenue gains that customers realize by purchasing the firm's product instead of the next-best alternative. By understanding how customers in a market segment actually use a product or service and realize value from its use, the business marketer is ideally equipped to set the price and develop a responsive strategy.

[51]This discussion is based on John Bloomer, Joe Zale, and John E. Hogan, "Battling Powerful Procurement Groups: How to Profitably Participate in Reverse Auctions," *SPG Insights* (Fall 2004), pp. 1–3; accessed at http://www.strategicpricinggroup.com on August 1, 2008.
[52]Ibid., p. 2.

Price setting is a multidimensional decision. To establish a price, the manager must identify the firm's objectives and analyze the behavior of demand, costs, and competition. Hypercompetitive rivalries characterize the nature of competition in many high-technology industry sectors. Although this task is clouded with uncertainty, the industrial pricing decision must be approached actively rather than passively. For example, many business marketing firms use target costing to capture a competitive advantage. Likewise, by isolating demand, cost, or competitive patterns, the manager can gain insights into market behavior and neglected opportunities. Dealing effectively with an aggressive competitor requires more than a willingness to fight—it requires a competitive strategy and an understanding of when to ignore a price attack, when to accommodate it, and when to retaliate.

Competitive bidding, a unique feature of the business market, calls for a unique strategy. Again, carefully defined objectives are the cornerstone of strategy. These objectives, combined with a meticulous screening procedure, help the firm to identify projects that mesh with company capability.

Discussion Questions

1. Describe the core benefits and add-on benefits that FedEx provides to its business customers.

2. A Pac-10 university library recently purchased 60 personal computers from Hewlett-Packard. Illustrate how a purchasing specialist at the university could use a total cost-in-use approach in evaluating the value of the Hewlett-Packard offering in relation to the value provided by its rivals.

3. Explain why it is often necessary for the business marketer to develop a separate demand curve for various market segments. Would one total demand curve be better for making the industrial pricing decision? Explain.

4. Evaluate this statement: To move away from the commodity mentality, companies must view their products as customer solutions, and then sell the products on that basis.

5. Compare and contrast *commodity value versus differentiation value*, highlighting the significance of each in setting a price.

6. The XYZ Manufacturing Corporation has experienced a rather large decline in sales for its component parts. Mary Vantage, vice president of marketing, believes that a 10 percent price cut may get things going again. What factors should Mary consider before reducing the price of the components?

7. A business marketing manager often has great difficulty in arriving at the optimum price level for a product. First, describe the factors that complicate the pricing decision. Second, outline the approach you would follow in pricing an industrial product. Be as specific as possible.

8. Rather than time to market, Intel refers to the product development cycle for a new chip as "time to money." Andrew Grove, Intel's

legendary leader, said, "Speed is the only weapon we have." What pricing advantages issue from a rapid product development process?

9. If a competitor's price cut threatens only a small portion of expected sales, the sales loss from ignoring the threat is probably much less than the cost of retaliation. Agree or disagree? Explain.

10. Many companies, including GE, Quaker Oats, and United Technologies, report millions of dollars of savings from using reverse auctions rather than traditional purchasing methods. Of course, business marketing strategists fear that these auctions will transform their products and services into commodities. Propose particular strategies that marketing managers might follow to deal with this challenging situation.

Internet Exercise

1. Hill-Rom is a leading B2B firm that dominates a niche in the health-care industry. Go to http://www.hill-rom.com and, first, describe the products and services that Hill-Rom offers to hospitals. Next, describe how Hill-Rom products or solutions might reduce the total cost-in-use for a hospital.

Price Like a Retailer, Not a Widget Maker[53]

Parker Hannifin Corporation is a leading manufacturer of component parts used in aerospace, transportation, and manufacturing equipment. The company makes several hundred thousand parts—from heat-resistant seals for jet engines and components used in the space shuttle to steel valves that hoist buckets on cherry pickers. When Donald Washkewicz took over as chief executive, he came to an unnerving conclusion: the pricing approach that the company had followed for years was downright crazy.

For as long as anyone at the company could recall, the firm used this simple approach to determine the prices for its thousands of parts: Company managers would calculate how much it cost to make and deliver each product and then add a flat percentage on top, usually aiming for around a 35 percent margin. Across divisions, many managers liked this cost-plus approach because it was straightforward and gave them broad authority to negotiate prices with customers.

But the chief executive feels that the firm, which generates over $9 billion in annual revenues, may be severely restricting its profit growth. No matter how much a particular product is improved, the company often ends up charging the same premium that it would for a standard product. And if the company finds a way to make a product less expensively, it ultimately cuts the product's price as well. "I was actually losing sleep," recalls Donald Washkewicz, who believes that the company should stop thinking like a widget maker or a cost-plus price setter and start thinking like a retailer by determining prices by what customers are willing to pay.

Changing the firm's pricing approach, however, is a complex task. The company has tens of thousands of products—(1) some are high-volume commodities and there are large, formidable competitors; (2) some have unique features, fill niches in the market, and have limited competition; and (3) many are custom-designed for a single customer.

Discussion Questions

1. Describe the process that you would follow in performing an audit of the firm's product line to identify those products that represent the best and worst candidates for profit-margin expansion.

2. Provide a set of specific pricing guidelines that managers should apply as the traditional cost-plus approach is phased out and a value-based approach to pricing is implemented.

---

[53]Timothy Aeppel, "Seeking Perfect Prices, CEO Tears Up the Rules," *The Wall Street Journal Online*, March 27, 2007, accessed at http://online.wsj.com/public/us on May 18, 2008.

Business Marketing Communications: Advertising and Sales Promotion

Advertising supports and supplements personal selling efforts. The share of the marketing budget devoted to advertising is smaller in business than it is in consumer-goods marketing. A well-integrated business-to-business marketing communications program, however, can help make the overall marketing strategy more efficient and effective. After reading this chapter, you will understand:

1. the specific role of advertising in business marketing strategy.

2. the decisions that must be made when forming a business advertising program.

3. the business media options, including the powerful role of online advertising.

4. ways to measure business advertising effectiveness.

5. the role of trade shows in the business communications mix and how to measure trade show effectiveness.

Let's consider the vital role that marketing communications can assume in business marketing strategy by exploring the stunning success of Bomgar Corporation.[1] While working as a network engineer for an information technology integrator in Mississippi, Joel Bomgar grew tired of driving around the region, moving from client to client, and solving the same basic problem. So, Joel began to work on the original version of the Bomgar Box—a remote information technology support system delivered on an appliance owned and controlled by the customer. Once developed, he then recruited two college friends, created a Web site, and set out to launch the new product, targeting small and medium-sized businesses. Reflecting on this critical milestone for the business, Joel recalls his chief fears: "My entire advertising budget consisted of my personal debit card. How could I possibly compete with all the billion-dollar corporations out there?"[2]

Joel decided to use Google AdWords (that is, paid search engine advertising) to drive qualified customer prospects to the firm's new Web site. Joel and his team chose keywords and developed targeted messages that highlighted the important features that differentiate Bomgar's products from the competition, including ease of implementation and effective security controls. Patrick Norman, vice president of e-commerce for Bomgar, observes: "With Google, this guy in Mississippi who'd built this new technology was able to put it out there, and suddenly the world was open to him. That just doesn't happen with traditional media."[3] Once a foundation was established, Bomgar expanded the scope of its marketing strategy by running ads on the Google Content Network that reaches 75 percent of Internet users. Next the team used site targeting to display advertising on specific Web sites that are frequented by information technology professionals. By 2008, 4,000 corporate customers from all 50 states and 48 countries have chosen the Bomgar virtual support solution.[4] In addition to a wealth of mid-size enterprises, current customers include Humana, Ethan Allen, Nissan, and UnitedHealth Group.

Communication with existing and potential customers is vital to business marketing success. Experience has taught marketing managers that not even the best products sell themselves: The benefits, problem solutions, and cost efficiencies of those products must be effectively communicated to everyone who influences the purchase decision. As a result of the technical complexity of business products, the relatively small number of potential buyers, and the extensive negotiation process, the primary communication vehicle in business-to-business marketing is the salesperson. However, nonpersonal methods of communication, including advertising, catalogs, the Internet, and trade shows, have a unique and often crucial role in the communication process. To maximize the return on promotional spending, business-to-business firms are developing integrated marketing campaigns that align marketing communications strategies to strategic objectives.[5]

The focus of this chapter is fourfold: (1) to provide a clear understanding of the role of advertising in business marketing strategy; (2) to present a framework for structuring advertising decisions—a framework that integrates the decisions related to

---

[1]This example is based on Google Content Network: Success Stories, "Remote Control," accessed on August 1, 2008 at http://www.adwords.google.com.

[2]Ibid., p. 1.

[3]Ibid., pp. 2–3.

[4]"About Bomgar," accessed on August 1, 2008 at http://www.bomgar.com.

[5] Don Schultz and Heidi Schultz, *IMC—The Next Generation* (New York: McGraw-Hill, 2004).

objectives, budgets, messages, media, and evaluation; (3) to develop an understanding of each business-to-business advertising decision area; and (4) to evaluate the valuable role of online advertising and trade shows in the promotional mix.

The Role of Advertising

Integrated Communication Programs

Advertising and sales promotion are rarely used alone in the business-to-business setting but are intertwined with the total communications strategy—particularly personal selling. Personal and nonpersonal forms of communication interact to inform key buying influentials. The challenge for the business marketer is to create an advertising and sales promotion strategy that effectively blends with personal selling in order to meet sales and profit objectives. In addition, the advertising, online media, and sales promotion tools must be integrated; that is, a comprehensive program of media and sales promotion methods must be coordinated to achieve the desired results.

Enhancing Sales Effectiveness

Effective advertising can make personal selling more productive. John Morrill examined nearly 100,000 interviews on 26 product lines at 30,000 buying locations in order to study the effect of business-to-business advertising on salesperson effectiveness.[6] He concluded that dollar sales per salesperson call were significantly higher when customers had been exposed to advertising. In addition to increasing company and product awareness, research indicates that buyers who had been exposed to a supplier's advertisement rated the supplier's salespeople substantially higher on product knowledge, service, and enthusiasm.[7] A primary role of business-to-business advertising is to enhance the reputation of the supplier.

Business-to-business advertising also increases sales efficiency. Increased spending on advertising leads to greater brand awareness for industrial products, which translates into larger market shares and higher profits.[8] One study used a tightly controlled experimental design to measure the effect of business-to-business advertising on sales and profits. For one product, sales, gross margin, and net profit were significantly higher with advertising, compared with the pretest period with no advertising.[9] In fact, gross margins ranged from four to six times higher with advertising than with no advertising.

Increased Sales Efficiency

The effect of advertising on the marketing program's overall efficiency is evidenced in two ways. First, business suppliers frequently need to remind actual and potential buyers of their products or make them aware of new products or services. Although

---

[6]John E. Morrill, "Industrial Advertising Pays Off," *Harvard Business Review* 48 (March–April 1970): pp. 4–14.

[7]Ibid., p. 6. For a comprehensive study of the relationship between brand awareness and brand preference, see Eunsang Yoon and Valerie Kijewski, "The Brand Awareness-to-Preference Link in Business Markets: A Study of the Semiconductor Manufacturing Industry," *Journal of Business-to-Business Marketing* 2 (4, 1995): pp. 7–36.

[8]"New Proof of Industrial Ad Values," *Marketing and Media Decisions* (February 1981): p. 64.

[9]"ARF/ABP Release Final Study Findings," *Business Marketing* 72 (May 1987): p. 55.

these objectives could be partially accomplished through personal selling, the costs of reaching a vast group of buyers would be prohibitive. Carefully targeted advertising extends beyond the salesperson's reach to unidentified buying influentials. A properly placed advertisement can reach hundreds of buying influentials for only a few cents each; the average cost of a business sales call is currently more than $200.[10] Sales call costs are determined by the salesperson's wages, travel and entertainment costs, and fringe benefits costs. If these costs total $800 per day and a salesperson can make four calls per day, then each call costs $200. Second, advertising appears to make all selling activities more effective. Advertising interacts effectively with all communication and selling activities, and it can boost efficiency for the entire marketing expenditure.

Creating Awareness

From a communications standpoint, the buying process takes potential buyers sequentially from unawareness of a product or supplier to awareness, to brand preference, to conviction that a particular purchase will fulfill their requirements, and, ultimately, to actual purchase. Business advertising often creates awareness of the supplier and the supplier's products. Sixty-one percent of the design engineers returning an inquiry card from a magazine ad indicated that they were unaware of the company that advertised before seeing the ad.[11] Business advertising may also make some contribution to creating preference for the product—all cost-effectively. In addition, advertising can create a corporate identity or image. Hewlett-Packard, Dell, IBM, and others use ads in general business publications such as *Business Week* and even television advertising to trumpet the value of their brand and to develop desired perceptions in a broad audience.[12]

Interactive Marketing Communications

The Internet changes marketing communications from a one-way to a two-way process that permits the marketer and the consumer to more readily exchange information.[13] Consumers receive and provide information by navigating Web sites, specifying their preferences, and communicating with business marketers.[14] To illustrate, Intel rolled out its new Xeon server processors through an online program called "Four Days of Dialogue."[15] Rather than renting conference facilities and asking customers to travel to a particular location to see the product, chip architects at Intel provided a 1-hour online session on four consecutive days to introduce and describe the technology. Customers could log in to ask questions or simply to monitor the

[10]Erin Anderson and Bob Trinkle, *Outsourcing the Sales Function: The Real Costs of Field Sales* (Mason, OH: Thomson Higher Education, 2005).

[11]Raymond E. Herzog, "How Design Engineering Activity Affects Supplies," *Business Marketing* 70 (November 1985): p. 143.

[12]David A. Aaker and Erich Joachimsthaler, "The Lure of Global Branding," *Harvard Business Review* 77 (November–December 1999): pp. 137–144.

[13]C. K. Prahalad and Venkat Ramaswamy, *The Future of Competition: Co-Creating Value with Customers* (Boston: Harvard Business School Press, 2004), pp. 1–17.

[14]David W. Stewart, "From Consumer Response to Active Consumer: Measuring the Effectiveness of Interactive Media," *Journal of the Academy of Marketing Science* 30 (Fall 2002): pp. 376–396.

[15]Beth Snyder Bulik, "B to B's Best Marketers 2007: Donald MacDonald, VP-Sales and Marketing Group, Intel Corp.," *B to B* (October 27, 2008), accessed at http://www.btobonline.com on July 29, 2008.

discussion. Intel received 22,000 unique visitors. According to Sandra Lopez, integrated marketing manager for business at Intel, the goal of the firm's online strategy is to "engage our audience in a continuous dialogue."[16] To advance this goal, Intel distributes its marketing messages throughout CNET.com (a product review forum for technology products), including blogs and reader forums.

What Business-to-Business Advertising Cannot Do

To develop an effective communications program, the business marketing manager must blend all communication tools (online and print formats) into an integrated program, using each tool where it is most effective. Business advertising quite obviously has limitations. Advertising cannot substitute for effective personal selling—it must supplement, support, and complement that effort. In the same way, personal selling is constrained by its costs and should not be used to create awareness or to disseminate information—tasks quite capably performed by advertising.

For many purchasing decisions, advertising alone cannot create product preference—this requires demonstration, explanation, and operational testing. Similarly, conviction and actual purchase can be ensured only by personal selling. Advertising has a supporting role in creating awareness, providing information, and uncovering important leads for salespeople; that is how the marketing manager must use it to be effective.

Managing Business-to-Business Advertising

The advertising decision model in Figure 15.1 shows the structural elements involved in managing business-to-business advertising. First, advertising is only one aspect of the entire marketing strategy and must be integrated with other components to achieve strategic goals. The advertising decision process begins with formulating advertising objectives, which are derived from marketing goals. From this formulation the marketer can determine how much it has to spend to achieve those goals. Then, specific communication messages are formulated to achieve the market behavior specified by the objectives. Equally important is evaluating and selecting the media used to reach the desired audience. The result is an integrated advertising campaign aimed at eliciting a specific attitude or behavior from the target group. The final, and critical, step is to evaluate the campaign's effectiveness.

Defining Advertising Objectives

Knowing what advertising must accomplish enables the manager to determine an advertising budget more accurately and provides a yardstick for evaluating advertising. In specifying advertising goals, the marketing manager must realize that (1) the advertising mission flows directly from the overall marketing strategy; advertising must fulfill a marketing strategy objective, and its goal must reflect the general aim and purpose of the entire strategy; and (2) the advertising program's objectives must respond

---

[16]Matthew Schwartz, "Ad Units Meet New Demands," B to B's Interactive Marketing Guide 2008, p. 17, accessed at http://www.btobonline.com on July 25, 2008.

FIGURE 15.1 | **THE DECISION STAGES FOR DEVELOPING THE BUSINESS-TO-BUSINESS ADVERTISING PROGRAM**

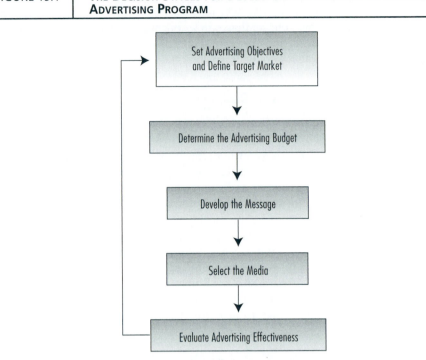

to the roles for which advertising is suited: creating awareness, providing information, influencing attitudes, and reminding buyers of company and product existence.

Written Objectives

An advertising objective must be measurable, realistic, and specify what is to be achieved and when. The objective must speak in unambiguous terms of a specific outcome. The purpose is to establish a single working direction for everyone involved in creating, coordinating, and evaluating the advertising program. Correctly conceived objectives set standards for evaluating the advertising effort. A specific objective might be "to increase from 15 percent (as measured in June 2010) to 30 percent (by June 2011) the proportion of general contractors associating 'energy efficiency' feature with our brand of commercial air conditioners." The objective directs the manager to create a message related to the major product benefit, using media that reaches general contractors. The objective also provides a way to measure accomplishment (awareness among 30 percent of the target audience).

Business advertising objectives frequently bear no direct relationship to specific dollar sales targets. Although dollar sales results would provide a "hard" measure of advertising accomplishment, it is often impossible to link advertising directly to sales. Personal selling, price, product performance, and competitive actions have a more direct relationship to sales levels, and it is almost impossible to sort out advertising's impact. Thus, advertising goals are typically stated in terms of *communication goals* such as brand awareness, recognition, and buyer attitudes. These goals can be measured; it is presumed that achieving them stimulates sales volume.

Target Audience   A significant task is specifying target audiences. Because a primary role of advertising is to reach buying influentials inaccessible to the salesperson, the business marketing manager must define the buying influential groups to be reached. Generally, each group of buying influentials is concerned with distinct product and service attributes and criteria, and the advertising must focus on these. Thus, the objectives must specify the intended audience and its relevant decision criteria.

Creative Strategy Statement   A final consideration is to specify the creative strategy statement. Once objectives and targets are established, the **creative strategy statement** provides guidelines for the company and advertising agency on how to position the product in the marketplace. Product position relates to how the target market perceives the product.

For example, if the commercial air conditioners cited earlier currently have an unfavorable product position with regard to energy efficiency but recent product development efforts have advanced performance, the firm might use the following creative strategy statement: "Our basic creative strategy is to reposition the product from that of a reliable air conditioner to a high-performance, energy-efficient air conditioner."

All creative efforts—copy, theme, color, and so forth—as well as media and tactics, should support the creative strategy statement. Planning an effective advertising campaign requires clearly defined objectives that provide a foundation for selecting media and measuring results.

Determining Advertising Expenditures

Collectively, business marketers spend billions of dollars on media advertising annually and the Web is winning a growing share of these dollars. The leading advertisers are shown in Table 15.1. Note the preponderance of telecommunications and high-tech firms on the top-10 list. In allocating advertising dollars, Hewlett-Packard, for example, has bumped up its online ad budget to 42 percent of its overall media spending.[17] Typically, business marketers use a blend of intuition, judgment, experience, and, only occasionally, more advanced decision-oriented techniques to determine advertising budgets. Some of the techniques business marketers most commonly use are rules of thumb (for example, percentage of past years' sales) and the objective-task method.

Rules of Thumb   Often, because advertising is a relatively small part of the total marketing budget for business firms, the value of using sophisticated methods for advertising budgeting is not great. In these cases, managers tend to follow simple **rules of thumb** (for example, allocate 1 percent of sales to advertising or match competition spending). Unfortunately, percentage-of-sales rules are all too pervasive throughout business marketing, even where advertising is an important element.

The fundamental problem with percentage-of-sales rules is that they implicitly make advertising a consequence rather than a determinant of sales and profits and can easily give rise to dysfunctional policies. Percentage-of-sales rules suggest that the business advertiser reduce advertising when sales volume declines, just when increased advertising may be more appropriate. Nevertheless, simple rules of thumb continue to be applied in budget decisions because they are easy to use and familiar to management.

---

[17]Ibid., p. 17.

TABLE 15.1 | **TOP BUSINESS-TO-BUSINESS ADVERTISERS**

Company	Total Advertising Expenditures (millions)
AT&T Inc.	$419.4
Verizon Communications Inc.	405.9
Sprint Nextel Corp	277.1
IBM	236.3
Hewlett-Packard Co.	219.6
Microsoft Corp.	213.6
Monster Worldwide	155.1
FedEx Corp	144.0
Citigroup	137.6
J.P. Morgan Chase & Co.	129.0

SOURCE: "Largest U.S. B-to-B Advertising Buyers," *Marketing News*, July 15, 2008, p. 25.

Objective-Task Method   The task method for budgeting advertising expenditures relates advertising costs to the objective it is to accomplish. Because the sales dollar results of advertising are almost impossible to measure, the task method focuses on the communications effects of advertising, not on the sales effects.

The **objective-task method** is applied by evaluating the tasks advertising will perform, analyzing the costs of each task, and summing up the total costs to arrive at a final budget. The process can be divided into four steps:

1. Establish specific marketing objectives for the product in terms of such factors as sales volume, market share, profit contribution, and market segments.

2. Assess the communication functions that must be performed to realize the marketing objectives and then determine the role of advertising and other elements of the communications mix in performing these functions.

3. Define specific goals for advertising in terms of the measurable communication response required to achieve marketing objectives.

4. Estimate the budget needed to accomplish the advertising goals.

The task method addresses the major problem of the rule-of-thumb methods—funds are applied to accomplish a specific goal so that advertising is a *determinant* of those results, not a consequence. Using the task approach, managers allocate all the funds necessary to accomplish a specific objective rather than allocating some arbitrary percentage of sales. The most troubling problem with the method is that management must have some instinct for the proper relationship between expenditure level and communication response. It is difficult to know what produces a certain level of awareness among business marketing buying influentials. Will 12 two-page insertions in *Purchasing* magazine over the next six months create the desired recognition level, or will 24 insertions over one year be necessary?

Budgeting for advertising must not ignore the political and behavioral aspects of the process. Nigel Piercy's research suggests that firms pay insufficient attention to budgeting technique because they operate through structures and processes that are often political in nature.[18] Piercy suggests that what actually determines advertising budgets are the power "interests" in the company and the political behavior of various parties in the budgeting process. An implication of this research is that the manager may be well served by focusing on budgeting as a political activity, and not simply as a technique-driven process.

Passing the Threshold   Several communications are often needed to capture the attention of buyers, which complicates the budgeting decision. Research suggests that a brand must surpass a threshold level of awareness in the market before meaningful increases can be made to its brand preference share. A small advertising budget may not allow the marketer to move the firm's brand beyond a threshold level of awareness and on to preference. Eunsang Yoon and Valerie Kijewski warn that "the communications manager having limited marketing resources will then be in danger of making the mistake of stopping the program prematurely, thus wasting past investment, rather than pressing on to pass the threshold awareness level."[19]

Because budgeting is so important to advertising effectiveness, managers must not blindly follow rules of thumb. Instead, they should evaluate the tasks required and their costs against industry norms. With clear objectives and proper budgetary allocations, the next step is to design effective advertising messages.

Developing the Advertising Message

Message development is a complex, critical task in industrial advertising. Highlighting a product attribute that is unimportant to a particular buying group is not only a waste of advertising dollars but also a lost opportunity. Both the appeal and the way that appeal is conveyed are vital to successful communication. Thus, creating business-to-business advertising messages involves determining advertising objectives, evaluating the buying criteria of the target audience, and analyzing the most appropriate language, format, and style for presenting the message.

Perception   For an advertising message to be successful, an individual must first be exposed to it and pay attention to it. Thus, a business advertisement must catch the decision maker's attention. Once the individual has noticed the message, he or she must interpret it as the advertiser intended. Perceptual barriers often prevent a receiver from perceiving the intended message. Even though the individual is exposed to an advertisement, nothing guarantees that he or she processes the message. In fact, the industrial buyer may read every word of the copy and find a meaning in it opposite to the one the advertiser intended.

The business advertiser must therefore contend with two important elements of perception: attention and interpretation. Buyers tend to screen out messages that are inconsistent with their own attitudes, needs, and beliefs, and they tend to interpret information in the light of those beliefs (see Chapter 3). Unless advertising messages

---

[18]Nigel Piercy, "Advertising Budgeting: Process and Structure as Explanatory Variables," *Journal of Advertising* 16 (2, 1987): p. 34.

[19]Yoon and Kijewski, "The Brand Awareness-to-Preferences Link," p. 32.

are carefully designed and targeted, they may be disregarded or interpreted improperly. Advertisers must put themselves in the position of the receivers to evaluate how the message appears to them.

Whether an ad uses technical wording appears to have some effect on readers' perceptions of both the industrial product and the ad.[20] Technical ads were shown to create less desire in some readers to seek information because such ads suggest "more difficulty in operation." Therefore, it is important to remember that technical readers (engineers, architects, and so on) respond more favorably to the technical ads and nontechnical readers respond more favorably to nontechnical ads. From a message-development viewpoint, the business advertiser must carefully tailor the technical aspects of promotional messages to the appropriate audience.

Focus on Benefits   A business buyer purchases benefits—a better way to accomplish some task, a less expensive way to produce a final product, a solution to a problem, or a faster delivery time. Advertising messages need to focus on benefits that the target customer seeks and persuade the reader that the advertiser can deliver them.[21] Messages that have direct appeals or calls to action are viewed to be "stronger" than those with diffuse or indirect appeals to action. Robert Lamons, an advertising consultant, observes:

> A good call to action can actually start the selling process. Promise a test report; offer a product demonstration; direct them to a special section of your Web site. . . . Compare how your product stacks up to others in the field. Everyone is super-busy these days, and if you can offer something that helps them expedite or narrow their search, you're giving them something money can't buy: free time.[22]

Understanding Buyer Motivations   Which product benefits are important to each group of buying influentials? The business advertiser cannot assume that a standard set of "classical buying motives" applies in every purchase situation. Many business advertisers often do not understand the buying motives of important market segments. Developing effective advertising messages often requires extensive marketing research in order to fully delineate the key buying criteria of each buying influencer in each of the firm's different target markets.

Selecting Advertising Media for Business Markets

Although the message is vital to advertising success, equally important is the medium through which it is presented. An integrated marketing communications program might include a blend of online, print, and direct-mail advertisements that deliver a consistent story across formats. Business-to-business media are selected by the target audience—the particular purchase-decision participants to be reached. Selection of media also involves budgetary considerations: Where are dollars best spent to generate the customer contacts desired?

---

[20]Joseph A. Bellizzi and Jacqueline J. Mohr, "Technical versus Nontechnical Wording in Industrial Print Advertising," in *AMA Educators' Proceedings*, Russell W. Belk et al., eds. (Chicago: American Marketing Association, 1984), p. 174.

[21]Steve McKee, "Five Common B2B Advertising Myths," *Business Week*, April 2007, accessed at http://www.businessweek.com on July 29, 2008.

[22]Robert Lamons, "Tips for Distinguishing Your Ads from Bad Ads," *Marketing News* (November 19, 2001): p. 10.

INSIDE BUSINESS MARKETING

Viral Marketing Campaigns Create Buzz

Viral marketing involves the use of electronic media to stimulate and encourage word-of-mouth or electronic message dissemination between individuals concerning a particular product or brand. For example, IBM launched an online campaign called "IBM Storage Scavenger Hunt Game," which sent information technology (IT) professionals scrambling around the Web to locate clues for freeing fictional characters from a virtual storage maze. The campaign featured online video in banner ads and e-mail featuring a call for help from IT characters Ned and Gil, who regularly appear in many IBM TV spots. The ads directed users to a landing page, where they were given clues for freeing Ned and Gil from the maze.

IBM's goal for the campaign was to reach storage-system decision makers in a fun and engaging way. It worked! The target audience became truly engaged in the campaign and participants were interested in solving the puzzle. "The IBM campaign resulted in click rates that were four to five times higher than average e-mail campaigns and twice as high as average banner ad campaigns.

SOURCE: Kate Maddox, "Video in Play as Ad Vehicle," B to B Interactive Marketing Guide 2008, accessed on August 1, 2008 at http://www.btobonline.com.

Online Advertising As business marketing strategists seek more effective ways to communicate with customers and prospects, they continue to shift more of the advertising budget to digital formats. For example, during a recent global interactive campaign, more than 220,000 visitors clicked through to a Hewlett-Packard microsite designed for small and mid-sized businesses.[23] A **microsite** is a specialized Web page a visitor lands on after clicking an online ad or e-mail. Similarly, both IBM and GE make extensive use of online videos to show how their products and services are helping customers around the world to solve business problems.

A Shift to Digital Online advertising spending by business-to-business firms exceeds $27 billion and will continue to grow at a rapid pace (see Table 15.2). Paid search engine advertising represents the prime format, accounting for 40 percent of total online spending, followed by display ads. Experiencing particularly rapid spending growth is the rich media/video format, particularly the online video category. "Video is a particularly compelling way to tell a brand or product story that can be very useful for b-to-b communications, as these businesses tend to be more complex and can require additional explanation," according to Andreas Combuechen, CEO–chief creative officer of Atmosphere BBDO.[24]

Motorola's Integrated Campaign Like many other firms, Motorola is shifting its emphasis from traditional advertising to a more integrated focus. A recent integrated marketing campaign demonstrates Motorola's mission-critical public

---

[23]"B to B's Best Brands – Hewlett-Packard," B to B's Best: 2007, p. 26, accessed at http://www.btobonline.com on June 15, 2008.

[24]Ellis Booker, "Economic Slowdown Will Accelerate Online Shift," B to B's Interactive Guide: 2008, p. 3, accessed at http://www.btobonline.com on August 1, 2008.

TABLE 15.2 | U.S. ONLINE ADVERTISING SPENDING

Format	$ in Millions
Search	$11,000
Display ads	5,912
Classified	4,675
Rich Media/Video	2,613
Lead/Generation	2,269
E-mail	481
Sponsorships	550
TOTAL	$27,500

SOURCE: "eMarketer," cited in B to B Interactive Marketing Guide, 2008, p. 4, accessed at http://www.btobonline.com on August 1, 2008.

safety solutions.[25] The campaign features a microsite at http://www.motorola.com/secondnature, targeted at police chiefs, fire chiefs, and municipal chief information officers. The campaign includes print and online ads, direct mail and e-mail, all of which are designed around a unifying goal: drive customer prospects to the microsite to observe Motorola's technology solutions at work in a virtual city environment.

Business Publications   More than 2,700 business publications carry business-to-business advertising. For those specializing in the pharmaceutical industry, *Drug Discovery & Development*, *Pharmaceutical Executive*, and *Pharmaceutical Technology* are a few of the publications available. Business publications are either horizontal or vertical. **Horizontal publications** are directed at a specific task, technology, or function, whatever the industry. *Advertising Age*, *Purchasing*, and *Marketing News* are horizontal. **Vertical publications**, on the other hand, may be read by everyone from floor supervisor to president within a specific industry. Typical vertical publications are *Chemical Business* or *Computer Gaming World*.

If a business marketer's product has applications within only a few industries, vertical publications are a logical media choice. When many industries are potential users and well-defined functions are the principal buying influencers, a horizontal publication is effective.

Many trade publications are **requester publications,** which offer free subscriptions to selected readers. The publisher can select readers in a position to influence buying decisions and offer the free subscription in exchange for information such as title, function, and buying responsibilities. Thus, the advertiser can tell whether each publication reaches the desired audience.

Obviously, publication choice is predicated on a complete understanding of the range of purchase-decision participants and of the industries where the product is used. Only then can the target audience be matched to the circulation statements of alternative business publications.

---

[25]Kate Maddox, "Video in Play as Ad Vehicle," B to B's Interactive Marketing Guide: 2008, p. 26, accessed at http://www.btobonline.com on August 1, 2008.

B2B TOP PERFORMERS

Search Engine Marketing at Google: The Right Message, the Right Time

To reach customers through all stages of the buying cycle, from awareness to retention, business-to-business firms are devoting a greater share of their advertising budgets to e-marketing campaigns, including keyword advertising through leading Internet search engines such as Google or Yahoo. As marketing managers face increased pressure to demonstrate the return on investment of each advertising dollar spent, keyword advertising provides compelling value—it delivers qualified leads in the form of potential customers searching on terms specifically related to your products and services. You pay only when users click on your ads. Keyword advertising provides the lowest average cost-per-lead of any direct marketing method.[1] Says Eric Grates, business service manager at Dow Chemical, "With click through rates ranging from 2.5 to 7 percent, the Google advertising program continues to be a key component of our overall marketing efforts."[2]

Russ Cohn, who leads Google's business-to-business service operations, offers some useful guidelines for successful keyword advertising:

1. Ensure that your Web site is search-crawler friendly by providing a clear hierarchy, text links, and information-rich content.

2. Understand that relevance to the user is the goal: The most successful ads connect customers to the information or solution they are seeking.

3. Create a relevant, targeted keyword list by choosing specific words that accurately reflect your Web site and advertised products.

4. Write clear and compelling ads that use the keywords and that isolate your unique value proposition.

5. Track results and measure everything.

   - Monitor click-through rates to make adjustments to the campaign.

   - Test different keywords and ad copy.

   - Use free conversion tracking tools to analyze which keywords are providing the best returns.

   - Calculate the return on investment.

---

[1]Russ Cohn, "Unlocking Keyword Advertising," *B2B Magazine*, accessed at http://www.b2bm.biz.com on November 2, 2005.

[2]"Google Named Top 5 Business-to-Business Media Property," accessed at http://www.google.com on May 5, 2003.

Characteristics of an Effective Print Ad   Recent research on the effectiveness of business-to-business print ads provides strong evidence that the marketing strategist should emphasize a "rational approach" and provide a clear description of the product and the benefits it offers to customers.[26] The effectiveness of ads is also enhanced by detailing product quality and performance information in a concrete and logical manner.

Advertising Cost   Circulation is an important criterion in the selection of publications, but circulation must be tempered by cost. First, the total advertising budget must be allocated among the various advertising tools, such as business publications, sales promotion, direct marketing (mail and e-mail), and online advertising. Of course, allocations to the various media options vary with company situation and advertising

---

[26]Ritu Lohtia, Wesley J. Johnston, and Linda Rab, "Business-to-Business Advertising: What Are the Dimensions of an Effective Print Ad?" *Industrial Marketing Management* 24 (October 1995): pp. 369–378.

mission. The allocation of the business publication budget among various journals depends on their relative effectiveness and efficiency, usually measured in cost per thousand using the following formula:

$$\text{Cost per thousand} = \frac{\text{Cost per page}}{\text{Circulation in thousands}}$$

To compare two publications by their actual page rates would be misleading, because the publication with the lower circulation is usually less expensive. The cost-per-thousand calculation should be based on circulation to the *target* audience, not the total audience. Although some publications may appear expensive on a cost-per-thousand basis, they may in fact be cost-effective, with little wasted circulation. Some publications also have popular Web sites that advertisers can use to create integrated marketing communications.

Frequency and Scheduling   Even the most successful business publication advertisements are seen by only a small percentage of the people who read the magazine; therefore, one-time ads are generally ineffective. Because a number of exposures are required before a message "sinks in," and because the reading audience varies from month to month, a schedule of advertising insertions is required. To build continuity and repetitive value, at least 6 insertions per year may be required in a monthly publication, and 26 to 52 insertions (with a minimum of 13) in a weekly publication.[27]

Direct Marketing Tools

Direct mail and e-mail are among the direct marketing tools available to the business marketer. Direct mail delivers the advertising message firsthand to selected individuals. Possible mailing pieces range from a sales letter introducing a new product to a lengthy brochure or even a product sample. Direct mail can accomplish all of the major advertising functions, but its real contribution is in delivering the message to a precisely defined prospect. In turn, says Internet marketing consultant Barry Silverstein, direct *e-mail* can have a substantial effect on creating and qualifying customer leads, *if* some important rules are strictly followed: "always seek permission to send e-mail" and "always provide the recipient with the ability to 'opt out.'"[28] Attention first centers on direct-mail advertising.

Direct Mail   Direct mail is commonly used for corporate image promotion, product and service promotion, sales force support, distribution channel communication, and special marketing problems. In promoting corporate image, direct mail may help to establish a firm's reputation of technological leadership. On the other hand, product advertising by direct mail can put specific product information in the hands of buying influentials. For example, as part of a successful integrated marketing campaign to change perceptions of UPS from a ground shipping company to a supply chain leader, the firm used direct mail to target decision makers—from shipping managers

[27]See Stanton G. Cort, David R. Lambert, and Paula L. Garrett, "Effective Business-to-Business Frequency: New Management Perspectives from the Research Literature," *Advertising Research Foundation Literature Review* (October 1983).

[28]Barry Silverstein, *Business-to-Business Internet Marketing*, 3rd ed. (Gulf Breeze, FL.: MAXIMUM Press, 2001), p. 171. See also Carol Krol, "E-Mail: Integrating Channels Key," B to B's Interactive Marketing Guide: 2008, p. 8, accessed at http://www.btobonline.com on August 1, 2008.

to front-office administrators. The direct-mail strategy had strong results, achieving a 10.5 percent response rate, with 36 percent of those responders buying services.[29]

Direct E-Mail   Because marketers are devoting a larger share of their advertising budgets to online marketing, IBM's customer relationship program, called *Focusing on You*, rests on a simple but powerful idea—ask customers what information they want and give it to them.[30] By giving the customer the choice, IBM learns about the customer's unique preferences and is better equipped to tailor product and service information to that customer's specific needs. The program relies on e-mail marketing, which is far less costly than direct mail. In fact, IBM found that sending customers traditional printed materials by mail was 10 times more expensive than e-mail communications. Moreover, e-mail campaigns often yield higher responses than direct-mail campaigns, and the results are generated more quickly. For example, a third of all responses to a particular IBM e-mail campaign were generated in the first 24 hours!

Let the Customer Decide   Pamela Evans, director of worldwide teleweb marketing at IBM, describes the value of interactive marketing:

> In the IBM software business, for example, we have a long sales cycle, and the Web gives us the opportunity for our prospects and customers to go online where we establish a relationship that we can then continue to nurture electronically. . . . The challenge as marketers we all face is determining how the customer wants to interact with us, and really taking advantage of the Web and the power . . . there for self-service.[31]

Firms that plan to fully integrate direct e-mail into their marketing communications strategy should make a special effort to build their own e-mail list. Often such information is already available from the firm's customer relationship management (CRM) system. From Chapter 4, recall that a goal of the CRM system is to integrate customer records from all departments, including sales, marketing, and customer service. As a result, if a customer responds to an e-mail (or direct-mail) campaign, the CRM system captures that information in a centralized database for all contact employees (salespersons, call center employees, marketing managers) to retrieve.

Other ways to create an e-mail list include offering an e-mail alert service or e-mail newsletter, asking for e-mail addresses in direct-mail campaigns, and collecting e-mail addresses at trade shows.[32] Business marketers must also realize that the response to an e-mail campaign can be immediate, so they must be prepared to acknowledge, process, and fulfill orders before the e-mail campaign is launched.

Measuring Advertising Effectiveness

The business advertiser rarely expects orders to result immediately from advertising. Advertising is designed to create awareness, stimulate loyalty to the company, or create a favorable attitude toward a product. Even though advertising may not directly

---

[29]Kate Maddox and Beth Snyder Bulik, "Integrated Marketing Success Stories," *B2B* 89 (July 7, 2004): p. 23.

[30]Silverstein, *Business-to-Business Internet Marketing*, p. 226.

[31]Carol Krol, "The Internet Continues to Reshape Direct," *BtoB*, accessed at http://www.b2bonline.com on October 10, 2005.

[32]Barry Silverstein, *Internet Marketing for Information Technology Companies*, 2d ed. (Gulf Breeze, FL.: MAXIMUM Press, 2001), p. 107.

precipitate a purchase decision, advertising programs must be held accountable, and marketing managers are facing increased pressure to demonstrate the actual returns on marketing expenditures.[33] Research suggests that firms that are adept at marketing performance measurement generate greater profitability and stock returns than their competitors.[34] Thus, the business advertiser must be able to measure the results of current advertising in order to improve future advertising and evaluate the effectiveness of advertising expenditures against expenditures on other elements of marketing strategy.

Measuring Impacts on the Purchase Decision

Measuring advertising effectiveness means assessing advertising's effect on what "intervenes" between the stimulus (advertising) and the resulting behavior (purchase decision). The theory is that advertising can affect awareness, knowledge, and other dimensions that more readily lend themselves to measurement. In essence, the advertiser attempts to gauge advertising's ability to move an individual through the purchase decision process. This approach assumes, correctly or not, that enhancement of any one phase of the process or movement from one step to the next increases the ultimate probability of purchase.

A study completed at Rockwell International Corporation suggests that business marketers should also measure the **indirect communication effects of advertising**.[35] This study revealed that advertising affects word-of-mouth communications (indirect effect), and such communications play an important role in buyer decision making. Similarly, the study showed that advertising indirectly affects buyers on the basis of its effect on overall company reputation and on the sales force's belief that advertising aids selling. The study suggested that advertising effectiveness measurement include a procedure for tracking and measuring advertising's effect on the indirect communication effects.

In summary, advertising effectiveness is evaluated against objectives formulated in terms of the elements of the buyer's decision process as well as some of the indirect communication effects. Advertising efforts are also judged, in the final analysis, on cost per level of achievement (for example, dollars spent to achieve a certain level of awareness or recognition).

The Measurement Program

A sound measurement program entails substantial advanced planning. Figure 15.2 shows the basic areas of advertising evaluation. The advertising strategist must determine in advance what is to be measured, how, and in what sequence. A preevaluation phase is required to establish a benchmark for a new advertising campaign. For example, a preevaluation study would be conducted to capture the existing level of awareness a firm's product enjoys in a defined target market. After the advertising campaign, the evaluation study examines changes in awareness against this benchmark. Five primary areas for advertising evaluation include (1) markets, (2) motives, (3) messages, (4) media, and (5) results.

---

[33]Diane Brady and David Kiley, "Making Marketing Measure Up," *Business Week*, December 13, 2004, pp. 112–113.

[34]Dan O'Sullivan and Andrew V. Abela, "Marketing Performance Measurement Ability and firm Performance," *Journal of Marketing* 71 (April 2007): pp. 79–93.

[35]C. Whan Park, Martin S. Roth, and Philip F. Jacques, "Evaluating the Effects of Advertising and Sales Promotion Campaigns," *Industrial Marketing Management* 17 (May 1988): p. 130.

FIGURE 15.2 | **THE PRIMARY AREAS FOR ADVERTISING EVALUATION**

AREA		FOCUS OF MEASUREMENT
Target Market Coverage	⟶	Degree to which advertising succeeded in reaching defined target markets
Key Buying Motives	⟶	Factors that triggered purchase decision
Effectiveness of Messages	⟶	Degree to which the message registered with key buying influentials in defined market segments
Media Effectiveness	⟶	Degree to which various media were successful in reaching defined target markets with message
Overall Results	⟶	Degree to which advertising accomplished its defined objectives

Web Metrics   For online advertising, attention likewise centers on defined communication objectives. Was the ad designed to drive visitors to the Web site to view an online video or to download information on a new product? This event is the "desired action" and the business marketing manager wants to measure site traffic to this action and evaluate all of the components of the Web site that lead visitors to take this action. "Pulling in information from search marketing campaigns allows b-to-b marketers to better understand what visitors searched for to find their site and what text-based ads elicited the highest click-through and conversion (action) rates. In turn, these data can help marketers optimize their sites with language that resonates with their target audiences and customize their home pages with links that are most important to their visitors,"[36] says Jim Sterne, president, Target Media.

Evaluation is Essential   The evaluation of business-to-business advertising is demanding and complex, but absolutely essential. Budgetary constraints are generally the limiting factors. However, professional research companies can be called on to develop field research studies. When determining the effect of advertising on moving a decision participant from an awareness of the product or company to a readiness to buy,

---

[36]Jim Sterne, "Must-have Web Metrics," *B to B*, March 10, 2008, accessed at http://www.btobonline.com on May 14, 2008.

the evaluations usually measure knowledge, recognition, recall, awareness, preference, and motivation. Measuring effects on actual sales are unfortunately not often possible.

Managing Trade Show Strategy

Business advertising funds are designated primarily for online, print, and direct-mail formats but these are reinforced by other promotional activities such as exhibits and trade shows, catalogs, and trade promotion. Special attention is given here to trade shows—an important promotional vehicle for business markets.

Trade Shows: Strategy Benefits

Most industries stage an annual business show or exhibition to display new advances and technological developments in the industry. The Center for Exhibition Industry Research indicates that some 1.5 million U.S. and Canadian firms place displays at trade shows each year and that 83 percent of trade-show visitors are classified as "buying influencers."[37] Exhibiting firms spend more than $21 billion annually on floor space at North American exhibitions, and the average company participates in more than 45 trade shows per year.[38] Generally, sellers present their products and services in booths visited by interested industry members. The typical exhibitor contacts four to five potential purchasers per hour on the show floor.

A trade-show exhibit offers a unique opportunity to publicize a significant contribution to technology or to demonstrate new and old products. According to Thomas Bonoma, "For many companies, trade-show expenditures are the major—and for more than a few, the only—form of organized marketing communication activity other than efforts by sales force and distributors."[39] Through the trade show:

- An effective selling message can be delivered to a relatively large and interested audience at one time (for example, more than 30,000 people attend the annual Plant Engineering Show).

- New products can be introduced to a mass audience.

- Customers can get hands-on experience with the product in a one-on-one selling situation.

- Potential customers can be identified, providing sales personnel with qualified leads.

- General goodwill can be enhanced.

- Free publicity is often generated for the company.

The cost of reaching a prospect at a trade show is approximately $250, much lower than the cost of making a personal sales call for many firms.[40] Furthermore,

---

[37]Douglas Ducante, "The Future of the United States Exhibition Industry—Flourish or Flounder," accessed at http://www.ceir.org on October 2002.

[38]Ruth P. Stevens, *Trade Show and Event Marketing* (Mason, OH: Thomson/South-Western, 2005), pp. 2–6.

[39]Thomas V. Bonoma, "Get More Out of Your Trade Shows," *Harvard Business Review* 61 (January–February 1983): p. 76.

[40]Stevens, *Trade Show and Event Marketing*, p. 16.

trade shows offer an excellent and cost-effective short-term method for introducing a product in new foreign markets.[41] An international trade fair enables a manufacturer to meet buyers directly, observe competition, and gather market research data. The entry time for exporting can easily be cut from six years to six months by attending foreign trade fairs.

Trade-Show Investment Returns

A recent study evaluated the effect of a trade show on the sales and profitability of a new laboratory testing device.[42] In a controlled experiment where new product sales could be traced to customers both attending and not attending the show, sales levels were higher among attendees. In turn, the proportion of customers who bought the product was higher among those who had visited the booth during the show. Importantly, there was a positive return on trade-show investment (23 percent) based on incremental profits related to the cost of the trade show. This research is one of the first studies to show that the returns from trade-show investments can indeed be measured.

Improving Sales Efficiency Another study demonstrated the powerful way personal selling and trade shows work together in an integrated marketing communications strategy.[43] The results demonstrate that follow-up sales efforts generate higher sales productivity when customers had already been exposed to the company's products at a trade show. The return-on-sales figures are higher among show attendees than nonattendees, illuminating the positive effects of trade shows on customer purchase intentions. Although dramatically enhancing performance, however, trade shows can be extremely costly and must be carefully planned.

Planning Trade-Show Strategy

To develop an effective trade-show communications strategy, managers must address four questions:

1. What functions should the trade show perform in the total marketing communications program?
2. To whom should the marketing effort at trade shows be directed?
3. What is the appropriate show mix for the company?
4. What should the trade-show investment-audit policy be? How should audits be carried out?[44]

Answering these questions helps managers crystallize their thinking about target audiences, about expected results, and about how funds should be allocated.

---

[41]Brad O'Hara, Fred Palumbo, and Paul Herbig, "Industrial Trade Shows Abroad," *Industrial Marketing Management* 22 (August 1993): p. 235.

[42]Srinath Gopalakrishna, Gary L. Lilien, Jerome D. Williams, and Ian K. Sequeira, "Do Trade Shows Pay Off?" *Journal of Marketing* 59 (July 1995): pp. 75–83.

[43]Timothy M. Smith, Srinath Gopalakrishna, and Paul M. Smith, "The Complementary Effect of Trade Shows on Personal Selling," *International Journal of Research in Marketing* 21 (March 2004): pp. 61–69.

[44]Bonoma, "Get More Out of Your Trade Shows," p. 79.

Trade-Show Objectives

The functions of trade shows in generating sales include identifying decision influencers; identifying potential customers; providing product, service, and company information; learning of potential application problems; creating actual sales; and handling current customer problems. In addition to these selling-related functions, the trade show can be valuable for building corporate image, gathering competitive intelligence, and enhancing sales force morale. Specific objectives are needed to guide the development of trade-show strategy and to specify the activities of company personnel while there. Once specific objectives are formulated, however, the exhibitor must evaluate alternative trade shows in light of the target market.

Selecting the Shows

The challenge is to decide which trade shows to attend and how much of the promotional budget to expend.[45] Clearly, the firm wants to attend those shows frequented by its most important customer segments, so it begins by soliciting ideas from salespeople and customers. A wealth of information can also be found in leading trade-show directories, like the *American Tradeshow Directory* (http://www.tradeshowbiz.com) or from a Web-based trade-show searchable database like http://www.ExhibitNet.com. Here information on each show is provided and exhibitors can promote their presence at the show on the site.

Some firms use the reports published by Exhibit Surveys, Inc., a company that surveys trade-show audiences. Two of the important measures Exhibit Surveys developed are the **net buying influences** and the **total buying plans**. The first measures the percentage of the show audience that has decision authority for the types of products being exhibited; the second measures the percentage of the audience planning to buy those products within the next 12 months. These measures are very useful to the business marketing manager when selecting the most effective shows to attend.

Many firms survey their target prospects before the trade show to learn which trade shows they will attend and what they hope to gain from attending. In this way the exhibitor can prepare its trade-show strategy to fit the needs of its potential customers. Others suggest that a firm rank-order various shows based on expected profitability.[46] The expected profitability is computed by calibrating a model of "lead efficiency" using the firm's historical sales lead and lead conversion-to-sale data, gross margin information, and total attendance at past shows. **Lead efficiency** is defined as the number of sales leads obtained at the show divided by the total number of show visitors with definite plans to buy the exhibitor's product or one similar to it.

Managing the Trade-Show Exhibit

To generate interest in an exhibit, business marketing firms run advertisements in business publications profiling new projects they will exhibit at the show. Trade-show strategies should also be linked to interactive marketing communications. This enables many exhibitors to schedule appointments with prospects and customers during the show.

Sales personnel must be trained to perform in the trade-show environment. The selling job differs from the typical sales call in that the salesperson may have only 5 to 10 minutes to make a presentation. On a typical sales call, salespersons

---

[45]Stevens, *Trade Show and Event Marketing*, pp. 58–62.

[46]Srinath Gopalakrishna and Jerome D. Williams, "Planning and Performance Assessment of Industrial Trade Shows: An Exploratory Study," *International Journal of Research in Marketing* 9 (September 1992): pp. 207–224.

FIGURE 15.3 | REPRESENTATION OF TRAFFIC FLOW MODEL AT TRADE SHOWS AS A SEQUENCE OF STAGES

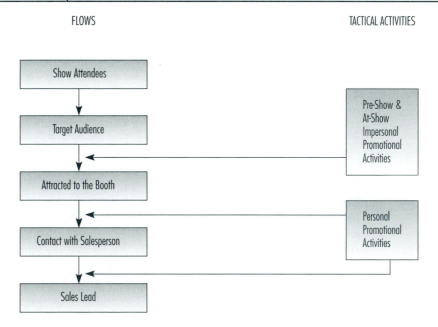

SOURCE: Srinath Gopalakrishna and Gary L. Lilien, "A Three-Stage Model of Industrial Trade Show Performance," Working paper #20-1992, Institute for the Study of Business Markets, Pennsylvania State University.

usually sell themselves first, then the company, and finally the product. At the trade show, the process is reversed.

There must be a system for responding effectively to inquiries generated at the show. Some business marketers find it effective to use a laptop to transmit information to corporate headquarters electronically. Headquarters staff then generate a letter and send out the required information by mail or e-mail. When prospects return to their offices after a show, the material is immediately available.

Evaluating Trade-Show Performance

The measurement of trade-show performance is very important in assessing the success of a firm's trade-show strategy. Srinath Gopalakrishna and Gary Lilien present a useful framework to assess performance by considering traffic flow through the firm's booth as a sequence of three stages.[47] Figure 15.3 illustrates the process and three different indices of performance—attraction, contact, and conversion efficiency for the three respective stages.

An important contribution of this framework is the link between performance indices and key decision variables the firm can control. Attraction efficiency is the proportion of *interested* visitors the booth is able to attract. Notice that the firm's target audience is the pool of visitors at the show who are interested in the firm's products,

---

[47]Srinath Gopalakrishna and Gary L. Lilien, "A Three-Stage Model of Industrial Trade Show Performance," *Marketing Science* 14 (Winter 1995): pp. 22–42.

which is usually smaller than the total number of attendees at the show. The booth's attraction power is a function of space (square feet), show promotion, use of attention-getting techniques, and so on. Similarly, contact and conversion efficiencies are modeled as a function of the number of booth personnel and their level of training.

For an individual firm, trade-show expenditures should be tied to concrete marketing communication goals to secure an adequate return on investment. To this end, business marketing managers must carefully evaluate each trade show and its expenses in terms of the likely effect on sales, profit, and corporate image. As with all other promotional vehicles, the planning and budgeting for trade shows must focus on specific objectives. Once these objectives have been determined, the rational approach will then identify what has to be done and how much will have to be spent.

Summary

Business-to-business marketers are developing integrated marketing communications strategies that align strategic business objectives with creative execution across a variety of media to achieve desired results. Because of the nature of the business-to-business buying process, personal selling is the primary technique for creating sales; advertising supports and supplements personal selling. Yet, advertising does perform some tasks that personal selling simply cannot perform. Advertising is able to reach buying influentials who are often inaccessible to sales personnel.

Advertising supports personal selling by making the company and product known to potential buyers. The result is greater overall selling success and firm performance. Effective advertising makes the entire marketing strategy more efficient, often lowering total marketing and selling costs. Finally, advertising can provide information and company or product awareness more efficiently than can personal selling. More than just an advertising medium, the Internet changes marketing communications from a one-way to a two-way process that permits the marketer to more readily exchange information with customers.

Managing the advertising program begins by determining advertising objectives, which must be clearly defined and directed to a specific audience. Once objectives are specified, funds are allocated to advertising efforts. Rules of thumb, though common, are not the ideal methods for specifying advertising budgets. The objective-task method is far more effective.

Advertising messages are created with the understanding that the potential buyer's perceptual process influences receptivity to the message. The most effective appeal is one that projects product benefits or the solution sought by the targeted buying influential.

Advertising media are selected on the basis of their circulation—how well their audience matches the desired audience of buying influentials. The Internet provides a powerful medium to communicate with target customers, and business-to-business firms are shifting a major share of the advertising budget to digital formats. Astute business marketers integrate the Web with other media and are using online videos to tell a brand or product story. Interactive marketing campaigns can be readily changed, personalized, and customized, making one-to-one marketing a reality.

Finally, advertising effectiveness must be evaluated against the advertising campaign's communication objectives. Readership, recognition, awareness, attitudes, and intention to buy are typical measures of business-to-business advertising performance. For online advertising, attention centers on the degree to which the ad moved potential customers to the desired action (for example, to download a new-product brochure).

Trade-show visitors tend to be buying influentials, and the cost of reaching a prospect here is far lower than through personal selling. A carefully planned and executed strategy is needed to secure promising returns on trade-show investments. Trade shows are an effective way to reach large audiences with a single presentation, but funds must be allocated carefully.

Discussion Questions

1. Although the bulk of the promotional budget of the business marketing firm is allocated to personal selling, advertising can play an important role in business marketing strategy. Explain.

2. Evaluate this statement: "The Internet changes marketing communications from a one-way process to a two-way process that permits the marketer and the consumer to now more readily exchange information."

3. Breck Machine Tool would like you to develop a series of ads for a new industrial product. On request, Breck's marketing research department will provide you with any data they have about the new product and the market. Outline the approach you would follow in selecting media and developing messages for the campaign. Specify the types of data you would draw on to improve the quality of your decisions.

4. Outline how you would evaluate the effectiveness and efficiency of a business firm's advertising function. Focus on budgeting practices and performance results.

5. Explain how a message in a business-to-business advertisement in the *Wall Street Journal* may be favorably evaluated by the production manager, unfavorably evaluated by the purchasing manager, and fail even to trigger the attention of the quality-control engineer.

6. Given the rapid rise in the cost of making personal sales calls, should the business marketer attempt to substitute direct-mail advertising or online advertising for personal selling whenever possible? Support your position.

7. Describe the role that online advertising might assume in the promotional mix of the business marketer. How can the business marketer use the Web to form close relationships with customers?

8. It is argued that business advertising is not expected to precipitate sales directly. If business advertising does not persuade organizational buyers to buy brand *A* versus brand *B*, what does it do, and how can we measure its effect against expenditures on other marketing strategy elements?

Internet Exercise

1. Intuit Inc, a leading provider of software for small and medium-sized enterprises created a Web site to help these businesses develop customized jingles. Go to http://www.thejinglegenerator.com and provide an assessment of this online initiative by Intuit.

Johnson Controls, Inc.[48]

Johnson Controls, Inc., provides control and automotive systems worldwide. The Controls Division offers mechanical and electrical systems that control energy use, air-conditioning, lighting, security, and fire safety for buildings. The company also provides on-site management and technical services for customers in a range of settings, including manufacturing installations, commercial buildings, government buildings, hospitals, and major sports complexes.

While serving a full range of market sectors from manufacturers to educational institutions, Johnson Controls has developed a suite of products and services for large retail chains, including department stores, discount stores, grocers, and "big box" supercenters. Most major shopping malls in North America are customers. Johnson Controls' products include a variety of control panels that manage HVAC equipment, transportation, airflow, lighting levels, energy consumption, and air quality—and even determine how many customers enter and exit a store. Behind the control systems is a Remote Operations Center for 24-hour monitoring: Many problems can be diagnosed and corrected online.

Johnson Controls has recently developed a product and service solution that targets the convenience store industry. The convenience store controller smartly manages a store's lighting, refrigeration, and HVAC, alerting store personnel to malfunctions. Building on its deep experience in working with large grocery chains, Johnson Controls can demonstrate to a convenience store chain how the system reduces energy costs, prevents food spoilage, improves occupant comfort, and lowers the cost of maintenance.

Discussion Questions

1. Outline the advertising strategy Johnson Controls might follow to promote the convenience store controller. What benefits would you emphasize in the body of an ad?

2. Develop a list of keywords you would use in promoting the product through Google's Internet search advertising program.

---

[48]"Johnson Controls, Retail Industry Solutions," accessed at http://www.johnsoncontrols.com on November 5, 2005.

Business Marketing Communications: Managing the Personal Selling Function

Business marketing communications consist of advertising, sales promotion, and personal selling. As explored in Chapter 15, advertising and related sales promotion tools supplement and reinforce personal selling. Personal selling is the most important demand-stimulating force in the business marketer's promotional mix. Through the sales force, the marketer links the firm's total product and service offering to the needs of business customers. After reading this chapter, you will understand:

1. The role of personal selling in relationship marketing strategy.

2. the skills and characteristics of high-performing account managers.

3. the nature of the sales management function.

4. selected managerial tools that can be applied to major sales force decision areas.

John Chambers, president and CEO at Cisco, says that "the customer is the strategy."[1] He began his career in the 1970s as an IBM salesperson. Today, he still spends 40 percent of his time working directly with customers, and he believes that the key to Cisco's success comes through continuous customer feedback. In fact, every night, 365 days a year, he receives voice-mail updates on 10 to 15 top-tier customer accounts. By developing leading-edge technology and staying close to the customer, Cisco continues on its astonishing growth path.

In the marketing operations of the typical firm, selling has been a dominant component and a major determinant of overall company success, highlighting the importance of a strong structural linkage between marketing and sales.[2] U.S. businesses, alone, spend $800 billion annually on personal selling, roughly three times the amount spent on advertising.[3] Personal selling is dominant in business markets because, compared with consumer markets, the number of potential customers is relatively small and the dollar purchases are large. The importance of personal selling in the marketing mix depends on such factors as the nature and composition of the market, the product line, and the company's objectives and financial capabilities. Business marketers have many potential links to the market. Some rely on manufacturers' representatives and distributors; others rely exclusively on a direct sales force. Each firm must determine the relative importance of the promotional mix components—advertising versus sales promotion versus personal selling.

Across all industries, the cost of an industrial sales call is much more than $200.[4] Computer firms report much higher costs; chemical producers have much lower ones. Of course, these figures vary, depending on a host of company, product, and market conditions. They do indicate, however, that significant resources are invested in personal selling in the business market. In fact, Erin Anderson and Bob Trinkle persuasively argue that few firms have a clear understanding of the real costs of field sales.[5] To maximize effectiveness and efficiency, the personal selling function must be carefully managed and integrated into the firm's marketing mix. To enhance productivity and respond to intense competition, sales strategists are using a host of new approaches and technologies.

Regardless of how a firm implements its sales strategy, the salesperson is the initial link to the marketplace and specific customers. The task of the salesperson is both complex and challenging. To meet all their customers' expectations, salespeople must have broad knowledge that extends beyond their own products. They must be able to talk intelligently about competitors' products and about trends in the customer's industry. They must know not only their customer's business but also the business of their customer's customers. This chapter first considers the lead role of the salesperson in executing relationship marketing strategies and serving key customer accounts. Attention then turns to the characteristics of high-performing account managers and the central features of the sales management process.

[1]Michele Marchetti, "America's Best Sales Forces: Sales to CEO," *Sales & Marketing Management* 151 (July 1999): p. 63.

[2]Christian Homburg, Ore Jensen, and Harley Krohmer, "Configurations of Marketing and Sales: A Taxonomy," *Journal of Marketing* 72 (March 2008): pp. 133–154; see also James Cross, Steven W. Hartley, and William Rudelius, "Sales Force Activities and Marketing Strategies in Industrial Firms: Relationships and Implications," *Journal of Personal Selling & Sales Management* 21 (Summer 2001): pp. 199–206.

[3]Deborah Kreuze, "How Effective is Personal Selling," *Insights from MSI* (Spring 2008): p. 3.

[4]"The Cost of Doing Business," *Sales & Marketing Management* 151 (September 1999): p. 56.

[5]Erin Anderson and Bob Trinkle, *Outsourcing the Sales Function: The Real Costs of Field Sales* (Mason, OH: Thomson Higher Education, 2005).

Relationship Marketing Strategy[6]

Assuming a central role in implementing the customer relationship marketing (RM) strategy for the business-to-business firm (see Chapter 4) is the salesperson. Firm-to-firm relationships in the business market involve multiple interactions among individuals, forming a network of relationships. To ensure that customers are as satisfied as possible, business marketers must effectively manage the complex web of influences that intersect in buyer-seller relationships.[7]

Figure 16.1 provides a model of interfirm relationship marketing. **Relationship marketing activities** represent dedicated relationship marketing programs, developed and implemented to build strong relational bonds. These activities influence three important drivers of relationship marketing effectiveness—relationship quality, breadth, and composition—each capturing a different dimension of the relationship and exerting a positive influence on the seller's performance activity.

Drivers of Relationship Marketing Effectiveness

Some customer relationships are characterized by extensive interactions and close bonds among members of the buying and selling organizations. By contrast, other relationships might be confined to a few relational ties that the salesperson has developed with members of the purchasing staff. Drawing on insights from social network theory, the following drivers of relational marketing effectiveness have been identified.

Relationship Quality **Relationship quality** represents a high-caliber relational bond with an exchange partner that captures a number of interaction characteristics such as commitment and trust. "Commitment represents a desire to maintain a valued relationship and, thus, an exchange partner's relationship motivation toward a partner. Trust involves the evaluation of a partner's reliability and integrity, which generates confidence in the partner's future actions that support cooperation."[8] Partners involved in high-quality, committed relationships are willing to disclose proprietary information, which enables sellers to identify the customer's unmet needs, cross-sell additional products more effectively, and price products properly, thereby enhancing profitability.

Relationship Breadth A key objective of the business marketer is to develop a keen understanding of a customer's needs in order to develop a value proposition that squarely addresses those needs. **Relationship breadth** represents the number of interpersonal ties that a firm has with an exchange partner. A seller that has forged more interpersonal ties with a customer can gain better access to information, identify profit-enhancing opportunities, and become more efficient in building and maintaining the relationship. Research indicates that multiple interfirm ties are particularly vital when serving customer organizations that have high employee turnover.[9]

[6]Unless otherwise noted, this section is based on Robert W. Palmatier, *Relationship Marketing* (Cambridge, MA: Marketing Science Institute, 2008).

[7]Christian Homburg and Ruth M. Stock, "The Link between Salespeople's Job Satisfaction and Customer Satisfaction in a Business-to-Business Context: A Dyadic Analysis," *Journal of the Academy of Marketing Science* 32 (Spring 2004): pp. 144–158.

[8]Robert W. Palmatier, "Interfirm Relational Drivers of Customer Value," *Journal of Marketing* 72 (July 2008): p. 77.

[9]Ibid., p. 86.

FIGURE 16.1 | A MODEL OF INTERFIRM RELATIONSHIP MARKETING

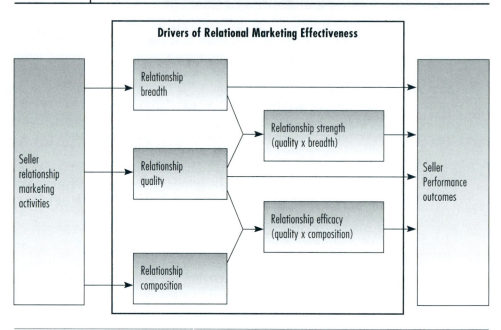

SOURCE: Robert W. Palmatier, *Relationship Marketing* (Cambridge, MA: Marketing Science Institute, 2008), p. 26. Copyright © Marketing Science Institute. All rights reserved. Reproduced by permission.

Relationship Composition   **Relationship composition** centers on the decision-making capability of relational contacts at the customer firm; a contact portfolio that includes high-level decision makers increases a seller's ability to effect change in customer organizations. For example, greater authority in the contact portfolio allows a salesperson to access information, adapt offerings, and reach influential decision makers. A competitor who has access only to contacts with less authority faces difficult odds in winning the account. Research suggests that building relationships with key decision makers generates the highest returns among customer organizations that are the most difficult to access.[10]

Relationship Strength   A clear portrait of a buyer-seller relationship will consider both relationship quality and relationship breadth. (See Figure 16.1.) Therefore, **relationship strength** reflects the ability of a relationship to withstand stress and/or conflict, such that multiple, high-quality relational bonds result in strong, resilient relationships. A service failure, like equipment failure or poor delivery service, creates conflict in a buyer-seller relationship. A customer relationship characterized by many cursory contacts (greater breadth, low quality) will afford little protection to the seller during this period of stress. However, based on confidence (trust), multiple, high-quality relationship ties (greater breadth, high quality) will support the seller during the service recovery process.

Relationship Efficacy   Representing the interaction between relationship quality and relationship composition, **relationship efficacy** captures the ability of an interfirm relationship to achieve desired objectives. High-quality relationships with

---

[10]Ibid., pp. 85–86.

members of the customer organization, coupled with a well-structured and diverse contact portfolio, gives sellers the means to execute responsive strategy. Robert W. Palmatier observes:

> A portfolio might encompass high-quality, broad relationships but it suffers if those contacts are restricted to one functional area with little decision-making (low composition) because the seller lacks access to divergent (nonredundant) information and cannot promote customer change.[11]

Relationship Marketing (RM) Programs

To strengthen relational ties with customers, three types of relationship marketing programs are employed.

- **Social RM programs** use social engagements (for example, meals, sporting events) or frequent, customized communication to personalize the relationship and highlight the customer's special status. The relational bonds that result from this specialized treatment are difficult for rivals to duplicate and may prompt customers to reciprocate in the form of repeat sales and positive recommendations of the seller to others.

- **Structural RM programs** are designed to increase productivity and/or efficiency for customers through targeted investments that customers would not likely make themselves. For example, the seller might provide an electronic order-processing interface of customized packaging for the customer. By offering unique benefits and, in the case of electronic ordering, a structural bond, these programs create competitive advantages and discourage customers from switching to competitors.

- **Financial RM programs** provide economic benefits, such as special discounts, free shipping, or extended payment terms, to increase customer loyalty. Because competitors can readily match the economic incentives, the advantages tend to be unsustainable.

Financial Impact of RM Programs[12]

Do RM programs pay off? A recent study measured the incremental profits generated by RM programs to isolate the return on investment (ROI).

Social   In evaluating the short-term financial returns of the different RM strategies, the study found that social RM investments have a direct and significant (approximately 180 percent) impact on profit—far greater than the impact of structural or financial RM programs. For the customer, social programs create a feeling of interpersonal debt, stimulating a pressing need to reciprocate and thereby generating immediate returns. Yet, Robert Palmatier observes: "Social programs may cause customers to think highly of the salesperson rather than the selling firm, which increases the risk that the selling firm loses the customer if the salesperson

[11]Palmatier, *Relationship Marketing*, p. 25.

[12]This section is based on Robert W. Palmatier, Srinath Gopalakrishna, and Mark B. Houston, "Returns on Business-to-Business Relationship Marketing Investments: Strategies for Leveraging Profits," *Marketing Science* 25 (September–October 2006): pp. 477–493.

leaves. Therefore, the selling firm should keep other avenues open for direct communication with customers."[13]

Structural   The financial impact of structural RM programs (for example, providing a value-enhancing linkage) depends on the frequency of interaction a firm has with customers. While break-even returns are achieved for customers with average interaction frequency, the return on structural RM investment is approximately 120 percent for those customers who receive frequent contact from the seller. As a result, the business marketing strategist should target those customers for whom structural solutions offer the most value. Moreover, while merely breaking even in the short term, structural linkages like electronic order processing should increase long-term profits because customers are inclined to take advantage of the value provided.

Financial   Since economic incentives often attract "deal-prone" customers and are easy for rivals to match, financial RM programs generally fail to generate positive economic returns. Of course, such programs (for example, special discounts) may represent a necessary response to a competitive threat that is needed to protect existing customer relationships. By contrast, social and structural RM programs are offensive weapons that provide greater financial returns and a more durable competitive advantage.

Targeting RM Programs[14]

Some customers are more receptive to relationship marketing initiatives than others. As purchasing managers emphasize cost-reducing and productivity-enhancing objectives, they carefully scrutinize the time and effort that can be invested in particular supplier relationships. **Relationship orientation** (RO) represents the customer's desire to engage in strong relationships with a current or potential supplier. "Customers tend to be more . . . open to relationship building when they face some risk, uncertainty, or dependence in the exchange process or are very motivated about the product or service category. In these situations, customers find the expertise, added flexibility, and risk-reduction benefits of a relationship valuable and likely welcome the seller's relationship efforts."[15]

Allocating RM Resources   Research demonstrates that the returns on RM investments improve if business marketers are able to target customers on the basis of their RO rather than size. For example, salespeople report higher returns for their RM efforts directed toward buyers with the highest self-reported RO than for those with the lowest RO. Importantly, the study reveals a separate strategy that can be used effectively for customers who demonstrate a *low* RO. These customers would shift 21 percent of their business to another supplier of similar products if the transaction were completely automated (that is, if no salesperson was involved). This suggests that the business marketer could drastically lower costs and better serve some customers by accurately detecting those with a low RO and offering them the option of using an electronic ordering interface. By properly aligning RM resources to the

---

[13]Palmatier, *Relationship Marketing*, p. 64.

[14]This section is based on Robert W. Palmatier, Lisa K. Scheer, Kenneth R. Evans, and Todd J. Arnold, "Achieving Relationship Marketing Effectiveness in Business-to-Business Exchanges," *Journal of the Academy of Marketing Science* 36 (June 2008): pp. 174–190.

[15]Palmatier, *Relationship Marketing*, p. 90.

needs of customers, the salesperson can direct attention to those customers who are most receptive to relationship-building efforts.

Managing the Sales Force

Effective management of the business-to-business sales force is fundamental to the firm's success. Sales management refers to planning, organizing, directing, and controlling personal selling efforts.[16] Sales force decisions are tempered by overall marketing objectives and must be integrated with the other elements of the marketing mix. Forecasts of the expected sales response guide the firm in determining the total selling effort required (sales force size) and in organizing and allocating the sales force (perhaps to sales territories). Techniques for estimating market potential and forecasting sales (discussed in Part III, "Assessing Market Opportunities") are particularly valuable in sales planning. Sales management also involves the ongoing activities of selecting, training, deploying, supervising, and motivating sales personnel. Finally, sales operations must be monitored to identify problem areas and to assess the efficiency, effectiveness, and profitability of personal selling units.

This section considers strategic components of sales force management: (1) methods for organizing the sales force, (2) key account management, and (3) the distinctive characteristics of high-performing account managers.

Organizing the Personal Selling Effort

How should the sales force be organized? The appropriate form depends on such factors as the nature and length of the product line, the role of intermediaries in the marketing program, the diversity of the market segments served, the nature of buying behavior in each market segment, and the structure of competitive selling. The manufacturer's size and financial strength often dictate, to an important degree, the feasibility of particular organizational forms. The business marketer can organize the sales force by geography, product, or market. Large industrial enterprises that market diverse product lines may use all three.

Geographical Organization   The most common form of sales organization in business marketing is geographical. Each salesperson sells all the firm's products in a defined geographical area. By reducing travel distance and time between customers, this method usually minimizes costs. Likewise, sales personnel know exactly which customers and prospects fall within their area of responsibility.

The major disadvantage of the geographical sales organization is that each salesperson must be able to perform every selling task for all of the firm's products and for all customers in the territory. If the products have diverse applications, this can be difficult. A second disadvantage is that the salesperson has substantial leeway in choosing which products and customers to emphasize. Sales personnel may emphasize products and end-use applications they know best. Of course, this problem can be remedied through training and capable first-line supervision. Because the salesperson is crucial in implementing the firm's segmentation strategy, careful coordination and control are required to align personal selling effort with marketing objectives.

---

[16]A comprehensive treatment of all aspects of sales management is beyond the scope of this volume. For more extensive discussion, see Mark W. Johnston and Greg W. Marshall, *Sales Force Management* (New York: McGraw-Hill/ Irwin, 2008).

Product Organization   In a product-oriented sales organization, salespersons specialize in relatively narrow components of the total product line. This is especially appropriate when the product line is large, diverse, or technically complex and when a salesperson needs a high degree of application knowledge to meet customer needs. Furthermore, various products often elicit various patterns of buying behavior. The salesperson concentrating on a particular product becomes more adept at identifying and communicating with members of buying centers.

A prime benefit of this approach is that the sales force can develop a level of product knowledge that enhances the value of the firm's total offering to customers. The product-oriented sales organization may also help identify new market segments.

One drawback is the cost of developing and deploying a specialized sales force. A product must have the potential to generate a level of sales and profit that justifies individual selling attention. Thus, a "critical mass" of demand is required to offset the costs. In turn, several salespersons may be required to meet the diverse product requirements of a single customer. To reduce selling costs and improve productivity, some firms have launched programs to convert product specialists into general-line specialists who know all the firm's products and account strategies. Often, as customers learn to use technology, they outgrow the need for product specialists and prefer working with a single salesperson for all products.

Market-Centered Organization   The business marketer may prefer to organize personal selling effort by customer type. Owens-Corning recently switched from a geographical sales structure to one organized by customer type. Similarly, Hewlett-Packard successfully used this structure to strengthen its market position in retailing, financial services, and oil and gas exploration.[17] Sales executives at *Fortune* 500 companies that use sales teams believe they are better able to secure customers and improve business results by adopting a more customer-focused sales structure.[18]

By learning the specific requirements of a particular industry or customer type, the salesperson is better prepared to identify and respond to buying influentials. Also, key market segments become more accessible, thus providing the opportunity for differentiated personal selling strategies. The market segments must, of course, be sufficiently large to warrant specialized treatment.

Key Account Management[19]

Many business marketing firms find that a small proportion of customers (for example, 20 percent) often account for a major share (for example, 80 percent) of its business. These customers possess enormous purchasing power by virtue of their size, and they are searching for ways to leverage their suppliers' capabilities to enhance the value they deliver to their own customers (see Chapter 2). In turn, many of these large buying firms have centralized procurement and expect suppliers to provide coordinated and uniform service support to organizational units that are geographically dispersed on a national or global scale. In exchange for a long-term volume commitment, these customers expect the business marketing firm to provide additional value-added services

---

[17] Thayer C. Taylor, "Hewlett-Packard," *Sales and Marketing Management* 145 (January 1993): p. 59.

[18] Vincent Alonzo, "Selling Changes," *Incentive* 170 (September 1996): p. 46.

[19] This section is based on Joseph P. Cannon and Narakesari Narayandas, "Relationship Marketing and Key Account Management," in Jagdish N. Sheth and Atul Parvatiyar, eds., *Handbook of Relationship Marketing* (Thousand Oaks, CA: Sage Publications, 2000), pp. 407–429.

(for example, new-product-development assistance) and support (for example, just-in-time delivery) that may not be available to other customers.

Unique Value Propositions   **Customer prioritization** represents the degree to which firms prioritize customers by developing different value propositions for its top-tier versus bottom-tier customers. A recent study reveals that customer prioritization leads to higher average customer profitability and a higher return on sales by (1) positively affecting relationships with top-tier customers without affecting relationships with bottom-tier customers and (2) reducing marketing and sales costs.[20]

Key Accounts versus Regular Accounts   Given the importance of these large customers, firms are rethinking how they manage their most important customers and how they organize internal operations to meet these customers' complex needs. To that end, many firms—Hewlett-Packard, Xerox, 3M, IBM, and Dow Chemical, for example—are establishing *key account* managers and creating customer teams composed of individuals from sales, marketing, finance, logistics, and other functional groups. Key account managers are typically responsible for several important customers and report to a senior executive. For some customers, the key account manager may work directly in the customer's facilities. For example, an IBM key account team occupies offices at Boeing and works solely on that account.

A **key account** represents a customer who

1. purchases a significant volume as a percentage of a seller's total sales;

2. involves several organizational members in the purchasing process;

3. buys for an organization with geographically dispersed units;

4. expects a carefully coordinated response and specialized services such as logistical support, inventory management, price discounts, and customized applications.[21]

Rather than calling them "key accounts," some companies describe such customers as strategic accounts or national accounts.

A Different Type of Relationship   Table 16.1 compares and contrasts the traditional selling paradigm with the key account selling paradigm. Key account customers purchase in very large volume, and the focus of exchange extends beyond a core product as the seller augments the offering through value-added services and support. For example, acting on behalf of Cisco, FedEx coordinates the delivery of Cisco components from geographically dispersed facilities to ensure a seamless installation in a customer's organization. Whereas traditional sales management objectives typically emphasize maximizing revenue, key account relationships involve multiple goals. To illustrate, firms may enter into a closer, long-term relationship to lower costs to both partnering firms by reducing the seller's marketing and logistics costs and reducing the buyer's acquisition and production costs.

Coordinated Action   To effectively deliver more value to an important customer, the interpersonal connections between the buying and selling firms must extend

---

[20]Christian Homburg, Mathias Droll, and Dirk Totzek, "Customer Prioritization: Does It Pay Off and How Should It Be Implemented?" *Journal of Marketing* 72 (September 2008): pp. 110–128.

[21]Frank V. Cespedes, *Concurrent Marketing: Integrating Products, Sales, and Service* (Boston: Harvard Business School Press, 1995), p. 187.

TABLE 16.1 | **Traditional Selling versus Key Account Selling**

	Traditional Selling Focus	**Key Account Selling Focus**
Sales Volume	Varies	Large volume of purchases by the customer, often across multiple business units of the seller
Nature of Product/ Service Offering	Core product/service	Core product/service *plus* customized applications and value-added services
Time Horizon	Short-term	Long-term
Benefits to Customer	Lower prices and higher quality	Lower total costs Broader set of strategic benefits
Information Sharing	Limited: Narrow focus on price and product features	Extensive: Broader focus as firms share strategic goals
Sales Force Objectives	Maximize revenue Satisfied customers	Become preferred supplier Lower customer firm's total costs Enhance learning in the relationship
Structure of Selling Center	Individual salesperson is primary link to customer organization	Many individuals from multiple functional areas on the selling side interact with counterparts in the customer organization
Structure of Buying Center	Purchasing manager and a few other individuals are involved in buying decision	Many individuals within the customer organization interact in making decisions and evaluating the relationship

SOURCE: Adapted with modifications from Joseph P. Cannon and Narakesari Narayandas, "Relationship Marketing and Key Account Management," in *Handbook of Relationship Marketing*, Jagdish N. Sheth and Atul Parvatiyar, eds. (Thousand Oaks, CA: Sage Publications, 2000), p. 409; and Frank V. Cespedes, *Concurrent Marketing: Integrating Products, Sales, and Service* (Boston: Harvard Business School Press, 1995), pp. 186–202.

beyond the salesperson–purchasing manager relationship. A key account relationship involves frequent interactions between a team of functional experts from both organizations. The key account manager assumes a lead role in coordinating selling center activities and facilitating these cross-firm communications among functional experts. Nurturing these interpersonal connections creates an atmosphere in which these specialized personnel can cooperatively identify new solutions that lower costs or advance performance. When uncertainty is high or important product adaptations are required, the interorganizational team should feature the active participation of key personnel from the customer organization who join with members of the selling organization to create the desired solution.[22]

Selecting Key Accounts[23]   If the business marketing firm can have close and important relationships with a rather small set of customers, each requiring a large investment, the choice of the key accounts is critical. Because key accounts possess buying power, demand special services, and are generally more costly to serve, the

---

[22]Ruth Maria Stock, "Interorganizational Teams as Boundary Spanners Between Supplier and Customer Companies," *Journal of the Academy of Marketing Science* 34 (October 2006): pp. 588–599.

[23]This section is based on Cespedes, *Concurrent Marketing*, pp. 193–198; see also George S. Yip and Audrey J. M. Bink, "Managing Global Accounts," *Harvard Business Review* 84 (September 2007): pp. 103–111.

account selection process must examine the sales and profit potential as well as the long-term resource commitments the relationship demands.

Frank V. Cespedes recommends a three-phase approach in selecting key accounts To be chosen, a potential customer must meet the screening requirements of all three phases.

> Phase 1: Centers on (a) the profit potential of a customer, measured in terms of incremental sales potential, and (b) the degree to which a customer values the firm's support services and is willing to pay a premium price for them. (*For example, if the product is critical to a customer's operations, support services are more valuable.*)

> Phase 2: Identifies customer accounts from Phase 1 that have unique support requirements that provide profitable organizational learning opportunities. (*For example, the goal here is to invest in support capabilities that are valued by multiple accounts.*)

> Phase 3: Considers the degree to which the transactions with the potential customer complement the economics of the seller's business. (*For example, some customers purchase higher-margin products than others or provide a better match to the firm's manufacturing capabilities.*)

Says Cespedes, "When there are clear criteria for determining the profit potential, learning benefits, and cost drivers associated with customers, the firm knows when (and when not) to incur the substantial commitments required for effective key-account relationships."[24]

National Account Success

Research suggests that successful national account units enjoy senior management support; have well-defined objectives, assignments, and implementation procedures; and are staffed by experienced individuals who have a solid grasp of their entire company's resources and capabilities and how to use them to create customer solutions.[25] Do key account management programs enhance profitability? Yes. A recent comprehensive study of U.S. and German firms demonstrates the clear performance advantages that firms with active key account management programs enjoy over peers without them. In turn, the research also indicates that successful programs provide the key account manager with ready access to resources and support across functional areas.[26] Successful national account programs also adopt a strong relationship marketing perspective and consistently demonstrate their ability to meet the customer's immediate and future needs.

To this point, we have examined the central role of personal selling in business marketing strategy and alternative ways to align the sales force to customer segments. Attention now turns to key milestones in managing an engagement with a particular customer.

---

[24]Ibid., p. 197.

[25]John P. Workman Jr., Christian Homburg, and Ove Jensen, "Intraorganizational Determinants of Key Account Management Effectiveness," *Journal of the Academy of Marketing Science* 31 (Winter 2003): pp. 3–21; see also Homburg, Droll, and Totzek, "Customer Prioritization."

[26]Christian Homburg, John P. Workman Jr., and Ove Jensen, "A Configurational Perspective of Key Account Management," Journal of Marketing 66 (April 2002): pp. 38–60; see also Roberta J. Schultz and Kenneth R. Evans, "Strategic Collaborative Communication by Key Account Representatives," *Journal of Personal Selling & Sales Management* 22 (Winter 2002): pp. 23–32.

B2B TOP PERFORMERS

Using Customized Strategies to Outmaneuver Rivals

Competitive cognition refers to the framework a manager uses to organize and retain knowledge about competitors and to direct information acquisition and usage.[1] Research suggests that competitive cognition influences individual performance. For example, in an intriguing study in the sports literature, research demonstrates that elite athletes (for example, members of the U.S. Olympic wrestling team) use extensive competitive plans that involve customized strategies and tactics to beat individual competitors, whereas poorer performers do not develop customized plans but rely, instead, on a more generic approach to competition.[2]

Building on this line of inquiry, a study explored the role of competitive cognition in the competitive crafting that salespeople do.[3] **Competitive crafting** involves salespeople's use of information and knowledge about competitors to create a business proposition for the customer. Examples of crafting include speeding up the selling cycle to counter a slow rival or broadening the scope of the product and service offered to outmaneuver a niche rival. The results of the study indicate that each additional act of crafting increases the likelihood of the salesperson winning the customer's business by fivefold!

---

[1]Beth A. Walker, Dimitri Kapelianis, and Michael D. Hutt, "Competitive Cognition," *MIT Sloan Management Review* 46 (Summer 2005): pp. 10–12.

[2]Daniel Gould, Robert C. Eklund, and Susan A. Jackson, "1988 U.S. Olympic Wrestling Excellence: I. Mental Preparation, PreCompetitive Cognition, and Affect," *The Sports Psychologist* 6 (December 1992): pp. 358–382.

[3]Dimitri Kapelianis, Beth A. Walker, Michael D. Hutt, and Ajith Kumar, "Those Winning Ways: The Role of Competitive Crafting in Complex Sales," Working paper (Tempe, AZ: Arizona State University, 2008).

Isolating the Account Management Process[27]

To explore the work that account managers perform, our focus is on complex sales situations in business markets, which are characterized by large dollar values, protracted sales cycles, customized solutions, and the involvement of many organizational members on both the buying and selling sides. Frequently, in these sales situations an account manager is assigned to a particular set of customers and then assembles an ad hoc team as customer requirements or opportunities dictate. For example, large information technology firms, such as IBM, reserve key account teams for a carefully chosen set of customers but rely on an assigned account manager to cover the majority of large-enterprise customers.

Assuming a central role in a particular engagement is the account manager who diagnoses what the customer needs, identifies the appropriate set of internal experts, recruits them onto the ad hoc team, and then orchestrates the selling center's activities to deliver a solution that matches customer needs. Let's examine how high-performing account managers undertake these activities and highlight how they differ from their peers. Recent studies that explored the characteristics of high-performing account managers at two *Fortune* 500 firms provide some valuable insights.

---

[27]This section draws on Michael D. Hutt and Beth A. Walker, "A Network Perspective of Account Manager Performance," *Journal of Business & Industrial Marketing* 21 (7, 2006): pp. 466–473.

FIGURE 16.2 | THE CYCLE OF ACCOUNT MANAGEMENT SUCCESS

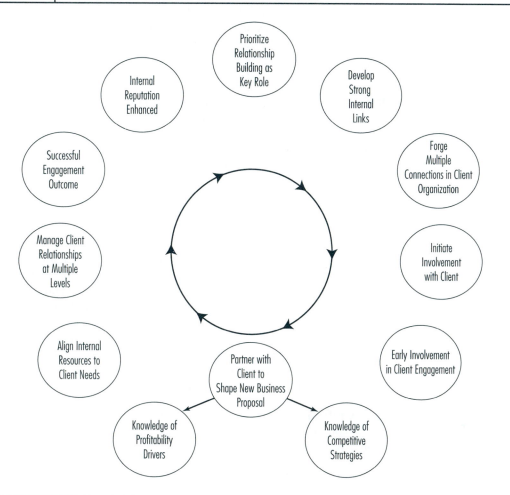

Account Management Success

For complex sales situations, account manager performance is contingent on securing access to the right people and the right information to solve novel problems for the customer. Figure 16.2 highlights the key milestones in a customer engagement and emphasizes the crucial role of relationship-building activities in the firm and in the client organization. High performers excel at relationship building. Capitalizing on these relationship connections, the account manager is better equipped to design a business proposal that aligns the firm's capabilities to customer goals. Moreover, observe that successful outcomes enhance the account manager's internal reputation, providing social capital the manager can invest in future customer engagements.

Building Internal Relationships   High-performing account managers form more cross-functional and cross-unit ties within the organization than their colleagues.

A diverse social network provides a manager with access to unique skills and knowledge. Account managers with ties to a number of distinct knowledge pools in the organization can draw on a large array of skills, knowledge, and resources—thereby enhancing their customer responsiveness. Research suggests that top-performing salespeople are able to "navigate their own organization to discover personnel, resources, or capabilities that may benefit them in specific sales situations. . . ."[28]

Forging Relationships Within the Customer Organization   Being centrally involved in a customer organization's buying system improves an account manager's ability to understand the customer's requirements and business goals. Compared with their peers, high performers possess more cross-functional ties and a larger network of contacts within the customer organization. Because complex sales situations involve a buying center that includes participants from multiple levels of the organizational hierarchy and diverse units, an account manager's communication network must go beyond the focal purchasing unit.

Managing the Customer Engagement Process   By developing a network of relationships both within the firm and within the customer organization, an account manager is ideally equipped to manage the customer engagement process. Through these connections account managers receive vital information about emerging customer opportunities, customer requirements and solutions, and competitive challenges (see Figure 16.2). Compared with low performers, high-performing account managers are more proactive in initiating involvement with the customer and tend to be involved in client engagements earlier in the purchasing process than their peers. Capitalizing on this early involvement, high performers are also more inclined to take an active role in shaping the client's request for proposals (RFP).

Aligning and Crafting   A successful client engagement hinges on both customer knowledge and competitive intelligence. High performers know more about client goals and the drivers of client profitability than low performers. When creating a customer solution, a salesperson must "act as a broker and assemble an ad-hoc team of experts, coordinating the efforts of people who may not have met one another before."[29] Drawing on this knowledge allows them to align the capabilities of the firm to the goals of the customer. High-performing account managers develop sound competitive intelligence and use this knowledge to outmaneuver their rivals in a particular client engagement.

Enhanced Internal Reputation   By building a strong network of relationships within both the firm and the customer organization, high-performing account managers—compared with their peers—are better able to diagnose customer requirements, mobilize internal experts, and choreograph the activities that are required to outmaneuver rivals and create the desired customer solution. Successful outcomes enhance the reputation of an account manager in the organization, thereby strengthening internal working relationships and assuring ready access to the right people and right information for future engagements.

[28]Christopher R. Plouffe and Donald W. Barclay, "Salesperson Navigation: The Intraorganizational Dimension of the Sales Role," *Industrial Marketing Management* 36 (May 2007): p. 529.

[29]Tuba Ustuner and David Godes, "Better Sales Networks," *Harvard Business Review* 84 (July–August 2006): p. 108.

Sales Administration

Successful sales force administration involves recruiting and selecting salespersons, then training, motivating, supervising, evaluating, and controlling them. The industrial firm should foster an organizational climate that encourages the development of a successful sales force.

Recruitment and Selection of Salespersons

The recruiting process presents numerous trade-offs for the business marketer. Should the company seek experienced salespersons, or should it hire and train inexperienced individuals? The answer depends on the specific situation; it varies with the size of the firm, the nature of the selling task, the firm's training capability, and its market experience. Smaller firms often reduce training costs by hiring experienced and more expensive salespersons. In contrast, large organizations with a more complete training function can hire less experienced personnel and support them with a carefully developed training program.

A second trade-off is quantity versus quality. Often, sales managers screen as many recruits as possible when selecting new salespersons. However, this can overload the selection process, hampering the firm's ability to identify quality candidates. Recruiting, like selling, is an exchange process between two parties. Sales managers are realizing that, for prospective salespersons, they need to demonstrate the personal development and career opportunities that a career with the firm offers. A poorly organized recruiting effort that lacks closure leaves candidates with a negative impression. A well-organized recruiting effort ensures that qualified candidates get the proper level of attention in the screening process. Thus, procedures must be established to ensure that inappropriate candidates are screened out early so that the pool of candidates is reduced to a manageable size.[30]

Responsibility for recruiting and selecting salespersons may lie with the first-line supervisor (who often receives assistance from an immediate superior), or with the human resources department, or with other executives at the headquarters level. The latter group tends to be more involved when the sales force is viewed as the training ground for marketing or general managers.

Training

To prepare new salespersons adequately, the training program must be carefully designed. Periodic training is required to sharpen the skills of experienced salespersons, especially when the firm's environment is changing rapidly. Changes in business marketing strategy (for example, new products, new market segments) require corresponding changes in personal selling styles.

The salesperson needs a wealth of knowledge about the company, the product line, customer segments, competition, organizational buying behavior, and effective communication skills.[31] All these must be part of sales training programs. Compared with their counterparts, top-performing sales organizations train new salespeople in

---

[30]Wesley J. Johnston and Martha C. Cooper, "Industrial Sales Force Selection: Current Knowledge and Needed Research," *Journal of Personal Selling & Sales Management* 1 (Spring/Summer 1981): pp. 49–53.

[31]William L. Cron, Greg W. Marshall, Jagdip Singh, Rosann Spiro, and Harish Sujan, "Salesperson Selection, Training, and Development Trends: Implications, and Research Opportunities," *Journal of Personal Selling & Sales Management* 25 (Spring 2005): pp. 123–136.

a broader range of areas: market knowledge, communication skills, listening techniques, complaint-handling skills, and industry knowledge.[32]

With the expansion in global marketing, firms need to include a sales training module that examines how to approach and respond to customers of different cultures. Such training would focus on the role of intercultural communication in developing global buyer-seller relationships.[33] Effective training builds the salesperson's confidence and motivation, thereby increasing the probability of success. In turn, training helps the business marketer by keeping personal selling in line with marketing program objectives. A successful training effort can reduce the costs of recruiting; many business-to-business firms have found that salesperson turnover declines as training improves. Clearly, a salesperson who is inadequately prepared to meet the demands of selling can quickly become discouraged, frustrated, and envious of friends who chose other career options. Effective training and capable first-line supervision can alleviate much of this anxiety, which is especially prevalent in the early stages of many careers.

Supervision and Motivation

The sales force must be directed in a way that is consistent with the company's policies and marketing objectives. Critical supervisory tasks are continued training, counseling, assistance (for example, time management), and activities that help sales personnel plan and execute their work. Supervision also sets sales performance standards, fulfills company policy, and integrates the sales force with higher organizational levels.

Orville Walker Jr., Gilbert Churchill Jr., and Neil Ford define **motivation** as the amount of effort the salesperson "desires to expend on each of the activities or tasks associated with his (her) job, such as calling on potential new accounts, planning sales presentations, and filling out reports."[34] The model presented in Figure 16.3 hypothesizes that a salesperson's job performance is a function of three factors: (1) level of motivation, (2) aptitude or ability, and (3) perceptions about how to perform his or her role. Each is influenced by personal variables (for example, personality), organizational variables (for example, training programs), and environmental variables (for example, economic conditions). Sales managers can influence some of the personal and organizational variables through selection, training, and supervision.

Motivation is related strongly to (1) the individual's perceptions of the types and amounts of rewards from various degrees of job performance and (2) the value the salesperson places on these rewards. For a given level of performance, two types of rewards might be offered:

1. **Internally mediated rewards:** The salesperson attains rewards on a personal basis, such as feelings of accomplishment or self-worth.

2. **Externally mediated rewards:** Rewards are controlled and offered by managers or customers, such as financial incentives, pay, or recognition.

---

[32]Adel I. El-Ansary, "Selling and Sales Management in Action: Sales Force Effectiveness Research Reveals New Insights and Reward-Penalty Patterns in Sales Force Training," *Journal of Personal Selling & Sales Management* 13 (Spring 1993): pp. 83–90.

[33]Victoria D. Bush and Thomas Ingram, "Adapting to Diverse Customers: A Training Matrix for International Marketers," *Industrial Marketing Management* 25 (September 1996): pp. 373–383.

[34]Orville C. Walker Jr., Gilbert A. Churchill Jr., and Neil M. Ford, "Motivation and Performance in Industrial Selling: Present Knowledge and Needed Research," *Journal of Marketing Research* 14 (May 1977): pp. 156–168; see also Steven P. Brown, William L. Cron, and Thomas W. Leigh, "Do Feelings of Success Mediate Sales Performance–Work Attitude Relationships?" *Journal of the Academy of Marketing Science* 21 (Spring 1993): pp. 91–100.

FIGURE 16.3 | **DETERMINANTS OF A SALESPERSON'S PERFORMANCE**

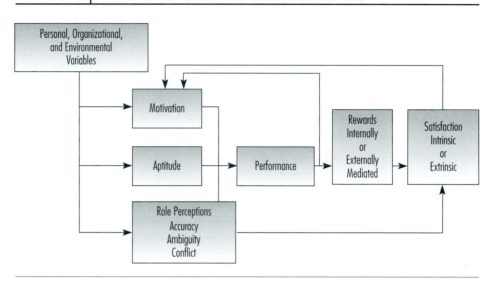

SOURCE: Orville C. Walker Jr., Gilbert A. Churchill Jr., and Neil M. Ford, "Motivation and Performance in Industrial Selling: Present Knowledge and Needed Research," *Journal of Marketing Research* 14 (May 1977): p. 158. Reprinted by permission of the American Marketing Association.

The rewards strongly influence salesperson satisfaction with the job and the work environment, which is also influenced by the individual's role perceptions. Job satisfaction declines when the salesperson's perception of the role is (1) *inaccurate* in terms of the expectations of superiors, (2) characterized by *conflicting* demands among role partners (company and customer) that the salesperson cannot possibly resolve, or (3) surrounded by *uncertainty* because of a lack of information about the expectations and evaluation criteria of superiors and customers.

Business marketers often use formal incentive programs to achieve specified customer service, sales, and profit results. Typically, an incentive program offers rewards for achieving a well-defined goal during a specified time frame. The rewards must be well conceived, based on what salespeople value, tied to achieving desired behavior, and recognize both individual and team behavior.[35] Frequently, recognition is a key ingredient in sales incentive programs and may run the gamut from Hewlett-Packard's quarterly award for a salesperson who was particularly astute in converting an objection into an order to the elaborate sales award presentations at IBM.

Organizational Climate and Job Satisfaction[36]   Churchill, Ford, and Walker, who contributed the model in Figure 16.3, also provide empirical support for some propositions that flow from the model. In examining job satisfaction in a cross section of industrial salespersons, the authors found that role ambiguity and role

[35]Katherine Morrall, "Motivating Sales Staff with Rewards," *Bank Marketing* 28 (July 1996): pp. 32–38.

[36]This section is based on Gilbert A. Churchill Jr., Neil M. Ford, and Orville C. Walker Jr., "Organizational Climate and Job Satisfaction in the Salesforce," *Journal of Marketing Research* 13 (November 1976): pp. 323–332. For related discussions, see R. Kenneth Teas and James C. McElroy, "Causal Attributions and Expectancy Estimates: A Framework for Understanding the Dynamics of Salesforce Motivation," *Journal of Marketing* 50 (January 1986): pp. 75–86; William L. Cron, Alan J. Dubinsky, and Ronald E. Michaels, "The Influence of Career Stages on Components of Salesperson Motivation," *Journal of Marketing* 52 (January 1988): pp. 78–92; and Jeffrey K. Sager, Charles M. Futrell, and Rajan Varadarajan, "Exploring Salesperson Turnover: A Causal Model," *Journal of Business Research* 18 (June 1989): pp. 303–326.

conflict undermine job satisfaction. Salespersons are likely to be anxious and dissatisfied when they are uncertain about the expectations of role partners or feel that role partners (for example, customers, superiors) are making incompatible and impossible demands.

An effective approach for reducing role ambiguity among new salespeople is training and socialization that offer sufficient information about role expectations and minimize potential confusion about performance requirements. Strategies that reduce role ambiguity are likely to boost sales performance and job satisfaction.[37] Moreover, a socialization program that provides newly hired salespersons with a realistic picture of their job strengthens their commitment to the organization.[38]

Job Satisfaction Really Matters   Salespersons tend to have a higher level of job satisfaction when (1) they perceive that their first-line supervisor closely directs and monitors their activities, (2) management provides them with the assistance and support they need to solve unusual and nonroutine problems, and (3) they perceive themselves to have an active part in determining company policies and standards that affect them. Job satisfaction also appears to be related more to the substance of the contact between sales managers and salespersons than to its frequency. Also, satisfied salespersons appear to be able to accept direction from a number of departments in the organization without a significant negative effect on job satisfaction—unity of command does not appear to be a prerequisite for high morale.

Direct Link to Customer Satisfaction   A recent study by Christian Homburg and Ruth M. Stock demonstrates a positive relationship between salespeople's job satisfaction and customer satisfaction.[39] Why? First, when they are exposed to a salesperson's positive emotions, customers experience a corresponding change in their own affective state. This phenomenon, rooted in the field of social psychology, is referred to as emotional contagion and has a positive influence on customer satisfaction. Second, the higher the salesperson's job satisfaction, the higher the quality of customer interaction, reflected by the salesperson's openness, flexibility, and customer orientation. The relationship between job satisfaction and customer satisfaction is particularly strong when customer interactions are frequent, customers assume a central role in the value-creation process, or innovative products or services are involved.

Turnover   Performance and individual differences in motivation, self-esteem, and verbal intelligence may also affect job satisfaction. Richard Bagozzi notes:

> Salespeople tend to be more satisfied as they perform better, but the relationship is particularly sensitive to the level of motivation and positive self-image of the person. Although management may have no direct control over the performance achieved by salespeople, they can influence the level of motivation and self-esteem through effective incentive and sensitive

[37]Steven P. Brown and Robert A. Peterson, "Antecedents and Consequences of Salesperson Job Satisfaction: Meta-Analysis and Assessment of Causal Effects," *Journal of Marketing Research* 30 (February 1993): pp. 63–77.

[38]Mark W. Johnston, A. Parasuraman, Charles M. Futrell, and William C. Black, "A Longitudinal Assessment of the Impact of Selected Organizational Influences on Salespeople's Organizational Commitment during Early Employment," *Journal of Marketing Research* 27 (August 1990): pp. 333–343.

[39]Homburg and Stock, "The Link between Salespeople's Job Satisfaction and Customer Satisfaction in a Business-to-Business Context," pp. 144–158.

supervisor-employee programs and thereby indirectly affect both performance and job satisfaction.[40]

Research suggests that sales manager leadership directly and indirectly influences salespersons' job satisfaction, which in turn affects sales force turnover.[41] In addition, another study indicates that salespeople who are managed by "high-performing" sales managers exhibit less role stress and are more satisfied than their colleagues.[42] Although some factors that influence job satisfaction and performance are beyond the control of sales managers, this line of research points up the importance of responsive training, supportive supervision, and clearly defined company policies that are congruent with the needs of the sales force.

Evaluation and Control

An ongoing sales management responsibility is to monitor and control the industrial sales force at all levels—national, regional, and district—to determine whether objectives are being attained and to identify problems, recommend corrective action, and keep the sales organization in tune with changing competitive and market conditions.

Performance Measures[43]   Sales managers use both behavior-based and outcome measures of salesperson performance. When a sales force control system is more **behavior based**, the sales manager monitors and directs the activities of salespeople, uses subjective measures to evaluate performance, and emphasizes a compensation system with a large fixed component. Behavior-based selling measures include the salesperson's knowledge of product applications and the company's technology and the clarity of the salesperson's presentations to customers. Behavior-based control systems are a good match when salespeople lack experience, companies need to control how salespeople present their products and services, and when salespeople are asked to perform a number of nonsales activities (for example, assisting with new product development).

By contrast, an **outcome-based** sales force control system involves less direct field supervision of salesperson activities and uses objective measures to evaluate performance and a compensation system with a large incentive component. Sales force outcome measures include sales results, market-share gains, new-product sales, and profit contributions. Outcome-based control fits when the skills and efforts of the sales force are the major determinants of sales results. "When sales reps make that big of a difference to the bottom line, it is worth it to give them autonomy and to pay them handsomely to do what they do," say Erin Anderson and Vincent Onyemah.[44]

Setting Performance Standards   The standards for evaluating salespersons offer ways to compare the performance of various salespersons or sales units (for example,

---

[40]Richard P. Bagozzi, "Performance and Satisfaction in an Industrial Sales Force: A Causal Modeling Approach," in *Sales Management: New Developments from Behavioral and Decision Model Research*, Richard P. Bagozzi, ed. (Cambridge, MA: Marketing Science Institute, 1979), pp. 70–91; see also Bagozzi, "Performance and Satisfaction in an Industrial Sales Force: An Examination of Their Antecedents and Simultaneity," *Journal of Marketing* 44 (Spring 1980): pp. 65–77.

[41]Eli Jones, "Leader Behavior, Work Attitudes, and Turnover of Salespeople: An Integrative Study," *Journal of Personal Selling & Sales Management* 16 (Spring 1996): pp. 13–23.

[42]Frederick A. Russ, Kevin M. McNeilly, and James M. Comer, "Leadership, Decision-Making, and Performance of Sales Managers," *Journal of Personal Selling & Sales Management* 16 (Summer 1996): pp. 1–15.

[43]This section is based on Erin Anderson and Vincent Onyemah, "How Right Should the Customer Be?" *Harvard Business Review* 84 (July–August 2006): pp. 59–67.

[44]Ibid., p. 64.

districts), as well as for gauging the overall productivity of the sales organization. Managerial experience and judgment are important in developing appropriate standards. Importantly, the standards must relate to overall marketing objectives, and they must take into account differences in sales territories, which can vary markedly in the number and aggressiveness of competitors, the level of market potential, and the workload.

Evidence suggests that a strict reliance on outcome measures and incentive compensation plans may not produce the desired sales or marketing performance results: "The alleged automatic supervisory power of incentive pay plans has lulled some sales executives into thinking that important sales outcomes could be reasonably accomplished without intense management reinforcement in noncompensation areas."[45] Often more effective is a more balanced approach that assigns a more prominent role to field sales managers and emphasizes behavior-based measures.[46]

Behavior-based measures also fit relationship selling—an important strategy in the business market. Relationship selling requires salespeople with a team orientation who can focus on activities such as sales planning and sales support, as well as on goals such as customer satisfaction.

Models for Business-to-Business Sales Force Management

To this point, our discussion has been concerned with (1) recruiting and selection, (2) training, (3) motivating and supervising, and (4) evaluating and controlling. Poor decisions in one area can create a backlash in other areas. One critical sales management task remains: deploying the sales force. The objective is to form the most profitable sales territories, deploy salespersons to serve potential customers in those territories, and effectively allocate sales force time among those customers.

Deployment Analysis: A Strategic Approach

The size of the sales force establishes the level of selling effort that the business marketer can use. The selling effort is then organized by designating sales districts and sales territories. Allocation decisions determine how the selling effort is to be assigned to customers, prospects, and products. All these are illustrated in Table 16.2.

Proper deployment requires a multistage approach to find the most effective and efficient way to assign sales resources (for example, sales calls, number of salespersons, percentage of salesperson's time) across all of the **planning and control units (PCUs)** the firm serves (for example, prospects, customers, territories, districts, products).[47] Thus, effective deployment means understanding the factors that influence sales in a particular PCU, such as a territory.

Territory Sales Response What influences the potential level of sales in a particular territory? Table 16.3 outlines eight classes of variables. This list shows the complexity

---

[45]David W. Cravens, Thomas N. Ingram, Raymond W. LaForge, and Clifford E. Young, "Behavior-Based and Outcome-Based Salesforce Control Systems," *Journal of Marketing* 57 (October 1993): p. 56.

[46]Richard L. Oliver, "Behavior- and Outcome-Based Sales Control Systems: Evidence and Consequences of Price-Form and Hybrid Governance," *Journal of Personal Selling & Sales Management* 15 (Fall 1995): pp. 1–15.

[47]David W. Cravens and Raymond W. LaForge, "Sales Force Deployment," in *Advances in Business Marketing*, vol. 1, Arch G. Woodside, ed. (Greenwich, CT: JAI Press, 1986), pp. 67–112; and LaForge and Cravens, "Steps in Selling Effort Deployment," *Industrial Marketing Management* 11 (July 1982): pp. 183–194.

TABLE 16.2 | **DEPLOYMENT DECISIONS FACING SALES ORGANIZATIONS**

Type of Decision	Specific Development Decisions
Set total level of selling effort	Determine sales force size
Organize selling effort	Design sales districts
	Design sales territories
Allocate selling effort	Allocate effort to trading areas
	Allocate sales calls to accounts
	Allocate sales calls to prospects
	Allocate sales call time to products
	Determine length of sales call

SOURCE: Reprinted by permission of the publisher from "Steps in Selling Effort Deployment," by Raymond LaForge and David W. Cravens, *Industrial Marketing Management* 11 (July 1982): p. 184. Copyright © 1982 by Elsevier Science Publishing Co., Inc.

TABLE 16.3 | **SELECTED DETERMINANTS OF TERRITORY SALES RESPONSE**

1. Environmental factors (e.g., health of economy)
2. Competition (e.g., number of competitive salespersons)
3. Company marketing strategy and tactics
4. Sales force organization, policies, and procedures
5. Field sales manager characteristics
6. Salesperson characteristics
7. Territory characteristics (e.g., potential)
8. Individual customer factors

SOURCE: Adapted from Adrian B. Ryans and Charles B. Weinberg, "Territory Sales Response," *Journal of Marketing Research* 16 (November 1979): pp. 453–465.

of estimating sales response functions. Such estimates are needed, however, to make meaningful sales allocations.

Three territory traits deserve particular attention in sales response studies: potential, concentration, and dispersion.[48] **Potential** (as discussed in Chapter 5) is a measure of the total business opportunity for all sellers in a particular market. **Concentration** refers to how much potential lies with a few larger accounts in that territory. If potential is concentrated, the salesperson can cover with a few calls a large proportion of the potential. Finally, if the territory is geographically **dispersed**, sales are probably lower because of time wasted in travel. Past research often centered on **territory workload**—the number of accounts. However, Adrian Ryans and Charles Weinberg report that workload is of questionable value in estimating sales response: "From a managerial standpoint, the recurrent finding of an association between potential and sales results suggests that sales managers should stress territory potential when making sales force decisions."[49]

Sales Resource Opportunity Grid   Deployment analysis matches sales resources to market opportunities. Planning and control units such as sales territories or districts

---

[48]Adrian B. Ryans and Charles B. Weinberg, "Territory Sales Response," *Journal of Marketing Research* 16 (November 1979): pp. 453–465; see also Ryans and Weinberg, "Territory Sales Response Models: Stability over Time," *Journal of Marketing Research* 24 (May 1987): pp. 229–233.

[49]Ryans and Weinberg, "Territory Sales Response," p. 464.

FIGURE 16.4 | **SALES RESOURCE OPPORTUNITY GRID**

<table>
<tr>
<td rowspan="2">PCU
Opportunity</td>
<td>High</td>
<td>

Opportunity Analysis
PCU offers good opportunity because it has high potential and because sales organization has strong position

Sales Resource Assignment
High level of sales resources to take advantage of opportunity

</td>
<td>

Opportunity Analysis
PCU may offer good opportunity if sales organization can strengthen its position

Sales Resource Assignment
Either direct a high level of sales resources to improve position and take advantage of opportunity or shift resources to other PCUs

</td>
</tr>
<tr>
<td>Low</td>
<td>

Opportunity Analysis
PCU offers stable opportunity because sales organization has strong position

Sales Resource Assignment
Moderate level of sales resources to keep current position strength

</td>
<td>

Opportunity Analysis
PCU offers little opportunity

Sales Resource Assignment
Minimal level of sales resources; selectively eliminate resource coverage; possible elimination of PCU

</td>
</tr>
<tr>
<td></td>
<td></td>
<td>High</td>
<td>Low</td>
</tr>
<tr>
<td></td>
<td></td>
<td colspan="2" align="center">Sales Organization Strength</td>
</tr>
</table>

SOURCE: Reprinted by permission of the publisher from "Steps in Selling Effort Deployment," by Raymond LaForge and David W. Cravens, *Industrial Marketing Management* 11 (July 1982): p. 187. Copyright © 1982 by Elsevier Science Publishing Co., Inc.

are part of an overall portfolio, with various units offering various levels of opportunity and requiring various levels of sales resources. A sales resource opportunity grid can be used to classify the business-to-business firm's portfolio of PCUs.[50] In Figure 16.4, each PCU is classified on the basis of PCU opportunity and sales organization strength.

PCU opportunity is the PCU's total potential for all sellers, whereas **sales organization strength** includes the firm's competitive advantages or distinctive competencies within the PCU. By positioning all PCUs on the grid, the sales manager can assign sales resources to those that have the greatest level of opportunity and capitalize on the particular strengths of the sales organization. For example, existing customers and prospects that are most appropriately positioned in the upper left cell of the grid represent the most attractive target while those in the lower right cell represent the least attractive.

---

[50]LaForge and Cravens, "Steps in Selling Effort Deployment," pp. 183–194.

At various points in deployment decision making, the sales resource opportunity grid is important for screening the size of the sales force, the territory design, and the allocation of sales calls to customer segments. This method can isolate deployment problems or deployment opportunities worthy of sales management attention and further data analysis.

Summary

Personal selling is a significant demand-stimulating force in the business market. Given the rapidly escalating cost of personal sales calls and the massive resources invested in personal selling, the business marketer must carefully manage this function and take full advantage of available technology to enhance sales force productivity. Relationship marketing (RM) activities represent dedicated relationship marketing programs, developed and implemented to build strong relational bonds with customers. These activities influence the three important drivers of RM effectiveness—relationship quality, breadth, and composition. To strengthen relational ties with customers, three types of RM programs are used: social, structural, and financial. Returns on RM investments improve when business marketers are able to target customers on the basis of their relationship orientation rather than size.

To manage the complex web of influences that intersect in buyer-seller relationships, an account manager must initiate, develop, and sustain a network of relationships, within both the firm and the customer organization. Compared with their colleagues, high-performing account managers excel at building relationships and develop a richer base of customer and competitor knowledge that they use to create superior solutions for the customer.

Managing the sales force is a multifaceted task. First, the marketer must clearly define the role of personal selling in overall marketing strategy. Second, the sales organization must be appropriately structured—by geography, product, market, or some combination of all three. Regardless of the sales force organization, an increasing number of business-to-business firms are also establishing a key account sales force so they can profitably serve large customers with complex purchasing requirements. Third, the ongoing process of sales force administration includes recruitment and selection, training, supervision and motivation, and evaluation and control.

A particularly challenging sales management task is deploying sales effort across products, customer types, and territories. The sales resource opportunity grid is a useful organizing framework for sales deployment decisions. Likewise, the business marketer can benefit by implementing a CRM system. Such tools can help the sales manager pinpoint attractive accounts, deploy the selling effort, coordinate activities across multiple sales channels, and build customer loyalty.

Discussion Questions

1. As drivers of relationship marketing effectiveness, compare and contrast relationship breadth and relationship composition.

2. Some customers are more open to relationship marketing initiatives than others. Under what conditions would customers tend to be more responsive to relationship-building efforts by the salesperson?

3. On the basis of return on investment, why do financial relationship marketing programs (for example, discounts) often fail to pay off?

4. When planning a sales call on a particular account in the business market, what information would you require about the buying center, the purchasing requirements, and the competition?

5. Some business marketers organize their sales force around products; others are market centered. What factors must be considered in selecting the most appropriate organizational arrangement for the sales force?

6. Christine Lojacono started as a Xerox sales rep several years ago and is now a key account manager, directing activities for five key accounts. Compare the nature of the job and the nature of the selling task for a key account manager with those of a field sales representative.

7. Explain how a successful sales training program can reduce the costs of recruiting.

8. Develop a list of skills and characteristics that distinguish between high performers and average performers in a sales organization. Next, describe the steps that a firm might take to improve the skill set of the average performers.

9. To make effective and efficient sales force allocation decisions, the sales manager must analyze sales territories. Describe how the sales manager can profit by examining (a) the potential, (b) the concentration, and (c) the dispersion of territories.

10. Research suggests that the greater the salesperson's satisfaction, the greater the customer satisfaction. Given the important relationship, what steps can a business-to-business firm take to nurture and sustain job satisfaction in the sales force?

Internet Exercise

1. Oracle, Inc., designs, develops, markets, and supports a family of enterprise application software products for large and medium-sized organizations. For example, the company provides enterprise application software for customer relationship management (CRM). Go to http://www.oracle.com, click on "Products," then on "Customer Relationship Management" to locate case studies of customers that have purchased the Oracle CRM product. Identify one of these customers and describe the benefits that the CRM system provided.

Account Management at YRC Worldwide: Choosing Customers Wisely

YRC Worldwide is a *Fortune* 500 company that provides a full range of transportation services for customers across all U.S. industry sectors. YRC's customers, which number more than 300,000, include industrial and consumer-goods manufacturers, large and small, as well as retailers, including those that operate on a regional or national scale. Whereas key account teams serve large corporate customers, YRC serves the majority of its customers through a network of local sales offices.

For example, in a metropolitan area, such as Seattle, Chicago, or Boston, account managers—working out of a fully staffed sales office and directed by a sales manager and area director—are assigned a particular section of the city and given responsibility for covering all of the customers within those boundaries. Depending on the concentration of business activity in an area, the number of potential customers that fall within an account manager's assigned territory might range from 300 to more than 1,500. Of course, the transportation services each customer requires are unique—some need guaranteed, time-definite delivery service or expedited delivery, whereas others are looking for the lowest-cost route. Moreover, the products involved are equally diverse, ranging from appliances or heavy machinery to apparel, component parts, or specialty chemicals.

Given the large number of potential customers they cover, coupled with the unique shipping requirements that each can present, account managers must give special attention to the most promising prospects, reaching others only if time permits.

Discussion Question

1. Develop a list of criteria an account manager at YRC could use to evaluate the relative attractiveness of 600 potential customers and isolate the "top-100" prospects. Assume that you have full access to any company information, including past purchasing behavior, revenue and profit data, customer satisfaction reports, and a complete demographic profile of each customer organization.

PART

V

EVALUATING BUSINESS MARKETING STRATEGY AND PERFORMANCE

Marketing Performance Measurement

Two business marketing managers facing identical market conditions and with equal resources to invest in marketing strategy could generate dramatically different results. Why? One manager might carefully monitor and control the performance of marketing strategy, whereas the other might not. The astute marketer evaluates the profitability of alternative segments and examines the effectiveness and efficiency of the marketing mix components to isolate problems and opportunities and alter the strategy as market or competitive conditions dictate. After reading this chapter, you will understand:

1. a system for converting a strategic vision into a concrete set of performance measures.

2. the function and significance of marketing control in business marketing management.

3. the components of the control process.

4. the distinctive value of "dashboards" for evaluating marketing strategy performance.

5. the importance of execution to the success of business marketing strategy.

Larry Bossidy and Ram Charan say, "When companies fail to deliver on their promises, the most frequent explanation is that the CEO's strategy was wrong. But the strategy by itself is not often the cause. Strategies most often fail because they aren't executed well."[1]

Managing a firm's marketing strategy is similar to coaching a football team: The excitement and challenge rest in formulating strategy. Should we focus on running or passing? What weaknesses of the opposition can we exploit? How shall we vary our standard plays? So too, the business marketer applies managerial talent creatively when developing and implementing unique marketing strategies that respond to customer needs and capitalize on competitors' weaknesses.

However, formulating effective strategy is only half of coaching or management. A truly great coach devotes significant energy to evaluating team performance during last week's game to set strategy for this week's. Did our strategy work? Why? Where did it break down? Similarly, a successful marketing strategy depends on evaluating marketing performance. The other half of strategy planning is **marketing control**, that is, checking actual against planned performance by evaluating the profitability of products, customer segments, and territories. James Harrington, Quality Advisor for Ernst & Young, puts the importance of marketing control in perspective: "Measurement is the first step that leads to control and eventually to improvement. If you can't measure something, you can't understand it. If you can't understand it, you can't control it. If you can't control it, you can't improve it."[2] Importantly, an effective control system should measure the key drivers of success in the business environment and focus attention on where improvements need to be made.[3]

According to a study conducted by the Chief Marketing Officer (CMO) Council, chief marketing officers face intense pressure from bottom-line-focused CEOs and demanding corporate boards to improve the relevance, accountability, and performance of their organizations. Measuring marketing performance, quantifying and measuring marketing's worth, and improving marketing's efficiency and effectiveness continue to rank among the top challenges faced by marketers. The CMO Council study found that for today's marketers, proving marketing's value is the number-one challenge above other challenges, such as growing customer knowledge and extracting greater value and profitability from customers.[4] Thus, the critical importance of an effective control system that provides key measures of performance is highlighted for all business marketers, whether small or large.

Information generated by the marketing control system is essential for revising current marketing strategies, formulating new ones, and allocating funds. As Roland Rust and his colleagues note, "the effective dissemination of new methods of assessing marketing productivity to the business community will be a major step toward raising marketing's vitality in the firm and, more importantly, toward raising the performance of the firm itself."[5] Thus, marketing control provides a critical foundation

---

[1]Larry Bossidy and Ram Charan, *Execution: The Discipline of Getting Things Done* (New York: Crown Business, 2002), p. 15.

[2]Amy Miller and Jennifer Cioffi, "Measuring Marketing Effectiveness and Value: The Unisys Marketing Dashboard," *Journal of Advertising Research* 44 (September /October 2004): p. 244.

[3]Robert S. Kaplan and David P. Norton, "Using the Balanced Scorecard as a Strategic Management System," *Harvard Business Review* 74 (January–February 1996): pp. 75–85.

[4]Laura Patterson, "Taking On the Metrics Challenge," *Journal of Targeting, Measurement and Analysis for Marketing* 15 (June 2007): p. 273.

[5]Roland T. Rust, Tim Ambler, Gregory S. Carpenter, V. Kumar, and Rajendra K. Srivastava "Measuring Marketing Productivity: Current Knowledge and Future Directions," *Journal of Marketing* 68 (October, 2004): 76–90.

for diagnosing and advancing firm performance, and the assessment of marketing performance is as important as the formulation and execution of marketing strategy. Importantly, the requirements for an effective control system are strict—data must be gathered continuously on the appropriate performance measures. Thus, an effective marketing strategy is rooted in a carefully designed and well-applied control system. Such a system must also monitor the quality of strategy implementation. Gary Hamel asserts that "implementation is often more difficult than it need be because only a handful of people have been involved in the creation of strategy and only a few key executives share a conviction about the way forward."[6]

This chapter presents the rudiments of a marketing control system, beginning with a framework that converts strategy goals into concrete performance measures. Next, it examines the components of the control process. Finally, it examines the implementation skills that ultimately shape successful business marketing strategies.

A Strategy Map: Portrait of an Integrated Plan[7]

A strategy map provides a visual representation of the cause-and-effect relationships among the components of a company's strategy. Recall that strategy maps were introduced in Chapter 6 to demonstrate how to align internal processes to support different marketing strategies. Figure 17.1 provides the strategy map for Boise Office Solutions—a $3.5 billion distributor of office and technology products, office furniture, and paper products that developed a distinctive customer relationship strategy, emphasizing customer solutions and personalized service. Leading firms widely use the strategy map concept, developed by Robert S. Kaplan and David P. Norton, because it isolates the interrelationships among four perspectives of a company that the authors refer to as a balanced scorecard[8] (see Chapter 6):

1. A **financial perspective** that describes the expected outcomes of the strategy, such as revenue growth, productivity improvements, or increased shareholder value.

2. The **customer perspective** that defines how the firm proposes to deliver a competitively superior value proposition to targeted customers.

3. The **internal perspective** that describes the business processes that have the greatest effect on the chosen strategy, such as customer relationship management (Chapter 4), innovation management (Chapter 9), or supply-chain management (Chapter 13).

4. The **learning and growth perspective** that describes the human capital (personnel), information capital (information technology systems), and organizational capital (climate) that must be aligned to the strategy to support value-creating internal processes.

---

[6]Gary Hamel, "Strategy as Revolution," *Harvard Business Review* 74 (July–August 1996): p. 82. See also, Gary Hamel and Liisa Välikangas, "The Quest for Resilience," *Harvard Business Review* 81 (September 2003): pp. 52–63.

[7]This section is based on Robert S. Kaplan and David P. Norton, *Strategy Maps: Converting Intangible Assets into Tangible Outcomes* (Boston: Harvard Business School Publishing, 2004).

[8]Kaplan and Norton, "Using the Balanced Scorecard," pp. 75–85.

FIGURE 17.1　|　**BOISE OFFICE SOLUTIONS STRATEGY MAP**

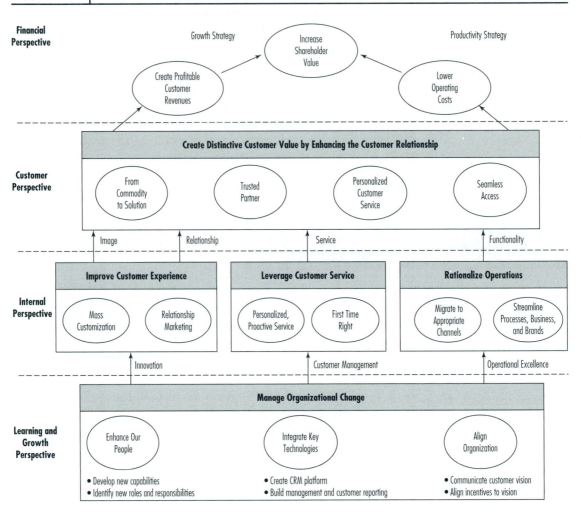

Using Boise Office Solutions as an illustrative case study, let's explore the six-step process that managers can use to build a tightly integrated strategy.[9]

Developing the Strategy: The Process

A strategy must provide a clear portrait that reveals how a firm will achieve its goals and deliver on its promises to customers, employees, and shareholders.[10] Boise Office Solutions sought a new strategy because the industry continued to consolidate

---

[9]Kaplan and Norton, *Strategy Maps*, pp. 355–360.

[10]Robert S. Kaplan and David P. Norton, "Having Trouble with Your Strategy? Then Map It," *Harvard Business Review* 78 (September–October 2000): pp. 167–176.

and more and more of its customers viewed office products as a commodity. Without a fresh strategy, company executives believed that these challenging forces would continue to shrink profit margins and put increasing pressure on shareholder value. Likewise, in a service-driven, price-sensitive business, Boise managers were uncertain which customers might contribute the most value over time and how to allocate marketing budgets among the diverse customers that it served—from small businesses to large corporate accounts.[11]

Step 1: Define the Financial Objectives and Establish Growth and Productivity Goals Strategy maps start with financial objectives for creating shareholder value through two paths: long-term revenue and short-term productivity. The long-term goal often establishes a stretch target that creates a value gap—the difference between a desired future state and current reality. Kaplan and Norton note that the size of the value gap must be established with care: "Executives must balance the benefits from challenging the organization to achieve dramatic improvements in shareholder value with the realities of what can possibly be achieved."[12] So, specific targets for revenue growth and productivity improvements should be established along with a corresponding time line (for example, achieve revenue growth of 15 percent by year 1 and 30 percent by year 3).

Boise adopted a new customer strategy driven by this strategic theme: *Create Distinctive Customer Value by Enhancing the Customer Relationship* (see Figure 17.1). The financial objectives were to increase shareholder value by emphasizing market segmentation and measuring revenue, profit contribution, and cost-to-serve by individual customer segment.

Step 2: Define the Customer Value Proposition for Target Customer Segments Achieving revenue growth goals requires explicit attention to generating revenue from new customers or increasing revenue from existing customers. Thus, the most important component of strategy is to develop and clarify the value proposition for customers in targeted segments. Recall that Chapter 6 presented four major value propositions and customer strategies: low total cost, product leadership, complete customer solutions, and system lock-in.

Boise adopted a customer solutions strategy that enhances value through one-to-one marketing, anticipates customers' needs to create customized service, and provides seamless access across sales channels (for example, sales force, Web, direct mail). A customer satisfaction survey assessed the core elements in the firm's new value proposition. The core objective, "to create distinctive value," was measured by

- The number of customers retained in targeted segments;
- The number of new customers acquired;
- Estimates of the lifetime value of customers.

Step 3: Establish the Time Line for Results To develop a coordinated plan, the high-level financial goals must be broken down into targets for particular functions or internal processes, like innovation management, so that organizational members unite behind the strategy and are comfortable with the overall target.

---

[11]Kaplan and Norton, *Strategy Maps*, pp. 355–360.
[12]Ibid., p. 353.

For Boise, operations management processes would reduce the costs of servicing customers, the customer management process would increase the number of relationship customers, and the innovation processes would create new offerings such as contract purchase plans. A time line for performance targets guided the efforts in each group.

Step 4: Identify the Critical Strategic Themes and Internal Processes with the Greatest Impact on the Strategy   This step identifies the key processes in delivering the customer value proposition and reaching the company's financial objectives.
Boise's internal process objectives emphasized three themes (see Figure 17.1):

- *Operational excellence:* Rationalize operations by moving more customers to an e-commerce channel to provide more convenient customer access and lower costs per customer contact.

- *Customer management:* Leverage customer service by personalizing the ordering process, making interactions easier for the customer, and meeting all the customer's needs in a single interaction.

- *Innovation management:* Redefine customer value expectations by creating new tools that customers can use to control spending on office supplies.

Once again, Boise developed measures—such as the percentage of customers in a target segment that used the e-commerce channel—for each of these themes. To illustrate, for operations, success at reaching cost reductions was measured by the percentage of business in targeted segments that came through e-channels; for innovation management, success was measured by the number of customers participating in new contract purchasing plans.

Step 5: Identify the Human, Information, and Organizational Resources Required to Support the Strategy   The learning and growth objectives assess how ready the organization is to support the internal processes that drive the strategy. This stage ensures that organizational members are aligned with the strategy and get with the training, information technology, and incentives to successfully implement it.
To introduce the strategy at Boise, every employee saw a video of the CEO describing the strategy, and more than 1,000 employees attended a 6-hour course on the new customer management initiative. Moreover, the firm installed a comprehensive customer relationship management (CRM) system and provided 1,500 customer service representatives and managers with 30 hours of training on it.[13] A video was likewise developed for customers to show them the benefits of the new strategy. Among the measures used were the percentage of employees trained for the new customer-centric strategy and the proportion of staff with incentives directly aligned to the strategy.

Step 6: Develop an Action Plan and Provide Required Funding for Each of the Separate Initiatives (Strategic Themes)   To reach financial targets and fulfill the strategic vision, several separate initiatives—involving different functions and

---

[13]Don Peppers and Martha Rogers, *Return on Customer: A Revolutionary Way to Measure and Strengthen Your Business* (New York: Currency/Doubleday, 2005), pp. 133–134.

processes in the company—must support the overall strategy in a coordinated fashion (see Figure 17.1). These initiatives create the performance results and form the foundation for successfully implementing the strategy. Rather than a series of stand-alone projects, these initiatives should be aligned to the overall strategy and managed as an *integrated* bundle of investments.

Strategy Results   Boise's new strategy allowed the firm to reduce costs, boost growth, and offer even their most price-sensitive customers an integrated solution that delivered greater value than lower-priced competitors. In turn, customer retention improved dramatically, and sales from the firm's most valuable customers expanded. Don Peppers and Martha Rogers describe how the strategy achieves profit targets:

> The firm now has good customer profitability data, which is yielding steady benefits on a customer-by-customer basis. For instance, relying on this data, Boise chose to discontinue working with one of its largest customers, a hospital group that apparently cost Boise money with every sale. And a senior executive visited another customer's headquarters, shared data to show that the company was one of Boise's least profitable accounts, and won a price increase over two years.[14]

Maps: A Tool for Strategy Making

Because a firm's strategy is based on developing a differentiated customer value proposition, the business marketing manager assumes a lead role in both strategy development and implementation. Fundamental to this role is the challenging job of coordinating activities across functions to create and deliver a superior solution for customers.

Translating Objectives into Results   The strategy map, coupled with the measures and targets from the balanced scorecard, provides a valuable framework for the strategist. First, the strategy map clearly describes the strategy, detailing objectives for the critical internal processes that create value and the organizational assets (for example, information technology, employee rewards) needed to support them. Second, the balanced scorecard translates objectives into specific measures and targets that guide critical components of the strategy. Third, to achieve financial or productivity goals, a set of well-integrated action plans must be designed that are carefully aligned to the overall strategy. Attention now turns to the central role of the control process in business marketing management.

Marketing Strategy: Allocating Resources

The purpose of any marketing strategy is to yield the best possible results. Resources are allocated to marketing in general and to individual strategy elements in particular to achieve prescribed objectives. Profit contribution, market-share percentage, number of new customers, cost-to-serve customers, and level of expenses and sales are

---

[14]Ibid., p. 135.

typical performance criteria; but regardless of the criteria, four interrelated evaluations are required to design a marketing strategy:

1. How much should be spent on marketing in the planning period? (This is the budget for achieving marketing objectives.)

2. How are marketing dollars to be allocated? (For example, how much should be spent on advertising? On personal selling?)

3. Within each element of the marketing strategy, how should dollars be allocated to best achieve marketing objectives? (For example, which advertising media should be selected? How should sales personnel be deployed among customers and prospects?)

4. Which market segments, products, and geographic areas are most profitable? (Each market segment may require a different amount of effort because of competitive intensity or market potential.)

Guiding Strategy Formulation

Evaluation outcomes provide the foundation for integrating the market strategy formulation and the marketing control system. Results in the most recent operating period show how successful past marketing efforts were in meeting objectives. Performance below or above expectations then signals where funds should be reallocated. If the firm expected to reach 20 percent of the OEM market but reached only 12 percent, a change in strategy may be required. Performance information provided by the control system might demonstrate that sales personnel in the OEM market were reaching only 45 percent of potential buyers; additional funds could be allocated to expand either the sales force or the advertising budget. On the other hand, since performance was below targets, as pointed out by the control system, the problem may not be with the strategy, but with the way it is being implemented. Thus, additional funds may be allocated to marketing efforts, but it may be necessary to also carefully examine how effectively the sales force is executing the sales strategy or whether the advertising was implemented effectively—perhaps the message is wrong or the advertising media were not appropriate.

Managing Individual Customers for Profit[15]

As explored in Chapter 4, business marketers should also focus on revenues from individual customers and isolate the cost-to-serve them. For relationship customers, attention should be given to the share-of-wallet the firm is attracting. **Share-of-wallet** represents the portion of total purchases in a product and service category (for example, information technology) that a customer makes from the firm (for example, Hewlett-Packard).

For customers with a more transactional focus, the business marketer should

- Develop a customer database that profiles the past purchasing patterns of customers;

- Determine the cost-to-serve each customer;

[15]Roland T. Rust, Katherine N. Lemon, and Das Narayandas, *Customer Equity Management* (Upper Saddle River, NJ: Prentice Hall, 2005), pp. 426–428.

- Set a revenue target and profit goal;

- Develop a customer contact plan that details the sales channel (for example, direct sales, telesales, Web-based contact) to be used;

- Monitor performance results and the relative effectiveness of different sales channels.

Marketing managers must weigh the interactions among the strategy elements and allocate resources to create effective and efficient strategies. To do so, a system for monitoring past performance is an absolute necessity. In effect, the control system enables management to keep abreast of all facets of performance.

The Marketing Control Process

Marketing control is a process management uses to generate information on marketing performance. Two major forms of control are (1) control over efficient allocation of marketing effort and (2) comparison of planned and actual performance. In the first case, the business marketer may use past profitability data as a standard for evaluating future marketing expenditures. The second form of control alerts management to any differences between planned and actual performance and may also reveal reasons for performance discrepancies.

Control at Various Levels

The control process is universal in that it can be applied to any level of marketing analysis. For example, business marketers must frequently evaluate whether their general strategies are appropriate and effective. However, it is equally important to know whether the individual elements in the strategy are effectively integrated for a given market. Further, management must evaluate resource allocation within a particular element (for example, the effectiveness of direct selling versus that of industrial distributors). The control system should work in any of these situations. The four primary levels of marketing control are delineated in Table 17.1. In short, measures of marketing performance should be used both to assess the overall business success and to examine the health of particular products, markets, or distribution channels.[16]

Strategic Control

Strategic control is based on a comprehensive evaluation of whether the firm is headed in the right direction. Strategic control focuses on assessing whether the strategy is being implemented as planned and whether it produces the intended results.[17] Because the business marketing environment changes rapidly, existing product/market situations may lose their potential and new product/market matchups provide important opportunities. Philip Kotler suggests that the firm periodically conduct a

---

[16]Bruce H. Clark, "A Summary Of Thinking On Measuring the Value of Marketing," *Journal of Targeting, Measurement and Analysis for Marketing* 9 (June, 2001): p. 361.

[17]Philip Kotler, "A Three-Part Plan for Upgrading Your Marketing Department for New Challenges," *Strategy & Leadership* 32 (May 2004): pp. 4–9.

TABLE 17.1 | LEVELS OF MARKETING CONTROL

Type of Control	Primary Responsibility	Purpose of Control	Tools
Strategic control	Top management	To examine whether the company is pursuing its best opportunities with respect to markets, products, and channels	Marketing audit
Annual plan control	Top management, middle management	To examine whether the planned results are being achieved	Sales analysis; market-share analysis; expense-to-sales ratios; other ratios; attitude tracking
Efficiency and effectiveness control	Middle management	To examine how well resources have been utilized in each element of the marketing strategy to accomplish a specific goal	Expense ratios; advertising effectiveness measures; market potential; contribution margin analysis
Profitability control	Marketing controller	To examine where the company is making and losing money	Profitability by product territory, market segment, trade channel, order size

SOURCE: Adapted from Philip Kotler, *Marketing Management: The Millennium Edition* (Englewood Cliffs, N.J.: Prentice-Hall, 2000), p. 698.

marketing audit—a comprehensive, periodic, and systematic evaluation of marketing operations that specifically analyzes the market environment and the firm's internal marketing activities.[18] An analysis of the environment assesses company image, customer characteristics, competitive activities, regulatory constraints, and economic trends. Evaluating this information may uncover threats the firm can counter and future opportunities it can exploit.

An internal evaluation of the marketing system scrutinizes marketing objectives, organization, and implementation. In this way, management may be able to spot where existing products could be adapted to new markets or new products could be developed for existing markets. The regular, systematic marketing audit is a valuable technique for evaluating the direction of marketing strategies.[19]

Marketing Performance Measurement (MPM) Strategies[20]   Many firms are now *strategically* developing performance measurement approaches to evaluate their marketing efforts: They have developed a marketing operations area that concentrates on maintaining a set of pragmatic *marketing performance* objectives and measures which

[18]Philip Kotler, *Marketing Management: The Millennium Edition* (Englewood Cliffs, NJ: Prentice Hall, 2000), pp. 708–709; and Michael P. Mokwa, "The Strategic Marketing Audit: An Adoption/Utilization Perspective," *Journal of Business Strategy* 7 (Winter 1986): pp. 88–95.

[19]For example, see Philip Kotler, William T. Gregor, and William Rogers III, "SMR Classic Reprint: The Marketing Audit Comes of Age," *Sloan Management Review* 20 (Winter 1989): pp. 49–62; and Mokwa, "The Strategic Marketing Audit," pp. 88–95.

[20]This section based on Michael Gerard, "The Best Technology Marketers Are Well Versed in MPM," *B to B* 93 (April 7, 2008): pp. 21–23.

become the marketing performance measurement (MPM) system. Very simply, **marketing performance measurement** is a business strategy that provides performance feedback to the organization regarding the results of marketing efforts, and it is often viewed as a specific form of market information processing for the organization.[21]

For example, IBM maintains MPM from a central marketing operations function, providing its global marketing board with an integrated view across all business units. This process is part of marketing's strategic planning and resource management process, ensuring that the marketing measurement and specific metrics line up with the company's strategic and business objectives. IBM executives assert that MPM allows them to better align marketing priorities to business priorities and to connect marketing expenditures to business performance. Also, consistent use of common metrics under a common structure allows IBM to restructure programs, shift emphasis on particular offerings, and move investments to higher-growth opportunities—in other words, to drive actionable results.

In a different approach, Intel identifies four top-level broad strategies each year. Then it determines key business strategies, marketing metrics, and targets, and puts these on a "dashboard." These metrics are monitored quarterly or monthly and do not usually change radically throughout the year. Lastly, Intel drills down to the project level and identifies tasks and management by objectives (MBOs), which are measured by activity (completed or not) or results. Intel's dashboard increases visibility, reinforces accountability and facilitates execution of key marketing strategies. Intel marketing managers believe that the dashboard has allowed them to sharpen marketing strategies and to more clearly understand how marketing programs can contribute to business success.

MPM Guidelines and Payoff To effectively develop their MPM strategy, business marketing strategists should follow four important guidelines:

1. If the firm does not have an MPM process, it should begin slowly and should not aim for perfection.

2. The MPM should use relevant metrics that drive action.

3. All marketing groups and the sales department should be included in the MPM process.

4. The MPM process should become part of the weekly, monthly, quarterly and annual reporting as well as a central component of the strategic planning process.

In a study conducted by Don O'Sullivan and Andrew V. Abela, MPM ability was shown to have a positive impact on firm performance in the high-tech sector.[22] The study found that firms with a strong MPM ability tend to outperform their competitors, as reported by senior marketers. The results also suggest that MPM ability has a positive influence on return on assets (ROA) and on stock returns. In addition, the research revealed

---

[21]Bruce H. Clark, Andrew V. Abela, and Tim Ambler, "An Information Processing Model of Marketing Performance Measurement," *Journal of Marketing Theory and Practice* 14 (Summer 2006): p. 193.

[22]Don O'Sullivan and Andrew V. Abela, "Marketing Performance Measurement Ability and Firm Performance," *Journal of Marketing* 71 (April 2007): p. 79.

that MPM ability has a significant, positive impact on CEO satisfaction with marketing. Development of MPM ability requires that marketers divert part of their budget and attention away from actual marketing programs and toward measurement efforts.

Annual Plan Control

In **annual plan control**, the objectives specified in the plan become the performance standards against which actual results are compared. Sales volume, profits, and market share are the typical performance standards for business marketers. **Sales analysis** is an attempt to determine why actual sales varied from planned sales. Expected sales may not be met because of price reductions, inadequate volume, or both. A sales analysis separates the effects of these variables so that corrective action can be taken.

Market-share analysis assesses how the firm is doing relative to competition. A machine-tool manufacturer's 10 percent sales increase may, on the surface, appear favorable. However, if total machine-tool industry sales are up 25 percent, a market-share analysis would show that the firm has not fared well relative to competitors.

Finally, **expense-to-sales ratios** are analyses of the efficiency of marketing operations—whether the firm is overspending or underspending. Frequently, industry standards or past company ratios provide standards of comparison. Total marketing expenses and expenses of each strategic marketing element are evaluated in relation to sales. Recall the discussion in Chapter 15 on advertising expenditures, which provided a range of advertising expense-to-sales ratios for business-to-business firms. These figures provide management with a basis for evaluating the company's performance.

Marketing Control: The Marketing Performance Dashboard

Many business marketers have adopted the practice of creating "dashboards" of key metrics that provide information on the performance of the marketing function. Dashboards may be configured in many ways, but they typically present marketers with a highly graphical capsule view of key performance and operational metrics.[23] **Dashboards** provide management with a feedback system to track progress on key metrics and connect marketing performance to business outcomes.[24]

A marketing performance dashboard graphically depicts a company's marketing and operational performance through the use of simple gauges and scales. They represent graphical overlays on databases, providing managers with visual clues about what's happening in real time. Marketing dashboards are an appropriate visualization of critical underlying performance data.[25] Business marketers are increasingly using dashboards because of the high level of attention senior management is devoting to marketing return-on-investment. Importantly, dashboards help companies improve performance because dashboard metrics center on the key outcomes expected from the marketing function. For example, Tektronix, a company that provides test and measurement equipment to high-tech firms, demonstrates the striking improvements that a performance dashboard can facilitate. Over the first 5 years of using the system, the company has achieved a 125 percent increase in responses to marketing programs and has seen a 90 percent increase in qualified sales leads. In addition, Tektronix has reduced its cost per lead by 70 percent. Moreover, the company's marketing forecast

---

[23]Richard Karpinski, "Making The Most of a Marketing Dashboard," *B to B* 91 (March 13, 2006): p. 17.

[24]Patterson, "Taking On the Metrics Challenge," p. 274

[25]Christopher Hosford, "Driving Business with Dashboards," *B to B* 91(December 11, 2006): p. 18.

accuracy now has a variance of 3 percent, down from a variance of 50 percent before the dashboard was developed.[26]

Which Metrics Matter?   The metrics to be included in a marketing dashboard will vary dramatically from one firm to the next, because each firm has different performance outcomes that are considered important.

> Marketers must accept that there's no one-size-fits-all dashboard they can use; they must customize the tool for themselves. After establishing what the company's true business drivers are, management must cull the myriad possibilities down to the three or four key ones that will be the most fruitful to follow. At least one of these drivers, such as share of wallet, should indicate performance relative to competitors. At least one, such as loyalty, should clearly measure the customers' experience. And one, such as customers' average annual expenditures or lifetime value, should measure the growth of retained customers' business. Finally, any driver on the dashboard must be one the company can manipulate. It might be informative for a supplier of hospital beds to track the number of elective surgeries in the US, but the company can't influence that number, so it's not a useful metric for them to follow—they cannot 'manipulate' the number of elective surgeries.[27]

Isolating Performance Drivers   There is both art and science in the creation of effective marketing dashboards. However, an effective dashboard maps out the relationships between business outcomes and marketing performance. One of the great challenges is determining where all the relevant data reside: The marketer has to define what the key performance metrics are and think about where to get the actual data to populate those metrics, according to one expert who designs marketing dashboards.[28] In addition, the information one really needs to make decisions almost always comes from multiple sources: internal sales and marketing data, as well as external partner or third-party data. A typical dashboard could include data from 6 to 10 sources, which presents a major challenge. Table 17.2 provides examples of the metrics used in the marketing dashboards by Cisco Systems, Cognos Corporation, and Adobe Systems. Note that each company employs a very different set of metrics. The dashboard elements for each firm reflect the importance that each particular element plays in the success of marketing strategy.

Desirable Dashboard Features   One expert in the development of marketing dashboards suggests that a good dashboard should accomplish several objectives. The dashboard should

1. Foster decision making: the metrics should suggest a course of action to be followed;
2. Provide a unified view into marketing's value to the business;
3. Enable better alignment between marketing and the business;
4. Translate complex measures into a meaningful and coherent set of information.[29]

---

[26]Kate Maddox, "Tektronix Wins for Best Practices," *B to B* 90 (April 4, 2005): p. 33.

[27]Gail J. McGovern, David Court, John A. Quelch, and Blair Crawford, "Bringing Customers into the Boardroom," *Harvard Business Review* 82 (November 2004): pp. 70–80.

[28]Karpinski, "Making The Most of a Marketing Dashboard," p. 18.

[29]Patterson, "Taking On the Metrics Challenge," p. 273.

TABLE 17.2 | **EXAMPLE OF MACROSEGMENTATION: AIRCRAFT INDUSTRY**

Cognos Corp	Adobe Systems	Cisco Systems
Market share	Marketing activities: Ad reach; Web site hits	Image
Financial analyst firm rankings	Operational measures: Brand awareness	Brand perception
Average revenue per sales rep	Cost per sale; Program-to-people ratio	Lead generation
Penetration of top global companies	Outcome-based metrics: Market share; Number of leads	Employee retention
Number of customers using a company solution year-to-date	Leading indicators: Brand loyalty; Lifetime value of a customer	Customer satisfaction

SOURCES: Kelly Shermach, "Driving Performance," *Sales & Marketing Management* 157 (December 2005): p. 18; Kate Maddox, Sean Callahan, and Carol Krol, "Top Trends," *B to B* 90 (June 13, 2005): p. 24; and Sandra Swanson, "Marketers: James Richardson," *B to B* 90 (October 24, 2005): p. 10.

Finally, a dashboard should be focused on two levels: The dashboard should (a) report operations metrics that are internally focused and (b) reflect execution metrics that mirror marketplace performance.[30]

Operations metrics can include such measures as a

> marketing budget ratio, which tracks marketing investment as a percent of total revenue; a program-to-people ratio that determines the percent of a marketing dollar spent on programs versus staff; and an awareness-to-demand ratio that evaluates the percent of marketing investment focused on awareness-building versus demand-generation. Execution metrics, on the other hand, determine how effectively the marketing strategy is being executed. Here the measures include efficiency and effectiveness around implementation: Is awareness building? Are we developing preference? Is the company gaining consideration? Are leads being generated, opportunities identified and qualified? Are deals being closed?[31]

Marketing performance dashboards are powerful control tools that provide management at all levels of the company with vital data concerning just how well marketing strategy is performing and how much value the marketing function is adding to the firm.

Efficiency and Effectiveness Control

Efficiency control examines how efficiently resources are being used in each element of marketing strategy (for example, sales force, advertising); **effectiveness control** evaluates whether the strategic component is accomplishing its objective. A good control system provides continuing data for evaluating the efficiency of resources used for a given element of marketing strategy to accomplish a given objective. Table 17.3 provides a representative sample of the types of data required. Performance measures

---

[30]Michael Krauss, "Marketing Dashboards Drive Better Decisions," *Marketing News* 39 (October 1, 2005): p. 7.
[31]Ibid., p. 7.

TABLE 17.3 | **ILLUSTRATIVE MEASURES FOR EFFICIENCY AND EFFECTIVENESS CONTROL**

Product

Sales by market segments
Sales relative to potential
Sales growth rates
Market share
Contribution margin
Percentage of total profits
Return on investment

Distribution

Sales, expenses, and contribution by channel type
Sales and contribution margin by intermediary type and individual intermediaries
Sales relative to market potential by channel, intermediary type, and specific intermediaries
Expense-to-sales ratio by channel, etc.
Logistics cost by logistics activity by channel

Communication

Advertising effectiveness by type of media
Actual audience/target audience ratio
Cost per contact
Number of calls, inquiries, and information requests by type of media
Dollar sales per sales call
Sales per territory relative to potential
Selling expenses to sales ratios
New accounts per time period

Pricing

Price changes relative to sales volume
Discount structure related to sales volume
Bid strategy related to new contracts
Margin structure related to marketing expenses
General price policy related to sales volume
Margins related to channel member performance

and standards vary by company and situation, according to the goals and objectives in the marketing plan.

Profitability Control

The essence of **profitability control** is to describe where the firm is making or losing money in terms of the important segments of its business. A **segment** is the unit of analysis management uses for control purposes; it may be customer segments, product lines, territories, or channel structures. Suppose a business marketing firm focuses on three customer segments: health-care organizations, universities, and local government units. To allocate the marketing budget among the three segments, management must consider the profit contribution of each segment and its expected potential. Profitability control, then, provides a methodology for linking marketing costs and revenues with specific segments of the business.

Profitability by Market Segment   Relating sales revenues and marketing costs to market segments improves decision making. More specifically, say Leland Beik and Stephen Buzby,

> For both strategic and tactical decisions, marketing managers may profit by knowing the effect of the marketing mix on the target segment at which marketing efforts are aimed. If the programs are to be responsive to environmental change, a monitoring system is needed to locate problems and guide adjustments in marketing decisions. Tracing the profitability of segments permits improved pricing, selling, advertising, channel, and product management decisions. The success of marketing policies and programs may be appraised by a dollar-and-cents measure of profitability by segment.[32]

Profitability control, a prerequisite to strategy planning and implementation, has stringent information requirements. To be effective, the firm needs a marketing–accounting information system.

An Activity-Based Cost System   The accounting system must first be able to link costs with the various marketing activities and must then attach these "activity" costs to the important segments to be analyzed. The critical element in the process is to trace all costs to the activities (warehousing, advertising, and so on) for which the resources are used and then to the products or segments that consume them.[33] Such an **activity-based cost (ABC) system** reveals the links between performing particular activities and the demands those activities make on the organization's resources. As a result, it can give managers a clear picture of how products, brands, customers, facilities, regions, or distribution channels both generate revenues and consume resources.[34] An ABC analysis focuses attention on improving activities that have the greatest effect on profits.

Robin Cooper and Robert Kaplan capture the essence of ABC:

> ABC analysis enables managers to slice into the business many different ways—by product or group of similar products, by individual customer or client group, or by distribution channel—and gives them a close-up view of whatever slice they are considering. ABC analysis also illuminates exactly what activities are associated with that part of the business and how those activities are linked to the generation of revenues and the consumption of resources. By highlighting those relationships, ABC helps managers understand precisely

[32]Leland L. Beik and Stephen L. Buzby, "Profitability Analysis by Market Segments," *Journal of Marketing* 37 (July 1973): p. 49; see also Fred A. Jacobs, Wesley Johnston, and Natalia Kotchetova, "Customer Profitability: Prospective vs. Retrospective Approaches in a Business-to-Business Setting," *Industrial Marketing Management* 30 (June 2001): pp. 353–363.

[33]Robin Cooper and Robert S. Kaplan, "Measure Costs Right: Make the Right Decisions," *Harvard Business Review* 66 (September–October 1988): p. 96. For a related discussion, see Robin Cooper and W. Bruce Chew, "Control Tomorrow's Costs through Today's Designs," *Harvard Business Review* 74 (January–February 1996): pp. 88–97.

[34]Robin Cooper and Robert S. Kaplan, "Profit Priorities from Activity-Based Costing," *Harvard Business Review* 69 (May–June 1993): p. 130; see also Robin Cooper and Robert S. Kaplan, "The Promise—and Peril—of Integrated Cost Systems," *Harvard Business Review* 76 (July–August 1998): pp. 109–118.

where to take actions that drive profits. In contrast to traditional accounting, activity-based costing segregates the expenses of indirect and support resources by activities. It then assigns those expenses based on the drivers of the activities, rather than by some arbitrary percentage allocation.[35]

ABC System Illustrated[36] ABC analysis highlights for managers where their actions will likely have the greatest effect on profits. The ABC system at Kanthal Corporation led to a review of profitability by size of customer (see Chapter 4). Kanthal, a manufacturer of heating wire, used activity-based costing to analyze its customer profitability and discovered that the well-known 80/20 rule (80 percent of sales generated by 20 percent of customers) was in need of revision. A 20/225 rule was actually operating: 20 percent of customers were generating 225 percent of profits. The middle 70 percent of customers were hovering around the break-even point, and Kanthal was losing 125 percent of its profits on 10 percent of its customers.

The Kanthal customers generating the greatest losses were among those with the largest sales volume. Initially, this finding surprised managers, but it soon began to make sense. You can't lose large amounts of money on a small customer. The large, unprofitable customers demanded lower prices, frequent deliveries of small lots, extensive sales and technical resources, and product changes. The newly revealed economics enabled management to change the way it did business with these customers—through price changes, minimum order sizes, and information technology—transforming the customers into strong profit contributors.

Using the ABC System An ABC system requires the firm to break from traditional accounting concepts. Managers must refrain from allocating all expenses to individual units and instead separate the expenses and match them to the activity that consumes the resources.[37] Once resource expenditures are related to the activities they produce, management can explore different strategies for reducing the resource commitments. To enhance profitability, business marketing managers need to figure out how to reduce expenditures on those resources or increase the output they produce. For example, a sales manager would search for ways to reduce the number of sales calls on unprofitable customers or find ways to make the salesperson more effective with them. In summary, ABC systems enable the business marketing manager to focus on increasing profitability by understanding the sources of cost variability and developing strategies to reduce resource commitment or enhance resource productivity.

Implementation of Business Marketing Strategy

Many marketing plans fail because they are poorly implemented. Implementation is the critical link between strategy formulation and superior organizational performance.[38] **Marketing implementation** is the process that translates marketing plans into action assignments and ensures that such assignments are executed in a

---

[35]Cooper and Kaplan, "Profit Priorities from Activity-Based Costing," p. 131; see also Robert S. Kaplan and Steven R. Anderson, "Time-Driven Activity-Based Costing," *Harvard Business Review* 82 (November 2004): pp. 131–138.

[36]This section is based on Cooper and Kaplan, "Profit Priorities from Activity-Based Costing," p. 130, and Cooper and Kaplan, "The Promise—and Peril—of Integrated Cost Systems," pp. 109–119.

[37]Cooper and Kaplan, "Profit Priorities from Activity-Based Costing," p. 130.

[38]Charles H. Noble and Michael P. Mokwa, "Implementing Marketing Strategies: Developing and Testing a Managerial Theory," *Journal of Marketing* 63 (October 1999): pp. 57–73.

INSIDE BUSINESS MARKETING

Tracking Marketing Success at Siemens

Inside a huge corporation—one with a multitude of products and services and thousands of employees serving its customers worldwide—what constitutes a marketing success? With so many transactions and interactions, and a seemingly endless supply of data components, the question to be asked is, "Can success be effectively defined, tracked, measured, and communicated?"

For Siemens AG, a leading global electronics and engineering company employing more than 417,000 people in 192 countries, this process became a strategic goal more than 5 years ago on the B2B side and has since resulted in a program that has been rolled out in nine countries, including the United States. Siemens, like most businesses, understood that it needed to justify its marketing and marketing-related technology budgets from the start so there would be no surprises to report to senior management at the end of each quarter and at year's end. Getting to this point is a logical step, but accomplishing it is less easy. Siemens realized its goal through a strategy that combined both art and science.

The company's "*marketing scorecard*" report of the enterprise-marketing division offers invaluable insight across the entire marketing continuum, including awareness, interest, consideration, evaluation, and ultimate purchase—and illustrates the return-on-investment (ROI) of individual efforts. Here is an example: Say a Webinar costs $70,000 to produce. E-mail efforts to generate awareness produce 4,654 impressions. From that group, 529 express genuine interest by responding to the e-mail message. From here, 54 leads are generated. The questions become, "What did it really cost to get someone to respond?" and "What is the cost per lead?" Analysis of the marketing scorecard may indicate that some leads are too expensive and therefore should be refined or aborted.

The beauty of the scorecard—which Siemens uses to report to management monthly and to the company quarterly—is that it offers key measurement elements on one sheet of paper. Marketers are able to see how many orders were placed and how many were confirmed with the sales organization. It shows in black and white what each marketing dollar is producing or *not* producing and helps to determine quickly where the winners are and which efforts should be continued, retested, or dropped.

What may seem like an "overnight success" story for Siemens actually took years of collaboration and data-driven strategy that have now become engrained in the culture. Both art and science have been skillfully combined to help Siemens manage, track, and fund its marketing efforts—proving that each sustained activity creates a beneficial impact on the bottom line.

SOURCE: Yvette Castanon, "Keeping Score," *Marketing Management*, 13 (September/October 2004): pp. 16–18.

---

manner that accomplishes a plan's defined objectives.[39] Special implementation challenges emerge for the marketing manager because diverse functional areas participate in both developing and executing strategy.

The Strategy-Implementation Fit

Thomas Bonoma asserts that "marketing strategy and implementation affect each other. Although strategy obviously affects actions, execution also affects marketing strategies, especially over time."[40] Although the dividing line between strategy and execution is a bit fuzzy, it is often not difficult to diagnose implementation

---

[39]Kotler, *Marketing Management: The Millennium Edition*, p. 695.

[40]Thomas V. Bonoma, "Making Your Marketing Strategy Work," *Harvard Business Review* 62 (March–April 1984): pp. 69–76.

problems and distinguish them from strategy deficiencies. Bonoma presents the following scenario:

> A firm introduced a new portable microcomputer that incorporated a number of features that the target market valued. The new product appeared to be well positioned in a rapidly growing market, but initial sales results were miserable. Why? The 50-person sales force had little incentive to grapple with a new unfamiliar product and continued to emphasize the older models. Given the significant market potential, management had decided to set the sales incentive compensation level lower on the new machines than on the older ones. The older models had a selling cycle one-half as long as the new product and required no software knowledge or support. In this case, poor execution damaged good strategy.[41]

Marketing strategy and implementation affect each other. When both strategy and implementation are appropriate, the firm is likely to meet its objectives. Diagnosis becomes more difficult in other cases. For example, the cause of a marketing problem may be hard to detect when the strategy is on the mark but the implementation is poor. The business marketer may never become aware of the soundness of the strategy. Alternatively, excellent implementation of a poor strategy may give managers time to see the problem and correct it.

Implementation Skills

Thomas Bonoma identifies four important implementation skills for marketing managers: (1) interacting, (2) allocating, (3) monitoring, and (4) organizing.[42] Each assumes special significance in the business marketing environment.

Marketing managers are continually *interacting* with others both within and outside the corporation. Inside, a number of peers (for example, R&D personnel) over whom the marketer has little power often assume a crucial role in strategy development and implementation. Outside, the marketer deals with important customers, channel members, advertising agencies, and the like. The best implementers have good bargaining skills and the ability to understand how others feel.[43]

The implementer must also *allocate* time, assignments, people, dollars, and other resources among the marketing tasks at hand. Astute marketing managers, says Bonoma, are "tough and fair in putting people and dollars where they will be most effective. The less able ones routinely allocate too many dollars and people to mature programs and too few to richer ones."[44]

Bonoma asserts that marketing managers with good *monitoring* skills exhibit flexibility and intelligence in dealing with the firm's information and control systems: "Good implementers struggle and wrestle with their markets and businesses until

---

[41]Ibid., p. 70.

[42]Ibid.

[43]Michael D. Hutt, "Cross-Functional Working Relationships in Marketing," *Journal of the Academy of Marketing Science* 23 (Fall 1995): pp. 351–357.

[44]Bonoma, "Making Your Marketing Strategy Work," p. 75.

they can simply and powerfully express the 'back of the envelope' ratios necessary to run the business, regardless of formal control system inadequacies."[45]

Finally, the best implementers are effective at *organizing*. Sound execution often hinges on the marketer's ability to work with both the formal and the informal organizational networks. The manager customizes an informal organization to solve problems and facilitate good execution.

The Marketing Strategy Center: An Implementation Guide[46]

Diverse functional areas participate to differing degrees in developing and implementing business marketing strategy. Research and development, manufacturing, technical service, physical distribution, and other functional areas play fundamental roles. Ronald McTavish points out that "marketing specialists understand markets, but know a good deal less about the nuts and bolts of the company's operations—its internal terrain. This is the domain of the operating specialist. We need to bring these different specialists together in a 'synergistic pooling' of knowledge and viewpoint to achieve the best fit of the company's skills with the market and the company's approach to it."[47] This suggests a challenging and pivotal interdisciplinary role for the marketing manager in the business-to-business firm.

The marketing strategy center (discussed in Chapter 6) provides a framework for highlighting this interdisciplinary role and for exploring key implementation requirements. Table 17.4 highlights important strategic topics examined throughout this textbook. In each case, nonmarketing personnel play active implementation roles. For example, product quality is directly or indirectly affected by several departments: manufacturing, research and development, technical service, and others. In turn, successful product innovation reflects the collective efforts of individuals from several functional areas. Clearly, effective strategy implementation requires well-defined decision roles, responsibilities, timetables, and coordination mechanisms.

On a global market scale, special coordination challenges emerge when selected activities such as R&D are concentrated in one country and other strategy activities such as manufacturing are dispersed across countries. Xerox, however, has been successful in maintaining a high level of coordination across such dispersed activities. The Xerox brand, marketing approach, and servicing procedures are standardized worldwide.[48]

The Marketer's Role To ensure maximum customer satisfaction and the desired market response, the business marketer must assume an active role in the

---

[45]Ibid.

[46]Michael D. Hutt and Thomas W. Speh, "The Marketing Strategy Center: Diagnosing the Industrial Marketer's Interdisciplinary Role," *Journal of Marketing* 48 (Fall 1984): pp. 53–61; and Michael D. Hutt, Beth A. Walker, and Gary L. Frankwick, "Hurdle the Cross-Functional Barriers to Strategic Change," *Sloan Management Review* 36 (Spring 1995): pp. 22–30.

[47]Ronald McTavish, "Implementing Marketing Strategy," *Industrial Marketing Management* 26 (November 5, 1988): p. 10; see also Deborah Dougherty and Edward H. Bowman, "The Effects of Organizational Downsizing on Product Innovation," *California Management Review* 37 (Summer 1995): pp. 28–44.

[48]Michael E. Porter, "Changing Patterns of International Competition," *California Management Review* 28 (Winter 1986): pp. 9–40.

| TABLE 17.4 | **INTERFUNCTIONAL INVOLVEMENT IN MARKETING STRATEGY IMPLEMENTATION: AN ILLUSTRATIVE RESPONSIBILITY CHART** |

Decision Area	Marketing	Sales	Manufac-turing	R&D	Purchasing	Physical Distri-bution	Tech-nical Service	Strategic Business Unit	Corporate-Level Planner
Product/ service quality									
Technical service support									
Physical distribution service									
National accounts management									
Channel relations Sales support									
Product/ service innovation									

NOTE: Use the following abbreviations to indicate decision roles: R = responsible; A = approval; C = consult; M = implement; I = inform; X = no role in decision.

strategy center by negotiating market-sensitive agreements and coordinating strategies with other members. While being influenced by other functional areas to varying degrees in the process, the marketer can potentially influence key areas such as the design of the logistical system, the selection of manufacturing technology, or the structure of a materials management system. Such negotiation with other functional areas is fundamental to the business marketer's strategic interdisciplinary role. Thus, the successful business marketing manager performs as an integrator by drawing on the collective strengths of the enterprise to satisfy customer needs profitably.

Looking Back

Figure 17.2 synthesizes the central components of business marketing management and highlights the material presented in this textbook. Part I introduced the major classes of customers that constitute the business market: commercial enterprises, governmental units, and institutions. The timely themes of organizational buying behavior and customer relationship management provided the focus of Part II. Part III discussed the tools for assessing market opportunities; it explored techniques for

B2B TOP PERFORMERS

Cross-Functional Relationships: Effective Managers Deliver on Promises

Ask an R&D manager to identify a colleague from marketing who is particularly effective at getting things done and he or she readily offers a name and a memorable episode to justify the selection. To explore the characteristics of high-performing cross-functional managers, detailed accounts of effective and ineffective interactions were gathered from managers at a *Fortune* 100 high-technology firm. Interestingly, the top-of-mind characteristics that colleagues emphasize when describing high performers are soft skills like openness rather than hard skills like technical proficiency or marketing savvy. Here's a profile:

- High-performing managers are revered by their colleagues for their *responsiveness*. Remembering effective cross-functional episodes, colleagues describe high performers as "timely," "prompt," and "responsive" (for example, "When I need critical information, I turn to him and he gets right back to me").

- Rather than a "functional mindset," high performers demonstrate *perspective-taking* skills—the ability to anticipate and understand the perspectives and priorities of managers from other units (for example, "He's a superb marketing strategist but he also recognizes

the special technical issues that we've been working through to get this product launched on schedule").

- When colleagues describe the *communication style* of their high-performing cross-functional counterparts, they focus on three consistent themes: openness, frequency, and quality. Interactions with high performers are described as "candid," "unencumbered," and characterized by a "free flow of thoughts and suggestions." Such high-quality interactions clarify goals and responsibilities.

By "delivering on their promises," effective managers develop a web of close relationships across functions. "He has really good personal relationships with a lot of people and he has a network—he really understands the mechanisms that you have to use to get things done."

SOURCE: Michael D. Hutt, Beth A. Walker, Edward U. Bond III, and Matthew Meuter, "Diagnosing Marketing Managers' Effective and Ineffective Cross-Functional Interactions," Working paper, Tempe, AZ.: Arizona State University, 2005. See also Edward U. Bond III, Beth A. Walker, Michael D. Hutt, and Peter H. Reingen, "Reputational Effectiveness in Cross-Functional Working Relationships," *Journal of Product Innovation Management* 21 (January 2004): pp. 44–60.

identifying market segments, and forecasting sales. Functionally integrated marketing planning provides a framework for dealing with each component of the business marketing mix, as detailed in Part IV. Special attention was also given to the special challenges and unique opportunities that rapidly developing economies present for business-to-business firms.

Once business marketing strategy is formulated, the manager must evaluate the response of target market segments to minimize any discrepancy between planned and actual results. This chapter, which constitutes Part V, explores the critical dimensions of the marketing control process, which is the final loop in the model presented in Figure 17.2: planning for and acquiring marketing information. Such information forms the core of the firm's management information system; it is derived internally through the marketing–accounting system and externally through the marketing research function. Evaluation and control enable the marketer to reassess business market opportunities and make adjustments as needed in business marketing strategy.

FIGURE 17.2 | **A FRAMEWORK FOR BUSINESS MARKETING MANAGEMENT**

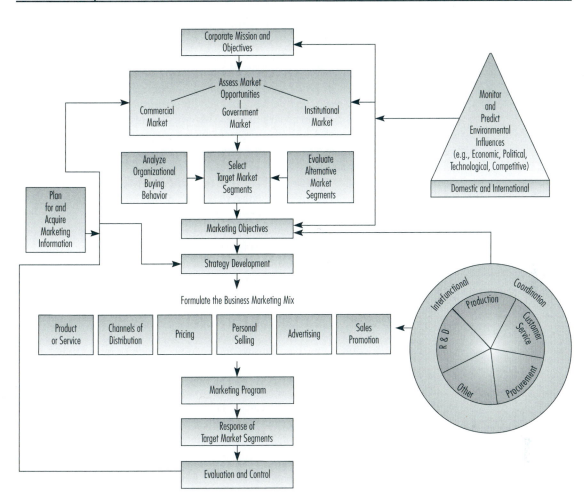

Summary

Central to market strategy is the allocation of resources to each strategy element and the application of marketing efforts to segments. The marketing control system is the process by which the business marketing firm generates information to make these decisions. Moreover, the marketing control system is the means by which current performance can be evaluated and steps can be taken to correct deficiencies. Used in conjunction with the balanced scorecard, the strategy map converts a strategy vision into concrete objectives and measures, organized into four different perspectives: financial, customer, internal business process, and learning and growth. The approach involves developing a customer strategy, identifying target market segments, isolating the critical internal processes the firm must develop to deliver value to customers in these segments, and selecting the organizational capabilities needed to achieve customer and financial objectives. A strategy map provides a visual representation of a firm's critical objectives and the cause-and-effect relationships among them that drive superior organizational performance.

An effective control system has four distinct components. Strategic control, which is operationalized through the marketing audit, provides valuable information on the present and future course of the firm's basic product/market mission. Annual plan control compares annual with planned results to provide input for future planning. Efficiency and effectiveness control evaluates whether marketing strategy elements achieve their goals in a cost-effective manner. Finally, profitability control seeks to evaluate profitability by segment. Marketing dashboards are effective tools for helping managers to isolate and monitor key performance metrics while providing top management with a compact profile concerning the impact of marketing strategies on overall company performance.

Many business marketing plans fail because they are poorly executed. Marketing implementation is the process that translates marketing plans into action assignments and ensures that such assignments are executed in a timely and effective manner. Four implementation skills are particularly important to the business marketing manager: (1) interacting, (2) allocating, (3) monitoring, and (4) organizing. Nonmarketing personnel play active roles in implementing business marketing strategy. This suggests a challenging and pivotal interdisciplinary role for the marketing manager.

Discussion Questions

1. Discuss why a firm that plans to enter a new market segment may have to develop new internal business processes to serve customers in this segment.

2. Not all customer demands can be satisfied profitably. What steps should be taken by a marketing manager who learns that particular customer accounts—including some long-standing ones—are unprofitable?

3. Describe the relationships between and among the four central perspectives represented in the balanced scorecard and included in a strategy map: financial, customer, internal business process, and learning and growth.

4. Last December, Lisa Schmitt, vice president of marketing at Bock Machine Tool, identified four market segments her firm would attempt to penetrate this year. As this year comes to an end, Lisa would like to evaluate the firm's performance in each of these segments. Of course, Lisa turns to you for assistance. First, what information would you seek from the firm's marketing information system to perform the analysis? Second, how would you know whether the firm's performance in a particular market segment was good or bad?

5. Susan Breck, president of Breck Chemical Corporation, added three new products to the firm's line 2 years ago to serve the needs of five NAICS groups. Each of the products has a separate advertising budget, although they are sold by the same salespersons. Susan requests your assistance in determining what type of information the firm should gather to monitor and control the performance of these products. Outline your reply.

6. Assume that the information you requested in question 5 has been gathered for you. How would you determine whether advertising and personal selling funds should be shifted from one product to another?

7. Hamilton Tucker, president of Tucker Manufacturing Company, is concerned about the seat-of-the-pants approach managers use in allocating the marketing budget. He cites the Midwest and the East as examples. The firm increased its demand-stimulating expenditures (for example, advertising, personal selling) in the Midwest by 20 percent, but sales climbed only 6 percent last year. In contrast, demand-stimulating expenditures were cut by 17 percent in the East, and sales dropped by 22 percent. Hamilton would like you to assist the Midwestern and Eastern regional managers in allocating their funds next year. Carefully outline the approach you would follow.

8. Your company produces electric motors for use in appliances, machinery, and a variety of other industrial applications. The CEO of the company wants the chief marketing officer (CMO) to create a dashboard of marketing indicators that could be reviewed by top management to evaluate the contribution of marketing to overall firm performance. What advice would you give to the CMO in terms of criteria he or she should use in designing the dashboard? That is, what will be required to make the dashboard effective?

9. Using the marketing strategy center concept as a guide, describe how a strategy that is entirely appropriate for a particular target market might fail because of poor implementation in the logistics and technical service areas.

10. Describe how the strategy implementation challenges for a marketing manager working at DuPont (an industrial firm) might be different from those for a marketing manager working at Pillsbury (a consumer-goods firm).

Internet Exercise

1. McKinsey & Company is a leading management consulting firm. The company publishes *McKinsey Quarterly*, an online journal that features the latest thinking on business strategy, finance, and management. Go to http://www.mckinsey.com, click on *McKinsey Quarterly*, and conduct a search for articles on "strategy implementation." Select a recent article on this topic and briefly outline the key insights that the article provides.

Intuit Leads in the Accounting Software Market[49]

Intuit, Inc. has developed a loyal customer base for its QuickBooks (small-business accounting) products, which simplify the difficult task of keeping accounting records. Once a customer becomes familiar with its products, the time it takes to transfer data or to learn a new application makes it quite difficult and inefficient to switch to a competing product.

The company has attracted a customer base of 3.5 million small-business clients who buy QuickBooks upgrades as their business requirements become more complex. "Intuit has loyal customers because it listens to users and incorporates their feedback to improve products. Few businesses understand their customers as well as Intuit." With 24 million small businesses already in existence and 600,000 new ones launched each year, Intuit has significant opportunities to grow.

Intuit's strategy centers on generating more revenue from its existing customers by adding a host of new services, attracting nonusers to its existing products, and entering new markets.

Discussion Question

1. As Intuit introduces new services and attempts to further strengthen the position of QuickBooks in the lucrative small-business market, what marketing performance metrics should marketing managers use to monitor the progress of its growth strategy and to make required adjustments?

---

[49]Irina Logovinsky, "When it Comes to Accounting Software: Intuit Has No Equal," *Morningstar* (August 15, 2008), accessed on August 25, 2008 at http://www.morningstar.com.

Case Planning Guide

PAGE	CASE #	CASE TITLE	1	2	3	4	5	6	7	8	9	10	11	12	13	14	15	16	17
										Relevant Chapters								
462	1	Columbia Industries, Inc.	★	★	★													★	
471	2	Clariant Corporation Marketing					★	★										★	★
486	3	Circuit Board Corporation					★	★		★	★								
499	4	3 M Canada: Industrial Business Division		★	★			★					★		★			★	★
515	5	FedEx Corp.: Structural Transformation through e-Business			★	★		★	★	★		★		★	★				
535	6	Clearwater Technologies						★		★						★			
541	7	Barro Stickney, Inc.											★					★	
547	8	We've Got Rhythm! Medtronic Corporation's Cardiac Pacemaker Business			★			★		★	★								
565	9	Total Quality Logistics: Sales Force Management		★	★							★				★		★	
583	10	Telezoo (A): Feast or Famine?					★	★		★				★					★
595	11	Van Leer Packaging Worldwide: The TOTAL Account (A)			★	★			★									★	★
607	12	Ethical Dilemmas in Business Marketing	★	★	★	★													

CASE

1

Columbia Industries, Inc.

Columbia Industries, Inc. (CI) was established in 1948 in Vancouver, British Columbia. It quickly grew to be the largest manufacturer of code-approved products to the construction industry for the purpose of connecting, adapting, reducing, and repairing pipes used in sewer and drain waste applications. CI product line included: couplings, flex-seal couplings, large diameter repair couplings, inflatable plugs, and a broad array of specialty couplings. In 1994, it opened a branch in Toronto and subsequently expanded internationally by opening another branch in Los Angeles, California, in 1997. The company employs over 950 people (550 people in Vancouver) and has annual sales of approximately $176 million ($102 million in Vancouver). The majority of its customers in served through a large network of specialized distributors, supply houses, and mass merchandisers.

On September 16, 1999, there would be a final meeting between the Plant Manager, the Industrial Engineer, and the Plant Engineer of the Vancouver operations. The meeting was expected to generate a sfinal recommendation to the company's general manager about the acquisition of seven new lift trucks. Lift trucks were used to move finished pallets of couplings, ceramic pipes, rubber hoses, and other production materials to and from the warehouse (see Exhibit 1).

The need to purchase new lift trucks had first come to their attention when the head mechanic, who was also the plant union leader, formally submitted the complaints of the lift truck drivers concerning the safety and performance of the Hyster lift trucks. They were concerned about the stability of the lift truck when it had a full load and the mast was fully extended to reach the 260-inch top shelf in the warehouse. A driver had recently experienced a near accident when lifting a roll of ceramic pipes to the top shelf in which the back of the truck lifted momentarily off the ground. In addition, the excessive maintenance costs of the Hyster high must lift trucks had come to the attention of the Plant Engineer.

Secondly, the Vancouver operation had experienced a rapid increase in sales and demands in the last few years. They were unable to address their customer's needs in a timely fashion due to limited lift trucks and plant capacity, which cost them several valuable customers.

Background

Mr. Jacques Debré, the Plant Manager, had been with the company for eighteen years. He had started his career there as an industrial engineer after graduating from college and had been promoted several times since then. For the past seven years he had been the Plant Manager at the Vancouver headquarters. Mr. Stuart West was the Industrial Engineer who was responsible for the efficient allocation of equipment and machinery, including lift trucks. He was responsible for the financial cost analysis concerning equipment justification and capacity planning. He had been with the company the past five years. Prior to his employment at Columbia Industries, Inc., he had extensive experience as an industrial engineer in other industries, and his opinion was held in high regard.

The Plant Engineer, Ms. Sandra Ogrosky, had been with the company for the last six years. She was responsible for maintaining the plant equipment and machinery and was very concerned with its reliability and minimal downtime for repairs. Two of her key functions were performance monitoring and productivity modeling and analysis. Therefore, the poor performance of the fork lifts had come to her attention. Due to rapid growth in recent years, it was even more critical to increase reliability and minimize downtime.

The Task

It came to the attention of the Plant Manager that seven new warehouse lift trucks were needed due to the high maintenance expense, high lift truck downtime, safety concerns, and the rapid expansion of the company. Clients, such as large homebuilders, made up the majority of CI's business, and for several years the significant population expansion had put increased demand on the homebuilders and indirectly on CI.

One of the Hyster lift trucks was several years old and had broken down twice in the last three months. Consequently, the company had to delay two large orders, which cost them one of their major clients. Both of the breakdowns had been due to problems with the transmission of the lift truck.

It had taken ten days to get one replacement transmission part rushed to them, and the other faulty part in the transmission had taken nearly a week. In the last three months the lift truck had cost them over $4,000.

Furthermore, CI had to rebuild the transmission in another of the Hyster lift trucks six months ago, costing them close to $2,000. Since then, they had not had any other problems with that particular lift truck.

Besides reliability and quick service, CI also had the requirements of maneuverability in order for the lift truck operators to safely maneuver through the narrow aisles and tight corners. And as mentioned previously, the lift truck drivers had complained to the labor union about safety problems surrounding the stability of the truck when the mast was fully extended and carried a full load of large diameter pipes.

Mr. West was given the task of finding seven lift trucks that would best meet the needs of the company. However, company policy required that the initial step be to approach the purchasing department with the task of narrowing the scope of possibilities down to five brands of lift trucks. The purchasing agent examined the qualifications of low down time, safety, good service, and maneuverability. He then studied the various offerings and narrowed the decision down to five brands. At this point he contacted the various companies and requested that each company send a salesman to meet with Mr. West and give him a quote.

The Presentations

The quotations were formally requested on June 1, 1999. The Yale quotation arrived first on June 6, 1999 (see Exhibit 2). The Yale distributorship sold a wide array of products from storage equipment to safety equipment and had just included lift trucks in their product line three months ago. Columbia Industries, Inc., frequently bought products from this company and had been very satisfied with the distributor's service. The salesman met with Mr. West and explained the features of the lift trucks. He then promised to send a demonstrator lift truck to CI. A week later the lift truck arrived. The lift truck operators liked the performance of the truck, but were uncertain concerning the function of several of the Fault Monitor Indicator Lights. It took them about one hour to ascertain how to operate the truck due to the difference in the Yale truck and the Hyster trucks they were used to working with; however, eventually they became confident in their ability to operate the machine and were impressed by its capabilities. The Yale salesman called Mr. West once a week from then on to see if the company had made a decision yet.

The Komatsu proposal arrived the same day as the Yale proposal (see Exhibit 3). However, a few days prior to the arrival, the Komatsu salesperson had spent considerable time presenting the Komatsu lift truck features and advantages to Mr. West. He then asked which other companies Mr. West was considering, and proceeded to list the faults of his competitors and their products. When Mr. West requested a demonstrator truck, the Komatsu salesperson appeared hesitant and replied that he would "see about it." After the proposal arrived, CI did not hear from the salesperson again.

The third quotation arrived on June 7 from Caterpillar, Inc (see Exhibit 4). The salesman gave a thorough presentation to Mr. West and asked him to explain what features the company was looking for in a lift truck. He then sent the demonstration truck to the plant three days later. He arrived with the truck and met the lift truck drivers. He quickly showed them how to operate the truck and answered their questions concerning the performance of the truck. At this point the lift truck mechanic arrived to examine the features of the truck. He and the Caterpillar salesman candidly began discussing the mechanics of the lift truck. The mechanic was surprised about the depth of knowledge the salesman had of the lift truck until he discovered the salesman used to be a lift truck mechanic several years ago. The Caterpillar salesman then met with Mr. West, Mr. Debré, and Ms. Ogrosky and explained in detail how the characteristics of the Caterpillar lift truck would benefit them and how it met all of their criteria. He reminded them that Caterpillar parts were easily available and that the service facility was only a few miles away. From that meeting on, he called Mr. West every two weeks and sent him recent articles about the Caterpillar lift trucks.

The fourth quotation received was from Hyster on June 9 (see Exhibit 5). Prior to this, the Hyster salesman met with Mr. West. Mr. Debré, and Ms. Ogrosky. He gave a very impressive presentation about the Hyster brand and the lift truck features. Ms. Sparrow then asked him about the features of the Hyster transmission and explained the problems the plant had with them. The salesman said he might be able to "get a deal" for the plant due to the previous problems they'd had with the Hyster lift trucks. The Hyster salesperson called every week from that point on.

The last quotation was from Toyota (see Exhibit 6). The salesman had been out of town so he and Mr. West were not able to meet until June 21. The salesman was very knowledgeable about lift trucks and his company. Originally, Mr. West had been very interested in this brand because he had read about the reliability and performance features of this lift truck. However, when Mr. West requested that a demonstration lift truck be sent to the plant, the salesman had seemed unsure and told Mr. West he would have to "check on it." A week later a demonstration Toyota lift truck arrived. The salesman was unable to get the lift truck Mr. West had requested, but sent one that was close to the required specifications. The lift truck operators were impressed with the performance and easy handling of the truck, but the lift truck operators were unable to test lifting the pipes to the maximum height needed because the lift on this model only expanded 112 inches, instead of the required 260 inches. The salesman called a few days later to see what Mr. West had thought of the lift truck, and then called him every two weeks to check on the progress of the decision.

On August 20, Mr. West and Ms. Ogrosky planned a meeting with the lift truck operators and the mechanic for CI to get their opinions about the performance of the various trucks. Following is a summary of their discussion:

- The lift truck operators were impressed with the performance of the Yale lift truck. It had a tight turning radius and was very responsive. However, they were still a little uncertain about all the features the truck offered and exactly how to use them. The operators were particularly pleased with the stability and safety of the truck when they tested it with the mast fully extended and with a full load. The mechanic seemed confident about his abilities to make repairs to the truck should it eventually need any.

- Komatsu did not send a demonstration truck.

- The Caterpillar lift truck was very maneuverable and had advanced features. The operators were excited about trying out the various features and enhancements and seemed confident about their abilities to operate the lift truck. The Caterpillar lift truck was tested with the mast fully extended with a full load and performed very well under these conditions. The mechanic was impressed with the truck and was confident that he could address any problems that might arise.

- The lift truck operators were pleased with the maneuverability of the Hyster trucks and were confident about their abilities to operate them. However, they were still concerned about the stability and safety of the trucks when there was a full load with the mast fully extended. Due to his prior experience repairing the Hyster trucks, the mechanic was confident about his abilities to make repairs to it. He was impressed with the new transmission Hyster now used and believed that it would be much more reliable than the previous one.

- The Toyota lift truck handled like the Hyster lift truck and the lift truck operators were very satisfied with its maneuverability and features. Due to the fact that Toyota sent a different model to CI, the drivers were unable to test the stability of the truck when the mast was fully extended with a full load. However, the mechanic felt that the lift truck would hold up under those conditions.

Mr. West and Ms. Ogrosky met on September 3rd to decide which lift truck to recommend to Mr. Debré. They created a chart to better compare the lift truck characteristics and to facilitate their decision-making process (see Exhibit 7). It was crucial to back their decision up with hard data and, they knew that Mr. Debré might be hesitant to purchase a new lift truck from a brand with which they had no previous experience. If he was not convinced the decision was a correct one, they would have to re-evaluate all of the options.

EXHIBIT 1 | **LIFT TRUCK AND WAREHOUSE**

EXHIBIT 2

June 6, 1999

Columbia Industries, Inc.
P.O. Box 120
Vancouver, British Columbia
Attention: Mr. Stuart West

Dear Mr. West:

Thank you for the opportunity to extend our business partnership with you. We are sure you will be excited about the special services and prices that we can offer you, due to the quantity of products we send to you and your proximity to our location.

We are giving you the quote for the Yale GC050ZG and the trade-in price for your Hyster lift truck. Our Yale truck is only $18,990 and we can offer you $2,110 for your trade-in. Let me remind you that we are able to get any parts you may need overnight to you and that we are available for any questions or problems you encounter.

Due to our close business relationship with your company, we will also extend your warranty free of charge from 12 months or 2,500 hours to 18 months or 3,750 hours.

Let me know if you have any questions. I am looking forward to talking further about this opportunity.

Signed
Yale Salesman

EXHIBIT 3

June 6, 1999

Columbia Industries, Inc.
P.O. Box 120
Vancouver, British Columbia
Attention: Mr. Stuart West

Dear Mr. West:

I enjoyed our discussion the other day and am sure that Komatsu will be the best choice for you. We surpass all of our competitors and also offer a more competitive price. I recommend the Komatsu FG255HT-12 for the uses we discussed. This model is only $18,400, which includes a one-year, or 2,250-hour warranty.

We are not able to send you a demonstration truck because our lift trucks are in such high demand, but I am sure this model would meet all your criteria and would surpass all the offerings our competitors could offer you.

I am looking forward to talking to you soon.

Signed
Komatsu Salesperson

EXHIBIT 4 |
___

June 7, 1999

Columbia Industries, Inc.
P.O. Box 120
Vancouver, British Columbia
Attention: Mr. Stuart West

Dear Mr. West:

After analyzing all of your requirements for a warehouse forklift, I am sure the Caterpillar FGC25K-HO will fulfill all of your criteria. This forklift has consistently ranked as one of the top two forklifts in its class for performance and durability. You should receive a recent article that I copied for you in the next week, which gives a detailed comparison of the warehouse forklifts in this class.

Unfortunately, we will not be able to give you a trade-in on your Hyster lift trucks, but I have enclosed the names and numbers of several companies in your area that should be able to help give you a fair price for your Hyster lift trucks.

Our Caterpillar lift truck sells for $19,550 with a 12-month or 3,000-hour warranty. The warranty can be extended if CI has this requirement.

I am looking forward to talking with you soon.

Signed
Caterpillar Salesperson

___

EXHIBIT 5 |
___

June 9, 1999

Columbia Industries, Inc.
P.O. Box 120
Vancouver, British Columbia
Attention: Mr. Stuart West

Dear Mr. West:

I enjoyed talking to you the other day and have come up with a good solution to your problems. First, I am sure that the Hyster H50 XM will give you all the capabilities that you need. It is similar to the models you have now, but the transmission has been replaced with a more durable one.

The price for the new Hyster forklift is $18,220. As you will see (from the demonstration model), it is one of the least expensive forklifts of this class on the market. We can add to this value by extending the warranty period to 36 months or 5000 hours at no charge to you.

Furthermore, we are also able to give you a very competitive trade-in price on your other Hyster truck. We will offer you a trade-in of $2,000.

I am glad I have the chance to work with you and am sure you will see the competitive offer we were able to extend to you.

Signed
Hyster Salesperson

EXHIBIT 6

June 23, 1999

Columbia Industries, Inc.
P.O. Box 120
Vancouver, British Columbia
Attention: Mr. Stuart West

Dear Mr. West:

Thank you for taking the time out of your busy schedule to spend such a lengthy time discussing all of the criteria you have for a new warehouse lift truck. I have given it considerable thought and am certain that the Toyota 5 FG 25 will fulfill all of your needs.

As you know, Toyota has obtained an incredible image as the industry leader in service and performance. We will ensure your complete satisfaction with our products and will have a quick response time should you ever experience any problems with your lift truck.

The Toyota 5 FG 25 is $19,220. In addition, we have included a 20-month or 4,500-hour warranty. We are unable to give you a trade-in on your Hyster lift truck, but I am sure the Hyster dealer near you might be able to help you with it.

We are sending you a similar model to the Toyota 5 FG 25 due to its availability. I am sure it will provide the performance you are looking for. I am looking forward to getting feedback from you about our lift truck and will talk to you in the next few weeks.

Signed
Toyota Salesman

EXHIBIT 7

Description	Caterpillar FGC25K-HO	Yale GC050ZG	Toyota 5 FG 25	Komatsu FG255HT-12	Hyster H50 XM
Capacity	5000 lbs.	5000 lbs.	5000 lbs.	5000 lbs	5000 lbs.
O/A Width	41.5"	42"	45.5"	41.7"	45.5"
Turning Radius	79"	78.7"	78.1"	77.6"	87.4"
Lowered Height	85"	84"	84.5"	85"	85.5"
Total Lift	262"	265"	265"	265.5"	263"
Lifting Speed:					
Empty	112 fhp	133 fhp	122 fhp	120 fhp	118 fhp
Loaded	104 fhp	117 fhp	108 fhp	106 fhp	104 fhp
Travel Speed	10.5 mph	10.9 mph	11 mph	10.3 mph	11.0 mph
Engine	Mitsubishi 4G64	General Motors	52 Net HP	Komatsu	Mazda 2.0 L
Transmission	Powershift	Powershift	Powershift	Toraflow	Powershift
Steering	Power	Power	Power	Power	Power
Delivery	TBA	TBA	TBA	TBA	TBA
Subtotal	$20,900	$19,390	$21,100	$18,400	$18,220
Minus Trade-In	_____	$2,110	_____	_____	$2,000
Freight	_____	$100	$100	_____	$100
Total	$20,900	$17,380	$21,200	$18,400	$16,320

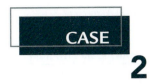

CASE

2

Clariant Corporation Marketing

Bradley W. Brooks, Queens University of Charlotte
David V. Rudd, Queens University of Charlotte

> Our specialty chemicals are used in many products you encounter every day. Pigments in paint, plastic, and leather in cars and in cosmetics. Photo-resists in video game displays. De-icing fluids for airports. Agro chemicals for food production and intermediate molecules for medicines. Special visual effects in plastic packaging. Even the active ingredient insect repellants. Clariant is "All Around You."
>
> —Promotional video (2001)

Swiss-based Clariant International Limited, like most specialty chemical companies, organizes its six global divisions around either the products they make, the products the chemicals are used on, or the industrial customers served. TLP (Textiles, Leather, and Paper) makes process chemicals for TLP producers. P&A (Pigments and Additives) makes colorants and other functional additives for many industries, including TLP. FUN (Functional Chemical) produces a plethora of "magic molecules." LSE (Life Sciences and Electronics) serves the needs of the electronics and booming pharmaceuticals industries. MB (Masterbatches) custom-blends pigments and/or additives into various substrates for use in the production of colored plastics. CEP (Cellulose Ethers and Polymerisates) provides specialty feed-stock chemicals plastics processing.

Clariant International Limited promises "Exactly Your Chemistry" for thousands of customers in four regions (Europe, the Americas, Asia/Australia, and Africa).

In September 2000, Vincent Thompson, vice president of operations for Clariant, frowned as he reviewed sales growth and contribution margin growth for the NAFTA region arm of Clariant International, Ltd. Sales and margin growth metrics were two of the company's most critical performance trends (Table 1). The data reflected the continued volatility that plagued the NAFTA arm for several years.

Vincent Thompson ended his review of the situation with questions about how Clariant could fully develop its potential for meeting its sales and profit growth goals. Thompson felt that Clariant should pursue overall structural changes to the sales and marketing functions, but he knew that such changes could be very costly and disruptive to the company and its operations. He wanted Clariant to redesign its sales force

TABLE 1 | **CLARIANT CORP. MARGIN CHANGES/SALES GROWTH BY DIVISION, 1998–2000***

Clariant North America	Margin Change (%)			Sales Growth (%)		
Division	2000	1999	1998	2000	1999	1998
Textiles, Leather, & Paper	(>100)	(68.0)	(19.6)	(7.7)	(9.1)	(6.8)
Pigments and Additives	21.4	(0.9)	51.3	(2.7)	(2.3)	(1.7)
Functional Chemicals	6.8	(7.3)	43.9	(12.0)	(3.9)	(14.1)
Life Science & Electronic	91.9	(4.2)	(78.6)	(9.8)	(5.3)	1.7
Masterbatches	26.5	370.4	26.5	(1.1)	12.9	(48.0)

*SOURCE: Internal tracking reports for Clariant Corporation.

to include cross-divisional account teams that could be assigned to the organization's most profitable customers. In doing so, Clariant would assign one account executive to serve as a single contact person for the customer and to manage the overall relationship. This account executive would then work with salespersons representing each product of interest for the specific customer (i.e., the account team). Such changes, of course, would be achieved at a great cost financially both in terms of direct expenses and disruptions in the organization's operations. It would also require a shift in the current culture within the sale force. Other Clariant executives argued that the firm should alter its training approach. Instead of an account team for certain customers, they argued that Clariant should retrain its individual sales force representatives to be capable of selling products from the company's various product divisions. They argued that this approach would be less disruptive than designing account teams. Of course, incentives for the sales representatives would also need to be modified under such an approach. Still other executives argued that actually implementing either of these changes would be too difficult and complicated. They believed that all Clariant really needed was to begin providing financial incentives to its sales representatives for referring their individual customers to other Clariant sales representatives (i.e., those representatives who sell other products that the specific customer purchases).

Thompson understood the concerns about costs and disruptions and was willing to consider each of the options. His main concern was for Clariant to position itself to be able to attack multiple growth strategies simultaneously while competing under increasing external pressures. The specialty chemical industry, however, was no easy environment in which to compete.

Chemical Industry Background

Hilfra Tandy wrote,

Chemical processes and products affect the lives of billions of people in both developed and less developed nations.[1] Most people, especially North Americans, would be hard pressed to find an element of their daily lives not impacted by the production or use of chemicals. From the plastic that protects their food,

---

[1]Tandy, Hilfra, "Core Industry Finds Cures for Old Sickness," *Financial Times Survey*, July 3, 2000, (I). London, UK.

to the plethora of emerging medicines, to special treatments for paper, leather, and textiles, to the rainbow of colors that grace the shelves, chemicals play a major role in bringing functionality, variety, and safety into people's daily lives. This phenomenon is not limited to the industrialized nations alone.

Worldwide, according to Tandy, the chemicals industry generates sales in the neighborhood of $1.7 trillion annually. As with many established industries, the chemicals industry divided over time into two major categories: commodity chemicals and specialty chemicals.

"Commodity" chemicals (83 percent of the market) are produced and sold in high volume in standard forms and configurations. Essential to most core manufacturing industries, commodity chemicals are used in a wide range of applications but serve the same function in most cases. Their appeal is in their functionality regardless of the application. Many commodity chemicals attract so much competition that price competition has driven much of the profitability out of the business. In fact, price competition is so fierce that the sales representatives of many of the commodity chemical producers often cut prices below their company's already low list prices to attract or retain a specific customer.

In response, several companies developed marketing campaigns that would differentiate their product offerings. For example, DuPont's "Better Living through Chemistry" campaign, BASF's "We don't make a lot of the products you buy; we make a lot of the products you buy better," and CIBA's "We are all around you" attempted to differentiate commodity chemical companies through advertising-supported market positioning.

Another common response to the increasing intensity of price competition of core products has been movement of manufacturing facilities to manufacturing-friendly parts of the world. Like firms in many industries, chemical companies shopped the world for places to process and produce their products that offer lower labor costs, special considerations on capital-goods costs, less stringent environmental regulations, and favorable tax structures. At the beginning of the 21st century, this movement toward global manufacturing, a worldwide tendency toward lower tariffs, as well as transportation and communication improvements that reduced time and space barriers in general, made the chemical industry one of the most widely distributed industrial activities on the face of the earth.

Globalization also brought new, low-cost, government-supported competitors, especially from China and India. Overcapacity in many commodity chemicals made it nearly impossible for any one company to sustain acceptable growth levels through internal expansion.

These circumstances led to grave concerns within the industry. Graham Copley, an investment-banking analyst speaking at an industry conference in early 2000, stated that the chemical industry had "failed to meet growth objectives for more than 30 years" and "the underlying earnings growth is poor."[2] With narrow margins, availability issues, and standard specifications, success in all commodities rests on three factors: economies of scale, cost reduction, and constant improvement in all aspects of the business.

Two of these factors can be acquired through mergers or acquisitions among like competitors. Economies of scale can be achieved for whole corporations by combining operations and eliminating duplication and, therefore, is generally limited by the

---

[2]Ibid.

TABLE 2 | **VALUE OF CHEMICAL INDUSTRY MERGERS AND ACQUISITIONS***

Year	1995	1997	1998	1999 (est.)
$ Billions in mergers and acquisitions	10	37	41	50

*Excluding oil and pharmaceuticals.
SOURCE: Hilfra Tandy, *Financial Times Survey of the Chemical Industry*, July 3, 2000, p. iii.

efficient sizing of individual production facilities. Table 2 shows the growth of mergers or acquisitions of $50 million or more in the chemicals industry. This pace of large-company and large-component mergers and acquisitions is expected to continue.

The Product Life Cycle in the Chemical Industry

A commodity chemical does not begin its product life as a low-margin, high-volume, tightly contested product. It typically begins as a specialty chemical designed to fulfill a specific customer's needs. Early in the product life cycle, a successful specialty chemical would be highly valued for improving the product or the process leading to the product. Specialty chemical companies and their direct customers are often willing to invest in research and development to find just the right combination of performance and cost to meet the immediate need. Decision makers are able to visualize a product need and to forecast demand sufficient to assure an adequate return on investment.

If the specialty chemical reaches the right target market and the end product delivers the promised performance or performance improvement, then growth follows. Because growth generated good returns, other firms would then introduce competitive products. New, competitive products can successfully enter the market through *differentiation* (providing superior performance or end-user benefits) or by *positioning* (creating the perception that one product is better than another). Successful product differentiation usually allows the maker of the superior product to charge a premium price and thus generate premium margins even as the product reached maturity.

Ultimately, however, as technology spreads and competitors gravitate toward similar best practices, pricing and customer service tend to become the deciding factors in buyer-seller-user relationships. Specialty chemicals developed to meet even a highly specialized market need usually become standardized commodity products. At the extreme, where all competitors face similar technologies and raw materials and labor costs, price becomes the principal competitive weapon. In such mature markets, customers are unwilling to pay a premium for a standardized product even with exceptional customer service support. Mature commodity markets are primarily driven by price, service, technical support, company relationships, and delivery reliability.

Markets eventually decline as the product is replaced with substitutes, as technology eliminates the need for the product, or as the end use product loses favor in the marketplace.

Thompson understood that the highest profit potential for any single product came either from exploiting pricing opportunities during the growth stage of the life cycle or from maintaining superior product differentiation or positioning throughout an extended maturity stage. Growth and profitability for a chemical firm, therefore, come from maintaining a mix of products at different stages in the product life cycle.

Managing a portfolio of different product lines has become a critical part of the overall business strategy of the company.

Structure of the Specialty Chemical Industry[3]

By late 2000, specialty chemical sales were rapidly approaching $400 billion worldwide. Specialty chemicals were more application- and end-use specific than commodity chemicals. The number of distinct end-user segments was nearly 50. With the rapid expansion of technology, the dizzying pace of product innovation, and the rapid globalization of commercial competition in general, specialty chemicals companies were under tremendous pressure for growth in both sales and profits.

Not surprisingly, the specialty chemical market was highly segmented itself. The top eight end-user segments (pharmaceuticals, agrochemicals, polymers, adhesives and sealants, food additives, flavors and fragrances, electronic chemicals, and photographic chemicals) accounted for less than two-thirds of total sales. This diversity added to the challenge of growth.

The specialty chemicals segment was even more active in the area of mergers and acquisitions than the overall chemical industries. Despite accounting for only 17 percent of total sales in 1999, the specialty chemical segment accounted for 21 percent of merger-and-acquisition activity as commodity chemical companies sought specialty products to bolster their margins.

Industrial globalization brought new competition to the specialty segment, and technology-driven change demanded introduction of more and more specialty products. In the last decade of the 20th century the specialty chemical segment had evolved into three distinct tiers:

Tier-one specialty chemical producers were divisions of major chemical firms specializing in particular chemicals or user segments. Typical tier-one company sales were tens of billions of dollars annually. Their parent corporations were eager to invest in these higher-margin opportunities.

Tier-two firms were spin-off businesses, divisions of large chemical companies spun off into separate entities in order to allow them to focus on their own particular portfolio of specialty chemicals. Tier-two sales were typically in the $3–5 billion range annually.

Tier-two companies had to generate investment capital externally.

Tier-three companies typically range from $1 billion to $2 billion in annual sales and generally had a narrower range of offerings than tier-two firms. Long-term survival depended on the uniqueness of their product offering, which also had to be highly valued and protected from direct competition within their user base.

Vincent Thompson commented on Clariant's position:

We, meaning both Clariant Corporation and our parent, Clariant Limited, fall into Tier Two. Tier Two is a precarious place to be. Above us are the resource-rich divisions of large companies. Below us are narrow-line specialists who survive by doing only what they do best—meaning they build

---

[3]Tandy, Hilfra, "Star Sector Struggles to Retain Status," *Financial Times Survey*, July 3, 2000. (IV). London, UK.

TABLE 3 | COST/EXPENSE PERCENT OF SALES RATIOS 2000*, CLARIANT LIMITED

	Percent of Sales
Sales	100%
—Cost of goods sold	66
Gross Profit	34
—*Sales expense*	8
—Marketing and distribution	6
—Research and development	4
—Admin & general overhead	5
Operating income	11

*This profit model is a rough approximation and is not to be used beyond the scope of this case.

lasting relationships with the best end-users in their particular segments and they compete fiercely on price when a major account is up for grabs. One of our managers characterized our position as being caught "between a herd of elephants and a pool of sharks." We certainly understand the pressure of being in the middle.

Clariant International Limited and Clariant Corporation

Clariant International Limited was formed in 1995 when selected specialty chemical divisions of Sandoz, with sales of approximately $1.5 billion, were spun off. Selected divisions of Hoechst-Celanese were added to the mix in 1997, bringing the total annual sales to approximately $5.5 billion worldwide. (See Table 3 for a year 2000 corporate breakdown of sales and expense ratios.) The NAFTA region accounted for approximately $1.1 billion, or 20 percent of worldwide sales.

On average it appeared that the increased cost to train the sales representatives to be able sell products across other divisions would probably increase the sales activities from its current 8 percent of sales to approximately 8.5 percent for the next two to three years and then to settle in at approximately 8.2 percent thereafter. Major expenses included cross-divisional product training and building and maintaining an informational infrastructure to keep everyone up to date on product and account information. Of course, a future sales expense to sales revenue ratio that is roughly equivalent to its current level but with increased actual sales levels could represent significant actual profit increases. Thompson, however, perceived this approach to pose a high level of risk because it would certainly not be a given that the company could achieve a sales increase within only three years that would be in proportion to the required increase in expenses.

By 2000, Clariant Limited, based in Switzerland, was organized into six global business units. Two of the six divisions were organized by end user: Textiles, Leather, & Paper (TLP) and Life Science and Electronic Chemicals (LSE). Two divisions were organized by functionality: Pigments and Additives (P&A) and Masterbatches (MB). Finally, two divisions were organized by chemical class: Functional Chemicals (FUN) and Cellulose Ethers and Polymerisates (CEP).

Although the exact composition of the product array in each division had varied significantly from year to year and division names had occasionally been changed, the basic alignment had persisted throughout the six-year history of Clariant Limited. In all, these six divisions contained 19 separate businesses. (See Table 4 for a breakdown of each division's costs and expenses as a percentage of sales.)

Until mid-2000, only five of the global business units had operations in Clariant Corporation's North American realm. In the summer of 2000, CEP was added to the Clariant product array as a result of the acquisition of British Tar Products (BTP) by Clariant Limited. The BTP acquisition also brought critical mass to the Life Sciences Intermediates part of the LSE unit and greatly enhanced the offerings in the TLP business unit for Clariant Corporation. Clariant Corporation was created coincident with the Sandoz spin-off to oversee Clariant's businesses in North America. Because of the size of North American markets and the level of development of the North American economies, performance in the region is especially important to the overall performance of Clariant Limited.

With a strong U.S. economy, performance expectations for Clariant Corporation were high. Going into 2000, the North American market contributed almost one-third of overall corporate sales. In the opinions of some at Clariant Limited's world headquarters, however, the specialty chemical businesses in North America should have generated more growth and profitability than it had. Overall sales figures indicated a broad general decline thought to have been caused in part by heightened competition from expanded production in China and other Far East countries. All five of Clariant Corporation's established divisions showed sales declines (see Table 1).

Contribution margin decreases in the Textiles, Leather, and Paper Division had accelerated an already precipitous decline. Extreme competitive price pressures, the growth of production capacity in Asia, and a general economic slowdown beginning in early 2000 had all contributed to the division's problems. Contribution margin had increased, however, in the other four divisions. Thompson wondered if the long, arduous, and difficult period of forming, consolidating, expanding, and integrating units that made up the global company was beginning to pay off. In light of increasing external pressures, he also wondered how Clariant could capitalize on its current margin growth strength and if there were ways to leverage the current technical, sales, and marketing capabilities to pursue growth. "Our current North American strategy," Thompson considered, "is to focus growth on fine chemicals and specialty chemicals while holding the line in price sensitive 'semi-specialties.' The nature of the industry

TABLE 4 | **OPERATING EXPENSES AND OPERATING INCOME PERCENT OF SALES RATIOS BY DIVISION 2000, CLARIANT LIMITED**

	TLP	P&A	FUN	LSE	MB	CEP*
Sales	100%	100%	100%	100%	100%	100%
Sales to other divisions	1	3	5	10	0	4
Net sales	99	97	95	90	100	96
Total Operating Expenses	82	78	82	75	87	88
Operating income	17	19	13	15	13	12

*CEP was added in summer 2000.

is that sitting still for too long will probably lead to a rapid degradation in both sales and profit performance."

At Clariant Corporation headquarters in Charlotte, North Carolina, it was believed that a portion of the lower-than-expected performance could be explained by the shift of production capacity from the United States to other countries (China, India, Mexico, etc.) in key customer industries such as textile fibers, fabric, and clothing production. Additionally, logistical and other difficulties related to integrating multiple divisions, multiple product lines, and multiple business operations into a cohesive whole had provided a difficult operating environment in the late 1990s.

Clariant Corporation president David Lawrence, in speaking to the different operating units on what he called a "Town Meeting" tour in spring of 2000, had divided the brief history of Clariant Corporation in three stages:

> The consolidation stage ran from 1995 to 1997. Emphasis was on sorting out all of the pieces, reorganizing the structure, aligning the Clariant Corporation structure with the Clariant Limited structure, and eliminating excess cost brought on by duplication. The integration stage ran from 1997 to 1999. Emphasis was on discovering and capitalizing on easily obtained internal opportunities ("low hanging fruit") for cross-divisional sales or inter- intra-divisional cost reductions. The growth stage is now underway. The aim is to aggressively attack the problems of growth and profitability using the technical, marketing, and sales capacities of the many operating units.

In setting the agenda for growth, Lawrence outlined a three-pronged strategy to achieve both the sales and profit performance:

A. Sales growth through strategic acquisitions to achieve targeted growth in high-margin segments,

B. Sales growth generated by cross-divisional sales of multiple Clariant lines to key, high-potential customers, and

C. Improving margins by emphasizing sales of higher-margin specialty products over the more established "semi-specialty" products (those nearing commodity status).

In implementing these strategies, especially the cross-divisional sales strategy, Clariant had invested significant time, energy, and money into the creation of cross-divisional product understanding among the various business units. Significant training investments were already being made in the various sales forces. Technologies were being implemented, including central databases of product information, product contact information, and "center of excellence teams." All of these activities contributed to the ability of a salesperson from a particular division to probe for and identify opportunities for other divisions. Customers having potential for sales from other Clariant divisions were then to be connected with the appropriate people. Some Clariant executives argued that the company should begin offering financial incentives for such referrals, pointing out that the incentives would be paid only if the referral actually resulted in additional sales. The cost, therefore, was negligible, because it would be incurred only when Clariant makes additional revenue and because it represented a marginal amount of the increase in profit. Their argument pointed out the low initial investment and, therefore, low risk of this approach.

To capture these potential cross-divisional opportunities, which often arose from a customer's pressing needs for new approaches to product development, a fledgling national accounts system was under development and had resulted in several promising contacts with high-potential customers, including a major packaged-goods marketer, a major multiline retailer, and a major athletic sportswear and footwear manufacturer. Recognizing that the core of Clariant Limited was its strong divisional structure and worldwide presence, the national accounts effort in North America started on an ad hoc basis. This meant that each opportunity for cross-divisional cooperation had to be formed, funded, and managed as a separate task force or team. Thompson commented: "I know that this is a good thing, but I wonder how well these cross-divisional and national accounts initiatives are working and how our ad hoc approach compares to that of the competition."

Marketing and Sales in Clariant Corporation

As with most tier-two specialty chemical companies, Clariant is almost constantly involved in adjusting the mix of its businesses, with frequent acquisitions, integrations, consolidations, and dispositions. Clariant Limited, and by natural extension Clariant Corporation, is a conglomeration of the pieces that had been put together over the past five years. Unlike DuPont or BASF, no attempt has been made to create a universal Clariant brand. Most of the products are still sold under their original trade names. (See Appendix A for examples of the mix of Sandoz [Sanda, Sando, Sodye], Hoechst [Hosta], and Clariant [CAS] trade nomenclature.)

Although somewhat oversimplified, Clariant's marketing strategy consists primarily of finding the right mix of product lines and running the plants at profitable levels. Pull-oriented marketing efforts, aimed at educating customers, potential customers, and prospects to the wide range of capabilities in the Clariant portfolio of businesses are then far less important than the push-related efforts from the sales forces.

Business unit and divisional level sales forces are provided annual sales objectives that reflected the need for the company to keep its production facilities operating at profitable levels. Clariant depends on a number of separate and distinct sales organizations. Each global business unit has its own sales force. If the global business unit had distinct separations among its product lines, along user lines, along industry lines, or among geographic concentration of applications, then the business-unit sales force would be further divided. A large percentage of the sales force is composed of a legacy of salespeople from the original companies that had formed Clariant.

As with most chemical companies, most salespeople are recruited from the technical ranks of key customers and come to the sales job with extensive knowledge of how the chemicals they sell are used. With its wide range of specialty chemical applications, the Clariant sales force has very diverse backgrounds.

Through this diversity, combined with the variety of organizing schemes for the six divisions, virtually every form of sales force organizing strategy exists somewhere in Clariant Corporation. Some salespeople report to regional sales managers who report, in turn, to product-line-specific sales and marketing managers. Some salespeople report directly to national sales and marketing managers.

A summer 2000 research report on specialty chemical companies showed that virtually all of the competitive sales forces were organized by product line, by user groups or industries, or by geography. In many cases, these three methods were combined into multitiered sales organizations reflecting the same complexity that Clariant Corporation faces.[4] Most elements of DuPont, for example, were organized by industry, with coverage depending on the size of the account. BASF had 17 divisions and 100 strategic business units, most of which were organized around a formal key account structure. CIBA, committed to delivery of value through innovation, productive relationships, and operational speed and simplicity, was organized around regional business structures. PP&G tended to be organized by industry within its product divisions.

Clariant's approach to handling national accounts differs significantly from that of its major competitors. Most major competitors have permanent teams assigned to manage the relationship with high-potential and high-profit accounts. These teams generally cut across division boundaries and place the account at the center of the marketing and sales effort. In at least one case, an executive VP was assigned at company headquarters to coordinate all contacts with the account and served as a first call point for problem resolution. This executive VP had only one responsibility: to maintain and build the account relationship.

Clariant Corporation, on the other hand, occasionally assembles account teams in response to specific account opportunities. In the case of a cooperative development project with a major packaged-goods marketer, an ad hoc account team was "assembled" in response to a request from the customer's marketing and technical staff. In the case of a major retailer, an account team was "assembled" in response to a developing marketing strategy involving the Masterbatches Division and its ability to quickly match colors across multiple product categories (and therefore multiple materials and production systems). Thompson oversaw the Clariant national account work as a part of his overall responsibilities for consolidated operations. He commented:

> Part of the challenge of the national accounts approach in Clariant comes from the fact that the local business unit sales forces feel that they (personally) "own" their customers. Forming a national account team means convincing multiple divisions to allocate their limited sales, technical, and marketing resources to the national team and to allow the national team access to key customers. The divisions have been very cautious regarding this proposed approach because of the difficulty in estimating just how much of these resources would actually be required, particularly since any given division couldn't be sure that it would benefit as much as other divisions would. Furthermore, the individual account's current salesperson also tends to resist such an approach. A common concern is a fear that if other Clariant salespeople were involved with the account it could mean losing some of the customer's current level of business to the other Clariant sales members. Another common fear is that another Clariant salesperson might not handle the account in the same manner that he/she would handle it, particular since the new sales member would not yet "know" the customer.

Leaving the divisional sales forces as they were and adding an additional layer of sales management in the form of an account executive would add $120,000 per account per year. Thompson estimated that there were 50 major accounts that would be eligible for account executives.

---

[4]Brooks, Bradley W., "Exploratory Research on Customer Preferences," Clariant authorized study, 2000. Unpublished.

TABLE 5	SALES AND MARKETING PERSONNEL AVERAGE TIME BUDGET, FALL 2000	
	Sales and Marketing Managers' Time (%)	**Salespersons' Time (%)**
Processing routine reorders	1	14
Generating new business for our product line	23	31
Identifying prospects for new business for Clariant beyond our product line	4	3
Handling customer service problems and concerns	15	17
Professional development	3	4
Administrative tasks	34	13
Other	20	18

SOURCE: Confidential survey of Clariant Corporation Sales Managers, September 2000.

Clariant Sales and Marketing Managers

When asked to describe the role of marketing in the overall sales and marketing effort, sales and marketing manager comments ranged from "none at all" to "product management and communications" and "very little" to "secondary to the sales activities." One perception of the way the company is organized to fulfill the need of high-margin or high-volume customers is that "most of the effort of the sales managers, product managers, territory reps, and customer service is focused on key customers." With regard to top customers, "We will do custom product development for them." Often, key managers are assigned to important customers along with the sales representatives. As was the case at many industrial firms, access to key customers is closely guarded by the salesperson calling on the account.

Table 5 reports statistics on time allocation from Clariant's marketing and sales managers. Thompson commented on these figures:

> Clariant salespeople don't spend much of their time identifying opportunities for new business for Clariant outside of their own division. Likewise, the sales and marketing managers don't seem to focus on Clariant-wide new business development. Are those good numbers or are they lower than they should be? Does our effort reflect the size of the potential opportunity?

Since most routine orders are placed through Clariant Corporation's Customer Service Organization, the low percentage of time spent on routine order processing by salespeople and sales managers is expected. The emphasis on divisional efforts is not surprising, since the bulk of the salesperson's compensation is comprised of a base salary and a commission or bonus based on sales performance of their accounts on the products that their business unit produces.

Our incentive system doesn't exactly support the cross-divisional selling initiative. Seventy-five percent of our upper-management bonuses are tied to our North American divisional sales, earnings, return on sales, and net working capital performance.

Twenty-five percent of our bonuses relate to the same performance metrics for our global division. Despite the prominence of divisional results in our incentive system, the cross-divisional selling issue has the attention of Clariant Corporation's top management. We have placed a lot of emphasis recently on the need for identifying high-potential opportunities for Clariant Corporation as a whole. We feel that success here is critical to the success of the firm as a whole. Is our initiative in its infancy or is it destined not to catch hold at all?

Customer Expectations

During the summer of 2000, Thompson had commissioned research comprised of in-depth surveys of 26 Clariant customers.[5] The results of this research are summarized in Table 6.

The customers were not informed that Clariant was the sponsor of the research, and no attempt was made to evaluate Clariant versus any of its competitors. Instead, the research delved into what the customers expected of their key specialty chemical suppliers, how they expected to get information about new products and opportunities, and what role the emerging Internet "marketplaces for chemicals" would play in their future relationships with these suppliers.

The written report that accompanied the survey results contained the following observations:

> . . . Not surprisingly, all purchasers listed quality, service (including technical support), and price as very important variables in their relationships with suppliers. Perhaps surprisingly, price came in third. It is not clear whether the Clariant sales force appropriately emphasizes the firm's quality and technical support capabilities, rather than price.
>
> . . . We found a willingness to pay more for "chemicals involved in a special application or where the chemical needed to be tweaked or modified." This seems consistent with the company's technical expertise and major commitment to pilot operations that routinely develops "magic molecules" for key customers. Clariant's speed of response, technical expertise, and wide range of production capabilities across all divisions give strength in this important area.
>
> . . . Customers demand predictable, reliable, dependable delivery performance. Will increased cross-divisional customer relationships create unrealistic expectations on the various divisions' operations?
>
> . . . We found that customers are willing to give existing suppliers more business in the interest of streamlining operations if they have multiple products that fit the customer's needs. These customers definitely want to deal with one liaison to their key suppliers and not myriad individual contacts. Furthermore, these same customers think that the suppliers bear major responsibility for informing them of new products and new opportunities. These findings seem to place a very high premium on the ability of all of the company's sales and marketing people to represent the whole of Clariant Corporation.
>
> . . . We found that customers do not perceive the Internet to be replacing the buyer-seller relationship. According to the May 8, 2000, issue of Business-to-Business Marketing magazine, four of the top ten Internet based

[5]Ibid.

TABLE 6 | KEY FINDINGS: INTERVIEWS WITH CLARIANT CUSTOMERS

Issue	Primary Finding	Extent of Finding
Describe the nature of your relationship with your specialty chemical suppliers	Positive, close, there are special suppliers they feel closer to.	22 of 26 described relationship as close . . . meaning regular contact, sharing important information and supplier understanding customer's business.
Length of supplier relationship	Most have maintained relationship for three or more years . . . and wish to remain with long-time suppliers.	7 of 26 are "constantly looking for information on new suppliers."
Important supplier attributes	Quality service (including technical support) Price	Quality is a given . . . miss quality and you lose the account. Some willingness to pay higher price to ensure quality, service, and delivery . . . really meant pay more if chemical is special.
Who defines quality?	The customer	25 of 26 say that their customers determine what quality means.
Attitude and behavior toward companies with multiple products that you need	Majority give advantage to current suppliers when evaluating new product needs.	20 of 26 prefer to work with current suppliers.
How do you prefer to hear about new products from the supplier and about additional products from other units of the supplier's company?	Want to negotiate with just a single contact. Dislike having to work with multiple representatives from same company. Prefer the supplier contact keep them informed of new and additional offerings.	12 of 26 want single contact. 24 of 26 want new and additional product opportunities to come from supplier rep.
How will relationship with suppliers change in the future and in the face of new technology (Internet markets, etc.)?	Half would purchase commodity chemicals from an e-commerce market. Technology should facilitate the relationship, not replace it. Purchasers need information in a more timely (read that NOW) manner than ever before.	Attitude toward technology is biased by personal style in relating to suppliers. The more the purchaser values the relationship, the less technology looms as a threat to the relationship. The more distant the relationship, the more technology will threaten the interaction.
Other findings	Large, sophisticated clients want to integrate the supplier into the product-development process to shorten timetables and to streamline problem solving.	

marketplaces were designed to facilitate the exchange of chemicals. Clariant's customers saw these exchanges as more appropriate for the purchase of commodity chemicals than specialty chemicals. They do, however, see technology as a boost to the process of purchasing chemicals. Affording customers a way to review the inventory availability on products of interest is seen as a boost for the relationship. Clariant's order processing and order fulfillment process involves the customer service reps taking the time to confirm availability and/or see if production schedules could be adjusted to meet the customer's needs. Customers knew that an order placed did not necessarily mean that the order could be filled. Often, a customer would probe the availability of a product and only provide a purchase order upon availability confirmation.

. . . We found that the most sophisticated customers are eager to involve suppliers in the product development process. For a specialty chemical company, if a customer's end product is designed around one of your products, the odds are very good that you will enjoy at least a short period as the preferred supplier for that product.

. . . Finally, we found that Clariant's customer's customer (i.e., the end user, the retailer, etc.) plays an important part in defining what quality really means and what is acceptable performance. Clariant's culture was heavily oriented toward the chemicals themselves, the technology and science behind the chemicals, and the use of the chemicals by its direct customers. This perspective is not unusual in primary raw material and component supplier industries. Do the Clariant sales and marketing people think past their direct customer to understand the end user's interest in Clariant's chemicals?

Pushing back from this array of reports, Thompson resolved to complete his review in time for the start of the strategic planning cycle in two weeks and develop his definitive recommendations to the president.

APPENDIX A | PARTIAL LISTING OF CLARIANT CORPORATION TRADE NAMES

Algepon	Anodal	Apretan
Aquanyl	Bactosol	Carbapon
Carta . . . 16 variations	CAS . . . 290 numeric variations	Cassofix
Catolix	Ceranine	Ceridust
Colanyl	Dalamar	Deniblack
Denivat	Derma . . . 7 variations	Diaformer
Diresul	Dispersogen	Dissolvan
Drimagen Drimalan Drimarene	Duasyn	Flexonyl Flexoprint
Fluowet	Foron	Gena . . . 6 variations
Genolub	Glyoxal	Graphtol
Genosorb	Glyoxylic	
Hosta . . . 33 variations	Humectol	Hydro
Imacol	Imerol	Lamprecide
Lana . . . 6 variations	Leuco . . . 4 variations	Lico . . . 7 variations
Lyocol Lyogen	Maroxol	Mercerol
Nipa . . . 9 variations	Novo . . . 3 variations	Nylo . . . 5 variations
Opti . . . 3 variations	Pheno . . . 3 variations	Sanda . . . or Sando . . . 44 variations
Sodye . . . 12 variations	Supronil	Tergolix
V-Brite V-Finer	Virtex Virwhite	Visco . . . 3 variations

SOURCE: Master product information directory, Clariant Corporation.

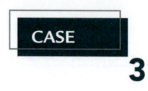

Circuit Board Corporation

John H. Friar, Northeastern University
Marc H. Meyer, Northeastern University

Maggie Adams sat in her office and replayed in her mind what she had just heard in the January 24, 2002, meeting of the board of directors of electronic component supplier Circuit Board Corporation (CBC). Maggie was the chairman of the board and the largest shareholder of the firm founded by her husband, Dieter. Dieter had passed away in June at the age of 67, and she had gone from being a part-time employee and secretary of the board to running the company. Maggie had been involved in the company since its founding but never had done much more than manage the insurance for the company. Dieter had been a one-man show, constantly yelling at people, running everything, and making all the decisions. He had grown the company to $30 million in sales and kept it afloat through some difficult periods. Now everyone was looking to her to make a decision, and she was getting conflicting and difficult advice.

In January 2001, the high-tech industry imploded. Most companies in the printed circuit-board industry had reported between 50 percent and 75 percent declines in quarterly revenue compared with the prior year. Excess capacity was rampant. Competitors were dropping prices and cutting their own margins just to keep their plants and equipment operating. Although many analysts had predicted a quick recovery, the unthinkable happened—terrorists crashed planes into the World Trade Towers, the Pentagon, and the Pennsylvania countryside on September 11. Forecasters began hedging their bets on any recovery, and CBC was in trouble—it had gone from making $1.2 million pretax in 2000 to losing $614,000 in 2001.

The discussion in the board meeting had caught Maggie by surprise. The company had been going through some very difficult times, but her president and CEO, Ben Cashman, had been assuring her that the market would rebound in the second quarter of 2002 and that they should invest to prepare for the turnaround. The outside board members, however, gave her three different recommendations, two of which were to get out of the business. Not only was the advice unexpected, but the fact that the outside board members even spoke up surprised her. All the outside directors were well-known businessmen and friends of Dieter. (See Exhibit 1 for a list.)

"Circuit Board Corporation" Case by John H. Friar and Marc H. Meyer, Northeastern University. The authors thank Edward Fitzgerald for his help in developing this case. Management cooperated in the field research for this case, which was written solely for the purpose of stimulating student discussion. All events and individuals are real, but they have been disguised at the organization's request.

EXHIBIT 1 | OUTSIDE BOARD MEMBERS

The board of directors consisted of Maggie Adams, Chairman, and Ben Cashman, CEO. They were also shareholders. The outside members did not own stock. They were:

Dane Lombard (Board Member): an expert in company turnarounds and asset redeployment. He was employed by Apollo Consulting.

Will Tatelman (Advisor to the Board): the company's auditor and principal at Tatelman & Associates. He attended at the request of Maggie Adams.

Don Armour (Board Member): a principal at Armour & Company. His expertise lay in mergers and acquisitions activities.

But Dieter had never really listened to them, so they had rarely done more than rubber-stamp his decisions. Now without Dieter there, they had started to express their opinions.

Maggie wanted to do what was right but was not sure what that meant. Maggie and her children controlled 86.5 percent of the company and in 2000 had paid themselves (including Dieter) a combined total of $1.8 million in salaries. The company also employed a number of other family members and friends who could never make the same level of pay for another company. She had to think about her lifestyle and that of her family and friends. But she also had to think about the employees and the other stakeholders in the company. Maggie explained:

> Dieter and I have been through recessions in the business that felt as tough as this one, and I bet lasted longer than this one is going to last. There was a time around here in the late '80s when everything dropped by 30 percent—businesses, houses, everything—and seemed to stay there for a good three years. In addition, before that, there was the recession during the mid '70s. That one seemed to go on for five years before business picked up. Dieter always figured a way to keep our customers, keep our staff, and preserve the business.

Company History

Dieter had started Circuit Board Corporation in 1961 during the early days of the computer industry. Dieter was pursuing an undergraduate technical degree after having returned from service in the Korean War when he started the company. His first significant production contract was to design and manufacture printed circuit boards for the early minicomputer companies.

A printed circuit board (PCB) was one of the building blocks in industrial and consumer electronics. It was the platform on which a variety of electronic components, such as chips, resistors, and capacitors, were mounted. Wiring between insert points needed to be present for these mountings to function. On the printed circuit board, that wiring was "printed" by bonding copper through electrolysis in specific predefined patterns on a fiberglass board. The residual wiring on the board provided the layout both for mounting and for holding electrical components, as well as the electrical interconnections between components. In short, the PCB was the subassembly for all larger electronic systems, including computers, medical equipment, instrumentation, and controls.

Dieter became a pioneer in the electrochemical production of printed circuit boards. Before him, computer manufacturers placed electronic subassemblies onto plastic boards with wires clipped to little posts to make electrical connections. At that time, a handful of engineers, one of whom was Dieter, were using electrically charged baths to bond copper to fiberglass plates. The new process offered far greater reliability for the printed circuit boards and far higher density (chips and circuitry per square inch) for packaging components. Dieter developed his process by using his mother's kitchen oven as a curing device for his first printed circuit boards.

When Dieter launched the company, most computer and electronics manufacturers were fabricating their own boards. Independent suppliers, however, became increasingly efficient and were proving a more cost-effective solution for a broad range of printed circuit-board applications. Likewise, computer and electronics manufacturers became more comfortable using suppliers for key electronic components, including printed circuit boards. These suppliers were demonstrating reductions in time to market, engineering/prototyping costs, and manufacturing ramp-up costs to win business. In 1979, 40 percent of all rigid printed circuit-board fabrication was being outsourced to suppliers like Dieter. By 1989, that figure was about 60 percent, and by 1995, 80 percent. By 2001, 98 percent of all printed circuit-board production was going to external suppliers. Industry analysts placed total bookings for printed circuit-board production worldwide at approximately $30 billion in 2000, with the U.S. market comprising about a third of that dollar volume.

From his humble origins in his mother's kitchen, Dieter had built a thriving, profitable company doing about $30 million a year in revenue at its peak in 2000, with a 100,000-square-foot fabrication plant on Route 128 outside of Boston. He had 240 employees working two full shifts a day, and sometimes another half shift for limited production of new prototype boards.

Technology Development

As the industry grew, several basic factors increased the complexity of the boards and their production processes. The first of these was the number of "layers" on a board. The simplest printed circuit board was a single-layer, single-sided assembly. Soon, PCB manufacturers began designing and manufacturing boards with more than one "layer," that is, sheaths of fiberglass each printed with application-specific wiring that were then bonded together very much like a book. Holes were drilled at specific points in each layer and wired to provide connections between components on different layers. By the end of the 1960s, companies were regularly manufacturing four-layer PCBs. By the late 1970s, manufacturers of industrial control systems and computers were demanding ever greater functionality in the electrical interconnect capability of the boards. Six-layer PCBs became standard, and the trend continued. By the following decade, PCB manufacturers enhanced their processes to make 12-layer board assemblies in volume. The number of layers continued to increase, driven by the complexity of applications, such as medical devices and telecommunications switches.

Beginning in the late 1970s, the market divided into three distinct product segments by functionality. The functionality within each of the segments, however,

EXHIBIT 2 | THE EVOLUTION OF PRINTED CIRCUIT-BOARD APPLICATIONS

	1960s	1970s	1980s	1990s	2001–
High Complexity Low Volume		Military	Instrumentation Controls	Telecom	Servers & Storage Medical Devices Telecom: Optical
		22-layer PCBs	24-layer PCBs	30-layer PCBs	30-50-layer PCBs
Medium–High Complexity Medium Volume	Defense 4-layer PCBs	Telecom Switches Repeaters	Large Computers, Fax Machines, Copiers	Servers & Storage Medical Devices, Instrumentation Controls	Military Security Medical Devices Video conferencing
		4–8 layer PCBs	4–12 layer PCBs	8–18 layer PCBs	12–24 layer PCBs
Low Complexity High Volume	Computers	Consumer Electronics Appliances, HiFi	TVs, Radios, PCs, Games, Calculators, Typewriters	Mobile Phones	Smart Appliances
	1 or 2 layers	1 or 2 layers	1 or 2 layers	1–4 layers	1–4 layers

changed dramatically over time. (See Exhibit 2 for a detailed breakout.) In 2001 the three product segments were:

The Low-End Segment: For simple applications requiring one- to four-layer boards; order size ranged from 50,000 to 100,000 in a given year from a customer. An example was PCBs for stereo equipment. In the final assembly, a dozen electronic components would be mounted on each board. The price per board as shipped to the customer could be as low as 10 cents and rarely exceeded $10 per board.

The Mid-Range Segment: For more complex applications requiring 12- to 24-layer board assemblies; the order size ranged from as few as 50 up to as many as 5,000 in a given year from a customer. An example of this type of application was a medical imaging system. Hundreds of components and processors would be mounted on these boards. The price per board as shipped to customers was in the range of $10 to $150. The supplier's design engineers might spend as much as 40 hours designing the wiring and related circuitry. Higher prices were justified because of additional costs in prototyping, production ramp, materials in the final production run, and inspection.

The High-End Segment: For the most complex applications, requiring 30- to 50-layer boards; the order quantity was between 5 and 50 boards a year. An example was a defense contractor that developed electronic-warfare jamming systems integrated into aircraft. Hundreds if not thousands of components might be "stuffed" onto these boards. A supplier might charge from several hundred dollars to thousands of dollars per board. Hundreds of hours of labor were required in designing, prototyping, and placing the PCB into limited production.

EXHIBIT 3 | **THE PRINTED CIRCUIT BOARD FABRICATION VALUE CHAIN**

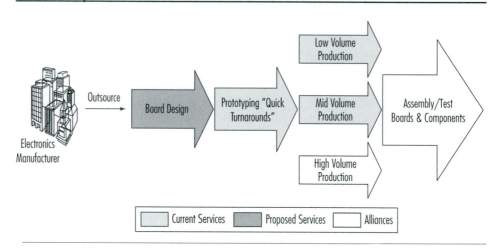

Another important factor in the development of the industry was the growth in technical services. These occurred in the front end of the fabrication process: designing the board, prototyping the design, and preproduction testing, which all focused on "quick-turns." Cycle times for developing complex electronics had shortened dramatically during the 1990s and showed no signs of slowing. For example, IBM's product-development cycles for its largest mainframes at the beginning of the 1990s were reported to be 72 months from start to commercial release. By the end of the decade, its newest mainframe—packed with highly complex printed circuit boards that connected all sorts of chips and electrical components—was developed in less than 18 months. An external supplier had to work fast and effectively with such customers as IBM.

Exhibit 3 shows the spectrum of activities generally considered by industry participants as the basic elements of the PCB business. At the front-end of that spectrum was the actual design of the printed circuit board itself, complete with the printed circuitry and various electrical components. Certain competitors had developed substantial board-design capabilities largely by acquiring boutique electronic design shops starting in 1995. These competitors were able to service major accounts by locating engineers close to their customers' engineering facilities.

Dieter's Business Approach

CBC had traditionally operated in the mid-range segment, providing boards to New England–based minicomputer companies. Dieter bought state-of-the-art equipment to keep pace with the industry, but he always did it as a follower. He would wait until his competitors had all upgraded their manufacturing processes before he would upgrade his own. Dieter also had a tendency to defer maintenance on the equipment and delay tool acquisition. On several occasions, equipment had broken down so that Dieter had to call up competitors to fulfill orders for CBC.

At the beginning of the 1980s, Dieter saw that volumes in the low end were beginning to explode and decided to diversify. By 1995, only 50 percent of CBC's revenues came from its traditional mid-range customers; the other 50 percent came from low-end consumer electronics manufacturers. By 1995 his company was a $20-million-a-year business. However, this low-end strategy got the company into financial trouble and led to the hiring of Ben.

By the early 1980s, offshore manufacturers had started low-complexity, high-volume fabrication. By the end of the decade, they dominated it. In this semi-automated, high-volume process, the offshore producers were able to quote substantially lower prices because of cheap labor. By 1995, the consumer electronics manufacturers had moved virtually all their business to Asian fabricators. Because of this foray into the low end, by 1995 CBC's profits had declined 90 percent. Deiter hired Ben in 1996 to help him turn the company around. Because of the financial hardships, Dieter had increased his practice of skimping on materials and maintenance. Things had gotten so bad by the time Ben first saw the plant that his immediate reaction was, "What a pit this is!"

Ben shed the unprofitable low-end business to refocus on the mid-range, more technologically complex segment of the market. Ben had the good fortune of making these moves when the electronics industry had explosive growth. Historically, the PCB market had grown about 6 percent a year, but from 1995 to 2000 it grew at 10 percent. By 2000, he had not only gotten the company back to profitability but also increased sales to $30 million. Even though Ben had gotten the company on reasonable footing in 2000, he knew that it still had more investments to make in process technology. Laser drilling, better solder masking for finishing printed circuitry, and semi-automated systems for electrical testing of finished boards were the major improvements needed to get to industry parity.

Current Competition

The competitive landscape had three types of players: the multiproduct electronics outsourcing giants, the publicly traded focused printed circuit-board suppliers, and the smaller, independent suppliers. (See the appendix for a description of the competitors.) Well-known electronics brands had increasingly turned to third-party contract manufacturers for systems assembly. The largest contract electronics manufacturers made everything from computers to networking switches to industrial controls to consumer electronics. Often, they would take over the existing plant as well as the salaries of plant employees from a brand-name producer and use that as a foundation for manufacturing not only the current products but, over time, those of the brand's competitors as well.

The next tier of PCB suppliers comprised publicly traded manufacturers that were focused almost exclusively on PCB production. The performance of the stocks of these companies during 2001 had not been good. Some examples were: Coretec's stock dropped 67 percent, Dynamic Details dropped 60 percent, Circuit World dropped 48 percent, and TTM Technologies dropped 22 percent. Only Merix had increased in value, rising 38 percent during 2001 as investors focused on its strong balance sheet.

The third tier consisted of independent suppliers. At the end of 2001, there were approximately 500 privately held independent printed circuit-board suppliers in North America alone. The industry was highly fragmented. Only 20 suppliers had annual revenues of more than $10 million. Many of the truly small suppliers went out of business in 2001.

All printed circuit-board suppliers had suffered during 2001. Orders were 50 percent below those of the prior year. Suppliers with strong design skills and a high-tech sales focus were impacted the least in the downturn. While excess capacity hurt margins in the lower segment of the business, companies making boards with 20-plus layers were able to maintain reasonable margins. If the industry turned around—and many expected it would within 9 to 12 months—the permanent reduction in total fabrication capacity meant that the survivors might expect even greater margins.

Management Team

Maggie had married Dieter in 1957 after she had graduated high school and he was in college. She was now 62 years old. She had started college as a part-time student in the 1980s but had just completed her BA in 2001. Although she had always spent a couple of hours a day at CBC, her main task was to have lunch with Dieter. Most of her other time had been occupied in maintaining the household and raising their two children. Dieter and Maggie loved to travel and socialize—they enjoyed cooking, fine wine, and the opera. Maggie had no business experience apart from that at CBC.

Maggie's son and daughter had both worked in the company from childhood. They both had undergraduate business degrees, but neither one played an active role in the management of the company. The son, Harry, nominally was a factory worker but made $150,000 a year regardless of the number of hours he worked. The daughter, Heidi, also made $150,000, but she was an administrative assistant to the sales manager. They were both paid much more than the managers they reported to.

Ben Cashman, 46, had an MBA and had known Dieter for 30 years. He had started his own television and intercom service business before Dieter hired him as president and COO of the company. Although Dieter had controlled everything when Ben came on board, he was hoping to eventually buy the company, as he knew Dieter was in his 60s and had never developed anyone to take over when he retired. Ben was given 2.5 percent of the company when he joined.

Current Situation

To survive the market stress of 2001, Ben felt they needed to get their financial house in order, and they needed to make strategic investments to stay competitive. (See Exhibits 4 and 5 for CBC's financials.) CBC went from about $2.5 million in bookings a month in 2000 down to about $1.8 million a month in 2001. Throughout the year, Ben had taken measures to reduce costs. One was to reduce head count in the plant. He had mostly an hourly workforce operating semi-automated processes for various stages of production and quality control. While painful to do, he estimated that each head-count reduction of 10 persons saved the company about $300,000 a year in operating expense. Once having 240 full-time employees, the company now had 135, going from essentially a two-and-a-half-shift operation to a single-shift operation. He felt that the integrity of the operation at a $20 million order rate could still be maintained even with only 100 people. Ben also felt that G&A was too high, running at about 10 percent of sales. He had asked all salaried employees to take a pay

EXHIBIT 4 | **INCOME STATEMENT**

		2000	2001	Projected 2002
Net sales		$29,316,885	$21,877,855	$18,300,000
Cost of sales		23,790,016	19,086,179	14,587,000
Gross margin		5,526,869	2,791,676	3,713,000
Operating Expenses				
	Selling	1,035,708	988,151	846,000
	G&A	2,630,723	2,351,482	1,711,000
	Income/Loss from			
	Operations	1,860,438	(547,957)	1,156,000
Interest Expense		708,381	659,684	564,000
	Other Income	13,096	593,743	25,000
	Income (loss) before tax	1,165,153	(613,898)	567,000

EXHIBIT 5 | **BALANCE SHEET**

Current Assets	2001	2000	Current Liabilities	2001	2000
Cash	141,144	92,244	Short-Term Debt	1,222,175	993,843
A/R	2,670,771	4,672,372	Accounts Payable	4,020,299	3,382,278
Notes Receivable	81,400	125,650	Accrued Expenses	388,355	886,542
Inventory	3,382,850	3,284,724	Total Current	5,630,829	5,262,663
Prepaid expenses	260,280	161,485			
Deferred/prepaid income tax	162,866	3,636	Capital leases	421,610	637,074
			Long-Term Debt	6,336,888	7,383,814
Total Current Assets	6,699,311	8,340,111	Deferred Income Taxes	−92,731	578,146
			Total Liabilities	12,296,596	13,861,697
Property, Plant, Equipment	20,224,430	18,605,375	Shareholder's Equity	3,748,489	3,723,591
Less Accumulated Depreciation	−11,028,378	−9,743,957			
Net	9,196,052	8,861,418			
Other Assets	149,722	383,759			
Total Assets	16,045,085	17,585,288	Total Liabilities and Equity	16,045,085	17,585,288

reduction in keeping with the current level of sales. Ben was determined to get G&A down to 7.5 percent of sales.

Weakness in 2001 sales had drained the company's cash. By the end of 2001, the balance sheet showed $4 million in accounts payable. Suppliers had essentially financed the business for the past six months. Ben knew that this situation would not last much longer, as they were threatening to sue for collection. Half the accounts were now more than 90 days past due. He knew that he had to cut trade debt in order to keep the suppliers from abandoning the company. The company was also behind in payments to one of Dieter's early partners, who owned 11 percent of the company. He and CBC had an agreement to repurchase all his shares at a set rate and price, but CBC had stopped doing so because of the lack of cash. He was also threatening to sue.

The company had more than $3 million in inventory by the close of 2001. Ben estimated that about half of that was truly productive in the sense that it comprised unfinished goods that could be directly rolled into new orders, but he never really investigated its true worth. The utility and value of the other half was not clear, being finished goods for products that manufacturers might never make. Many suppliers had purchased materials under the reasonably positive expectations in the last half of 2000, only to be left "holding the bag" as conditions worsened and orders plummeted. Ben had cut accounts receivables by approximately half from the prior year, largely through tenacious efforts to get the company paid faster. Ben was not sure how much of the remaining accounts receivable he could collect because many of his customers were also in financial distress.

The projections on the income statement showed no marked improvement in sales for 2002. Ben saw no reason for the industry to turn around—not yet at least. However, he felt a strong rebound could again bring sales back up to the $30 million level in a single year. CBC, moreover, was adding new types of customers. Military electronics, videoconferencing systems, new generations of mobile phones, biometric systems, security devices, and security-enhanced routers and switches were potential growth opportunities for technologically advanced suppliers. It seemed that the tragic events of "9/11" were driving the business: People wanted to travel less and required security-enhanced systems of all shapes and forms. The American defense agencies and their contractors, moreover, strongly preferred that U.S. companies only make all subassemblies for them.

However, the company had fallen behind its competitors in the high-end multilayer board business. To compete effectively in defense and other emerging high-end applications, Ben felt that the company would have to invest $2 million over the next two or three years to improve the company's fabrication technology. The manufacturing process was capital intensive. Like other PCB manufacturers, CBC had to continually invest in process technologies to meet demands for density and quality. CBC had no patents of its own. The second half of 2001 had been so difficult that the company had temporarily stopped process improvements. In addition, Ben wanted to spend another $2 million over two or three years to buy several board designer shops to execute an upstream design services.

On the revenue side, Ben thought the business was still worth pursuing. As electronics manufacturers consumed their inventories during the first half of 2002, and industry experts began forecasting a general turnaround later in the year, Ben believed that better days were ahead. A leading industry analyst projected that electronic component sales would rise by 5 percent in 2002 as electronics manufacturers were beginning to "recharge" their pipelines. In fact, during the last quarter of 2001, there had been a slight uptick in sales for both CBC and most of its competitors (Exhibit 6). Ben remained cautious, however. That uptick could just as easily reverse because consumer confidence and industrial spending remained low compared with prior years' levels. Ben hoped that the electronics industry would stabilize and that bookings for 2002 would come in at around $18 million.

EXHIBIT 6 | **TURBULENCE IN THE MARKET**

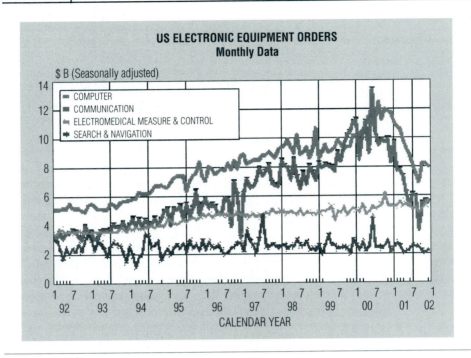

SOURCE: http://www.census.gov/indicator/www/m3/pastpressreleases/prel/2002/feb02prel.pdf

Board Meeting

To start the board meeting, Ben had gone over all the moves CBC had made over the past six months to respond to the market conditions. He summarized his opinion:

> CBC is a survivor of 2001 and so is positioned to take advantage of the rebound. Needham & Co. is predicting that because others have left the industry and capacity is down, that inventory will be used up by the second quarter. The market will then turn around, so we only have to hang in there for a couple more tough months. We can be profitable at $20 million in sales now with the cutbacks, but we can also grow back to $30 million as in 2000.

Don Armour, the mergers and acquisition specialist, was even more aggressive than Ben:

> Now is the time to take advantage of the situation to not only be a survivor but to grow even larger. There are many financially struggling companies out there that we can buy up cheaply. People are willing to make deals. We should set our sights even higher! Why not look to $100 million in sales?

Dane Lombard, the turnaround specialist, was next to jump in and was heated in his response:

Don't be foolish in going after pipe dreams—get the most you can now because the market is not going to turn around. Needham has been predicting a rebound for six months and keeps pushing out the date. Henderson Ventures and DLouhy Merchant both predict there will be no recovery until 2003 at the earliest. We do not have the money needed to invest in bringing us back to industry parity, plus our balance sheet is awful. In fact, we are not worth as much as an entity as we would be if we sell off the pieces separately.

Maggie looked to Ben and asked where the money would come from to do the investments he wanted. Ben had hired consultants in turnaround financing to give guidance in restructuring CBC's debt and to help find some outside investors. Ben reported:

The consultants have analyzed us and think that there is a possibility of finding some outside investors if the industry rebounds. I have held off on going ahead because they advise that any investors would want to put their money mainly into the company rather than into buying out the existing shareholders. The investors would also demand complete control of ownership and shed all non-productive employees. In effect, Maggie, your ownership position would be almost worthless. Plus, you and your family will be out of the company.

Will Tatelman, the company's auditor and Maggie's personal counsel, chimed in:

Maggie, you have to protect your own interests. You can work a deal to get ownership of the building for your shares, and then you can lease the plant back to the company. I have read two recent forecasts, one by Kaufman & Co., which said it is impossible to predict what will happen in the economy because of the risks of further terrorism and escalating military conflict, but they are saying there will be no recovery for a long time. The other by Wells Fargo is saying there would be no recession so this quarter's numbers will show we are already in recovery. So no one knows and you would be wise to protect yourself.

Ben agreed that Maggie should consider creating a sale/leaseback deal on the company's building before investors came in. The building was valued at $5 million and had a $3.5 million mortgage. The only tenant was CBC, but if CBC was successfully restructured, the rent would be a nice annuity with current rents going for $10 a square foot. The sale would take the mortgage off of CBC's books and turn the cost of the building into a rental expense. Of course, if the market did not turn around, Maggie could be stuck with a $3.5 million mortgage and a building worth much less.

Maggie had responded:

You know, this business has provided for me and my family for 40 years. At this point in my life, I want stable income. What else can we do?

Another alternative Ben put forward was to take the company into Chapter 11 bankruptcy, which would allow it to renegotiate all its bills with its creditors. This would buy time for the company until the market turned around. The downside was that the creditors got to go over CBC's books, which would make known how much money Maggie and her family had been taking out of the business. Although reduced from the 2000 peak, they were still much overpaid for the work they did. One of the banks that had given CBC a large credit line already was putting pressure on Ben to get Maggie and her family out of the business.

The final alternative put forward, and the one Ben wanted, was to bet on the recovery and to convince the creditors that they would be paid in full if they stuck by the company for a while longer. This would not provide any of the investment needed to make the company competitive again, but it did allow Maggie and her family to maintain control of the company.

Ben recommended staying the course—he was convinced the recovery was right around the corner. The outside board members, however, suggested otherwise. Maggie was left to make the first real business decision of her life.

Appendix: Competitor Information

The competitive landscape facing Circuit Board Corporation could be divided into three tiers of companies: the multiproduct electronics outsourcing giants, the publicly traded focused printed circuit-board suppliers, and the smaller, independent focused suppliers. The major board-making contract manufacturers were:

- Flextronics: With operations throughout the world, it made both rigid and flexible circuit boards (on flexible connectors) and assembled them up to the completed product stage.

- Sanmina-SCI: Sanmina-SCI was primarily a North American operation and made only rigid boards. During the 1990s, Sanmina bought several dozen independent board suppliers. They assembled boards, including backplanes and systems. One of these was an independent focused printed-circuit board manufacturer much like Circuit Board Corporation. Altron, however, had ramped up into a $200-million-a-year business targeting complex, multilayer printed circuit-board applications. Sanmina had mothballed 9 of its 12 printed circuit-board fabrication plants during 2001. This removed $800 million of annual printed circuit-board production capacity. Much of that was a permanent removal.

The next tier of suppliers comprised publicly traded manufacturers focused almost exclusively on printed circuit-board production.

- Coretec: Roughly a $100 million Canadian company with a strategy of providing rapid turnaround to electronics manufacturers. They were setting up a multisite, time-zone spread operation to be close to the various customers. Coretec still needed to set up an operation east of the Mississippi. Its target applications were multilayer, medium-volume applications, the proclaimed strategy of Circuit Board Corporation.

- TTM Technologies: A merger of two independents, Pacific Circuits (a medium- volume producer) and Power Circuits (quick turnaround prototypes) merged together with venture money to focus on the multilayer, medium-volume market. The investors then took the company public. TTM was a direct competitor with Circuit Board Corporation. It was doing about $100 million in annual revenue.

- Dynamic Details: This was the largest firm of the group, with about $400 million in orders per year. DDI had also focused at the front end of the value chain, buying many small engineering firms and board companies. One of these was Automata, a $45 million company. DDI specialized in critical needs, extremely fast turnaround, multilayer, complex applications. It was the industry leader in the "quick turn," something to which Circuit Board Corporation aspired.

- Merix: Another $100 million company, Merix was known as the technology leader in the downstream areas of board fabrication. It had a fine-tuned process to achieve the highest layer counts and the greatest density of wiring, and it could use various exotic materials. Merix could regularly manufacture mid-20-layer boards for its telecommunications customers, and could shoot into 30–40-layer boards when required. Merix also offered upstream design services as shown in Exhibit 3. It was proceeding with plans to complete a new highly automated fabrication plant in Wood Village, Oregon. On the other hand, while Merix's sales had approached $250 million in 2000, it garnered only $25 million in sales during the third quarter of 2001. However, it had a strong balance sheet and had used these assets to invest in plant and equipment and buy other companies. This allowed it to continue adding capacity in anticipation of a turnaround in demand.

- Circuit World: strictly a medium-volume board producer with limited prototyping capability. It was about a $30 million company.

3M Canada: Industrial Business Division

R. Chandrasekhar wrote this case under the supervision of Professor Terry Deutscher solely to provide material for class discussion. The authors do not intend to illustrate either effective or ineffective handling of a managerial situation. The authors may have disguised certain names and other identifying information to protect confidentiality.

Ivey Management Services prohibits any form of reproduction, storage or transmittal without its written permission. Reproduction of this material is not covered under authorization by any reproduction rights organization. To order copies or request permission to reproduce materials, contact Ivey Publishing, Ivey Management Services, c/o Richard Ivey School of Business, The University of Western Ontario, London, Ontario, Canada, N6A 3K7; phone (519) 661-3208; fax (519) 661-3882; e-mail cases@ivey.uwo.ca.

Version: (A) 2006-09-27

In May 2006, the Industrial Business Division (IBD) of 3M Canada Company had a new mandate. It had to step up its annual organic growth rate of three to five per cent in recent years to 12 to 15 per cent by 2008. The target had to be met independently of growth from ongoing acquisitions. Mahesh Yegnaswami, the IBD national accounts manager, had to recommend a plan of action to the vice- president (IBD) on how the division, the second largest in 3M Canada by sales, would achieve this target.

IBD sold products to business customers, not to individual consumers. Its products had two types of end user applications—production plants and servicing facilities—and two respective customer groups—original equipment manufacturers (OEMs) and maintenance, repair and overhaulers (MROs). Products catered to the OEMs were high-value items becoming part of the finished product (e.g. adhesives used in furniture making). Those catered to the MROs were consumables of low value (e.g. masking tapes used in paint shops). Growth at IBD was slow because the OEM segment, on which the division was concentrating so far, had become mature, with limited prospects of expansion. IBD had not concentrated on the MRO segment because it was fragmented, with little brand loyalty. The stock keeping units (SKUs) numbered around 10 million for the industry, most of them commoditized. However, MRO was growing. The large players within it, some of them mega-corporations, were, in fact, growing at a double digit rate.

Yegnaswami stated:

There are two ways of reaching the target—finding new customers for existing products, and launching new products aimed at new and existing customers. Both approaches take a long time to produce results. However, changing the customer focus from OEM to MRO gives us additional sales in the targeted time-frame. But IBD has had exposure only to a few segments of MRO. The division had commissioned a benchmarking study that showed that IBD's share of distributor sales was a mere two per cent of the distributors' revenue. Based on that study, we have recently identified ten distributors (see Exhibit 1), considered winners, for a close examination of their growth drivers and business processes. They are the industrial equivalents of consumer "Big Box" stores and can take IBD into the big league.

The questions before Yegnaswami were the following: How should IBD engage and hold on to the large distributors? How should it restructure its sales model to serve the new MRO channel?

3M Company

3M Company was founded in 1902 and had grown to become a global enterprise with employees numbering over 69,000, companies in over 60 countries, and plants in 139 locations worldwide. Its preliminary business charter was to mine a mineral deposit for grinding-wheel abrasives.[1] In 1922, Minnesota Mining and Manufacturing Company, as the company was then known, developed the world's first water-proof sandpaper. It marked the beginning of regular innovations with practical applications for which 3M was to be well-known in later years. To date, the company has a total of 50,000 patents worldwide, spread over 13 technology platforms ranging from abrasives to polymers. 3M has not, as a policy, outsourced production, although it encouraged subsidiaries worldwide, including 3M Canada, to pursue independent regional alliances—for third party distribution, licensed manufacturing and exclusive supplier status—to enhance local revenues and margins.

Since 2000, the management had been driving productivity through programs like Six Sigma, Lean Manufacturing and Global Sourcing. New products were a significant part of 3M's growth portfolio and efforts were underway to shorten the time to market from six to seven years to 18 months. The cost of sales was declining and margin as percentage of sales was expanding over the years (see Exhibit 2) indicating that operational efficiencies had taken root at 3M.

Strategy - Focus on Sales

The year 2006 heralded a shift in strategy at 3M. George Buckley, who took over as chairman, president and chief executive officer of the company on December 7, 2005, spearheaded the change by saying: "It's more fun growing grapes than working a

---

[1] www.mmm.com/About3M/History referenced July 6, 2006.

wine press."[2] The spotlight moved from margin expansion to top line growth. Investments priorities were redirected, from productivity gains and cost savings towards market development and promotion. The new strategy was comprised of four elements: growing the core business, pursuing acquisitions, concentrating on emerging business opportunities and doubling investments in emerging markets.

The general guidelines for growing the core business, of which IBD was one part, were the following:

- Drive scale in large markets

- Take higher relative share in small markets

- Go for customization

- Manage customer retention

- Develop local and differentiated products

- Extend private labeling

- Fill in product white spaces

- Plan for cannibalization

Said Yegnaswami:

These guidelines are consistent with the change in customer focus that IBD is seeking. The opportunity for driving scale and market share is larger in MRO because of four reasons. First, it is a big market, estimated to be of the order of Cdn$14 billion in Canada. Second, the large distributors are growing faster than the rate of growth of MRO market. Third, there are vacant spaces in most product lines waiting to be filled. And, finally, private labeling is an opportunity area with potential for both revenue and margins.

Structure

3M Company's business had been grouped into seven divisions: Health Care, Transportation, Display and Graphics, Consumer and Office, Industrial, Electro and Communications, and Safety and Security Services (see Exhibit 3). Each was a strategic business unit (SBU) with its own manufacturing and marketing facilities. Bringing together common or related technologies, each SBU had worldwide responsibility for product lines within it. As a result, line managers reported both to global heads of the business of which they were a part and also to country heads. While the business managers "owned" the product, the frontline sales force "owned" the customer. 3M had also introduced the concept of account managers for the company's OEM customers whose product requirements cut across SBUs. The account managers presented a common face for ordering and both delivery and billing while preempting the inconvenience of a salesperson from each division of 3M calling on the same customer.

---

[2]Begleiter David, Miner Jason and Sheehan James in "Growing Grapes: More Aggressive Growth," Deutsche Bank Securities Inc Equity Research report dated May 22, 2006.

Effective January 2006, the Transportation division had been merged with Industrial. This had been done to realize synergies in common markets, sales channels and customers, technologies, manufacturing facilities, and selling processes.

Industrial Business Division

IBD served a broad range of industrial markets, from appliances and electronics to paper and packaging. The products included tapes, a wide variety of coated and nonwoven abrasives, adhesives, specialty materials, and supply chain execution software solutions. The acquisition of Cuno Incorporated in the United States in August, 2005 added a new category of filtration products to its range. Tapes and adhesives represented 50 to 60 per cent to the division's turnover, and abrasives 40 to 50 per cent. Filtration was a future growth area. Person to person interaction was the basis of IBD's sales model. Sales were relationship-driven.

According to Yegnaswami,

> Several initiatives have been under way at IBD for some time to generate top line growth. These are independent of the decision to focus on MRO. The division has identified nine product opportunities, based on existing technology platforms, as having growth potential. Among them are composite conductors, liquid filtration, paint preparation, and supply chain execution software. The provision of a single face to the customer, bringing the complete line of potential 3M products and technologies together, is also perceived as a sales stimulus. These are larger corporate initiatives which the division has also been pursuing in Canada.

3M Canada

Set up in 1951, 3M Canada was the U.S. company's first overseas subsidiary. A year later, it opened a 145,000 sq ft manufacturing and packaging plant in London, ON, making tapes, adhesives and abrasives. The company had three more plants in Canada—in Ontario at Brockville and Perth and in Manitoba at Morden. Individual product managers were responsible for production, quality, sales, marketing and profitability of specific products. A central management committee provided coordination at the top. Each product group was autonomous, while having access to the experience and knowledge pool of the global organization and benefiting from close involvement in the marketing strategies of over 50 divisions in 3M Company.

IBD had two major customer segments—OEM and MRO.

OEM

OEMs were medium to large enterprises with an industry focus and a strong manufacturing core. Of late, a decline in Canadian manufacturing was affecting the OEM segment. Characterized by downsizings, plant closures and layoffs, the decline had set in for two reasons: a rising Canadian dollar and a growing trend towards offshoring. The Canadian dollar had risen 32.96 per cent (from 0.637 per U.S. dollar in April 2002 to 0.847 in May 2006), eroding the edge of Canadian manufacturers who earned sales in U.S. currency but incurred expenses in Canadian currency. High North American labor costs had become a powerful incentive since 2002 for off-shoring production. An hour of labor and benefits in Canada cost US$11 at the minimum wage level. The same hour in an area of interior China cost less than US$0.15. A similar ratio prevailed for skilled technical positions such as engineers, programmers, scientists and managers. The number of employees in the manufacturing sector in Canada had declined from 2.285 million in April 2002 to 2.207 million in April 2005.[3] On the positive side, the off-shoring trend was forcing Canadian manufacturers, including 3M Canada, to become competitive. It was also compelling businesses like IBD to look beyond the OEM segment for customers and revenue.[4]

Yegnaswami said:

> Vendors are always the first to be affected, and the last to recover, from a slow-down in the industry of which an OEM is a part. That makes OEM, in its nature, a volatile customer group. 3M has stayed the course through initiatives like product innovation, new product introduction, getting "specified" for in-process usage, building relationships with business customers and working with them closely to reduce their costs of operations. It also helps that the business customer is the end user. Tracking the customer needs is easier with an OEM.

MRO

Loosely defined, MRO meant "non-critical" items, used in the general repair and maintenance of plant, equipment and facilities. Given such a scope, distributors controlled the MRO market more than suppliers. This was a psychological entry barrier for a brand driven supplier like 3M. There were other disincentives. Products could not be specified, brand loyalty was minimal and price was an important business driver. To the discomfiture of suppliers like 3M, several of IBD's products were being progressively pushed into the MRO category because of growing commoditization. There were, however, a number of specialized items closely identified with suppliers like 3M.

For a better internal understanding of the MRO market, 3M Canada had categorized distributors into four types: National, Special, General and Niche (see Exhibit 4). The National category was the fastest growing, due to ongoing consolidation, among other reasons. The Special and Niche categories brought to bear some singular IBD competencies—like technical skill, vertical specialization and product knowledge—in their dealings with the customer. In a sense, Special and Niche customers served as an extension of the sales force of vendors like 3M. Being a product-driven company with a strong R&D orientation, 3M had found a natural fit with the ethos of the Special and Niche categories. The company had, in fact, grown the two categories over the years. The 3M component of their individual businesses was high. Set up by qualified technocrats working earlier with companies like 3M, they generally had a flat organization structure and were quick-footed. Also, generally speaking, they focused more on the regional OEM market. However, they were not extending their footprints geographically as rapidly as the large National category.

---

[3]http://www.statscan.ca/subject/labor/employment/employmentbyindustry referenced July 24, 2006.

[4]http://www.bankofcanada.ca/en/rates/can_us_close.html referenced August 2, 2006.

Yegnaswami stated:

> Our sales representatives have been accustomed to dealing with store managers as individuals, one to one, in the Special and Niche categories. Now they have to deal with large corporations driven by networks, procedure and protocol. The profiles are vastly different. Instead of interfacing with one branch and one customer, they have to coordinate the requirements of 40 or 50 branches of the same customer. Instead of dealing with one product in which they have the expertise, they are answerable to varied requirements of a mega-distributor.

Trends in MRO

- National distributors numbered about a dozen in Canada. They were growing at double digit rates. They secured large contracts wherein by low unit margins, integral to a commodity business, were offset by high volumes. National players had a vast sales infrastructure in terms of branches, delivery centers and sales forces (inside and outside). Securing volumes was crucial to their profitability because their fixed costs were high. They also catered to the supply needs of OEM.

- Special and Niche stores were thus losing their traditional competitive edge because of two reasons. Large players were building up domain expertise by acquiring product/process skills. They were making inroads into niche players' customers. Secondly, as technologies were going off patent, manufacturing was open to all. The absence of legacy expenses (such as R&D) lowered costs for new entrants. Products were becoming commoditized. Product specialization, a major plus for a Niche player, no longer carried a premium. Generic sales skills, rather than technical knowledge, were crucial to getting sales. Staffed by no more than eight to 10 people, operating no more than three to four branches, restricted to one or two verticals, and with no succession planning in place, Special and Niche stores were becoming vulnerable to takeovers.

- Growth by acquisition was common. Consolidation was a major trend. But there were still as many distributors as there were ten years ago. For every traditional distributor disappearing due to acquisition, a new boutique distributor was opening up, focusing on a narrow market in which it would quickly develop expertise. Consolidation was evident even on the demand side. Customers were consolidating their purchases and reducing the number of distributors with whom they would do business.

- E-commerce was gathering ground. It was, however, still limited to transactional elements like order processing and bill payment. It had not led to large scale disintermediation or elimination of MRO companies' sales forces. The physical medium of a salesperson was still crucial to retaining customers.

Said Yegnaswami:

> It is obvious that IBD has to change tack in several ways. First, we have to redirect our efforts from OEM to MRO. Second, within MRO, we have to shift emphasis from Special and Niche players to large National players. I think we

also need to get closer to the end users of MRO supplies—the maintenance foreman or the tools engineer—in manufacturing enterprises, large and small. In OEM, the customer (the manufacturer) is the end user. In MRO, the customer (the distributor) is not the end user. Connecting with the end user, in whatever form, is necessary to get closer to the customer. We must find ways of connecting with the end user in MRO. This calls for a change of mindset in our sales force.

Sales Organization

IBD had 35 sales people—10 located in Western Canada, 10 in Quebec and 15 in Ontario. They had both geographic and product specialization, but not customer-specialization. 3M, as a policy, took people only at entry levels and promoted from within. It did not encourage lateral inductions. Sales people moved along a hierarchical ladder from S1 to S5 grades based on performance.

Customers were perceived as ongoing, not one-off, at 3M. Maintaining an existing business account and generating repeat business were key indicators of sales performance. Customer defections (known as 'leakages' within 3M) averaged five per cent of sales. The annual compensation of each salesperson had a large fixed component. Sales achieved in excess of targets carried a reward that moved in geometric progression. New business development carried an incentive. Notwithstanding its reputation as an innovative company, 3M was conservative in some ways. It groomed people from within, slowly and steadily, giving them time to grow and develop. Employee compensation was oriented towards staying the course.

Since early 2006, Yegnaswami had tracked the large National accounts in MRO in order to learn about them. He said:

> There are some takeaways. We know for sure that some of the National accounts are growing at double digit. They themselves see opportunities for IBD to grow with them. These are large organizations, larger than 3M Canada, with complex buying processes, unlike the Niche stores we deal with. What is clear is that our present way of doing business does not work with National accounts. For this segment, we need a different model of going to market.

The traditional way of doing business at IBD had three characteristics. First, the division sold products at the premium end of the market. Second, its sales force had product specialization. Finally, IBD sales representatives excelled in relationship-building. The new model required different attributes—selling products at the low-end of the market; a well-rounded business perspective that provided a common company face to the customer; and managing the dynamics of a distribution channel.

Said John Mann, vice president (marketing & business development), Unisource Canada:

> We have, of late, seen 3M turning its attention to MRO. As a product-driven company, 3M has been traditionally good at what it does. But to succeed in its new endeavor, the company needs to do four things well. First, it must put in place effective supply chain processes. 3M must know what is on the floor and what is not and manage the replenishment process. Second, 3M should

be able to provide technical support to the end user. A distributor's role is limited to buying commodities in bulk, breaking them down into packaging units, bundling them with others and delivering to the end user. Provision of technical back-up would be the responsibility of the supplier. Third, 3M should offer "total solutions." A good beginning here would be to break down the silos within its ranks among various divisions and loosen up its product discipline. Finally, 3M is a large organization and a bureaucracy. Quicker decision-making is imperative if it is serious about MRO.

The industrial business was changing in terms of product applications, service delivery mechanisms, customer expectations and logistics requirements. But the 3M business model had not changed. It had stood the test of time and there was a comfort level with it in the organization. This was a major challenge for some line managers at 3M.

The Big Three Issues

As he began to prioritize the areas requiring change, Yegnaswami narrowed them down to three: sales model, logistics and marketing programs.

Sales Model

The traditional focus of 'what to sell' had to be replaced by 'how to sell'. IBD had to make a transition from the current product/division centric model to a customer/account centric model—without forfeiting product expertise, the hallmark of 3M. One alternative was to build a cadre of 'channel' specialists to complement the product specialists at IBD. For example, IBD could add a salesperson in each of Western Canada, Ontario and Quebec to cultivate and build relationships with National players in the region, or reassign one from the existing cadre. The idea would be to develop this employee into a well-rounded businessperson presenting a single face to the MRO channel.

Outsourcing sales would be another option. IBD could team up with independent sales agents and manufacturers' representatives for specific product categories (like adhesives). The latter would have their own sales force and would work on a base commission (of two per cent on existing business and five per cent extra on additional sales). The agents dealt with complementary product lines and would not take more than one supplier in the same category. However, Yegnaswami was concerned that outsourcing would introduce an additional layer in 3M's interface with the customer.

Growth in volumes could be driven by private labels. In general, the penetration of private labels in MRO was low, at about one to two per cent of sales. But the National distributors wanted to grow their private label business in order to increase their clout with manufacturers and build their own equity in the trade. For 3M, private label business was a means of moving the tonnage in the market, although it would not enhance the 3M brand or its market share because the products would not carry the 3M label. IBD was open to the idea of using some of its plant capacity to manufacture private labels. But using private labels to supply MRO would mean a full-scale commitment. Yegnaswami thought to himself: "Are we ready to move into private labels?"

Channel conflict was another source of concern. It was draining sales force productivity without adding to revenue. For example, a distributor would approach 3M for price reductions on items that it had negotiated as part of an offering to an OEM.

But the OEM might already be buying these items from 3M through a Niche distributor who would now be deprived of this particular portion of business. The net result would be a switch of business which meant delicate negotiations involving 3M salespeople and their customers without any overall gain in terms of new business for 3M. Channel conflicts would only increase if MRO accounts were developed by IBD.

The challenges before IBD were typical of its counterparts at 3M's subsidiaries in the mature markets of the United States and Western Europe. But Canada was unique because of its low population density and wide distances separating geographies. One alternative was to provide a dedicated toll number to each individual MRO distributor which the latter could use to readily speak to a specially designated inside salesperson for any of its product/service requirements during business hours.

Logistics

Supply chain management could be strengthened by linking an incentive program with reduction in supply chain costs of the large National Player. A recent study by Hagemeyer (see Exhibit 5) on channel costs had shown that the price of goods constituted only 39 per cent of the total costs. The other 61 per cent (25 per cent were costs of procurement and 36 per cent the cost of inventory), represented a large area of opportunity for supply chain savings. This was an area of opportunity for 3M to work closely with MROs and, by progressively lowering their costs, get a progressively increasing share of their business.

Another notable area for improvement for IBD was to strive to be the "best in class" in logistics fulfillment, standardizing SKUs, and just-in-time delivery. These were "quick fixes" but necessary to maintain the competitive edge (see Exhibit 6).

Marketing Programs

Traditionally, marketing programs at 3M were aimed at the "Regional Specialist" segment of distributors. They were not working with the National players. Customized programs now needed to be created, taking into account the constraints and protocols as established by the National players. A paradigm shift was thus necessary in the way marketing programs were being designed, launched and executed.

It was clear that there would be no additional resources available to IBD. Growth had to be achieved with the existing field sales force alone.

With the strength of its corporate brand, and of the technology behind its products, 3M had been traditionally operating at premium price points. This had led to some high margins. Growth in sales, to the targeted extent, would be possible by adding new lower price points. There were white spaces to be filled. Yegnaswami had two apprehensions here. How would it impact the brand? How would it impact on margins?

Conclusion

As he was putting together the plan, a thought occurred to Yegnaswami: "Why not continue the way we are?" IBD was doing okay. With the combination of Transportation business with IBD, effective January 2006, it had become the largest business at 3M.

EXHIBIT 1 | CANADIAN **MRO** MAJORS

#	Company	Value Proposition	No of stores	Competitive advantage	Sales in 2004		Future Strategy
					Cdn$ mn	% growth over '03	
1	Wolseley Canada	• Integrated supply • Automated vending • Single source • E-commerce • Mobile warehouse	238	• Second largest distributor of plumbing and heating products in Canada • The Ferguson "legacy of leadership" program in the United States, a training initiative	748[1]	12.4	• Acquire companies • Open new distribution centers • Improve customer service • Generate operating efficiencies • Enhance product offerings
2	Acklands-Grainger	• Authorized warranty repair facility • Value-added services • Customization	160	• 116 years in business • Broad-line supplier of facilities maintenance products	720	11.1[2]	• Penetrate customer accounts • Improve employee knowledge of products through SAP roll out
3	Century Vallen	• Using innovation to add value to supply chain • Reducing customer's total cost of product ownership	32	• Part of Hagemeyer N.V. • Niche in petroleum industry supplies • A bulk of customers comprises small to medium-sized electrical contractors	NA	3.7[3]	• Restore profitability and 'fix the business' in short term • Stick to professional products and services (PPS) segment • Pursue acquisitions
4	Fastenal	• "In-plant" site in or near customer facility selling solely to that customer	112	• Focused on fasteners • Customer convenience through stores in small, medium and large markets • Centrally located distribution centers • The Fastenal School of Business, set up for employee development	91[4]		• Open new stores at the rate of 13–18 per cent every year, consistent with historical average • Focus on store locations with an 'industrial-leaning' retail look and feel. • Upgrade store formats

(continues)

EXHIBIT 1 | CANADIAN MRO MAJORS (*CONTINUED*)

5	Home Depot Supply	• Associate know-how • Merchandising selection	123	• Parent company in United States aiming to become the world's largest diversified wholesale distributor, with sales of US$28 billion, by 2010 • Acquired Hughes Supply Inc, dealing with contractors' supplies and MRO items, in March 2006 • Firming up Canadian launch	US$3,250 (of Hughes Supply Inc)	• Expand product adjacencies • Open new stores • Launch eco-friendly products • Establish platforms catering to the Pro-market • Deliver compelling customer productivity • Ensure low-cost provider status
6	Unisource Canada	• Single-source Just-in-Time supply • Focused on printing, packaging and imaging supplies • Third-party logistics (3PL) business model	19			
7	Guillevin International Co		115	• Second largest wholesale distributor of electrical materials in Canada	50	
8	Tenaquip Industrial Distribution	• First company in Canada to distribute industrial product through a catalogue • Integrated Supply programs	8			

(continues)

EXHIBIT 1 | CANADIAN **MRO** MAJORS (*CONTINUED*)

#	Company	Value Proposition	No of stores	Competitive advantage	Sales in 2004		Future Strategy
					Cdn$ mn	% growth over '03	
9	Weber Supply Co Inc.	• Among the first distributors in North America to employ radio frequency technology to manage inventory • Among early converts in 1995 to e-commerce	12	• 150 year history – now into third generation in business • Balancing the use of technology with 'high touch' approach of promoting personal relationships with customers	153[5]		• Strengthen presence in Ontario • Look for regional alliances on both supply and demand side • Sell more to each existing customer
10	Richelieu Hardware Ltd	• Everything under one roof	29	Hardware supplies for furniture industry	350	12.2	• Acquire for synergy • Improve product mix • Develop targeted marketing programs • Expand into United States

[1] Wolseley Canada's turnover in 2004 was 445.7 million pounds (396.4 million pounds in 2003) as per page 65 of the company's 2004 annual report. On conversion, it will be Cdn$748 million.

[2] SEC filings 10K–2004, p. 16.

[3] Includes United States, Mexico and Canada operations comprising Hagemeyer NA.

[4] The store sites located outside the United States contributed approximately six per cent of the company's consolidated net sales of US$1523.3 million in 2005 with approximately 83 per cent of this amount attributable to Canadian operations.

[5] Sales of over US$100 million a year in late 1990s, according to the recorder May 11, 2005.

EXHIBIT 2 | **3M Company Financials**

(In mn US $)	2005	2004	2003
	Income statement		
Net sales	21,167	20,011	18,232
Less Operating expenses			
– Cost of sales	10,381	9,958	9,285
– Selling, gen. and admn.	4,535	4,281	3,994
– R&D	1,242	1,194	1,147
– Other expenses	—	—	93
Operating income	5,009	4,578	3,713
Less			
– Interest	26	23	56
– Income taxes	1,694	1,503	1,202
– Minority interest	55	62	52
Net income	3,324	2,990	2,403
	Balance sheet as on December 31		
Assets			
Cash and cash equivalents	1,072	2,757	1,836
Accounts receivables	2,838	2,792	2,714
Inventories	2,162	1,897	1,816
Other current assets	1,043	1,274	1,354
Investments	272	227	218
Plant and equipment (net)	5,593	5,711	5,609
Goodwill	3,473	2,655	2,419
Intangible assets	486	277	274
Prepaid expenses and others	3,574	3,118	1,360
	20,513	**20,708**	**17,600**
Liabilities			
Short term borrowings	1,072	2,094	1,202
Accounts payable	1,256	1,168	1,087
Accrued expenses	1,458	1,354	1,316
Other current liabilities	1,452	1,455	1,477
Long term debt	1,309	727	1,735
Other debt	3,866	3,532	2,898
Stockholders' equity (net)	10,100	10,378	7,885
	20,513	**20,708**	**17,600**

(continues)

EXHIBIT 2 | **3M COMPANY FINANCIALS (CONTINUED)**

Financial Ratios

As % of sales			
— Cost of sales	49.0	49.8	50.9
— Selling, gen and admn.	21.4	21.4	22.2
— R&D	5.9	5.9	6.0
— Operating income	23.7	22.9	20.4

SOURCE: 3M annual reports 2005 (pages 24 and 37); 2003 (pages 25 and 39).

EXHIBIT 3 | **3M COMPANY—FINANCIAL DATA BY SEGMENT**

Business segment (amounts in mn US$)	Net sales			Operating income			Op. income (% of sales)		
	2005	2004	2003	2005	2004	2003	2005	2004	2003
Health Care	4,373	4,230	3,995	1,215	1,123	1,027	27.8	26.5	25.7
Transportation	1,772	1,674	1,531	461	426	388	26.0	25.5	25.4
Display and Graphics	3,558	3,416	2,970	1,159	1,133	886	32.6	33.2	29.8
Consumer and Office	2,986	2,861	2,607	576	542	460	19.3	18.9	17.6
Industrial	**3,806**	**3,444**	**3,070**	**735**	**610**	**425**	**19.3**	**17.7**	**13.8**
Electro & Communications	2,333	2,224	2,101	463	342	288	19.8	15.4	13.7
Safety and Security	2,292	2,125	1,928	553	491	437	24.1	23.1	22.7
Unallocated/Other	47	37	30	153	89	198	—	—	—
Total	**21,167**	**20,011**	**18,232**	**5,009**	**4,578**	**3,713**	**3.6**	**22.8**	**20.4**

EXHIBIT 4 | INDUSTRIAL DISTRIBUTORS LANDSCAPE (SEGMENTATION AS PER 3M CANADA)

	Large National	General	Special	Niche
End-Markets	Multiple	Multiple	Multiple	Single
Core Capabilities	Integrated Supply Commodity Skills Vendor Managed Inventory National Contracts	Integrated Supply	Product Specialisation (e.g. adhesives, abrasives, safety etc.)	High level market/ product knowledge
Value Propositions	Product Bundling Costs-out Logistics Product Specialisation	Goes wherever business goes	Technical knowledge. An extension of Vendor's sales force	Industry/market expertise. An extension of Vendor's sales force
Primary Sales tool	Sales Representatives Call Centres Branches/Store fronts Catalogues Flyers Web sites	Sales Representatives Some Catalogues & flyer	Sales Representatives	Sales Representatives
Typical geographic coverage	National	Regional	Regional	Regional
Approximate number in segment	See Exhibit 1	20–40	20–40	About 10

SOURCE: Company files.

Exhibit 5 | Channel Costs

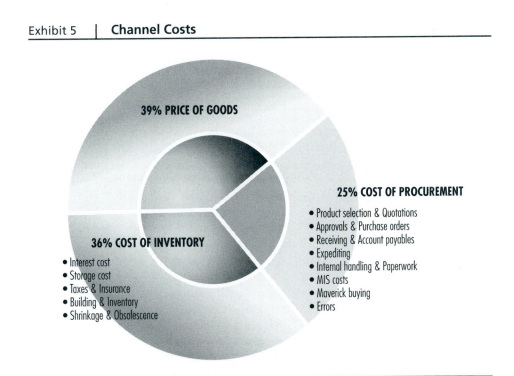

SOURCE: Picture Courtesy Hagemeyer, MRO4All

EXHIBIT 6 | **3M IBD—PRODUCTS & SALE INFLUENCE FLOW CHART**

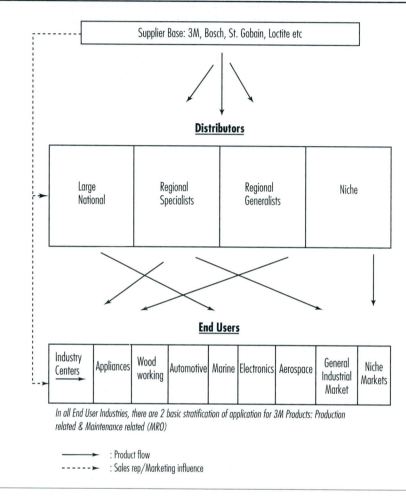

Supplier Base: 3M, Bosch, St. Gobain, Loctite etc

Distributors

| Large National | Regional Specialists | Regional Generalists | Niche |

End Users

| Industry Centers | Appliances | Wood working | Automotive | Marine | Electronics | Aerospace | General Industrial Market | Niche Markets |

In all End User Industries, there are 2 basic stratification of application for 3M Products: Production related & Maintenance related (MRO)

⟶ : Product flow

┈┈⟶ : Sales rep/Marketing influence

SOURCE: Company files.

CASE

5

FedEx Corp.: Structural Transformation through e-Business

"[FedEx] has built superior physical, virtual and people networks not just to prepare for change, but to shape change on a global scale: to change the way we all connect with each other in the new Network Economy."[1]

"[FedEx] is not only reorganizing its internal operations around a more flexible network computing architecture, but it's also pulling-in and in many cases locking-in customers with an unprecedented level of technological integration."[2]

Since its inception in 1973, Federal Express Corporation ("FedEx"[3]) had transformed itself from an express delivery company to a global logistics and supply-chain management company. Over the years, the Company had invested heavily in IT systems, and with the launch of the Internet in 1994, the potential for further integration of systems to provide services throughout its customers' supply-chains became enormous. With all the investment in the systems infrastructure over the years and the US$88 million acquisition of Caliber Systems, Inc., in 1998, the Company had built a powerful technical architecture that had the potential to pioneer in Internet commerce. However, despite having all the ingredients for the makings of a successful e-business, the Company's logistics and supply-chain operations were struggling to shine through the historical

Pauline Ng prepared this Case under the supervision of Dr Ali F. Farhoomand for class discussion. This Case is not intended to show effective or ineffective handling of decision or business processes.

This Case is part of a project funded by a teaching development grant from the University Grants Committee (UGC) of Hong Kong.

Ref. 99/57C

[1] 1999 Annual Report
[2] Janah, M. and Wilder, C., "Special Delivery", *Information Week*, URL: http://www.FedExcorp.com/media/infowktop100.html, 1997.
[3] The Company was incorporated as "Federal Express Corporation" in 1971. In 1994, the Company was renamed "FedEx Corporation" and subsequently renamed "FDX Corporation" in 1998 and then "FedEx Corporation" in 2000. However, throughout the case, the Company is referred to as "FedEx" to avoid confusion.

image of the Company as simply an express delivery business. Furthermore, competition in the transportation/express delivery industry was intense and there were reports that FedEx's transportation volume growth was slowing down, even though they were poised to take advantage of the surge in traffic that e-tailing and electronic commerce (EC) were supposed to generate. Hence, on 19 January, 2000, FedEx announced major reorganisations in the Group's operations in the hope of making it easier to do business with the entire FedEx family. The mode of operation for the five subsidiary companies was to function independently but to compete collectively. In addition to streamlining many functions, the Group announced that it would pool its sales, marketing and customer services functions, such that customers would have a single point of access to the whole Group. The reorganisation was expected to cost US$100 million over three years. Was this simply a new branding strategy or did FedEx have the right solution to leverage its cross-company synergies and its information and logistics infrastructure to create e-business solutions for its customers?

The Express Transportation and Logistics Industry

FedEx invented the air/ground express industry in 1973. Although UPS was founded in 1907 and became America's largest transportation company, it did not compete with FedEx directly in the overnight delivery market until 1982. Competition began with a focus on customer segmentation, pricing and quality of service. For most businesses, physical distribution costs often accounted for 10–30 per cent of sales or more. As competition put pressure on pricing, businesses began to look at ways to cut costs yet improve customer service. The solution was to have a well-managed logistics operation to reduce the length of the order cycle and thus generate a positive effect on cash flow.

The growth of the express transportation and logistics industry was brought about by three main trends: the globalisation of businesses, advances in information technology (IT) and the application of new technology to generate process efficiencies, and the changing market demand for more value-added services. As businesses expanded beyond national boundaries and extended their global reach to take advantage of new markets and cheaper resources, so the movement of goods created new demands for the transportation and logistics industry. With this, the competitiveness of transportation companies depended upon their global network of distribution centres and their ability to delivery to wherever their customers conducted business. Speed became of significance to achieve competitiveness, not only for the transportation companies but also for their customers. The ability to deliver goods quickly shortened the order-to-payment cycle, improved cash flow, and created customer satisfaction.

Advances in IT promoted the globalisation of commerce. The ability to share information between operations/departments within a company and between organisations to generate operational efficiencies, reduce costs and improve customer services was a major breakthrough for the express transportation industry. However, of even greater significance was the way in which new technology redefined logistics. At a time when competition within the transportation industry was tough and transportation companies were seeking to achieve competitive advantages through value-added services, many of these companies expanded into logistics management services. Up until the 1980s, logistics was merely the handling, warehousing and transportation of goods. By combining the functions of materials management and physical distribution, logistics took on a new and broader meaning. It was concerned with inbound as well as outbound material flow, within companies as well as the movement of finished goods from dock-to-dock. With this, the transportation industry responded by placing emphasis not only on the physical transportation, but also on the co-ordination and control of storage and movement of parts and finished goods. Logistics came to include value-added activities such as order processing, distribution centre operations, inventory control, purchasing, production and customer and sales services. Interconnectivity through the Internet and Intranets and the integration of systems enabled businesses to redefine themselves and to re-engineer their selling and supply-chains. Information came to replace inventory. Just-in-time inventory management helped to reduce costs and improve efficiency. With the advent of IT, express transportation became an aggregation of two main functions: the physical delivery of parcels, and the management and utilisation of the flow of information pertaining to the physical delivery (i.e., control over the movement of goods).

FedEx Corp.

FedEx was the pioneer of the express transportation and logistics industry. Throughout the 27 years of its operation, FedEx's investment in IT had earned the Company a myriad of accolades. Since 1973 FedEx had won over 194 awards for operational excellence. Fundamental to the success of the FedEx business was the vision of its founder.

The Visionary behind the Business

"If we're all operating in a day-to-day environment, we're thinking one to two years out. Fred's thinking five, ten, fifteen years out."

—William Conley, VP, FedEx Logistics, Managing Director Europe

Fred Smith, Chairman, President and Chief Executive Officer of FedEx Corporation, invented the express distribution industry in March 1973. By capitalising on the needs of businesses for speed and reliability of deliveries, FedEx shortened lead-times for companies. Its next-day delivery service revolutionised the distribution industry. The success of FedEx's distribution business in those early days rested on Smith's commitment to his belief that the opportunities open to a company that could provide reliable overnight delivery of time-sensitive documents and packages were excellent. Despite losses in the first three years of operation due to high capital investments in the physical transportation infrastructure of the business, FedEx began to see profits from 1976 onwards. To compete on a global basis, the key components of the physical infrastructure had to be in place to connect the world's GDP. The underlying philosophy was that wherever business was conducted, there was going to have to be the movement of physical goods.

Under Smith's leadership, the Company had set a few records with breakthrough technology. In the 1980s, FedEx gave away more that 100,000 sets of PCs loaded with FedEx software, designed to link and log customers into FedEx's ordering and tracking systems. FedEx was also the first to issue hand-held scanners to its drivers that alerted customers of when packages were picked up or delivered. Then in 1994, FedEx became the first big transportation company to launch a Website that included tracking and tracing capabilities. Very early on, Smith could foresee that the Internet was going to change the way businesses would operate and the way people would interact. By applying IT to the business, FedEx leapfrogged the rest of the industry. Smith was the visionary who forced his company and other companies to think outside of the proverbial one. The core of FedEx's corporate strategy was to "use IT to help customers take advantage of international markets"[4]. By 1998, FedEx was a US$10 billion company spending US$1 billion annually on IT developments plus millions more on capital expenditure. It had an IT workforce of 5,000 people.

Building the Transportation and Logistics Infrastructure

In the early years of the FedEx transportation business, Smith insisted that the Company should acquire its own transportation fleet, while competitors were buying space on commercial airlines and sub-contracting their shipments to third parties. The strategy of expanding through acquiring more trucks and planes continued. By the tenth year of operation FedEx earned the accolade of being the first US company to achieve the US$1 billion revenues mark within a decade without corporate acquisitions and mergers.

FedEx was quoted as being the inventor of customer logistics management.[5] As early as 1974, FedEx started logistics operations with the Parts Bank. In those days, a few small set-ups approached FedEx with their warehousing problems and decided on the idea of overnight distribution of parts. With those propositions, FedEx built a small warehouse on the end of its sorting facilities at Memphis. This was FedEx's first attempt at multiple-client warehousing. Customers would call up and order the despatch of parts and the order would be picked up on the same day. That was also FedEx's first value-added service beyond basic transportation. From there, the logistics side of the business snowballed.

Throughout the next three decades, FedEx's transportation business growth was attributable to a number of external factors that FedEx was quick to capitalise on. These included:

- Government deregulation of the airline industry, which permitted the landing of larger freight planes, thus reducing operating costs for FedEx.

- Deregulation of the trucking industry, which allowed FedEx to establish a regional trucking system to lower costs further on short-haul trips.

- Trade deregulation in Asia Pacific, which opened new markets for FedEx. Expanding globally became a priority for FedEx.

- Technological breakthroughs and applications innovations promoted significant advances for customer ordering, package tracking and process monitoring.

- Rising inflation and global competition gave rise to greater pressures on businesses to minimise the costs of operation, including implementation of just-in-time inventory management systems, etc. This also created demands for speed and accuracy in all aspects of business.

---

[4] Garten, 1998.

[5] Bruner, R. F. and Bulkley, D., "The Battle for Value: Federal Express Corporation versus United Parcel Service of America, Inc. (Abridged)," University of Virginia Darden School Foundation, 1995.

As of January 2000, FedEx served 210 countries (making up more than 90 per cent of the world's GDP), operated 34,000 drop-off locations and managed over 10 million square feet of warehouse space worldwide. It had a fleet of 648 aircraft and more than 60,000 vehicles, with a staff of nearly 200,000. It was the world's largest overnight package carrier, with about 30 per cent of the market share.

Building the Virtual Information Infrastructure

"We are really becoming a technology company enabled by transportation."

— David Edmonds, VP, Worldwide Services Group, FedEx[6]

Even as early as 1979, a centralised computer system—Customer, Operations, Service, Master On-line System (COSMOS)—kept track of all packages handled by the Company. This computer network relayed data on package movement, pickup, invoicing and delivery to a central database at Memphis headquarters. This was made possible by placing a bar-code on each parcel at the point of pickup and scanning the bar-code at each stage of the delivery cycle.

In 1984, FedEx started to launch a series of technological systems, the PowerShip programme, aimed at improving efficiency and control, which provided the most active customers (over 100,000) with proprietary on-line services [see **Exhibit 1** for a chronological list of FedEx systems]. In summary, these PowerShip systems provided additional services to the customer, including storing of frequently used addresses, label printing, on-line package pick-up requests, package tracking, and much more.

The emergence of electronic data interchange (EDI) and the Internet allowed companies to build one-to-one relationships with their customers. This was the perfect scenario for many manufacturers: the ability to match supply to demand without wastage. FedEx took advantage of such new technologies and started to track back along the supply-chain to the point of raw materials. As they did so, they identified points along the supply-chain where they could provide management services. Often, these services included transportation, order processing and related distribution centre operations, fulfilment, inventory control, purchasing, production and customer and sales services. The ability to interconnect and distribute information to all the players in a supply-chain became the focus of FedEx's attention. For many of its customers, logistics was viewed as a key means for differentiating their products or services from those of their competitors [see **Exhibit 2** for examples of some customer solutions]. In other words, logistics became a key part of strategy formulation. As businesses were placing more emphasis on the order cycle as the basis for evaluating customer service levels, FedEx's role in providing integrated logistics systems formed the basis of many partnership arrangements. By helping them to redefine sources and procurement strategies so as to link in with other parties in the supply-chain, such as raw materials suppliers, customers were outsourcing their supply-chain management functions to FedEx, functions that were seen as peripheral to the core of their business [see **Exhibits 3 and 4** for FedEx's coverage of the supply chain through

[6] Krause, K., "Not UPS with a Purple Tint," *Traffic World*, URL: http://www.trafficworld.com/reg/news/special/s101899.html, October 1999.

integrated systems]. By improving, tightening and synchronising the various parts to the supply-chain, customers saw the benefits of squeezing time and inventory out of the system. Tighter supply-chain management was no longer viewed as a competitive advantage but a competitive imperative.

Businesses sought ways to improve their return on investment and became interested in any business process that could be integrated and automatically triggered (e.g., proof of delivery and payment) as opposed to being separately invoked. So not only was FedEx pushing its customers for integration, but its innovative customers were also demanding greater integration. Some customers had even jumped ahead of FedEx. Cisco, for example, had developed an extranet that allowed its customers to order FedEx services without leaving the Cisco Website. By integrating its services within the supply-chain of its customers, and thus generating increases in customer loyalty and in customers' switching costs, FedEx managed to effectively raise the barriers to entry for competitors.

The Internet refined the COSMOS system. Whenever new information was entered into the system by FedEx or by customers through the Internet, all related files and databases were automatically updated. For example, when a FedEx customer placed an order through fedex.com, the information would find its way to COSMOS, FedEx's global package-tracking system. The courier's Route Planner—an electronic mapping toll—would facilitate the pickup and delivery of the order from the customer. A product movement planner would schedule the order through the Company's global air and courier operations. The customer would be able to track the status of the shipment through PowerShip or FedEx Ship. The COSMOS system handled 54 million transactions per day in 1999.[7]

In 1998, FedEx decided to overhaul its internal IT infrastructure under Project GRID (Global Resources for Information Distribution). The project involved replacing 60,000 terminals and some PCs with over 75,000 network systems. The decision to go with network computers was made to avoid the "desktop churn" found with PCs.[8] The network computers linked over a global Internet Protocol network aimed to enhance the quality and quantity of services FedEx could deliver to its customers. For example, FedEx employees at any location at any time could track a package through the various steps in the FedEx chain. Other applications planned to be launched included COSMOS Squared, which allowed Non-Event Tracking, a feature that triggered alerts when scheduled events, such as the arrival of a package, did not occur. Through a 24-hour, seven-day operation called the Global Operations Command Centre, the central nervous system of FedEx's worldwide system in Memphis, FedEx was able to provide efficient gathering and dissemination of real-time data. The operation housed huge screens covering the walls that tracked world events, weather patterns and the real-time movement of FedEx trucks and aircraft. New systems were also introduced to predict with greater accuracy the amount of inbound traffic. This system allowed FedEx to prioritise the hundreds of variables involved in the successful pickup, processing and delivery of a parcel. Senior managers at FedEx believed that having current and accurate information helped them to reduce failure in the business.

---

[7] ICFAI, FedEx: Excellence Through Information Technology, www.icfai.org (accessed 3 September 2007).

[8] "Desktop churn" refers to the rapid obsolescence of PCs as new applications eat up processing power.

As well as the data centre in Memphis, FedEx operated other centres in Colorado Springs, Orlando, Dallas-Fort Worth, Singapore, Brussels and Miami.

Also in 1999, FedEx signed an agreement with Netscape to adopt Netscape software as the primary technology for accessing its corporate intranet sites. FedEx's intranet included more than 60 Websites, created for its end users and in some cases by its end users. Customers could build integrated Websites using FedEx Applications Programming Interfaces (API) or FedEx intraNetShip[9] (free downloads from fedex.com) and incorporate a link that would allow them to track packages directly from their own site. Over 5000 Websites fed hundreds of thousands of tracking requests through to the fedex.com site.

> "Our API solutions are designed to give global visibility and access across the supply-chain, from manufacturing to customer service to invoicing. We've managed to wipe out those irritating WISMO (Where Is My Order) calls because we've seamlessly linked our customers to their customers."
>
> — Mike Janes, former VP, Electronic Commerce & Logistics Marketing, FedEx[10]

At the beginning of 1999, FedEx launched an enhancement to its package-tracking service. Customers could query and receive package status information for up to 25 shipments simultaneously, and forward this information on to up to three e-mail recipients. Furthermore, users in France, Japan, Italy, Germany, the Netherlands and Portuguese- and Spanish-speaking countries could access this information on-line in their native languages through fedex.com.

FedEx claimed to have the largest on-line client server network in the world that operated in real-time. Information became an extremely critical part of its business.

> "We're in the express transportation business, but we've discovered how to lock up a lot of value in the information that we have."
>
> — Mark Dickens, VP, Electronic Commerce & Customer Services[11]

> "… even when on the physical side of the business, we outsource, for instance, the pick-up or the delivery or the warehousing activity for a customer, we have never outsourced the information. Protecting the brand has always been very, very critical for us."
>
> — William Conley

The benefits of these services were not limited to FedEx's customers. For FedEx, its on-line services, which in 1999 handled 60 million transactions per day, saved FedEx the cost of 200,000 customer service employees. In turn, the Company reported spending 10 per cent of its US$17 billion annual revenue on IT in 1999.

---

[9] ICFAI, FedEx: Excellence Through Information Technology, www.icfai.org (accessed 3 September 2007).

[10] Gentry, C., "FedEx API's Create Cinderella Success Stories", October 1998, URL: http://www.fedex.com/us/about/api.html.

[11] Janah, M. and Wilder, C., "Special Delivery," *Information Week*: www.FedExcorp.com/media/infowktop100.html, 1997.

Information had allowed FedEx to lower its costs such that the cost to customers of using FedEx in 1999 was lower than it was 25 years ago.

Going beyond delivery services, FedEx aimed to fully integrate its corporate partners every step of the way along the supply-chain. Fundamental to FedEx's strategy for establishing its e-business and logistics operations was how well it could forge technology links with customers.

> "It's all about integration, whether it's inside FedEx, with our technology partners, or with our customers."
>
> — Laurie Tucker, Senior VP, Logistics Electronic Commerce & Catalog[12]

> "Integration of Internet services with our transportation offerings is not an addition to our core business; it is our core business."
>
> — Dennis Jones, CIO[13]

> "When it comes to managing synergies across businesses, we've found that seamless information integration is a critical component."[14]

Management and Operations Issues

Branding and Business Structure Up Until 19 January, 2000

In the first 21 years of business, FedEx operated under the corporate name of Federal Express Corporation. Its customers came to recognise it as "FedEx" in short and the brand took off as the Company grew and expanded its service offerings under the purple and orange flag. Hence in 1994, it seemed natural that the Company should change its brand name to "FedEx".

The Parts Bank was given official recognition when it became a division of FedEx Corp. in 1988 and became known as Business Logistics Services (BLS). It operated as a separate and independent company. In line with the express transportation side of the business, BLS developed expertise in the high-value, high-tech industries. It was involved in the express inbound, outbound and redistribution of goods. However, it focused mainly on the small parcel business. FedEx based its solutions on just-in-time logistics. As the business grew, concern was raised that the logistics business was not generating revenue for the express transportation business, but rather feeding this through to other carriers. Hence in 1994, BLS was renamed FedEx Logistics, and it became mandatory for the logistics business to include FedEx transportation as part of its solution to customers. In 1996, the division changed its name yet again, to FedEx Logistics and Electronic Commerce (FLEC). The Company started to focus

---

[12] Janah, M. and Wilder, C (1997)

[13] Cone, E. and Duvall, M., "UPS Keeps Truckin'; FedEx: A Documented Success", Inter@ctive *Week*, 16 November, 1999.

[14] 1999 Annual Report.

its resources on doing business on the Internet, and the name change was to reflect the changes in the marketplace.

Following the acquisition of Caliber Systems, Inc. in 1998, five separate subsidiary companies were formed: Federal Express, RPS, Roberts Express, Viking Freight and FDX Logistics. The latter four were Caliber businesses. Each subsidiary was managed independently and was responsible for its own accounts [see **Exhibit 5**]. However, Caliber and FedEx's logistics operations were fundamentally different in that they had completely distinct customer bases and service offerings. Caliber developed expertise in moving raw materials, plates of steel and steel bars and managing work-in-progress. It would manage the manufacturing of cars and fork-lift trucks. Caliber provided an elaborate logistics operation concentrating mainly on high-priced goods industries, and it provided a fuller supply-chain solution than FLEC did, whereas FLEC was primarily focused on finished goods, transportation logistics and reverse logistics (i.e., handling returns). One was concentrating its business at the front-end of the supply chain (e.g., receiving, work-in-progress) while the other was more involved in the back-end operations of the supply-chain (i.e., warehousing, transportation). Hence the two operations continued to operate independently of each other. Logistics systems and applications were also developed independently. Caliber Logistics became a subsidiary company under FDX Logistics, while FLEC continued as a division within Federal Express, the express transportation arm.

The acquisition served to reinforce FedEx's commitment to becoming more than just an express delivery company. Yet commentators and customers continued to associate the FedEx brand with transportation, and FedEx fought to transform the image of the Company outside of this mould. One solution was to rename the Company. With the acquisition, the Company created a holding company, "FDX Corporation". However, FedEx did very little to promote it new FDX corporate brand. Furthermore, its transportation subsidiary continued to operate under the Federal Express name with the purple and orange FedEx brand on its trucks and vans. The FedEx brand lived on, but with no advertising or aggressive promotion of FDX, the name did not resonate in the marketplace. While the likes of UPS had the advantage of promoting just one brand—UPS—to sell the entire company and its many service offerings, FedEx was trying to promote five different subsidiary companies with completely unrelated names and business logos under the FDX banner through distinctly separate sales and customer service teams. Furthermore, with two separate logistics businesses within the Group, separate sales forces selling services offered by different parts of the Company, separate customer services staff to deal with different queries and IT resources spread across the Group, customers were confused and resources were duplicated.

Despite the confusion, by 1999 FedEx purported to offer companies "total one-stop shopping" for solutions at all levels of the supply-chain. Each subsidiary continued to operate independently, with separate accounting systems and customer service staff, while competing collectively. However, while maintaining the autonomy of each subsidiary company, the challenge for FedEx was how to bring the companies closer together to create those synergies. Providing customers with a single point of access to the whole Group was the ultimate goal. In practical terms, the task was to decide how each of the subsidiary companies should leverage its skills and services to a broader audience.

Events Leading Up to the January 2000 Reorganisation

FedEx needed to address a number of factors that would affect the prospects of the Company.

FedEx's Performance

In the year ending 31 May, 1999, the Company had out-performed analyst expectations, posting record earnings of 73 per cent, an increase of 28 per cent over the previous year.[15] Net income had risen 30 percent to US$221 million. However, results took a downturn in the following financial year. For the first quarter ended 31 August, 1999, FedEx announced that rising fuel prices had severely impacted upon the Company's net income, causing it to miss its first-quarter target. With no sign of improvements in fuel prices and with the US domestic market growth slowing down, FedEx warned that earnings for the second quarter and the full fiscal year may fall below analyst expectations. Bearing in mind that the express transportation business (mainly Federal Express and RPS) accounted for over 80 per cent of the Group's revenue, and that the US market accounted for approximately US$10 billion of the Group's revenue, both trends had a significant negative impact on net income.

Sure enough, FedEx reported that for the quarter ended 30 November, 1999, operating income was down by 10 per cent on the previous year and net income was down by six per cent. The Company was not achieving the level of US domestic growth as expected. Rising fuel prices continued to erode operating income. However, operations other than express transportation (i.e., Viking Freight, Roberts Express, FDX Logistics and Caribbean Transportation Services) achieved revenue and operating income increases of 27 per cent and 12 per cent respectively in the second quarter. With the adverse fuel prices alone, the Company anticipated that operating income could be down by more than US$150 million for the year ending 31 May, 2000. This called for some immediate remedial action.

Other trends within the express transportation and logistics market were also putting pressure on the Company to re-think its business strategy.

The Internet Market and e-Tailing

The Internet changed the basis for competition for most businesses. Its low cost and diversity of applications made it appealing and accessible. The Internet levelled the playing field such that, once a company was on-line, as long as it fulfilled its orders to the expectations of its customers, the size of the company was of no significance. The impact of the Internet on FedEx was twofold. Firstly, it opened up opportunities in logistics management for FedEx as businesses were using the Internet to re-engineer their supply-chains. So long as customers were satisfied, it really did not matter whether the goods were warehoused or not, whether the goods came directly from a factory in some distant location or whether the goods had been made to order. Integration with customer supply-chains was the key.

---

[15] Gelsi, S., "FDX Posts Stronger-than-Expected Profit," CBS MarketWatch, 30 June, 1999, URL:http://cbs.marketwatch.com/archive.../current/fdx.htm?source=&dist=srch, February 2000.

Secondly, the express transportation needs associated with the growth in e-tailing (expected to reach US$7 billion in 2000) and business-to-business EC (expected to reach US$327 billion by 2002) presented enormous opportunities for companies such as FedEx.[16,17]

FedEx was sure that it had the right business model to take advantage of these opportunities.

> "We're right at the centre of the new economy. … Businesses are utilising the Internet to re-engineer the supply-chain. In the new economy, the Internet is the neural system. We're the skeleton œ we make the body move."
>
> — Fred Smith[18]

But so were its competitors.

The Competition

In January 2000, CBS MarketWatch Live reported that FedEx's express delivery business was maturing and was not growing as fast as it used to.[19] Furthermore, the industry was loaded with companies, local and global, that provided a myriad of transportation services to a wide range of businesses. Competition was fierce. All major transportation and delivery companies were betting big on technology. Although FedEx pioneered the Web-based package-tracking system, such systems became the industry norm rather than a competitive advantage.

The four leading companies in the international courier business were DHL, FedEx, UPS and TNT. Between them they held more than 90 per cent of the worldwide market.[20]

UPS

Since 1986, UPS had spent US$9 billion on IT and had formed five alliances in 1997 to disseminate its logistics software to EC users. However, while FedEx developed all its IS software in-house, UPS made a point in stating that it was not a software developer and that companies taking that route were "trying to go a bridge too far."[21]

In early 1998, UPS formed a strategic alliance with Open Market, Inc., a US-based provider of Internet software, to deliver a complete Internet commerce solution providing integrated logistics and fulfilment. They were also working with IBM and Lotus to standardise formats on their Website.

In 1999, UPS raised US$5.47 billion through its initial public offering, the largest in the US IPO history. The company shipped more than 55 per cent of goods ordered over the Internet and offered over the full range of logistics solutions to its customers.

---

[16] Lappin, T., "The Airline of the Internet," *Wired*, 4 (12), December 1996, URL:http://www.wired.com/wired/4.12/features/ffedex.html

[17] Erwin, B., Modahl, M. A. and Johnson, J., "Sizing Intercompany Commerce," *Business Trade & Technology Strategies*, 1 (1), Forrester Research, Cambridge, MA, 1997.

[18] Collingwood, H., 1999.

[19] Adamson, D., "FDX Corp. Changes Name to FedEx," CBS MarketWatch Live, 19 January, 2000.

[20] Murphy, D. and Hernly, K., "Air Couriers Soar Despite Mainland Gloom," *South China Morning Post*, 30 May, 1999.

[21] Blackmon, D. A., "Ante Up! Big Gambles in the New Economy: Overnight Everything Changed for FedEx," *The Wall Street Journal Interactive Edition*, URL: http://www.djreprints.com/jitarticles/trx0001272701443.html, 4 November, 1999.

DHL

In 1993, DHL announced a four-year US$1.25 billion worldwide capital spending pro-gramme aimed at investing in handling systems, automation, facilities and computer tech-nology. The company launched its Website in 1995. It was 25 per cent owned by Deutsche Post and 25 per cent owned by Lufthansa Airlines. Plans were under way for an initial public offering in the first half of 2001. Though the company dominated the UK market, it pro-jected an increase in worldwide turnover of 18 per cent to US$5.26 billion.[22]

TNT

In 1998, TNT launched a Web Collection facility on the Internet. Later the same year, TNT launched the world's first global Price Checker service on its Website that allowed customers to calculate the price of sending a consignment from one place to another anywhere in the world. Other applications were under development that would allow customers to integrate with TNT's on-line services. Then in 1999, TNT launched QuickShipper, a one-stop on-line access to TNT's entire range of distribu-tion services, from pricing to delivery. This new service was to be integrated with existing on-line tools such as Web Collection and Price Checker.

Also in March 1999, TNT launched the express industry's first dedicated cus-tomer extranet, Customised Services environment. This offered regular customers easy access to detailed and personalised shipment information through the use of user IDs and passwords. With this came a host of service offerings.

While FedEx had pioneered many logistics solutions that had helped it to achieve economies of scale faster than its competitors, the advantages were quickly eroding as newer technologies became even more powerful and less expensive.

The January 2000 Announcement

"All of your transportation and logistics needs can now be met by one organi-sation—FedEx Corporation."[23]

On 19 January, 2000, FedEx announced three major strategic initiatives:

- A new branding strategy that involved changing the Company's name to "FedEx Corporation," and extending the "FedEx" brand to four of its five subsidiary companies. The subsidiary companies became:

  - FedEx Express (formerly Federal Express)

  - FedEx Ground (formerly RPS)

  - FedEx Custom Critical (formerly Roberts Express)

  - FedEx Logistics (formerly Caliber Logistics)

  - Viking Freight (no change) [See **Exhibit 6**.]

---

[22] Exelby, J., "Interview—DHL UK Foresees Tough Market," URL: http://biz.yahoo.com/rf/000117/mq.html, 17 January, 2000.

[23] Corporate Overview, FedEx Corporation, URL: http://www.fedexcorp.com/aboutfdx/corporateoverview.html, 20th January, 2000.

- Major reorganisations such that there would be one point of access to sales, customer services, billing and automation systems. With these consolidations, the Company announced intentions to form a sixth subsidiary called FedEx Corporate Services Corp. in June 2000 [see **Exhibit 7** for new Group structure]. The new subsidiary would pool together the marketing, sales, customer services, information technology and electronic commerce resources of the Group. The invoicing functions would also be combined for all the companies.

- Introduction of a new low-cost residential delivery service, FedEx Home Delivery, to be launched in the US.

Of significance was the merging of the two logistics operations (Caliber Logistics and FLEC) into FedEx Logistics. The two companies seemed to complement each other in terms of their service offerings and customer base. Both had a few of the same customers but many different ones. Furthermore, Caliber's presence was mainly in North America and Europe, while FLEC had expanded into other continents. FedEx Logistics brought together all the splintered operations of logistics in all the subsidiary companies, streamlining costs, presenting one menu of logistics service offerings to customers, and aligning R&D of systems upon common, agreed platforms. This reorganisation also brought about another major change in operations. It was no longer mandatory for the logistics business to use FedEx transportation as part of its solutions to customers. Being "carrier-agnostic" meant that FedEx Logistics would use FedEx transportation where it fitted, both in terms of cost and in terms of geographic coverage. The decision would also rest on customer preference and the kind of goods being transported. For example, Caliber was transporting fork-lift trucks, cars and steel plates that FedEx did not have the physical capacity to handle.

Combining the two operations brought together the IT expertise and the know-how of the logistics business. Under one CIO, standards were set for the development of systems on a worldwide basis, including vendor selection. In the past, regions developed their own solutions and operated in isolation. However, the Internet forced the Company to consolidate its systems and solutions as customers demanded global solutions. Through the IT groups located in Memphis, Leiden (Holland) and Singapore, the Company resolved to develop global systems for worldwide implementation, with functions such as multiple currencies and multiple languages. FedEx Logistics forecast a 70 per cent growth rate in the year ending 31 May, 2000. However, the business so far failed to generate any profit. The company aimed to build on its expertise in the five market segments: health care, industrial, high-tech, automotive and consumer.

The Company anticipated having to spend US$100 million on these changes over three years. The intention was to take advantage of one of its greatest assets, the FedEx brand name; the name that customers could count on for "absolutely, positively" reliable service and cutting-edge innovation. The value of the brand had been ignored, particularly when the Company decided to change its corporate name to FDX in 1998. Realising its mistake, the renaming of the Company as FedEx Corporation and the extension of the brand to its subsidiaries fell in line with its intention to provide customers with an integrated set of business solutions. Customers wanted to deal with one company to meet their transportation and logistics needs.

Each subsidiary company was to continue operating independently, but collectively the Group would provide a wide range of business solutions. It was this collective synergy of solutions that FedEx believed would form the competitive advantage of the Company in the future. For customers, the benefits included easier means of doing business with FedEx. There was to be one toll-free telephone number, one Website, one invoice and account number, one sales team, one customer service team and a streamlined customer automation platform to handle electronic transactions for small and large businesses [see **Exhibits 6 and 7** for details of the changes following reorganisation]. The new organisation was aimed at helping businesses of all sizes to achieve their shipping, logistics, supply-chain and e-business objectives. However, analysts questioned whether the new Group structure would work, given that there would still be different teams of delivery and pick-up staff for the different operations. Hence, one person could pick up one package sent by ground and another person could pick up another package sent by express from the same company. Companies such as UPS, on the other hand, would have one person pick up both types of packages.

In addition to these changes, FedEx anticipated growth in consumer EC and planned to start a new service called FedEx Home Delivery (within the FedEx Ground subsidiary company) to meet the needs of businesses specialising in business-to-consumer e-tailing. FedEx had been successful in providing services to the business-to-business EC market. Now it aimed to achieve the same leadership status in the business-to-consumer EC market. However, expanding the residential delivery business was one segment that FedEx consciously made a decision not to pursue throughout the 1990s. This gave UPS the opportunity to lead in residential delivery services.

In late 1997, Smith was quoted as saying,

> "We've made huge investments in our networks, and now that bow wave has passed. We think we have a good chance of harvesting a lot of that investment."[24]

In the two years that followed, the results of the Company showed little signs of a harvest. Was the January restructuring going to bring in the harvest? The announcement certainly served to tell investors that they were making some major changes to address some competitive issues. However, analysts took a pragmatic view to the announcement, saying that, "the proof is in the pudding."[25]

> "Our biggest challenge is to correctly manage everything that's on our plate."

— Fred Smith[26]

Was the reoganisation going to leverage the power of the networks and the information and logistics infrastructures that FedEx had built? Did it provide the right ingredients to achieve the objectives of creating value for FedEx customers while at the same time improving profitability for FedEx? Given the speed at which technology and the marketplace were changing, would the new organisation structure be adaptable to the changing business environment? Were there better alternative solutions that the Company could have considered?

---

[24] Grant, L., "Why FedEx is Flying High," 10 November, 1997, URL: http://pathfinder.com/fortune/1997/971110/fed.html.

[25] Bazdarich, C.," "What's in a Name?: Traders Swayed by Nominal Changes," CBS MarketWatch, 21 January, 2000, URL:http://cbs.marketwatch.com/archive … st.htx?source=htx/http2_mw&dist=na, February 2000.

[26] Collingwood, H., 1999.

EXHIBIT 1 | **FEDEX'S RECORD OF SYSTEMS INNOVATIONS**

1979   COSMOS (Customer Oriented Services and Management Operating System), a global shipment tracking network based on a centralised computer system to manage vehicles, people, packages, routes and weather scenarios on a real-time basis. COSMOS integrated two essential information systems: information about goods being shipped and information about the mode of transportation.

1980   DADS (Digitally Assisted Dispatch System) co-ordinated on-call pickups for customers. It allowed couriers to manage their time and routes through communication via a computer in their vans.

1984   FedEx introduces the first PC-based automated shipping system, later named FedEx PowerShip; a standalone DOS-based system for customers with five or more packages per day. The customer base was immediately transformed into a network that allowed customers to interact with the FedEx system and download software and shipping information.

1984   PowerShip Plus, a DOS-based shipping system integrated with customers' order-entry, inventory-control and accounting systems, for customers who ship more than 100 packages per day.

1985   FedEx was the first to introduce bar-code labelling to the ground transportation industry.

1986   The SuperTracker, a hand-held bar-code scanner system that captures detailed package information.

1989   FedEx launches an on-board communications system that uses satellite tracking to pinpoint vehicle location.

1991   Rite Routing demonstrates the value of a nationwide, centralised transportation management service.

1991   PowerShip PassPort, a Pentium-class PC system that combines best of PowerShip and PowerShip Plus for customers who ship more than 100 packages a day. (1,500 users)

1993   MultiShip, the first carrier-supplied customer automation system to process packages shipped by other transportation providers.

1993   FedEx ExpressClear Electronic Customs Clearance System expedites regulatory clearance while cargo is en route.

1993   PowerShip 3, a client-server shipping system for customers who ship three or more packages per day.

1994   The FedEx Website debuts at www.fedex.com, the first to offer on-line package status tracking so that customers can actually conduct business via the Internet.

1994   DirectLink, a software that lets customers receive, manage and remit payments of FedEx invoices electronically.

1995   FedEx Ship, a Windows-based shipping and tracking software allows customers to process and manage shipping from their desktop. (650,000 users) It extended the benefits of PowerShip to all FedEx's customers, providing software and toll-free dial-up to the FedEx network.

1995   FedEx launches the AsiaOne network, a transportation routing system.

1996   FedEx became the first company to allow customers to process shipments on the Internet with FedEx interNetShip, available through www.fedex.com. (65,000 users). This allowed customers to create shipping labels, request courier pick-ups and send e-mail notifications to recipients of the shipments, all from the FedEx Website.

1996   FedEx VirtualOrder, a software that links Internet ordering with FedEx delivery and on-line tracking. It also puts customers' catalogues on their Websites for them.

1997   FedEx introduces e-Business Tools for easier connection with FedEx shipping and tracking applications.

(continues)

EXHIBIT 1 | **FEDEX'S RECORD OF SYSTEMS INNOVATIONS (*CONTINUED*)**

1998   FedEx Ship for Workgroups, a Windows-based software housed on a server that lets users share information, such as address-book information, access to shipping logs and a tracking database. The server can be connected to FedEx via either modem or the Internet.

1998   PowerShip mc, a multi-carrier electronic shipping system.

1999   The FedEx Marketplace debuts at www.fedex.com, providing easy access to on-line merchants that offer fast, reliable FedEx express shipping.

1999   The EuroOne network was launched to link 16 cities to FedEx's Paris hub by air and another 21 cities by road-air. Like AsiaOne, this was a transportation routing system.

1999   FedEx MarketPlace, a convenient link to on-line shopping. Through this new portal, shoppers had one-click access to several top on-line merchants that utilised FedEx's delivery services, including Value America, L. L. Bean, and HP Shopping Village (Hewlett-Packard's consumer EC Website).

1999   FedEx made a deal with Netscape to offer a suite of delivery services at its Netcenter portal. This entailed automatically integrating Netscape with the FedEx site. Although customers of Netscape could choose not to use FedEx, the use of an alternative shipper meant that they would not benefit from the efficiencies of the integrated systems. Considering the Netscape Netcenter had more than 13 million members, the deal was a winner for FedEx.

(NB. PowerShip had 850,000 on-line customers worldwide; PowerShip, PowerShip 3 and PowerShip PassPort were hardware-based products.)

EXHIBIT 2 |

Dell Computers pioneered the direct selling model in the computer industry and succeeded because it was able to keep inventory very low. FedEx provided the system to track and monitor the assembly of each PC on order. Because the assembly line could be in any one of five manufacturing locations around the world, however, FedEx described itself as the conveyor belt for that manufacturing line. FedEx was a key partner for Dell, allowing customised, built-to-order products to be delivered within days of a customer placing an order, a huge advantage in an industry whose components become obsolete at the rate of two per cent per month.

Five years ago, **National Semiconductor Corp.** decided to outsource its warehousing and distribution to FedEx. By 1999, virtually all of NatSemi's products, manufactured by six factories (three being subcontractors) were shipped directly to FedEx's distribution warehouse in Singapore. Hence, FedEx had control over the goods, the warehouse and the despatch of orders (via FedEx transportation, of course). Having complete visibility of NatSemi's order systems allowed FedEx to reduce the average customer delivery cycle from four weeks to two days, and distribution costs from 2.9 per cent of sales to 1.2 per cent. FedEx could pack and fulfil orders without NatSemi having to notify them. In effect, it became the logistics department of NatSemi. Furthermore, this arrangement enabled NatSemi to dispense with seven regional warehouses in the US, Asia and Europe. NatSemi reported savings in the region of US$8 million over the five-year period [see **Exhibit 4**].

For **Omaha Steaks**, when orders were received, they would be relayed from Omaha Steaks' IBM AS/400 to its warehouse and simultaneously to FedEx by dedicated line. FedEx would generate the tracking and shipping labels and the orders would be delivered to one of FedEx's regional hubs for onward delivery.

Cisco Systems was a Silicon Valley Internet hardware maker that transacted 80 per cent of its business over the Web. At the end of 1999, FedEx had signed an agreement with Cisco to co-ordinate all of Cisco's shipping over the next two years, and to gradually eliminate Cisco's warehousing over the following three years. How could this be possible? Cisco had factories in the US, Mexico, Scotland, Taiwan and Malaysia. The finished parts were stored in warehouses near the factories awaiting completion of the whole order before it was despatched to the customer. But Cisco did not want to build more warehouses, pay for reshipping and hold massive volumes of inventory in transit. So the solution was to merge the orders in transit. As soon as parts were manufactured, they would be shipped to customers. Once all the parts had arrived at the customer's site, assembly would take place, thus doing away with warehousing. (This was known as the "merge-in-transit" programme offered to companies such as Micron Computers.) FedEx created a unique system for Cisco that would automatically select routes and pick the most effective and economical mode of transportation, which included carriers other than FedEx's fleet of trucks and planes. Just as critical, however, was that the real-time information status of the synchronisation operation was constantly available on the Internet.

EXHIBIT 3 | FEDEX SOLUTIONS FOR THE ENTIRE SUPPLY-CHAIN

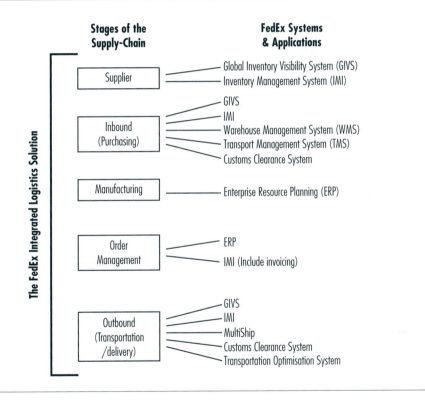

EXHIBIT 4 | **EXAMPLE OF INTEGRATED CUSTOMER ORDER PROCESS MANAGEMENT: NATIONAL SEMICONDUCTOR**

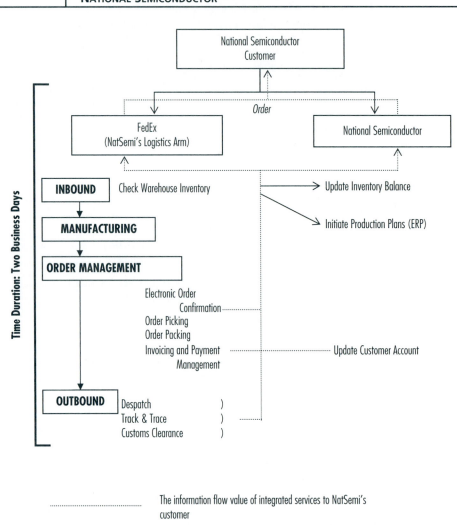

.... The information flow value of integrated services to NatSemi's customer

EXHIBIT 5 | **SUBSIDIARY COMPANIES OF FEDEX FOLLOWING THE ACQUISITION OF CALIBER SYSTEMS INC. IN 1998**

- **Federal Express** was the world leader in global express distribution, offering 24–48-hour delivery to 211 countries that comprised 90 per cent of the world's GDP. In 1998, FedEx was the undisputed leader in the overnight package delivery business. It had a fleet of 44,500 ground vehicles and 648 planes that gave support to the US$14 plus billion business. It had 34,000 drop-off locations, and 67 per cent of its US domestic shipping transactions were generated electronically. Goods shipped ranged from flowers to lobsters to computer components. This company was constantly running in crisis mode, seeking to move packages through all weather and conditions to fulfil shipments overnight. The underlying philosophy that ensured high service levels was that every package handled could make a difference to someone's life. The company handled nearly three million shipments per day in 1998.

- **RPS** was North America's second-largest provider of business-to-business ground small-package delivery. It was a low-cost, non-union, technology-savvy company aquired with the Caliber purchase. The company specialised in business-to-business shipments in one to three days, a service that FedEx could not attract because it was unable to offer prices low enough to attract enough volume. Being a 15 year-old company, RPS prized itself on having one of the lowest cost models in the transportation industry. It employed only owner-operators to deliver its packages. In terms of volume and revenue growth, RPS out-performed FedEx. For the future, plans were to grow RPS's business-to-consumer delivery service to take advantage of the growth of electronic commerce, thus carving a niche in the burgeoning residential delivery market. In 2000, the company owned 8,600 vehicles, achieved annual revenues of US$1.9 billion and employed 35,000 people, including independent contractors. It handled 1.5 million packages per day.

- **Viking Freight** was the first less-than-truckload freight carrier in the western United States. The company employed 5,000 people, managed a fleet of 7,660 vehicles and 64 service centres, and shipped 13,000 packages per day.

- **Roberts Express** was the world's leading surface-expedited carrier for non-stop, time-critical and special-handling shipments. The service offered by Roberts Express has been likened to a limousine service for freight. In 1999, the company handled more than 1,000 shipments per day. It was the smallest company within the FedEx Group. Urgent shipments could be loaded onto trucks within 90 minutes of a call and shipments would arrive within 15 minutes of the promised time 96 per cent of the time. Once loaded, shipments could be tracked by satellite every step of the way. Goods such as works of art or critical manufacturing components often required exclusive-use truck services. Exclusivity allowed customers greater control but at a price. This service was an infrequent necessity for most customers. Roberts had exclusive use of a handful of FedEx aircrafts, but the company still had to pay for use and for crew time.

- **Caliber Logistics** was a pioneer in providing customised, integrated logistics and warehousing solutions worldwide. The acquisition of Caliber in January 1998 brought with it over-the-road transportation and warehousing capabilities. Since the acquisition, FedEx tried to move away from traditional logistics offerings to providing total supply-chain management solutions, and Caliber Logistics was renamed FDX Logistics. To the customer, this meant that FedEx could provide warehousing services, but only if this was part of a bigger deal. In September 1999, FedEx bought its first freight forwarder, Caribbean Transport Services (formerly GeoLogistics Air Services). Caribbean had a strong overseas network. FDX Logistics was the parent company of FedEx Supply-chain Services and Caribbean Transportation Services.

EXHIBIT 6 | **BEFORE AND AFTER THE REORGANISATION**

Before	After
Multiple brands under FDX umbrella	A single branding system leveraging the power of the FedEx brand so more customers can use FedEx reliability as a strategic competitive advantage
Separate sales force with directed cooperation	A single, expanded sales force especially targeting small and medium-sized businesses, cross-selling a wide portfolio of services and pricing schemes
Multiple invoices and account numbers	A single invoice and single account number from FedEx
Multiple automation platforms offering all FDX services	Streamlined customer automation systems to handle electronic transactions and database management needs for small and large businesses
Separate customer service, claims trace functions	Single customer service, claims and trace functions by calling 1-800-Go-FedEx® (800-463-3339) or visiting its Website at www.fedex.com.

EXHIBIT 7 | **GROUP STRUCTURE**

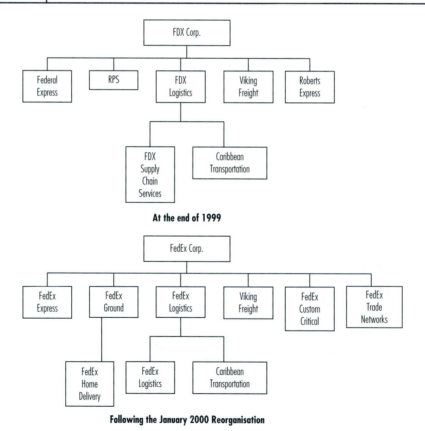

At the end of 1999

Following the January 2000 Reorganisation

Clearwater Technologies

Susan F. Sieloff, Northeastern University
Raymond M. Kinnunen, Northeastern University

At 9:00 A.M. on Monday, May 2004, Rob Erickson, QTX Product Manager; Hillary Hanson, Financial Analyst; and Brian James, District Sales Manager; were preparing for a meeting with Mark Jefferies, Vice President of Marketing, at Clearwater Technologies. The meeting's objective was to establish the end-user pricing for a capacity upgrade to the QTX servers Clearwater offered.

No one was looking forward to the meeting because company pricing debates were traditionally long and drawn out. Because there had already been several meetings, everyone knew that there was no consensus on how to determine the appropriate price, but company policy insisted on agreement. Only one price proposal went forward, and it had to represent something everyone could accept.

When Jefferies called the meeting, he commented:

> We've struggled with this pricing issue for several months. We can't seem to all agree on the right price. Finance wants the price as high as possible to generate revenue. Sales wants it low to sell volume. Product management wants the price to be consistent with the current product margin model. We've debated this for quite a while, but we need to finalize the third quarter price book update before June in order to get it into print and out to the sales force. We need to get this done.

Clearwater Technologies, Inc. History

Clearwater Technologies, Inc. was a small, publicly traded technology firm outside Boston. It was the market share leader in customer relationship management (CRM) servers for sales staffs of small- to medium-sized companies. Four MIT graduates had founded the company when they saw an opportunity to meet a market need that larger firms ignored. Unlike the CRM systems from Oracle or SAP, Clearwater customized the QTX for companies with sales forces of 10 to 30 people. Clearwater had been first to market in this particular segment, and QTX sales represented $45 million of its $80 million sales in 2004.

The QTX product line represented Clearwater's core franchise. Clearwater's premium-priced products were renowned for high reliability in performance supported by free lifetime technical support. The QTX line held 70 percent of its mature market. To date, competition in this market had been minimal, because no competitor had been able to match Clearwater's general functionality, and Clearwater held a U.S. patent on a popular feature that directed faxed documents to a specific salesperson's e-mail rather than a central fax machine.

Since 1999, Clearwater had used the cash generated by the QTX line to support engineering-intensive internal product development and to buy four other companies. None of these other businesses had achieved a dominant market position or profitability, so maximizing the QTX cash flow remained a priority.

The QTX Product

QTX was a sales support server that allowed multiple users to simultaneously maintain their sales account databases. These databases covered contact information, quote histories, copies of all communications, and links to the customers' corporate database for shipping records. The basic QTX package consisted of a processor, chassis, hard drive, and network interface, with a manufacturing cost of $500. The package provided simultaneous access for 10 users to the system, referred to as 10 "seats." Each seat represented one accessing employee. The product line consisted of 10-, 20-, and 30-seat capacity QTX servers. Each incremental 10 seats required $200 of additional manufacturing cost. Yearly sales were at the rate of 4,000 units across all sizes. In initial sales, approximately 30 percent of customers bought the 30-seat unit, 40 percent bought the 20-seat unit, and 30 percent bought the 10-seat unit. Customers who needed more than 30 seats typically went to competitors servicing the medium-to-large company market segment.

Clearwater set a per-seat Manufacturer's Suggested Retail Price (MSRP) that decreased with highter quantity seat purchases, reflecting the customer perception of declining manufacturing cost per seat. Clearwater also saw this as advantageous because it encouraged customers to maximize their initial seat purchase.

Clearwater typically sold its products through Value Added Resellers (VARs). A VAR was typically a small local firm that provided sales and support to end users. The value added by these resellers was that they provided a complete solution to the end user/customer from a single point of purchase and had multiple information technology products available from various vendors. Using VARs reduced Clearwater's sales and service expense significantly and increased its market coverage.

These intermediaries operated in several steps. First, the VAR combined the QTX from Clearwater with database software from other suppliers to form a turnkey customer solution. Second, the VAR loaded the software with customer-specific information and linked it to the customer's existing sales history databases. Finally, the VAR installed the product at the customer's site and trained the customer on its use. Clearwater sold the QTX to resellers at a 50 percent discount from the MSRP, allowing the

VARs to sell to the end user at or below the MSRP. The discount allowed the VARs room to negotiate with the customer and still achieve a profit (Table 1).

TABLE 1

Number of Seats	MSRP to End User	VAR Price	Unit Cost*	Unit Margin**
10	$8,000	$4,000	$500	87.5%
20	$14,000	$7,000	$700	90.0%
30	$17,250	$8,625	$900	89.6%

* Unit cost reflects additional $200 for memory capability for each additional 10 seats.

** $\text{Margin} = \dfrac{\text{VAR Price} - \text{Unit Cost}}{\text{VAR Price}}$

The Upgrade

Initially, the expectation had been that the 30-seat unit would be the largest volume seller. In order to gain economies of scale in manufacturing, reduce inventory configurations, and reduce engineering design and testing expense to a single assembly, Clearwater decided to manufacture only the 30-seat server with the appropriate number of seats 'enabled' for the buyer. Clearwater was effectively 'giving away' extra memory and absorbing the higher cost rather than manufacturing the various sizes. If a customer wanted a 10-seat server, the company shipped a 30-seat capable unit, with only the requested 10 seats enabled through software configuration. The proposed upgrade was, in reality, allowing customers to access capability already built into the product (Table 2).

TABLE 2

Number of Seats	Original Unit Cost	Original Unit Margin	Actual Unit Cost	Actual Unit Margin
10	$500	87.5%	$900	77.5%
20	$700	90.0%	$900	87.1%
30	$900	89.6%	$900	89.6%

Clearwater knew that many original customers were ready to use the additional capacity in the QTX. Some customers had added seats by buying a second box, but because the original product contained the capability to expand by accessing the disabled seats, Clearwater saw an opportunity to expand the product line and increase sales to a captive customer base. Customers could double or triple their seat capacity by purchasing either a 10- or a 20-seat upgrade, and getting an access code to enable the additional number of seats. No other competitor offered the possibility of an upgrade. To gain additional seats from the competitor, the customer purchased and installed an additional box. Because customers performed a significant amount of acceptance testing, which they would have to repeat before switching brands, the likelihood of changing brands to add capacity was low.

The objective of this morning's meeting was to set the price for the two upgrades.

As QTX product manager Rob Erickson stopped to collect his most recent notes from his desk, he reflected:

> What a way to start the week. Every time we have one of these meetings, senior management only looks at margins. I spent the whole weekend cranking numbers and I'm going in there using the highest margin we've got today. How can anybody say that's too low?

He grabbed his notes, calculator, and coffee and headed down the hall.

From the other wing of the building, financial analyst Hillary Hanson was crossing the lobby towards the conference room. She was thinking about the conversation she had late Friday afternoon with her boss, Alicia Fisher, Clearwater's CFO. They had been discussing this upcoming meeting and Alicia had given Hillary very clear instructions.

> I want you to go in and argue for the highest price possible. We should absolutely maximize the profitability on the upgrade. The customers are already committed to us and they have no alternative for an upgrade but with us. The switching costs to change at this point are too high since they've already been trained in our system and software. Let's go for it. Besides, we really need to show some serious revenue generation for the year-end report to the stockholders.

Hillary had not actually finalized a number. She figured she could see what the others proposed and then argue for a significant premium over that. She had the CFO's backing so she could keep pushing for more.

From the parking lot, Brian James, the district sales manager, headed for the rear entrance. He, too, was thinking about the upcoming meeting and anticipating a long morning.

> I wish marketing would realize that when they come up with some grandiose number for a new product, sales takes the hit in the field. It's a killer to have to explain to customers that they have to pay big bucks for something that's essentially built in. It's gonna be even tougher to justify on this upgrade. At least with the QTX, we have something the buyer can see. It's hardware. With the upgrade, there isn't even a physical product. We're just giving customers a code to access the capability that's already built into the machine. Telling customers that they have to pay several thousand dollars never makes you popular. If you think about it, that's a lot of money for an access code, but you won't hear me say that out loud. Maybe I can get them to agree to something reasonable this time. I spent the weekend working this one out, and I think my logic is pretty solid.

Price Proposals

Once everyone was settled in the conference room, Rob spoke first:

> I know we have to come up with prices for both the 10-seat and 20-seat upgrades, but to keep things manageable, let's discuss the 20-seat price first.

Once that number is set, the 10-seat price should be simple. Because the margin on the 30-seat unit is the highest in the line, I think we should use that as the basis to the price for the upgrade.

He went to a white board to show an example:

If a customer is upgrading from a 10-seat unit to a 30-seat unit, they are adding two steps of capacity costing $200 each to us, or $400. $400/1−0.90 $4,000 to the reseller, and $8,000 to the end user. We keep the margin structure in place at the highest point in the line. The customer gets additional capacity, and we keep our margins consistent.

He sat down feeling pleased. He had fired the first shot, had been consistent with the existing margin structure, and had rounded up the highest margin point in the line. Brian looked at Rob's calculations and commented:

I think that's going to be hard for the customer to see without us giving away information about our margins, and we don't want to do that, since they are pretty aggressive to begin with. However, I think I have solved this one for us. I've finally come up with a simple, fair solution to pricing the upgrade that works for us and the customers.

He walked over to a white board and grabbed a marker:

If we assume an existing 10-seat customer has decided to upgrade to 30-seat capability, we should charge that customer the difference between what the buyer has already paid and the price of the new capacity. So ...

New 30-seat unit	$17,250
Original 10-seat unit	$8,000
Price for 20-seat upgrade	$9,250

It's consistent with our current pricing for the QTX. It's fair to the customer. It's easy for the customer to understand and it still makes wads of money for us. It also is easy for the customer to see that we're being good to them. If they bought a 20-seat box in addition to the 10-seat box they already have, it would be costing them more."

He wrote:

New 20-seat unit $14,000

A new unit provides customers with redundancy by having two boxes, which they might want in the event of product failure, but the cost is pretty stiff. Upgrading becomes the logical and affordable option.

Hillary looked at the numbers and knew just what she was going to do.

> That all looks very logical, but I don't see that either of you has the company's best interests at heart. Brian, you just want a simple sale that your sales people and the customers will buy into, and Rob, you are charging even less than Brian. We need to consider the revenue issue as well. These people have already bought from us; are trained on our hardware and software and don't want to have to repeat the process with someone else. It would take too long. They've got no desire to make a change and that means we've got them. The sky is really the limit on how much we can charge them because they have no real alternative. We should take this opportunity to really go for the gold, say $15,000 or even $20,000. We can and should be as aggressive as possible.

All three continued to argue the relative merits of their pricing positions, without notable success. Jefferies listened to each of them and after they finished, he turned to a clean white board and took the marker.

> I've done some more thinking on this. In order to meet the needs of all three departments, there are three very important points that the price structure for these upgrades must accomplish:
>
> 1. The pricing for the upgrades shouldn't undercut the existing pricing for the 30-seat QTX.
>
> 2. We want to motivate our buyers to purchase the maximum number of seats at the initial purchase. A dollar now is better than a potential dollar later. We never know for sure that they will make that second purchase. If we don't do this right, we're going to encourage customers to reduce their initial purchase. They'll figure they can add capacity whenever, so why buy it if they don't need it. That would kill upfront sales of the QTX.
>
> 3. We don't want to leave any revenue on the table when buyers decide to buy more capacity. They are already committed to us and our technology and we should capitalize on that, without totally ripping them off. Therefore, while Hillary says 'the sky's the limit,' I think there is a limit and we need to determine what it is and how close we can come to it.

> If we assume that those are the objectives, none of the prices you've put together thus far answers all three of those criteria. Some come close, but each one fails. See if you can put your heads together and come to a consensus price that satisfies all three objectives. OK?

Heads nodded and with that, Jefferies left the conference room. The three remaining occupants looked at one another. Brian got up to wipe the previous numbers off the white boards and said:

> OK, one more time. If our numbers don't work, why not and what is the right price for the 20-seat upgrade?

CASE 7

Barro Stickney, Inc.

With four people and sales of $5.5 million, Barro Stickney, Inc. (BSI) had become a successful and profitable manufacturers' representative firm. It enjoyed a reputation for outstanding sales results and friendly, thorough service to both its customers and principals. In addition, BSI was considered a great place to work. The office was comfortable and the atmosphere relaxed but professional. All members of the group had come to value the close, friendly working relationships that had grown with the organization.

Success had brought with it increased profits as well as the inevitable decision regarding further growth. Recent requests from two principals, Franklin Key Electronics and R. D. Ocean, had forced BSI to focus its attention on the question of expansion. It was not to be an easy decision, for expansion offered both risk and opportunity.

Company Background

John Barro and Bill Stickney established their small manufacturers' representative agency, Barro Stickney, Inc., ten years ago. Both men were close friends who left different manufacturers' representative firms to join as partners in their own "rep" agency. The two worked very well together, and their talents complemented each other.

John Barro was energetic and gregarious. He enjoyed meeting new people and taking on new challenges. It was mainly through John's efforts that many of BSI's eight principals had signed on with BSI. Even after producing $1.75 million in sales this past year, John still made an effort to contribute much of his free time to community organizations in addition to perfecting his golf score.

Bill Stickney liked to think of himself as someone a person could count on. He was thoughtful and thorough. He liked to figure how things could get done, and how they could be better. Much of the administrative work of the agency, such as resource allocation and territory assignments, was handled by Bill. In addition to his contribution of

This case was written by Tony Langan, B. Jane Stewart, and Lawrence M. Stratton Jr., under the supervision of Professor Erin Anderson of the Wharton School, University of Pennsylvania. The writing of the case was sponsored by the Manufacturers' Representatives Educational Research Foundation. The cooperation of the Mid-Atlantic Chapter of the Electronic Representatives Association (ERA) is greatly appreciated. Copyright by Erin Anderson.

$1.5 million to total company sales, Bill also had a Boy Scout troop and was interested in gourmet cooking. In fact, he often prepared specialties to share with his fellow workers.

A few years later, as the business grew, J. Todd Smith (J.T.) joined as an additional salesperson. J.T. had worked for a nationally known corporation, and he brought his experience dealing with large customers with him. He and his family loved the Harrisburg area, and J.T. was very happy when he was asked to join BSI just as his firm was ready to transfer him to Chicago. John and Bill had worked with J.T. in connection with a hospital fund-raising project, and they were impressed with his tenacity and enthusiasm. Because he had produced sales of over $2 million this past year, J.T. was now considered eligible to buy a partnership share of BSI.

Soon after J.T. joined BSI, Elizabeth Lee, a school friend of John's older sister, was hired as office manager. She was cheerful and put as much effort into her work as she did coaching the local swim team. The three salespeople knew they could rely on her to keep track of orders and schedules, and she was very helpful when customers and principals called in with requests or problems.

Most principals in the industry assigned their reps exclusive territories, and BSI's ranged over the Pennsylvania, New Jersey, and Delaware area. The partners purchased a small house and converted it into their present office located in Camp Hill, a suburb of Harrisburg, the state capital of Pennsylvania. The converted home contributed to the familylike atmosphere and attitude that was promoted and prevalent throughout the agency.

Over the years, in addition to local interests, BSI and its people had made an effort to participate in and support the efforts of the Electronics Representative Association (ERA). A wall of the company library was covered with awards and letters of appreciation. BSI had made many friends and important contacts through the organization. Just last year BSI received a recommendation from Chuck Goodman, a Chicago manufacturers' rep who knew a principal in need of representation in the Philadelphia area. The principal's line worked well with BSI's existing portfolio, and customer response had been quite favorable. BSI planned to continue active participation in the ERA.

Each week BSI held a five o'clock meeting in the office library where all members of the company shared their experiences of the week. It was a time when new ideas were encouraged and everyone was brought up to date. For example, many customer problems were solved here, and principals' and members' suggestions were discussed. An established agenda enabled members to prepare. Most meetings took about sixty to ninety minutes, with emphasis placed on group consensus. It was during this group meeting that BSI would discuss the future of the company.

Opportunities for Expansion

R. D. Ocean was BSI's largest principal, and it accounted for 32 percent of BSI's revenues. Ocean had just promoted James Innve as new sales manager, and he felt an additional salesperson was needed in order for BSI to achieve the new sales projections. Innve expressed the opinion that BSI's large commission checks justified the additional effort, and he further commented that J.T.'s expensive new car was proof that BSI could afford it.

BSI was not sure an additional salesperson was necessary, but it did not want to lose the goodwill of R. D. Ocean or [its] business. Also, while it was customary for all principals to meet and tacitly approve new representatives, BSI wanted to be very sure that any new salesperson would fit into the close-knit BSI organization.

Franklin Key Electronics was BSI's initial principal and had remained a consistent contributor of approximately 15 percent of BSI's revenues. BSI felt its customer base was well suited to the Franklin line, and it had worked hard to establish the Franklin Key name with these customers. As a consequence, BSI now considered Franklin Key relatively easy to sell.

A few days previously, Mark Heil, Franklin's representative from Virginia, perished when his private plane crashed, leaving Franklin Key without representation in its D.C./Virginia territory. Franklin did not want to jeopardize its sales of over $800,000 and was desperate to replace Heil before its customers found other sources. Franklin offered the territory to BSI and was anxious to hear the decision within one week.

BSI was not familiar with the territory, but it did understand that there were a great number of military accounts. This meant there was a potential for sizable orders, although a different and specialized sales approach would be required. Military customers are known to have their own unique approach to purchase decisions.

Because of the distance and the size of the territory, serious consideration was needed as to whether a branch office would be necessary. A branch office would mean less interaction with and a greater independence from the main BSI office. None of the current BSI members seemed anxious to move there, but it might be possible to hire someone who was familiar with the territory. There was, of course, always the risk that any successful salesperson might leave and start his or her own rep firm.

In addition to possibilities of expanding its territory and its sales force, BSI also wanted to consider whether it should increase or maintain its number of principals. BSI's established customer base and its valued reputation put them in a strong position to approach potential principals. If, however, BSI had too many principals, it might not be able to offer them all the attention and service they might require.

Preparation for the Meeting

Each member received an agenda and supporting data for the upcoming meeting asking them to consider the issue of expansion. They would be asked whether BSI should or should not expand its territory, its sales force, and/or its number of principals. In preparation, they were each asked to take a good hard look at the current BSI portfolio and to consider all possibilities for growth, including the effect any changes would have on the company's profits, its reputation, and its work environment.

It was an ambitious agenda: one that would determine the future of the company. It would take even more time than usual to discuss everything and reach consensus. Consequently, this week's meeting was set to take place over the weekend at Bill Stickney's vacation lodge in the Poconos, starting with a gourmet dinner served at 7 p.m. sharp.

Before the meeting, Bill Stickney examined the sources of BSI's revenue and the firm's income for the previous year. He also estimated the future prospects for each of BSI's lines, considering each line's market potential and BSI's level of saturation in each market. Finally, he estimated the costs of hiring a new employee both in the current sales territory and in the Washington/Virginia area. Immediately before the meeting, Elizabeth finished compiling Bill's data into four figures (see pages 597–599).

Figure 1 evaluates the amount of sales effort (difficulty in selling) necessary to achieve a certain percentage of sales in BSI's portfolio (return). Difficulty in selling is measured by the level of marketing investment required for growth. Stickney's estimates are shown on the vertical axis. Return for this investment is measured by the

FIGURE 1 | **RETURN VERSUS DIFFICULTY IN SELLING**

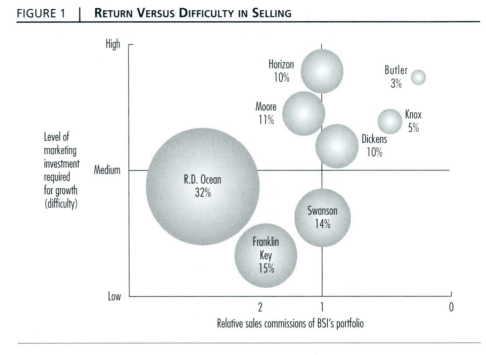

relative sales commissions as a percent of BSI's portfolio shown on the horizontal axis. If BSI's time were evenly divided among its eight principals, each would receive 12.5 percent of the agency's time. The x-axis shows each principal's time allocation as a proportion of 12.5 percent of the "par" time allocation. The area of each ellipse reflects each principal's share of BSI's commission revenue.

Bill Stickney presented the following additional comments as a result of his research:

1. Swanson's products are being replaced by the competition's computerized electronic equipment, a product category the firm has ignored. As a result, the company is losing its once prominent market position.

2. Although small amounts of effort are required to promote Ocean's product line to customers in the current sales territory, Ocean is extremely demanding of both BSI and other manufacturer's representative firms.

3. According to a seminar at the last ERA meeting, the maximum safe proportion of a rep firm's commissions from a single principal should be 25–30 percent. Also, at the meeting, one speaker indicated that if a firm commands 80 percent of a market, it should focus on another product or expand its territory rather than attempt to obtain the remainder of the market.

4. The revenue for investment for the manufacturer's representative firm comes from one or more of several sources. These sources include reduced forthcoming commission income, retained previous income, and borrowed money from a financial institution. Most successful firms expand their sales force or sales territory when they experience income growth and use the investment as a tax write-off.

FIGURE 2 | BARRO STICKNEY, INC., ESTIMATION OF COST OF ADDITIONAL SALES REPRESENTATIVE

Compensation Costs for New Sales Representative
Depending on the new sales representative's level of experience, BSI would pay a base salary of $15,000–$25,000 with the following bonus schedule:

  0% firm's commission revenue up to $500,000 in sales
20% firm's commission revenue first $0.5 million in sales over $500,000
25% firm's commission revenue for the next $0.5 million in sales
30% firm's commission for the next $0.5 million in sales
40% firm's commission sales above $2 million

Estimate of Support Costs[1] for the New Representative[2]

Search applicant pool, psychological testing, hiring, training,[3] flying final choice to principals for approval[4]	$28,000
Automobile expenses, telephone costs, business cards, entertainment promotion	22,000
Insurance, payroll taxes (social security, unemployment compensation)	16,000
Total expenses	$66,000

Incremental Expenses for New Territory

Transportation (additional mileage from Camp Hill to Virginia)	$02,000
Office equipment and rent (same regardless of headquarter's location)	4,000
Cost of hiring office manager[5]	18,000
Total increment expenses	$24,000

[1]Rounded to the nearest thousand.   [2]In current territory.   [3]Excludes the lost revenue from selling instead of engaging in this activity (opportunity cost).   [4]Although rep agencies are not legally required to show prospective employees to principals, it is generally held to be good business practice.   [5]Discretionary.

FIGURE 3 | BARRO STICKNEY, INC., STATEMENT OF REVENUE (TOTAL SALES REVENUE 1988, $5.5 MILLION)

Principal	Estimated Market Saturation	Product Type	Sales/ Commission Rate	Share of BSI's Portfolio	Commission Revenue
R. D. Ocean	High	Components	5.00%	32%	$96,756
Franklin Key	High	Components	5.00	15	45,354
Butler	Low	Technical/ computer	12.00	3	9,070
Dickens	Low	Components	5.00	10	30,236
Horizon	Medium	Components	5.50	10	30,237
Swanson	High	Components	5.25	14	42,331
Moore	Medium	Consumer/ electronics	5.25	11	33,260
Knox	Low	Technical/ communications	8.50	5	15,118

FIGURE 4	BARRO STICKNEY, INC., STATEMENT OF INCOME (FOR THE YEAR ENDING DECEMBER 31, 1988)

Revenue

Commission income	$302,362

Expenses

Salaries for sales and bonuses (includes Barro Stickney)	130,250
Office manager's salary	20,000
Total nonpersonnel expenses[1]	128,279
Total expenses	$278,529

Net income[2]	$23,833	(7.9% of revenue)

[1]Includes travel, advertising, office supplies, retirement, automobile expenses, communications, office equipment, and miscellaneous expenses.

[2]Currently held in negotiable certificates of deposit in a Harrisburg bank.

We've Got Rhythm! Medtronic Corporation's Cardiac Pacemaker Business

The legacy of Medtronic Corporation, the company that created the cardiac pace-maker industry, is a proud one. Starting from its earliest pacemakers, which had to be carried outside the body, Medtronic had achieved dramatic improvements in the functionality, size and reliability of these devices. In so doing it had extended the lives, and improved the quality of life, for hundreds of thousands of people in whom pacemakers had been implanted. The pacemaker has been designated as one of the ten most outstanding engineering achievements in the world over the past 50 years, along with the digital computer and the Apollo 11 moon landing.[1]

Medtronic, which in 1995 booked operating profit of $300 million on revenues of $1.7 billion, had been founded in 1957 in Minneapolis, Minnesota by Earl Bakken, a researcher and inventor who had to his credit patents on several of the crucial tech-nologies that led to the modern heart pacemaker. Pacemakers were small, battery-powered devices which, when implanted within a patient, helped a malfunctioning heart to beat in a steady, fixed rhythm. Because Medtronic was the first entrant into the pacemaker field and built a strong technological lead, it enjoyed a substantial por-tion (over 70%) of the market share for cardiac pacing through the 1960s.

Building upon Medtronic's legacy of leadership was not easy, however. In the face of increasing competition, rapid technological change and tightening market and reg-ulatory demands for product quality, Medtronic saw its market share cut by more than half between 1970 and 1986. Though it had invested heavily in technology and product development over this period, much of that investment had been unproductive. Many projects failed to produce product designs that could be launched competitively, and

[1] This citation was made by the National Society of Professional Engineers in 1984.

Professor Clayton M. Christensen prepared this case as the basis for class discussion rather than to illustrate either effec-tive or ineffective handling of an administrative situation. Some of the data and names in this case have been disguised to protect the proprietary interests of the company.

the features and functionality of most of the products the company was able to launch, lagged the competition. Several key employees left the company, seeing greater opportunity to develop their new pacemaker product ideas in new start-ups rather than within Medtronic. These competitors proved much faster than Medtronic at developing new products that advanced the state-of-the-art in pacemaking. Medtronic was also pummeled by two major product recalls related to product quality problems. Observers felt the company would have lost even more of the market during this period, were it not for its strong worldwide salesforce and the lingering legacy of its brand reputation amongst surgeons, the primary customer group.

Management changes which were initiated in the late 1980s, however, had sparked a dramatic reversal in the company's fortunes, and by 1996 the company had regained its position of product and market leadership. By all accounts, it was in front and pulling away from its competitors. On a pleasant Minneapolis spring afternoon in 1996, several members of the team that managed this turn-around—Steve Mahle, president of the Brady Pacing Business; Mike Stevens, general manager of the Pulse Generator & Programming Systems (PGPS) Division; Bill Murray, general manager of the MicroRel component manufacturing subsidiary; Director of Marketing Paula Skjefte (pronounced Sheftee); and Director of Product Development Technology Don Deyo—gathered to assess the progress they had made since they had taken the helm of the troubled division in the late 1980s. They were also anxious to understand whether the management structure and the processes, values, and resources they had created to achieve this turn-around, were capable of maintaining the company's successful momentum in the future. This case recounts their achievements and concerns.

Medtronic's Brady Pacing Business

Medtronic's Brady Business Unit designed and built pacemakers that delivered a rhythm of electrical impulses, to remedy a disorder called Bradycardia, in which the heart's electrical system does not generate pulses to cause the heart to beat rapidly enough to sustain the body's normal activity, as described in Appendix 1.[2] Amongst its other businesses, Medtronic also had a Tachy cardia Business Unit, whose products addressed the opposite malfunction—when the heart's electrical system generated too many beats. Because of the prevalence of Bradycardia relative to other disorders in cardiac patients, the Brady Business Unit historically had delivered most of Medtronic's revenues, and an even larger share of its profits. Consequently, the health and vitality of the Brady Business strongly affected the corporation's overall financial performance.

The Brady Business Unit worked hand-in-glove with the component divisions of Medtronic in product development efforts, as shown in Exhibit 1. The Promeon Division, for example, developed new technologies to power pacemakers. In the early years of the industry's history in particular, battery technology had been a pivotal selling point because the battery could not be replaced: once it was depleted, a new pacemaker had to be implanted. Another division, MicroRel, designed and fabricated the critical hybrid microelectronic circuits in Medtronic's pacemakers. Located in Tempe, Arizona, it supplied proprietary circuitry to all of Medtronic's businesses.

---

[2] The term "brady" derives from a Latin root meaning "slow." The opposite cardiac pacing disorder, tachycardia, took its name from a Latin root meaning "fast."

EXHIBIT 1 | A PARTIAL ORGANIZATION CHART OF MEDTRONIC

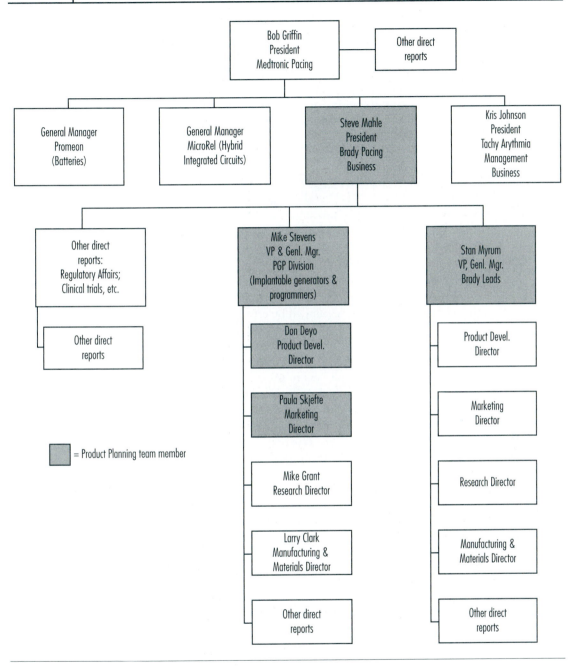

Work with MicroRel was viewed as a crucial connection in the development of new pacemakers, because of the increasing importance that integrated circuit (IC) technology played within these devices. Perhaps the most critical division for the Brady Business was the Pulse Generators & Programming Systems (PGPS), headed by Mike Stevens. Unlike the other two component divisions that shared their services and output with other parts of Medtronic, PGPS focused on developing new products for

Bradycardia pacing, by translating customer and market-based inputs into product designs, and then worked closely with manufacturing to produce the final products. This involved design and assembly of the pacemaker as well as the programming unit, which typically sat on a table in the cath lab or operating room where the implantation was performed. Programming units allowed physicians to tailor the firmware in the pacemaker so that the frequency of the pulses it generated and a number of other attributes of the device matched the needs of each individual patient. The leads which carried electrical impulses from the pulse generator to the wall of the heart were designed by a separate leads group within the Brady pacing Business Unit, headed by Warren Watson.

How the Pacemaking Leader Lost Its Rhythm

Product development at Medtronic historically had been supervised by its functional managers, who were intimately involved with each development effort during the company's early years. However, as the company grew, the functional managers became increasingly absorbed by operating responsibilities in their own functional organizations, making coordination across functions, in practice if not intent, a lower priority. The company responded by creating a group of project managers to coordinate the work of various functional groups. While this helped, most major decisions still had to be passed by the functional managers—"A legacy of how decisions had been made that still lingered in the organization," according to a long-time employee. The project managers' job was to try and get decisions to be made by the functional leadership—they only had minor authority to make decisions themselves.

"Planning new products is actually a lot more difficult in a business like this than it looks," reflected another experienced executive. "In some businesses the problem is a lack of great ideas. But in our situation—with rapidly changing technological possibilities, some darned good competitors and thousands of cardiologists out there with ideas for all kinds of new features, the opposite is true: We've always had *too* many ideas for new products. In our functional organization, without a single, coordinated process or person to articulate a product plan or strategy, development projects just started everywhere. When you had a good idea, you'd mock up something—either a real prototype or something on paper—and carry it around with you. Then when you'd run into Earl Bakken or another powerful manager in the hall, you'd corner him, pull your idea out of your pocket, and try to get him to support it. If his reaction seemed positive, then you would use that leverage, to get a few friends to help you push it along. At some point you'd go to the engineering manager to get formal resources.

"The problem with this system was *not* that we were working on bad ideas. Most of them were technically sound and made market sense," commented Don Deyo, an experienced engineer and currently Director of Product Development and Technology. "We were trying to do too many things, and no project got the focus and attention needed to get it done right. It was taking too long to get anything to market. We never got good at releasing new products, because you only get good at things you do a lot. Those that we did introduce often followed the lead of competitors. That's what happens when you continually try to respond to every new idea to come along."

The problem then fed on itself," reflected Mike Stevens, general manager. "The development people would tell me that they could never get anything to market because marketing kept changing the product description in the middle of the projects.

And the marketing people would say that it took so long for engineering to get anything done, that by the time they got around to completing something, the market demands would have changed. When customer requirements evolve faster than you can develop products, it becomes a vicious spiral."

In environments like that, it is *very* difficult to plan product families," Stevens continued. "If the company launched a product that subsequently could be modified or extended to create derivative models, it was a stroke of luck." Because of the *ad hoc* way in which new product development projects were conceived, Medtronic's project pipeline was made up of incongruous development cycles. Projects were separated according to whether they were single or dual-chamber platforms. Each new model had largely its own unique circuitry, components, testing programs, casing, and battery. Due to the high costs of developing all these parts of the pacemaker, project managers battled each other for resources.

Although the company's reputation and strong salesforce relationships with surgeons kept disaster at bay, the company's performance suffered as a result of its disabilities in development. Between 1970 and 1986, it was almost always a competitor, not Medtronic, that introduced major new improvements to the market. For example, Cordis introduced the world's first programmable pacemaker in 1972; Medtronic followed in 1980. Cardiac Pacemakers Inc., a Medtronic spin-off, pioneered the first pacemaker with a long-life lithium battery in 1974. Even though the technology was available from a third-party supplier, Medtronic did not get its lithium battery-powered product out the door until 1978.

Although Medtronic introduced its first dual-chamber pacemaker during this period, it did not follow it with an improved dual chamber device for another eight years. Deyo explained, "We were working on next-generation dual chamber products during all of those eight years. The problem was that just as we'd get ready to announce a new product, a competitor would come out with something better. So we'd force the funnel open again to allow for this new input, re-scope the project, and try to leap ahead of the competitor. Then just as we'd get ready with the improved version, a competitor would come in ahead of us with an even better product; and so on."

"I got so that I just didn't want to answer the phone because I was afraid there would be a salesman on the line wanting to know when we were going to come out with a product that was comparable to something a competitor had introduced," recalled Paula Skjefte, director of marketing. "I just couldn't give him an answer."

Field product failures compounded the problems caused by Medtronic's long development cycle. Its Xytron pacemaker line was recalled in 1976 after several units failed following implantation. And a few years later, physicians found that the leads on some pacemakers they had implanted had disintegrated, so that the pacemaker's output was not getting transmitted to their patients' hearts. In total, Medtronic was forced to issue four different product advisories to warn that certain models were susceptible to malfunction. The result of these factors was a massive loss of share, from 70% in 1970 to 29% in 1986, as shown in Exhibit 2. Still, however, due to significant growth in the market, the company continued to report record sales and profits over this period, and for many in the company there was no cause for alarm.

"Medtronic was a really nice Minneapolis company," Don Deyo noted. This reflected in many ways the values of Medtronic's founder, who had a genuine reverence of every employee's contributions to the company's success. "But somehow in the mid-1970s, Deyo noted, "This attitude got out of hand. We dominated the market, and were very profitable. Because there was so little pressure on the business, we lost our intensity and willingness to focus our efforts."

EXHIBIT 2 | **CHANGES IN THE MARKET SHARES OF LEADING PACEMAKER MANUFACTURERS**

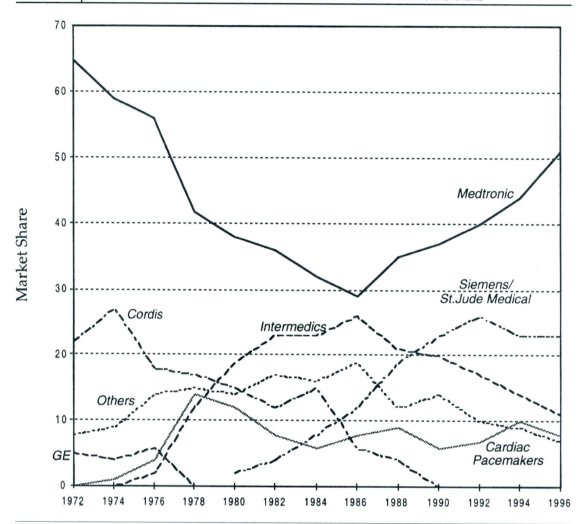

NOTES: Over this period, ownership of several of these companies changed hands. Intermedics was acquired by Sulzer in the early 1990s. St. Jude Medical acquired the pacemaker business of Siemens; and Cardiac Pacemakers, a division of Eli Lilly, was spun off along with other of Lilly's medical device companies, into an independent corporation called Guidant.

SOURCE: Casewriter's estimates, synthesized from data provided by the company, by investment analysts, and by David Gobeli and William Rudelius, in "Managing Innovation: Lessons from the Cardiac-Pacing Industry," *Sloan Management Review* (26), Summer, 1985, pp. 24–43.

A Home Run Saves the Day

The company's decline was arrested in 1986—more by good fortune than any change in management practice, however. In the early 1980s a project leader, Ken Anderson, championed an idea for a "rate-responsive" pacemaker—a device which could sense when changes in body activity required the heart to beat faster or slower, and stimulated the heart to beat accordingly. Although most cardiologists Anderson spoke to thought the idea was impractical, and despite the indifference of most of Medtronic's staff, Anderson won the support of the general manager, and the two of them set up a dedicated team to pursue the idea. Its product, dubbed

Activitrax, worked—technologically and in the marketplace. Cardiologists found its single-chamber design easy to implant, and its effect was nearly as good for patients as a dual chamber pacemaker. Patients reported feeling stronger, because it would cause their hearts to beat more rapidly when they were working hard or exercising. And they reported feeling more rested in the morning, because *Activitrax* paced their hearts to beat more slowly when they were asleep.

The dramatic *Activitrax* therapeutic breakthrough literally saved Medtronic, because no other new platform products were ready for introduction until 1992. It did not, however, alter the way the company developed products.

The Turnaround in Product Development

Though Medtronic's market position was helped by the success of Activitrax and by a serious product recall suffered by a principal competitor, the most dramatic changes in the company's market position were instigated when Mike Stevens was assigned to be vice president for product development of the PGPS Division in 1987. Stevens' career with Medtronic had begun in 1973, when Motorola decided to shut down its hybrid circuit manufacturing operation near Phoenix. Stevens and several other employees of the Motorola facility decided to continue the operation and obtained financing from Medtronic, which had been a major customer.

Stevens had watched Medtronic's struggles in product development from a supplier's viewpoint. "Though I didn't have a background in product development, I saw much of Medtronic's problem as Management 101. We had very strong functional roles. People were being measured by cost centers, and there was no accountability for the delay or failure of a new product. I felt the basic values and ethics of the company were still really strong. But what needed work were its *processes*. I felt if we could get those straightened out, then we could bring the Brady business back to its past glory."

Stevens summarized key elements of his management philosophy as follows:

1. Commitments are sacred. The more responsibility you give to people to control their destiny, the more you can and must hold them accountable.

2. Create a sense of urgency by contrasting the excitement of bringing new therapy to patients, versus the consequences if your competitors are there first with better solutions. Don't waste time with excess travel or off-site meetings.

3. Are happy employees productive, or are productive employees happy? Stevens believed the latter, whereas Medtronic management had been acting as if the former were true.

4. Do nothing that separates management and employees. Management means responsibility, not status.

5. You only get what you measure.

6. Focus on gaining market share. Over time, this is the most accurate measure of your success.

Managers in the PGPS Division got a taste of Stevens' belief that commitments are sacred when, shortly after arriving at Medtronic, he held management to the project milestones they had agreed upon at the beginning of fiscal year 1988.

Their incentive compensation was tied to these objectives, and 1988 was the first year in memory that management did not receive year-end bonuses that were tied to objectives.

Measuring Product Development Performance

Stevens implemented his measurement philosophy by focusing on four measures of product development performance, which corresponded to the achievements he wanted the organization to focus upon. These are described in the following table.

Focus	Measure	Stevens' Comments
Speed	Cycle time	"This is the time required to get a new product into the market. If I measure this, there isn't much else I need to measure. It forces you to do the other things right in product development, because you can't make mistakes, and you can't waste time."
Cost	Fully allocated unit product costs	"The reason we focus on fully allocated cost, rather than just viewing functional costs or direct product costs, is that it gets you thinking about market share, and the impact that unit volumes can have on your financial success. This is healthy thinking."
Innovativeness	Product performance relative to competitors	"This translates into market share, pure and simple."
Product Quality	Field performance– defects per million	"In our business, you can't afford a field failure— because our patients count on us, and doctors can choose to go elsewhere."

Most people in PGPS welcomed Stevens' attitude. One commented, "I was just getting started as a project manager, and Mike was a breath of fresh air. His priorities were clear; I knew where he stood. He had a very different management style: very firm, assertive, thoughtful and focused. He was execution-oriented, and really held people accountable.

Processes and Practices

"This isn't a story about great management," Stevens emphasized. "It's a story about putting into place a set of processes that helped a great team of people be as productive as they could be." The processes Stevens instituted had the following features:

1. Speed   "Being fast to market eliminates *so* many other problems," commented Steve Mahle, who took over as president of the Brady Pacing Business in 1990. "The slowest part of our process was actually in deciding what needed to be done. We used to spend *lots* of time debating what we should do. One of Mike's greatest achievements was in cleaning up the front end. He did this by articulating very clearly what our strategy was, so that there was a well-defined criteria that could guide these decisions. Then he created a process to get those decisions made."

Exhibit 3 describes the process by which new products were defined. An assessment of the competitive and customer environment was combined with a technology assessment, to define the business objectives of each new product, and to clarify what the financial and competitive contributions of the new product needed to be. Stevens, who by 1991 had become division general manager, reviewed new product ideas according to their potential for meeting those business objectives. His staff, comprised of the managers of the division's marketing, research, development, technology, finance, human resources and manufacturing functions, participated in this review with Stevens.

2. Platform Strategy   Since product ideas in the earlier regime had originated in disparate parts of the organization and were approved and funded in independent decisions, it was quite common that products that required significant investments of time and money were not leveraged with derivative products that could extend their life and market reach. The highly successful Activitrax model, for example, did not spawn a single derivative product that offered different features, performance, or price points to the market. To devise an effective product line architecture built around product platforms, Mahle established a product planning team comprised of himself, Mike Stevens, Paula Skjefte, Don Deyo and Stan Myrum, Vice president and general manager of the business unit's leads division. This team defined a platform strategy around three key elements.

The first element was that the initial platform product had to be designed to accommodate the full range of derivative models from it, without significant redesign.

EXHIBIT 3	**PROCESS BY WHICH NEW PRODUCT CONCEPTS WERE DEFINED AT MEDTRONIC**

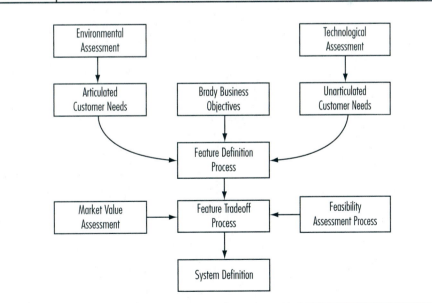

NOTE: Throughout this process, as customers' needs were balanced against business objectives and technological feasibility, the marketing members of the Medtronic development teams repeatedly sought customers' feedback to the tradeoffs that were being contemplated.

"In other words," Stevens explained, "We designed the highest-performance, most fully featured version of the product at the outset." Medtronic then created derivatives by de-featuring and de-rating certain elements of that design, so that it could address other tiers of the market as well.

The second element of the platform strategy was enabled by the first. Historically, Medtronic had introduced new pacemaker features on its single-chamber models first, because they were technologically simpler to design and build. Once the features were accepted and the technology perfected in the single-chamber platform, the features were then moved up-market onto the dual chamber platform. "The effect of this," Paula Skjefte noted, "Was to force a lot of our lead physicians to continue focusing on single-chamber devices just so they could utilize our newest features. Once we began designing the platform to accommodate the full range of derivative models we planned to spin off from it, we didn't face the same constraint—it was just as easy to put the most advanced features on the dual chamber model. This gave us a much clearer progression from basic, simple devices for the low-end of the market to high-performance, fully featured models at the high end.

Skjefte continued, "The way we used to play in the low-end of the market was to discount the price of our old model, after we had introduced a new one. This was ironic. Because we were reducing the cost of our products with each generation, we sold our high-cost models at the lowest prices, and our low-cost, newest models at the highest prices." The result was that there was little incentive to maintain a strong presence in lower tiers of the market. Under the new strategy, Medtronic addressed lower price points in its market with the simplest versions of its new lower-cost platforms. Hence, even as Medtronic was assuming a leadership role in features and functionality in higher tiers of the market, it strengthened its position in the low end as well.

The third aspect of Medtronic's platform strategy was to change the way platforms were defined. Formerly, Medtronic had thought of platforms in terms of physical architecture. Hence, it was inconceivable that a dual-chamber device could have been levered off of a single-chamber device platform. The projects were executed by completely different teams, and their designs therefore diverged from the very beginning. Under the new strategy, advances in microelectronics technology enabled so many of the most important capabilities to be designed into the hybrid circuit, that the circuit design constituted the platform. This circuit could then be modified quite readily, often through firmware modifications, to enable or disable particular features in the design of derivative products.

"I couldn't say whether Medtronic's decision to integrate backward into hybrid circuit production by starting MicroRel was good luck or good management," Stevens reflected. "But at this point the expertise we have developed in circuit design and production is an enormous advantage. Our competitors outsource their hybrid circuits. But we have found that the hybrid is so integral to our functionality and our standards in quality and specifications, that suppliers just can't meet what we need. We can outsource things that are a little bit more modular—things that aren't so integral to the essence of our product. And being vertically integrated helps with speed. We can go down to MicroRel and shift priorities if something needs to be done quickly. We are also vertically integrated with our battery development and manufacturing."

Medtronic faced two particular challenges in implementing its platform strategy, Stevens reflected. "First, we learned that we needed to have the technology building blocks in place, before we could begin a platform project. Product development is not technology development—you can't have the uncertainties of advanced technology development on the critical path of a rhythmically executed product development project. Technology takes time to put into place, and it requires consistency in strategy and management methods, to tie advanced technology development with product development in a consistent, useful way. The second challenge we encountered was that platform projects required *much* more interaction and coordination amongst various individuals and groups in the company—within engineering, and across engineering, manufacturing, marketing and finance—than other projects. You can't have a 'one-size-fits-all' habit of organizing and managing development teams, if you're really serious about a platform strategy."

Indeed, Stevens' decision to vest platform development teams with much greater decision making authority—essentially making project managers the peers of functional managers—had a pervasive and sometimes disruptive impact on many in the organization. Heavyweight project managers with dedicated teams—from research, development and marketing—oversaw the development of every platform. Other project managers, working under the supervision of the platform manager, took responsibility for derivative projects extending off of each platform. This represented a significant shift in the job of the company's functional managers. Their charge became providing trained, capable people to staff projects, and developing new technology platforms. "It became very clear, very quickly," observed Bill Murray, an electrical engineer-turned-project manager, "That project management was the path for career advancement. Even some of the functional managers left their positions to become project managers."

3. Project Documentation   Previous agreements to initiate a project were often made verbally. "It was amazing how many misunderstandings and disagreements seemed to survive those verbal contracts," Don Deyo recalled. "You could leave a meeting thinking you had agreed on something, and learn a few months later that you hadn't. Then when we had to change something, the marketing and engineering people were always accusing each other of violating an earlier agreement. It's amazing in a set-up like that, how easy it is legitimately and honestly to find someone else at fault." One way Stevens implemented his credo that commitments are sacred was to require two documents to be written at the start of the development phase of each project: A *Product Description* document, written by marketing, which detailed the customer requirements, product definition and clinical performance expectations of the product; and the *Product Specification* document, written by engineering. This detailed the technical and cost specifications that the product would have to meet, in order to meet the Product Description. Stevens required marketing to sign off on the Product Specification, certifying that there was a technical specification corresponding to each requirement in the Product Description. Similarly, Engineering had to sign off on the Product Description, as a double-check that marketing and engineering were synchronized.

4. Phase Definition   Stevens and Mahle defined a system of phases and project reviews, to which all projects would be subject. Projects started in a *business analysis phase*, in which the Product Description was written and the financial benefits of the project to Medtronic were estimated. Following review of the business case, the project would enter the *demonstration phase*. Here, the technological feasibility of the project was probed, to avoid putting the necessity of inventing something on the critical path of development program. Rapid prototyping was emphasized in this phase, to identify problems and possible solutions as quickly as possible. If a product idea required a technology that was not well developed, Medtronic would shelve the idea, preferring to wait until the approach had been developed and proven in other markets. The Product Specification was prepared during this phase, and consistency with the Product Description was verified.

The major executive review came after the demonstration phase, where the proposed product's technological potential, competitive activity and market needs, and its volume, profit and return on investment projections were rigorously reviewed. "I call this our *Commitment Review*," noted Mahle. "I believe that language conveys intent. We had been plagued by waffling and compromise, and weren't doing what we said we would do." At one commitment review on a critical product, in fact, Mahle asked the team to stand up and make a verbal pledge to deliver to the customers and patients what they had said they would. "I believe in the power of personal commitment. Management tools are important, but tools alone won't do it."

Following the commitment review, projects went into the *development, or commitment phase* of the process. "In the first two phases we have a lot of product ideas falling out or getting canceled, because we decide the market or technology just isn't there," Stevens commented. "But once projects enter the commitment phase, we expect 100% of them to be technically and commercially successful. There is no narrowing of the funnel after that."

The Product Planning Team, which as noted above was responsible for establishing the product line architecture, also had responsibility for conducting the major phase reviews for each project.

5. Rhythm   "There's a lot of uncertainty in new product development," noted Stevens. "You don't want to create additional uncertainty by the way you manage. The more predictability you can build into the development environment, the more productive your efforts will be." Stevens implemented this philosophy in two steps. First, he and Mahle fixed a date each month, a year in advance, when phase reviews would be held. Project teams approaching a review milestone thus could always count on Mahle and Stevens being available, to review their progress. Second, the management team established a schedule, far into the future, according to which new products would be developed and launched. "Of course we don't know what these specific products will be," said Stevens. "But we know the technology will always change, and we know the competition will always be trying to get ahead. It's like publishing a train schedule. It helps people to know when the next projects are scheduled to leave the station."

In retrospect, one benefit of setting a "train schedule" in advance was that there was less clamoring amongst Medtronic's marketers to revise objectives to include additional functionality or features after projects had begun. "In our troubled days," recalled Mahle, "No one knew when the next project was going to be started, let alone finished. Because of this, whenever a competitor came out with something, or an important physician came up with an important new idea, our marketing people were desperate to revise the charter of the product currently under development, to include that feature. If they didn't get it on this train, when would they ever get it? Once we had a train schedule, they could relax. If we froze the spec and their feature or idea didn't make it on this one, they knew that in another 18–24 months, another train would be leaving the station, and they could get their idea on that one."

6. Market Inputs   Medtronic also systematized the ways in which the company got input from customers, by revitalizing two eight-person physician review boards which had previously been functioning but which had lost their impact on company policy, for each of Medtronic's pacemaker lines. These boards met twice each year to give inputs on the performance of existing models, and suggest what functionality and features the company might incorporate in new models. "A big challenge with these boards," noted Paula Skjefte, was that "There is a strong tendency just to have experts on our boards. Life would be easier if we did that, but we wouldn't be getting the whole picture. Joe Average Cardiologist only spends about 2% of his practice on pacemakers. He's just not interested in spending a whole day on our board advising us about pacemakers. We want to be able to satisfy all the customers, from the experts who want do their own programming, to the cardiologists who just want to get the pacemaker going with no hassle. Taking the pulse of the less demanding end of the market is actually a huge challenge." Once these boards were properly constituted and functioning, they became critical to Medtronic's ability to define the right pacing systems to meet clinical and customer needs.

Results to Date

The result of the Medtronic team's efforts to put discipline into the Brady Pacing Division's product development operations have been remarkable, as summarized in Exhibits 2 and 4. The time required to develop new platform products was reduced by 75% between 1986 and 1996. Fully allocated product cost per unit fell 30%. Manufacturing defects per million units dropped by a factor of 4; and the number of field failures over the life of an implant dropped by 90%. And the company's share of the Brady Pacemaker market increased from 29% in 1986, to 51% in 1996. Medtronic was the leader in every segment of the market.

From July 1995 to July 1996, Medtronic replaced 100% of its products with new models. It was able to access every segment of the market, and became the highest-volume competitor in each—with ten derivative products built around a single platform technology.

"What's interesting," Paula Skjefte observed, "is now to see some of our competitors doing the same thing as we did in the past. There is a vicious cycle that almost got us, and is starting to hurt them. It looks like this: 1. When their share starts to decline, they start arguing over what needs to be done and how to do it. They start more and more projects into the system, to placate these diverse opinions. 2. Because they aren't focused, it causes delays, and Medtronic gets its product out first. 3. They have to redirect their project to respond to our product, which slows them down. 4. They panic because we are getting way ahead, and try to make sure that the flagship product they are trying to launch has all the features and functions that will boost it ahead of the competition. 5. This takes even longer—forcing them either to introduce products that are not functionally competitive, or to rush something into the market that is potentially faulty, just to get something out there. 6. The effect of this is that they spend all the money requires to develop and launch products, but it is wasted because it does not generate profitable revenue."

Stevens added, "People ask us what the secret is, to make a development organization work effectively. I tell them there aren't any magic bullets that kill the problems. It's just discipline. You need to do what you say needs to be done. You need to be in it for the long haul, There are no quick fixes. It's interesting how many people leave these conversations and then go off in search of an easier answer from some guru somewhere. It's amazing that the obvious isn't so obvious."

EXHIBIT 4	IMPROVEMENTS IN NEW PRODUCT DEVELOPMENT PERFORMANCE AT MEDTRONIC, 1986–1996

Year	Platform Name	Time* req'd to develop platform	# of derivative models designed from this platform	Fully allocated manufacturing cost* per unit	Manufacturing defects* per million units	Manufacturing throughput time (days)
1986	Activitrax	160	1	140		30
1987						
1988						
1989						14
1990				120		
1991						
1992	Elite	140	1			
1993					270	
1994				110	150	8
1995	Thera	100	41	100	100	7

NOTE: To protect the company's proprietary interests, numbers in the third, fifth and sixth columns, whose headings are denoted by an asterisk (*), are indexed, where 1995=100.

Challenges for the Future

Success brought a new set of challenges to the Medtronic team, however. Internally, it was becoming clear that the job of changing company practices and culture would never be finished. Stevens noted, for example, that Medtronic's career path system constituted one of the most vexing challenges to implementing improvements. "When your best people are moving on every two or three years, you can never just sit back and say, 'It's working.' Because we're always losing the people we've trained, the understanding of what we're doing and why we're doing it has a very short half-life. We have to keep training and teaching and coaching. I suppose that someday these values and processes will become so ingrained that working this way will just be a part of our culture. But we sure aren't there yet. And probably by the time it gets deeply ingrained here, we'll need to unlearn this because something even better has come along."

"The new marketing challenges are formidable as well," Skjefte remarked. "We've always measured the performance of our products in terms of their therapeutic benefit—the extent to which the pacemaker can mimic the normal functioning of the heart's electrical system. Now we have dual chamber pacemakers whose rate varies with the patient's activity, whose batteries have a life far longer than the life expectancy of most implant recipients. Fifteen years ago pacemakers were not programmable. Today, our most advanced models have 200 parameters, which can be reprogrammed non-invasively using RF (radio frequency) technology. Today our models can sense and store all kinds of data about irregularities and other abnormal events in a patient's heart. Doctors can download this data with RF technology, simply by placing a device near the patient's chest. How much more do we need? I worry that we're getting to the point that "better" will no longer be valued as "better" by the mainstream cardiologists. How do you develop a stream of improved products if customers are genuinely happy with the performance and features in the products that they have today? In the future we'll need to change the rules of the game. We've got to figure out how to add value in different ways."

"Catching up to competitors was a very different challenge than it is now, to stay a generation *ahead* of them—because now we're the ones needing to define what the product generations must be," Don Deyo added.

Fortunately for Medtronic, experts continued to forecast strong growth for the pacemaker market into the foreseeable future, thanks to the bulge in the population most likely to need pacemakers created by the aging of the relatively prosperous "baby boom" generation in Western Europe, Japan and North America. In addition to this growth, the large potential markets for pacemakers in other parts of Asia, Latin America and Eastern Europe, where economic growth was making advanced medical technology more affordable, defined even greater growth possibilities. This was especially true if the price of pacemakers (currently priced between $2,000 and $7,500, depending upon features and functionality) could be reduced significantly.

It also appeared in 1996 that the industry's competitive landscape had stabilized. Whereas 15 firms had entered the world pacemaker industry between 1965 and 1980, by 1996 only five of them remained. Medtronic claimed half of the market; St. Jude Medical (formerly Siemens) held 23%; Sulzer Intermedics 11%; and Guidant (recently divested by Eli Lilly) and Biotronik, a German firm focusing primarily in developing regions of the world, each accounted for 8%). Though several of these competitors were reeling from the rapid pace of product development that Medtronic had set, they were capable companies with substantial financial depth. In North America in particular, efforts of managed care providers to purchase larger volumes from fewer, highly capable suppliers with broad product lines, had substantially raised the barriers to future would-be entrants into the industry.

"We've set some very different goals," added Steve Mahle. "We want to bring pacing to less developed countries. This will be a challenge to Medtronic, because our culture won't allow us to bring them substandard therapy just to make it affordable. We've got to find a way to bring them *appropriate* therapy at an affordable price. This will likely involve *very* advanced technology, and a massive effort at physician education. And we've got to figure out how to do all of this profitably.

"In developed countries, where we do 95% of our volume, our goal is to see that every patient has access not just to pacemaking therapy, but to *optimum* therapy—where the technology in their pacemakers is matched to their disease. For example, ten years ago only 30% of patients were receiving dual chamber pacemakers. Today we're at 50%, but 70% really need them. This requires that we no longer just sell devices," Mahle continued. "We have to educate physicians, and help insurance providers understand that they should reimburse patients for devices that provide optimum therapy.

Skjefte described another dimension of the marketing challenge: "Now that we've taken the technological lead, we've got to work much more closely with our customers to understand how to make *them* more successful and profitable by using our products. This means not just the *physician* customers—cardiologists, electrophysiologists and surgeons—but hospital management, payors and buying groups.

Helping these customers become more profitable by using Medtronic devices loomed as a huge challenge, because the priority each placed on various aspects of a pacing system was different, and because the customers themselves often weren't structured to understand what was profitable for them. As an example, Medtronic had recently lost a major account, the Intermountain Cardiology Clinic in Salt Lake City, to a competitor which had undercut Medtronic's pacemaker price by nearly $1,000 per device. Although the Medtronic device was easier to program as the pacemaker was being installed, those responsible for maximizing the profitability of the clinic's "cath lab" (the operating room where pacemakers were implanted) determined that they would nonetheless maximize the cath lab's profitability by using the less expensive pacemaker.

The follow-up of patients with newly implanted pacemakers at this clinic was managed by a different out-patient profit center, however, and for *them*, use of the competing pacemaker proved much *more* expensive. All new pacemakers required some adjustments a few weeks after implantation, to address unique aspects of each patient's disease and lifestyle. Because Medtronic's product recorded data about the patient's heart functions within the pacemaker itself and allowed physicians to download and analyze this data and adjust the pacemaker easily through an RF device held close to the patient's chest, all necessary adjustments could be done in a single, 30-minute visit. The competitor's system, in contrast, required the patient to visit the out-patient clinic twice for adjustments, taking approximately 1.5 hours per visit. In addition, during the time between these visits (about two weeks) the patient had to carry a $500 "holter monitor" on his or her belt 24 hours per day, which recorded the heart functions as detected by a set of electrodes taped to the patient's chest. These additional monitoring and adjustment costs overwhelmed the money saved by purchasing the cheaper pacemaker. But because the savings and added expenses were incurred within two different profit centers of the clinic, it took enormous effort for Medtronic's salesforce to win back the business.

"These customers not only speak a different language than our traditional physician customers, but their knowledge and preferences are very heavily influenced by what pieces of the therapeutic puzzle they have responsibility for. Somehow we've got to restructure our sales and marketing teams to better understand and address their concerns."

Appendix: The Cardiac Pacemaker

Rhythmic contractions of the heart which pump blood through the body are stimulated by electrical impulses from the nervous system. Cardiac pacemakers either supplement or entirely replace the heart's own malfunctioning electric system. The heart contains four chambers—the right body and left atria (singular: atrium) and the right and left ventricles. Blood flows from the veins of the body into the right atrium where it collects, and then is pumped into the right ventricle. The blood is pumped from the right ventricle to the lungs to obtain oxygen, and is then pumped into the left ventricle. The blood, now refreshed with oxygen, is then pumped from the left ventricle through arteries to all parts of the body.

To initiate the proper sequence of contractions, a normal electrical impulse originates in the sinoatrial (SA) node in the right atrium. This impulse then spreads throughout both atria and stimulates atrial contraction. The electrical signal continues on to the ventricles through the atrioventricular (AV) node which delays the signal approximately 1/10 of a second to allow for the ventricles to fill with blood. When the ventricles complete their contraction, the signal is initiated once again in the SA node, creating a steady rhythm of heart beats.

Heart conditions necessitating a cardiac pacemaker can result from malfunction in any stage of this electrical system. Problems usually arise within the SA node and/ or the AV conduction pathways, resulting in a slow, fast, or irregular heart rhythm. When the SA node malfunctions, the proper electrical impulses will not be generated to contract the atria and the ventricles at correct intervals. Patients with this condition suffer from Sinus Bradycardia: Their hearts beat at a persistently slow rate. When the AV node and its neurological pathways malfunction, the electrical signal that has just stimulated atrial contraction is blocked from initiating ventricle contraction. Consequently, a patient suffering from atrioventricular blockage would have a normal atrial beat but the ventricular rate would be too slow.

As diagrammed below, the main body of the pacemaker is called the pulse generator, comprised primarily of electrical circuitry and the battery. An insulated wire called the lead connects this circuitry to the inside wall of one of the heart's chambers. The electrical impulse is created by the pulse generator and then delivered to the heart's muscle through the lead.

The first pacemakers employed a single-chamber system: They had one lead which was attached to the right ventricle. These devices paced the heart at a fixed rate (usually 70 to 80 beats per minute), independently of the heart's intrinsic rhythm and changes in body activity. Because the heart and the implantable pacemaker were operating independently, the pacing was called "asynchronous."

The next generation of single-chamber pacemakers, which Medtronic invented in the mid-1960s, paced the heart on "demand," meaning that if the heart beat on its own, the pacemaker did not send a pacing impulse to the heart.

In 1981, Intermedics Corporation, an industry entrant whose founders included several former Medtronic employees, introduced the first dual-chamber pacemaker. This design utilized two leads—one in the right atrium and one in the right ventricle, which could sense and record the activity of both chambers and make sure that their contractions were synchronized. The dual-chamber pacemaker was capable of varying the heart rate by sensing or "tracking" atrial activity and then pacing the ventricle accordingly. Synchronizing atrial-ventricular contractions afforded the patient more flexibility in activity.

THE CARDIAC PACEMAKER

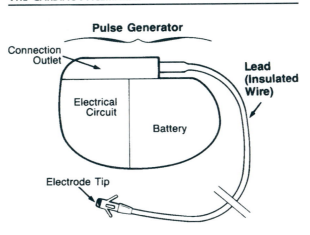

Pacemakers were implanted beneath the patient's skin near the heart, in a relatively simple proceedure. Immediately prior to implantation, most pacemakers were placed in a programming device which typically sat on a table in the cath lab or operating room where the implantation was performed. This allowed the physician to program the firmware in the pacemaker so that the frequency of the pulses it generated and a number of other attributes of the device, could be tailored to the needs of each individual patient.

The lead on the single-chamber design was implanted into the right ventricle relatively easily. Attaching the lead of the dual-chamber pacemaker, however, required much greater surgical skill, because the locations in the atrium were tricky to access, and attaching the lead to the smooth atrial chamber wall was difficult. This difficulty, coupled with its higher cost, had kept the dual chamber pacemaker's share of the total market at about 20% throughout the 1980s, despite its superior functionality. Device and procedural innovations in the 1990s had reduced these barriers, however, so that use of dual chamber devices became much more common.

Total Quality Logistics: Sales Force Management

David W. Rosenthal, Miami University

In June 2005, Ken Oaks, President, Debbie Strawser, Human Resources Director, and Kerry Byrne, Executive Vice President, sat in Total Quality Logistics' (TQL) conference room to discuss the company's sales management practices and organization. They expected the sales force to roughly double in size in the coming year and wanted to be prepared for that growth.

TQL offered freight brokerage services to companies that needed to send or receive shipments by truck. Its brokers were responsible for finding truck shipments or "loads," matching them with trucks, referred to as "carriers," and coordinating the entire process to make certain that the carriers picked up the loads and delivered them in good condition and on time.

Since Ryan Legg, CEO, and Ken Oaks had founded the company in Milford, Ohio, in 1997, it had grown to employ roughly 130 salespeople. The three executives were concerned that the sheer size of the firm could begin to erode the quality of service they provided. Kerry Byrne described the management team's thinking regarding the sales organization:

> What we really need is to break the sales organization down. It was 20 sales-people, then it was 40, then 60. It is really hard to push the accountability down; there is no one to push it to. It is too much for the high-level sales managers to cover, just too many people.

For much of the company's history Oak or Legg had maintained direct oversight of every broker. Although the company was still small, such direct management had become impossible. It was important to ensure that the salespeople continued to perform according to the company's best practices because the company relied on its reputation for integrity and outstanding service as differentiating features in the highly competitive freight brokerage field. (Exhibit 1 presents the company's sales organization.)

Reprinted by permission from the *Case Research Journal*. Copyright © 2007 by the *Case Research Journal* and David W. Rosenthal. All rights reserved.

I am grateful for the insightful comments and suggestions made by David Walsh, Brett Smith and Don Saunders of Miami University, and for the efforts of the reviewers and Editor of the *Case Research Journal*. Special thanks to the management and employees of Total Quality Logistics.

EXHIBIT 1 | **TOTAL QUALITY LOGISTICS, INC. SALES ORGANIZATION**

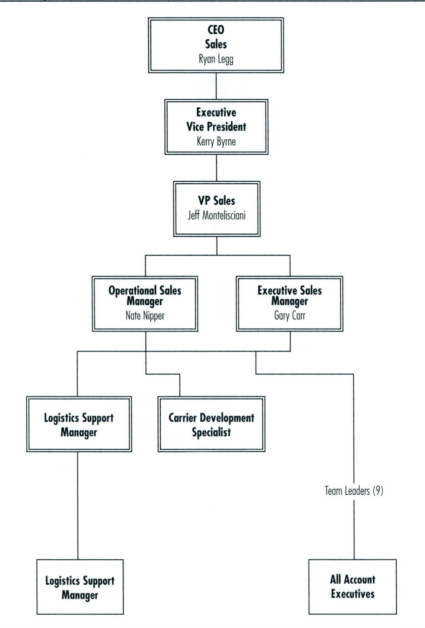

SOURCE: Company records

TQL's managers considered the availability of qualified employees, their training, support, and management to be the major constraints to the company's continued growth. Management expected company revenues to exceed $150 million in 2005. The number of employees was approaching 200, and they believed it was important to structure management practices and the organization of the sales force to lay the groundwork for even more growth.

Recently, the company had organized the brokers into nine teams, designating each with a color and assigning an experienced broker to oversee the team. However, the team leaders had not yet been assigned formal duties or responsibilities or given any formal authority. Today's meeting was to decide what, if any, formal structure the company would implement. One option was to establish a new layer of sales management, making the nine team leaders salaried managers. At the other end of the spectrum, they could decide that no changes were necessary at this time. Other options fell between the two extremes; for example, adding a smaller number of managers or creating specialized positions for training.

The Freight Brokerage Industry

Simply stated, freight brokers provided a service. They matched loads with carriers. For example, JTM Meats, a food processor in Cincinnati, might need to ship a truckload of frozen meats to the Jewel T supermarket distribution center in Chicago, Illinois. JTM would call and inform its TQL Account Executive (AE) that it had a shipment that would be ready at a certain time and needed to be delivered by a certain time. The AE would set a price for handling the shipment and then find a carrier who was willing and able to transport the load to Chicago in the allotted time. The AE would negotiate a fee for this service with the carrier. TQL earned its money by charging JTM Meats more than it cost TQL to contract with a carrier to make the delivery.

Once the carrier had delivered the shipment, the AE would likely be involved in arranging another load for the carrier to bring back to Cincinnati or some other destination. Shippers did not always have the time, expertise, or communications network to find the best carriers or to negotiate the best terms for a given load. Similarly, having delivered a load, a carrier could find itself with an empty truck, many miles from home, with no prospects for a new shipment.

Brokers created value for shippers and carriers by developing a network of contacts, making the appropriate connections, and negotiating rates that included a fee for their services.

The freight brokerage market was large and growing. Industry estimates were that third-party brokerage companies controlled approximately 20 percent ($50 billion) of the $255 billion truckload and less-than-truckload (LTL) freight market. The freight brokerage industry was highly fragmented; a broker was often simply an individual with a telephone, a computer, and the necessary personal relationships to connect a carrier and a load. Large companies such as C. H. Robinson had the advantage of offering international, inter-modal, warehousing, consulting, and other third-party logistics (3PL) services. Other firms often specialized by geographic region, type of freight (e.g., produce versus dry goods) or carrier (refrigerated or "reefer" versus liquid or bulk).

The trucking industry was similarly fragmented. Industry estimates indicated that there were more than 320,000 trucking companies in the U.S., of which 82 percent operated fewer than 20 trucks.

TQL's Background

Ken Oaks and Ryan Legg met in 1990. Ken was a buyer and selling agent for the Castellini Company, a Cincinnati-based produce wholesaler, and Ryan was a freight broker with RWI, a Castellini subsidiary.

Oaks described his start and the motivation for founding TQL:

Ryan and I talked all the time about starting our own thing, whatever it would be, mainly because we were both selling and we weren't making commission. We were both doing great at selling and every year our numbers were way up, but we didn't feel that we were being compensated properly. We loved our jobs and the business, and we finally decided that there was definitely room for more people in this industry.

Legg elaborated:

I used to give a lot of freight to freight brokers and I had a terrible time with them. I'd visit them and see that their business was successful but I often found that they gave horrible service and they just weren't very ethical. You couldn't get hold of them on weekends and they didn't really follow up to make sure the truck and shipment actually arrived on time, but they were still doing business. Ken agreed, and that's when he said, "Well, I know we can do that." We decided that being on the customer side, we knew what they expected, and we weren't getting that service.

The company had revenue of $1 million in 1997, which was a little more than Legg and Oaks had expected in their first year. Revenue jumped 48 percent from 2001 to 2002, to $32 million, which was sufficient for TQL to be named the fastest growing Tri-State (Ohio, Kentucky, Indiana) private company, according to Cincinnati Business Courier research. The company expected to double the number of employees from 170 (2004) to 350 (2005). Revenue reached nearly $50 million in 2003 and over $100 million for 2004. (See Exhibit 2 and Exhibit 3.)

EXHIBIT 2 | **TQL EMPLOYEE GROWTH***

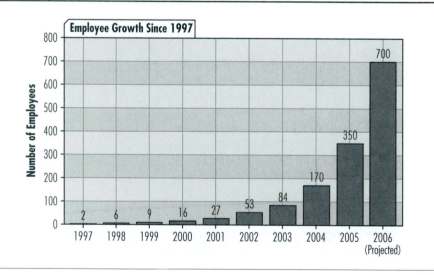

SOURCE: Company records.

*2005 entry is anticipated number at year-end.

EXHIBIT 3 | **TQL REVENUE GROWTH***

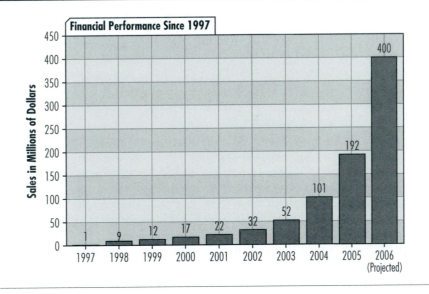

SOURCE: Company records.

*2005 entry is anticipated number at year-end.

The company had over 1,000 customers including Fortune 500 companies such as Wal-Mart, Super Valu, Kroger, Fleming, Conagra, Sara Lee, Publix supermarkets, Spartan stores and Chiquita. Customers also included small and medium-sized businesses such as JTM Food Group, Gilardi Foods, Hillshire Farms and Kahns. The company contracted for a wide variety of loads ranging from frozen dinners, produce, and general commodities to heavy equipment and lumber. TQL brokered shipments to and from the 48 contiguous states plus Canada and Mexico.

The TQL Advantage

TQL's founders believed its competitive advantage stemmed from three factors.

Honesty

The owners attributed the company's growth to hard work and an emphasis on honesty. "Reputation is everything in this line of work, so we do absolutely everything possible to keep ours," said Oaks. "There are lots of unethical people in this industry. They'll over promise, saying that a truck will be there in a couple hours when they have no idea where it is."

The company had formalized its commitment to maintaining an excellent reputation by establishing its **"Five Winning Principles"**:

1. **Pledge integrity.**
   Commit to the highest ethical standards, and don't compromise them. Ethical and professional behavior is the bedrock of our company.

2. **Exceed expectations.**

   Seek to achieve not only what is asked, but also use creativity to provide solutions above and beyond what is expected. There is little traffic on the extra mile.

3. **Recognize the value of teamwork.**

   Fidelity to a team ethic results in personal achievements beyond one's individual capabilities and respects differences among individuals. The only way we can be the one-stop source providing the best overall service for our clients is to pool the talents of our people.

4. **Be forthright about conflict.**

   Inform clients of real or perceived conflicts. Always choose the harder right over the easier wrong.

5. **Maintain balance in life and business.**

   To be our most productive, we must maintain a healthy balance among our priorities for clients, family, faith, community, and self.

Evidence of the company's commitment to its reputation was also clear in a number of industry ratings and certifications that noted TQL as being in the top one percent of all companies registered in integrity, pay practices, and credit worthiness, and as having the best practices among logistics industry members.

Access and Communication

Prior to founding TQL, Legg and Oaks found it difficult to get a straight answer from brokers, and that brokers were often unavailable when needed most. At TQL, dispatchers took calls through nights, weekends and holidays, and the company expected brokers to be on call for a customer at all times. The company's ability to deal with problems quickly had helped it land one of its major customers, JTM Food Group. In 2000, JTM Director of Distribution Paul Burton received a cold call from Oaks on a day when Burton needed help. "I had had problems moving some loads, and he made that the most important part of his day," Burton said. "I started him out with a problem, and he solved it." Burton was so impressed that he used the company as JTM's major freight broker, to the tune of about $1 million of business annually.

A conversation with one of TQL's freight brokers in a rare off-the-phone moment amplified the founders' perspective:

At TQL, a customer gets a one-on-one relationship with their broker. They know they are going to talk to the same guy, every time. If they have a question, they are going to call my cell phone and they know that I am going to be available 24–7–365. I am personally responsible for any problems with a customer's load. Every load has a specific broker, a person, attached to it. Loads are not let out to a group of dispatchers like you might find at a large trucking company, where if you have a problem you would first have a hassle just to find the person responsible for that piece of business. With TQL, you know who you are dealing with, every time. That allows us to get to know the customer, and their specific needs and the little details of providing the best service to them. For example, I might know that the load is supposed to be there by 9:00 a.m., but if I get it there just a few minutes early, I can get off-loaded immediately rather than having to wait. That is good for everybody.

We communicate with everyone in the channel. We offer 24/7 dispatch to make sure your truck is on the road. We make "check calls" every morning between 8:00 and 9:00 a.m. so that we know where every shipment is. We have cell phone numbers for every driver. We are going to make sure that load gets there on time and in good shape if it is humanly possible. And if it isn't, you are going to know about it ahead of time.

Carrier Business Practices

As a brokerage company, TQL dealt with customers and with carriers as well. TQL management considered the relationships with the carriers from dispatcher all the way to the individual truck drivers to be as important as their relationships with their customers. Oaks commented:

> From experience on the truck side, we know how to treat truckers and drivers. A lot of brokers talk very badly to drivers, and that's another part of the business that you've got to take care of.

> On the Load Program it will show the history we have with them, how many loads we've done, and what their on-time percentage is. (The Load Program was the company's custom database that included data on all carriers and customers served by TQL. The Load Program was a sophisticated customer relationship management system that kept track of all contact information, history of transactions, pricing, payments, call data, performance measures, credit ratings, locations, broker assignments, and other pertinent comments and conditions.)

The Load Program software required certain fields for each transaction, and therefore controlled the information generated and the activities of the sales force. The records generated by the Load Program were used to document contracts, to account for payments and commissions, for reference in case of claims, and for research and analysis. Every transaction was recorded in the Load Program. Further, no carrier not certified by management could be used by a broker, and all of the certified carriers were listed in the Load Program, along with the necessary contact information.

Legg added:

> The carriers' dispatchers decide whether to take a load or not. It is based on the money, what we're paying on the load, where it's going, and probably the commodity. They also look at our history with them, and how quick we've paid the company.

> Here's an example of something unethical brokers will do. They'll have a load picked up on Friday to be delivered Tuesday. The run is only two days long, but the receiver can't unload it until Tuesday—and the broker knows that. Well, they don't tell the carrier this, so the trucker is expecting to drop it on Sunday or first thing Monday. So, Saturday or Sunday the broker will call the carrier and say, "Gosh, they don't have enough room until Tuesday!" But it's

already on a truck and, the truck is already almost there. The trucker says, "You need to pay me $250 for the extra time and labor!" But the broker says, "Well, I can't do that, but I'll give you $50." The driver maybe had plans to go home, or had to reload for one of their best customers, and they would never, ever have taken that load to deliver on Tuesday. We don't do that.

Ken and I realized from the very beginning how important carriers are, and a lot of brokers don't. They think they'll just find another truck. Well, in this day and age, there are credit agencies and if you treat carriers wrong it'll catch up to you. Money is a big thing with the carriers, particularly the smaller firms. They don't have a lot of cash or credit, many times, so they need to be paid immediately. A good, ethical broker would pay in 20–30 days, but on average it would probably be 45 days before the carrier would get paid. But we pay all of our trucks right away up until 21 days. Plus, after they pick up a load we'll advance them 40 percent of the fee for fuel or costs. Some brokers will not do that. If they break down on the side of the road and need money for a tire, we'll give them an advance on the load.

And, it is not just the credit. If you have a carrier that has 40 trucks running our lanes (routes), and we treat them right and talk to their drivers and are personal with the drivers, they're going to want to haul for us. Truck drivers talk to people all day on the road, and if they like someone they're going to tell the dispatcher they want to haul for them. The dispatchers want their drivers to be happy, so if a dispatcher gets a load from a broker who treated a driver badly, they're not going to haul for them. And we want drivers to haul for us. You want a great relationship with CEOs of our customers, but we treat truck drivers the same way.

The Selling Task

Four elements made up the selling task: customer acquisition, finding a carrier, rate negotiation, and project management.

Customer Acquisition

The broker position at TQL was almost entirely comprised of telephone sales. Brokers identified potential customers, researched them—often on-line or through industry references—and made cold calls to introduce TQL and solicit loads. Once a broker had identified and contacted a potential customer, the account was "protected" for a 90-day period, after which it became open for other brokers to call, unless the original broker had been successful in generating a load. If a load had been forthcoming, the broker kept that account permanently.

The prospecting phase of the selling process often took multiple calls just to break through and have a conversation with the person responsible for truck shipments. Decision makers at shippers could receive as many as 40–50 calls per day from competing sales people asking for their freight business. The initial contact call involved qualifying the customer for truckload shipments, type of freight, etc., and then sending the TQL Customer Packet, which included information on TQL certifications, insurance, practices, and accomplishments. A few days later, the broker would contact the customer again, and begin asking for loads. It often took as many as 20 calls before a first-time customer would agree to ship with TQL. Most often, however, the first shipment would occur as the result of a customer emergency.

Legg described the customer acquisition process:

> They'll look at our rates, and usually when they give us a shot it'll be when they're in a bind. They're not going to say, "Okay, here's some business." It takes some time to build rapport; probably five or ten phone calls. You do the typical sales routine to let them know you are available and interested in them, and usually it's an afternoon when a truck falls out on them (can't make a pick up), and they'll call us. That's how you get your foot in the door. Beautiful thing about this business, there are always problems.

> Once we get in the door, they won't take away all of the business from the competitor and give it to us, but they'll keep us in the loop. If that guy got ten loads a week, now they're getting nine and we're getting one. Then it's up to the broker to keep calling, and to provide better communication, better service, and more attention to gain a greater share.

Finding Carriers

The broker's second focus involved finding trucks to handle the freight on specific lanes. Legg described the firm's treatment of truckers:

> We actually deal with (carriers) from JB Hunt, huge, to a guy who has two trucks. But what we do with those guys as far as services, we treat them the way we would want to be treated. We don't lie to them, we don't mislead them. We tell them this is the deal, either I know or I don't know, no maybes or gray areas, all black and white.

> We have our primary carriers, the guys we use day in and day out, with whom we have built rapport. We've done business with them, we know the drivers, we know how they perform. We're probably talking to them just as much as a customer. We go to them first. We know they'll be on top of it. If they can't handle it then we'll go to our secondary carriers. We still know everything is fine, we just don't talk to them every day.

A variety of industry conditions had combined over the previous three years to limit the availability of trucks. New regulations limited the number of hours drivers could spend on the road. Weakness in the economy and fuel price increases had driven less profitable trucking firms out of business. TQL brokers generally believed that the major constraint to growth on a day-to-day basis was finding more trucks. Company policy required that top managers evaluate all carriers before brokers could use them. Once managers certified carriers, the Load Program listed them as available for use.

Rate Negotiation

There were considerable variances in the prices charged to customers and in the payments made to carriers. Lanes that easily supported consistent front-haul and back-haul opportunities permitted lower payments to truckers. Length of haul played a role as well.

Commodity type also affected pricing. Because of its perishability, produce generated high shipping costs and high carrier payments. Contracts, ongoing relationships, timing, availability of trucks, and a myriad of other factors all played into the negotiations and price setting. On average, however, a load resulted in about $2,000 cost to the shipper. Industry estimates were that brokers earned about a 7–10 percent gross margin, although TQL generally tried to maintain somewhat higher margins because of its service levels.

TQL brokers were effectively in charge of their own pricing. Stories abounded about taking a load for a shipper below the trucking cost in order to gain a new customer, or to remind an established customer of the value of dealing with TQL. Similarly, if there had been a problem with an earlier shipment, a broker might quote a low price as a "make good." Similarly, a broker might pay a carrier a greater-than-normal fee to entice them to take an unattractive load, or to make up for a previous problem. In the long run, however, the brokers tried to strike a balance based on fairness, quality service, and mutually beneficial relationships.

Project Management

The fourth part of the selling task involved monitoring the load. Brokers were in contact with drivers at least twice a day, and often more, keeping track of the pickup, progress along the route, conditions of the truck and load. They also provided directions, and relayed information to customers and receivers as needed. Effectively, each load was a "project" and the broker played the role of "project manager" to assure a satisfactory conclusion. Oaks described the company's dedication to service:

> While our prices are often higher than our competitors', we can save customers money—not on the transaction but on the efficiency. We save the time of the guys at the warehouse in loading and unloading. If we say our truck is going to be there at three, it is going to be there at three o'clock, or else you get a call way before three letting you know it's going to be there at four. So, we keep in contact with the drivers and dispatchers the whole time, and make sure we know exactly what is going on so we can get the information to the customer. That way, they won't be throwing their money out the window for labor or whatever.

The Broker (Account Executive) Position

The Account Executive (AE), or broker, was the key player in TQL's business. Account Executive Trainees (AETs) received training on company policy, use of the Load System, and some general selling guidelines and principles, including the number of daily calls TQL expected them to make (120). After the initial training phase, which consisted of about two weeks, each AET began working with a specific AE. AETs assisted in managing that AE's customer base, prospecting, communicating with customers, tracking truck locations, and coordinating pickups and deliveries.

The "apprenticeship" the AETs served under their respective AEs was an important training stage. AETs worked closely with their AEs and learned by doing. The AEs provided close supervision because their actual accounts and carrier relationships were on the line. The relationships were usually close and supportive, and by the time the AET was ready to strike out on his/her own, he/she had developed a good working knowledge of the business, critical relationship-building skills with carriers and customers, problem-solving abilities, and a network of colleagues upon whom they could call for advice or assistance.

Once AEs reached a certain sales level, the company assigned an assistant. As AEs attained higher levels of sales, additional assistants joined their teams. The team grew as sales warranted. Some salespeople had teams of seven or more and earned over $600,000 a year themselves. Generally, assistants and trainees handled the carrier procurement and some project management sides of the brokerage task, leaving the cold calling, solicitation of loads, and customer relationship building to the AEs. Experienced AEs generally spent about 40 percent of their time on solicitation of loads and relationship building with existing accounts, another 40 percent on project management and problem resolution, and ten percent each on prospecting new accounts and carrier procurement. New AEs often spent 90 percent of their time cold calling new accounts for loads.

Over the years, some AETs had found that they were more skilled at finding trucks and managing the relationships with carriers than at developing loads. Other skilled candidates had been uncomfortable with the uncertainty of entirely commission-based compensation. As a result, the company had created the Logistics Coordinator (LC) position. An LC supported an AE by selling loads to carriers, negotiating, tracking, updating information, managing calls, and solving problems on the carrier side of the business. LCs worked with specific AEs and were included as an integral part of their team. The company generally paid LCs straight salary, but they could also earn bonuses based on team performance.

Recruitment and Selection

The characteristics the company sought in a candidate included: PC skills, typing, exceptional phone skills, teamwork skills, written and verbal communication skills, organization, customer service orientation, sense of urgency, attention to detail, a strong work ethic (giving 110 percent at all times), dependability, focus, ability to multi-task, strong determination, and an entrepreneurial spirit.

Oaks expressed the desired attitude through an email provided to trainees:

> If you asked me how Ryan and I became so successful so fast, I would reply as follows: In the beginning, we were in early, we worked late every night, we worked all day Saturday and part of Sunday (and that was just selling, we did the billing after that). We were there when no other brokers were. We called prospects multiple times all through the day until 7:00 p.m. We were in calling our prospects every Saturday and Sunday to see if anyone else fell out on them and, if so, we stayed until we got them covered. We were willing to do whatever it took to get business established. We never missed work because we were a little sick, and would have missed only if we were extremely sick. The customers and prospects were amazed at our dedication to them, and we built relationships. We built our base and then expanded it from there.
>
> Now it is up to you.
>
> If you think getting established is easy, you are mistaken. It takes incredibly hard and long work. Ask Jeff M., Nathan, Mike N., Royce, Tony, David, Fuhrman

and others—they have mirrored our ways. This is also how they became successful so quickly. They were in your shoes once. They are no smarter than you. Pay your dues, especially in the beginning, if you want to excel.

Over the years, we have had to let a few salespeople go, and they all shared one common belief—they just weren't having any luck getting accounts. They failed to realize that luck has nothing to do with success. These individuals did not go the extra mile to build a customer base. Nobody ever saw them on a Saturday when they were not scheduled to work, and rarely were they here after 5:00 p.m. or before 8:00 a.m. during the week. Success doesn't "happen," it is a result of hard work, perseverance, and dedication. Make your own bed.

One more thing: The successful people did not ever, ever make excuses such as, "I'm getting offered loads and can't get trucks cheap enough," or, "I'm so depressed because I can't get sales." They never had time to feel sorry for themselves because they were constantly on the phone hustling, **doing it!**

In its recruiting literature, the company claimed "TQL Only Hires the Best of the Best" and indicated that a "target potential candidate for TQL possesses one or more of the following:"

Background in sports (college preferable)	Sales experience
Military "special forces" background	Leadership experience
Transportation/Logistics background	College experience (degree)
Former traffic manager	Strong work ethic
Former dispatcher	Hunger for success

The company recruited primarily from local and regional colleges through an established network of contacts among faculty members and career placement offices. It also solicited candidates from employees and advertised open positions in local and regional media.

The recruitment and selection process consisted of five phases. Candidates submitted a resume and an HR manager interviewed them via telephone. In this call, the interviewer asked the candidate to sell something. Interviewers were reportedly almost combative in this process. TQL required multiple letters of recommendation. Candidates had to pass a geography test (naming all 50 states on a map) with 100 percent accuracy. Candidates had a short time to develop a list of potential customers and to provide statistics on the trucking industry. Lastly, they visited the facility to interview in person. A committee comprised of Legg, Oaks, and Vasseur conducted nearly all interviews and had to come to a consensus to make an offer.

The management team believed that the five-phase process did a good job of weeding out weak candidates, and preparing those chosen for the tasks inherent in the AE position. The telephone interview tested selling and communication skills, telephone demeanor, and assertiveness. The letters of recommendation required diligence and timeliness. The geography test focused on learning shipping lanes. The research assignment also required a timely return and tested the candidate's ability to identify potential new business and to use appropriate research resources.

Management believed the company's four percent turnover rate, high levels of compensation, and growth were indicators that the hiring process was successful.

Compensation

AEs earned commission on the difference between the rates they negotiated with customers and carriers. For example, a customer might need a load delivered from St. Louis, Missouri, to Atlanta, Georgia. The AE for that account would negotiate a price and terms of the pickup and delivery, etc. If the shipping cost were $2,000, the AE might then negotiate a payment of $1,800 with a carrier. The AE would then receive a 30 percent commission on the $200 difference, for a total commission of $60.

AETs received a straight salary but had the goal of moving to commission-only compensation within a year, along with promotion to the AE position. TQL paid AE commissions equal to 30 percent of gross profit on loads, payable when the customer paid. The company could also charge an AE's commission account for 30 percent of any costs paid by TQL in the event of a customer bad debt or cargo claim not collected from the carrier. Recently, the company had cut the commission rate to 25 percent, but it continued to pay the old rate in some instances.

In 2003, ten out of 41 salespeople made over $100,000, and 22 of the 41 were new salespeople in 2003. The average sales executive commission among first-year brokers was $70,000, second year—$100,000, and third year—$115,000.

The benefits package was relatively standard and included a company cell phone, vacation, health insurance, dental coverage, life insurance, disability coverage, and retirement.

Physical Facilities

The company was growing rapidly, roughly doubling in size each year, and a year before, had moved into a new, 30,000 square foot facility in Milford, Ohio. In the intervening year, it had been necessary to double the size of the building, and the new extension had just opened a few weeks ago.

The new facilities were very different from the cramped conditions of the previous location. There, desks had been jammed into whatever space was available, and the place was dark, cramped, piled with files, records, and the accumulated junk of years.

The new building largely consisted of a vast, open expanse of waist-high dividers that did nothing to obstruct the view. Teams of brokers and assistants worked in "bays" around multiple phones and computer screens. The buzz of phone conversations, computer keyboards, and shared discussions across the maze was evidence of the rapid pace and high energy level.

The general atmosphere was light and open. Two sides of the rectangular space were glass, providing views of the surrounding countryside. The other two sides of the perimeter were comprised of offices for accounting, IT services, training rooms, meeting rooms, executive offices, a large lunchroom and even an exercise facility. Management specifically wanted to provide employees with amenities to make it easy for them to stay on site.

Sales Organization

As the company grew, Ryan Legg and Ken Oaks looked to senior AEs to take on additional responsibilities. On January 1, 2004, the company promoted Jeff Montelisciani to Vice President of Sales. He was the company's top salesperson at the time. His duties included the continued coverage of his major accounts, but also extensive travel in support of new customer development and ongoing customer support. Montelisciani traveled over half the time, and his customer visits were an important part of the process of gaining new, large accounts. Other brokers had the opportunity to get into the field and actually meet their customers only rarely. However, in a number of instances, the personal face-to-face interaction with Montelisciani or Legg had proved to be the difference in obtaining trial business from a customer. Montelisciani also was responsible for advising other AEs and for decisions when questions of policy or problem resolution occurred.

Nate Nipper was the company's top salesperson on September 13, 2004, when he was promoted to the position of Operational Sales Manager. Nipper was responsible for handling claims and insurance issues. The company handled all insurance claims as part of its "one-stop shopping" service. Essentially, TQL guaranteed that a customer's load would arrive on time and in good condition. If the carrier damaged or lost a load, TQL would pay the customer the load's value or the appropriate adjustment and would then seek redress from the carrier, insurance company, or other responsible party. This practice significantly reduced customer risk, and was another reason customers regarded TQL's service highly. However, it also added a great deal of potential risk exposure when TQL contracted to handle a load. As a result, the company was very careful about the carriers it used, the insurance the carriers had, and the value and types of loads it would accept. For example, the company would not accept a load of cigarettes because of the high value and the potential for loss. On matters related to the area of insurance, all AEs reported to Nipper.

Gary Carr was also one of the company's top ten AEs and had been with the company for a number of years when Legg and Oaks promoted him to the position of Executive Sales Manager on January 1, 2005. His combination of performance and long-standing relationships made him an obvious choice to become manager. Legg and Oaks had asked him to take on some of the sales management duties including providing input on hiring decisions, handling customer problems and issues beyond the abilities of less-experienced AEs, providing training, instruction, and mentoring. On maters related to general sales or sales management, all AEs reported to Carr.

Montelisciani, Nipper, and Carr all received a compensation mix of salary and bonuses. Their salaries were proportional with their prior level of sales commissions, and they could earn bonuses based on corporate attainment of income targets. Their new compensation plan allowed them to earn total pay that was consistent with their compensation levels as AEs.

Kerry Byrne had joined the company in March, 2005. He had been in client management with 5/3 Bank in Cincinnati for 15 years and had a background in both personal and corporate finance. He and Oaks had known each other since grade school. He had been instrumental in the construction of TQL's initial business and financial plans, and was a natural choice to join the company to contribute both financial and client service perspectives.

J. J. Blum had also been a top AE and rose to the position of Training Manager in summer 2004. He was responsible for the formal portion of the training program and for managing the Logistics Coordinators.

Discussion of an Additional Management Level

In late 2004, the management team had begun discussing the idea of creating a more formal sales management organization. The managers were concerned that the company was growing too large for the direct AE-management contact that had been the practice. While there were, as yet, no serious signs of weakening performance, the general consensus was that it was only a matter of time before sheer numbers made the current structure untenable.

By late January 2005, the management team had decided to experiment with the sales force structure by breaking the sales force into a number of teams. A "team captain" would head each team, and there would be a backup. Management had selected individuals who had shown leadership, who were successful, and who had "credibility on the floor" to fill the positions.

Management selected teams based on several factors including commodity focus and existing relationships. Several teams dealt exclusively with produce, others with mostly dry goods, and others mostly with frozen goods. One of the goals was to generate more interaction within teams. Organizing by commodity made sense because each commodity tended to use different types of trucks, and different lanes. TQL had also taken care to support natural groupings that already existed. For example, an AE who had a couple of assistants and a logistics coordinator would all be on the same team.

The initial team meetings took place in late February. Captains met with their team members to discuss the new structure and how the teams would work together. In addition, some captains suggested social gatherings, while others focused on team members coming to them with questions or problems.

By May, the experiment had been underway for over two months and Byrne, Strawser and Oaks met to discuss future steps the company would take in managing the sales force. Kerry Byrne summed up the purpose of the meeting:

> Up to now, the team concept has been a purely volunteer thing. Captains don't have formal responsibilities, and they don't receive any additional compensation. What we are trying to do is solidify this and create some structure that makes sense for us in going forward. The discussion is about what the actual job will look like. What do we think that we want them to do? How will we compensate them? Part of the problem is that the team captains still have their own individual books of business, and most of them are pretty successful. That makes it hard to continue paying them at their current levels if they stop selling in order to manage.

The existing managerial roles had evolved more or less on an "as needed" basis, and reflected specialized duties rather than day-to-day supervision. Oaks observed:

> The managers we have now are all specialized. Nate is great at taking claims, Gary is great at handling the scheduling and customer complaints and general supervision, Jeff is great at working on acquiring large, new customers. If we want to, we can bring someone up, possibly to take care of all the first-year guys, mentor those guys, and be the coach. We can't expect one guy to be able to be good at all of that. Why don't we just go ahead and do what we are doing; bring up guys, have them in charge of particular things, and still have the teams?

Debbie Strawser, Human Resources Director, was concerned, however, about the impact of growth and the increasing span of control. First, she was worried over training, both initial and ongoing.

> We have a lot of class work that first six months. The second six months we do one 4-hour class on prospecting and that is the only classroom piece they get. Sales is an area where I think you need some one-on-one, me sitting with you and saying, 'You know what, here's how you might have done that better.' We are doing some of that, but nobody has enough time to do as much as needs to be done. From six to twelve months, they are not getting enough direction. They are not getting enough mentoring.

Byrne agreed, and added his concern over the continuing development of experienced brokers:

> It is a basic sales management issue. How do we enhance productivity? And it is a big problem. With as many people as we have now, we are kind of throwing them out of the nest. They are off the training program and on their own, but they are not getting a lot of direction. It is just sink or swim. Can we provide some more coaching during that 6–12 month period? Also, there is the experienced $4,000 per week guy—how do we get him to $6,000 or $7,000? We *completely* ignore those folks because they are doing okay. At $4,000 and they have been here for a year and a half? They could probably do a whole lot better than that. We just haven't had the resources and the structure in place to have somebody spend time pushing them and coaching.

Oaks agreed that training should be a company focus, but was more concerned about ongoing mentorship and "developing the top folks." He had had a recent conversation with a friend on the subject. This friend pointed out the obvious math, "If you increase a guy who is doing $10,000 by 20 percent, what do you get? If you increase someone who is doing $4,000 by 20 percent what do you get?" Ken believed that the company practice of creating "manager specialists" should continue. However, he was concerned about who might fill a high-end training position, and the reception that person might receive. He concluded, "In fact, nobody here would be right for that spot."

Byrne supported that view:

> That's right, because this is a tough crowd. Their attitude would be, "this has to be the right person for me, somebody who has an understanding of the transportation industry." It has to be somebody with credibility.

Strawer's second concern was that the span of control was growing so large that managers could no longer handle their managerial functions effectively. The sheer volume of work created by the increasing numbers of account executives, trainees and logistics coordinators was becoming overwhelming. She had drafted a "job description" to point out the duties and responsibilities of a potential sales manager (Exhibit 4). In general, these tasks included involvement in recruiting and selection, evaluation and promotion of trainees, assignments of personnel and accounts, scheduling, monitoring adherence to policies, and some customer contact and support. She noted:

> I'm still worried about span of control. We are okay today, but I am worried that shortly we are going to get beyond a good span of control. As we get bigger, somehow we are going to have to divide it up a little. When we have 100 brokers out there, one person is not going to be able to handle it.

EXHIBIT 4 | **EXECUTIVE SALES MANAGER JOB DESCRIPTION**

(DRAFT)

Responsibilities include (but not limited to):

- Weekend and after hour shifts
- DAT/Transcore
- Cincinnati Reds tickets
- Phase five interviewer
- Sales interns and co-ops
- Sales meetings with brokers
- Role playing with assistants two weeks before they are approved to start cold calling
- Periodic fill in on sales trips with brokers
- Daily sales operations
- Monitor phone times of brokers
- Convention/associations coordinator involving customers
- Inactive customers: contact why no business
- Customer list/inactive prospects
- First delivered load/contact customer
- Customer contracts review
- Daily attendance
- Working on advertising options
- Customer rate confirmations (being turned in)

The following should be directed to the Executive Sales Manager, Gary Carr. (In case of absence contact Nate Nipper.)

- Carriers/customers asking for a manager
- Questions on lanes/rates/quotes
- Questions on after hour shifts
- All attendance issues: late, sick, weather, etc.
- Questions on inactive customers/prospects
- Any new customer/prospect calling in on customer service
- Problem carrier approval
- Waiving comcheck fees
- Cincinnati Reds ticket requests

SOURCE: Company records

Another issue was that of compensation. If the company created a new layer of management, the additional overhead would be a significant cost to the firm. Top performers who would be candidates for a management position simply earned so much in commission that the company could not afford to pay them at the same level for management duties. The time required to be a successful broker limited the ability to take on additional managerial roles at a significant level. Views on captains' compensation ranged from zero, to recognition, to travel incentives, to a $10,000 salary increment. One thought was to make this role a qualifying "stepping stone" to be promoted to the next "official" sales management position. There had been some discussion among the management about the need to create a "career path" for senior brokers, reflecting concern that over time brokers would "burn out" from their normal duties.

Conclusion

As the meeting ended, the three executives returned to their offices, to other meetings and responsibilities. Each considered the meeting to have been a good exchange of ideas, but they had finalized nothing. The questions were still on the table. Should they formalize the management function over the sales force, creating nine new management positions? If so, how should they pay the managers, and what would happen to their accounts? Should they maintain the informal "team captains" positions, and wait for the sales force to grow further before selecting a captain to move into a new position? Might they take a middle route and add a smaller number of managers, perhaps to deal with specific functions? Were there other things that they should change in their sales management system? For that matter, things were going so well, did they really need to do anything at all? They were all agreed on one thing, the company would continue to grow rapidly and they didn't want to be unprepared. Another meeting would be scheduled in a few weeks to continue the discussion and come to a consensus on a direction.

CASE

10

Telezoo (A): Feast or Famine?

Marie-Louise Murville heard a series of loud noises outside her offices on the Northern Virginia side of the Potomac River. As she peered out her office window, she saw fireworks erupting in a myriad of colors over the Washington and Jefferson monuments. Murville, the newly appointed vice president of marketing and business development at Telezoo, realized that she had forgotten Independence Day because she had been completely immersed in the preparation of her presentation for the upcoming board meeting. She sat and enjoyed the celebration's grand finale while pondering the fate of her own company. Would telezoo.com (Telezoo) fade into obscurity as another dot-com casualty or would it make an indelible impression on the procurement decision-making process in telecommunications?

The company had recently burned through a significant amount of capital with a limited positive return on investment. In addition, as recently as April 2000, the capital markets had come to reject the hype initially given to Internet stocks. Although the founding team had accomplished a great deal, they and the board understood from the beginning that to maximize the company's potential, seasoned general management, marketing, sales, and finance executives would need to join the company. Ideally, a CEO would be hired first to build the team, but as the market exuberance faded, and the sources of fresh investment capital dried up, Telezoo faced a dilemma. A seasoned CEO would only join a startup that had plenty of cash in the bank; yet, new investors would only be interested in companies with full management teams already in place. Murville had been working closely with the management team and the board for six months as a venture capitalist. Despite the increasingly critical cash/market changes, she decided to join the risky startup, a choice that provided the necessary executive skills and gave reassurance to both a prospective CEO and investors that Telezoo was a wise investment. Once on board, Murville immediately began assessing the situation. She was intent on developing new product and marketing strategies that would allow Telezoo to better allocate its limited resources and realize its dream.

Murville first envisioned the use of the Internet for B2B e-commerce in researching and writing her 1994 London Business School master's thesis on electronic catalog sites and services. The thesis was developed around the time Mosaic was introduced and before Netscape was conceived. Six years later, she now had an opportunity to implement her original vision. Although she was certain about the fundamental business model, she was not at all sure how to turn the compelling value proposition into revenue and profits.

Company History

Telezoo.com was formed in October 1998 by the husband-and-wife team of Elias Shams and Sharmine Namazi-Narwani. Shams had invested his share of the proceeds from the sale of Yurie Systems to Lucent Technologies earlier in 1998. Given his telecommunications experiences, he was eager to start his own company. Shams and Narwani, a journalist, discussed many of the opportunities available in the telecommunications industry. They focused on the complex and highly inefficient procurement process. Shams recalled his many frustrations in purchasing and selling telecommunications equipment. From the buyer's perspective, it was difficult to find timely and accurate product information from the thousands of vendors and consultants in the market. From the seller's perspective, it was difficult to identify and reach prospective customers during the brief window of opportunity when buyers were actively engaged in the search process for new equipment.

Because the telecom market space was so fragmented and inefficient, Shams and Narwani used the metaphors of the "jungle" and the "zoo" to describe the telecommunications industry. They decided that Telezoo, through the use of the Internet, would "tame telecommunications" by providing a better procurement solution for the $1.3 trillion that was spent annually for telecommunications equipment and services.

Shams and Narwani quickly recruited and hired a core team of six developers and operations personnel to develop functional requirements, build a user-friendly Web site, and integrate information from content providers and telecommunications suppliers (see Exhibit 1: Organizational Chart and Exhibit 2: Management Team Overview).

EXHIBIT 1 | **ORGANIZATIONAL CHART**

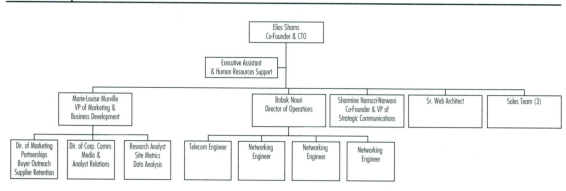

SOURCE: Telezoo Investor Memorandum, April 2001.

EXHIBIT 2 | **MANAGEMENT TEAM OVERVIEW**

Elias Shams, Chairman and CTO

For more than a decade, Elias Shams has worked in the technology arena, holding positions in software engineering, network design and implementation, customer support, RFP preparation, sales, marketing, and global business development. He has been employed by well-known companies such as Yurie Systems, Newbridge Networks, and SAIC. Shams has extensive experience in project management, marketing and sales support, and has designed ATM networking, Local Area Networks (LAN), and Wide Area networks (WAN) for the U.S. defense, transportation, and labor departments and the Federal Aviation Administration as well as commercial organizations. Shams has developed multimillion dollar proposals specializing in cost analysis, design, implementation, integration, and installation. He has provided technical assistance and a wide range of solutions in networking and telecommunications for clients. He holds a B.S. in electrical engineering from the University of Maryland and a master's in telecommunications from George Washington University.

Sharmine Namazi-Narwani, Vice President of Strategic Communications

As co-founder and vice president of Strategic Communications at Telezoo, Sharmine Namazi-Narwani oversees all aspects of strategic communications including investor relations for Telezoo. Prior to Telezoo, Narwani was conference director for the London-based "Women in Business: Linking North America, Europe and the Middle East." The conference brought together women business owners and executives from three continents to forge networking relationships on an international level and provide foundations for trade and investment opportunities between participants. Narwani worked as a journalist for several print and television media organizations, including the Reuters news agency, where she covered breaking news in the Middle East. Narwani held senior communications and development posts at two separate D.C.-based interest groups, where she worked on U.S. foreign policy issues. Her educational background reinforced her interest in political conflict resolution and diplomacy. Narwani holds a BA with a concentration in political science from Sarah Lawrence College and an MA in international affairs from Columbia University.

Marie-Louise Murville, Vice President of Marketing and Business Development

Marie-Louise Murville has more than 16 years of senior management experience guiding the development of early-stage companies into market leaders. As vice president, she oversees marketing, strategic partnerships, distribution, and content deals. Before joining Telezoo, Murville worked in venture capital for six years at Lazard Technology Partners in Washington, D.C., Charles River Ventures in Boston, and Alta Berkeley Associates in London, England. In addition, she was president of a networking-based information services company in Annapolis, MD, a successful turn-around effort that involved strategic acquisitions. After a five-year stint with Arthur D. Little as a consultant, Murville envisioned the use of the Internet for B2B e-commerce in her 1994 London Business School master's thesis on electronic catalog sites and services. Murville graduated from the Massachusetts Institute of Technology, earning both a BS and MS in Mechanical Engineering.

Babak Nouri, Director of Operations

As director of operations at Telezoo, Babak Nouri oversees the day-to-day operations of Telezoo. Before joining Telezoo, Nouri was a manager for Xpedior. At Xpedior, Nouri oversaw a team of 20 consultants that served numerous telecommunications companies including MCI WorldCom, Verizon, and eSpire. While in this role, he also served as a consultant at both MCI WorldCom and Bell Atlantic. For both of these clients, Nouri was relied upon for his expertise on Internet technologies, telecommunications infrastructure, and business process and how improvements in these areas could enhance a company's top- and bottom-line numbers.

Doug Humphrey, Board of Directors

Doug Humphrey is one of the Washington Metropolitan region's most respected entrepreneurs. He is chairman, chief executive officer, and founder of Cidera, Inc. (formerly known as SkyCache, Inc.). Prior to founding Cidera, Humphrey founded DIGEX, a national Internet service provider that was acquired by Intermedia Communications in July 1997. During his tenure at DIGEX, Humphrey served as chief executive officer and chief technology officer from 1991 to 1997. An authority in the ISP satellite content broadcast arena, Humphrey is a frequent speaker at Internet conferences.

Esther Smith, Board of Directors

Esther Smith is well known in the Washington region as the founder of both the *Washington Technology* newspaper and the *Washington Business Journal*. She is widely regarded as one of the first to recognize Washington as a center of technology, and as a practical visionary who has pioneered organizations, programs, and alliances to strengthen the region as a global cluster. Among many other successful ventures, Smith was CEO and president of *TechNews Inc.*, the predecessor to *Post-Newsweek Business Information, Inc.*, before the *Washington Post* acquired it. She is currently a partner with Qorvis Communications (formerly The Poretz Group investor relations).

Kevin Burns, Board of Directors

Kevin Burns founded Intersolv, formerly Sage Software, in 1982 and served as its president and CEO until October 1996, at which time he was made chairman of the board. Under Burns's leadership, the company grew to $200 million in annual revenues, with more than 1,000 employees and a public market value of $400 million. Burns led the company's transition from IBM mainframes to the client/server environment and expanded its distribution to include Europe and Asia. Before founding Intersolv, Burns served in senior sales, marketing, and development management positions at Cincom Systems, a database management software company. He serves on the board of directors of Cyveillance, Essential Technologies, Hardball Software, Merant, Object Design, and Terascape.

SOURCE: Telezoo Investor Memorandum, April 2001.

They invested $1 million of their own personal funds during 1998 and 1999 to finance the early development of the venture. To control expenses, Shams located the company's operations in the basement of their Washington, D.C., home. After the first-round of funding, they relocated operations to their current office space in Arlington, Virginia. Telezoo.com was launched in March 1999.

Traditional Procurement Process

It is estimated that the telecommunications market spends $1.3 trillion to purchase goods and services. Roughly $900 billion is spent for business-to-business or business-to-government purchases. Small, medium, and large businesses and government agencies tend to purchase telecommunications equipment during periods of expansion or to improve the performance of existing equipment. The individuals involved in the procurement decision range from technical staff, like network administrators and telecommunications engineers, to executive management, such as CEOs and CTOs. Given the complexity of these decision-making units, it is very difficult for telecommunications equipment/service providers to identify and reach key decision makers. In addition, traditional marketing channels might not be suitable or cost-effective for these more complex sales.

The initial requirements for telecommunications equipment can be from the very general (good performance) to the very specific (must have 10 × capacity). Specificity is often a function of the needs requirement and the importance of the product/service to the operation of the network. After the needs are identified, either an internal group of engineers or a consulting firm will search to identify the suppliers' products and determine whether these requirements can be met. For example, categories can range from wireless infrastructure to include network security, optical networking, caching, LAN and WAN infrastructure, conferencing, satellite communications, and voice, data, and video services. A host of services is also required to install, maintain, and upgrade the equipment.

Given the rapid changes in the telecommunications industry, buyers find themselves having to compare solutions using up-to-the-moment and often incomplete information. Their decisions are fraught with risk as the cost is high, and there is the possibility that the technology will change very quickly. Information is typically gathered through a wide variety of independent and company sources, including articles in trade journals, marketing brochures, and company Web sites. The information was out there. The problem is not the availability of information on the Internet; rather it is the ability to find, interpret, and act on the information.

Once the information was gathered, buyers would typically contact and qualify sellers through phone calls or visits with the supplier or its business partners. Both brand and performance specifications were typically considered in the evaluation process. Once the requirements were established, a request for proposal (RFP) was released. After the RFPs were reviewed, appointments were typically set with a select group of potential vendors to discuss in detail the final requirements and cost estimates. Following this intensive review, the buyer would select the most attractive proposal and sign a firm contract. The size of an order can range from $5,000 to $5 million, and the buying process can last from two weeks to 18 months. The procurement process is

TABLE 1 | **TRADITIONAL CUSTOMER PROCUREMENT PROCESS**

Customer Purchase Process

Marketing & Sales Channels	Awareness/ Branding	Gather Info & Contact Companies	Compare solutions/ vendors	Proposal (scope out project)	Buy	Post Sales Review
Face-to-Face		Sales Presentation, Proposal, Decision, Install, & Acct Mgmt by Sales Rep				
Business Partners						
Telechannel		Info Requested via 800# & Appt Set with Rep				
Print Advertising, Direct Mail, Banner Ads		Client Becomes Familiar with Brands and Products				

Cost Per Sale

SOURCE: Telezoo Internal Document, June 2001.

summarized in Table 1. From that table, it should also be noted that there are a number of channels through which product-related information can flow, customer contact can be enacted, and products/services installed and maintained.

Traditional Sales Channels

Telecommunications equipment providers sold through a wide variety of distribution channels. The majority of the marketing budget, especially for the larger suppliers, was allocated to the field sales force, which had been seen as critical given the complex and dynamic nature of the products. More than 38.5% of large suppliers' marketing expenses were allocated to the field sales force. The next-largest expense was call centers that handle inbound and outbound telemarketing (9%). New methods of telecommunications marketing included targeted (opt-in) e-mail, which allowed buyers to receive e-mails from specific suppliers and hyperlinks/banner advertisements on Web pages. As isolated customers were more easily reached due to technological innovation, suppliers could now attract segments of one. Sellers could develop tailored offerings and communications strategies to meet the requirements of a single buyer. The key differentiator to such targeted efforts lay in the ability to capture the buyer information. Conventional wisdom had long predicted that if you waited for the RFP, the order was lost. Through targeted messages, buyers could be supplied specific product and supplier information as they began the search process. Another gain from the evolution of technology was that new channels emerged as potential outlets for the supplier to reach new customers. These new channels became important as large suppliers looked to the low end of the marketplace that they tended to ignore in the past due the cost inefficiencies of selling directly to that part of the market. The mantra for the telecommunications equipment supplier was to determine what channels afford a low-cost solution to reach potential customers. See Exhibit 3 to learn how the average telecom provider allocated its marketing budget.

EXHIBIT 3	MARKETING BUDGET ALLOCATION

Marketing Channel	% of Budget
Field Sales	38.5%
Inside Sales (Local)	5.0%
Marketing Support	5.0%
Indirect Labor and Allocated Expenses	2.0%
Telemarketing (from national call center)	9.0%
VAR Management	1.0%
Commissions to VARs	8.0%
Partnerships with Other Suppliers	2.0%
Training (Education of End-Users and Partners)	2.0%
High-end Direct Mail	2.0%
Low-end Direct Mail	4.0%
Opt-in E-mail	1.0%
Hyper links/Banner Ads	1.0%
Print Ads- Corporate	5.0%
Print Ads- Product Specific	5.0%
Radio/TV/Sponsorships	1.0%
Trade Shows (with Booth)	3.0%
Public Relations	3.5%
Market/Industry Research Reports	1.5%
Promotions/Giveaways	0.5%
Total Sales and Marketing Expense	**100.0%**

SOURCE: Telezoo Internal Document, May 2001.

The Telezoo Solution

Telezoo was originally developed as an interactive catalog that compared product descriptions and features from a wide variety of vendors across a broad section of product categories. All this information was available through one central repository. The Telezoo Web site was organized hierarchically by product category and allows for quick searching. That solution addressed the large amount of time spent during the information-gathering stage of the procurement process. A key advantage was that Telezoo permitted an apples-to-apples comparison among the vast array of product and service offerings.

The initial pricing model called for free buyer memberships. Suppliers, however, were charged a subscription fee and $100 CPM (cost per thousand impressions) advertising rates. These rates are relatively high because of the highly targeted placement focusing on "serious" buyers of specific types of telecommunications equipment. Recall that visitors to the Telezoo site were not casual shoppers; they had a need and are looking to purchase specific products. For example, a data storage manufacturer could place a highly targeted advertisement in Telezoo's storage area. The company's site also expected to license its proprietary content for a fee to other potential content providers in the telecommunications arena.

EXHIBIT 4	AN EXAMPLE OF TELEZOO'S AUTOMATED PROCUREMENT PROCESS AT WORK

1. Tella Global IP Network Provider fills out on-line request for proposal (RFP) and submits to Telezoo.com

2. Telezoo filters RFP against its supplier database.

   Time Spent: 2 hours

3. Telezoo identifies and confers with five vendors: Nortel, Foundry, CISCO, Extreme, Sycamore.

4. Telezoo negotiates potential deals with the two best prospects, Extreme & Foundry.

   Time Spent: 1 week

   Telezoo Transaction Fee: $350,000

SOURCE: Telezoo London Presentation, February 2001.

To add more value to their content and to complement the buying decision-making process, Telezoo developed proposal-generating tools. Specifically, tools were used to assist in the "Contact/Qualify Companies" and "Pre-sales/Proposal" phases of the process. Shams and Narwami developed the first Internet-based Request for Proposal (RFP) and Request for Quote (RFQ) processes that allowed buyers to quickly request more information or receive quotes from select suppliers. As buyers reviewed competing products, Telezoo allowed them to construct the RFP or RFQ on-line with the information gathered from the site.

For compiling and having this information available from one location, Telezoo added a transaction fee of 5%. Suppliers that completed Telezoo-generated transactions successfully would be charged the fee. The procurement process under the Telezoo model is shown in Exhibit 4.

Telezoo's Value Proposition

Telezoo offered benefits to the buyer and the seller and added value to both telecom buyers and suppliers in several key areas.

Telezoo buyers had the ability to:

- View unbiased information on multiple suppliers

- Compare similar products in an apples-to-apples format

- Receive customized bids from multiple suppliers

- Save time and effort in the procurement life cycle

Telezoo suppliers provided:

- Cost-effective access to qualified sales leads

- A shortened sales cycle

- Increased consideration rates, especially for smaller suppliers
- Data mining on customer buying behavior through market intelligence tools.

Market Opportunity

The total telecommunications marketplace was estimated to be $1.3 trillion in annual expenditures. Based on Telezoo's original revenue model, a 5% transaction fee would generate a market potential of approximately $65 billion. During her first week on the job, Murville eliminated residential from the target market, focusing exclusively on business purchases. Of the $900 billion that comprised the business-to-business or business-to-government purchases, Telezoo focused on the entire spectrum of telecommunications products, from complex, high-end components, such as LAN/WAN infrastructure, data storage, and optical networking, to lower-end commodity products such as phones and cables. Yet Telezoo was more appropriately utilized for complex high-end products, which account for $139 billion. Using the same 5% figure, this market was estimated to be approximately $7 billion.

Competition

Telezoo competed against a number of on-line and off-line competitors. (The competitive field is categorized in Table 2.) Shams and Narwani thought that Telezoo was uniquely positioned in the industry as a comprehensive business-to-business procurement solution (Exhibit 5).

TABLE 2 | **COMPETITOR CATEGORIES**

Category	Main Companies	Comments
Aggregators	VerticalNet	Broad industry coverage with content and commerce offerings
Niche Players	Databid, Simplexity, Telecomsmart, Telebright	Mainly target residential, SOHO, and small business buyers
Infomediaries	ZDNet, CMPNet	Magazines with online content offerings
Online Resellers	Telcobuy.com	Mostly spare parts delivery and re-orders with limited geographic coverage
Consortiums	E2Open	Focus on supply chain efficiencies and collaboration
Telecom Market Research Firms	Gartner Group, Ogilvy, Harte Hanks	Provide value-added information gathering & analysis of secondary data

SOURCE: Telezoo Internal Memorandum, April 2001.

EXHIBIT 5　| COMPETITIVE MATRIX

	online catalog/directory	normalized data	product comparisons	solution focused	white papers	product positioning/categorization	brand awareness	lead generation	lead qualification	lead tracking	transaction capability	online/offline technical consultations	direct contact with buyer	datamining services/tools	market/product intelligence	competitive analysis	high value – complete sales & mktg cycle	high cost
				Education				Branding			Sale				Analysis			$$
telezoo	×	×	×	×	×	×	×	×	×	×	×	×	×	×	×	×	×	
Harte Hanks						×	×	×	×	×			×	×	×			×
Gartner Group			×	×	×	×	×	×						×	×	×		×
Ogilvy						×	×	×										×
Double Click							×	×							×			×
Seller Field Sales				×	×	×	×	×	×	×	×	×	×					×
Network+Interop			×	×	×	×	×	×	×			×	×					
Newmediary				×			×						×					

	TZ	HH	GG	OG	DC	SFS	NI	NM
Brand Awareness	X	X	X	X	X	X	X	X
Supplier Directory	X						X	X
Supplier Product Catalog	X	X				X		
Product Comparisons	X	X	X	X	X	X	X	
Normalized product comparisons	X							
White Papers	X		X			X	X	
Lead generation	X	X	X	X	X	X	X	X
Lead qualification	X	X				X		
Lead routing	X	X				X		
Lead tracking	X					X		
Live expert technical/project consulting	X		X			X	X	
Facilitated, Direct supplier/buyer contact	X	X				X	X	
Current Market Intelligence Reports	X	X						

Marketing Strategy

Telezoo's initial marketing strategy focused on customer acquisition using traditional marketing channels. Because Telezoo had to build its inventory of value-added content and product descriptions, the initial effort concentrated on acquiring suppliers. Once their product data base was compiled, marketing shifted its emphasis to a more balanced effort of targeting buyers and suppliers.

To maximize its exposure to the industry, Telezoo placed a series of advertisements in many of the top telecommunications magazines. The advertisements touted the value-added benefits for buyers. To complement the mass media, a direct-mail campaign was targeted to suppliers. The message both reinforced the benefits of Telezoo to suppliers and also emphasized end-user benefits.

An important component of the overall marketing strategy was to be very visible at trade shows, which provided an opportunity to meet a targeted group of buyers and suppliers under one roof. Company representatives attended trade shows such as Networld+Interop and Supercomm in both foreign (Brazil, Switzerland) and domestic locations (Las Vegas, Atlanta). The company also relied heavily on public relations efforts that would allow them to cost-effectively reach a large customer base.

Year One Results (March 1999 to March 2000)

Through the efforts of the founders, industry leaders such as *Forbes*, which ranked Telezoo in the top five globally, *Business Week*, *Legg Mason*, and a number of other well-regarded magazines and investment banks recognized Telezoo as a leading telecommunications marketplace. Shams and Narwani thought that these respected editorial and financial groups had validated the usefulness of their business proposition. Although Narwani was able to generate very positive press, Telezoo was unable to convert accolades into financial success. The company was particularly unsuccessful in generating revenue through transaction fees, which were a large component of their revenue model. In fact, the company had not recorded any completed transactions at all, while spending close to $1.5 million on an annualized basis on their sales and marketing programs. Telezoo had a very good product that was recognized by leaders in the field, but unfortunately, the marketplace was either not hearing the company's message or had chosen not to respond to it. It was becoming clear that the company would not be able to sustain itself at the current rate it was going.

At the close of May 2000, Telezoo had fewer than 5,000 unique visitors per month and nine firm contracts with suppliers. Most important, the company had less than $60,000 in revenue and wanted to build on the supplier base to acquire more buyers. Yet, they struggled with the need to minimize their costs as they built the business. The executive search firm hired to recruit a seasoned CEO was progressing, but the leading candidate, even if the offer was extended and accepted, would be unavailable until September. Meanwhile, the burn rate continued, and a quest for a fresh infusion of capital was in full swing.

Murville was brought to Telezoo in July 2000. In addition to the Master of Science and Management degree she had earned from London Business School, Murville held both a BS and MS in mechanical engineering from MIT. With more than 16 years of senior management experience guiding the development of early-stage companies into market leaders. Murville worked for a number of blue chip venture capitalists and had performed some successful turnaround efforts for growing organizations. She was given a great deal of latitude to bring a fresh perspective to the company's strategic direction. Her first objective was to assess the situation and present her fresh findings and recommendations at the next board meeting. Adding to the pressure, investors were no longer willing to bet on a concept. They needed to see a clear path to profitability, and, at this point, Telezoo's path to profits was not easily understood. In preparation for the board meeting, Murville asked herself the following questions:

1. What was the true market for Telezoo?

2. How can Telezoo differentiate itself from the growing field of competitors?

3. How can Telezoo generate revenues without hiring additional people or advertising?

4. How viable is the original transaction fee model?

5. How could the quantity versus quality of partners be balanced?

6. How could she provide additional assurance to the board and potential investors that a sustainable business model existed?

7. How could Telezoo stay in business?

CASE

11

Van Leer Packaging Worldwide: The TOTAL Account (A)

On June 21, 1995 at 12:34 Claude Hoareau, Business Unit Manager of Van Leer Steel Drums, a division of Van Leer France, received a copy of a message faxed from the Lubricants department at Groupe TOTAL to Van Leer's headquarters in the Netherlands. It read:

> "[We] are still very concerned by the proposed unit prices in France, and outside of France, which look rather high. Please investigate the possibility of further improvement. We would still like to continue our European relationship and do hope that you may be in a position to offer some improvements."

TOTAL was one of the largest French multinationals and the world's ninth oil company. A loss of the TOTAL account would be a serious blow to Hoareau and to Van Leer France. Hoareau had expected this account to supply 6% of expected sales in 1995.

The message was disheartening news for Hoareau, especially as he had spoken to TOTAL's buyer, Paul Laveissiere, earlier that morning and had faxed to Amstelveen,

> "As far as Van Leer France is concerned we are not in too bad a position. The final decision will be based on the proposal for Europe and not only for France. Laveissiere is totally unhappy with our last proposal, mainly due to the UK situation, aren't we interested in TOTAL UK?"

The issue was also of great concern to Johan Ten Cate, Manager of International Accounts at Van Leer's corporate headquarters in the Netherlands, to whom the fax had been addressed. Ten Cate himself wondered whether a loss of TOTAL was not a symptom of the problem that Van Leer encountered in serving and retaining even larger global accounts. Some of these companies had already been in touch with him, "showing their teeth" and demanding significant global discounts and other benefits.

This case was written by David Weinstein, Professor of Marketing at INSEAD, with the assistance of Alain Debenedetti, Research Assistant. It is intended to be used as a basis for class discussion rather than to illustrate either effective or ineffective handling of an administrative situation.

Van Leer

Royal Packaging Industries Van Leer was founded in 1919 by Bernard Van Leer. From the outset, the company's capital belonged entirely to The Van Leer Foundation, a philanthropic association subject to Royal Dutch decree and legislation, funding special programs for socially and culturally impaired children. Van Leer began manufacturing steel drums in the Netherlands in 1925, launching into closure systems in 1927. By the 1930s the company was already the European leader for both of these products and by the 1940s it had established its presence in seven countries, across three continents.

In the '60s and '70s Van Leer expanded its product lines to flexible packaging, using paper and plastic materials, which facilitated the group's penetration into the consumer goods sector. The '80s marked a whole new expansion phase via a series of acquisitions, broadening Van Leer's scope of activities. In 1992, a new milestone was set in the company's mass consumer goods packaging with the acquisition from Unilever of 4P, its packaging subsidiary.

Van Leer's worldwide sales for 1994 reached NFL 3.958 billion (approximately $2.5 billion), a 3% growth from 1993. Profits soared that year to NFL 67 million. The company employed some 16,000 people across the globe, half of them in Europe. Van Leer held 25% of the world's large steel drum sales that year. Exhibit 1 includes Van Leer's consolidated financial statements for 1994.

EXHIBIT 1 | **VAN LEER'S CONSOLIDATED FINANCIAL STATEMENTS FOR 1993–1994**

AS AT DECEMBER 31, 1994 (AFTER PROFIT APPROPRIATION)

(NLG. 000)	1994		1993	
Assets employed:				
Tangible fixed assets				
Cost value	3,325,879		3,443,947	
Accumulated depreciation	(1,881,311)		(1,898,492)	
		1,444,568		1,545,455
Financial fixed assets				
Minority participations	4,360		1,117	
Loans	7,102		9,445	
		11,462		10,562
Total fixed assets		1,456,030		1,556,017
Current assets				
Stocks	534,256		508,867	
Debtors	717,320		668,125	
Cash and banks	39,588		49,715	
Total current assets	1,291,164		1,226,707	
Creditors	(714,169)		(645,072)	
Net working capital		576,995		581,635
Net capital employed		2,033,025		2,137,652

Financed by:

Medium and long-term loans	662,331		400,201	
Banks	161,812		498,801	
		824,143		899,002
Provisions for liabilities and charges				
Unfunded pension liabilities and similar obligations	263,547		263,005	
Deferred taxes	139,438		140,791	
Sundry	141,528		152,759	
		544,513		556,555
Capital and reserves				
Shareholder's equity	502,464		514,958	
Third party interest in subsidiaries	161,905		167,137	
Total shareholders, funds		664,369		682,095
Financing capital		2,033,025		2,137,652

FOR THE YEAR ENDED DECEMBER 31, 1994

(NLG. 000)	1994	1993
Net sales to third parties	3,957,640	3,844,497
Movements in stocks	15,327	(28,906)
Proceeds of production	3,972,967	3,815,591
Consumption direct materials	(1,798,180)	(1,638,026)
Value added	2,174,787	2,177,565
Operating costs	(1,968,712)	(1,979,966)
Gross operating result	206,075	197,599
Interest expenses	(63,840)	(75,927)
Foreign exchange results	(5,806)	4,518
Operating profit before taxation	136,429	126,190
Taxation on operating profit	(41,459)	(44,484)
Net operating profit	94,970	81,706
Net extraordinary expenses	(13,102)	(18,961)
Profit after taxation	81,868	62,745
Third party interest	(14,844)	(15,252)
Net income	67,024	47,493

Products, Countries and Clients

In 1994, industrial packaging activities represented 46.3% of Van Leer's total sales, the main industrial end uses being industrial liquids such as chemicals and lubricants. Steel drum production accounted for 35% of Van Leer's global sales and for 74% of its industrial packaging division.

Steel drums being a very voluminous product, they were historically manufactured close to the clients' production sites. Van Leer's traditional approach to new international markets was dictated by a simple motto: "Wherever you need us, we go". Van Leer relied on its client relationships to set up factories abroad, giving it a foothold both in strong economies as well as in emerging markets. In 1994, a score of new contracts led Van Leer to set up operations in Russia, China and Costa Rica.

Van Leer was the only player in the steel drum industry to operate on such a worldwide scale, boasting a solid presence across five continents: 130 factories in 41 countries. In 1994, 57.9% of Van Leer's sales were in Europe, 22.5% in North America and Mexico, 7.9% in Australia and the Far East, 6.4% in Central and South America, and 5.3% in Africa.

Van Leer's client base was highly diversified. The company prided itself on being both a supplier for large multinational concerns, especially large chemical and oil giants, smaller multinationals and at the same time local family-owned businesses. Exhibit 2 presents some of the steel drum sales figures by major clients.

Organization

Van Leer's management genuinely reflected its international aspirations, with every executive board member being of a different nationality (see Exhibit 3). The company was organized in autonomous Strategic Business Units, some spanning product categories and others, geographical area (see Exhibit 4). Each business unit acted as a profit center with the objective of exploiting opportunities in its own area of responsibility. The business unit's performance was evaluated in this light, and financial rewards, in bonus and other payments, were granted accordingly. A manager's annual bonus could reach up to 30% of his or her annual income, some of it based on SBU performance and the rest on the BU performance. This structure had been designed to fit the international and diverse Van Leer markets.

The Steel Drum Market

The steel drum market developed in tandem with the oil extraction and refinery boom, since steel drums were the most practical way to transport and ship oil. The market was characterized by its numerous suppliers, primarily local companies serving local manufacturing sites using standard drums, but also companies developing highly specific products. The most frequently used drum was the 213 liter format, Van Leer having a market share of approximately 25% for this item.

In 1995, the steel drum market reached 150 million units sold worldwide. On the whole, the market was growing very slightly at a rate of approximately 1% a year. Nonetheless, there appeared to be significant growth disparities among regions. In Europe, which accounted for one third of the world market, consumption had been

EXHIBIT 2 | **STEEL DRUM SALES BY SELECTED GLOBAL CLIENT IN 1995 (IN NFL '000, 000s)**

	Steel Drums Europe	North America	South America	Asia	Africa	Australia	Worldwide
Shell Oil/Chemical	36.20	1.00	1.00	7.00	4.10	0.60	49.90
ICI	31.60	4.50	-	0.50	0.70	3.90	41.20
Dow Chemical	13.60	6.50	0.60	9.00	-	0.30	30.00
Mobil	14.20	2.40	-	6.10	-	6.60	29.30
BASF	18.30	9.60	0.20	1.00	-	-	29.10
Dow Coming	2.20	18.90	-	-	-	-	21.10
Elf/Atochem	16.50	1.00	-	1.50	-	-	19.00
PPG	5.50	12.00	-	-	-	-	17.50
Burmal/Castrol	8.70	4.50	-	2.20	-	1.40	16.80
Esso/Exxon	13.40	-	0.40	1.90	-	0.30	16.00
DSM (Chemical & Resin)	15.30	-	-	-	-	-	15.30
Rhone Poulenc	13.30	0.60	0.40	-	-	0.30	14.60
AKZO/Nobel	12.70	1.30	0.20	0.30	-	-	14.50
BP	11.60	-	-	1.00	1.90	-	14.50
Texaco	4.10	-	6.60	3.80	-	-	14.50
Bayer	7.60	0.80	4.00	0.70	-	-	13.10
Witco	6.30	6.50	-	-	-	-	12.80
Rohm and Haas	5.00	7.30	0.40	-	-	-	12.70
Monsanto	2.30	7.30	0.20	-	0.40	-	10.20
Total Oil/Chem/Bostik	5.90	1.90	-	-	2.20	-	10.00
Hoechst	9.60	-	-	-	-	-	9.60
Union Carbide	2.70	2.90	-	0.90	0.60	-	7.10
Arco	1.80	-	-	5.20	-	-	7.00
IFF	5.50	1.20	0.20	-	-	-	6.90
Dupont	2.20	3.90	0.40	-	-	-	6.50
Cyanamid/Agrar	1.20	2.80	-	-	-	-	4.00
TOTAL	**267.30**	**96.90**	**14.60**	**41.10**	**9.90**	**13.40**	**443.20**

EXHIBIT 3 | **PERSONAL BACKGROUNDS OF VAN LEER'S BOARD MEMBERS**

Willem de Vlugt (b.1942)

Chairman and CEO of Van Leer since 1992 and an executive board member since 1989.
A Dutch national who joined Van Leer in 1968 and held executive positions in the US, France, Argentina and Brazil. Between 1977 and 1983, de Vlugt served in general management positions in the coatings divisions of Akzo Nobel, the Dutch chemicals group. He then returned to Van Leer, where, prior to joining the Executive Board, he served as president and CEO of Van Leer Containers, including the industrial container activities in the US.

André Saint-Denis (b.1944)

CFO since 1992. A Canadian national who held several managerial positions at Air Canada, Alcan, Canadian and Kinburn Corp in both Canada and Switzerland. Prior to joining Van Leer in 1992, Mr Saint Denis served as vice-president finance and treasurer of Le Groupe Vidéotron Ltée in Montreal.

Francisco de Miguel (b.1944)

Francisco de Miguel was appointed to the Executive Board in 1995 with a special brief for the industrial packaging activities of Van Leer. Mr de Miguel; a Spaniard, joined Van Leer in 1968 and held several position in Spain and Brazil. Prior to joining the Executive Board he was responsible for Van Leer's operations in Latin America.

Christian Betbeder (b.1942)

A member for the Executive Board since 1995, Christian Betbeder was responsible for the development for the consumer packaging business. Prior to joining Van Leer in 1983, Mr Betbeder, a French national, served in various managerial positions in France. Before joining the board, Betbeder headed the strategic business in Flexibles, including Van Leer's activities in strength films, metallised products and industrial flexibles.

EXHIBIT 4 | **ORGANIZATION STRUCTURE VAN LEER GROUP (JAN 95)**

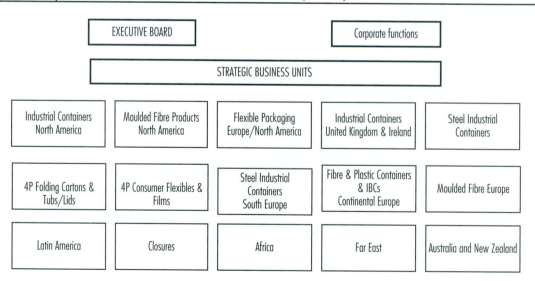

decreasing at an annual rate of 1 to 2% since 1989. In the US, consumption had remained stable for the past ten years and no changes were anticipated. US consumption consistently accounted for 20–25% of worldwide consumption. The outlook for emerging markets such as China and Latin America was, however, optimistic.

The steel drum industry was unique in that it included both new and reconditioned drums. The cost of a reconditioned drum was about 70 to 80% of a new one, including collection, cleaning, repair and reassembly, and it could be reused several times.

The cost structure of a steel drum was as follows: steel—50%, labor just under 10%, paint and lacquers—9%, closures—8%, transport—6% and overhead and depreciation about 17%. Given the proportion of steel content, drum makers followed the price of steel vigilantly, attempting to pass on price increases to their customers through escalation clauses in drum supply contracts. Between the first quarter of 1994 and the final quarter of 1995 the price of steel shot up from $355 to $590 per ton.

Competition

In 1994, Van Leer was the only truly global steel drum manufacturer in the world. Competitors either stayed mainly within their territories or formed international alliances, in an effort to compete for multinational accounts. In Europe, Van Leer held a market share of 37% in 1995. One European competitor was Blagden, the British company holding 20% of the European market. While being second in new drums, Blagden led in reconditioned drums with a market share in Europe of 35%. Another major competitor in Europe was Gallay-Mauser, the Franco-German organization holding the No. 3 position in Europe, with 12% market share, and the No. 1 position in France and Germany.

Other types of containers were increasingly competing with steel drums, especially since the price of steel surpassed the $450 per ton threshold. At this level, steel drum manufacturers were no longer able to transfer the rising costs of steel to their clients. Hence, plastic and fiber packaging became viable substitutes for many applications. The result was that some steel drum manufacturers had to close down while the slightly more fortunate ones had to bite the bullet and increase productivity.

Customer Needs and Differentiation

The drum is a critical product for any chemical or oil company. It not only stores but also facilitates transportation of goods, especially since drums may use pallets for storage and transportation and may be rolled. With many customers going through reengineering and rationalization of their logistics, steel drum manufacturers were expecting pressure from their clients, in the form of demand for lower prices, better quality, as well as trying to shift the inventory of empty drums upstream.

Product differentiation in steel drums was difficult as the manufacturing process was widely accessible and easy to imitate. However some clients had specific needs of cleanliness, internal coatings of the drums, closure standards, external color and drum size mix, allowing price premiums. Traditionally, Van Leer managers had felt that their organization's global presence was a source of differentiation, assuring customers with standards of quality, service and responsiveness that local manufacturers could not match.

Van Leer's Strategy

Van Leer's management was sensitive to the following trends: global client companies were (1) transferring production to cheaper and emerging economies, (2) consolidating their purchasing into the hands of fewer suppliers in order to achieve price advantages, and (3) seeking to rationalize the range of their packaging material. According to Van Leer senior executives, these trends would result in both a lower demand for steel drums in parts of Europe and a smaller number of competitors. They felt that these pressures would require both an efficient cooperation among the business units of Van Leer on international contracts, and a review of the product range.

The position of Manager of International Accounts was created in October, 1994 as Van Leer's response to pressure by international accounts. Ten Cate, an executive with more than 30 years experience in the company, was appointed to this position. Although Ten Cate did not have formal authority over local mangers, he commanded extensive knowledge, experience, personal networking and respect inside the Van Leer organization, in the packaging industry and within the client base. Management expected his background, together with his personal sensitivity and negotiating skills, to enable Ten Cate to contribute to Van Leer's continued success with international accounts as their purchasing process evolved.

The TOTAL Account

Groupe TOTAL was the ninth largest oil concern in the world and one of the largest and most visible French companies. Its sales reached $27 billion in 1994. TOTAL was well established in a number of fields and its activities were quite diversified: oil and natural gas extraction, refinery and distribution, crude oil and oil derivatives, trading, production of chemical products such as resins, paints and inks and more. Established across five continents, TOTAL was still a growing empire, operating in 80 countries and boasting sound financial health and many years of experience in all its fields of activity.

TOTAL Lubricants was one of the company's profit centers. The division was broken down into three units: two departments devoted to selling automobile and industrial lubricants and the third functioning as a cost center. The latter was called FAL (Manufacturing Purchasing Logistics) and was "selling" the products and services that it sourced-in, at internal transfer prices, to the other two "selling" departments. The Purchasing department was in turn subdivided into three units: Packaging, Raw Materials and special Materials.

In the final months of 1994, TOTAL went through a worldwide reengineering effort at the initiative of its president. Consolidating international purchasing was part of this scrutiny, through which the company expected to reduce the types of drums bought, thus standardizing and cutting costs. A senior executive at TOTAL commented:

> "We were hoping, through the consolidation, to also instill genuine collaboration between TOTAL and its suppliers, in the form of advice, assistance, technical information and perhaps deeper forms of collaboration, involving R & D."

Jean-Claude Delvallée, who managed Purchasing, embarked on the reengineering effort together with an internal TOTAL consultant, Michel Chouarain, who joined the Lubricants department temporarily for the duration of the reengineering project. Chouarain would participate, with Delvallée, in implementing purchasing strategy as well as in negotiating with major suppliers. Their message was that every supplier would have to: (1) offer goods on an international scale, (2) factor in TOTAL's international standards requirements, (3) keep track of sales volumes and negotiate globally via a single representative. A third purchasing manager, Hal Swinson, who represented TOTAL in North America, joined the two in the contact with global suppliers.

As in many international companies, globalizing purchasing activities was not an easy task. Globalization typically came after a competitive price had been reached locally, based on local competitive conditions and the establishment of personal relationships. In some cases global contracts would indeed obtain significant price reductions, beyond the ability of local organizations. However, market conditions in other markets could provide better local conditions than global purchasing would obtain. This phenomenon created resistance by some countries to comply with a global arrangement negotiated by headquarters. Commenting on this, a senior manager at TOTAL said:

> "We too have our problems of globalization. As local purchasing has an effect on local performance evaluation, we risk interfering with local relationships with suppliers. Clearly a manager would not like headquarters to impose prices and relationships on him or her, especially when these could potentially hurt local performance. Like all organizations, TOTAL will find the way to overcome this local resistance."

December 13, 1994

December 13, 1994 was the day it all started. A seemingly innocent letter arrived at Van Leer France signed by TOTAL's Delvallée. In it, he explained that TOTAL had decided to pursue a global purchasing policy for steel drums, for all its subsidiaries worldwide. Under this new approach, TOTAL announced that it would soon be contacting Van Leer to explore possibilities for "potential collaboration". The letter also said,

> "We also inform you that our Request For Quote [RFQ] which would have been applicable starting January 1995 is now frozen, and ask you to maintain current drum prices through March 31, 1995."

Hoareau, the Business Unit Manager of Steel Drums at Van Leer France, authorized his commercial director, to whom TOTAL's letter had been addressed, to issue the following response:

> "We thank you for associating our group with the globalizing of Group TOTAL's needs. We are clearly at your service and will cooperate fully with your analysis. Nevertheless you certainly know that our industry has been subject

to the spectacular price hikes of steel [the price of steel rose by 15% in 1994]. That is why we were forced to readjust our prices starting January 1, 1995. We cannot endanger our operation's survival and regret that we are unable to satisfy your request for a price freeze. We ask that you consider the price we quoted in response to your recent RFQ as applicable starting January 1, 1995. We trust that you will understand our reasoning."

Meeting in Amstelveen

Ten Cate hosted the meeting with TOTAL at Van Leer's worldwide headquarters in Amstelveen on January 13, 1995. Beforehand he had collected the necessary data pertaining to Van Leer's sales volume to TOTAL in different countries, as grounds for the discussion. The UK and France were clearly the two major European countries in TOTAL's steel drum purchasing. TOTAL was represented by Delvallée, Chouarain, and also by the American, Swinson. Hoareau came over from France to join the meeting.

Swinson, who was responsible for Purchasing in the US, was TOTAL's most active spokesperson. After having outlined the company's activities, he presented the highlights of the global steel drum purchasing plan, akin to the one already implemented in the United States. TOTAL was seeking to obtain (1) best prices at each location, based on the overall purchasing volume for the group, (2) all quoted prices would be firm for one year, with a multi-year proposal including cost escalation clauses for raw material starting only in the second year, (3) an annual rebate based on global purchasing levels, and (4) suppliers were asked to include information on their quality assurance and drum collecting facilities.

Later Ten Cate commented on this meeting,

"It was strange that the most active member of the three TOTAL executives was Swinson. Delvallée continued to act as the "old friend and elder statesman" sitting back and leaving Swinson the stage. Chouarain was totally silent and gave me the impression that he would rather not be there and was forced by someone to be present at this meeting."

Preparation of the Proposal

On January 17, 1995, following the meeting in Amstelveen, Ten Cate dispatched a message to all Van Leer subsidiaries, launching the preparation of his proposal to TOTAL. This note first contained a copy of TOTAL's presentation (see Exhibit 5) and TOTAL's European steel drums consumption plan for 1995:

Germany	45,000
Spain	17,000
France	458,000
Italy	23,000
UK	316,000
Sweden	13,000

EXHIBIT 5 | **TOTAL GLOBAL PURCHASE PROGRAM STEEL DRUMS**

Elements of Proposal:

• Best prices at each location based on the total purchasing volume for the group.

• Purchasing data and names of local contracts provided for supplier to verify specifications, ordering patterns, etc.

• All prices to be quoted on a "delivered" basis.

• A multi-year proposal is encouraged, with price increases for raw material only in years two, three. . . .

• As an incentive to TOTAL, a yearly rebate proposal based on various purchase levels is encouraged.

• Along with the proposal, supplier is asked to include information on their:

– Quality Assurance programs

– Drum recovery and reconditioning program

Total Ranked 9th in the World*

OVERALL RANKING		RANKING BY CRITERIA	
1. SHELL	(NL/UK)	Oil reserves	6th
2. EXXON	(US)	Gas reserves	12th
3. MOBIL	(US)	Oil production	10th
4. BP	(UK)	Gas production	15th
5. CHEVRON	(US)	Refining Capacity	8th
6. AMOCO	(US)	Product Sales	7th
7. TEXACO	(US)		
8. ELF	(FR)		
9. TOTAL	(FR)		
10. ARCO	(US)		

APRIL 1994
*EXCLUDING NATIONAL OIL COMPANIES FROM PRODUCING COUNTRIES AND ENI, PIW-DECEMBER 1993

Additionally, the note indicated that his proposal to TOTAL would include six European countries and establish a cumulative discount policy on all purchasing in Europe. Emphasizing the importance of this market for Van Leer, which meant 872,000 new drums per annum, Ten Cate instructed all the subsidiaries to contact their local TOTAL representatives for specifics on drum types and quantities they anticipated.

Ten Cate knew that TOTAL was having similar discussions with Van Leer's competitors. Van Leer's UK steel drum manager told him that (1) the relationship between Van Leer's management and TOTAL's in the UK was very strong, (2) Van Leer UK's price was competitive, and (3) Van Leer UK felt that TOTAL *in Paris* would not be able to "impose a supplier" on their UK subsidiary.

Based on his discussions with Van Leer subsidiaries, and on his knowledge of the market, Ten Cate was hoping that the competition would not offer more than comparable international discounts, while maintaining existing market prices.

Ten Cate was impressed by the attitude of Van Leer France to the situation. Hoareau took TOTAL's reengineering effort very seriously, especially in view of a new manager, Paul Laveissiere, designated to succeed Delvallée. Unlike the British, the French thought that this was not "business as usual" and the new purchasing team at TOTAL represented a real threat. Ten Cate had not met the new purchasing manager and relied on Hoareau for information and impressions.

CASE

12

Ethical Dilemmas in Business Marketing

Individuals in marketing and sales positions are frequently confronted by ethical problems and dilemmas. The scenarios presented below were real situations faced by individuals during their first year on the job after graduation from college. After reading each scenario you should decide what action you would have taken.

1. I presently sell a line of industrial compressors to customers and the standard sales pitch indicates that they are the best for the money available in the market. Unfortunately, I also know that this isn't true. However, they make up 40 percent of my line and I cannot successfully make my quota without selling at least $85,000 worth per month. It's probably okay, because all salespersons say theirs are the best.

   Would you take the same selling approach?

2. My field sales manager drinks excessively and has accompanied me on sales calls hung over and smelling of alcohol. This behavior does not enhance my professional reputation with my customers or the company. I have decided not to say anything, as the field sales manager writes my review and can dramatically influence my success or failure in this, my first selling assignment.

   Would you report the sales manager to upper level management?

3. I am working for a large company that is heavily involved in defense contracts. I have recently been transferred to a new division that builds nuclear weapons. These are weapons of which the public is not aware and of which I do not personally approve. However, our work is entirely legal and classified top secret. I have decided to stay with the company because I find my work challenging and I am not directly involved with any phase of the actual nuclear component of the project.

   If you had similar attitudes, would you stay with the company?

4. I recently had the opportunity to buy a new . . . computer, printer, and software for $1,000 from our MIS Director. He apparently received these items "free" with a large computer order for the company. I would be doing mostly work

---

These scenarios were developed by Professor John B. Gifford and Jan Willem Bol, Miami University. They were part of a study of the ethical problems recent business school graduates faced on their first job. Copyright by John B. Gifford.

for the company at home on the computer. I decided to accept his offer and paid him $1,000 cash.

What action would you have taken?

5. After a business dinner with an important client in California, he implied that he wanted to go out and "do the town" plus. . . . Although I wasn't sure what the "plus" might involve, there was a 50/50 chance he wanted an affair on the side. I said I was tired, and retired alone for the evening. I also lost the account which had been a 90 percent sure thing.

What action would you have taken?

6. By coincidence, your salesperson and your distributor are both pitching your product to the same prospect. The distributor, however, does not know this yet. You know that when he finds out he will offer a competitor's product that will most certainly undercut your price. Your salesperson is totally dependent on commission.

Should you ask your salesperson to back off?

7. A buyer for a large government institution (a good prospect with potentially high volume) offers you information about the sealed bids of competitors. You know the practice is questionable, but he is a good friend and no one is likely to find out. Besides, you are below quota, and need the commission badly.

Will you accept his offer?

8. An industrial customer has indicated that our lubricants were priced about 5 percent higher than those being offered by our competition. He indicated that if I would drop my price 7½ percent, he would cancel his order with our competition and buy from me. This will mean a $1,400 commission for me personally. I agreed.

What action would you have taken?

9. As an industrial salesperson, you are in the office of a prospect to provide a verbal price on a project. You and your sales manager have determined that a specific price is the right price for your organization and you believe you will win the contract. However, as the prospect walks out of his office you see a copy of your competitor's proposal on his desk with a substantially lower price. You will need to give him your price now, as he walks back into the room.

Will you change your price?

10. I have a set quota of goods that I must sell every month. Sometimes it becomes necessary to overstock my customers in order to meet my quota. Most of the customers are not very sophisticated, and don't even know how much inventory they should carry.

Is this an appropriate sales tactic?

NAME INDEX

A

Aaker, David A., 210, 214, 372, 386
Abela, Andrew V., 398, 445
Abell, Derek F., 220
Adams, Arthur J., 143, 146
Aeppel, Timothy, 37, 382
Agrawal, Anupam, 333
Alghalith, Nabil, 310
Allen, Philip, 132
Alonzo, Vincent, 414
Alsop, Stewart, 72, 324
Ambler, Tim, 436, 445
Ames, B. Charles, 12
Anderson, Erin A., 78, 290, 291, 297, 386,
    408, 425
Anderson, James C., 10, 11, 94, 106–109, 111,
    297, 298, 359, 364
Anderson, Matthew G., 39–42, 44
Anderson, Scott, 73
Anderson, Steven R., 99, 451
Andzulis, James K., 306
Anthony, Scott D., 243
Armstrong, J. Scott, 146
Arndt, Michael, 187, 188
Assael, Henry, 263
Athaide, Gerard A., 248
Auerbach, Jon G., 277
Avery, Susan, 42, 75

B

Baatz, Elizabeth, 40
Bagozzi, Richard P., 425
Baker, Walter, 361
Balasubramanian, Sridhar, 261
Balinski, Eric W., 132
Banting, Peter, 81
Baptista, João P. A., 124, 125, 216, 239
Barclay, Daniel W., 420
Barnes, Hank, 309
Bartolini, Andrew, 38, 72
Batchelor, Charles, 334
Bearden, William O., 154
Belk, Leland L., 450
Bell, Marie, 6
Bellizzi, Joseph A., 76, 128, 392

Bello, Daniel C., 69
Belonax, Joseph J., 76
Bennion, Mark J., Jr., 136
Bens, Kartrina J., 304, 305, 314
Berman, Dennis K., 140
Berry, Leonard R., 265, 275
Beutin, Nikolas, 106, 216, 217, 359, 360, 362
Bharadwaj, Sundar R., 262
Bhattacharya, Arindam K., 14, 181, 182, 189
Bink, Audrey J. M., 76, 416
Bitner, Mary Jo, 264, 269
Blackman, Douglas A., 25
Bloch, Nicholas, 72
Bloomer, John, 379
Boewadt, Robert J., 367
Bogosian, Joseph H., 194
Boles, James, 76
Bolton, Ruth N., 105
Boomgar, Joel, 384
Bond, Edward U., III, 159, 456
Bonner, Joseph M., 247
Bonoma, Thomas V., 80, 400, 452, 453, 454
Booker, Ellis, 393
Bossidy, Larry, 436
Boughton, Paul D., 378
Bourde, Marc, 18, 73, 74
Bowman, Douglas, 92, 110
Bowman, Edward H., 454
Bowman, Robert J., 338
Boyd, Harper W., Jr., 221, 222
Boyson, Sandor, 339
Bradley, Peter, 344
Bradtke, Thomas, 181–185, 187, 189
Brady, Diane, 398
Brentani, Ulrike de, 277
Brewer, Peter C., 330, 335, 341
Brickman, Chris, 354
Brodie, Roderick J., 271
Bromley, Philip, 158
Brooks, R., 139
Brown, Eryn, 314
Brown, Robert, 158
Brown, Shona L., 240, 244, 245
Brown, Steven R., 422
Brown, Susan P., 434

Brunell, Tom, 334
Bulik, Beth Snyder, 386, 397
Bunn, Michele D., 67
Burdick, Richard K., 70, 81, 131
Burgelman, Robert A., 234, 236
Burn, Darryl, 267
Bush, Victoria D., 422
Butaney, Gul T., 67
Buzby, Stephen L., 450
Byrne, John A., 155
Byron, Ellen, 25

C
Calantone, Roger, 251
Callahan, Sean B., 73, 323, 448
Callioni, Gianpaolo, 353
Cannon, Joseph P., 93, 94, 96, 414, 416
Carbone, James, 19, 40, 46, 70, 75, 288
Cardozo, Richard N., 125, 127
Carpenter, Gregory S., 8, 436
Castanon, Yvette, 452
Cavusgil, S. Tamer, 195, 201
Cespedes, Frank V., 106, 107, 139, 218, 284, 361, 415, 416
Chambers, John, 9, 92
Chapman, Timothy L., 56
Charan, Ram, 138, 436
Chew, W. Bruce, 369, 450
Choffray, Jean-Marie, 82, 85, 248
Choi, Thomas Y., 340
Chopra, S., 333
Christensen, Clayton M., 126, 220, 226, 236, 241, 242
Christopher, Martin, 337
Churchill, Gilbert A., Jr., 422, 423
Cioffi, Jennifer, 436
Clark, Ann Hojbjerg, 124
Clark, Bruce H., 443, 445
Clark, Don, 89
Clark, Kim B., 239, 240
Clemes, Michael, 267
Cohn, Russ, 395
Coles, Gary L., 135
Collins, David J., 158
Comer, James M., 425
Conlon, Ginger, 314
Cooper, Martha C., 421
Cooper, Robert G., 246, 247, 248, 250, 251, 252

Cooper, Robin, 103, 368, 369, 450, 451
Copacino, Bill, 330
Corey, E. Raymond, 75, 76, 284
Corsi, Thomas, 339
Cort, Stanton G., 396
Court, David, 447
Coviello, Nicole E., 271
Cowell, Donald, 272, 273, 274, 275
Cravens, David W., 426, 428
Cressman, George E., Jr., 363, 374, 375, 376, 377
Cron, William L., 421, 422, 423
Cross, James, 408
Crow, Lowell E., 86
Culley, James D., 135
Czinkota, Michael R., 190, 192

D
Danaher, Peter J., 271
D'Aveni, Richard A., 359, 370
Davenport, Thomas H., 35, 198
Davidow, William H., 268, 271, 272
Davies, Greg, 47
Davis, Donna, 37
Dawes, Philip, 80
Day, George S., 8, 77, 92, 93, 95, 102, 104, 112, 163, 191, 220, 236, 304, 305, 314, 371
De Meyer, Arnoud, 333
Dean, Joel, 372
DeBonis, Nicholas, 132
Debruyne, Marion, 248
Delaney, Laura, 192
Deligonul, Seyda, 195
Dell, Michael, 323
Desai, Mihir A., 195
Deschamps, Jean-Phillippe, 369
Deshpande, Rohit, 8
Devinney, Timothy M., 339
Dickson, Peter R., 81, 82
Dolan, Robert J., 363, 367, 368, 372, 373
Doney, Patricia M., 94
Donnelly, James H., 268
Donthu, Naveen, 65
Dorf, Bob, 107
Dougherty, Deborah, 454
Dowst, Somerby, 70
Doyle, Peter, 136

Dozbaba, Mary Sigfried, 70
Drakšaitė, Aura, 338
Droll, Mathias, 415
Dubinsky, Alan J., 423
Ducante, Douglas, 400
Durvasula, Srinivas, 270
Dyer, Jeffrey H., 112, 114, 193

E
Edgett, Scott J., 246, 250, 251
Eggert, Andreas, 11, 97, 98, 106, 216, 362
Eisenhardt, Kathleen M., 240, 244, 245, 253
Eklund, Robert C., 418
El-Ansary, Adel, 422
Ellinger, Alexander B., 306
Elliot, Stuart, 25
Elliott, Heidi, 288
Ellram, Lisa, 346
Engardio, Pete, 14, 187
Erickson, Tamara J., 238
Evans, David, 276
Evans, Kenneth R., 412, 417

F
Fadell, Tony, 234
Faherenwald, Bill, 334
Fahey, Liam, 9
Fang, Eric (Er), 262
Faris, Charles W., 65, 67
Farley, John U., 8
Farrell, Mark A., 82
Fearon, Harold E., 38, 49, 50
Fehle, Frank, 215
Ferguson, Brad, 338
Ferguson, Renee Boucher, 312
Ferguson, Tim, 4
Ferguson, Wade, 215
Ferrin, Bruce, 346
Fiqueiredo, Bruna, 182
Fisher, Marshall, 339
Fites, Donald V., 199
Flynn, Anna E., 38
Foley, C. Fritz, 195
Ford, David, 81
Ford, Neil M., 422, 423
Fornell, Claes, 188
Foster, Thomas A., 346

Fournier, Susan, 215
Frambach, T., 372
Frankwick, Gary L., 156, 157, 454
Fraser, Cynthia, 136
Fredette, Michael, 36
Freytog, Per Vagn, 124
Friedman, Lawrence G., 282, 283, 284, 285, 287
Friscia, Tony, 334
Frost, Raymond, 321
Fujino, Michimosa, 235
Furey, Timothy R., 283
Fürst, Andreas, 110
Futrell, Charles M., 423, 424

G
Gale, Bradley T., 215, 359
Gamble, Robert H., 341
Ganesan, Shankar, 8
Garda, Robert A., 129
Gardner, Alston, 76
Garren, Jeffrey E., 181
Garrett, Paula L., 396
Gatignon, Hubert, 135
Gebhardt, Gary F., 8
Gentry, Julie, 350
George, William R., 268
Gerard, Michael, 444
Gertz, Dwight L., 124, 125, 216, 239
Ghemawat, Pankaj, 197, 200
Ghingold, Morry, 65, 67, 78
Gillilard, David I., 69
Gilmore, Thomas N., 159
Glazer, Rashi, 73
Godes, David, 420
Gonzalez, Gabriel R., 84
Good, David J., 305
Gooley, Toby, 349
Gopalakrishna, Srinath, 401, 402, 403, 411
Gothfredson, Mark, 74
Gould, Daniel, 418
Green, Jeremy, 140
Gregor, William T., 444
Gremler, Dwayne D., 264, 269
Grewal, Dhruv, 35, 138, 265, 347, 371
Griffin, Abbie, 233, 237, 238, 248
Gronroos, Christian, 268
Gross, Andrew, 81

Grove, Andy, 309
Guiltinan, Joseph P., 275
Gummesson, Evert, 267
Gupta, Ajay, 56

H
Hackett, James P., 256
Haley, George T., 185
Hamel, Gary, 154, 160, 162, 164, 238, 437
Hamilton, David P., 194
Hamm, Steve, 277
Hancock, Maryanne Q., 364
Hancock, William A., 374
Hannon, Neal J., 315
Hansotia, Behram J., 223
Harlan, Robert K., 46, 74
Hardt, Chip W., 4, 37, 42, 74
Harper, Doug, 297
Harris, Jeanne G., 35
Harris, Nicole, 44
Hartley, Steven W., 408
Hauser, John, 233
Hawes, Jon M., 131
Hawker, Charlie, 18, 73, 74
Hayes, Simon, 112, 114
Hebda, John, 237, 238
Heide, Jan B., 67, 72, 73
Hemerling, James W., 14, 181–185, 187, 189
Henderson, John C., 312
Herzog, Raymond E., 386
Heskett, James L., 269, 274
Hesseldahl, Arik, 31
Hill, Ruth, 280
Hines, James, 195
Hoffman, K. Douglas, 37
Hoffman, William, 318, 334
Hofman, Debra, 334
Hogan, John, 373, 379
Holcomb, Mary Collins, 346
Hollis, Judith, 36
Homburg, Christian, 67, 106, 110, 111, 156, 216, 217, 359, 360, 362, 408, 409, 415, 417, 424
Hook, Jeff, 112
Hosford, Christopher, 446
Houston, Mark B., 245, 411
Howard, John A., 67, 86
Howell, Jane M., 236
Hubbard, Katrina J., 77
Huffman, Nicole P., 67

Hult, G. Tomas M., 195
Hunt, Shelby D., 16, 37, 92, 94, 298
Hutt, Michael D., 4, 11, 81, 84, 115, 116, 156, 157, 158, 159, 219, 234, 237, 245, 248, 418, 453, 454, 456

I
Inampudi, Srikant, 44
Ingram, Thomas N., 422, 426

J
Jacobs, Fred A., 450
Jacobson, Robert, 214, 372
Jacoby, David, 182
Jackson, Barbara Bund, 96
Jackson, Donald W., Jr., 70, 81, 131
Jackson, Ralph W., 272
Jackson, Susan A., 418
Jacques, Philip, 398
Jana, Reena, 256
Jap, Sandy D., 319, 377, 378
Jarboe, Greg, 323
Jaworski, Bernard J., 8
Jayachandran, Satish, 154, 209
Jensen, Ore, 156, 408, 417
Jeuland, Abel P., 372
Joachimsthaler, Erich, 386
Jobber, Damd, 190
Jobs, Steve, 234
John, Roland H., 364
Johnson, James C., 350
Johnson, M. Eric, 332
Johnson, Mark W., 243, 413, 424
Johnson, Michael D., 105
Johnson, Paul, 225
Johnston, Wesley J., 76, 77, 80, 84, 85, 395, 421, 450
Jones, Daniel J., 274
Jones, Eli, 425
Jones, Thomas O., 216, 269
Jubak, Jim, 31

K
Kahl, Steven, 338
Kahney, Leander, 233
Kale, Prashant, 112, 114, 193
Kalkoffen, Malte, 19, 20
Kalkota, Ravi, 306
Kanter, Rosabeth Moss, 92, 114, 116, 324

Kapelianis, Dimitrios, 84, 219, 248, 418
Kaplan, Robert S., 10, 99–101, 103, 138,
    167–174, 436, 437, 438, 439, 450, 451
Karpinski, Richard, 446, 447
Katrichis, Jerome M., 81
Katz, Paul B., 39–42, 44
Kearney, A. T., 80
Keedy, Jennifer, 319
Keiningham, Timothy L., 217
Keith, Janet E., 70, 81, 131
Keller, Kevin Lane, 5, 209–213
Keon, Shawn, 193
Kesseler, Jim, 321, 322
Kijewski, Valerie, 385, 387
Kiley, David, 398
Kim, W. Chan, 136
King, Ronald H., 83, 84
Kippola, Tom, 225
Kirca, Ahmet H., 154
Kleinschmidt, Elko J., 246, 247, 248, 251, 252
Kohli, Ajay K., 8, 35, 82, 262
Kopczak, Laura Rock, 332
Kosnik, Thomas J., 193
Kotchetova, Natalia, 450
Kotler, Philip, 23, 129, 443, 444, 452
Kovar, Joseph, 277
Krapfel, Robert, 94
Krauss, Michael, 448
Kreuze, Deborah, 408
Krisher, Tom, 17
Krishnan, M. S., 188, 216
Krishnan, R., 35, 138, 265, 371
Krishnan, Vish V., 261
Krohmer, Harley, 156, 408
Krol, Carol, 73, 396, 448
Kuester, Sabine, 67
Kuglin, Fred A., 112
Kumar, Nirmalya, 359
Kumar, V., 8

L
Laczniak, Gene R., 79
Lafley, A. G., 138
LaForge, Raymond W., 426, 428
LaLonde, Bernard J., 346
Lambert, David R., 396
Lambert, Douglas M., 331, 345
Lamons, Bob, 133, 209, 221
Lamons, Robert, 392

Lamont, Judith, 309
Lapide, Larry, 137
Larréché, Jean-Claude, 221, 222
Laseter, Timothy M., 39, 74, 129
LeBlanc, Ronald P., 86
Lee, Don Y., 80
Lee, Hau, 336
Leenders, Michael R., 38, 49, 50
Lehmann, Donald R., 131, 212, 213
Leigh, Thomas W., 422
Lemon, Katherine N., 105, 108, 139, 171, 442
Leonhardt, David, 258
Levy, Michael, 347
Lewin, Jeffrey E., 65, 77, 84, 85
Li, Tiger, 251
Liakko, Timo, 80
Lichtenthal, J. David, 4, 77, 78
Ligos, Melinda, 47
Liker, Jeffrey K., 340
Lilien, Gary L., 78, 80, 82, 83, 85, 248,
    401, 403
Lim, Jeen-Su, 158
Lin, Chia Chia, 202
Lin, Jason, 202
Liukko, Timo, 128
Lococo, Edmond, 53
Lodish, Leonard M., 297
Logovinsky, Irma, 460
Lohtia, Ritu, 395
Lovelock, Christopeher, 267
Loveman, Gary W., 269
Lucke, Tom, 373
Lunsford, Dale. A., 272
Lusch, Robert F., 262
Lynch, David F., 306
Lysonski, Steven, 270

M
Madden, Thomas J., 215
Maddox, Kate, 73, 393, 394, 397, 447, 448
Magee, John F., 238
Magnusson, Liz, 133
Mahajan, Vijay, 372
Maidique, Modesto A., 236
Maier, E. B., 294
Makridakis, Spyros, 142, 144
Malter, Alan J., 8
Mangalindan, Mylene, 46
Mange, Paul O., 56

Marchetti, Michele, 408
Marn, Mike, 361
Marsh, Peter, 354
Marshall, Greg W., 413, 421
Marshall, Jeffrey, 203
Martin, Karla L., 158
Marvel, Matthew R., 237, 238
Mast, Kenneth E., 131
Mathews, Anna Wilde, 351
Mauborgne, Renée, 136
McBurney, Peter, 140
McCaney, Kevin, 52
McCann, Joseph E., 159
McConville, Daniel J., 349
McCormick, Aislinn, 310
McElroy, James C., 423
McGovern, Gail J., 447
McKee, Steve, 392
McKenna, Regis, 209, 219, 370
McNeilly, Kevin M., 425
McQuiston, Daniel H., 81, 82, 290, 297
McTavish, Ronald, 454
McWilliams, Gary, 199
McWilliams, Robert D., 78
Mehrotra, Anuj, 295
Mehta, Stephanie N., 49
Mehta, Subhash C., 270
Mendel, Arthur H., 377
Menezes, Melvin A. J., 294
Menon, Ajay, 106, 216, 217, 359, 360, 362
Mentzer, John T., 141
Morrill, John E., 385
Meyer, Arnoud De, 333
Meyer, Christopher, 258, 259, 260
Meyer, Marc H., 239, 250
Michaels, Ronald E., 423
Micheau, Victoria A., 141
Midgley, David, 80
Milford, Maureen, 280
Millar, Victor E., 18
Miller, Amy, 436
Miller, Chris, 320
Minahan, Tim A., 44–46, 75
Miner, Ann S., 244
Mintzberg, Henry, 233
Mirani, Robert, 143
Mitchell, Vincent-Wayne, 125
Mittal, Vikas, 103

Moenart, Rudy, 248
Mohr, Jacqueline J., 392
Mokwa, Michael P., 158, 444, 451
Mollenkopf, Diane, 267
Möller, Kristian, 258
Moltzen, Edward, 277
Momin, Zafar, 19, 20
Monroe, Kent B., 369, 373, 374
Montgomery, David B., 371
Montgros, Xavier de, 353
Montoya-Weiss, Mitzi M., 251
Moon, Mark A., 141
Moore, Deanne, 143
Moore, Jeffrey A., 224–226, 228, 370
Moorman, Christine, 244
Morgan, Neil A., 163
Morgan, Robert M., 16, 92, 94, 298
Moriarty, Mark A., 143, 146
Moriarty, Rowland T., 76, 132
Morrall, Katherine, 423
Morris, Michael H., 272
Mosquet, Xavier, 19, 20
Moyer, Reed, 367
Mulcahy, Ann, 9
Mummaleni, Venkatapparao, 4
Murphy, Elena Epatko, 22
Murshed, Feisal, 103

N
Nagle, Thomas T., 359, 363, 364, 365, 366, 374, 375, 376, 377
Narayanan, V. G., 99, 100, 138
Narayandas, Das, 92, 94, 110, 217, 360, 442
Narayandas, Narakesari, 414, 416
Narus, James A., 10, 11, 94, 106–109, 111, 297, 298, 359, 364
Narver, John C., 8
Naumann, Earl, 78
Nayak, P. Ranganath, 369
Neidell, Lester A., 272
Neilson, Gary L., 158
Nielsen, Jacob, 304
Neisser, U., 83
Nevens, T. Michael, 239
Noble, Charles H., 158, 451
Norton, David P., 10, 100, 167–173, 436, 437, 438, 439

O

O'Brien, Louise, 333
O'Connell, Patricia, 9
O'Hara, Brad, 401
O'Heir, Jeff, 298
Ohmae, Kenichi, 194
Ohmae, Kenneth, 113
Ojola, Mary D., 308
Oke, Adegoke, 277
O'Leary, Bay, 377
Oliver, Richard L., 216, 426
Olshavsky, Richard W., 86
Olson, Eric M., 154
O'Marah, Kevin, 334
Onyemah, Vincent, 425
Oosthuizen, Pierre, 272
Ormiston, Charles, 72
O'Shaughnessy, John, 131
Osmonbekov, Talai, 69
O'Sullivan, Dan, 398, 445

P

Page, Albert L., 219
Palmatier, Robert W., 92, 94, 262, 409, 410,
    411, 412
Parasuraman, A., 265, 275, 424
Park, C. Whan, 398
Parkhe, Arvind, 195
Parsons, Simon, 140
Patten, Carol, 324
Patterson, Laura, 436, 446, 447
Patterson, Paul G., 80
Patton, W.E., III, 83, 84
Peppers, Don, 107, 258, 304, 440, 441
Perreault, William D., Jr., 93, 96
Peterson, Robert A., 424
Phillips, Stephen, 74
Piercy, Nigel, 391
Pitt, Leyland, 272
Plank, Richard F., 346
Plouffe, Christopher R., 420
Porter, Ann Millen, 22, 34, 75
Porter, Michael E., 18, 165–167, 171, 198, 199,
    201, 238, 311, 322, 454
Poueymirou, Roger, 377
Powers, Elizabeth, 158
Prahalad, C. K., 216, 239, 261, 263,
    316, 386

Puryear, Rudy, 74
Puto, Charles P., 83, 84

Q

Quelch, John A., 447
Quinn, James Brian, 24, 25, 164, 233, 234

R

Rab, Linda, 395
Rajala, Risco, 258
Rajendra, K. Srivastava, 9
Ramani, Girish, 8
Ramaswamy, Venkat, 216, 261, 263,
    316, 386
Rands, G., 117
Rangan, V. Kasturi, 6, 94, 132, 284, 292, 293,
    294, 295, 296
Ranstad, Evan, 199
Raynor, Michael E., 226, 236, 241
Reichheld, Frederick E., 92, 104, 105, 110, 111,
    270
Reid, David A., 158
Reinartz, Werner, 8, 276, 366
Reinecke, Nicholas, 37, 42, 74
Reingen, Peter H., 81, 115, 116, 156, 157, 159,
    234, 237, 245, 456
Richard, Pierre J., 339
Richardson, James, 448
Richey, Keith, 214
Rickard, David, 109, 259, 260
Rigby, Darrell K., 104, 105, 111
Ring, Peter Smith, 116, 117
Ritterkamp, James J., Jr., 374
Roberts, Dexter, 187, 188
Roberts, Karl, 319
Robertson, Thomas S., 135, 136
Robinson, Patrick J., 65, 67
Rogers, Martha, 107, 258, 304, 440, 441
Rogers, William, III, 444
Ronchetto, John R., Jr., 81, 234, 237
Ronkainen, Ilka A., 190, 192
Roos, Gina, 10
Root, Franklin R., 190
Rosenbloom, Bert, 282
Rostky, George, 367
Roth, Martin S., 398
Roussel, Philip A., 238
Rozin, Randall S., 133

Rudelius, William, 408
Rudzki, Robert A., 332
Ruekert, Robert W., 247
Rukstad, Michael G., 158
Rule, Eric, 193
Rumar, Dave, 311
Russ, Frederick A., 425
Rust, Roland T., 108, 139, 271, 436, 442
Ryan, Jim, 7
Ryans, Adrian R., 427

S
Saad, Komol N., 238
Sager, Ira, 25
Sager, Jeffrey K., 423
Samuel, David M., 76
Sanders, Nada, 142
Sands, Jeff, 138
Sarkees, Matthew, 103
Sashi, C. M., 377
Sasser, W. Earl, Jr., 216, 269, 270
Satpathy, Aurobind, 44
Saunders, John, 136
Savitz, Eric J., 21
Sawhney, Mohanbir, 46, 260, 261, 263
Scheer, Lisa K., 94, 412
Schefter, Phil, 104, 105, 111
Schnedler, David E., 124, 131
Schroeder, Bill, 82
Schiff, Larry, 109, 110, 111, 270
Schultz, Dan, 384
Schultz, Heidi, 384
Schultz, Roberta J., 305, 417
Schwager, Andre, 250, 258, 259, 260
Schwartz, Matthew, 5, 387, 389
Scott, Stan, 78
Segalo, A. Michael, 142, 144
Seigel, Jason, 74
Selnes, Fred, 105
Serwer, Andy, 164
Shaikh, Muzaffar A., 223
Shankar, Satish, 72
Shapiro, Benson P., 76, 102, 218
Sharma, Arun, 35, 138, 265, 295, 347, 371
Shaw, Gordon, 158
Shaw, Wade H., 305
Shear, Herbert, 343

Sheffi, Yossi, 337
Shermach, Kelly, 448
Sherman, Stratford, 155
Sherry, John F., Jr., 8
Shervauie, Tadasadduq A., 9
Sheth, Jagdish N., 67, 82, 83, 85, 86, 223
Shirouzu, Norihiko, 235
Shostack, G. Lynn, 264
Siemplenski, Michael, 219
Silverstein, Barry, 284, 396, 397
Simko, Stephen, 301
Simpson, James T., 83
Singh, Anant, 44
Singh, Habir, 112, 114, 193
Singh, Jagdin, 421
Sirkin, Harold L., 14, 181, 206
Slagmulder, Regine, 368
Slater, Stanley F., 8, 154
Slatter, Stuart St. P., 377
Smith, Frank O., 313
Smith, Gerald E., 363, 364, 365, 366
Smith, Paul M., 401
Smith, Timothy M., 401
Smock, Doug, 68
Sonnack, Mary, 124, 249, 250
Spekman, Robert, 94, 322
Speh, Thomas W., 4, 158, 330, 335, 341, 343, 352, 454
Spiller, Peter, 37, 42, 74
Srivam, Ven, 94
Stafford, Edwin R., 115, 116
Stallkamp, Thomas W., 332
Steenkamp, Jan-Benedict E.M., 94, 262
Stephenson, Susie, 54
Sterne, Jim, 399
Stevens, Ruth P., 400, 402
Stewart, David W., 386
Stewart, Thomas A., 172, 333
Stock, James, 343
Stock, Ruth M., 111, 366, 408, 409, 416, 424
Stone, Brad, 31
Strauss, Judy, 321
Stump, Rodney L., 248
Summe, Gregory L., 239
Summers, John O., 86

Swanson, Sandra, 448
Swartz, Gordon S., 132

T
Tabrizi, Behnam N., 253
Takahashi, Dean, 24
Tanzer, Andrew, 344
Taylor, Alex, III, 199, 219
Taylor, Thayer C., 414
Teas, R. Kenneth, 423
Tellis, Gerald J., 233
Thedinger, Bart, 127
Theocharides, Theo, 18, 73, 74
Thomas, Robert J., 145
Thomke, Stefan, 124, 249, 250, 251
Thurm, Scott, 55
Tichy, Noel M., 155
Totzek, Dirk, 415
Toupin, Lorie, 330
Trebilcock, Bob, 22
Trinkle, Bob, 290, 291, 386, 408
Troy, David, 310
Tsai, Jessica, 125
Tuli, Kapil R., 262
Tuttle, Al, 289

U
Uchitelle, Louis, 187
Ulaga, Wolfgang, 11, 97, 98, 106, 216, 276, 362, 366
Ungerman, Drew, 354
Usha, C. V., 185
Ustener, Tuba, 420
Uttal, Bro, 239, 268, 271, 272
Utterback, James M., 239

V
Valikangas, Liisa, 437
Van de Ven, Andrew H., 116, 117
Van Hoek, Remko, 276, 348
Van Mieghan, J. A., 333
van Rossum, Wouter, 10, 11, 107, 364
Varadarajan, Rajan, 209, 423
Vargo, Stephen L., 262
Venkatesh, R., 82
Venkatraman, N., 312
Verhllen, Theo M., 372
Verhoof, Peter, 105
Veverka, Mark, 106

Vigoroso, Mark, 46
Vojak, Bruce, 237, 238
von Hippel, Eric, 124, 248, 249, 250, 251
Vorhies, Douglas W., 163
Vuori, Risto, 80, 128

W
Wailgum, Thomas, 22
Walker, Beth A., 84, 115, 116, 156, 159, 219, 245, 248, 418, 454, 456
Walker, Orville C., Jr., 221, 222, 247, 422, 423
Walker, Richard, 52
Walton, James A., 233
Ward, James C., 156, 157
Washburn, Stewart A., 143
Weber, John A., 143
Weber, Rick, 186
Webster, Frederick E., Jr., 5, 8, 79, 85, 154, 155, 209, 210
Weinberg, Charles B., 427
Weiss, Allen M., 67, 72, 73
Weitz, Barton A., 67, 78, 297
Welch, Jack, 155
Wensley, Robin, 163
Werner, Curt, 309
West, Douglas C., 141
Westerland, Mika, 258
Wheelwright, Steven C., 142, 239, 240
Whinston, Andren W., 306
Whitaker, Jonathan, 188
White, Erin, 215
Whitelock, Jerry, 190
Williams, Jerome D., 401, 402
Willis, Raymond E., 143
Wilson, David T., 4, 65, 78, 83
Wilson, Dominic F., 125
Wilson, Elizabeth J., 83, 136
Wind, Yoram, 65, 67, 78, 85, 125, 127, 136, 372
Wojcik, Philip J., 364
Womack, James, 274
Wong, M. Anthony, 78, 80
Wood, Donald F., 350
Woodside, Arch G., 76, 77, 80, 128, 136
Workman, Daniel, 6
Workman John P., Jr., 417
Worthen, Ken, 73
Wren, Brent M., 83

Y
Yip, George S., 76, 416
Yoder, Stephen Kreider, 227
Yoon, Eunsang, 248, 385, 397
Young, Dave, 181–185, 187
Yu, Larry, 104

Z
Zahorik, Anthony J., 271
Zale, Joe, 379

Zarley, Craig, 277
Zaltman, Gerald, 82
Zawala, Craig, 361
Zeithaml, Valarie A., 108, 139, 264, 265, 268, 269, 271, 275
Zimmerman, Eileen, 9
Zou, Shaoming, 201

SUBJECT INDEX

A

Accessory equipment, 24
Account management, 418–420
  building internal relationships, 419
  cycle of account management success, 419
  key account management, 414–417
  national account success, 417
  YRC Worldwide, case study, 431
Action plan (marketing strategy), 440
Activity-based costing (ABC), 99, 450
  calculating logistics costs, 346
Advertising, 383–400. *See also* business marketing
    communications
  defining objectives, 387–389
  determining expenditures, 389
  developing the message, 391
  formal advertising by government, 52
  Johnson Controls, Inc., case study, 406
  role in business marketing strategy, 385–387
  measuring advertising effectiveness, 397–400
  selecting advertising media, 392–397
  specifying target audience, 389–391
  stages in advertising program development,
    388
Advisory support, 25
Allegiance Healthcare Corporation, 108
Alliances. *See* strategic alliances
Annual plan control (marketing strategy), 446
Apple Computer
  face-off of BlackBerry and iPhone in business
    market, 31
  iPhone, triumph of supply chain
    management, 22
  iPod, development of, 234
Ariba, Inc., 45, 59
Assets
  intangible, 172
  strategic, 164
autonomous strategic behavior, 234–236
Avnet, supply chain management, 332

B

BASF, building strong brand with services, 221
B2B (business-to-business) e-commerce, 304,
  307. *See also* e-commerce;

e-commerce strategies
B2C (business-to-customer) e-commerce, 307
B2M (business-to-machine) e-commerce, 308
Balanced scorecard, 167, 437
  customer perspective, 170
  financial perspective, 168–170
  internal business process perspective, 171
  learning and growth, 172
  strategy map, 173–175, 438
benchmarking to competitors in channel design
    process, 294
benefits contributing to customer value, 360
Best practices in customer relationship
    management, 109
Bidding, competitive, 377–379
BlackBerry, face-off with iPhone, 31
Boeing
  sales forecasting and collaboration with
    Alcoa, 141
  supplier collaboration, 42
Boomgar Corporation, 384
Boundary-spanning connections, 115
Brands, 5, 209–215
  brand equity, 210
  corporate brand personality traits, 214
  defined, 210
  steps in brand-building, 210–212
  systems model for managing, 212–215
Brazil, rapidly developing economy, 14, 72, 181
Bribery dilemma in global markets, 194
Budgeting for advertising, 389–391
Bundling services, 275
Business market segmentation, 122–150
  bases of segmentation, 127
  benefits of, 125
  choosing market segments, 136–138
  defining channel customer segments and needs
    by segment, 293
  defining customer value proposition for
    segments, 439
  estimating segment demand, 139–142
  implementing segmentation strategy, 139
  isolating market segment profitability, 138
  macrolevel bases of segmentation, 128–131
  microlevel bases of segmentation, 131–136

profitability analysis by segment, 449
recognizing new market opportunities, 126
requirements for, 125
services market, 271
value-based segmentation, 368
Business marketing, 4
consumer marketing versus, 14–17
market-centered organizations, 56, 57
business marketing channels, managing
281–302
channel administration, 296–298
channel design, 292–296
channel of distribution, 282
considerations with Internet marketing, 320
direct channels, 283
indirect channels, 284
integrated multichannel models, 285
Internet as channel alternative, 321
managing customer contact points, 285
multichannel integration map, 286
participants in business marketing channel,
287–292
SunPower Corporation case study, 301
using customer relationship management
(CRM) systems, 286
Business marketing communications
advertising, 384
managing business-to-business advertising,
387–397
measuring advertising effectiveness,
397–400
managing the personal selling function,
407–431
role of advertising, 385–387
trade show strategy, 400–404
Business marketing management, 5
framework for the process, 28, 457
Business marketing strategies, 26, 153–179
building the strategy plan, 167–175
business-level strategy, 155
components of a business model, 160–165
corporate strategy, 155
developing, process of, 438–443
functional strategy, 155
functionally integrated planning, 158–160
for global markets, 180–207
hierarchy of strategies in large organizations,
154
Intuit, Inc., case study, 460

marketing control, 443–451
marketing's strategic role in strategy
development, 154–160
strategic positioning, 165–167
strategy formulation and the hierarchy,
156–158
strategy map, 437
Business markets
characteristics of, 13
characteristics of customers, 17
classifying goods for, 22–25
commercial enterprises as consumers, 21,
34–47
consumer-goods markets versus, 7
customers, categories of, 6
defined, 4
government market, 47–53
institutional market, 53–57
organizational buyers, 33–60
Business mission, 163
Business model, 160–167
components of, 162
core strategy, 163
customer interface, 162
strategic positioning, 165–167
strategic resources, 164
value network, 164
Business process outsourcing, 183
Business publications, advertising in, 394–396
Businesses as customers, 6
Business-level strategy, 155
Business-to-business e-commerce. 304, 307. See
also e-commerce; e-commerce strategies
Business-to-business logistical management,
349–354
Business-to-business logistical service, 346–349
Business-to-customer (B2C) e-commerce, 307
Business-to-machine (B2M) e-commerce, 308
Buyer, 80
Buyers, organizational, 33–60. *See also*
purchasing
commercial enterprises, 34–44
e-procurement, 44–47
governments, 47–53
Buyer-seller relationships, managing, 95–98. See
also customer relationship management
evaluating relationships, 112
transactional exchange, 95
collaborative exchange, 96

strategy guidelines for marketers, 97
switching costs considered by buyers, 96
Buying behavior, organizational, 63–90
   consumer-driven innovation at Johnson
      Controls, 64
   environmental forces in, 71–73
   individual forces in, 82–84
   forces influencing, summary of, 71
   group forces in, 77–81
   major elements of buying behavior, 85
   major stages of buying process, 65
   organizational buying process, 65–71
   organizational forces in, 73–77
Buying center, 77–81, 86
   identifying patterns of influence, 80
   identifying powerful members, 81
   involvement of participants at stages of
      procurement process, 79
   predicting composition of, 79
   roles of members in procurement process,
      79–81
   structure of, as microsegmentation basis, 135
Buying decision approaches (organizational)
   new-task buying situations, 67
   modified rebuy situations, 69
   straight rebuy situations, 68
Buying motivations, understanding for commer-
      cial customers, 21
Buying organizations, macrolevel characteristics,
      128–131
   product/service application, 129
   value in use, 129
Buying process, organizational, 65–71
   key buying influentials, 11
   modified rebuy, 69
   new-task buying situation, 67
   search process, 66
   straight rebuy approach, 68
   supplier selection and performance review, 66

C
Callaway Golf, 43
Canon, global stategy, 199
Capacity (service businesses), 266
Capital investment requirements, advantages in
      RDEs, 184
Caterpillar
   global strategy, 199
   logistics service, 354

Causal analysis, 144
CBBE (customer-based brand equity), 210
Central and eastern Europe, rapidly developing
      economies, 72, 181
Centralization of procurement, 75
Challenges in services marketing. *See* marketing
      challenges for services
Channel administration, 296–298
   building trust, 298
   dealer advisory councils, 297
   selection of channel members, 296
   margins and commissions, 298
   motivating channel members, 297
   partnership with channel members, 297
Channel design, 292–296
   assessing firm's channel capabilities, 294
   benchmarking to competitors, 294
   channel structure, 292
   creating channel solutions for customers' la-
      tent needs, 295
   crucial points in channel transformation, 295
   defining customer segments, 293
   evaluating and choosing channel options, 295
   identifying customers' channel needs by
      segment, 293
Channel of distribution, 282
Channel participants, 287–292
   distributors, 287–290
   factors influencing choice of intermediaries,
      292
   manufacturers' representatives, 290–292
   members providing services, 277
Channel structure, 292
Chief purchasing officer (CPO), 37
China, 14, 181. *See also* rapidly developing
      economies
   capabilities advantage of workforce, 187
   government subsidies, 184
   growing role as market, 186
   rapidly developing economy, 72
   risks in manufacturing and selling, 203
Cisco Systems, 34, 92
   career path for CEO, 9
   gorilla power in high tech markets, 225
   management by FedEx of parts shipments, 25
   strategic alliances, 112
   TelePresence technology, 231
Close working relationships,
Closed bidding, 377

Cognition, 83

Collaborative advantage, 92

Collaborative customers, 97

Collaborative exchange, 93, 96

Collaborative Planning Forecasting and
    Replenishment (CPFR), 145

Collaborative relationships, 96, 108
  value drivers in, 97

Commercial enterprises, 34–44
  as customers in business market, 6, 21
  classifying, using NAICS, 36
  distribution by size, 35
  geographical concentration of manufacturers
    in U.S., 35

Commercial Service of the Department of
    Commerce, 191

Commissions
  manufacturers' representatives, 290
  margins and commissions in marketing
    channels, 298

Commodity value, 364

Competitive bidding, 377–379

Complex modified rebuy, 70

Complexity management, 40

Competition, 370
  responding to price attacks by competitors,
    374–377

Competitive bidding, 377–379

Competitive cognition, 418

Competitor orientation, 248

Compliance program (for government
    contractors), 49

Compression strategy (product development),
    253

Configuration (in global market), 197

Consumer-goods markets
  business markets versus, 7
  Dell Computer customers, 6
  e-commerce, 304

Consumer marketing, business marketing versus,
    14–17

Contract manufacturing, 192

Contracting (global market entry strategy), 191

Contracts, government, 49

Control of marketing strategy. *See* marketing
    control

Coordination (in global market), 197, 202

Core business, Internet enabling focus on, 312

Core processes, 164

Core competencies, 164

Core participants in strategic alliances, 114

Core strategy, 163

Corporate strategy, 155

Cost advantages in RDEs, 183–186
  hidden cost or RDE operations, 185

Cost determinants, 368–370
  classifying costs, 369
  target costing, 368

Cost reductions with SCM, 336

Cost-reimbursement contracts, 50

Cost in use for customers, 361

Costs of serving the customer, 102, 348

CPO (chief purchasing officer), 37

Creative strategy statement (advertising), 389

CRM. *See* customer relationship
    management

Cross-functional relationships in marketing, 11

Custom-built products, 218

Custom-designed products, 219

Customer contact points, managing in channels,
    285

Customer experience, 258–260

Customer experience management, 260

Customer interface (business model), 162

Customer perspective (balanced scorecard), 170

Customer prioritization, 415

Customer relationship management (CRM),
    104–112, 143
  acquiring the right customers, 104
  crafting the right value proposition, 107–109
  CRM systems, coordinating sales channels,
    286
  defined, 104
  diversifying the customer portfolio, 106
  help from CRM technology, 105
  new-market disruption in CRM technology,
    243
  steps in creating a CRM strategy, 105
  tracking customer response to advertising, 397

Customer relationships, managing, 9, 91–120
  CRM (customer relationship management),
    104–112
  managing buyer-seller relationships, 95–98
  measuring customer profitability, 99–103
  relationship marketing, 92–95
  strategic alliances, 112–117

Customer solutions approach to services,
    260–263

Customer value, 216–218, 359–362
benefits, 360
cost in use, 361
differentiation through value creation, 362
sacrifices, 360
Customer value proposition, 10–14
characteristics of business markets, 13
deciding what matters most, 11
defined, 11
defining for target segments, 439
global market perspective, 14
illustration of, Sonoco, 11
marketing's cross-functional relationships, 11
working relationships, 12
Customer service, offshore outsourcing, 188
Customer service segmentation, 137
Customer-based brand equity (CBBE), 210
Customer-benefit concept (services), 272
Customer-linking capability, 8
partnering with customers, 10
Customers
benefits from business use of Internet, 311
benefits from supply chain management, 336
characteristics of business market
customers, 17
communication with, Internet capabilities, 322
groups presenting greatest growth
opportunities, 220
input into product design, 250
judgments about brands, 211
managing as assets, 8
price sensitivity and customer satisfaction, 366
relationship with manufacturers'
representatives, 290
requirements, meeting with Internet strategy,
323
customer satisfaction and loyalty, business
services, 268

D

Dashboard, marketing performance, 446–448
Dealer advisory councils, 297
Dealers and distributors (commercial
enterprises), 21
Deciders, 80
Deere & Company
profit impact of inventory management, 353
service offerings, 263
Defense procurement, 51

Delivery system, services, 274
Dell, Inc.
business and consumer markets, 6
competition for global PC market, 199
diversified customer portfolio, 106
Internet and e-commerce in corporate
strategy, 304
Internet marketing content, 73, 88
legendary success with e-commerce, 314
supply chain management, 333
Delphi method (forecasting), 143
Demand, 13
combining several forecasting techniques, 146
CPFR, collaborative approach to estimating
demand, 145
determinants of, 363–365
estimating demand for market segments,
139–142
price elasticity of demand, 366
qualitative techniques of forecasting, 142–144
quantitative techniques of forecasting, 144
Deployment of the sales force, 426–429
geographical organization, 413
Derived demand, 13
Development process factors in new product
success, 252
Development projects, types of, 239
Differentiation of products and services, 163,
201, 263
through value creation, 362
Differentiation value, 364
Direct channels, 283
Direct goods, 46
Direct marketing tools, 396
Discontinuous innovations, 224
Disintermediation, 320
Disruptive innovation model, 240–243
disruptive strategies, 241
low-end strategy tests, 242
new-market strategy tests, 242
final litmus test, 243
Distinctive value proposition, 167
Distribution channels, 282. *See also* business
marketing channels, managing
Distribution, services, 277
Distributors, 287–290
classification of, 289
choosing a distributor, 289
distributor as valuable partner, 289

effects of Internet marketing on, 320
responsibilities of, 288
DLA (Defense Logistics Agency), 51
DOD (Department of Defense) procurement by, 51
Dow Chemical, Internet and e-commerce in corporate strategy, 304
Dow Corning
    award-winning ad for its Web-based business model, 134
    business market segmentation, 132, 133
DuPont
    advertising of products to final consumers, 29
    market segmentation analysis, 135
    running Ford's paint shop, 261

E
E-commerce, 25, 304–312
    B2B and retail, 304
    B2M (business-to-machine), 308
    defining, 305–307
    strategic role of, 309–312
    support by intranets and extranets, 307–309
    types of, 307
E-commerce strategies, 312–325
    channel considerations with Internet marketing, 320
    delineating e-commerce objectives, 314–316
    effect of Internet on pricing strategy, 322
    Internet as channel alternative, 264, 321
    Internet strategy implementation, 316–319
    objectives of Internet marketing strategies, 314–316
    questions to guide strategy formulation, 313
    W.W. Grainger case study, 327
E-government, 48
E-mail marketing, 397
E-procurement, 44–47
    buying direct and indirect goods, 45
    defined, 45
    enhancement of buyer's capabilities, 45
    evaluation of suppliers' performance, 47
    measurable benefits delivered by, 45
    reverse auctions, 46
EACs (Export Assistance Centers), 191
Economic influences on buying behavior, 72
Economic value, 363
Efficiency and effectiveness controls, 448
Elasticity, price elasticity of demand, 11, 366

Employees, motivating, 110
End-market focus, 367
Entering goods, 23, 46
Entrepreneurship. *See also* innovation and product development
    conditions supporting, 237
    motivations of corporate entrepreneurs, 238
Environmental forces in buying behavior, 71–73
Environmentally responsible supply chain, 354
Ericcson, 337
Ethics
    bribery dilemma in global markets, 194
    gift-giving in business marketing, 47
Evaluative criteria, 82
Evoked set of alternatives, 86
Executive judgment (demand forecasting), 142
Expenditures for advertising, 389–391
Expense-to-sales ratio, 446
Experiential strategy (rapid development), 253
Experimentation and probing the future (product innovation), 245
Export Assistance Centers (EACs), 191
Exporting, 190
Extensive problem solving, 66
Extranets, 308

F
Facilitating goods, 23, 24
Fast-paced product development, 252
Feasible set of alternatives, 86
FedBizOpps (FBO), 52
Federal government buying, 52
Federal Supply Schedule Program, 51
Federated Insurance, targeting small businesses, 149
FedEx, 35, 258
    customer profitability, 139
    integrated technologies linking customers and SCM, 339
    management of Cisco's parts shipments, 25
    supply chain management, 339
Financial benefits from supply chain management, 337
Financial objectives, defining for marketing strategy, 439
Financial perspective (balanced scorecard), 168–170
Fixed-price contracts, 50

Flexible response throughout supply chain, 116
Focus, unique, 166
Focused strategy, 227
Forecasting. *See* demand
Formal advertising (government), 52
Foundation goods, 23, 24
Fuji Photo Film Company, 193
Functional strategy, 155
Future, probing into (product innovation), 245

G
Gatekeepers, 79
GE (General Electric), 155
  branding campaign, 209
  career path of CEO, 9
  customer input into product design, 251
  Kanthal supplier and GE's customer
    profitability, 99
  quality initiative, 215
GE Aircraft Engines, 196, 267
GE Capital, 154
GE Healthcare, 54, 186
  using Web to create new services, 316
GE Medical, Internet selling, 77
General Services Administration (GSA),
    procurement by, 51
Geographical organization of sales force, 413
Gift-giving in business marketing, 47
Global industries, 197
Global market perspective, 14
Global markets, 180–207
  access through the Internet, 312
  capabilities advantage in workforces in RDEs,
    187
  capturing global advantage in RDEs, 181
  choosing mode of entry, 195
  cost advantages in moving to RDE sourcing,
    183–186
  entry options, 190–195
  global strategy, 201–203
  market access advantages in RDEs, 186
  multidomestic versus global strategies,
    195–200
  outsourcing decision, 189
  unique risks in RDEs, 188
Global strategy, 196, 200, 201–203
Goods, classifying for business market, 22–25
  categories of goods, 22
  entering goods, 23

  facilitating goods, 23, 24
  foundation goods, 23, 24
Google, search engine marketing,
    384, 395
Governments, 47–53
  as business market customers, 6
  e-government, 49
  federal buying, 52
  government contracts, 49
  IBM's sales program for, 48
  influences on government buying, 49
  marketing strategy for, 53
  publications for potential vendors, 50
  purchasing organizations and procedures,
    50–52
  volume of purchases by government
    units, 47
Grainger. *See* W.W. Grainger, Inc.
Green supply chain, 354
Group forces in organizational buying behavior,
    77–81
Group purchasing (institutions), 55
Growth and productivity goals, defining for
    marketing strategy, 439
Growth stage, 169
GSA (General Services Administration),
    procurement by, 51

H
Harley-Davidson, 14
Harvest stage, 170
Hewlett-Packard (H-P), 124
  advantage in high tech markets, 225
  challenges from diverse, demanding
    customers, 120
  home base for businesses, 201
  Internet marketing content, 73
  inventory management, 353
  main street strategy, 228
  tornado strategy, 227
  Web site for medical customers, 309
High-cost-to-serve customers, 101
Home base for a business, 201
Honda, 17
  global strategy, 201
  HondaJet, 235
  strategic procurement, 39, 74
  supplier relationships, 340
Hypercompetitive rivalries, 370

I

IBM
  best practices in customer relationship
    management, 109
  building trust in channels, 298
  collaboration with channel partners through
    the Internet, 284
  collaborative relationships with customers, 95
  customer solutions, 74
  diversified customer portfolio, 106
  key account management, 76
  e-procurement, 44
  managing relationships in supply chain, 19
  selling to government units, 48
  service offerings, 258, 269, 277
Ideas for new products, sources of, 248–251
IDEO, 249
Implementation of marketing strategy. *See*
    marketing implementation
Improvisation (product innovation), 244
India, 14, 72, 181. *See also* rapidly developing
    economies
  capabilities advantage of workforce, 187
  unique risks in, 188
Indirect channels, 284
Indirect communication effects of advertising,
    398
Indirect goods, 45
Induced strategic behavior, 234
Industrial services, 219
Influencers, 79
Information processing, 83
Innovativeness of organization, 135
Innovation and product development,
    232–256
  autonomous strategic behavior, 234–236
  conditions supporting entrepreneurship, 237
  disruptive innovation model, 240–243
  induced strategic behavior, 234
  innovation winners in high-technology
    markets, 243–245
  management practices and innovation, 233
  managing technology, 238–245
  new product development process, 246–251
  product championing and the informal
    network, 236
Institutional market, 6, 53–57
  group purchasing, 55
  purchasing practices, 56

  purchasing procedures for institutional
    buyers, 54
  targeted marketing strategy for, 54
Installations, 24
Intangible assets, 172
Interactive or real-time marketing, 265
Integrated multichannel models, 285
Integration in strategic alliances, 116
Intel Corporation
  advantage in high tech markets, 225
  advertising, shift to online media, 25
  cost of operations in China, 186
  Motion C5 Mobile Clinical Assistant, 89
  partnering with customers, 10
  use of representatives, 291
Interaction structure (buying center), 86
Interfunctional involvement in marketing
    decision making, 158–161
Intermediaries. *See also* channel participants;
    manufacturers' representatives
  disintermediation, 320
  effect of Internet marketing on, 320
  securing good intermediaries for marketing
    channel, 296
Internal business process perspective (balanced
    scorecard), 171
Internal processes impacting marketing strategy,
    440
International Circuit Technology, 70
International markets. *See* global markets
International orientation in product innovation,
    252
Internet. *See also* e-commerce; e-commerce
    strategies
  benefits to businesses, 311
  delivering services through, 277
  interactive marketing communications, 386
  Internet strategy implementation, 316–319
  Internet marketing objectives, 314–316
  targeting buying influentials, 77
Interorganizational e-commerce, 307
Intranets, 307
Intraorganizational e-commerce, 307
Intuit, Inc., 178, 460
Inventory management, 345, 352
  inventory in rapidly changing markets, 353
  just-in-time (JIT) systems, 343
  profit impact of, 353
  reduction or elimination of inventories, 352

iPhone, 22, 31
iPod, 234
ISO-9000 standards, 215

J
J.M. Smucker Company, 11, 16
Job satisfaction (sales force), 423–425
Johnson Controls, Inc., 64
    advertising strategy case study, 406
    supply chain management, 330, 333
Joint ventures, 193–195
Just-in-time (JIT) systems, 343, 352
    supplier relationships and, 344

K
Kanthal, customer profitability of GE
Key account management, 414–417
    key accounts versus traditional
        accounts, 415
    selecting key accounts, 416
Key buying influentials, 11

L
Landed cost, 183
Latent needs of customers, creating channel
        solutions for, 295
Lead efficiency, 402
Lead user approach to product ideas, 249
Lean consumption, 274
Learning and growth, 172
Legal considerations in pricing, 373
Leveraged buy, 40
Licensing (global market entry strategy), 191
Limited problem solving (in modified rebuy), 69
Limited structure (product innovation), 244
Linked buy, 40
Logistics, 341–354
    calculating costs of, 346
    business-to-business logistical management,
        349–354
    business-to-business logistical service,
        346–349
    controllable elements in logistics system, 345
    just-in-time (JIT) systems, 343
    logistical system elements, 344
    managing flows, 342
    managing at TransPro, 357
    sales-marketing-logistics integration, 343
    strategic role of, 343

supply chain management versus, 342
    total-cost approach to logistics management,
        344
Lotus Notes, 226
Low-cost-to-serve customers, 101
Low-end disruptive strategy test, 242

M
Macrosegmentation, 127
    aircraft industry example, 130
    macrolevel characteristics of buying
        organizations, 128–131
Main street strategy, 228
Maintenance and repair support, 25
Management contracts, 192
Management judgment (demand forecasting), 142
Management system, 167
Manufactured materials and parts, 24
Manufacturers' representatives, 290–292
    commission basis, 290
    experience in markets they serve, 291
    factors influencing choice of, 292
    rep-customer relationship, 290
    securing good representatives, 296
Maps, strategy, 173–175, 441, 438
Margins and commissions (marketing channels),
        298
Market access in rapidly developing economies,
        186
Market orientation, 8
Market-centered organizations, 56, 57, 414
Market-driven firms, distinctive capabilities, 8
Market segment, defined, 125. *See also* business
        market segmentation
Market-share analysis, 446
Marketing audit, 444
Marketing challenges for services, 263–267
    differences in goods and services, 264
    nonownership of services, 266
    perishability of services, 266
    simultaneous production and
        consumption, 265
    tangibility versus intangibility, 264
    variability of services, 265
Marketing communications. *See* business
        marketing communications
Marketing control, 438, 443–451
    annual plan control, 446
    efficiency and effectiveness control, 448

marketing audit, 444
marketing performance dashboard, 446
marketing performance dashboard, 446–448
marketing performance measurement (MPM) strategies, 444–446
profitability control, 449–451
strategic control, 443
Marketing implementation, 451–456
implementation skills, 453
interfunctional involvement in, 455
marketing strategy center, 454
strategy-implementation fit, 452
Marketing, integration with sales and logistics, 343
Marketing mix for business services, 271–277
developing new services, 277
pricing services, 275
segmentation, 271
service packages, 272–275
services distribution, 277
services promotion, 276
Marketing performance measurement (MPM) strategies, 444–446
Marketing strategy. *See* business marketing strategies; strategy guidelines
Marketing strategy center, 160, 454
Marketing synergy, 251
Marketing tasks for managers, 9
Market-sensing capability, 8
McDonald's
supply chain for McNuggets, 39
use of raw materials, 24
Media selection for advertising, 392–397
Message development for advertising, 391
Mexico, rapidly developing economy, 14, 72, 181
Microsegmentation, 127
illustration of, 136
key criteria segmentation basis, 131
organizational innovativeness as basis, 135
personal characteristics of decision makers as basis, 136
price versus services tradeoffs example, 132
purchasing strategies as basis, 133
structure of decision-making unit as basis, 135
summary of selected microlevel bases, 131
value-based strategies as basis, 132
Microsoft
advantage in high tech markets, 225
diversified customer portfolio, 106

strategic alliance with Cisco Systems, 112
targeting SMB customers, 178
value-based selling tools, 43
Minority subcontracting program (government contracts), 49
Mobile Clinical Assistant (Motion C5), 89
Modified rebuy, 69
Motion Computing, Inc., 89
Motivation, sales force, 422–425
Motivations for buying, commercial consumers, 21
Motorola
centralized procurement, 75
e-procurement, 46
supplier involvement in product development, 74
supply chain management, 334
MPM (marketing performance measurement) strategies, 444–446
Multichannel models, integrated, 285
Multidomestic industries, 197
Multidomestic versus global strategies, 195–200

N
NAFTA (North American Free Trade Agreement), 36
NAICS (North American Industrial Classification System), 36, 127
National account success, 417
Negotiated contract buying (federal government), 52
Negotiated outcomes in collective decisions, 156
Net buying influences, 402
Net margin, 102
New-market disruptive strategy test, 242
New product development. *See* innovation and product development
New product strategy, 248
New-task buying situation, 67
Nokia, 337
Nondefense procurement (federal government), 51
North American Free Trade Agreement (NAFTA), 36
North American Industrial Classification System (NAICS), 36, 127

O
Objective-task method (advertising budgeting), 390
OEMs. *See* original equipment manufacturers

Online advertising, 393
   evaluation of, Web metrics, 399
   search engine marketing, 395
Online open bid format, 378
Online sealed bid format, 377
Open bidding, 378
Operating resources, 68
Operating costs, advantages in RDEs, 183
Operational linkages, 93
Oracle Corporation
   CRM software solutions, 119
   multichannel strategy, 285
Organizational buyers. *See* buyers, organizational
Organizational buying behavior. *See* buying
      behavior, organizational
Organizational climate and job satisfaction,
      423–425
Organizational forces influencing buying
      behavior, 73–77
Original equipment manufacturers (OEMs), 21
Outsourcing decision, 189
Overshooting mainstream technology users'
      needs, 240

P
Packages, service, 272–275
Parker Hamlin Corporation, pricing study, 382
Partnering with customers, 10
Partnerships in supply chain management, 332
Patching (strategy in dynamic markets), 245
PC market, global battle for, 199
PCUs (planning and control units), 426
   PCU opportunity, 428
Penetration (pricing), 372
Performance
   marketing performance dashboards,
      446–448
   marketing performance measurement (MPM)
      strategies, 444–446
   purchases affecting, 43
   performance review of selected supplier, 66
   sales force performance measures, 425
Peripheral participants in strategic alliances, 115
Perishability of services and managing demand/
      capacity, 275
Personal selling function, managing, 407–431
   account management process, 418–421
   relationship marketing strategy, 409–413
   managing the sales force, 413–418

models for B2B sales force management,
      426–429
   sales administration, 421–426
Phillips Electronics, 337
Philips Lighting Company, 136
Planning and control units (PCUs), 426
   PCU opportunity, 428
Points of difference, 11
Points of parity, 11
Pragmatists (technology customers), 225
Price elasticity of demand, 11, 366
Price sensitivity, customer satisfaction and, 366
Price versus service tradeoffs, importance to
      buyers, 132
Pricing services, 275
Pricing strategy, 358–382
   competition, 370
   competitive bidding, 377–379
   cost determinants, 368–370
   demand determinants, 363–365
   effects of Internet on, 322
   legal considerations, 373
   Parker Hamlin Corporation case study, 382
   price attacks by competitors, 374–377
   price objectives, 362
   pricing new products, 372
   product line considerations, 373
   value in business markets, 359–371
   value-based pricing, 365–368
Print advertising, business publications, 394–396
Private exchanges, 44, 319
Problem solving
   extensive, 66
   limited, 69
   routine, 68
Process (new product development), 246
   matching to development task, 253
Processes
   core, 164
   internal processes impacting marketing
      strategy, 440
Procter & Gamble (P&G), 25
   Internet initiative, working with Cisco, 34
Procurement. *See* purchasing
Product advantage, 251
Product development. *See also* innovation and
      product development
   determinants of new product success, 251
   fast-paced development, 252

major drivers of new product performance, 247

managing technology, 238–245

new product development process, 246–251

product championing and the informal network, 236

supplier involvement in, 42

Product families, 239

Product life cycle, pricing across, 371–374

economic value of new products, 373

new products, 372

Product lines

considerations in pricing, 373

types of, 218

Product market, defining, 219

Product organization (sales force), 414

Product positioning, 221–223

Product/market scope, 163

Product/service application in macrolevel segmentation, 129

Products, managing for business market, 208–231

building strong B2B brand, 209–215

planning industrial product strategy, 221–223

product quality and customer value, 215–218

product policy, 218–221

product support strategy, 218

technology adoption life cycle, 223–228

Profit focus, 10

Profit management tool, target pricing as, 369

Profitability

customer profitability, 99–103

impact of inventory management, 353

levels of logistics service, 348

market segment, 138

service, 276

Profitability control (marketing strategy), 449–451

Promotion of Web sites for e-commerce, 324

Promotional strategies for services, 276

Proprietary or catalog products, 218

Psychological contracts, 115

Purchase decision, impacts of advertising on, 398

Publications for potential government vendors, 50

Purchasing

centralization of procurement, 75

centralization versus decentralization, 76

e-procurement, 44–47

goals of the purchasing function, 38

government buying, 47–53

growing influence of, 73

institutional buying, 53–57

levels of procurement development, 40–43

organization of, 37

organizational position of, 75

purchases affecting performance, 43

segmenting purchase categories, 43

strategic priorities, 73

strategic procurement, 39

understanding total cost, 39

Purchasing situation in macrosegmentation, 130

Q

Quality, 215

elimination of inventories in TQM programs, 352

service quality, 268–271

R

Rapid product development, 252

Rapidly developing economies (RDEs), 72, 181–190

capabilities advantage of workforces, 187

capturing global advantage in, 181

cost advantages in, 183–185

following key customers to, 187

hidden costs of RDE operations, 185

making the outsourcing decision, 189

market access advantages, 186

risk management in, 203

Raw materials, 24

Raytheon, purchasing strategies, 133

Readiness, measuring strategic readiness, 173

Real-time communication (product innovation), 244

Recruitment and selection of salespersons, 421

Regression, 144

Relational strategies in services marketing, 271

Relationship commitment, 94

Relationship marketing, 16, 92–95, 409–413

drivers of relationship marketing effectiveness, 409–411

evaluating relationships, 112

nature of relationships, 94

relationship marketing (RM) programs, 411–413

strategic choices in, 94

types of relationships, 93
value-adding exchanges, 94
Relationship orientation (RO), 412
Representatives for manufacturers. *See* manufacturers' representatives
Research in Motion Ltd. (R.I.M.), 31
Resources
   allocating for marketing strategy, 441–443
   identifying for marketing strategy, 440
   resource commitments (new product development), 247
   strategic, 164
Responsibility charting, 159
Responsive marketing strategy, 82
Reverse auctions, 46, 52, 319
   strategic approach to, 379
Rewards (sales force), 422
Risk, managing in emerging markets, 203
Risk-reduction strategies, 83
RM (relationship marketing) programs, 411–413
Robinson-Patman Act, 373
Routine problem solving, 68
Russia, increasing importance in global market, 14
Ryder Truck Company, 308

S

SafePlace Corporation, 280
Sales. *See* personal selling function, managing
sales administration, 421–426
   evaluation and control, 425
   recruiting and selecting salespersons, 421
   supervision and motivation, 422–425
   training, 421
Sales analysis, 446
Sales force composite (forecasting technique), 143
Sales force
   models for sales force management, 426–429
   role of, impact of Internet strategies on, 324
   service-savvy, 276
Sales force management, 413–421
   key account management, 414–417
   models for B2B sales force management, 426–429
   national accounts success, 417
   organizing personal selling effort, 413
Sales resource opportunity grid, 427
Salesforce.com, 243

Sales-marketing-logistics integration, 343
SBU (strategic business unit), 155
Schwinn, case study, 206
SCM. *See* supply chain management
Scorecard. *See* balanced scorecard
Sealed Air Corporation, 60
Search process in organizational buying, 66
Segments, 449
   profitability by market segment, 450
Segmentation of business market. *See* business market segmentation
Segmentation of purchase categories, 42, 43
Selective processes (in cognition), 83
Selling tools, value-based, 43
Service bundling, 275
Service concept, 273
Service delivery system, 274
Service offer, 273
Service packages, 272–275
Service personnel, 275
Service, product, 218
Service recovery, 269
Services, 25, 257–280
   building strong brand with (BASF), 221
   challenges in marketing services, 263–267
   customer experience, 258–260
   customer experience management, 260
   industrial services, 219
   marketing mix for business services, 271–277
   SafePlace Corporation (case study), 280
   service quality, 268–271
   solution-centered perspective, 260–263
Set-aside program (government contracts), 49
SGA (strategic global alliance), 192
Share-of-wallet, 442
Siemens, tracking marketing success, 452
Skimming (pricing), 372
Small and medium-sized businesses (SMB)
   business market for Dell Computers, 6
   Federated Insurance targets SMB sector, 149
   importance as IT customers, 106
   Microsoft targets SMB sector, 178
Smucker Company. See J.M. Smucker Company
Social ingredients in strategic alliances, 116
Solutions, customization via Internet marketing, 304, 311, 316, 321
Solutions approach to services, 260–263
Sonoco, customer value proposition, 11
Sony, relationships with suppliers, 119

Southeast Asia, rapidly developing economies, 72, 181
Staples, customized solutions via Internet, 321
Steelcase, Inc., 256
Straight rebuy purchasing situation, 68
Strategic alignment, 171, 173
Strategic alliances, 112–117
    accessing complementary skills, 112
    benefits of, 113
    determinants of alliance success, 114–116
    social ingredients in alliance success, 116
Strategic assets, 164
Strategic business unit (SBU), 155
Strategic control (marketing strategy), 443
Strategic factors in new product success, 251
Strategic global alliance (SGA), 192
Strategic new-task decisions, 67
Strategic positioning, 163–167
Strategic priorities in purchasing, 73
Strategic readiness, measuring, 173
Strategic resources, 164
Strategic themes, critical, 440
Strategy guidelines for marketers
    buyer-seller relationship management, 97
    buying center members, 81
    key account management for centralized procurement
    modified rebuy situations, 70
    new-task buying situation, 68
    responsive marketing strategy, 82
    straight rebuy situations, 66
Strategy map, 167, 173–175, 437
Strategy plan, building, 167–175
Subjective technique (demand forecasting), 142
SunPower Corporation, 301
Suppliers
    evaluation by organizational buyers, 47
    involvement in new product development, 42
    selection of and performance review by organizational buyers, 66
    value drivers in key supplier relationships, 96
Supplies, 25
Supply chain, 17–22
    commercial enterprises as consumers, 21
    iPhone, triumph of supply chain management, 22
    integration through use of Internet, 312
    managing relationships in, 19
    sales forecasts, vital to smooth functioning of, 141
Supply chain management (SCM), 18, 36, 329–357
    benefits to final customer, 336
    breakdown of supply chain, 337
    business-to-business logistical management, 349–354
    business-to-business logistical services, 346–349
    calculating logistics costs, 346
    concept of, 331–333
    financial benefits perspective, 337
    goals of, 335
    information and technology drivers, 336
    logistics as critical element, 341–345
    logistics management at TransPro, 357
    making supplier relationships work, 340
    SCM software, 338
    stages in adoption of, 334
    successful supply chain practices, 340
Sustain stage, 170
Sustaining innovation, 240
Switching costs, 96, 367

T
Tablet PC for nurses, 89
Target audience for advertising, 389
Target costing, 368
Technical synergy (in new product development), 252
Technological influences on buying behavior, 72
Technology adoption life cycle, 223–228
    bowling alley analogy for technology market, 226
    strategies for, 225
    types of technology customers, 224
Technology enthusiasts, 224
Territory sales response, 426
Third-party logistics, 353
Thought-worlds, 156
3M, 155, 177
    business plan, 158
    encouraging innovation, 234
    product championing, 236
    Web site for custom Post-it Notes, 315
Touchpoints (customer experience), 259

Time compression in order-to-delivery cycle, 335
Time line for marketing strategy results, 439
Time pacing (product innovation), 245
Time segmentation (pricing), 372
Time series techniques (forecasting), 144
Tornado strategy, 227
Total buying plans, 402
Total cost approach to logistics management, 344
Total cost of ownership (TCO), 40
  calculating logistics costs, 346
Total cost in use, 361
Total cost and value of a good or service, 39
Toyota
  identifying suppliers for innovativeness, 134
  supplier relationships, 19, 340
Trade show strategy, 400–404
  benefits of, 400
  evaluating performance, 403
  investment returns, 401
  managing exhibits, 402
  planning strategy, 401
  selecting shows, 402
Training (sales force), 421
Transaction costs, reduction with Internet use, 311
Transaction customers, 98
Transactional exchange, 93, 95
Transactional relationships, 95, 108
Transportation, 350–352
  logistical service and, 350
  performance criteria, 351
  speed of service, 351
TransPro, logistics management, 357
Trust, building in marketing channels, 298
Turf issues and thought-world views, 156

U
Unit cost reduction goal of SCM, 116
Unbundling strategy, 107
Unique focus, 166
UPS
  e-commerce technology, 310
  UPS Solutions, 261
Users (buying center), 79
Users (commercial enterprises), 21

V
Value, 106, 174, 175
  customer value, 216–218, 359–362
Value-adding exchanges, 94
Value analysis, 40
Value buy, 40
Value-based pricing, 361, 365–368
Value-based segmentation, 368
Value-based selling tools, 43
Value-based strategies in microsegmentation, 132
Value drivers in collaborative relationships, 97
Value network, 164
Value proposition, crafting, 107–109. *See also* customer value proposition
  bandwidths of industry relationships, 107
  distinctive value proposition, 167
  flaring out by unbundling, 107
  flaring out with augmentation, 108
  flexible service offerings, 109
  instituting best processes, 109
  key value propositions and customer strategies, 170
  learning to retain customers, 111
  motivating employees, 110
  in strategic alliances, 114
  unique value propositions for key accounts, 415
Value in use, 129
Vietnam, 182
Visionaries (technology customers), 225

W
W. W. Grainger, Inc., 7, 317
  Internet and e-commerce strategies, 327
Walt Disney Company, 75
Warehousing function, outsourcing, 350
Waste reduction through supply chain management, 335
Web, synchronizing with marketing strategy, 314
Web sites, 316–319. *See also* e-commerce; e-commerce strategies
  B2B, borrowing from consumer sites, 318
  Internet catalogs, 319
  private exchanges, 319
  promotion of, 324
  reverse auctions on, 319
  successful design, 318
  W.W. Grainger example, 317

Wendy's International, Inc., 36
Whale curve of cumulative profitability, 100

X
Xerox Corporation, 238
    career path for CEO, 9

global strategy, 199
joint venture with Fuji Film, 193

Y
YRC Worldwide, account management, 431